MACHINE INTELLIGENCE 10

Intelligent Systems: Practice and Perspective

Machine Intelligence
Editor-in-Chief: Donald Michie

Volumes 1–7 are published by
Edinburgh University Press
and in the United States by
Halsted Press (a subsidiary of John Wiley & Sons, Inc.)

Volumes 8–10 are published by
Ellis Horwood Ltd., Publishers, Chichester
and in the United State by
Halsted Press (a subsidiary of John Wiley & Sons, Inc.)

To the memory of
John Gaschnig
June 6, 1950 — March 4, 1982

MACHINE
INTELLIGENCE 10

Edited by

J. E. HAYES
Research Associate
University of Edinburgh

DONALD MICHIE
Professor of Machine Intelligence
University of Edinburgh

and

Y-H PAO
Dively Distinguished Professor of Engineering, and
Professor of Electrical Engineering and Computer Science
Case Western Reserve University, USA

ELLIS HORWOOD LIMITED
Publishers · Chichester

Halsted Press: a division of
JOHN WILEY & SONS
New York · Brisbane · Chichester · Toronto

First published in 1982 by

ELLIS HORWOOD LIMITED
Market Cross House, Cooper Street, Chichester, West Sussex, PO19 1EB, England

The publisher's colophon is reproduced from James Gillison's drawing of the ancient Market Cross, Chichester.

Distributors:

Australia, New Zealand, South-east Asia:
Jacaranda-Wiley Ltd., Jacaranda Press,
JOHN WILEY & SONS INC.,
G.P.O. Box 859, Brisbane, Queensland 40001, Australia

Canada:
JOHN WILEY & SONS CANADA LIMITED
22 Worcester Road, Rexdale, Ontario, Canada.

Europe, Africa:
JOHN WILEY & SONS LIMITED
Baffins Lane, Chichester, West Sussex, England.

North and South America and the rest of the world:
Halsted Press: a division of
JOHN WILEY & SONS
605 Third Avenue, New York, N.Y. 10016, U.S.A.

© 1982 J. E. Hayes, D. Michie, Y-H Pao/Ellis Horwood Ltd.

British Library Cataloguing in Publication Data
Machine intelligence. — 10
1. Artificial intelligence — Periodicals
001.53'5'05   Q335

The Library of Congress cataloged this serial as follows — 67–13648

ISBN 0–85312–431–0 (Ellis Horwood Limited)
ISSN 0076–2032
ISBN 0–470–27323–2 (Halsted Press)

Typeset in Press Roman by Ellis Horwood Limited.
Printed in Great Britain by Unwin Brothers Ltd., of Woking.

PREFACE

The year of the first MI Workshop, 1965, was a milestone for more reasons than one, not least for the appearance of a paper entitled "A machine-oriented logic based on the resoluton principle". It was appropriate and a cause for pleasure that the author of that paper, J. A. Robinson, was the opening contributor to the scientific proceedings of MI-10, held in November 1981 at Case Western Reserve University, Cleveland, USA.

Among prominent guests at MI-10 first mention must be made of Bill Price of the US Air Force Office of Scientific Research, the Workshop's sponsors, to whom warmest thanks are due. Tribute is also due to the deft organisation of local arrangements by George Ernst, who as an outstanding pioneering worker in our field contributes a paper with R. J. Hookway.

Followers of this series will know that Machine Intelligence 9 was held near Leningrad under the co-sponsorship of the Fredkin Foundation and the USSR Academy of Sciences, whose All-Union Council for Artificial Intelligence acted as host. The Council's scientific secretary, Leo Mikulich, had been a much appreciated visiting worker in Edinburgh some years earlier. He now attended the Tenth Workshop as bearer of good wishes from the Soviet Academy of Sciences and AI community, in addition to contributing the paper which appears as Chapter 19 in the present volume.

Through the good offices of Professor Yoh-Han Pao, co-director of the Workshop, we were further honoured by the presence of Professor P. J. Chu, who directs the Institute for Automation of the Chinese Academy of Sciences in Beijing, and of Dr Tibor Vamos from Budapest, Director of the Computer and Automation Institute of the Hungarian Academy of Sciences, and President of the International Federation for Automatic Control. Science, it is often proclaimed, is international. Often, alas, the attempt to make it so goes no further than proclamation. Co-operation and the reasoned approach can be effectively nourished only by action; and as with nourishment of other kinds repetition is desirable at more or less regular intervals. One of the aims of the MI Workshop is to contribute, in however small a measure, to this process.

All workers in AI have been saddened by the tragic death of John Gaschnig. The paper he gave at the Workshop appears as Chapter 15 of this volume, which is dedicated to his memory.

DONALD MICHIE
May 1982

CONTENTS

vii

CONTENTS

MECHANISED REASONING

1

On generating and using examples in proof discovery

A. M. Ballantyne and W. W. Bledsoe
Departments of Mathematics and Computer Science
University of Texas at Austin, Austin, Texas

Abstract

This paper describes some work on automatically generating finite counter-examples in topology, and the use of counterexamples to speed up proof discovery in intermediate analysis, and gives some examples theorems where human provers are aided in proof discovery by the use of examples.

INTRODUCTION

This paper is divided into two parts: the first part on counterexamples, their automatic generation and use as filters to speed up proofs; and the second part on using examples as a positive force in theorem proving whereby the examples suggest lines of attack rather than act as filters to prune bad subgoals.

1. COUNTEREXAMPLES

Although one of the earliest and most influential experiments in automatic deduction (Gelernter 1959) made extensive use of examples, relatively few attempts to incorporate examples into automatic theorem proving have been made since then. This lack of attention to an important topic is unfortunate, for, we feel that in the human prover, the creation and manipulation of examples plays as important a role in the problem solving process as does his strictly deductive faculties. To quote Gelernter:

> "The creative scientist generally finds his most valuable insights into a problem by considering a model of the formal system in which the problem is couched. In the case of Euclidean geometry, the semantic interpretation is so useful that virtually no one would attempt the proof of a theorem in that system without first drawing a diagram; if not physically then in the mind's eye."

Gelernter manually supplied the program with examples for the various problems attempted. He postponed investigating the problem of automatically

3

generating examples. In general, the problem of constructing counterexamples is very difficult. For example, when attempting to generate a counterexample to the sentence $\forall x P(x)$, it clearly does not suffice to try to prove $\exists x^- P(x)$. What is really required is a proof of the higher order statement $\exists P \exists x^- P(x)$. Proving this statement is equivalent to finding an interpretation of P that falsifies $\forall x P(x)$. In other words, the generation of counterexamples often requires finding instantiations for higher order variables ranging over sets, functions, and predicates. Although, in theory, higher order proof procedures (Huet 1972, Minor 1979) should be applicable, in practice they have so far been of little use.

EXPERIMENTAL RESULTS

We now present the results of two rather different experiments dealing with counterexamples. The first experiment deals with the construction of finite counterexamples to false conjectures in elementary point set topology. A program was constructed that incrementally tried to build an interpretation for a finite collection of sets. The second experiment deals primarily with using counter-examples as a subgoal filter in analysis. In this project, interpretations for universally quantified function and constant symbols were supplied manually. The computer then extended that interpretation to include the skolem functions and constants that arose as a result of quantifier elimination.

1.1 Generating Counterexamples in Topology

In [5] and [1], efforts at producing a topology theorem prover are described. In [1] we describe a method of representing some topological theorems which seems to have enough power of expression to be of real value to a mechanical topologist. With some reflection it also appears that this representation can be used as the basis for a program which finds finite (finite topological spaces) counterexamples to some statements which are not theorems. This process is analogous to constructing a Venn diagram and then interpreting the circles in the diagram by adding points.

When a student attacks a homework exercise from a textbook, he usually is assured that what he is trying to prove is, in fact, valid. When he is forced to step out of this rather narrow circle of confidence, he must take a different approach to the problem. Now, instead of driving for a proof, he must in addition, look rather carefully for a counterexample. What follows are some observations on what such a search entails.

First, let us comment briefly on **Resolution**. What Resolution amounts to is a search for a counterexample. If the algorithm produces □ then we know that no counterexample is to be had. If, on the other hand, the program grinds for ever, then we have a counterexample. If the program halts in some finite time without producing □, then we also have a counterexample. A resolution program will usually terminate without producing □ only when the Herbrand universe is finite. In this case the Herbrand universe with the correct interpretation is a counterexample. Most interesting statements have an infinite Herbrand universe.

One could describe Resolution as a brute force enumerative approach to finding a counterexample. In passing we mention that Roach and Siklossy [11] have implemented a program which refutes conjectures which arise in simulated robot tasks. This program does not explicitly construct a counterexample, but instead disproves a conjecture by showing its absence from a finite enumeration of the consequences of the hypotheses.

In general, the approaches used by mathematicians are quite a bit cleverer than either of these. Effective human problem solvers encode the problem well and bring a lot of knowledge to bear. From now on in this section we will be using very elementary point set topology as a basis for our discussions. Suppose we had the following definition:

Definition — Let (X, τ) be a topology. Then a set $A \subset X$ is said to be regularly open if $\bar{A}^\circ = A$. In other words, a point set is regularly open if we take its closure and then from that take its interior, we get A back.[†] Clearly any regularly open set is open. The natural question to ask is whether the terms open and regularly open are equivalent. More exactly, is

(I) $\forall A [\mathrm{OPEN}(A) \rightarrow \mathrm{REGOPEN}(A)]$ a theorem?

In looking for a counterexample to this theorem, one's first inclinination is to look to the standard topology E^1 (the real numbers with the usual topology), and within this context to look at the most familiar open set, the open interval $]a, b[$ for some $a, b \in R$. Unfortunately we have $\overline{]a,b[}^\circ = [a,b]^\circ =]a,b[$. That is, when we close $]a,b[$ we pick up the points a, b but then promptly lose them when we take the interior. So we need to be a little more clever. We need to find an open set that picks up some other set of points when we take its closure and doesn't let go of all those points when we apply the interior operator. After some fiddling the natural choice of a set A is made by taking an open interval $]a, b[$ and deleting from it some point c to get the two intervals $]a, c[$ and $]c, b[$. Now when we close up A we pick up the points a, b, c and when we take the interior we drop a, b and keep c. Diagramatically we have

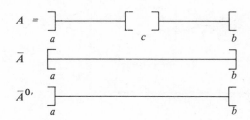

[†] For any set A, A° denotes the interior of A (the largest open subset of A), $\bar{A}$ denotes the closure of A, and A' denotes the complement of A, $X - A$.

5

In a certain sense we could have picked a simpler $A^* \subseteq R$, namely $R \cap \{x_0\}'$ for any $x_0 \in R$. This set A^* is a simpler counterexample in that its closure picks up one point and loses none when we take the interior. Although both choices A and A' are perfectly satisfactory, the second is preferable for the reason that it is the meagerest counterexample obtainable, in the sense mentioned above, once we have fixed our topological space to be E^1.

Actually E^1 is a much more complicated topology than we need. If we abstract from our second counterexample, what we really have is a set A which is not all of X but whose closure is X. Since X is both open and closed this assures us that $X \neq A$. Diagramatically we have

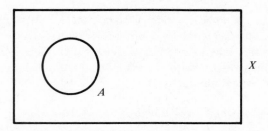

In our second counterexample we knew that A^* was not equal to X since we put x_0 in $A^{*'}$. In our abstracted counterexample we will do the same thing — that is, we will start off with some arbitrary open set A and put an arbitrary point, call it x_0, in A'. Since we don't really care what A is, we assign it the simplest value possible. Since $A = \phi$ will not do, we give A the value $\{p_0\}$ for some point p_0. These assignments are consistent with the axioms of topology, hence we have created for a counterexample the following small topology and an assignment to A within that topology. We denote open sets with a circle and closed sets with a rectangle. Note that the set $\{p_0\}$ had to be an open set since from our statement (I) we know that A must be open.

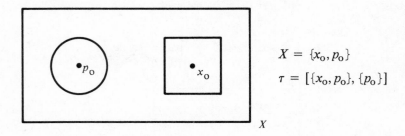

$$X = \{x_0, p_0\}$$
$$\tau = [\{x_0, p_0\}, \{p_0\}]$$

This last example's structural simplicity and apparent ease of construction would, offhand, indicate that we could write a program which would have to know only the rudiments of topology to be able to construct such simple counterexamples.

The system described in [1] attempts to prove a theorem. Essentially that program (let us call it GRAPHER) uses the statement of a theorem to draw a picture from which it tries to prove the theorem. If GRAPHER were trying to prove

(II) $\text{OPEN}(A) \longrightarrow \text{REGOPEN}(A)$

where A is a skolem constant, it would rewrite the theorem in the following way. Defining REGOPEN yields

(i) $\text{OPEN}(A) \longrightarrow \bar{A}^o = A$

and defining = yields

(ii) $\text{OPEN}(A) \longrightarrow A \subset \bar{A}^o \wedge \bar{A}^o \subset A$

Using knowledge internal to the program, GRAPHER constructs a diagram which contains the objects mentioned in the theorem and relationships between those objects. The link '$\longrightarrow$' in the diagram below denotes inclusion. The small 'o's hanging off some sets signify that they are open sets, while the small 'c's indicate closed sets. From the hypothesis $\text{OPEN}(A)$ GRAPHER constructs the following diagram. Note that all objects $(A, \bar{A}, \bar{A}^o)$ mentioned in the theorem appear in the diagram. GRAPHER uses its fairly extensive knowledge of the interior (^{o}) and closure ($\bar{}$) operators to draw the arcs appearing in the diagram.

The first half of the conclusion is proved immediately from the graph which the program constructs.

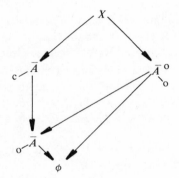

NOTE: The little o's indicate that the set is open; c means the set is closed.

The GRAPHER tries to prove the second conclusion of (ii) and rewrites it as follows

(iii) $\text{OPEN}(A_o) \wedge x_o \in \bar{A}^o \longrightarrow x_o \in A$

The arc $\bar{A}^o \longrightarrow \{x_o\}$ is added to the current graph but to no avail. The program makes a few other unsuccessful probes and then gets suspicious. Maybe (iii) is not true! So now GRAPHER tries to assert the negation of the conclusion; i.e. $x_o \notin A_o$ which is immediately rewritten as $x_o \in A'_o$. All these facts are incorporated into the picture until we finally have

7

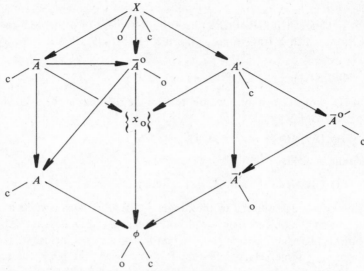

There do not appear to be any contradictions in the diagram, so the program tries to assign values to the various objects in the diagram subject to the constraints imposed by the relations depicted in the graph and the axioms of topology. Basically, what the algorithm does is to start from the bottom of the diagram and work upwards — assigning the smallest possible value to each object. For the time being we will informally step through the program's actions. Later we will give a more precise specification of the algorithm.

When we view the graph we see that the two smallest objects, excluding ϕ, and $\{x_0\}$, are A and $\bar{A}'$. The GRAPHER always starts to work on the least complicated set for reasons which, if not clear now, should become clear later.

(1) The algorithm tries to assign A the smallest possible value which is ϕ.

(2) This choice for A is substituted for A throughout the graph. All possible reductions are performed. This means that $\bar{A} = \bar{\phi} = \phi$. This causes trouble though, for we have $x_0 \in \bar{A}$; in other words $x_0 \in \phi$. So $A = \phi$ is not a viable choice.

(3) The program realizes that it must put a point in A. It uses the only point so far discussed. It therefore tries to assign the value $\{x_0\}$ to A. But the program immediately detects x_0's simultaneous presence in A and A'. Hence this too is an impossible assignment.

(4) The program now discards x_0, 'activates' another point p_0, and gives A the value $\{p_0\}$. So far, this choice appears to be okay. At this time our partial assignment to X is $\{x_0, p_0\}$.

(5) We now move 'up' the graph and find the smallest superset of A. Since from the graph we have both $A \subset \bar{A}$ and $A \subset \bar{A}^{\circ}$ and also $\bar{A}^{\circ} \subset \bar{A}$, we operate on $\bar{A}^{\circ}$ next. Since we see that $\bar{A}^{\circ}$ is constrained to contain at least x_0 and p_0, $\{x_0, p_0\}$ is our first assignment to $\bar{A}^{\circ}$. At this time the open sets are $\{p_0\}$ and $\{p_0, x_0\}$.

8

(6) The program continues to work up the graph. The set which is immediately above $\bar{A}^o$ is $\bar{A}$. We assign to $\bar{A}$ the minimal assignment, that is, $\{x_o, p_o\}$.

(7) At last the program works its way up to X. X also gets the value $\{x_o, p_o\}$. The values of the other sets now fall out immediately. We are finally left with

$A = \{p_o\}$
$X = \{x_o, p_o\}$ *NOTE:* The symbol X denotes
$\tau = \{\{x_o, p_o\}, \{p_o\}\}$.   the whole space.

Diagrammatically we have

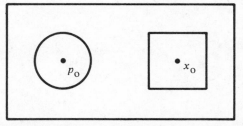

X

which was what we constructed as counterexample II. It appears that the human and the program are doing pretty much the same sort of thing.

Some notes on the algorithm

The program starts at the bottom of the graph and works its way upward. The notion of upward is well defined since the graph can contain no loops. If there ever arises a chain of inclusions of the form $A_0 \subseteq A_1 \subseteq \ldots A_n \subseteq A_0$ then the links corresponding to those relations are removed and the diagram notes the fact that $A_0 = A_1 = \ldots = A_n$.

If the sets A and A' appear in the graph, the algorithm will only attempt to assign values to A, the reason being that we would have to know what X is before we could give A' a meaningful value. The assignment to X is essentially the last important assignment. The assignments occur primarily in a depth-first fashion. For example, if our graph were

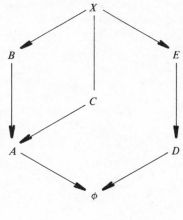

9

the algorithm would traverse the graph in the order

$$A\,B\,C\,D\,E\,X.$$

When the set A has several subsets B,C in the graph, B,C must be assigned values before A. To illustrate this, suppose the graph looked as follows:

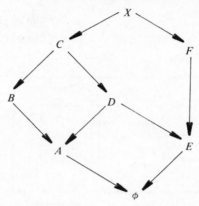

then our order of assignment goes

$$A\,B\,E\,D\,C\,F\,X.$$

The reason behind this peculiar order is that at each choice point we assign the smallest value to a set with respect to the restrictions implied by the graph. One of the most crucial restrictions is the values of a set's subsets.

Let A be a set to which we want to assign a value, call it $v(A)$. Let $A_1,\ldots,A_n$ be the immediate subsets of A. Then our initial choice of a value for A is

$$v(A) = \bigcup_{i=1}^{n} v(A_i).$$

Whenever a choice $v(A)$ for A is made, a new copy of the graph is made with that $v(A)$ substituted for A throughout. The REDUCE operations described in [5] are applied to the nodes of this modified graph and the search begins from where we left off. For example, suppose we have

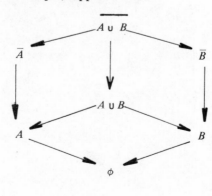

and we assign to A the value ϕ. Then ϕ is substituted for A throughout the graph, and we wind up with

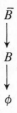

$$\bar{B}$$
$$\downarrow$$
$$B$$
$$\downarrow$$
$$\phi$$

since $\bar{\phi} = \phi$ and $B \cup \phi = B$.

If an assignment causes a contradiction then we back up (as in MICRO-PLANNER) to our last assignment and try to add another point. We use the next available point in POINTLIST (the list of points available to GRAPHER) that does not cause a contradiction. For example, the program never tries to add p to A if $p \in A'$. If the program cannot add a new point, it backs up to the next choice point and tries again. The program never tries to add two new points to a node. It appears to be the case that if *one* new point is not sufficient, then no finite number of new points will work.

At all times the program is keeping track of the topology τ. Whenever open sets are assigned values, they are put into the topology, and all finite unions and intersections of the new set with previous sets are added also.

Having described these basic principles, we can look at what the algorithm does with some other examples.

Theorem $\forall A \; \forall B [\overline{A \cap B} = \bar{A} \cap \bar{B}]$

The program rewrites this as

$$\overline{A \cap B} \subseteq \bar{A} \cap \bar{B} \wedge \bar{A} \cap \bar{B} \subseteq \overline{A \cap B} \quad \text{where } A,B \text{ are skolem constants.}$$

The first conjecture is proved immediately from the graph, leaving only the second. The program rewrites this as

$$x_0 \in \bar{A} \cap \bar{B} \longrightarrow x_0 \in \overline{A_0 \cap B} \quad \text{for } x_0 \text{ another skolem constant.}$$

The hypothesis is asserted and the conclusion attempted. A failure here evokes an attempt at a counterexample. Now the program asserts

$$x_0 \notin \overline{A \cap B}.$$

In other words,

$$x_0 \in \overline{A \cap B}\,'.$$

We now have the following graph

11

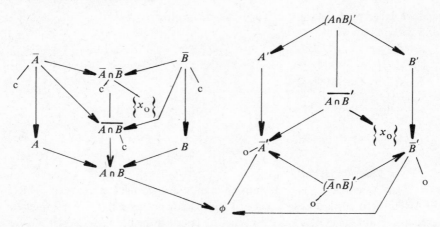

The program's first step is to assign $A \cap B$ the value ϕ. By the reductions mentioned in [5] this forces the assertion $A \subseteq B'$ and $B \subseteq A'$. The program now tries to assign A the value ϕ. This produces a contradiction since $\overline{A} = \overline{\phi} = \phi$ and we have $x_0 \in \overline{A}$. So the program tries the next point, x_0. At this point the graph contains the following substructure.

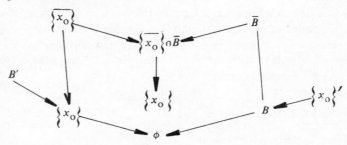

Before the program can assign $\overline{A} = \{\overline{x_0}\}$ a value, it must first assign $\{\overline{x_0}\} \cap \overline{B}$ a value. Obviously the minimal value is $\{x_0\}$. The next set to which the program tries to assign a value is $\overline{B}$. But before it can do so B must have a value. Since B can have neither the value ϕ nor $\{x_0\}$ (Why?) it is given the value $\{p_0\}$. Now $\overline{B}$ is assigned the value $\{x_0, p_0\}$ and X is assigned the same value. So we have the, by now familiar, topological space

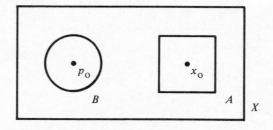

We present another example in detail to show the versatility of the program.

Let us try to extend our knowledge of regularly open sets. As Bledsoe mentions in [2], one of the natural steps to undertake is to test for closure with respect to some function. Specifically, if P is a n-ary predicate and f is some defined n-ary function, then P is closed with respect to f if

$$\forall A_1, \ldots, A_n [P(A_1) \wedge \ldots \wedge P(A_n) \longrightarrow P(f(A_1, \ldots, A_n))] .$$

When dealing with sets, some of the most obvious functions to consider are $\cup$, $\cap$. This would seem especially true in topology since topology is nothing more than a family of sets closed with respect to union and intersection (with some cardinality restrictions). So, going back to our notion of regularly open set, two possible theorems pop into mind

1. $\mathrm{REGOPEN}(A) \wedge \mathrm{REGOPEN}(B) \longrightarrow \mathrm{REGOPEN}(A \cap B)$
2. $\mathrm{REGOPEN}(A) \wedge \mathrm{REGOPEN}(B) \longrightarrow \mathrm{REGOPEN}(A \cup B)$.

Indeed, the GRAPHER establishes the truth of (1) immediately. The second conjecture is more difficult. After the program has defined the main concepts, we have (2) in the restated form

2′. $\mathrm{OPEN}(A) \wedge \overline{A}^{\mathrm{o}} = A \wedge \mathrm{OPEN}(B) \wedge \overline{B}^{\mathrm{o}} = B \longrightarrow$
$$\mathrm{OPEN}(A \cup B) \wedge \overline{A \cup B}^{\mathrm{o}} = A \cup B .$$

The first conclusion is immediately verified, and the second is redefined as

$$A \cup B \subseteq \overline{A \cup B}^{\mathrm{o}} \wedge \overline{A \cup B}^{\mathrm{o}} \subseteq A \cup B .$$

The first inclusion relation is also immediately verified. The program grinds on the second conclusion, redefining it as:

$$x_0 \in \overline{A \cup B}^{\mathrm{o}} \longrightarrow x_0 \in A \cup B .$$

The hypothesis is asserted, but we have failure on the conclusion. Now the program tries for a counterexample and it asserts $x_0 \in (A \cup B)'$, or, as the GRAPHER prefers to say, $x_0 \in A' \cap B'$. At this point our computer-produced graph contains the following subgraph (using the fact that $\overline{A \cup B} = \overline{A} \cup \overline{B}$ to deduce that $x_0 \in (\overline{A} \cup \overline{B})^{\mathrm{o}}$):

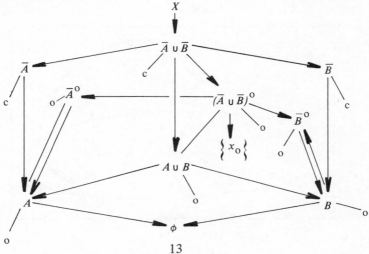

13

Note that the fact $x_0 \in A' \cap B'$ dictates that $x_0 \in A'$ and $x_0 \in B'$. The graph that the machine constructs does contain these facts. We do not draw them in here for the graph is already complicated enough. The complimentary pair of arcs between A and $\bar{A}^o$ indicate equality. Now the program begins by assigning to A the value ϕ. When ϕ is substituted for A throughout and the reductions are made, then the graph reduces to a graph containing nodes pertaining to B only. This reduced-graph contains the fact that $x_0 \in B$ and $x_0 \in B'$ hence $A = \phi$ is impossible.

The program tries to put the point x_0 into A, but this does not work since $x_0 \in A'$. A is now given the value $\{p_0\}$. Of course $\bar{A}^o$ gets the same value and the program tentatively assigns $\bar{A}$ the same value.

The GRAPHER now tries to give B a value. The possibilities ϕ, $\{x_0\}$, $\{p_0\}$ are easily eliminated. (Note that if $B = \{p_0\}$ then $B = A$ and we are back to the case where the graph talks only about A.) Now B gets the value $\{p_1\}$. Hence $\bar{B}^o$ gets the same value. $\bar{B}$ also gets the same value. This choice for $\bar{B}$ fails since it means that $\overline{A \cup B}$ (which is the same as $\bar{A} \cup \bar{B}$) is equal to $\{p_0, p_1\}$. But from the graph we know that $x_0 \in \bar{A} \cup \bar{B}$. So the program realizes that it must give another point. The first point in the list to try is x_0, and so for the time being $\bar{B} = \{p_1, x_0\}$ looks good. Let us recap our assignments so far:

$$A = \bar{A}^o = \{p_0\}$$
$$B = \bar{B}^o = \{p_1\}$$
$$\bar{A} = \{p_0\}$$
$$\bar{B} = \{p_1, x_0\} \ .$$

At this point our space $X = \{x_0, p_0, p_1\}$, and our open sets are $A, B, \bar{A}', \bar{B}'$ and all possible unions. In other words

$$\tau = \{\{p_0\}, \{p_1\}, \{p_0, p_1\}\}, \{p_1, x_0\}\} \ .$$

Hence the closed sets, call them τ', are $\{\{p_1, x_0\} \{p_0, x_0\}, \{x_0\}, \{p_0\}\}$. Thus we have the following topology:

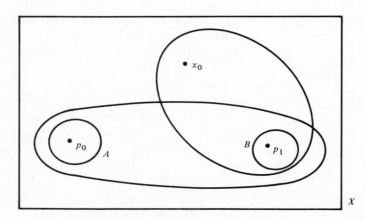

We have $A \cup B = \{p_0\} \cup \{p_1\} = \{p_0, p_1\}$. Hence $\overline{A \cup B} = \overline{A} \cup \overline{B} = \{p_0\} \cup \{p_1, x_0\} = \{p_0, p_1, x_0\}$ and $\overline{A \cup B} = (\overline{A} \cup \overline{B})^\circ = \{p_0, p_1, x_0\}^\circ = \{p_0, p_1, x_0\}$.

But notice that in this topology, $\overline{B}^\circ = \{x_0, p_1\}$ violates the restriction in the graph that $B \subset \overline{B}^\circ$. So GRAPHER looks at its last assignment, which was the assignment of $\{x_0, p_1\}$ to $\overline{B}$ and tries to re-do it. It finds that it cannot re-do $\overline{B}$ so it looks at the assignment of $\{p_1\}$ to B. There is nothing GRAPHER can do to this assignment since by its rules, if one new point won't work, two new points won't work. The next assignment that GRAPHER can undo is the assignment of $\{p_0\}$ to $\overline{A}$. GRAPHER makes the tentative assignment $\{p_0, x_0\}$ to $\overline{A}$ and proceeds as before. This time everything works and we have the following space and topology:

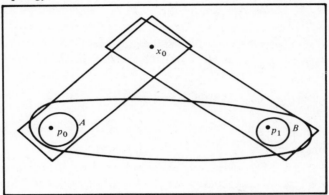

We would like to present one more counterexample that was generated after the previous work was done. The algorithm had evolved some in the meantime, but is sufficiently like the algorithm mentioned to make the following example meaningful.

The computer was asked if every subspace of a normal space is normal. For those who have forgotten, a topological space is normal if every two disjoint closed sets can be separated by open sets. In response to the query, the machine printed the following four point space as a counterexample.

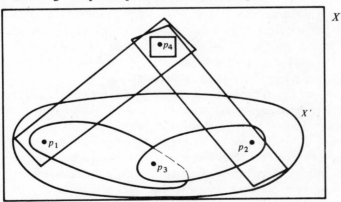

Note that X with the indicated topology has no pairs of disjoint closed sets and hence is normal. However, if we drop the point p_4 to form the subspace X', we now have the two disjoint closed sets $\{p_1\}$ and $\{p_2\}$. But every open set that contains p_1 also contains p_3, and every open set that contains p_2 also contains p_3, hence $\{p_1\}$ and $\{p_2\}$ cannot be separated by open sets. We were pleasantly surprised by the appearance of this example since the standard textbook counter-examples are quite complicated. For example, if Ω is the first uncountable ordinal and ω the first infinite ordinal, then the space $X = [0,\Omega] \times [0,\omega]$ is normal. If we form X' by dropping off the corner point (Ω, ω) then X' is not normal (X' is called the **Tychonoff plank**). Other examples are formed by embedding some non-normal space in a cube (which is always normal).

Conclusion

Although this experiment required that the program discover interpretations for sets and families of sets (topologies), it nevertheless succeeded in this difficult task by

1. considering only interpretations consisting of finite families of finite sets;
2. using considerable knowledge about elementary topology to organize the search.

While we feel that (2) is a necessary prerequisite for a successful example builder. we do not feel that (1) is a fundamental limitation. We believe that humans use a relatively small, albeit well organized body of knowledge about infinite sets to aid them in the construction of examples over infinite domains. For instance, a human can use various sets like the rationals, the primes, the integers, the ordinals, etc., manipulating them somewhat in the manner that we manipulated points and finite sets in the above examples to make up counterexample sets with certain required properties.

1.2 Counterexamples in Analysis

The following experiment deals with the utilization of counterexamples to improve the performance of a theorem prover working in intermediate analysis. In this project the emphasis was not so much on the automatic construction of counterexamples as it was on the elimination, by means of counterexamples, of false subgoals arising in the proof of theorems.

In [6] we report on a program which proves theorems in anlaysis. Even with considerable knowledge about inequalities built into the program, many seemingly elementary theorems proved formidable. Example 7 of that paper details a particularly difficult problem, the intermediate value theorem. In this section we will discuss our choice of counterexamples used as well as the techniques developed to automatically extend these examples to include the skolem functions that the proof procedure places in the theorem. The development of techniques to generate the interpretations for these skolem functions proved quite challenging. Finally, we will discuss how these counterexamples simplified the search space.

The Intermediate Value Theorem

Let f be a continuous function on the closed interval $[a,b]$. If $f(a) \leqslant 0$ and $f(b) \geqslant 0$ then there exists an x where $f(x) = 0$. Symbolically the theorem reads

IMV $\text{Cont}[f,a,b] \wedge a \leqslant b \wedge f(a) \leqslant 0 \wedge f(b) \geqslant 0 \longrightarrow \exists x (f(x) = 0)$.

In order to prove this theorem, the prover was given four lemmas. Two of the lemmas, LUB1 and LUB2, are parts of the least upper bound axiom instantiated for this particular theorem. The other two lemmas, L1 and L2, are simple facts about continuous functions. These lemmas will be described in greater detail shortly. Partly to motivate the difficulty of this theorem, and partly to give a preview of the benefits of the use of counterexamples, we present the proof tree of the intermediate value theorem that was generated by the program.

The Proof Tree

We use here an and-or proof tree, to represent the proof of Theorem 1. Figure 2 gives an overview of the proof and Figs, 3, 4, and 5 give details of the portions α , β , and γ of Fig. 2.

In these figures the symbol X indicates branches which have been discarded (pruned) by the use of counterexamples or by the use of the higher-subgoal failure mechanism [6]. Double lines indicate successful branches.

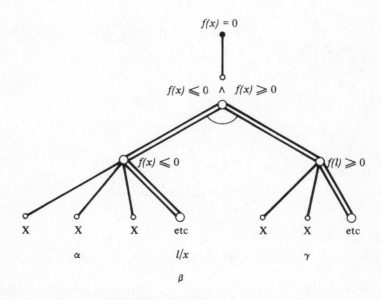

Fig. 2 – The counterexample tree for Theorem 1.

In Fig. 3 the tree is extended *below X* on some branches, in order to indicate to the reader the amount of computation saved by the use of counterexamples. The notation 'etc.' in Fig. 3 indicates places where even further calculations would be needed to fail these branches, if counterexamples were not used for that purpose.

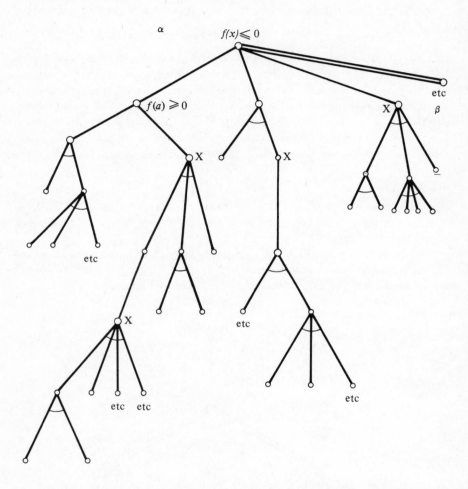

Fig. 3 – The counterexample tree, showing failure branches for the first half of the proof.

A casual look at Figs. 2 and 3 shows that large portions of the tree have been pruned away.

Before we look at some of the branches which were pruned, we need to discuss the counterexamples which were used for this purpose.

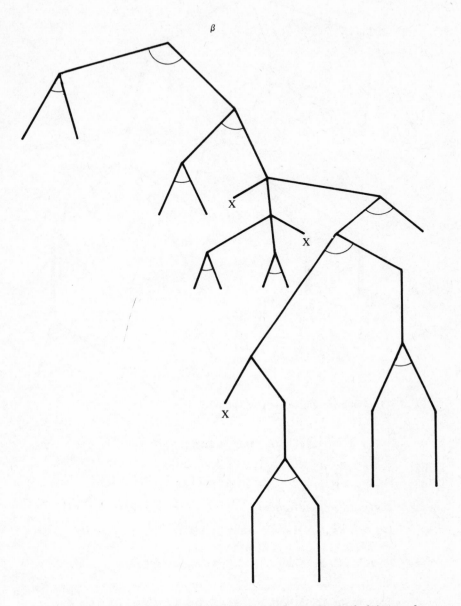

Fig. 4 – The proof tree, showing success branches for the first half of the proof.

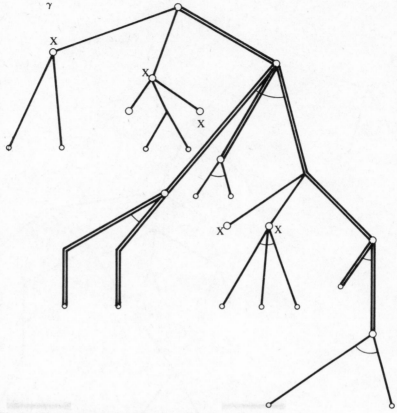

Fig. 5 – The counterexample tree (last half of the proof).

The Proof

We will describe in some detail the lemmas mentioned previously. The lemmas

LUB1: $(x \leqslant b \wedge f(x) \leqslant 0 \to x \leqslant l)$

LUB2: $((z_y \leqslant b \wedge f(z_y) \leqslant 0 \to z_y \leqslant y) \to l \leqslant y)$

are parts of the skolemized form of

LUB: $([\exists u \, \forall t(t \leqslant b \wedge f(t) \leqslant 0 \to t \leqslant u) \wedge \exists r(r \leqslant b \wedge f(r) \leqslant 0)]$
$\longrightarrow \exists l [\forall x(x \leqslant b \wedge f(x) \leqslant 0 \to x \leqslant l)$
$\wedge \forall y(\forall z(z \leqslant b \wedge f(z) \leqslant 0 \to z \leqslant y) \to l \leqslant y)])$

which is the instance of the least upper bound axiom obtained by instantiating the set variable in the axiom with the set $\{z : z \leqslant b \wedge f(z) \leqslant 0\}$. The lemmas

L1: $\forall x(a \leqslant x \leqslant b \wedge 0 < f(x) \to \exists t(t < x \wedge \forall s(t < s \leqslant x \to 0 < f(s))))$
  skolemized $(a \leqslant x \leqslant b \wedge 0 < f(x) \to t_1(x) < x \wedge (t_1(x) < s \leqslant x \to 0 < f(s)))$

L2: $\forall x(a \leqslant x \leqslant b \wedge f(x) < 0 \to \exists t(x < t \wedge \forall s(x \leqslant s < t \to f(s) < 0)))$
  skolemized $(a \leqslant x \leqslant b \wedge f(x) < 0 \to x < t_2(x) \wedge (x \leqslant s < t_2(x) \to f(s) < 0))$

20

represent the facts about the continuity of f needed for the proof. The reader should note that the constants a, b, f are the same as those in the IMV theorem.

To provide an example (counterexample) we must give an interpretation to the constants a, b, f that satisfy the hypotheses of the IMV theorem. We decided to limit all function interpretations to be linear. We chose to use two different counterexamples (henceforth referred to as CE's):

CE 1 (trivial) $a = b = 0$
$$f(x) = 0$$
CE 2 (robust) $a = 0, b = 1$
$$f(x) = 2x - 1$$

Although these counterexamples were manually presented to the computer, programs were written which, when given a set of constraints such as those appearing in the hypothesis of IMV, would generate counterexamples satisfying those constraints. The function symbols are interpreted by piecewise linear functions.

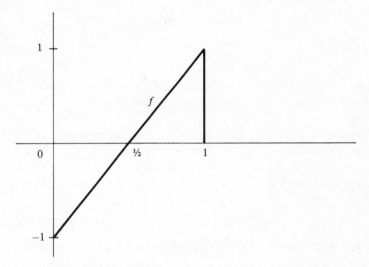

Providing values for a, b and f gives only part of a counterexample. In order to be useful, the interpretations CE1 and CE2 must be extended to include the skolem functions l, t_1, t_2 and z. The reason for this will become clear when we view the counterexamples in action. An interesting question is what values to use for these symbols. Since l is the least upper bound of the set $\{z : z \leqslant b \wedge f(z) \leqslant 0\}$, in CE 2, l would be the least upper bound of the set $\{z : z \leqslant 1 \wedge 2z - 1 \leqslant 0\}$ or, simplified, $\{z : z \leqslant \frac{1}{2}\}$. Clearly l must take on the value $\frac{1}{2}$. It was decided that the computer should be able to discover these values itself. Notice that the skolem functions in question are all derived from the lemmas that were added to the hypothesis of the theorem. Since they are lemmas, they should themselves be provable. In particular, they should be provable when instantiated with the

21

values of a, b, f given in the counterexamples. Proving the lemmas should then provide values for the skolem constants and functions.

To see this, remember that the skolem constant l arose as a result of skolemizing an expression of the form $\exists l P(l)$ in the hypothesis of the IMV theorem yielding $P(l)$ where l is a constant. If we are trying to prove $\exists l P(l)$ on the other hand, $\exists l P(l)$ is now presented as a conclusion and hence skolemized as $P(L)$ where L is a variable. Proving $P(L)$ yields a value for L which is the value given to the skolem constant l in the counterexample. We will illustrate this principle with the automatic discovery of an interpretation for l. Remember that LUB1 skolemized in the hypothesis is

LUB1 (hypothesis) $x \leqslant b \land f(x) \leqslant 0 \to x \leqslant l$.

The same LUB1 skolemized for the conclusion reads

LUB1 (conclusion) $x_L \leqslant b \land f(x_L) \leqslant 0 \to x_L \leqslant L$

Instantiating the last expression with CE 2 values for f, a and b gives

LUB1 (conclusion) $x_L \leqslant 1 \land 2x_L - 1 \leqslant 0 \to x_L \leqslant L$

which simplifies to

$$x_L \leqslant \tfrac{1}{2} \to x_L \leqslant L .$$

Solving for L yields $\tfrac{1}{2} \leqslant L$. Applying the same process to LUB2 yields the solution $L \leqslant \tfrac{1}{2}$. Combining the two values gives the final value $L = \tfrac{1}{2}$, which is what we expected.

The problem of discovering values for skolem functions of one argument or more is more involved. Again, we will illustrate this by discovering a value for the function t_1. The function t_1 arises in the lemma L1.

As before, we will prove L1 and hence must first reskolemize L1 in the conclusion position

L1 (conclusion) $a \leqslant x_0 \leqslant b \land 0 < f(x_0) \to t < x_0 \land (t < s_t \leqslant x_0 \to 0 < f(s_t))$

Instantiating L1 (conclusion) with the values for a, b, f and simplifying yields

L1 (conclusion) $\tfrac{1}{2} < x_0 \leqslant 1 \to t < x_0 \land (t < s_t \leqslant x_0 \to \tfrac{1}{2} < s_t)$

which is equivalent to

$$\tfrac{1}{2} < x_0 \leqslant 1 \to t < x_0 \land (s_t \leqslant \tfrac{1}{2} \to x_0 < s_t \lor s_t \leqslant t)$$

Solving for t yields $\tfrac{1}{2} < t < x_0$ when $x_0 > \tfrac{1}{2}$, i.e., the hypothesis holds. We translate this to the average of the interval or

$$t_1(x) = \frac{x + \tfrac{1}{2}}{2}$$

when interpreting the value of t as a value for the function t_1. When $x_0 \leqslant \tfrac{1}{2}$ any value for t will work. Experience showed that $t_1(x) = \tfrac{1}{4}$ worked well in this case (note that this is unfortunately not automatic). Considerable effort was spent in automating this step entirely. In one set of experiments, we delay interpreting t_1 until a subgoal is encountered for which the prover desires a counterexample. The subgoal is then requantified (unskolemized). The quantified subgoal is then skolemized as a conclusion and the variable that corresponds to t_1 is solved for. This particular approach does have the nice property that the prover is not forced to exclude possible values for the skolem functions early in the proof. It does have the definite disadvantage that solving for these quantities (such as t_1) involves much of the theorem proving machinery we try to avoid by using counterexamples. Note also that the process of requantifying subgoals of a theorem is not as straightforward as one might expect [4].

In a similar fashion we chose values for the remaining skolem functions. To consolidate these results we present both counterexamples.

CE 1 $a = b = l = 0$,

        $f(x) = z_x = t_1(x) = t_2(x) = 0$,   for all x ,

CE 2 $a = 0$, $b = 1$, $l = \frac{1}{2}$,

        $f(x) = 2x - 1$,   (see Fig. 6, p. 00)

$$z_x = \frac{x+1}{2} ,$$

$$t_1(x) = \begin{cases} \dfrac{x+\frac{1}{2}}{2} & \text{for } x > \frac{1}{2} \\ \frac{1}{4} & \text{for } x \leqslant \frac{1}{2} , \end{cases}$$

$$t_2(x) = \begin{cases} \dfrac{x+\frac{1}{2}}{2} & \text{for } x < \frac{1}{2} \\ \frac{3}{4} & \text{for } x \geqslant \frac{1}{2} . \end{cases}$$

We note that CE 2 tells us that whenever proving IMV, any substitution for x must evaluate to $\frac{1}{2}$ in the example, since instantiating the value of f into the conclusion yields

$2x = 1$

which, of course, simplifies to the result $x = \frac{1}{2}$. Knowing this value for x greatly limits the substitutions that need to be considered when proving IMV.

To see these CE's in action let us consider a subgoal from Fig. 3.

SG 1 $(a \leqslant b \wedge f(a) \leqslant 0 \wedge f(b) \geqslant 0 \rightarrow f(a) \geqslant 0)$.

            H

We have already remarked that both CE 1 and CE 2 satisfy H, so for this

23

example we need only check that $f(a) \geqslant 0$ is falsified. CE 2 does indeed falsify $f(a) \geqslant 0$. Using CE 2, SG 1 becomes

$$(0 \leqslant 1 \wedge -1 \leqslant 0 \wedge 1 \geqslant 0 \rightarrow -1 \geqslant 0)$$

which is false. (By the way, this subgoal SG 1 comes from trying to prove the subgoal $f(x) \leqslant 0$ by using the hypothesis $f(a) \leqslant 0$.)

Note that the validity or invalidity of the instantiated subgoals can now be declared by means of a linear arithmetic package (the SUP–INF [3] procedure in this prover). Notice that in order to use linear arithmetic, all constant and function symbols must be eliminated by instantiating with the counterexample. This is the reason why initial interpretation of f,a,b had to be extended to include the skolem constants and functions.

1.3 Subgoals Encountered

We will now list *all* subgoals encountered in a computer run which proved Theorem 1. Since the hypothesis H and the lemmas are satisfied for both counterexamples, we need only apply CE 1 and CE 2 to the conclusion of each subgoal. Accordingly, with the following examples, we will list the subgoals without showing H or the lemmas.

It can be noted that both of the CE's fail to falsify SG 6, SG 7, and SG 14. This should be the case since these are not false but are (partly) repetitions of 'higher subgoals'. In the actual proof each of these is rejected by the 'higher subgoal failure' mechanism [6].

SG 1 $f(a) \geqslant 0$

     CE 1: $0 \geqslant 0$ T

     CE 2: $-1 \geqslant 0$ F

SG 2 $(f(z_y) \geqslant 0 \wedge y < l)$

     CE 1: $(0 \geqslant 0 \wedge y < \frac{1}{2})$ F

     CE 2: $2\dfrac{y + \frac{1}{2}}{2} - 1 \geqslant 0 \wedge y < \frac{1}{2}$ F

SG 3 $[(a \leqslant x2 \leqslant b \wedge x2 \leqslant x < t_2(x2) \wedge f(x2) < 0) \wedge f(x) \geqslant 0]$

     CE 1: $[(0 \leqslant x2 \leqslant 0 \wedge x2 \leqslant 0 < 0 \wedge 0 < 0) \wedge 0 \geqslant 0]^{\dagger}$ F

     CE 2: $0 \leqslant x2 \leqslant 1 \wedge x2 \leqslant \frac{1}{2} \wedge \ x2 < \frac{1}{2} \rightarrow \frac{1}{2} < \dfrac{x2 + \frac{1}{2}}{2}$

                    $\wedge (x2 \geqslant \frac{1}{2} \rightarrow \frac{1}{2} < \frac{3}{4}) \wedge 2 \cdot x2 - 1 < 0) \wedge 0 \geqslant 0]$.

---

† The variable x from the theorem is replaced by 0 when CE 1 is used, and by $\frac{1}{2}$ when CE 2 is used. As was mentioned above, these additional instantiations for x can be inferred once the values for a, b and f have been given.

This simplifies to

$$[(0 \leqslant x2 < \tfrac{1}{2} \wedge (x2 < \tfrac{1}{2} \rightarrow \tfrac{1}{2} < x2)] \qquad\qquad\qquad\text{F}$$

SG 4 $\quad [((t_1(x) < x \rightarrow f(s) \leqslant 0 \wedge t_1(x) < s \leqslant x) \wedge a \leqslant x \leqslant b) \wedge f(x) \geqslant 0] \qquad \text{T}$
$$\text{CORRECT PATH}^{\ddagger}$$

CE 1: $\quad [((0 < 0 \rightarrow \quad \text{etc.} \qquad\qquad\qquad] \qquad\qquad\qquad\qquad \text{T}$

CE 2: $\quad [((\tfrac{1}{4} < \tfrac{1}{2} \rightarrow 2 \cdot s - 1 \leqslant 0 \wedge \tfrac{1}{4} < s \leqslant \tfrac{1}{2}) \wedge 0 \leqslant \tfrac{1}{2} \leqslant 1) \wedge 0 \geqslant 0] \qquad \text{T}$

This simplifies to

$$[\tfrac{1}{4} < s \leqslant \tfrac{1}{2}]$$

which is true (i.e., there exists an s for which $\tfrac{1}{4} < s \leqslant \tfrac{1}{2}$).

Henceforth, we will omit $a \leqslant x \leqslant b$ and $f(x) \geqslant 0$ in the subgoals because they evaluate to $0 \leqslant \tfrac{1}{2} \leqslant 1$ and $0 \geqslant 0$ which are true. We will also omit CE 1.

SG 5 $\quad [t_1(x) < x \rightarrow t_1(x) < a \leqslant x]$

CE 2 $\quad [\tfrac{1}{4} < \tfrac{1}{2} \rightarrow \tfrac{1}{4} < 0 \leqslant \tfrac{1}{2}] \qquad\qquad\qquad\qquad\qquad\qquad\qquad\qquad \text{F}$

SG 6 $\quad [t_1(x) < x \rightarrow [(t_1(s) < s \rightarrow f(s1) \leqslant 0 \wedge t_1(s) < s1 \leqslant s)$
$$\wedge a \leqslant s \leqslant b] \wedge t_1(x) < s \leqslant x]^{\dagger}$$

CE 2: $\quad$ Note $t_1(x) < x$ reduces to true, and is omitted.

$$\left(s > \tfrac{1}{2} \rightarrow \left[\left(\frac{s + \tfrac{1}{2}}{2} < s \rightarrow s1 \leqslant \tfrac{1}{2} \wedge \frac{s + \tfrac{1}{2}}{2} < s1 \leqslant s \right) \right] \right.$$

$$\wedge \, 0 \leqslant s \leqslant 1] \wedge \tfrac{1}{4} < s \leqslant \tfrac{1}{2})$$

$$\wedge \, (s \leqslant \tfrac{1}{2} \rightarrow [(\tfrac{1}{4} < s \rightarrow s1 \leqslant \tfrac{1}{2} \wedge \tfrac{1}{4} < s1 \leqslant s)$$

$$\wedge \, 0 \leqslant s \leqslant 1] \wedge \tfrac{1}{4} < s \leqslant \tfrac{1}{2})]$$

This is true, as can be seen by putting $s = s1 = \tfrac{1}{2}$.

SG 7 $\quad [t_1(x) < x \rightarrow [x2 \leqslant s < t_2(x2) \wedge a \leqslant x2 \leqslant b \wedge f(x2) < 0]$
$$\wedge \, t_1(x) < s \leqslant x]^{\ddagger}$$

CE 2: $\quad x2 \leqslant \tfrac{1}{2} \rightarrow \quad x2 \leqslant s < \dfrac{x2 + \tfrac{1}{2}}{2} \wedge 0 \leqslant x2 \leqslant 1 \wedge x2 < \tfrac{1}{2}$

$$\wedge \, \tfrac{1}{4} < s \leqslant \tfrac{1}{2}] \qquad\qquad \text{T}$$

$$\wedge \, [x2 > \tfrac{1}{2} \rightarrow [x2 \leqslant s < \tfrac{3}{4} \wedge 0 \leqslant x2 \leqslant 1 \quad x2 < \tfrac{1}{2}]$$

$$\wedge \, \tfrac{1}{4} < s \leqslant \tfrac{1}{2}]$$

---

‡ This subgoal is true, it is on a correct path of the proof, and therefore cannot be falsified.

† This subgoal is true and cannot be falsified by either CE. However, it is (partly) a copy of SG 4 and in the actual proof it is rejected by the 'higher subgoal failure' mechanism [6].

‡ This too is rejected by the 'higher subgoal failure' mechanism.

SG 8 $[((t_1(x) < x \to y < l \land t_1(x) < z_y \leqslant x) \land a \leqslant x \leqslant b) \land f(x) \geqslant 0]$
(CORRECT PATH)

    CE 2: $\frac{1}{4} < \frac{1}{2} \to y < \frac{1}{2} \land \frac{1}{4} < \dfrac{y + \frac{1}{2}}{2} \leqslant \frac{1}{2} \ \land T \ \land T$ T

           $[0 < y < \frac{1}{2}]$

SG 9 $[t_1(x) < x \to [f(z_y) > 0 \land a \leqslant z_y \leqslant b] \land z_y \leqslant x \land y < l]$

    CE 2: $\frac{1}{4} < \frac{1}{2} \to \ 2 \cdot \dfrac{y + \frac{1}{2}}{2} > 1 \land 0 \leqslant \dfrac{y + \frac{1}{2}}{2} \leqslant 1 \ \land \dfrac{y + \frac{1}{2}}{2} \leqslant \frac{1}{2} \land y < \frac{1}{2}$

           $[y > \frac{1}{2} \land -\frac{1}{2} \leqslant y \leqslant \frac{3}{2} \land y \leqslant \frac{1}{2} \land y < \frac{1}{2}]$ F

SG 10 $f(l) \geqslant 0$ (CORRECT PATH)

    CE 2: $0 \geqslant 0$ T

SG 11 $[t_1(x1) < l \leqslant x1 \land a \leqslant x1 \leqslant b \land f(x1) > 0)]$

    CE 2: $\left[\left(x1 > \frac{1}{2} \to \left[\dfrac{x1 + \frac{1}{2}}{2} < \frac{1}{2} \leqslant x1 \land 0 \leqslant x1 \leqslant 1 \land x1 > \frac{1}{2}\right]\right)\right.$

           $\land\, (x1 \leqslant \frac{1}{2} \to [\frac{1}{4} < \frac{1}{2} \leqslant x1 \land 0 \leqslant x1 \leqslant 1 \land x1 > \frac{1}{2}])]$

           $[(x1 > \frac{1}{2} \to F) \land (x1 \leqslant \frac{1}{2} \to \frac{1}{2} < x1 \leqslant 1)]$

           $[x1 \leqslant \frac{1}{2} \land (x1 \leqslant \frac{1}{2} \to \frac{1}{2} < x1 \leqslant 1)]$

           $[x1 \leqslant \frac{1}{2} \land \frac{1}{2} < x1]$ F

SG 12 $[(l < t_2(l) \to l \leqslant b < t_2(l)) \land a \leqslant l \leqslant b]$

    CE 2: $[(\frac{1}{2} < \frac{3}{4} \to \frac{1}{2} \leqslant 1 < \frac{3}{4}) \land 0 \leqslant \frac{1}{2} \leqslant 1]$ F

SG 13 $[(l < t_2(l) \to f(s) \geqslant 0 \land l \leqslant s < t_2(l)) \land a \leqslant l \leqslant b]$
(CORRECT PATH)

In the following we will omit $a \leqslant l \leqslant b$, which is true under both CE's.

    CE 2: $[(\frac{1}{2} < \frac{3}{4} \to s \geqslant \frac{1}{2} \land \frac{1}{2} \leqslant s < \frac{3}{4}) \land 0 \leqslant \frac{1}{2} \leqslant 1]$

           $[\frac{1}{2} \leqslant s < \frac{3}{4}]$ T

SG 14 $[l < t_2(l) \to [f(x1) > 0 \ t_1(x1) < s \leqslant x1 \ a \leqslant x1 \leqslant b] \ l \leqslant s < t_2(l)]$

    CE 2: $\left[\frac{1}{2} < \frac{3}{4} \to \left(x1 > \frac{1}{2} \to \left[x1 > \frac{1}{2} \land \dfrac{x1 + \frac{1}{2}}{2} < s \leqslant x1 \land 0 \leqslant x1 \leqslant 1\right]\right.\right.$
$\left. \land \frac{1}{2} \leqslant s < \frac{3}{4}\right)$

           $\land\, (x1 \leqslant \frac{1}{2} \to [x1 > \frac{1}{2} \land \frac{1}{4} < s \leqslant x1 \land 0 \leqslant x1 \leqslant 1]$
$\land \frac{1}{2} \leqslant s < \frac{3}{4})]$ T

To see that this is true, put $x1 = s = \frac{3}{4}$. It too is rejected by the 'higher subgoal failure' mechanism.

26

2. USING EXAMPLES TO GUIDE PROOF DISCOVERY

It has long been recognized that examples play a crucial role in theorem proof discovery by mathematicians. For example when presented with a new theorem a mathematician might say, "let me try a couple of examples", or "let me draw a picture to get a 'feel' for the problem".

Such examples, or models, do more than serve as counterexamples to filter out bad, or unproductive lines of attack. Such examples are often imprecisely made in the beginning, with a good deal of 'slack', so that they can be altered and fine tuned as the proof proceeds.

It is not clear to us how such 'positive' examples work. Indeed, it might be that they are only 'negative' examples which show in one presentation, many lines of attack that will *not* succeed. But in any case, it seems important to better understand the role of examples in proof discovery, and to bring that expertise to bear in automatic theorem proving (ATP).

One of the problems with using examples in ATP, is the *generation* of such examples, especially if this is to be done automatically. This is usually equivalent to proving a theorem in higher order logic. (For example if we require a continuous function f on an interval $[a,b]$ which is negative at a and positive at b, this is equivalent to proving the higher order theorem, $\exists a \, \exists b \, \exists f \, (a < b_\wedge f$ is continuous on $[a,b]_\wedge f(a) < 0_\wedge f(b) > 0))$. It would seem to be foolish to require the proof of a higher order theorem as part of the proof of a main theorem which itself is only first order. However, necessary (and useful) examples are such, that the corresponding higher order theorems are often rather simple compared to the proof of the main theorem. Thus, it would appear that a *little* work in generating examples can result in a *lot* of saving in the proof of the main theorem. Indeed, a *balance of work* seems in order whereby, about as much power is used to generate examples as used in the main proof.

With this in mind it seems appropriate for more research to be expended on the automatic generation of examples, especially examples associated with proof discovery. The work of Rissland and Soloway [10] seems to be a correct step in this direction.

Let us return to the question, voiced earlier: "how do examples help us determine successful lines of attack in proof discovery?". One answer would be that examples allow us to *conjecture* lemmas which can be proved and which, in turn, help establish the proof of the main theorem. Such conjectures are derived from patterns derived from the examples used. 'Good' examples, which somehow best model the hypotheses of the theorem, more powerfully suggest good conjectures. Lenat's work on the automatic generation of conjectures in mathematics [12] seems quite appropriate to this work.

The following describes some instances where a human prover used examples to help in the discovery of proofs.

What we give is 'protocols', descriptions of some of the thoughts that led us to choose particular examples, and how these examples affected our proof search. Four example–theorems, Th 1, Th 2, Th 3 and Th 4, are used in this presentation.

No attempt is made here to automate this process, of using examples to guide proof discovery (*not* in using counterexamples to prune the proof tree which has been partially automated). But we feel that such automation must eventually take place if we are to ever get truly effective automatic provers.

Theorem 1. (Suggested by R. Shostak). If f is a function from the non-negative integers to the non-negative integers, $f(0) = 0$, and $f(f(n)) < f(n+1)$ for each n, then f is the identity function.

Proof and Commentary

First we try a few cases to get a feel for the problem.

$$f(0) = 0 \ .$$
$$f(1) > f(f(0)) = f(0) = 0 \ , \quad f(1) \geqslant 1 \ .$$

These two results suggest that $f(n) \geqslant n$, and we should probably prove this first, but we first try $f(2)$.

$$f(2) > f(f(1)) \ ? \qquad \text{No immediate result.}$$

Let us try to prove $n \leqslant f(n)$ by induction. Let k be the first integer for which $f(k) < k$. Then

$$f(f(k-1)) < f(k) < k \ .$$

$$k-1 \qquad k$$

No luck. But the picture suggests that we should centre our attention on the k for which $f(k)$ is *smallest* (and for which $f(k) < k$). That is let $E = \{n: f(n) < n\}$, $L = \inf_{n \in E} f(n)$, and let k be such that $f(k) = L$. Thus

(1) $n \leqslant k \rightarrow f(n) \geqslant n$ or $f(n) \geqslant L$.

Then $f(f(k-1)) < f(k) = L$.

Case 1. $f(k-1) < L$.

Contradiction of (1), because $L \leqslant k-1$.

Case 2. $f(k-1) \geqslant L$.

Since $f(f(k-1)) < L$, this is a contradiction of (1), (with $f(k-1)$ for n). Thus

(2) $n \leqslant f(n)$ for all n.

We now try to prove $f(n) \leqslant n$. But first try to make an example where $f(n) > n$ for some n.

n	0	1
$f(n)$	0	2

$f(2) < f(f(1)) = f(2)$, contradiction.

n	0	1	2
$f(n)$	0	1	3

$f(3) < f(f(2)) = f(3)$, contradiction.

n	0	1
$f(n)$	0	3

$f(2) < f(f(1)) = f(3)$, no information.

But note that $2 \leqslant f(1)$, and hence if we had monotonicity, $(n \leqslant m \rightarrow f(n) \leqslant f(m))$, then we would have $f(2) \leqslant f(f(1)) < f(2)$, contradiction. So let us digress to prove monotonicity: $f(n) \leqslant f(n+1)$.

Let k be a value for which $f(k+1) < f(k)$. Then, using (2),

$$f(f(k)) < f(k+1) < f(k) \leqslant f(f(k)) .$$

Contradiction. Thus

(3) $(n \leqslant m \rightarrow f(n) \leqslant f(m)) .$

Now we can finish the proof of $f(n) \leqslant n$. Let k be a value for which $k < f(k)$. Then $k+1 \leqslant f(k)$, and by (3),

$$f(k+1) \leqslant f(f(k)) < f(k+1) ,$$

contradiction. Therefore,

(4) $f(n) \leqslant n$ for all n ,

and hence $f(n) = n$ for all n, by (2) and (4).

Theorem 2. (Suggested by D. Chester). Let f be a real valued function on $[a,b]$ with the property that for each closed subinterval $[x,y]$ of $[a,b]$, if g is the restriction of f to $[x,y]$, then

    (i) g is bounded,
    (ii) g attains its maximum and minimum on $[x,y]$
    (iii) g attains every intermediate value between $g(x)$ and $g(y)$,
    (iv) for any z in Range (g), the set $f^{-1}(z) = \{x : g(x) = z\}$ contains both its lub and glb.

Then f is continuous on $[a,b]$.

Proof and Commentary

This is a good example because: (1) it is new, most people haven't seen it before; (2) it is not trivial, but it can be proved by good mathematicians in an hour or less.

Conditions (iii) and (iv) are unusual and appear to pack the weight of the proof. For this reason we decided to try for an indirect proof wherein we negate the conclusion and show that one of the hypotheses fails.

So we assume that f is discontinuous at some point x_0 in $[a,b]$. There are basically two types of discontinuities: those where the function jumps and those like

$$f(x) = \begin{cases} \sin \dfrac{1}{x} & \text{for } x \neq 0 \\ 0 & \text{for } x = 0 , \end{cases}$$

where $\lim_{x \to x_0} f(x)$ does not exist. We try the first (simpler) case first.

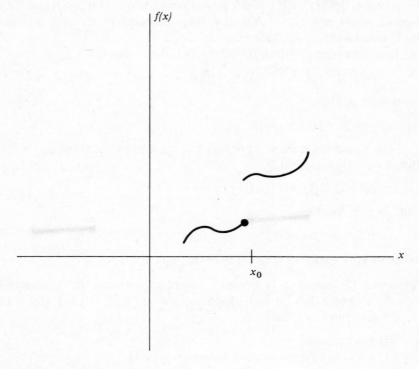

Fig. 6

This seems, from the picture, to 'leave a hole' in the range of f, that is, to fail condition (iii). This example has not given much help in our search for a proof, so we consider the second kind of discontinuity, and rely on 'the old standby'

$$f(x) = \begin{cases} \sin \dfrac{1}{x} & \text{for } x \neq 0 \\ 0 & \text{for } x = 0 . \end{cases}$$

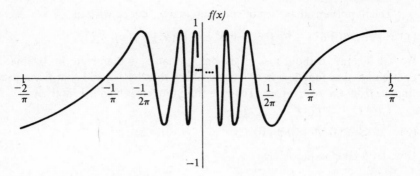

Fig. 7

This turns out to be an excellent choice because we see that f satisfies conditions (i)–(iii), but fails on (iv). It fails on (iv) because for the subinterval $[0, 1]$, and $z = 1$, we have that

$$f^{-1}(z) = \frac{2}{\pi}, \frac{2}{5\pi}, \frac{2}{9\pi}, \ldots \ .$$

That is $f(x) = 1$ for $x = \dfrac{1}{(\pi/2) + 2\pi n}$, $n = 0, 1, 2, \ldots$.

So $\inf f^{-1}(z) = 0$, but $0 \notin f^{-1}(z)$

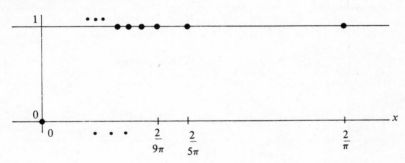

Fig. 8

We wonder at this point whether we could use this example as a guide to produce a proof of the theorem itself, that is that

(i) $_\triangle$ (ii) $_\triangle$ (iii) $_\triangle$ f is not continuous $\rightarrow \sim$(iv).

What is needed is to produce a sequence $x_1, x_2, \ldots$, like the $\dfrac{2}{\pi}, \dfrac{2}{5\pi}, \dfrac{2}{9\pi}, \ldots$ in Fig. 8, for which

$$f(x_n) = f(x_{n+1}) \neq f(x_0) \quad \text{for } n = 1, 2, 3, \ldots,$$
$$\lim_{n \to \infty} x_n = x_0.$$

31

The hypothesis that f is not continuous at x_0 can be written

(1) $\sim [\forall \epsilon > 0 \exists \delta > 0 \; \forall y \; (|x_0 - y| < \delta \to |f(x_0) - f(y)| < \epsilon)]$

We will assume, without loss of generality, that $x_0 = 0$ and $f(x_0) = 0$ (since the continuity of a function is not changed by shifting it), and that f is not continuous *from the right*, at x_0. (The case from the left is handled similarly).

Thus (1) becomes

(2) $\qquad \exists \epsilon > 0 \; \forall \delta > 0 \exists y (0 < y < \delta_\triangle \; |f(y)| \geqslant \epsilon)$.

If we let δ take on the values

$$1, \frac{1}{2}, \frac{1}{3}, \ldots, \frac{1}{n}, \ldots$$

then (2) gives a sequence

$$y_1, y_2, y_3, \ldots$$

of y values for which

$$0 < y_n < \frac{1}{n} \quad \text{and} \quad (f(y_n) \geqslant \epsilon \; \text{or} \; f(y_n) \leqslant -\epsilon).$$

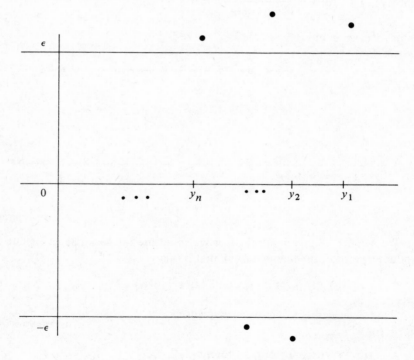

Fig. 9

32

For each n, we now use (iii) to obtain a point x_n for which

$$0 < x_n \leqslant y_n, \quad (f(x_n) = \epsilon \quad \text{or} \quad f(x_n) = -\epsilon).$$

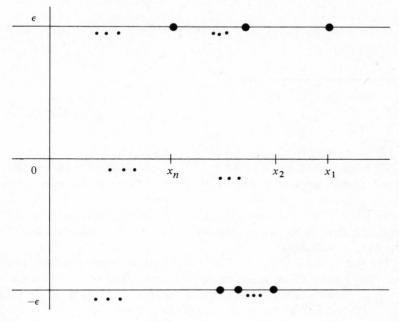

Fig. 10

And since there are infinitely many of the points $(x_n, f(x_n))$, then either $0 = \inf f^{-1}(\epsilon)$ or $0 = \inf f^{-1}(-\epsilon)$. But $0 \notin f^{-1}(\epsilon)$, $0 \notin f^{-1}(-\epsilon)$, in contradiction of (iv), and the proof is complete.

The similarity between Fig. 8 from the example, and Fig. 10 from the general proof is striking. And it is quite clear that the example chosen has led us directly to the proof in the general case.

Theorem 3. If f is monotone and differentiable on $[a,b]$, then f' is continuous on $[a,b]$.

Proof and Commentary

Without loss of generality we assume that f is non-decreasing. (Being monotone is either non-decreasing or non-increasing.)

Our first impulse is to draw a 'picture', one in which the hypotheses hold but f' is *not* continuous. (We reason that trying to draw such a picture will help to see why it cannot be done.)

If f' is to be discontinuous at a point x_0 in $[a,b]$, then we first try to draw it so that f' has a *jump* at x_0

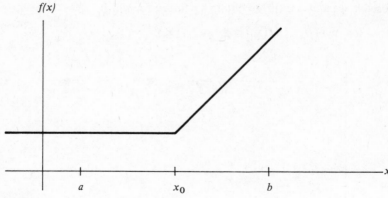

Fig. 11

We might as well let $f'(x) = 0$ for $x \leqslant x_0$, and $f'(x) = 1$ for $x > x_0$. But for this, $f'(x_0)$ does not seem to exist. Let's check that: yes, for this example $f'(x_0)$ does not exist.

So this example did not refute Theorem 3. It, in fact, seems to support Theorem 3, because we see no easy way to draw a function for which $f'(x_0)$ exists and f' has a jump at x_0.

The next thought we have is that f' can be discontinuous for another reason, other than a jump (because we are reminded that $f(x) = \sin(1/x)$ has a non-removable discontinuity at $x = 0$ but no jump there). So maybe we can define f in the spirit of $\sin(1/x)$, so that it is monotone, differentiable, but f' is not continuous at $x = 0$.

We also recall here that

$$f(x) = \begin{cases} x^2 \sin \dfrac{1}{x}, & x \neq 0 \\ 0 & x = 0 \end{cases}$$

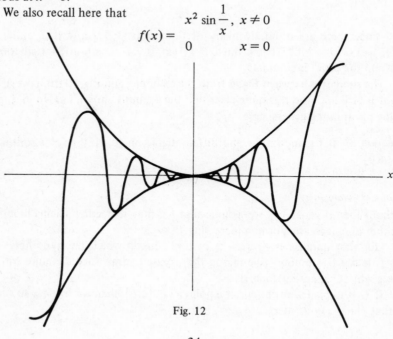

Fig. 12

is differentiable at $x = 0$, with $f'(0) = 0$. This comes to mind because of the need for f to be differentiable. But, alas, it is not monotone. Can we tilt a little so it becomes monotone and retains differentiability?

How about adding x?

$$f(x) = x + x^2 \sin \frac{1}{x}, \text{ and } f(0) = 0)$$

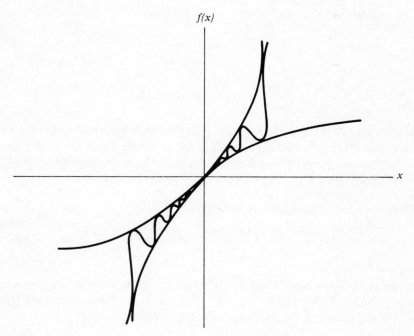

Fig. 13

Let's check this:

$$f'(x) = \begin{cases} 1 + 2x \sin \frac{1}{x} - \cos \frac{1}{x}, & \text{for } x \neq 0 \\ 1 & \text{for } x = 0. \end{cases}$$

But f is not monotone because

$$f'\left[\frac{1}{7\pi}\right] = 1 - 2 = -1 < 0.$$

Maybe we can make it steeper. Let

$$f(x) = \begin{cases} 2x + x^2 \sin \frac{1}{x}, & \text{for } x \neq 0 \\ 0 & \text{for } x = 0. \end{cases}$$

35

Then

$$f'(x) = \begin{cases} 2 + 2x \sin\dfrac{1}{x} - \cos\dfrac{1}{x}, & \text{for } x \neq 0 \\ 2 & \text{for } x = 0 . \end{cases}$$

Check that $f'(x)$ is always non-negative (at least near $x = 0$). In fact, for $0 < x \leqslant \frac{1}{2}$, we have

$$f'(x) = 2 + 2x \sin\frac{1}{x} - \cos\frac{1}{x}$$

$$\geqslant 1 + 2x \sin\frac{1}{x}$$

$$\geqslant 1 + 2x(-1)$$

$$= 1 - 2x \geqslant 0 .$$

Similarly $f'(x) \geqslant 0$ for $x \in [-\frac{1}{2}, \frac{1}{2}]$, and hence f is monotone in $[-\frac{1}{2}, \frac{1}{2}]$.

Hence, Theorem 3 is false; our attempt to prove it has led to the above counterexample. Notice how the analysis of the well known example, $x^2 \sin(1/x)$ let us straightforwardly to the eventual counterexample.

Theorem 4. Let f be continuous on R. If

$$\forall x \in [0, 1] \lim_{n \to \infty} f(nx) = 0, \text{ then } \lim_{x \to \infty} f(x) = 0 .$$

Proof and Commentary

The proof does not come immediately, so we decide to see what happens when the continuity hypothesis is omitted. Thus we try to build a function (non-continuous) for which the statement fails. Let us make f so that

$$\forall x \in [0, 1] \lim_{n \to \infty} f(nx) = 0 ,$$

but

$$\forall x \in R \quad y > x \ (f(x) = 1) .$$

That would be easy if we had a sequence $x_1, x_2, x_3, \ldots$ of $x_n \in [0, 1]$ for which

$$nx_i \neq mx_j$$

for all $n, m, i, j, i > 0, j > 0$, because then we could define

$$f(x) = \begin{cases} 1 & \text{for } x = nx_i, n \leqslant i \\ 0 & \text{otherwise .} \end{cases}$$

It would then follow that

(1) $$\lim_{n \to \infty} f(nx) = 0 ,$$

but

(2) $$\lim_{x \to \infty} \sup f(nx) = 1 .$$

The function f is well defined because x cannot be nx_i and mx_j at the same time, for $i > 0, j > 0$. So it remains to show that such a sequence $x_1, x_2, x_3, \ldots$ exists. And this is the case using a Hamel basis.[†]

Now that we have this example, how does it help us to prove the theorem when we restore the continuity of f?

Let us see whether we can alter this example in such a way that it becomes continuous, but retains properties (1) and (2) (and hence the theorem would be false).

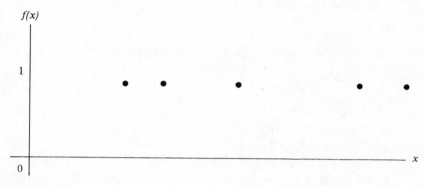

Fig. 14

maybe we can 'smooth it out'.

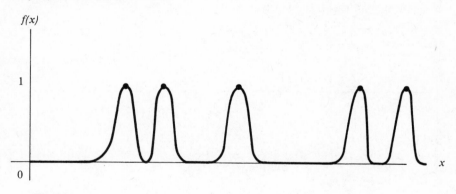

Fig. 15

But this seems impossible, because if $f(x) = 1$, then for some i and some $n \leqslant i$,

$$x = nx_i .$$

And, in any neighbourhood $(x - \delta, x + \delta)$ of x, there are points z for which $f(z) = 0$. To see this, we need only consider the interval $(x_i - \delta/n, x_i + \delta/n)$ about x_i.

† The reals can be partitioned into an infinite number of subsets such that no member of one is a rational multiple of any member of another [13].

37

So, we cannot alter f in this way and apparently the theorem is true. Let us prove it, using this example as a guide.

We will show that: if f is continuous and

(3) $\lim\limits_{x \to \infty} \sup f(x) > \epsilon > 0$,

then

(4) $\exists x \in [0,1]\ \forall N \in w\ \exists n \geq N(f(nx) \geq \epsilon)$.

To do this we will define a sequence

$C_0, C_1, C_2, \ldots$

of closed intervals, with $C_N = [a_N, b_N]$, and an increasing sequence

$k_0, k_1, k_2, \ldots$

of integers, for which

$C_{N+1} \subseteq C_N$,   and $f(k_N x) \geq \epsilon$

for all N, and for all $x \in C_N$.

Let $C_o = [0,1]$, $K_o = 1$. For each $N \geq 1$ use (3) to select $x_{N+1} \in R$ for which $x_{N+1} > x_N + 1$ and $f(x_{N+1}) > \epsilon$, and use the continuity of f to select $\delta > 0$ such that

$f(z) \geq \epsilon$ for $z \in (x_{N+1} - \delta, x_{N+1} + \delta)$.

Now select an integer k for which

$ka_N \leq x_{N+1} - \delta, kb_N > x_{N+1} - \delta$

and let

$$a' = \frac{x_{N+1} - \delta}{k},\ b' = \min\left(b_N, \frac{x_{N+1} + \delta}{k}\right)$$

$$a_{N+1} = a' + \frac{b' - a'}{3},\ b_{N+1} = b' - \frac{b' - a'}{3},$$

$$C_{N+1} = [a_{N+1}, b_{N+1}],\ k_{N+1} = k.$$

The fact that $K_{N+1} > K_N$ follows from the fact that $x_{N+1} > x_N + 1$ and $C_N \subseteq [0,1]$.

Thus $C_{N+1} \subseteq C_N$, for each N, and for each $y \in C_N, k_N y \in (x_{N+1} - \delta, x_{N+1} + \delta)$, and hence

$f(K_N y) \geq \epsilon$.

Since the intervals, C_N, are closed, bounded, and nested, they have a point x_o in common, for which

$$f(K_N x_o) \geqslant \epsilon$$

for each N. Therefore (4) holds and the proof is finished.

It should be noted that the selection of the points x_N and the open intervals $(x_N - \delta, x_N + \delta)$ for which $f(z) \geqslant \epsilon$ for $z \in (x_N - \delta, x_N + \delta)$, was motivated by the example wherein we were unable to ensure

$$f(z) \geqslant 1$$

near the points nx_i.

It should also be noted that examples played roles in other ways in the proof. For example in determining exactly how to define the numbers a', b', a_N, b_N, we used examples (not shown here) to experiment until the right choice was made. We feel that such low level experimentation is used many times within a proof.

REFERENCES

[1] Ballantyne, A. N., Bennett, M., & Bennett, W. (1973). Graphing methods for topological proofs. *Dept. Memo ATP 7*, Austin: Department of Mathematics, University of Texas at Austin.

[2] Bledsoe, W. W. (1973). Discussions on theorem proving. Univ. of Texas, Math. Dept. *Memo ATP 10*, Austin: Department of Mathematics, University of Texas at Austin.

[3] Bledsoe, W. W. (1974). The Sup-Inf Method in Presburger Arithmetic, *Dept. Memo ATP 18*, Department of Mathematics, University of Texas at Austin.

[4] Bledsoe, W. W., & Ballantyne, M. (1978). Unskolemizing, *Dept. Memo ATP-41A*, Austin: Department of Mathematics, University of Texas at Austin.

[5] Bledsoe, W. W., & Bruell, P. (1974). A man-machine theorem proving system. *Art. Int.*, 5, 51–72.

[6] Bledsoe, W. W., Bruell, P., & Shostak, R. (1978). A prover for general inequalities, *Dept. Memo ATP-40*, Austin: Department of Mathematics, University of Texas at Austin.

[7] Gelernter, H. (1959). Realization of a geometry theorem-proving machine, *Proc. Int. Conf. Information Processing*, Paris UNESCO House, 273–282.

[8] Huet, Gerard, (1972). Constrained resolution, a complete method for higher order logic, PhD. Thesis, *Report 1117*, Cleveland: Jennings Computing Center, Case Western Reserve University.

[9] Minor, J. T. (1979). Proving a subset of second-order logic with proof procedures. PhD Thesis, Austin: Department of Computer Science, University of Texas, Austin.

[10] Rissland, E., & Soloway, E. (1980). Generating examples in LISP: data and programs, *COINS Technical Report 80-07*, Amherst: Department of Computer and Information Science; University of Massachusetts at Amherst.

[11] Siklossy, L. & Roach, J. (1973). Proving the impossible is impossible: disproofs based on hereditary partitions. *IJCAI-73*, (Stanford), 383–387, Menlo Park: Stanford Research Institute.

[12] Lenat, D. B. (1977). The uniquity of discovery. *Art. Int.*, 9, 17–18.

[13] Hewitt, E., & Stromberg, K. (1965). *Real and Abstract Analysis*, New York: Springer-Verlag.

2

A first-order formalisation of knowledge and action and action for a multi-agent planning system

K. Konolige

Artificial Intelligence Center
SRI International, USA

1. INTRODUCTION

We are interested in constructing a computer agent whose behaviour will be intelligent enough to perform cooperative tasks involving other agents like itself. The construction of such agents has been a major goal of artificial intelligence research. One of the key tasks such an agent must perform is to form plans to carry out its intentions in a complex world in which other planning agents also exist. To construct such agents, it will be necessary to address a number of issues that concern the interaction of knowledge, actions, and planning. Briefly stated, an agent at planning time must take into account what his future states of knowledge will be if he is to form plans that he can execute; and if he must incorporate the plans of other agents into his own, then he must also be able to reason about the knowledge and plans of other agents in an appropriate way. These ideas have been explored by several researchers, especially McCarthy & Hayes (McCarthy & Hayes 1969) and Moore (Moore 1980).

Despite the importance of this problem, there has not been a great deal of work in the area of formalizing a solution. Formalisms for both action and knowledge separately have been examined in some depth, but there have been few attempts at a synthesis. The exception to this is Moore's thesis on reasoning about knowledge and action (Moore 1980), for which a planner has been recently proposed (Appelt 1980). Moore shows how a formalism based on possible-world semantics can be used to reason about the interaction of knowledge and action. In this paper we develop an alternative formalism for reasoning about knowledge, belief, and action; we show how this formalism can be used to deal with several well-known problems, and then describe how it could be used by a plan constructing system.

1.1 Overview and Related Work

We seek a formalization of knowing and acting such that a description of their interaction satisfies our intuitions. In the first section, we present a basic formalism for describing an agent's static beliefs about the world. We take a *syntactic* approach here: an agent's beliefs are identified with formulas in a first-order language, called the *object language* (OL). Propositional attitudes such as knowing and wanting are modelled as a relation between an agent and a formula in the OL. By introducing a language (the *metalanguage*, or ML) whole prime object of study is the OL, we are able to describe an agent's beliefs as a set of formulas in the OL, and express partial knowledge of that theory. An agent's reasoning process can be modelled as an inference procedure in the OL: from a base set of facts and rules about the world, he drives a full set of beliefs, called his *theory of the world.*

The syntactic approach to representing propositional attitudes is well-known in the philosophy literature, and in the artificial intelligence field McCarthy (McCarthy 1979) has developed a closely related approach. The formalism developed here differs mainly in that it explicitly identifies propositional attitudes as relations on sentences in an object language, and uses provability in the OL as the model of an agent's reasoning process. We are able to present quite complex deductions involving the beliefs of agents (see the *Wise Man Puzzle* in Appendix A, for example) by exploiting the technique of **semantic attachment** to model directly an agent's reasoning process. We are indebted to Weyhrauch (Weyhrauch 1980) for an introduction to this technique, and for the general idea of using ML/OL structures to represent agents.

Finally, our work differs from McCarthy's in its careful axiomatization of the relation between ML and OL, and incorporates solutions to several technical problems, including reasoning about *belief-nesting* (beliefs about beliefs; Creary (Creary 1979) has also described a solution, and a cleaner approach to representing quantified OL expressions in the ML. (This latter subject is not directly relevant to this paper, and will be reported in (Konolige 1981).)

An alternative to the syntactic approach to representing propositional attitudes is the *possible-world* approach, so called because it utilizes Kripke-type possible-world semantics for a modal logic of knowledge and belief. Moore (Moore 1980) has shown how to reason efficiently about propositional attitudes by using a first-order axiomatization of the possible-world semantics for a modal logic. Our objections to the possible-world approach are twofold: first, the possible-world semantics for representing propositional attitudes is complex and at times unintuitive; to deduce facts about an agent's knowledge, one must talk about the possible-worlds that are compatible with what the agent knows. Ultimately, we suspect that the syntactic approach will prove to be a simpler system in which to perform automatic deduction, but further research in both areas is needed to decide this issue. A second objection is that it seems to be difficult to modify possible-world semantics for the modal logic to model adequately inference processes other than logical deduction. The possible-world approach uses the modal axiom that every agent knows the consequences of his knowledge, and this is obviously not true, if only because real agents have resource limitations on their reasoning processes. The syntactic approach does not suffer from this criticism, because it is possible to describe explicitly in the ML the inference procedure an agent might use.

The second part of this paper integrates the syntactic approach to representing knowledge and belief with a *situation calculus* description of actions (McCarthy & Hayes 1969). We concentrate on many of the interactions between knowledge and action presented in Moore's thesis (Moore 1980). Simply stated, Moore's account is that an agent's beliefs in any situation arise from at least three sources: direct observation of the world, persistence of beliefs about previous situations, and beliefs about what events led to the current situation. By formalizing this assumption, he shows how to model in an intuitively plausible way the knowledge an agent needs to perform actions, and the knowledge that he gains in performing them. Although we subscribe to his notions on how knowledge and action should interact, for the reasons stated above we feel that the possible-world approach Moore uses to formalize these ideas, while elegant, may not have the same intuitive appeal as the syntactic approach.

The main contribution of this paper is to show that the syntactic approach, when integrated with a situation calculus description of actions, can adequately formalize Moore's criteria for the interaction of knowledge and belief. An important benchmark is to formalize the idea of a test: an agent can perform an action and observe the result to figure out the state of some unobservable property of the world. We conclude the second section with just such an example.

In the third section we consider the application of these results to a planning system, in particular one that would require an agent to take account of other agents' plans in forming his own. We come to the conclusion that such a planning system may not be significantly different from current situation calculus planners in its method of search, but does require considerably more sophistication in the deductions it performs at each node in that search.

2. AGENTS' BELIEFS AND FIRST-ORDER THEORIES

In this section we lay the basic groundwork for our syntactic approach to representing and reasoning about agents' beliefs. We will model an agent's beliefs about the world as a set of statements (or *theory*) in some first-order language with equality. This is not to say that an agent actually represents the world as a set of first-order statements; we are not concerned here with the details of the internal representation of a computer or human agent with respect to its environment. All we seek is a way of modelling the beliefs of an agent in a manner that will make reasonable predictions about the agent's behaviour, and still be formally tractable. To this end we assume that we can represent an agent's beliefs about the world as a set of statements in a first-order language, and model the derivation of new beliefs by an agent as an inference process in those statements.

Consider an example from the blocks-world domain; let A_0 be the name of an agent. A_0 will have some set of beliefs about the state of the blocks-world. We represent A_0's beliefs as a list of well-formed formulas (wffs) in a first-order

43

language with equality. We call this list of wffs A_0's *theory of the world*. For example, suppose A_0 believes that block B is on block C, and that he is holding block D. Then we would have:

>A_0's Theory of the Blocks-World
>$ON(B,C)$
>$HOLDING(A_0,D)$

where ON and $HOLDING$ have the appropriate interpretations.

Besides specific facts about the state of the world, A_0 also has some general rules about the way the world is put together. For instance, A_0 may know the rule that if any block x is on any block y, then the top of y is not clear. Using this rule together with specific beliefs about the world, he may be able to deduce that C is not clear. This can be modelled as a process of extending A_0's initial set of beliefs about the world to include the deduced information:

>A_0's Facts and Rules about the World $\Rightarrow$ A_0's Theory of the World
>$ON(B,C)$ $\qquad\qquad\qquad\qquad\qquad\quad$ $ON(B,C)$
>$HOLDING(A_0,D)$ $\qquad\qquad\qquad\quad$ $HOLDING(A_0,D)$
>$\forall xy\, ON(x,y) \supset {\sim} CLEAR(y)$ $\qquad$ $\forall xy\, ON(x,y) \supset {\sim} CLEAR(y)$
>$\qquad\qquad\qquad\qquad\qquad\qquad\qquad$ ${\sim} CLEAR(C)$
>$\qquad\qquad\qquad\qquad\qquad\qquad\qquad$ . . .

Thus an agent's theory of the world will be the closure of a set of facts and rules about the world, under some suitably defined inference procedure. We will call the set of basic facts and rules from which all other beliefs are derived the *base set* of the theory. Note that the inference procedure that derives the consequences of the base set need not be logical deduction; it is readily demonstrated that people do not know all the consequences of their beliefs, that they derive contradictory consequences, etc. We recognize that the problem of deriving the consequences of beliefs for more realistic inference procedures is a thorny and unsolved one, and do not intend to pursue it here. For the purposes of this paper we have chosen logical deduction as the inferential procedure: an agent will be able to deduce the logical consequences of his beliefs.

2.1 Metalanguage and Object Language

If we were always to have complete knowledge of an agent's beliefs, then it would be possible to use a simple list of facts and rules to represent the base set of those beliefs. However, it is often the case that our knowledge is incomplete; we may know that an agent either believes fact P or fact Q, but we don't know which. Such a description of an agent's beliefs cannot be modelled by a list of facts. So the modelling process must be extended to a *description* of an agent's beliefs. Since beliefs are wffs in a first-order language, a *metalanguage* can be used to describe a collection of such wffs (Kleene 1967). The basic idea is to have terms in the metalanguage to denote syntactic expressions in the first-order language used to encode an agent's beliefs. The latter first-order language is called the *object language*, or OL, since it is the object of study of the metalanguage (ML). Predicates in the metalanguage are used to state that an expression of the object language is in an agent's theory of the world. The full expressive power of the metalanguage is available for describing a given theory of the object language.

It is natural to choose a first-order language for the metalanguage, since we will be interested in proof procedures in the ML as well as the OL. Let ML be a sorted, first-order language with variables restricted to range over particular sorts. The domain of discourse of the ML will be both the syntactic expressions of the OL, as well as the domain of discourse of the OL. Thus the ML will be able to state relationships that hold between OL expressions and the actual state of the world.

A basic division of sorts of the ML is between terms that denote individuals in the world, and terms that denote expressions in the OL. Among the former will be terms that denote agents (A_0, A_1, . . .) and agents' theories of the world; all these will be called T_I terms. We will use the function *th* of one argument, an agent, to denote that agent's theory of the world.

The other major sort of terms will denote *formulas* of the OL; these will be referred to as T_F terms. Restricting our attention for the moment to sentential formulas of OL, there will be terms in ML that denote propositional letters in OL, and constructors in ML for putting together more complicated formulas from these letters. For example, P' in ML denotes the propositional letter P of the OL,[†] and the ML term $and(P',Q')$ denotes the sentence $P \wedge Q$ of the OL. These ML constructors from an *abstract syntax* (McCarthy 1962) for OL expressions.

Writing names of formulas using *and*, *or*, *not*, and *imp* as constructors is somewhat cumbersome. For the most part we will use a syntactic abbreviation, enclosing an OL formula in **sense quotes**,[‡] to indicate that the standard ML term for that formula in intended. For example, we will write:

$$\ulcorner P \wedge Q \urcorner \quad \text{for} \quad and(P',Q')$$
$$\ulcorner P \supset (Q \vee R) \urcorner \quad \text{for} \quad imp(P',or(Q',R'))$$
and so on.

The rule for translating sense-quote abbreviations into T_F terms of the ML is to replace each predicate symbol P of the sense-quote expression by the ML term symbol P', and each Boolean connective by the corresponding ML Boolean constructor. As more sorts are introduced into the ML we will extend the sense-quote convention in various ways.

Finally, we introduce the ML predicates *TRUE*, *FACT*, and *PR*, each of which has an OL formula as one of its arguments. *TRUE*(f), where f is an OL formula, means that f is actually true in the world under consideration. It is often

---

[†] The general convention will be to use primed terms in ML to denote the corresponding unprimed formulas in OL.

[‡] They are called sense-quotes to indicate that the sense of the expression is wanted, rather than its truth-value. In (Kaplan 1971) these are called **Frege quotes**.

45

the case that we will want to describe a certain condition actually holding in the world, independent of whether some agent believes it or not; for instance, this is critical to our reasoning about events in the next section, where events are defined as transformations from one state of the world to another.

We intend *TRUE* to have the normal Tarskian definition of truth, so that the truth-recursion axioms are valid. Let the variables f and g range over OL expressions. Then we can write the metalanguage axioms for truth-recursion in the object language as follows:

$$\forall f \sim TRUE(f) \equiv TRUE(not(f))$$
$$\forall fg \, TRUE(f) \vee TRUE(g) \equiv TRUE(or(f,g))$$
$$\forall fg \, TRUE(f) \wedge TRUE(g) \equiv TRUE(and(f,g)) \qquad (TR)$$
$$\forall fg \, TRUE(f) \supset TRUE(g) \equiv TRUE(imp(f,g)).$$

$FACT(t,f)$, where t is an OL theory, means that f is one of the base set formulas of the theory (from which the rest of the theory will be derived by deduction). Using *FACT*, agent A_0's previously exhibited beliefs about the world could be described by the following ML predicates:

$$FACT(th(A_0), \ulcorner ON(B,C) \urcorner)$$
$$FACT(th(A_0), \ulcorner HOLDING(A_0,D) \urcorner)$$
$$FACT(th(A_0), \ulcorner \forall xy \, ON(x,y) \supset \sim CLEAR(y) \urcorner).$$

The last *FACT* predicate describes a rule that agent A_0 believes.

One special type of *FACT* that we will make frequent use of is a formula known to all agents. We define the predicate *CFACT* on OL expressions to mean that a true expression is a *FACT* for all agents, that is, a *Common FACT*:

$$\forall f \, CFACT(f) \supset \forall a \, FACT(th(a), f) \wedge TRUE(f). \qquad (CF1)$$

CF1 doesn't completely axiomatize what we intend a common fact to be, however, since it doesn't say that every agent knows that every agent knows that every agent knows f, etc. But a fuller characterization of *CFACT* must wait until the technical machinery for describing belief-nesting is developed in a later subsection.

$PR(t,f)$ means that f is provable in the theory t. As discussed previously, we will assume that *PR* gives the closure of sentences in OL that can be generated by logical deduction from an original set of *FACT*s. A simple axiomatization of *PR* can can be given for Hilbert-style (assumption-free) proofs. There is only one rule of inference, *Modus Ponens*:

$$\forall tfg \, PR(t, imp(f,g)) \wedge PR(t,f) \supset PR(t,g) \qquad (MP)$$

that is, from $P \supset Q$ and P in the OL, infer Q. Since every *FACT* is an initial theorem of the theory, we assert that each of these is provable:

$$\forall tf \, FACT(t,f) \supset PR(t,f). \qquad (FP)$$

And in each theory the logical axioms of a Hilbert system need to be asserted; we assume a sufficient set for the sentential case.

MP and the Hilbert axioms will be used in ML proofs of the provability of OL statements; these axioms simulate a Hilbert-type proof system for an OL theory. This simulation is necessary because in general there will be an incomplete ML description of the OL theory, rather than a simple list of *FACT*s for that theory. In those special cases when a list of *FACT*s is available, it is possible to run the proof procedure on the OL theory directly. That is, since the intended meaning of the *PR* predicate is provability in the OL theory, we can check whether the *PR* predicate holds in the ML by running a theorem-prover in the OL. It also isn't necessary to use a Hilbert system, and we will feel free to exploit any system of natural deduction that is sound. The technique of using a computable model of the intended interpretation of a predicate to determine the truth of formulas involving the predicate is called *semantic attachment* (Weyhrauch 1980), and it will be used extensively to simplify proofs in later sections.

The provability predicate *PR* does not have the same characteristics as *TRUE*, and this is important in representing beliefs. For example, the fact that P is not provable doesn't imply that $\sim P$ is provable. If we identify provability with belief, $\sim PR(th(A_0), \ulcorner P \urcorner)$ asserts that P is not one of A_0's beliefs about the word, but this does not imply $PR(th(A_0), \ulcorner \sim P \urcorner)$, i.e., that A_0 believes $\sim P$. Also, it is possible to express that either A_0 believes that C is clear, or he believes that C is not clear:

$$PR(th(A_0), \ulcorner CLEAR(C) \urcorner) \lor PR(th(A_0), \ulcorner \sim CLEAR(C) \urcorner) \ ;$$

this says something quite different from $PR(th(A_0), \ulcorner CLEAR(C) \lor \sim CLEAR(C) \urcorner)$; the latter is a tautology that every agent believes, while the former says something a lot stronger about A_0's beliefs about the world.

Parallelling the truth recursion axioms *TR*, we can state rules for the provability of compound OL expressions in terms of their immediate subexpressions. Because of the nature of provability, the axioms for negation, disjunction, and implication, unlike their truth-theoretic counterparts, are not equivalences.

$$\begin{aligned}
\forall tsf \sim PR(t,f) &\subset PR(t, not(f)) \\
\forall tsfg [PR(t,f) \lor PR(t,g)] &\supset PR(t, or(f,g)) \\
\forall tsfg [PR(t,f) \land PR(t,g)] &\equiv PR(t, and(f,g)) \\
\forall tsfg [PR(t,f) \supset PR(t,g)] &\subset PR(t, imp(f,g)) \ .
\end{aligned} \qquad (PR)$$

These are all deducible from the logical axioms in the Hilbert proof system; for instance, the last assertion is just a restatement of *Modus Ponens*.

Another interesting connection between the *PR* and *TRUE* predicates can be drawn by looking at models of the OL. Suppose we have used *FACT* and *PR* to describe an agent's theory T of the world. There will be some set of models that satisfy T, i.e., for which all of T's theorems hold. The actual world will be one of these models just in case all T's theorems hold for the world. This condition is statable in the ML as:

$$\forall f PR(T,f) \supset TRUE(f) \ .$$

47

In general this assertion will not be valid, that is, an agent's beliefs need not correspond to the actual world. By introducing the predicate *TRUE* in the ML, we are able to state the correspondence between a given theory of the world and the actual state of affairs in the world.

2.2 Knowledge and Belief

The *PR* and *TRUE* predicates can be used to state our fundamental definitions of knowing and believing for an agent. $BEL(a,f)$ means that agent a believes f; $KNOW(a,f)$ means that agent a knows f. Then we have the definitions:

$$\forall af\, BEL(a,f) \equiv PR(th(a),f)$$
$$\forall af\, KNOW(a,f) \equiv BEL(a,f) \wedge TRUE(f) \ . \tag{$B1$}$$

That is, we identify belief with provability in an OL theory, and knowledge as a belief that actually holds in the world. In model-theoretic terms, a sentence is known to an agent if the sentence holds in all of his models, and the actual world is a model for that sentence. The definition of a common fact in *CF1* means that all common facts are known to all agents.

We already know that the inference process used in deriving new beliefs from old ones is only approximated as logical consequence, yet we should still expect this approximation to correctly model some of the characteristics we attribute to belief. For instance, if a rational agent believes that $P \supset Q$, and he doesn't believe Q, then it should be the case that he doesn't believe P. Translating to the above notation yields the sentence:

$$BEL(A_0, \ulcorner P \supset Q \urcorner) \wedge {\sim}BEL(A_0, \ulcorner Q \urcorner) \supset {\sim}BEL(A_0, \ulcorner P \urcorner) \ .$$

To illustrate the use of axioms for belief and provability given so far, we exhibit a natural deduction proof of this sentence in ML.

1.	$BEL(A_0, \ulcorner P \supset Q \urcorner)$	given
2.	$PR(th(A_0), \ulcorner P \supset Q \urcorner)$	$1, B1$
3.	${\sim}BEL(A_0, \ulcorner Q \urcorner)$	given
4.	${\sim}PR(th(A_0), \ulcorner Q \urcorner)$	$3, B1$
5.	$PR(th(A_0), \ulcorner P \urcorner) \supset PR(th(A_0), \ulcorner Q \urcorner)$	$2, PR$
6.	${\sim}PR(th(A_0), \ulcorner P \urcorner)$	$4,5$ contrapositive
7.	${\sim}BEL(A_0, \ulcorner P \urcorner)$	$6, B1$

This particular proof in the ML cannot be done by semantic attachment to the OL, because it involves reasoning about what isn't provable in the OL theory.

At this point we have presented the basic ideas and definition for a syntactic approach to representing and reasoning about agent's beliefs. The rest of this section is devoted to exploring various technical issues that arise when extending the previous analysis to talking about individuals.

2.3 Individuals

By restricting ourselves to the case of sentential formulas in OL, we have been able to present the basic concepts for representing the beliefs of an agent more simply. Additional complications arise when dealing with terms in the OL that denote individuals rather than truth-values. But a ML encoding of these terms is necessary in order to express such concepts as *agent A_0 knows who B is*.

To talk about the individuals that the OL refers to, we introduce an additional sort into the ML, whose denotation will be the *function terms* of the OL. This sort will be called T_T, and consists of the following members:

(1) variables $\alpha, \beta, \ldots$;
(2) $\{f^n(t_1, \ldots, t_n)\}$, where $t_i \in T_T$ [n-ary OL function];
(3) $\eta(t)$, where $t \in T_I$ [the 'standard name' function];   (TT)
(4) nothing else.

The ML variables α, β, $\ldots$, range over OL function terms. For example, we can state that A_0 believes a particular block is on C by asserting the ML expression:

$$\exists \alpha \; BEL(A_0, ON'(\alpha, C')) \,.$$

In this expression there are two ML terms in T_T, namely, α and C'. C' is a 0-ary function (or constant) in T_T that denotes the constant term C in OL.[†] ON' is a type of ML term that hasn't been used explicitly before; it is a member of T_F because it names an OL formula. It takes two arguments, each of which is an ML term denoting an OL term, and constructs an OL formula that is the OL predicate ON of these arguments. So the ML term $ON'(\alpha, C')$ denotes the OL expression $ON(\mathcal{A}, C)$ where $\mathcal{A}$ is the OL term denoted by α.

It is now possible to give a full definition of T_F terms:

(1) variables $f, g, \ldots$;
(2) $\{f^n(t_1, \ldots, t_n)\}$, where $t_i \in T_F$ [Boolean constructors, e.g., *and*];
(3) $\{g^n(t_1, \ldots, t_n)\}$, where $t_i \in T_T$ [predicate constructors, e.g., ON'];
(4) nothing else.

and T_I terms:

(1) variables $x, y, \ldots$;
(2) $\{f^n(t_1, \ldots, t_n)\}$, where $t_i \in T_I$ [individual constants and functions];
(3) $\Delta(t)$, where $t \in T_T$ [the denotation function];
(4) nothing else.   (TI)

We will also find it convenient to extend the notion of sense-quote abbreviations to handle ML terms involving T_T variables. The previous rules are expanded in the following way: all function symbols in the sense-quote expression are replaced by their primed forms, while any symbols used as variables in the surrounding ML expression remain unchanged. For example, the sense-quote expression in $\exists \alpha \; KNOW(A_0, \ulcorner ON(\alpha, b(C)) \urcorner)$ is to be understood as a syntactic

---

† We extend the prime convention to cover ML terms in T_T as well as T_F; that is, t' in ML denotes the unprimed term t in OL.

abbreviation for the ML term $ON'(\alpha, b'(C'))$. We have not yet said what happens to T_I variables in sense-quote expressions; this must wait until standard names are explained in the next subsection.

The introduction of T_T terms into the ML completes the descriptive power of ML for OL expressions. It also lets us handle some of the well-known denotational puzzles in the philosophy literature. One of the simplest of these is the Morningstar–Eveningstar description problem. Both Morningstar and Eveningstar are actually the planet Venus seen at different times of the day. An agent A_0 believes that they are not the same; further, he doesn't have any knowledge about either being the planet Venus. Let MS, ES, and $VENUS$ be OL terms that denote the Morningstar, the Eveningstar, and Venus, respectively. The following set of ML formulas describes this situation:

$$TRUE(\ulcorner ES = VENUS \urcorner)$$
$$TRUE(\ulcorner MS = VENUS \urcorner)$$
$$BEL(A_0, \ulcorner MS \neq ES \urcorner)$$
$$\sim BEL(A_0, \ulcorner ES = VENUS \urcorner)$$
$$\sim BEL(A_0, \ulcorner MS = VENUS \urcorner) \ .$$

It is perhaps easiest to explain this set of sentences in model-theoretic terms. The intended interpretation of the OL terms, ES, MS, and $VENUS$ is the same object, namely the planet Venus. The two $TRUE$ predicates establish this, since they assert that these three terms denote the same individual in the world. On the other hand, the first BEL predicate asserts that in the models of A_0's theory of the world, MS and ES denote different individuals. This means that the actual world cannot be among the models of this theory. Further, the last two BEL predicates assert that ES and MS are not provably equal to $VENUS$ in this theory; hence there will be some models of the theory for which $ES = VENUS$ holds, some for which $MS = VENUS$ holds, and some for which neither holds. From this we conclude that not only is A_0 mistaken as to the equality of ES and MS, he also is unsure about whether either is the same as $VENUS$. McCarthy (1979) lists some other philosophical puzzles that can be handled in a syntactic formulation.

2.4 Knowing Who Someone Is

One of the problems that any formal treatment of belief must confront is that of describing when an agent knows who or what something is. For example, the following two English sentences say something very different about the state of A_0's knowledge:[†]

(1) "A_0 knows who murdered John."
(2) "A_0 knows that someone murdered John."

The police would certainly be interested in talking to A_0 if the first statement were true, while the second statement just means that A_0 read the local tabloid.

[†] A similar problem appears in (Quine 1971).

We might paraphrase the first statement by saying that there is some individual who murdered John, and A_0 knows who that individual is. The second statement can be true without A_0 having any knowledge about the particular individual involved in the murder.

How is the distinction between the two sentences above to be realized in this formalism? The second sentence is easy to represent:

$$BEL(A_0, \ulcorner \exists \, x \, MURDERED(x, JOHN) \urcorner) \, . \qquad (W1)$$

This simply says that A_0 believes in the existence of an individual who murdered John. It might be supposed that the first sentence could be represented in the following way:

$$\exists \, \alpha \, BEL(A_0, \ulcorner MURDERED(\alpha, JOHN) \urcorner) \qquad (W2)$$

$W2$ says that there is a $MURDERED$ predicate in A_0's theory of the world relating some individual (α's denotation) and John. Unfortunately, this isn't quite strong enough; if the denotation of α is the OL term $murderer(JOHN)$, then $W2$ is virtually a tautology, and doesn't say that A_0 knows who murdered John. Indeed, if the OL expression in $W1$ is skolemized, it becomes obvious that $W1$ and $W2$ are equivalent.

What seems to be going on here is that different names have a different status as far as identifying individuals is concerned. "Bill" is a sufficient description for identifying John's murderer, whereas "John's murderer" is not. The question of what constitutes a sufficient description is still being debated in the philosophical literature. But for the purposes of this paper, it will suffice if we have a name that is guaranteed to denote the same individual in every model of the OL. By asserting a predicate involving this name in A_0's theory of the world, it will be possible to encode the fact that A_0 believes that predicate for the given individual. Names that always denote the same individual are called *standard names*.

The formal method of establishing standard names is straightforward. Consider the set of all individuals involved in the situation we wish to consider.[†] Include in the OL a set of constant symbols, the *standard name symbols*, to be put in one-one correspondence with these individuals. The language OL will be partially interpreted by specifying this correspondence as part of any model of the language; this means that the only models of OL we will consider are those that are faithful to the standard name mapping.

In the metalanguage, we introduce the *standard name function* η of one argument (see the definition of T_T terms above). This function returns the standard name of its argument. Generally we will use lowercase Greek letters from the later part of the alphabet as ML variables for OL standard names $[\mu, \nu, \ldots]$. The metalanguage statement of "A_0 knows who the murderer of John is" then becomes:

$$\exists \, x\mu \, (\eta(x) = \mu) \wedge KNOW(A_0, \ulcorner MURDERED(\mu, JOHN) \urcorner) \, . \qquad (W3)$$

† We restrict ourselves to countable sets here.

51

Because μ denotes a standard name, the only models of this statement are those in which the same individual x murdered John. This is in contrast to $W1$ and $W2$ above, which allow models in which any individual murdered John. An immediate consequence is that $W1$ and $W2$ are derivable from $W3$, but not the other way round.

So in order to assert that A_0 knows who or what some individual B is, we write in the ML:[†]

$$\exists\, x\mu\; (\eta(x) = \mu) \wedge KNOW(A_0, \ulcorner B = \mu \urcorner)\ .$$

By modifying the sense-quote translation rules slightly, it is possible to write OL expressions involving standard names much more compactly. The modification is to assume that any ML variable of type T_I occurring within a sense-quote gets translated to the standard name of that variable. With this rule, for example, the above assertion comes out as $\exists x\, KNOW(A_0, \ulcorner B = x \urcorner)$.

We will use the predicate $KNOWIS(a,\beta)$ to mean that the agent a knows who or what the OL term denoted by β refers to. The definition of $KNOWIS$ is:

$$\forall a\beta\, KNOWIS(a,\beta) \equiv \exists x\, KNOW(a, \ulcorner \beta = x \urcorner)\ . \qquad (KW)$$

Note that the property of being a standard name is a relation between a term of the OL and models of this language, and hence cannot be stated in the OL. The use of a metalanguage allows us to talk about the relation between the OL and its models.

One of the proof-theoretic consequences of using standard names is that every theory can be augmented with inequalities stating the uniqueness of individuals named by standard names. In the metalanguage, we write:

$$\forall xy\, x \neq y \supset \forall t\, PR(t, \ulcorner x \neq y \urcorner)\ . \qquad (SN)$$

Formally, the definition of a standard name can be axiomatized in the ML by introducing the denotation function Δ.[‡] $\Delta(\alpha)$, where α denotes an OL term, is the denotation of α in the actual world; it is the inverse of the standard name function, since it maps an OL term into its denotation. There is an intimate relation between the denotation function and equality statements in OL formulas describing the world:

$$\forall \alpha\beta\, TRUE(\ulcorner \alpha = \beta \urcorner) \equiv \Delta(\alpha) = \Delta(\beta) \qquad (D1)$$

that is, two OL terms are equal in the actual world just in case they denote the same individual; $D1$ can be viewed as a definition of the intended interpretation of equality. The prime purpose of the denotation function is to tie together the

---

† This analysis essentially follows that of (Kaplan 1971), with the extension of standard names to all individuals in the domain, rather than just numbers and a few other abstract objects. There are problems in using standard names for complex individuals, however (see Kaplan 1971).

‡ This is Church's denotation predicate in function form (Church 1951); since a term can have only one denotation, it is simpler to use a function.

denotation of terms in the OL and the ML. For standard names, it can be used to state that the denotation of a standard name is the same individual in all situations, something that cannot be done with equality predicates in the OL:

$$\forall x \; \Delta(\eta(x)) = x \; . \tag{D2}$$

For example, by asserting $\eta(VENUS) = VENUS'$ in ML, we fix the denotation of the OL term $VENUS'$ to be the individual denoted by the ML term $VENUS$ in all models of the OL.

The introduction of standard names with fixed denotations across all models makes the task of relating the OL to the ML easier. By introducing this 'common coin' for naming individuals, we are able to write expressions of the OL that represent beliefs without constantly worrying about the subtle consequences of the denotational variance of terms in those expressions. Standard names will play an important role in describing belief-nesting (beliefs about beliefs), in describing executable actions, and in simplifying the deduction process.

2.5 The Object Language as Metalanguage

In this subsection we extend the OL to include a description of another object language OL'. Thus extended, the OL can be viewed as a metalanguage for OL'. The reason we want to do this is that it will be necessary for representing an agent's view of a world that is changing under the influence of events. In the next section we will show how an agent can model the way in which the world changes by describing what is true about different states of the world connected by events. But to describe these states of the world, or *situations*, the agent's theory must talk about sentences of another language holding in a given situation.

Before trying to extend the formal apparatus of the OL to describe another OL, it is helpful to examine more closely the relation between the ML as a means of studying the OL and as a means of describing the actual world. This is because the structure of an ML/OL pair will be very similar no matter what the depth of embedding; and the simplest such structure to study is obviously the topmost one. Although we initially characterized the ML's domain of discourse as including that of the OL, it appears that we have not made much use of this characterization. In describing the models of OL, however, it was necessary to pick out the model that was the actual world; this was done with the predicate *TRUE*. And it was impossible to state the definition of a standard name without appealing to terms in the ML that referred to individuals in the actual world. So, in fact, we have already used the ML to characterize the actual state of the world and the individuals that populate it.

We have stated that agent's beliefs are represented as first-order therories of the world. The ML is, by the above argument, just such a theory; but whose theory of the world is it? One useful interpretation is to take what we will call the *egocentric view*: a theory in the ML is identified as the theory of a particular agent. That is, suppose we were to build a computer agent and invest him with an ML/OL structure as a way of representing other agent's beliefs. Then the nonlogical axioms of the ML would constitute the computer agent's theory of the world. The interpretation of the ML predicate *TRUE* would be "what the computer agent believes about the world", and of the predicate *KNOW*, "what another agent believes that agrees with what the computer agent believes." In this interpretation, there is no sense of absolute truth or knowledge; the beliefs of one agent are always judged relative to those of another.

Suppose we identify the agent A_0 with the ML; what interpretation does the OL theory $th(A_0)$ have? Interestingly enough, it is A_0's introspective description of his own beliefs. Unlike other agent's theories of the world, $th(A_0)$ shares an intimate connection with formulas that hold in the ML. For a rational agent, it should be the case that if he believes P, then he believes that he believes P. We can state this connection by the following rule of inference:

> Belief attachment: If the agent a is identified with the ML, then from $TRUE(f)$ infer $BEL(th(a),f)$.

Introspection will be useful when we consider planning, because a planning agent must be able to reflect on the future state of his beliefs when carrying out some plan.

If the metalanguage is intended to describe the actual world, then it is reasonable to ask what the relation is between models of the ML and models of its OL, and whether this connection can be formalized in the ML. We start by adding predicate symbols to the ML whose intended meaning is a property of the actual world, rather than of the OL and its models. Consider such a predicate P of no arguments, and let its intended meaning be "222 Baker Street Apt 13 is unoccupied:" that is, the actual world satisfies P just in case this apartment is indeed unoccupied. In the OL there is also a predicate symbol P of no arguments whose meaning we wish to coincide with that of the ML predicate P. The fact that these symbols are the same is an orthographic accident; they come from different languages and there is thus no inherent connection between them. However, because the ML can describe the syntax and semantics of the OL, it is possible to axiomatize the desired connection. Let P' be the ML term (in T_F) denoting the OL predicate P. Then P in the ML and OL have the same meaning if:

$$P \equiv TRUE(P') \tag{R1}$$

is asserted in the ML. For suppose the actual world satisfies P in the ML; then $TRUE(P')$ must also hold, and hence by the meaning of *TRUE*, the actual world is also a model for P in the OL. Similarly, if the actual world falsifies P in the ML, $TRUE(not(P'))$ must hold, and the actual world falsifies P in the OL also. So the proposition named by P' holds just in case Apt. 13 at 222 Baker Street is unoccupied, and thus the meanings of P in the ML and P in the OL coincide.

For predicates that have arguments, the connection is complicated by the need to make sure that the terms used in the ML and OL actually refer to the same individuals. So, for example, if P is an ML predicate of two arguments that we wish to mean the same as the OL predicate P, we would write:

$$\forall \alpha \beta \, TRUE(\ulcorner P(\alpha,\beta) \urcorner) \equiv P(\Delta(\alpha),\Delta(\beta)) \; ; \qquad (R2)$$

that is, since the denotation function Δ gives the individuals denoted by the OL terms α and β, P in the ML agrees with P in the OL on these individuals. Using standard names, $R2$ could be rewritten as:

$$\forall xy \, P(x,y) \equiv TRUE(\ulcorner P(x,y) \urcorner) \qquad (R3)$$

since, by $D2$, $\Delta(\eta(x)) = x$, $\Delta(\eta(y)) = y$. Note that the standard name convention for sense-quotes is in force for $R3$.

Using $TRUE$ and equivalence, axioms like $R3$ cause predicate symbols to have a 'standard meaning' across the ML and OL, in much the same way that $D2$ formalizes standard names using the denotation function and equality. But while nonstandard names are a useful device for encoding an agent's beliefs about individuals that the agent may have misidentified (recall the Morningstar–Eveningstar example), nonstandard predicates don't seem to serve any useful purpose. So we will assume that for every predicate symbol P in ML, there is a function symbol of the form P' whose denotation is the OL predicate P, and there is an axiom of the form $R2$ equating the meaning of these predicates.

To make the OL into a metalanguage for OL$'$, we simply introduce sorts that denote OL$'$ expressions into the OL, in exactly the same way that it was done for the ML. In addition, the various axioms that tie the ML and OL together (MP, $D1$, etc.) must also be asserted in the OL. Unfortunately, this also means that the ML itself must have a new set of terms denoting terms in the new OL; the machinery for describing embedded ML/OL chains rapidly becomes confusing as the depth of the embedding grows. So in this paper we will supply just enough of the logical machinery to work through the examples by introducing two conventions; readers who want more detail are referred to Konolige (1981).

We will extend the convention of sense-quote abbreviation to include ML variables of the sort T_F (denoting formulas of the OL). When these occur in sense-quotes, they are to be translated as the *standard name* of the variable; hence they denote the name of an expression. To take an example, we will complete the axiomatization of $CFACT$:

$$\forall f \, CFACT(f) \supset CFACT(\ulcorner CFACT(f) \urcorner) \qquad (CF2)$$

$CF2$ asserts that if f is a common fact, then every agent knows it is a common fact. The sense-quote term $\ulcorner CFACT(f) \urcorner$ denotes the OL expression $CFACT(f')$, where f' is the standard name of the OL$'$ expression corresponding to f.

Finally, every axiom is a common fact:

$$CFACT(\ulcorner A \urcorner), \; A \text{ an axiom.} \qquad (CF3)$$

In practice, we hope that the depth of embedding needed to solve a given problem will be small, since the complexity needed for even the three-level structure of ML, OL, and OL$'$ is substantial. Also, the technique of semantic attachment can be used to reduce the complexity of reasoning about embedded structures by attaching to a particular level of an embedded structure and reasoning in that language. In Appendix A we use embedded ML/OL structures to solve the wise man puzzle, which involves reasoning to a depth of embedding of three (ML, OL, and OL'); we exploit semantic attachment to simplify the reasoning involved.

3. THE INTERACTION OF ACTIONS AND BELIEFS

The previous section laid the groundwork for a syntactic treatment of knowledge and belief in a static world. This must be integrated with a formal treatment of actions in order to accomplish our original task of formalizing the interaction of knowledge and action. We examine the following two questions:

- What knowledge is required by an agent successfully to perform an action?
- What knowledge does an agent gain in performing an action?

The methodology we will use is to apply the *situation calculus* approach (McCarthy and Hayes 1969) first to formally describe the way in which the world changes as events occur. It will then be assumed that this formal system is a reasonable approximation to the way an agent reasons about changes in the world: this means that it becomes part of an agent's rules about the world. By simply attributing a facility for reasoning about events to agents, it turns out that we are able to answer both these questions formally, and that this formalization corresponds well with our intuitions about real agents. This is essentially the same method that was used by Moore (Moore 1980); here, we show that it can be successfully carried out for a syntactic formalization of knowledge and belief.

Once the formal requirements for reasoning about events have been specified, we consider how an agent might plan to achieve a goal using his knowledge of actions. We conclude that planning is inherently a process of self-reflection: that is, in order to construct a plan, an agent must reflect on what the state of his beliefs will be as the plan is undergoing execution. Such a self-reflection process is represented naturally by an ML/OL structure in which the planning agent is identified with the ML, and his future states are theories of the OL. We will show how it is possible to construct plans within this representation, and extend it to include plans that involve other cooperative agents.

3.1 Situations

In the situation calculus approach, events are taken to be relations on *situations*, where situations are snapshots of the world at a particular moment in time. It is natural to identify situations with models of a language used to describe the world; in this case, we will use the language OL of the previous section, because the ML for describing models of the OL is already laid out. In the ML, situations will be named by terms, generally the constants $\{S_0, S_1, \ldots\}$. A formula f of the OL holds in a situation s when the situation satisfies f; the ML predicate $H(s, f)$

will be used to indicate this condition. If the situation S_0 is singled out as being the actual world (and the initial world for planning problems), then $TRUE$ can be defined in terms of H:

$$\forall f\, TRUE(f) \equiv H(S_0, f) \ . \tag{H1}$$

Since H describes satisfiability in a model, the truth-recursion axioms TR are valid for H as well as $TRUE$.

If we consider agents to be part of domain of discourse, then their beliefs can change from one situation to the next, just as any other inessential property of an agent might. But if an agent's beliefs change from situation to situation, then the theory that is used to model these beliefs must also change. One way to represent an agent's changing beliefs is to ascribe a different theory to an agent in each situation to model his beliefs in that situation. In the ML, we will write $ths(a,s)$ to denote agent a's beliefs in situation s; if S_0 is taken to be the actual world, then it is obvious that $\forall a\, ths(a, S_0) = th(a)$.

But we might now ask what situation the expressions in each of these theories are about. Suppose that the OL sentence P is a member of $ths(A_0, S_1)$, and thus one of A_0's beliefs in situation S_1. We would naturally want P to be property that A_0 believes to hold of situation S_1 (and not S_0 or some other situation). That is, $ths(a,s)$ represents agent a's beliefs *in* situation s, *about* situation s. In informal usage we will call the situation we are focussing on the *current situation*, and say 'the agent a in situation s' when we are referring to the agent's beliefs in that situation. Later we will show how to represent an agent's beliefs about situations other than the one he is currently in.

For each situation, an agent's beliefs in that situation are specified by a theory. Given this arrangement, we define the new predicates B and K as similar to BEL and $KNOW$, but with a situation argument:

$$\forall asf\, B(a,s,f) \equiv PR(ths(a,s), f)$$
$$\forall asf\, K(a,s,f) \equiv B(a,s,f)\, H(s,f) \ . \tag{B2}$$

$B(a,s,f)$ means that in situation s agent a believes that f holds in s; K is similar, with the condition that f actually holds in s. Note that the underlying predicates $FACT$ and PR do not have to be changed, since they are defined on theories of OL rather than models. Thus the properties of BEL and $KNOW$ described in the previous section also hold for B and K in any particular situation. BEL and $KNOW$ can be defined as B and K in the situation S_0.

Several extensions to the formalism presented in the first section must be made to deal with situations. A new denotation function δ takes a situation argument as well as an OL term; $\delta(s, \alpha)$ is the denotation of α in situation s. $\Delta(\alpha)$ gives the denotation of a α in situation S_0, and is definable as $\delta(S_0, \alpha)$. The appropriate forms of $D1$ and $D2$ are:

$$\forall s\alpha\beta\, H(\ulcorner s, \alpha = \beta \urcorner) \equiv \delta(s, \alpha) = \delta(s, \beta)$$
$$\forall sx\ \delta(s, \eta(x)) = x \ . \tag{D3}$$

This last says that standard names always have the same interpretation in every situation. Nonstandard names can change their denotation in different situations, e.g., the block denoted by "the block A_0 is holding" may be changed by A_0's actions.

Finally, we require the appropriate versions of $R1$-$R6$, where these axioms are appropriately generalized to refer to all situations.

3.2 Observables

Following Moore (Moore 1980), we recognize three ways that an agent can acquire beliefs in a situation:

- He can observe the world around him.
- His beliefs about past situations persist in the current situation.
- He can reason about the way in which the current situation arose from events that occurred in previous situations.

In the next few subsections we describe how an agent's beliefs persist and how he reasons about events; here we formalize what it means for a property of the world to be observable.

It is certainly true that there are many properties of the world we live in that are not directly observable; for example, consider a gas oven whose pilot light is completely encased and hence not visible. Whether this pilot light is on or off isn't an observable property, but there are other observations that could be made to test what the state of the pilot light is, e.g., by turning on the oven and observing whether it lights. What we actually consider to be observable depends on how we formalize a given problem domain; but it is important for a planning agent to be able to make the distinction between properties of the world he can observe directly, and those he must infer.

One of the reasons that it is handy to have a separate theory representing the beliefs of an agent in each situation is that we then have a way of describing the effect of observable properties on an agent's beliefs. Formally, we can state that a property is observable by asserting that in every situation, subject to certain preconditions that are required for the felicitous observation of the property, an agent knows whether that property holds or not. For example, in the OL let o be an oven, and let $LIT(o)$ mean that o is lit. Then $LIT(o)$ is asserted to be observable by:

$$\forall aos \, H(s, \ulcorner AT(a,o) \urcorner) \supset [K(a,s, \ulcorner LIT(o) \urcorner) \lor K(a,s, \ulcorner \sim LIT(o) \urcorner)]; \ (O1)$$

that is, if the agent is actually at the oven, he knows either that it is lit, or that it is not lit. Recall from the previous section on knowledge and belief that $O1$ says something very strong about the state of a's knowledge, and is not derivable from the tautology $K(a,s, \ulcorner LIT(o) \lor \sim LIT(o) \urcorner)$.

3.3 Events Types

Event types are relations on situations; a given event type describes the possible states of the world that could result from an event occurring in any initial state.

58

We will use the three-place predicate EV in the metalanguage to describe event types: $EV(e, s_i, s_f)$, where e is an event type and s_i and s_f are situations, means that s_f results from an event of type e occurring in s_i. An event is an instance of an event type,[†] but generally we will not have to distinguish them for the purposes of this paper, and we will use 'event' for 'event type' freely.

Generally the events of interest will be agents' actions, and these will be constructed in the ML using terms representing actions, agents, and the objects involved in the action (the *parameters* of the action). If act is an action, then $do(a, act)$ is the event of agent a performing this action. Consider the situation calculus axiomatization of a simple blocks-world action, $puton(x, y)$, where the parameters of the action are blocks:

$$\forall axys_i s_f\, EV(do(a, puton(x, y)), s_i, s_f) \supset H(s_i, \ulcorner CLEAR(y) \urcorner) \wedge$$
$$H(s_i, \ulcorner HOLDING(a, x) \urcorner) \wedge$$
$$H(s_f, \ulcorner ON(x, y) \urcorner) \wedge$$
$$H(s_f, \ulcorner \sim HOLDING(a, x) \urcorner)$$
$$(PO1)$$

$$\forall axys_i s_f\, EV(do(a, puton(x, y)), s_i, s_f) \supset$$
$$[\forall f\, SAF(f) \wedge f \neq \ulcorner CLEAR(y) \urcorner \wedge f \neq \ulcorner HOLDING(a, x) \urcorner \supset$$
$$H(s_i, f) \equiv H(s_f, f)]$$
$$(PO2)$$

The form of $PO1$ is conditional, so the right-hand side describes the conditions under which situations s_i and s_f are related by the event of a putting x on y. The first two conjuncts on the right-hand side are essentially preconditions for the event to occur, since they state conditions on the intial situation s_i that must be satisfied for EV to hold. The preconditions are that $CLEAR(\eta(y))$ and $HOLDING(\eta(a), \eta(x))$ must hold in situation s_i; note that the standard names for the parameters are indicated by the sense-quote convention. If the preconditions are not met, then there is no situation s_f that is the successor to s_i under the event e. The rest of the conjuncts describe which formulas of the OL are to hold in the new situation s_f.

$PO2$ specifies that all formulas of a certain type that hold in s_i are also to hold in s_f. It is thus a *frame axiom* for the event e, describing which aspects of the situation s_i remain unchanged after the event occurs. The predicate SAF stands for *Simple Atomic Formula*; it picks out those formulas of the OL that are composed of atomic predicates over standard names. Although SAF applies only to non-negated atomic formulas, the frame axiom carries over negated atomic formulas as well, since $H(s, not(f))$ is equivalent to $\sim H(s, f)$.[‡] Among

---

[†] For example, "Borg's winning of Wimbledon yesterday was fortuitous" is a statement about a single event, but "Borg winning Wimbledon has happened five times" describes an event type that had five particulat instances.

[‡] The axiomatization of events given here is a standard one in the AI literature on formal planning, and there are well-known problems involving the use of frame axioms like the one above. We are not attempting to add any new insight to this particular aspect of planning; but we are interested in having a formal description of events to integrate with our theory of belief, and this seems to be the best formulation currently available.

the nicer features of this axiomatization is that events whose outcomes are conditional on the initial state can be easily described. For instance, consider the event of an agent turning on a gas oven that has a pilot light. If the pilot light is on, the oven will be lit; if the pilot light is off, the oven will have whatever status, lit or unlit, it had before the event occurred (the oven may already have been on). Let $PL(o)$ be an OL predicate meaning "the pilot light of oven o is on"; and let $LIT(o)$ mean "oven o is lit". Then the event of an agent turning on o can be described as:

$$\forall as_i s_f o \, EV(do(a, light(o)), s_i, s_f) \supset$$
$$H(s_i, \ulcorner AT(a,o) \urcorner) \wedge$$
$$H(s_i, \ulcorner PL(o) \urcorner) \supset H(s_f, \ulcorner LIT(o) \urcorner) \wedge \qquad (LT1)$$
$$H(s_i, \ulcorner \sim PL(o) \urcorner) \supset [H(s_f, \ulcorner LIT(o) \urcorner) \equiv H(s_i, \ulcorner LIT(o) \urcorner)]$$

$$\forall as_i s_f o \, EV(do(a, light(o)), s_i, s_f) \supset$$
$$[\forall f SAF(f) \wedge f \ne \ulcorner LIT(o) \urcorner \supset H(s_i, f) \equiv H(s_f, f)] \; .$$
$$(LT2)$$

The second conjunction of $LT1$ gives the result of the event on case the pilot light is on: the oven will be lit. The third conjunction says that if the pilot light is off, the oven will be lit in s_f just in case it was lit in s_i, i.e., its status doesn't change. $LT2$ is the frame axiom.

3.4 Reasoning about Situations and Events

The axiomatization of events as relations on situations enables us to talk about what is true in the world after some events have occurred starting from an initial situation (which we will generally take to be S_0). What it doesn't tell us is how an agent's beliefs about the world will change; nothing in the PO or LT axioms gives any insight into this. It might be suspected that, as events are described by axioms as changing the actual state of the world, this description might be extended to cover agents' *theories* as well, e.g., changing A_0's theory in situation S_0 ($ths(A_0, S_0)$) into his theory in situation S_1 ($ths(A_0, S_1)$).[†] But there is no obvious or well-motivated way to make modifications to axioms like PO and LT so that they take into account agents' beliefs about a situation rather than what actually holds in the situation.[‡] What is needed here is a principled way of deriving the changes to an agent's beliefs that result from an event, given a description of the event as a relation on situations. Credit for the recognition of

---

† Indeed, it might be though that the most widely known AI planning system, *STRIPS*, has just such a mechanism in its add/delete list approach to describing events. However, closer examination reveals that because *STRIPS* makes the assumption that it has a *partial model* in the sense of (Weyhrauch 1980), and it is actually slightly less descriptive than the situational approach described above (Nilsson 1980).

‡ There is one proposal that is suggested by the our use of H to refer to the actual situation and PR to statements that an agent believes about a situation, namely, to replace all predicates involving H with the corresponding ones involving PR. However, it can be shown that the substitution of $PR(ths(A_0, s), \ldots)$ for $H(s, \ldots)$ yields counterintuitive results for A_0's beliefs.

this problem belongs to Robert Moore, and we will formalize the solution he presented in his thesis, the main points of which follow.

The solution to this difficulty lies in making the observation that agents are reasoning entities. Consider how agent A_0 might reason about some event E; let us suppose the event is that agent A_0 turned on the oven in situation S_0, and that the result was that the oven was not lit in situation S_1. What should A_0's beliefs be in situation S_1? First, by observation, he knows that the oven isn't lit. He also believes (in S_1) that the current situation resulted from the event E occurring in situation S_0. So A_0 reasons as follows: if, in situation S_0, the pilot light of the oven had been on, then in S_1 the oven would be lit, since he turned it on. But the oven isn't lit; hence the pilot light couldn't have been on in S_0, and remains not on in S_1.

There are several important things to note about this analysis. The first is that, as suggested previously, A_0's beliefs in situation S_1 comes from only three sources: observation ("the oven is not lit"), persistence of beliefs about previous situations ("if in S_0 the pilot light had been on ... "), and beliefs about the way events change the world. This latter is equivalent to having some form of $LT1$ as part of A_0's beliefs in situation S_1. From these three sources A_0 is able to generate a new set of beliefs for S_1.

The second thing to note is that none of A_0's reasoning in S_1 could have taken place unless he believed that S_1 resulted from S_0 via the event E. Beliefs about what sequence of events led to the current situation play a very important role in reasoning about that situation, and, like other beliefs, they can be mistaken or inferred from other evidence. Suppose, for example, that A_0 suddenly sees the oven become lit. He might infer that the only way that could happen when it wasn't previously lit would be for an agent to turn it on; this is inferring that the situation where the oven is lit is connected by a certain event with a previous situation where the oven wasn't lit. We will not be concerned with this kind of inference here, although we note the possibility of doing *event recognition* in this framework. The events we are interested in are actions, and the assumption we will make for the remainder of this paper is that an agent knows what action it is that he performs in executing a plan.

A third aspect of this reasoning that is unusual is that the axiomatization of events is being used in a different way than a planning program would normally consider doing. Typically, a planner uses an event description like $LT1$ to form plans to light the oven, and the side condition that the pilot light be on is one of the things that can go wrong with the plan, and so must be taken into account as a subgoal. However, in the above example A_0 has used $LT1$ to reason about a property of the world that is not available to his direct observation, that is, as a *test*. This is an important characteristic for any formalism that combines a description of agent's beliefs with a description of events; a single description of an event should suffice for an agent to reason about it either as a means of effecting a change in the world, or as a test that adds to his beliefs about the world.

Finally, the precondition that A_0 be at the oven to turn it on translates naturally in this analysis into a precondition on A_0's beliefs in situation S_0. If A_0 is to reason that situation S_1 is the successor to S_0 under the event E, he must believe that he was actually at the oven in situation S_0. For if he doesn't believe this, then he cannot use $LT1$ to infer anything about the results of his action.

We might summarize the analysis of this section in the following way: by making the simple assumption that an agent reasons about the way in which situations are related by events, we are able to characterize in a natural way the belief preconditions required for executing an action, and the effects of actions on the subsequent belief state of an agent. The interaction of observation and reasoning about situations gives an agent the power to plan actions that perform tests, as well as change the state of the world.

3.5 Formalizing Agents' Reasoning about Events

We now give a formalization that implements the ideas just laid out. The first requirement is that we be able to describe an agent a in situation s reasoning about other situations, especially the one just preceding. Since the formulas of $ths(a,s)$ all refer to properties of situation s, we must enrich the OL so that formulas in the OL can refer to different situations. Using the techniques of belief-nesting of the previous section, we add to the OL the predicate H corresponding to the ML predicate of the same name. The OL expression $H(S_1, \ulcorner P \urcorner)$ means that the OL' formula P holds in situation S_1, regardless of what theory this formula appears in.[†] With the addition of the H predicate to the OL, the notion that all formulas in $ths(a,s)$ refer to properties of s can be formalized as:

$$\forall sf \, PR(th(a,s),f) \equiv PR(th(a,s), \ulcorner H(s,f) \urcorner) \ . \tag{H2}$$

$H2$ can be paraphrased by saying that an agent believes P in situation s just in case he believes that P holds in situation s. Given $H2$, it is possible to describe agents' theories as consisting purely of formulas in H; but the added level of embedding puts this technique at a disadvantage with respect to using other predicates from OL to describe an agent's beliefs about the current situation.

It is also possible to formalize the notion that beliefs about previous situations persist, or are carried over into succeeding situation. Suppose that in situation S_n an agent has a belief of the form, "in a previous situation S_i, P was true". Then if S_{n+1} is the successor to S_n under some event, this belief is still valid. Formally, we can assert this with the ML axiom:

$$\forall s_i s_f e \, EV(e,s_i,s_f) \supset [\forall asf \, B(a,s_i, \ulcorner H(s,f) \urcorner) \supset B(a,s_f, \ulcorner H(s,f) \urcorner)] \ . \tag{H3}$$

† We will take $S_0, S_1, \ldots$ to be standard names for situations in all languages. It will be assumed that standard names are always used to name situations.

The antecedent of the implication says that s_i and s_f must be connected by some event for beliefs to be carried over from s_i to s_f; this is necessary because we don't want agents to inherit beliefs from their future states. By phrasing the beliefs in terms of the predicate H, $H3$ carries over beliefs about all situations previous to and including s_i.

One of the consequences of $H3$ is that once an agent forms a belief about a situation, he holds that belief about that situation for all time. Since beliefs can be mistaken, it might happen that an agent observes something that forces him to revise his previously held beliefs. In that case, $H3$ is too strong, and the resultant theory will be inconsistent. We recognize that the general problem of reconciling inconsistent beliefs that arise from different sources (called *belief revision*) is a hard one, involving both conceptual and technical issues, and it is not part of this research to say anything new about it.[†] Nevertheless, it is worthwhile to note that because the ML has terms that refer to agents' theories in different situations, it may be possible to describe a belief revision process formally in the ML.

3.6 An Example of a Test

Given the preceding techniques for describing what an agent believes to hold in situations other than the one he is currently in, we can show formally that A_0 can use the LT axioms as a test to figure out whether the pilot light is on or not. In the initial situation S_0, we will assume that A_0 knows he is at the oven O (where O is the standard name for the oven), and realizes that it is not lit:

Initial Conditions in the ML

(1) $K(A_0, S_0, \ulcorner AT(A_0, O) \wedge {\sim}LIT(O) \urcorner)$ given

(2) $K(A_0, S_1, \ulcorner EV(do(A_0, light(O)), S_0, S_1) \urcorner)$ given

The style of proof we will exhibit will be natural deduction, with assumption dependencies noted in square brackets in the justification for a line of the proof. Given the initial conditions, we next show that A_0 can observe whether or not the oven is lit in situation S_1:

(3) $\forall f SAF(f) \wedge f \neq \ulcorner LIT(O) \urcorner \supset$
$$H(S_0, f) \equiv H(S_1, f) \qquad \text{2, B2, LT2}$$

(4) $SAF(\ulcorner AT(A_0, O) \urcorner)$ definition of SAF

(5) $H(S_1, \ulcorner AT(A_0, O) \urcorner)$ 1, 3, 4, B2

(6) $K(A_0, S_1, \ulcorner LIT(O) \urcorner) \vee K(A_0, S_1, \ulcorner {\sim}LIT(O) \urcorner)$ 5, O1

Line 3 comes from the frame axiom for *light*, and lets us infer that A_0 is still at the oven in situation S_1 (line 5). The observation axiom $O1$ is then invoked to assert that A_0 will know what the state of the oven is in that situation.

Throughout this proof, we will be interested in two theories of the OL:

---

† Doyle (Doyle 1978) worked on this problem under the rubric "Truth Maintenance", and more recent work in nonmonotonic reasoning also considers this problem.

$ths(A_0,S_0)$ and $ths(A_0,S_1)$. Assertions in the ML involving A_0's beliefs can be reasoned about by using semantic attachment to the appropriate OL theory. For example, line 1 above is attached to the following statements in $ths(A_0,S_0)$:

A_0's Theory in Situation S_0

(7) $AT(A_0,O) \land \sim LIT(O)$ 1, B2, semantic attachment
(8) $H(S_0,\ulcorner \sim LIT(O) \urcorner)$ 1, B2, H2, semantic attachment

Line 7 is the attachment of line 1 to A_0's theory in S_0. Line 8 is derived from line 1 by the use of $H2$; it is useful because it will persist as a belief in the successor situation S_1. Generally, beliefs that an agent derives about the current situation can be inherited into succeeding situations by expressing these beliefs with the H predicate.

At this point we do reasoning by cases. First assume the right disjunct of line 6; then for A_0's beliefs in situation S_1 we have:

A_0's Theory in Situation S_1

(9) $\sim LIT(O)$ [9]: assumed, semantic attachment
(10) $\sim H(S_1,\ulcorner LIT(O) \urcorner)$ [9]: 9, $H2$ semantic attachment
(11) $EV(do(A_0,light(O)),S_0,S_1)$ 2, semantic attachment
(12) $H(S_0,\ulcorner PL(O) \urcorner) \supset H(S_1,\ulcorner LIT(O) \urcorner)$ 11, $LT1$
(13) $\sim H(S_0,\ulcorner PL(O) \urcorner)$ [9]: 10,12 contrapositive
(14) $H(S_0,\ulcorner \sim PL(O) \urcorner)$ [9]: 13, TR for H

The first part of the result is derived by line 14, namely, that if A_0 observes that the O is not lit in situation S_0, then he knows that the pilot light was not on in situation S_0. This sequence of steps is interesting because it illustrates the inter-mixture of proof techniques in the ML and OL. Lines 9, 10, and 11 come from statements in the ML about $ths(A_0,S_1)$. Line 10 is derived from line 9 in the ML by the application of axiom $H2$. Line 11 says that A_0 believes that S_1 is the result of the $light(O)$ action occurring in S_0, and follows directly from line 2 and semantic attachment. Line 12 follows from line 11 and the event axiom $LT1$; it is assumed that A_0 believes this axiom. Finally, 13 and 14 follow, given that the truth-recursion axioms for H are made available in all theories in the OL.

The left disjunct of line 6 can be reasoned about in the following way (since lines 11 and 12 did not involve any assumptions, they can be used in this part of the proof also):

A_0's Theory in Situation S_1

(15) $LIT(O)$ [15]: assumed, sem. att.
(16) $H(S_1,\ulcorner LIT(O) \urcorner)$ [15]: 15, $H2$, sem. att.
(17) $\sim H(S_0,\ulcorner LIT(O) \urcorner)$ 8, $H3$, TR for H, sem. att.
(18) $\sim [H(S_1,\ulcorner LIT(O) \urcorner) \equiv H(S_0,\ulcorner LIT(O) \urcorner)]$ [15]: 16,17
(19) $H(S_0,\ulcorner \sim PL(O) \urcorner) \supset H(S_1,\ulcorner LIT(O) \urcorner) \equiv$
$H(S_0,\ulcorner LIT(O) \urcorner)$ 11, $LT1$
(20) $\sim H(S_0,\ulcorner \sim PL(O) \urcorner)$ [15]: 18,19 contrapositive
(21) $H(S_0,\ulcorner PL(O) \urcorner)$ [15]: 20, TR for H

Here again, the first few lines (15, 16, and 17) are established by reasoning at the ML about $ths(A_0,S_1)$. Line 17 comes from an instance of axiom $H3$, which enables an agent's beliefs to persist through a sequence of situations. Line 19 comes from A_0's knowledge of $LT1$, and line 20 is the key step: it establishes that under the assumption of O being lit in S_1, the pilot light was on in S_0. Finally, the frame axiom $LT2$ will carry the pilot light's status in S_0 forward into S_1:

A_0's Theory in Situation S_1

(22) $\forall f\, SAF(f) \wedge f \neq \ulcorner LIT(O) \urcorner \supset H(S_0,f) \equiv H(S_1,f)$ $11, LT1$

(23) $SAF(\ulcorner PL(O) \urcorner)$ definition of SAF

(24) $H(S_0, \ulcorner PL(O) \urcorner) \equiv H(S_1, \ulcorner PL(O) \urcorner)$ $22, 23$

(25) $PL(O)$ $[15]: 21, 24, H2$

(26) $\sim PL(O)$ $[9]: 14, 24, H2$

Line 25 is under the assumption of the left disjunct of line 6, and line 26 is under the right disjunct. In the ML we can derive several results from the preceding proof structure:

In the ML

(27) $B(A_0,S_1, \ulcorner PL(O) \urcorner) \vee B(A_0,S_1, \ulcorner \sim PL(O) \urcorner)$ $6, 20, 21$

(28) $B(A_0,S_1, \ulcorner LIT(O) \urcorner) \supset B(A_0,S_1, \ulcorner PL(O) \urcorner)$ $15, 25$

(29) $B(A_0,S_1, \ulcorner \sim LIT(O) \urcorner) \supset B(A_0,S_1, \ulcorner \sim PL(O) \urcorner)$ $9, 26$

Line 27 says that in S_1, A_0 will either believe that the pilot light is on, or he will believe that is not on. Thus, by performing the action of lighting the oven, A_0 gains knowledge about the state of an unobservable, the pilot light. This is the desired result of agent A_0 using $LT1$ to perform a test of an unobservable property.

Lines 28 and 29 give belief analogues to the LT axioms, which described the event of lighting the oven solely in terms of the actual situations before and after the event. These assertions show how the beliefs of A_0 change under the influence of the event $do(a, light(O))$. By suitably generalizing the preceding proof, it can be shown that 28 and 29 hold for all agents and initial situations.

$$\forall a o s_i s_f \; EV(do(a, light(o)), s_i, s_f) \wedge K(a, s_i, \ulcorner AT(a,o) \wedge \sim LIT(o) \urcorner) \supset$$
$$B(a, s_f, \ulcorner LIT(o) \urcorner) \supset B(a, s_f, \ulcorner PL(o) \urcorner) \qquad (LT3)$$
$$B(a, s_f, \ulcorner \sim LIT(o) \urcorner) \supset B(a, s_f, \ulcorner \sim PL(o) \urcorner).$$

$LT3$ is valid under the condition that $LT1$ is assumed to be believed by all agents. $LT3$ is one description of the way in which an agent's beliefs change in a situation that results from an oven-lighting event; it would be most useful to a planner as a lemma to be invoked if the state of the pilot were to be tested as a step in a plan. Another lemma about oven-lighting that would be useful to a planner would be one in which the belief preconditions to an action were made explicit; this would be used to plan actions that light the oven.

65

4. PLANS AND PLANNING

In the previous section we saw how to characterize the changes to an agent's beliefs produced by his observation of events. In this section we will consider how to use these results as part of the deductions that an agent needs to do to construct workable plans, i.e., plans that will accomplish their goals.

Consider how an agent might go about constructing workable plans. Using his description of various events (PO, LT, and others) he can try to find a sequence of actions that lead to the desired goals being true in some final situation. If we identify the planning agent with the ML, then a plan would be a sequence of situations connected by actions performed by that agent, such that the goals are true in the final situation. This doesn't seem to involve the planning agent in any reasoning about his beliefs; all he needs to do is describe how the actual world changes under the influence of his actions.

This isn't the whole story, though. The plan that is derived must be an *executable* plan; that is, if the plan is a sentence of actions, the agent must be able to execute each of those actions at request time. For instance, the action description $light(oven(John))$ will not be executable if A_0 doesn't know which oven is John's. For a plan to be executable by an agent, the agent must know what action is referred to by each of the *do*-terms in the plan. According to a previous section, this means that the agent must have the standard name for the action in his theory. But what are standard names for actions? Following Moore (Moore 1980), we take the viewpoint that actions can be analysed as a general procedure applied to particular arguments, e.g., *puton* is a general procedure for putting one block on top of another, and $puton(A,B)$ is that procedure applied to the two blocks A and B. If we assume that all agents know what general procedure each action denotes, then the standard names for actions are simply the terms formed by the action function applied to the standard names of its parameters.[†] The condition that actions be executable forces the planning agent to make the critical distinction between his beliefs at planning time and his beliefs at execution time. A planning agent may not know, as he forms his plan, exactly what action a particular *do*-term in his plan denotes; but if he can show that at the time he is to execute that action, he will know what it is, then the plan is an executable one. Plans of this type occur frequently in common-sense reasoning; consider a typical plan A_0 might form to tell someone what time it is. The plan has two steps: first A_0 will look at his watch to find out what the time is, and then he will communicate this information to the requestor. At planning time, A_0 doesn't really know what the second action

---

† Actually, the condition that the parameters be standard names is too strong. Standard names have the property that every agent knows whether two individuals named by standard names are the same or not in every situation, but this condition is not strictly necessary for an action to be executable. Consider the action of requesting information from the telephone operator; surely it is not required that an agent be able to differentiate the operator from every other individual in his beliefs. If he were to dial the operator on two separate occasions, he would not necessarily be able to tell if he talked to the same operator or not.

is, because he doesn't know the time, and the time is an important parameter of the communication act. Yet he can reason that after looking at his watch, he will know the time; and so the plan is a valid one.

By this argument, an agent must analyse at planning time what the future states of his beliefs will be as he executes the plan. Thus the planning process intrinsically forces the agent into introspection about his future beliefs. Since we have identified the planning agent with the ML, it is natural to represent his future beliefs during the execution of the plan as OL theories in the situations that the planning process gives rise to. If the planning agent is A_0, then these theories are $ths(A_0, S_0)$ (the initial situation), $ths(A_0, S_1)$, etc., where each of the S_i results from its predecessor via the execution of the next action in the plan. A_0's planning process is basically a simulation of the plan's execution in which he reasons about the changes that both the actual world and his set of beliefs will undergo during the course of the plan's execution. By figuring out what his future states of belief will be, he can decide at planning time whether an action of the plan will be executable.

For A_0 to take other agents' plans into account in forming his own, he must be able to represent their future states of belief, in addition to his own. But this doesn't involve any additional representational complexity, since A_0 is already keeping track of his own beliefs during the simulated execution of the plan. In Konolige and Nilsson [1980] an example of a multi-agent plan is presented; currently we are working on formalizing such plans in the framework presented here.

Actually, this planning process bears a strong resemblance to typical implementations of a situation calculus approach to planning (Warren 1974). In these systems, events are axiomatized along the lines of PO and LT, and the planner searches for a sequence of situations that leads to the goal by doing theorem-proving with the event axioms; the search space is essentially the same in either approach. The main difference is in the relative complexity of reasoning that the two planning systems must be able to handle. In the approach described here, the effect of actions on the agent's beliefs in each situation greatly increases the deductive complexity of the planner and the work that it must do at each node in the search space of plans. The usefulness of lemmas such as $LT3$ that describe the effects of actions on an agent's belief state now becomes apparent: by summarizing the effect of actions on an agent's beliefs, they reduce the complexity of the deductions that must be performed at each step in the plan. Further savings can be realized by using the method of belief attachment described in the previous section: from $H(s,f)$ at the ML, infer $K(A_0,s,f)$. Most of the work of figuring out A_0's future states of knowledge can be performed by reasoning about H at the metalevel, rather than K, and this is considerably simpler. Finally, it should be noted that the executability requirement acts as a filter on plans. Thus a reasonable search strategy would be to first find a plan that works without taking into account its executability (and hence the future belief states of the planning agent), and then test it for executability.

5. CONCLUSION

To summarize the contributions of this paper: we have defined a syntactic approach to the representation of knowledge and belief in which the key element is the identification of beliefs with provable expressions in a theory of the object language. The technique of *semantic attachment* to the intended interpretation of the metalanguage provability predicate has been advanced as a method of simplifying proofs by directly modelling an agent's inference procedure, rather than simulating it.

To unify a formalization of knowledge and action, we have shown how to take Moore's account of their interaction and formalize it within the syntactic framework. The benchmark example was a presentation of a *test* in which an agent uses his knowledge of observable properties of the world and the way actions affect the world to discover the state of an unobservable property. Finally, we pointed out how the formalization could be used in a planning system.

While this paper is a step towards showing that the syntactic approach can be extended to an adequate formalization of the interaction of knowledge and action, there is still much work to be done in constructing a practical planner for a multi-agent environment that uses this formalism. Two areas in particular are critical. First, a suitable system for doing automatic deduction in the framework has to be worked out. Although we have advocated semantic attachment as a means of simplifying proofs, we have not yet explored the problem of controlling a deduction mechanism that uses this technique. The second area also involves control issues: how can a planner be designed to search the space of multi-agent possible plans efficiently? One of the ideas suggested by this paper is to derive lemmas of the form of $LT3$ that show the effect of actions on an agent's beliefs. With such lemmas, a planning system would have compiled the necessary results for contructing new brief states from previous ones.

ACKNOWLEDGEMENTS

This research is a direct outgrowth of research conducted with N. Nilsson (Konolige and Nilsson 1980), and still reflects his influence. S. Rosenschein and N. Nilsson read previous drafts of this paper, and their criticisms and comments have contributed to the final form. Also, I have benefited from talks with P. Hayes, R. Moore, R. Weyhrauch, C. Talcott, and all the members of the planning group at the Artificial Intelligence Center at SRI. This research is supported by the Office of Naval Research under Contract No. N00014-80-C-0296.

APPENDIX: THE WISE MAN PUZZLE

This is a solution to a simple version of the wise man puzzle, for whose statement we quote from McCarthy *et al.* (1980):

> A king wishing to know which of his three wise men is the wisest, paints white dots on each of their foreheads, tells them that at least one spot is

white, and asks each to determine the colour of his spot. After a while the smartest announces that his spot is white, reasoning as follows: "Suppose my spot were black. The second wisest of us would then see a black and a white and would reason that if his spot were black, the dumbest would see two black spots and would conclude that his spot is white on the basis of the king's assurance. He would have announced it by now, so my spot must be white."

We will simplify this puzzle by having the king ask each wise man in turn if he knows what colour his spot is, staring with the dumbest. The first two say* "no", and the last says that his spot is white.

In formalizing the puzzle, we will take the three wise men to be A_0, A_1, and A_2, in order of increasing stupidity.[†] We will reason about the puzzle from A_0's point of view, and show that A_0 knows that his spot is white after hearing the replies of the other two. We will not be concerned with the axiomatization of the speech act performed by the agents; it will be assumed that A_0's model of the world changes appropriately to reflect this new information.

There are three situations in the puzzle: the initial situation S_0, the situation S_1 just after A_2 speaks, and the situations S_2 just after A_1 speaks. The frame axioms for these situation are simply that every agent knows he knew in the previous situation; these frame axioms are common knowledge.

We will identify A_0 with the ML, so that goal is to show: $H(S_2, \ulcorner W(A_0) \urcorner)$ in the ML. $W(a)$ is the predicate whose meaning is 'a's spot is white'. The initial conditions of the problem are:

(1) $W(A_1) \wedge W(A_2)$
(2) $CFACT(\ulcorner W(A_0) \vee W(A_1) \vee W(A_2) \urcorner)$
(3) $CFACT(\ulcorner K(A_2, S_0, \ulcorner W(A_0) \urcorner) \vee K(A_2, S_0, \ulcorner \sim W(A_0) \urcorner) \urcorner)$
(4) $CFACT(\ulcorner K(A_2, S_0, \ulcorner W(A_1) \urcorner) \vee K(A_2, S_0, \ulcorner \sim W(A_1) \urcorner) \urcorner)$
(5) $K(A_1, S_0, \ulcorner W(A_0) \urcorner) \vee K(A_1, S_0, \ulcorner \sim W(A_0) \urcorner)$
(6) $CFACT(\ulcorner \sim K(A_2, S_0, \ulcorner W(A_2) \urcorner) \urcorner)$
(7) $CFACT(\ulcorner \sim K(A_1, S_1, \ulcorner W(A_1) \urcorner) \urcorner)$

Line 1 says that A_0 observes white spots on A_1 and A_2; line 2 asserts that it is common knowledge that at least one spot is white. The next two lines state it is common knowledge that A_2 can observe whether the other two agent's spots are white or not. Line 5 says that A_1 knows the colour of A_0's spot. And the last two lines express the effect of the first two agent's answers to the king on everyone's knowledge. This axiomatization will be sufficient to prove that A_0 knows his spot is white in S_2.

The first step in the proof is to show that A_1 knows, in situation S_1, that either his own or A_0's spot is white; this by reasoning about A_2's answer to the king. We will attach to A_1's theory in situation S_1 (that is, $ths(A_1, S_1)$), and do our reasoning there:

† A_0, A_1 and A_2 are standard names for the wise men.

A_1's Theory in Situation S_1

(8) $\sim K(A_2,S_0,\ulcorner W(A_2)\urcorner)$	6, semantic attachment
(9) $K(A_2,S_0,\ulcorner W(A_0) \vee W(A_1) \vee W(A_2)\urcorner)$	3, semantic attachment
(10) $K(A_2,S_0,\ulcorner(\sim W(A_0) \wedge \sim W(A_1)) \supset W(A_2)\urcorner)$	9
(11) $K(A_2,S_0,\ulcorner \sim W(A_0) \wedge \sim W(A_1)\urcorner) \supset$	
$\qquad\qquad\qquad\qquad K(A_2,S_0,\ulcorner W(A_2)\urcorner)$	10, MP
(12) $\sim K(A_2,S_0,\ulcorner \sim W(A_0) \wedge \sim W(A_1)\urcorner)$	8,11 contrapositive

In these lines, we have used the fact that everyone knows that everyone knows common knowledge assertions. At line 12, A_1 realizes that A_2 doesn't know that both A_0 and A_1 lack white dots; if he did, he would have announced the fact.

Now A_1 uses the common knowledge that A_2 can observe the colour of A_0's and A_1's dots to reason that one of the latter has a white dot:

A_1's Theory in Situation S_1

(13) $K(A_2,S_0,\ulcorner \sim W(A_0)\urcorner) \wedge$	
$\qquad\qquad K(A_2,S_0,\ulcorner \sim W(A_1)\urcorner)$	[13]: assumption
(14) $K(A_2,S_0,\ulcorner \sim W(A_0) \wedge \sim W(A_1)\urcorner)$	[13]:13, PR
(15) $\sim K(A_2,S_0,\ulcorner \sim W(A_0)\urcorner) \vee$	
$\qquad\qquad \sim K(A_2,S_0,\ulcorner \sim W(A_1)\urcorner)$	13;12,14 contradiction
(16) $\sim K(A_2,S_0,\ulcorner \sim W(A_0)\urcorner)$	[16]: assumption
(17) $K(A_2,S_0,\ulcorner W(A_0)\urcorner) \vee$	
$\qquad\qquad K(A_2,S_0,\ulcorner \sim W(A_0)\urcorner)$	3, semantic attachment
(18) $K(A_2,S_0,\ulcorner W(A_0)\urcorner)$	[16]: 16,17
(19) $\sim K(A_2,S_0,\ulcorner \sim W(A_1)\urcorner)$	[19]: assumption
(20) $K(A_2,S_0,\ulcorner W(A_1)\urcorner) \vee K(A_2,S_0,\ulcorner \sim W(A_1)\urcorner)$	4, semantic attachment
(21) $K(A_2,S_0,\ulcorner W(A_1)\urcorner)$	[19]: 19,20
(22) $K(A_2,S_0,\ulcorner W(A_0)\urcorner) \vee K(A_2,S_0,\ulcorner W(A_1)\urcorner)$	15,16,18,19,21
(23) $H(S_0,\ulcorner W(A_0) \vee W(A_1)\urcorner)$	22, $B2$
(24) $W(A_0) \vee W(A_1)$	23, frame axioms, $R1$

We first show here that A_2 doesn't know A_0's spot is black, or he doesn't know that A_1's spot is black (line 15). Assertions that follow from assumptions are indicated by a square bracketing of the assumption line number in their justification. Next we do an analysis by cases of line 15; in either case, line 22 holds: A_2 either knows A_0's spot is white, or he knows A_1's spot is white. From this A_1 concludes that either he or A_0 has a white spot (line 24). Note that the frame axioms were needed to show that the W predicate doesn't change from situation S_0 to situation S_1.

At this point we are through analysing A_1's theory of situation S_1, and go back to the ML to reason about situation S_2. By line 5, A_1 knows the colour of A_0's dot, so we assume that he knows it is black:

At the Metalevel

(25) $K(A_1, S_0, \ulcorner \sim W(A_0) \urcorner)$	[25]: assumption
(26) $K(A_1, S_1, \ulcorner \sim W(A_0) \urcorner)$	[25]: 25, frame axioms
(27) $K(A_1, S_1, \ulcorner \sim W(A_0) \supset W(A_1) \urcorner)$	24, frame axioms
(28) $K(A_1, S_1, \ulcorner W(A_1) \urcorner)$	[25]: 26, 27, MP
(29) $\sim K(A_1, S_1, \ulcorner W(A_1) \urcorner)$	7, $CF1$
(30) $\sim K(A_1, S_0, \ulcorner \sim W(A_0) \urcorner)$	25, 28, 29, contradiction
(31) $K(A_1, S_0, \ulcorner W(A_0) \urcorner)$	5, 30
(32) $H(S_0, \ulcorner W(A_0) \urcorner)$	31, $B2$

Under the assumption that A_1 knows A_0's spot is black, we derive the contradiction of lines 28 and 29. Therefore, by line 5, it must be the case that A_1 knows A_0's spot to be white. This is the conclusion of line 32; since this is one of A_0's beliefs, we are done.

REFERENCES

Appelt, D., (1980). A planner for reasoning about knowledge and belief, *Proceeding of the First Annual Conference of the American Association for Artificial Intelligence*, Stanford, California.

Church, A., (1951). A formulation of the logic of sense and denotation, *Structure, Method and Meaning*, (Ed. Henle, P., *et al.*). New York: Liberal Arts Press.

Cohen, P. R., & Perrault, C. R., (1979). Elements of a plan-based theory of speech acts, *Cognitive Science*, 3, 52-67.

Creary, L. G., (1979). Propositional attitudes: Fregean representation and simulative reasoning, *IJCAI-6 (Tokyo)*, 176-181.

Doyle, J., (1978). Truth maintenance systems for problem solving, *Memo AI-TR-419*, Cambridge, Mass.: Artificial Intelligence Laboratory, MIT.

Kaplan, D., (1971). Quantifying in, *Reference and Modality*, 112-144, (Ed. Linsky, L.). Oxford: Oxford University Press.

Kleene, S. C., (1967). *Mathematical Logic*, New York: John Wiley.

Konolige, K., & Nilsson, N., (1980). Multiple agent planning systems, *Proceeding of the First Annual Conference of the American Association for Artificial Intelligence*, Stanford, California.

Kowalski, R., (1979). *Logic for Problem Solving*. New York: North-Holland.

McCarthy, J., (1962). Towards a mathematical science of computation, *Information Processing, Proceedings of the IFIP Congress*, 62, 21-28. Amsterdam: North-Holland Publishing Company.

McCarthy, J., & Hayes, P. J., (1969). Some philosophical problems from the standpoint of artificial intelligence, *Machine Intelligence*, 4, 463-502. (Eds. Meltzer, B., and Michie, D.). Edinburgh: Edinburgh University Press.

McCarthy, J., *et al.* (1978). On the model theory of knowledge, *Memo AIM-312*, Stanford: Computer Science Department, Stanford University.

McCarthy, J., (1979). First order theories of individual concepts and propositions, *Machine Intelligence*, 9, 120-147, (Eds. Hayes, J. E., Michie, D., and Mikulich, L. I.). Chichester: Ellis Horwood; and New York: Halsted Press.

Moore, R. C., (1977). Reasoning about knowledge and action, *IJCAI-5*, Cambridge Mass., 223-227. Pittsburgh: Department of Computer Science, Carnegie-Mellon University.

Moore, R. C., (1980). Reasoning about knowledge and action, *Artificial Intelligence Center Technical Note 191*. Menlo Park: SRI International.

Nilsson, N. J., (1980). *Principles of Artificial Intelligence*. Menlo Park: Tioga Publishing Co.

Quine, W. V. O., (1971). Quantifiers and propositional attitudes, *Reference and Modality*, 101-101, (Ed. Linsky, L.). Oxford: Oxford University Press.

Warren, D. H. D., (1974). WARPLAN: A system for generating plans, *DAI Memo 76*. Edinburgh: Department of Artificial Intelligence, University of Edinburgh.
Weyhrauch, R., (1980). Prolegomena to a theory of mechanized formal reasoning, *Artificial Intelligence*, 13.

3

Knowledge-based problem-solving in AL3

I. Bratko
Institute Jozef Stefan and Faculty of Electrical Engineering
University of Ljubljana

1. INTRODUCTION

AL3 (Advice Language 3) is a problem-solving system whose structure facilitates the implementation of knowledge for a chosen problem-domain in terms of plans for solving problems, 'pieces-of-advice', patterns, motifs, etc. AL3 is a successor of AL1 and AL1.5 (Michie 1976, Bratko & Michie 1980a, 1980b, Mozetic 1979). Experiments in which AL1 was applied to chess endgames established that it is a powerful tool for representing search heuristics and problem-solving strategies. The power of AL1 lies mainly in the use of a fundamental concept of AL1: piece-of-advice. A piece-of-advice suggests what goal should be achieved next while preserving some other condition. If this goal can be achieved in a given problem-situation (e.g. a given chess position) then we say that the piece-of-advice is 'satisfiable' in that position. In this way AL1 makes it possible to break the whole problem of achieving an ultimate goal into a sequence of subproblems, each of them consisting of achievement of a subgoal prescribed by some piece-of-advice. The control structure which chooses what piece-of-advice to apply next consists of a set of 'advice-tables', each of them being specialized in a certain problem-subdomain. Each advice-table is a set of rules of the form

if precondition *then* advice-list

If more than one rule-precondition is satisfied then simply the first rule is chosen. Advice-list is an ordered list of pieces-of-advice. Advice-list is interpreted so that the first satisfiable piece-of-advice in the list is executed. The satisfiability is checked by simple depth-first search.

This comparatively simple control structure has several advantages: simplicity, neatness of solutions, susceptibility to formal proofs of correctness of strategies. However, its disadvantage is that it is difficult to implement problem-solving strategies which make extensive use of higher-order concepts, such as plans, and which also do 'meta-level' reasoning about plans and pieces-of-advice themselves.

It is sometimes desirable that the system be able to create a new piece-of-advice, or in a case of its failure, modify it according to the cause of the failure.

AL 1.5 removed some minor defects of AL1. One improvement was to allow recursive calls of pieces-of-advice within a piece-of-advice. But the basic control structure of AL1 was preserved.

AL3 is an attempt at facilitating the use of higher-order concepts by providing a more flexible control structure over the basic mechanisms of AL1. Experiments with AL3, described in this paper, were implemented in PROLOG (Pereira, Pereira & Warren 1978). The problem-domain used in these experiments is a chess ending: king and pawn *vs.* king and pawn with passed pawns. Examples of using AL3 in another chess ending are described in Bratko & Niblett (1979). Although these experiments demonstrate how AL3 can be used for knowledge-based problem-solving using higher-order concepts, at this stage they should not be considered as completed. Many questions need further investigation, such as: in what ways, in general, can different plans be merged for achieving a desired combined effect? Examples of related research, also using plans for chess problem-solving, are Tan (1977), Pitrat (1977), and Wilkins (1979).

2. EXAMPLE: SOLVING A CHESS STUDY

As an illustration of the way AL3 uses problem-solving knowledge, consider the chess endgame study in Fig. 1. The Black pawn on h5 is threatening to run down to h1 and promote into a queen. White can try to stop this threat with his king, but the king on h8 is too far to catch the Black pawn. Another idea for White

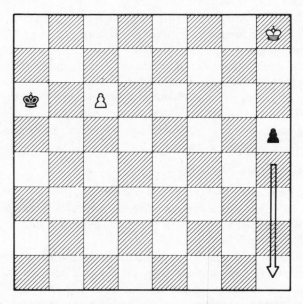

Fig. 1 – A study by Reti. White to move: can White draw? The Black pawn is threatening to run to square h1 and promote into a queen as indicated by the arrow.

is to queen his own pawn. But if the White pawn moves ahead, the Black king can easily move closer to stop the pawn and capture it if necessary. The position looks lost for White. However, there is a surprising plan for White which preserves the draw.

The following is a simplified trace of AL3's behaviour when solving the problem of Fig. 1. The problem is stated by an initial query 'Can White draw?' and the following hypothesis, $H0$, is investigated:

$H0$: White can draw?

This causes another hypothesis to be generated

$H1$: Black can win?

and a logical relation between both hypotheses is provided:

$H0 \Leftrightarrow \mathrm{not}(H1)$

That is: $H0$ is logically equivalent to $notH1$. This logical relation is called a 'fact' about our problem.

Now the system may consider the hypothesis $H1$, and one *method* for solving problems in the system's knowledge-base suggests a plan for Black: push Black pawn toward h1 while preserving a *holding-goal* "Black pawn alive and not White pawn successfully promoted" until a *better-goal* is achieved: "Black pawn promoted". Call this plan *BPQ* (Black pawn queens). This and subsequent plans are illustrated in Fig. 2. A hypothesis about plan *BPQ* is now generated

$H2$: Plan *BPQ* succeeds?

together with the fact

$H2 \Rightarrow H1$

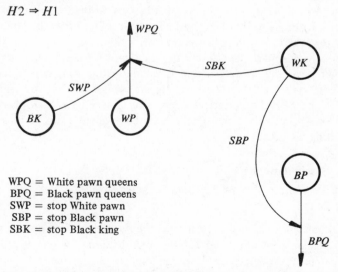

WPQ = White pawn queens
BPQ = Black pawn queens
SWP = stop White pawn
SBP = stop Black pawn
SBK = stop Black king

Fig. 2 – Illustration of plans for White and Black in the position of Fig. 1.

75

A method which 'knows' how to refute plans now proposes: try to refute plan *BPQ* by either destroying its holding-goal or its better-goal. Thus two refutation plans are proposed for White:

1. Plan *SBP* (Stop Black pawn): move White king toward the Black pawn path.
2. Plan *WPQ* (White pawn queens): promote White pawn by pushing it toward square c8.

Two corresponding hypotheses and a logical relation are:

$H3$: *SBP* refutes *BPQ*?
$H4$: *WPQ* refutes *BPQ*?
$H3 \vee H4 \Rightarrow \mathrm{not}(H2)$

There is a lemma in the knowledge-base which recognizes on the basis of distances among pieces that $H3$ is false. But another lemma, about pawn races, establishes that $H4$ is true. This gives, using logical relations among hypotheses: $H2$ is false. Thus the simple plan for Black, *BPQ*, (push Black pawn and queen) does not succeed.

One method in the knowledge-base, considering this failure and the cause for the failure, proposes a refinement of plan *BPQ*, obtaining plan *BPQ*1. The skeleton of *BPQ*1 is *BPQ*, but in the meantime Black king has, if necessary, to stop the White pawn by moving toward the White pawn path. Now either of the White's counter plans *WPQ* and *SBP* refutes the plan *BPQ*1.

The repertoire of simple ideas for White is now exhausted, but more complicated ideas can still be tried. First, plan *WPQ* is refined, obtaining plan *WPQ*1. The skeleton of *WPQ*1 is *WPQ* refined by the idea of bringing the White king toward the White pawn path in order to prevent Black's plan *SWP* (stop White pawn). It turns out that *WPQ*1 also does not refute *BPQ*1. But there is one more idea for White: a disjunctive combination of plans *WPQ*1 and *SBP*. The plan, based on this idea, *WPQ*1 *or* *SBP*, does refute Black's plan *BPQ*1. The solution that saves the White position is finally: White king moves diagonally from h8 to f6 or e5, all the time pursuing the idea of the 'or' combination of plans *WPQ*1 and *SBP*. The diagonal White king moves serve *both* plans. Then, depending on Black's reactions, one of the component plans refutes Black's *BPQ*1, ensuring the draw.

3. OVERVIEW OF AL3

The overall structure of the AL3 system is shown in Fig. 3. The main modules of the system are:

(1) a knowledge-base which contains *methods* that 'know' how to solve particular problems, and *lemmas* (or theorems) about the problem-domain that, hopefully, can be applied during the problem-solving process;

(2) a current-knowledge-pool (CKP) containing the already known *facts* and *hypotheses* about the problem being solved, and other objects that are relevant to the problem;

(3) the *control module* which decides what method, or lemma, to activate next.

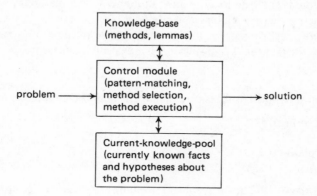

Fig. 3 – The AL3 System.

3.1 Knowledge-base

Methods in the knowledge-base are, in the terminology of Waterman & Hayes-Roth (1978), pattern-directed executional modules. They can be thought of as specialized subroutines for solving particular kinds of subproblems, or for providing a suggestion about how to solve a (sub)problem. For example, one method for the problem-domain of the king and pawn *vs.* king and pawn chess ending says: If one side (say White) is planning to promote his pawn, then a counter-plan for Black is: stop the advancing White pawn by bringing the Black king in front of the pawn. Together with this, a hypothesis is generated that this Black's plan refutes White's plan, and the following fact is provided: If the hypothesis is true then White's plan fails. The necessary precondition for this method to be executed is the existence of a hypothesis that White can promote his pawn.

Each method is defined by (1) its precondition, (2) a procedure for its execution, and (3) its characteristics. The characteristics include, for example, an estimate of how difficult is the method to execute; that is: how much computational resource will be spent on the execution of the method.

Preconditions are predicates on the current-knowledge-pool (CKP). They are implemented so that they do not only return the truth value. In the case that the precondition is satisfied, the 'context' which satisfies the precondition is also returned as a by-product of testing for the precondition. Context is simply a part of CKP.

77

When a method is executed, the context is used as input for the method's procedure. The results of the execution can be: new hypotheses, new facts, new plans for solving the problem, or other objects. These results are then used to update the CKP.

A special class of methods is called *lemmas* to indicate that by them we implement theorems about the problem-domain. Formally there is no distinction between methods and lemmas. The only difference is that methods may generate new hypotheses whereby lemmas generate only facts.

Facts are propositional calculus formulae made of hypothesis names. Thus for example, the fact that a hypothesis H is true can be represented by a formula:

H

The fact that if hypothesis $H1$ is true then $H2$ is false can be represented by

$H1 \Rightarrow not(H2)$

3.2 Current-knowledge-pool

CKP contains:

- hypotheses about the problem including the user's definition of the problem which is to be solved,
- user's query, called a 'target', which is to be proved or disproved, together with the currently known facts about the problem,
- plans, pieces-of-advice, and other objects that are in any respect relevant to the problem-solving task and have thus been generated so far during the problem-solving process.

3.3 Control module and executional cycle of AL3

The control module supervises the problem-solving process which consists of a sequence of executional cycles. To carry out each executional cycle the control module does the following: it analyses the current target and checks if enough facts about the problem are already known to imply an answer. If not, then the control module matches the preconditions of the methods and lemmas against the CKP to find a set of methods and lemmas applicable to CKP. This set is called the *conflict set*. A method or a lemma in the conflict set is then selected on the basis of a cost-benefit criterion. The selected method will, hopefully, produce new facts so as to most economically further the problem-solving process.

A PROLOG code for the top level of operation of AL3, including the main executional cycle, is given in Fig. 4. Notational conventions are those of the Edinburgh implementation of PROLOG (Pereira, Pereira, & Warren 1978). For solving a problem, the target is initialized by the user's query, and an upper limit on computational resources that may be spent on solving this problem is specified. The PROLOG procedure

solve(Target, Resources, Answer, Explanation)

78

produces an answer: "yes", "no", or "unknown" if it was not found before the Resources were exhausted. It also produces an Explanation of the Answer. Explanation is a list of notes supplied by the methods when activated during the problem-solving process. The main executional cycle is preformed by the procedure

applyknbase(Target, Resources, Target1, Resources1, Note)

It updates the target with new facts (producing Target1) and Resources, obtaining Resources1, i.e. resources left for the rest of the task.

```
problem:-
    initialize (Target, Resources),
    solve (Target, Resources, Answer, Explanation),
    display (Target, Answer, Explanation).

solve (Target,_,yes,nil) :-
    proved (Target).

solve (Target,_,no,nil) :-
    disproved (Target).

solve (Target, Resources, unknown, nil) :-
    exceeded (Resources, Target).

solve (Target, Resources, Answer, [Note | Exp1]) :-
    applyknbase (Target, Resources, Target1, Resources1, Note),
    solve (Target1, Resources1, Answer, Exp1).

applyknbase (T, Res, T1, Res1, Note) :-
    selectmethod (T, Mname, Context),
    execute (Mname, Context, Facts, Note, Spent),
    update (T, Facts, T1),
    subtract (Res, Spent, Res1).
```

Fig. 4 – PROLOG code for the top level operation of AL3.

4. REPRESENTATION OF TARGET AND FACTS

Target and facts are propositional calculus formulas. A target, T, can be thought of as a formula that the system is trying to prove or disprove. If T is a theorem then T has been proved; if not(T) is a theorem then T has been disproved; if T is neither of these then new facts, F, when found, are used as new axioms. The target T is updated by F giving a new target, $T1$:

$$T1 \equiv (F \Rightarrow T) \ .$$

Now the goal becomes to prove or disprove $T1$.

In the system, target, and facts are, to enable efficient manipulation, represented as sets of clauses (also called 'lines') of the form

$$a_1, a_2, \ldots, a_m \Rightarrow b_1, b_2, \ldots, b_n$$

meaning

$$a_1 \wedge a_2 \wedge \ldots \wedge a_m \Rightarrow b_1 \vee b_2 \vee \ldots \vee b_n \ .$$

All a_i and b_j are hypothesis names. The logical connective between clauses is conjunction. Any propositional formula can be converted into this form by Wang's algorithm (e.g. Raphael 1976). This form will be referred to as the 'c-form'.

Sometimes we will use the set notation in the following way. Capital letters A, B, ... will denote sets of hypothesis names. If $A = \{a_1, \ldots, a_m\}$ and $B = \{b_1, \ldots, b_n\}$ then

$$A \Rightarrow B$$

represents the line

$$a_1, \ldots, a_m \Rightarrow b_1, \ldots, b_n \ .$$

In this notation, a target in the c-form will be written as

$$\begin{bmatrix} A_1 \Rightarrow B_1 \\ A_2 \Rightarrow B_2 \\ \ldots\ldots\ldots \\ \ldots\ldots\ldots \end{bmatrix}$$

If $A_i = \phi$ then it represents the truth value "true". If $B_i = \phi$ then it represents the truth value "false".

A line $A \Rightarrow B$ is a *tautology* if

(1) A is false, or
(2) B is true, or
(3) $A \cap B \neq \phi$.

A target is *proved* if all its lines are tautologies (i.e. the target is a theorem).

A target can be decomposed into a product of its 'subtargets', where the subtargets themselves have the form of a target, e.g.:

$$T = T1 \times T2$$

The multiplication rule is:

$$T1 = \begin{bmatrix} A_1 \Rightarrow B_1 \\ \ldots\ldots\ldots \\ A_m \Rightarrow B_m \end{bmatrix}$$

$$T2 = \begin{bmatrix} C_1 \Rightarrow D_1 \\ \dots\dots \\ C_n \Rightarrow D_n \end{bmatrix}$$

$$T = T1 \times T2 = \begin{bmatrix} A_1 \cup C_1 \Rightarrow B_1 \cup D_1 \\ A_1 \cup C_2 \Rightarrow B_1 \cup D_2 \\ \dots\dots\dots\dots \\ A_1 \cup C_n \Rightarrow B_1 \cup D_n \\ A_2 \cup C_1 \Rightarrow B_2 \cup D_1 \\ \dots\dots\dots\dots \\ A_m \cup C_n \Rightarrow B_m \cup C_n \end{bmatrix}$$

A target

$$T = T_1 \times T_2 \times \dots \times T_N$$

is a theorem if at least one of its subtargets T_i is a theorem. The multiplication operation is associative and commutative. These properties provide a basis for different strategies of problem decomposition.

An easy way of updating the target by new facts is through the use of multiplication. The principle is: to update a target T with facts F, we have T and F represented in the c-form by

and
$$[\text{true} \Rightarrow T]$$
$$[F \Rightarrow \text{false}] \quad .$$

The updated target is then

$$[F \Rightarrow \text{false}] \times [\text{true} \Rightarrow T] = [F \Rightarrow T] \quad .$$

It may be advantageous to keep the target in the product form delaying the multiplication, or to carry out the multiplication only on part of the target. For example, complete multiplication on a target

$$F1 \times F2 \times T$$

may result in a bulky and difficult to manipulate new target with many lines. Instead, a partial multiplication of $F1 \times F2 = F$ may reduce the number of lines, giving a handy new target represented by the product $F \times T$.

Another reason for keeping the target in the product form is that if the subtargets consist of basically disjoint sets of hypotheses then the product of the subtargets corresponds to a natural decomposition of the problem. Each subtarget then corresponds to a comparatively independent subproblem. This enables the system to focus its attention on subproblems themselves.

Facts of the form "Hypothesis a is true" or "a is false" can be added by simply substituting the value of a into the lines of the target and applying

81

simplification rules for logical expressions. Facts of more complex forms are transformed into the c-form and then added as a new multiplication factor. Thus for example a fact

$$a \Rightarrow b$$

is properly transformed into the c-form by the following operations. Factor to be added is

$$(a \Rightarrow b) \Rightarrow \text{false} \ .$$

Its c-form is obtained by the following transformations (using Wang's algorithm):

$$(\text{not}(a) \lor b) \Rightarrow \text{false} \ .$$

This is equivalent to

$$\text{not}(a) \Rightarrow \text{false} \quad \text{and}$$
$$b \Rightarrow \text{false}$$

giving finally

$$\left[\begin{array}{l} \text{true} \Rightarrow a \\ b \Rightarrow \text{false} \end{array} \right]$$

Table 1 presents some useful transformations of typical forms of facts into a corresponding c-form representation.

The goal of the problem-solving process is to either prove the target or disprove it, that is, to demonstrate that the target is a theorem or that its negation is a theorem. Both alterations can be dealt with by keeping, during the problem-solving process, two targets: *positive* and *negative* target. If the positive target becomes a theorem then the initial target has been proved; if the negative target becomes a theorem then the initial target has been disproved. For example, assume that the initial goal was to answer the question: Is hypothesis h true or false? Then the corresponding positive and negative targets in the c-form are [true $\Rightarrow h$] and [$h \Rightarrow$ false] respectively. New facts are, when generated, added multiplicatively to both positive and negative targets.

After inserting a truth value for a hypothesis name or after carrying out a multiplication operation, targets may become messy and redundant. They can be tidied up by applying the following simplification rules:

(1) Delete tautological lines.
A line $A \Rightarrow B$ is a tautology if $A \cap B \neq \phi$.
A line false $\Rightarrow B$ is a tautology.
A line $A \Rightarrow$ true is a tautology.

(2) Delete lines that are implied by other lines.
A line $A \Rightarrow B$ *implies* another line $A1 \Rightarrow B1$ within the same subtarget if $A \subseteq A1$ and $B \subseteq B1$.

Table 1 — Some useful transformations of facts into the c-form.
For a given fact F, the right-hand side constructs in the table
are logically equivalent to $F \Rightarrow$ false.

Fact	Fact in the c-form
$a \lor b \lor c \lor \ldots$	$\begin{bmatrix} a \Rightarrow \text{false} \\ b \Rightarrow \text{false} \\ c \Rightarrow \text{false} \\ \ldots\ldots\ldots \end{bmatrix}$
$a \land b \land c \land \ldots$	$[a, b, c, \ldots \Rightarrow \text{false}]$
$a \lor b \lor c \lor \ldots \Rightarrow h$	$\begin{bmatrix} h \Rightarrow \text{false} \\ \text{true} \Rightarrow a, b, c, \ldots \end{bmatrix}$
$a \land b \land c \land \ldots \Rightarrow h$	$\begin{bmatrix} h \Rightarrow \text{false} \\ \text{true} \Rightarrow a \\ \text{true} \Rightarrow b \\ \text{true} \Rightarrow c \\ \ldots\ldots\ldots \end{bmatrix}$
$a \lor b \lor c \lor \ldots \Leftrightarrow h$	$\begin{bmatrix} \text{true} \Rightarrow h, a, b, c, \ldots \\ a, h \Rightarrow \text{false} \\ b, h \Rightarrow \text{false} \\ c, h \Rightarrow \text{false} \\ \ldots\ldots\ldots\ldots \end{bmatrix}$
$a \land b \land c \land \ldots \Leftrightarrow h$	$\begin{bmatrix} h, a, b, c, \ldots \Rightarrow \text{false} \\ \text{true} \Rightarrow a, h \\ \text{true} \Rightarrow b, h \\ \text{true} \Rightarrow c, h \\ \ldots\ldots\ldots \end{bmatrix}$

(3) Insert truth values for hypothesis names whose truth value is implied by
the targets.

The truth value of a hypothesis h is implied if h appears in the same side
of all the lines of a positive (sub)target and in this same side of all the
lines of a negative (sub)target. The value is:

(a) if h appears on the left then h is true;

(b) if h appears on the right then h is false.

This decision is based on the fact that positive and negative targets cannot
both be theorems.

5. EXAMPLE: SEARCHING AND/OR GRAPHS IN AL3

This section presents a detailed example to illustrate the whole basic AL3 machinery at work. In the example we use a miniature knowledge-base for searching AND/OR graphs. The knowledge-base does not contain any heuristics to guide the search. It consists of one lemma, GOALTEST, and one method, EXPAND, whose detailed PROLOG definition is in Fig. 5. The preconditions for both is the existence of a hypothesis H:

goal(X) ?

where X is a node in the AND/OR graph being searched, and goal(X) means that there exists a solution subgraph for X. If X is a terminal node which 'trivially' satisfies the goal-condition then the lemma returns the fact H is true.

```
    /*** Lemma GOALTEST ***/

precond (goaltest, [H,X] ) :-
  hyp (H,goal (X)).

exec (goaltest, [H,X] , [ [H] => false] ) :- goalnode (X),!.

exec (goaltest,_, [true => false] ).

    /*** Method EXPAND ***/

precond (expand, [H,X] ) :-
  hyp (H, goal (X)).

exec (expand, [H,X] , Fact) :-
  findall (Y,succ (X,Y),Ylist),
  (Ylist=[ ],!,Fact = [true => [H] ];
    findall (Hname,newhyp (Hname,Ylist),Hlist).
  getfact(H, Hlist,X,Fact)).

newhyp (Hname,Ylist) :-
  member (Y,Ylist),
  genhyp (Hname,goal (Y)).

getfact H, Hlist,X, [((H|Hlist] => false) | Lines] ) :-
  andnode (X),!,
  findall (true => [H,H1], member (H1,Hlist), Lines).

getfact (H, Hlist,X, [(true => [H|Hlist]) | Lines] ) :-
  ornode (X),!,
  findall ([H,H1] => false, member (H1,Hlist), Lines).
```

Fig. 5 – PROLOG code of a knowledge-base for searching AND/OR graphs. The base assumes that the control module prefers lemmas to methods.

Let $Y_1, \ldots, Y_n$ be the successor nodes of a node X. The method EXPAND, when executed on the context [H,X], generates hypotheses $H_1, H_2, \ldots, H_n$ of the form

goal(Y_i) ?

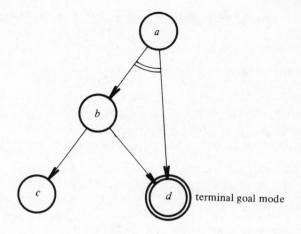

terminal goal mode

```
Current Knowledge Pool          Next execution cycle
=================               ================

Positive Target                 Conflict set (method names : contexts)

true=> [h:0]                    1 expand : [h:0,a]

Negative Target                 Which? 1.

[h:0] =>false                   Executed expand on context [h:0,a]

Hypotheses                      New facts

1 hyp (h:0,goal (a))            [h:0,h:1,h:2] =>false
                                true=> [h:0,h:1]
                                true=> [h:0,h:2]


Current Knowledge Pool          Next execution cycle
=================               ================

Positive Target                 Conflict set (method names : contexts)

true=> [h:0,h:1]                1 goaltest : [h:1,b]
true=> [h:0,h:2]                2 goaltest : [h:2,d]
                                3 expand : [h:1,b]
Negative Target                 4 expand : [h:2,d]

[h:0,h:1,h:2] =>false           Which? 1.

Hypotheses                      Executed goaltest on context [h:1,b]

1 hyp (h:0,goal (a))            New facts
2 hyp (h:1,goal (b))
3 hyp (h:2,goal (d))            true=>false
```

Fig. 6 – Part of trace, produced by AL3, when searching the AND/OR graph in top of the figure.

85

In addition, new facts are generated, namely: If X has AND successors then the facts are:

$$H \Leftrightarrow H_1 \wedge \ldots \wedge H_n$$

If X has OR successors then the facts are

$$H \Leftrightarrow H_1 \vee \ldots \vee H_n$$

The PROLOG code in Fig. 5 generates these facts already transformed into a proper form according to the transformation rules in Table 1. Fig. 6 is part of the trace, produced by AL3, when solving the problem

goal(a) ?

for the AND/OR graph in top part of Fig. 6.

6. CONCEPTS MANIPULATED BY AL3

In principle, the AL3 system as described in the previous sections is not limited to any special formalism for representing methods for problem-solving, or to any special class of concepts to be used for solving problems. In this section we present a formalism and a number of concepts that are useful for solving combinatorial problems in general and chess problems in particular. These concepts were used in the experiments with AL3 on chess endgames.

6.1 Piece-of-advice

A fundamental concept of AL1, piece-of-advice, proved to be extremely valuable, not only for representing knowledge, but also because it provides a good formal basis for precise definition of other concepts. A *piece-of-advice*, A, is a five-tuple

$$(X, BG, HG, MCX, MCY)$$

where X is the side (White or Black) to which A belongs, BG and HG are predicates on positions called *better-goal* and *holding-goal* respectively, MCX and MCY are predicates on moves, called *move-constraints* for side X and side Y respectively. Throughout the paper we use X and Y to represent both sides. Thus X can be either White or Black, and Y is always the opponent of X. Besides a mere selection of a subset of legal moves, move-constraints can impose an ordering on the moves that are selected. This becomes important for practical reasons when searching a game-tree.

A tree T is called a forcing-tree for a piece-of-advice

$$A = (X, BG, HG, MCX, MCY)$$

in a position Pos, iff T is a subtree of the game-tree rooted in Pos, such that:

(1) for every node p in T: $HG(p)$;
(2) for every nonterminal node p in T: not $BG(p)$;
(3) for every terminal node p in T: $BG(p)$ or p is a Y-to-move position from which there is no legal move that satisfies MCY;

(4) there is exactly one move in T from every X-to-move nonterminal node in T; that move must satisfy MCX;

(5) all legal moves from any nonterminal Y-to-move position in T that satisfy MCY are in T.

A piece-of-advice A is *satisfiable* in a position Pos iff there exists a forcing-tree for A in Pos. We write:

$$sat(A, Pos)$$

In fact, a piece-of-advice defines a subgame with two possible outcomes: win or loss. Legal moves of this subgame are defined by the move-constraints, and terminal positions of the subgame are defined by predicates better-goal and holding-goal. A position Pos is won for side X with respect to the subgame corresponding to a piece-of-advice A if $sat(A,Pos)$; otherwise it is lost for X with respect to A.

Note an important detail in the above definition of forcing-tree: if (1) $HG(Pos)$ and $not(BG(Pos))$, and (2) Y-to-move in Pos, and (3) no Y-move in Pos satisfies MCY then Pos is terminal node of a forcing tree. This interpretation of the 'no-move' condition ensures the following relation for any piece-of-advice and any position:

$$sat((X, BGX, HGX, MCX, MCY), Pos) \Leftrightarrow$$
$$not\ sat((Y, not(HGX), not(BGX\ and\ HGX), MCY, MCX), Pos)$$

This relationship will be referred to as 'inverse-advice relationship'. However, this definition sometimes necessitates that the test for stalemate in chess is explicitly stated in the goals of a piece-of-advice to avoid anomalous behaviour.

Some other useful relations concering the satisfiability of related pieces-of-advice are given in Bratko & Niblett (1979).

6.2 Plans

A *plan*, P, is a quadruple

$$(X, BG, HG, MCX)$$

where X is the side to which P belongs, BG and HG are predicates on positions called better-goal and holding-goal, and MCX (move-constraints for side X) is any schema for selecting and/or ordering X moves. An example of such move-constraints is a White king 'macromove' between two specified squares not exceeding a specified length, e.g.:

$$macromove(white\text{-}king, c2, e1, length \leqslant 3)\ .$$

This macromove denotes the set of all possible king-paths between squares c2 and e1 of the length of at most 3 moves (see Fig. 7). A plan with such move-constraints allows any legal White king move along this macromove.

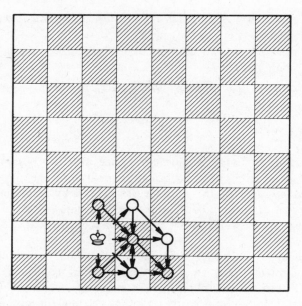

Fig. 7 – White king macromove from c2 to e1 in at most 3 moves.

Move-constraints can also prescribe an ordering of moves. For example the above king macromove can be ordered with respect to increasing length of the king-paths.

We say that a plan $P = (X, BG, HG, MCX)$ *succeeds* in a position *Pos* iff

$$\text{sat}(A, Pos)$$

where A is a piece-of-advice

$$A = (A, BG, HG, MCX, \text{anymove}) \ .$$

We write

$$\text{suc}(P, Pos) \Leftrightarrow \text{sat}(A, Pos) \ .$$

Let *Px* and *Py* be two plans

$$Px = (X, BGX, HGX, MCX)$$
$$Py = (Y, BGY, HGY, MCY) \ .$$

Then plan *Py* *refutes* plan *Px* in a position *Pos* iff

$$\text{not sat}(A, Pos)$$

where A is a piece-of-advice

$$A = (X, BGX \text{ or not}(HGY), HGX, MCX, MCY) \ .$$

We write

$$\text{ref}(Py, Px, Pos) \Leftrightarrow \text{not sat}(A, Pos) \ .$$

An equivalent definition is

$$\text{ref}(Py, Px, Pos) \Leftrightarrow \text{sat}(A1, Pos)$$

where $A1 = (Y, \text{not}(HGX), \text{not}(HGX) \text{ or not}(BGX) \text{ and } HGY, MCY, MCX)$. The equivalence of these two definitions can be proved by using the inverse-advice relationship.

Note that it is possible that a plan Py does not succeed (i.e. its better-goal is not attainable), but Py may still refute a plan Px.

6.3 "Or" combination of plans

Let $P1$ and $P2$ be plans

$$P1 = (X, BG1, HG1, MCX1)$$
$$P2 = (X, BG2, HG2, MCX2) \ .$$

A plan

$$P = P1 \text{ or } P2$$

is called an 'or-combination' of $P1$ and $P2$. The better-goal of P is $BG1$ or $BG2$. Precise combinations of the goals and move-constraints of $P1$ and $P2$ can be defined by the following AL3 method for investigating the success of or-plans.

Method OREXPAND
Precondition

$$\text{hypothesis}(H, \text{suc}(P1 \text{ or } P2, Pos)),$$
$$P1 = (X, BG1, HG1, MCX1)$$
$$P2 = (X, BG2, HG2, MCX2)$$

Action

1. Generate hypotheses: $\text{hypothesis}(Ha, \text{suc}(P1, Pos))$,
   $\text{hypothesis}(Hb, \text{suc}(P2, Pos))$
2. If Y-to-move in Pos then generate all legal successor positions $Pos_1, \ldots,$ Pos_n of Pos, else generate legal successor positions $Pos_1, \ldots, Pos_n$ such that the moves $Pos \rightarrow Pos_i$ satisfy either $MCX1$ or $MCX2$ or both. The ordering of $Pos_1, \ldots, Pos_n$ is: rough ordering by the criterion "first satisfy both move-contraints", and fine ordering as prescribed by $MCX1$ and $MCX2$.
3. Generate:
   $\text{hypothesis}(H1, \text{suc}(P1 \text{ or } P2, Pos_1))$
   . . . .
   $\text{hypothesis}(Hn, \text{suc}(P1 \text{ or } P2, Pos_n))$
4. Return facts
   (a) if X-to-move in Pos then
      $$Ha \vee Hb \Rightarrow H1 \vee H2 \vee \ldots \vee Hn$$
      $$Ha \vee Hb \vee H1 \vee \ldots \vee Hn \Leftrightarrow H$$
   (b) if Y-to-move in Pos then
      $$Ha \vee Hb \Rightarrow H1 \wedge H2 \wedge \ldots \wedge Hn$$
      $$Ha \vee Hb \vee (H1 \wedge \ldots \wedge Hn) \Leftrightarrow H \ .$$

6.4 Modification of plan by plan

Let $P1$ and $P2$ be two plans for side X. The modification of $P1$ by $P2$ is a plan $P = P1 \bmod P2$, such that the goal of P is the same as the goal of $P1$, but the sequence of steps of $P1$ may be interrupted by inserting steps of $P2$. An AL3 method for investigating the success of a modified plan is:

Method MODEXPAND
Precondition

> hypothesis$(H, \text{suc}(P1 \bmod P2, Pos))$,
> $P1 = (X, BG1, HG1, MCX1)$,
> $P2 = (X, BG2, HG2, MCX2)$

Action

1. Generate: Hypothesis$(Ha, \text{suc}(P1, Pos))$.
2. If Y-to-move in Pos then generate all legal successors $Pos_1, \ldots, Pos_n$ of Pos else generate legal successors $Pos_1, \ldots, Pos_n$ satisfying $MCX1$ or $MCX2$ or both. The ordering of $Pos_1, \ldots, Pos_n$ is: rough ordering by "first satisfy both move-constraints", then "satisfy $MCX1$" then "satisfy $MCX2$"; fine ordering as prescribed by $MCX1$ and $MCX2$.
3. Generate:
   > hypothesis$(H1, \text{suc}(P1 \bmod P2, Pos_1))$
   > ....
   > hypothesis$(Hn, \text{suc}(P1 \bmod P2, Pos_n))$
4. Return facts:
   (a) if X-to-move in Pos then
   > $Ha \Rightarrow H1 \lor \ldots \lor Hn$
   > $Ha \lor H1 \lor \ldots \lor Hn \Leftrightarrow H$
   (b) if Y-to-move in Pos then
   > $Ha \Rightarrow H1 \land \ldots \land Hn$
   > $Ha \lor (H1 \land \ldots \land Hn) \Leftrightarrow H$.

7. A KPKP KNOWLEDGE-BASE

Here we outline a small AL3 knowledge-base for the king and pawn *vs.* king and pawn chess ending with both pawns passed (pawns not on the same file or on adjacent files). Correct play in this ending can be very difficult, as indicated by many chess studies from this domain (e.g. Averbach & Maizelis 1974). An example is in Fig. 1.

The KPKP knowledge-base contains two lemmas. One, CATCHPAWN, decides whether a king can stop a running opponent's pawn. The other, PAWNRACE, decides which pawn wins a pawn-race.

The methods in the base implement basic motifs of the KPKP ending with passed pawns, and some more general, "meta-level" ideas about plans. The following is an informal description of the most important methods. Appropriate facts generated by the methods are obvious. At present the KPKP knowledge-base is not complete in the sense of producing correct play in all positions from this domain.

Method WIN

To win it is necessary to queen the pawn and not allow the opponent's pawn to queen successfully.

Method DRAW

To investigate the question "Can one side draw?", consider the question" Can the other side win?".

Method PUSH

One plan for queening is to push the pawn.

Method STOPPAWN

One way of preventing an opponent's plan to queen the pawn is to stop it by the king. It is assumed that the capture of that pawn implies that the pawn has been stopped.

Method RACE

One counter-plan against a queening plan is to queen own pawn.

Method STOPKING

If an opponent's plan consists of a king-macromove, then it may be refuted by a king's intervention: own king-macromove intersecting the opponent's king-macromove.

Method MODIFYPLAN

If a plan $P1$ fails against an opponent's plan R then $P1$ may be successfully improved in the following way: find a plan, $P2$, which, hopefully, refutes the plan R, and propose a new plan: $P1$ modified by $P2$, i.e. $P = P1 \bmod P2$. To find $P2$, AL3 solves a local subproblem with its own local target of refuting R. To solve the local subproblem AL3 may use all the knowledge in the knowledge-base.

Method ORPLAN

If two plans, $R1$ and $R2$, are known not to refute an opponent's plan P, then the or-combination of $R1$ and $R2$, i.e. $R = R1 \; or \; R2$, may refute P.

Method SEARCH

This method converts a hypothesis of the form suc($Plan, Pos$) or ref($Plan1, Plan2, Pos$) into sat(A, Pos) where A is a corresponding piece-of-advice, and checks the satisfiability of A by searching the game-tree. This method can be very expensive and is therefore used only occasionally.

Method EXPAND

Expands a hypothesis of the form suc($Plan, Pos$) by generating successor positions of *Pos*, subject to move-contraints in *Plan*, and hypotheses that *Plan* succeeds in the successor positions. New facts are generated according to who is to move in *Pos* and according to the form of *Plan* (see expansion rules for *P1 mod P2* and *P1 or P2* in the previous section).

To illustrate how this knowledge-base works, consider the position in Fig. 8. AL3 is asked the question "Can White win in this position?". Fig. 9 shows the current-knowledge-pool at the moment when AL3 has found a correct plan for White to win. This is: queen the White pawn by pushing it and in the mean-time stop the Black pawn with the White king if necessary.

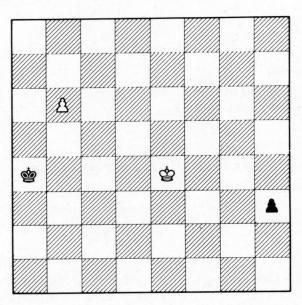

Fig. 8 — White to move, can White win? Correct is Ke4–f3 stopping the Black pawn. After that, the White pawn cannot be stopped.

8. DISCUSSION

There are several ways of looking at the AL3 system. One possible view is that AL3 is a theorem-prover which accepts a problem in the form of a formula to be proved or disproved. If the formula is neither a theorem nor a contradiction then AL3 tries to find new facts about the problem. The new facts are then used as additional axioms for proving or disproving the initial formula. In this sense each executional cycle aims at producing the most useful new axioms, such that they bring the formula as close as possible towards a theorem or a contradiction.

Another view of AL3 is that AL3 is a problem-solver which uses a special formalism for problem representation. This formalism can be thought of as a generalization of two known schemas for problem-representation: the state-space representation and the AND/OR graph representation (e.g. Nilsson 1971). With

```
Current Knowledge Pool
===================

Postive Target

[h:4,h:5] => [h:0,h:1,h:2,h:3,h:8]

Negative Target

[h:0,h:1,h:4,h:5] => [h:2,h:3]

Facts

1  h:3 is false
2  h:5 is true
3  h:7 is true

Hypotheses

1  hyp (h:0,canwin (w,pos))
2  hyp (h:1,suc (p:1,pos))
3  hyp (h:2,suc (p:2,pos))
4  hyp (h:3,ref (p:3,p:2,pos))
5  hyp (h:4,ref (p:4,p:2,pos))
6  hyp (h:5,ref (p:5,p:2,pos))
7  hyp (h:6,suc (p:5,pos))
8  hyp (h:7,ref (p:6,p:5,pos))
9  hyp (h:8,suc (p:2 mod p:6,pos))

Plans

1  plan (p:1,w,queenwin (w),alive (w) & (not queendraw (b)),any)
2  plan (p:2,w,queenwin (w),alive (w) & (not queendraw (b)),push (w))
3  plan (p:3,b,stopped (w),nil,macro (b,k,path (w,p)))
4  plan (p:4,b,queendraw (b),alive (b),any)
5  plan (p:5,b,queendraw (b),alive (b),push (b))
6  plan (p:6,w,stopped (b),nil,macro (w,k,path (b,p)))
```

Fig. 9 — AL3's current-knowledge-pool at the moment when a correct plan has been found for the position in Fig. 8. The symbol "pos" denotes that position. Goals in the plans mean: queenwin(w): White pawn has queened and position is won for White; queendraw(b): Black pawn queened and position not lost for Black; alive(w): White pawn not captured; etc.

respect to the logical relationships among the nodes in the problem space, the state-space representation could be called an 'OR-graph' representation, because all the sibling nodes in the state-space are disjunctively related. In this sense, the AND/OR-graph representation is a generalization of the state-space representation. Further, AL3's representation is a generalization of AND/OR-graph representation, and could be therefore called a 'general graph' representation, 'general' because it allows any logical relationship between the neighbouring nodes in the problem-space. This logical relationship is defined by new facts that can be any propositional calculus formula.

AL3, viewed as above, solves problems by searching a problem-space that does not consist of objects, defined by the problem-domain itself (e.g. rules of the game), but also of higher-order concepts like plans, macromoves, and pieces-of-advice. There is no formal distinction in the knowledge-base of AL3 between rules of the game and knowledge about how to solve problems.

Very little has been said about the control module of AL3 which implements the overall problem-solving strategy. One such strategic decision is whether to keep the current target in the form of a product or to carry out the multiplication, or to do the multiplication only partially, on some of the subtargets. In the experiments with AL3, described in this paper, the control module used the following simple strategy:

1. Carry out every multiplication in the target immediately.
2. Find 'interesting' hypotheses by simply counting the number of hypothesis occurrences in the left- and right-hand sides of the lines in the target. Hypotheses with high frequencies are interesting. Include in the conflict set only lemmas and methods that are applicable to interesting hypotheses, and that produce 'complementary' facts (that is: if an interesting hypothesis tends to occur on the left-hand side in the target then a complementary fact contains this hypothesis on the right-hand side).
3. Choose a lemma or a method from the conflict set in the following order of preference: first lemmas, then easy methods, then difficult methods (methods in the knowledge-base are characterised by 'easy' or 'difficult').

Design of more sophisticated control strategies seems to be necessary for solving larger-scale problems. One way of improving the above simple strategy is to delay (partially) the multiplication operation when updating the target and thus control the growth of the target. Another improvement, aiming at the reduction of the possibly very time-consuming matching of method-preconditions against the complete CKP is to limit this matching to a 'window' in CKP only. The window consists of the hypotheses dealt with in the previous executional cycle and their neighbouring hypothesis. Thus the window provides a mechanism for focusing AL3's attention to a part of CKP.

Another interesting problem for further experiments is concerned with the inclusion of more 'meta-knowledge' into the knowledge-base to facilitate more sophisticated reasoning about plans and pieces-of-advice. Such knowledge could provide rules for deciding whether a given plan, $P1$ say, is more specific than another plan, $P2$; then if yes and if $P2$ is known to fail then $P1$ also fails. Even very simple 'meta-methods' in the KPKP knowledge-base are sufficient for discovering concepts like a joint action of a king and a pawn. For example, if White's plan is to queen his pawn by pushing the pawn, and a Black king-macromove refutes this plan by stopping the White pawn, the White's plan can be modified by a White king-macromove preventing the Black king-macromove. This effectively results in the idea: support the advancement of the White pawn by the White king.

Acknowledgements

The author would like to thank Professor Donald Michie for encouragement and support, T. B. Niblett for collaboration at the previous stages of this research, and the Edinburgh PROLOG development group (L. Byrd, F. Pereira and D. Warren) for their continuous advice on the PROLOG implementation of AL3. The following institutions made this work possible by providing financial and other support: the Science Research Council, UK; the Machine Intelligence Research Unit, University of Edinburgh, UK; the Faculty of Electrical Engineering and Jozef Stefan Institute, Ljubljana, Yugoslavia.

References

Averbach, Y., & Maizelis, I., (1974). *Pawn Endings*. London: Batsford.
Bratko, I., & Michie, D., (1980a). A representation for pattern-knowledge in chess end-games, in *Advances in Computer Chess 2*, 31–56, (ed. Clarke, M. R. B.). Edinburgh: Edinburgh University Press.
Bratko, I., & Michie, D., (1980b). An advice-program for a complex chess-programming task, *Computer Journal*, 23, 353–350.
Bratko, I., & Niblett, T., (1979). Conjectures and refutations in a framework for chess end-game knowledge, in *Expert Systems in the Microelectronic Age*, 83–102, (ed. Michie, D.). Edinburgh: Edinburgh University Press.
Michie, D., (1976). An advice-taking system for computer chess. *Comp. Bull.*, 11, 12–14.
Michie, D., (1980). Problems of the conceptual interface between machine and human problem-solvers, *Experimental Programming Reports No. 36*. Edinburgh: Machine Intelligence Research Unit, University of Edinburgh. To appear in *Prospects for Man: Computers and Society*. Toronto: York University.
Mozetic, I., (1979). Advice Language and the AL 1.5 program system. Work report and manual. Ljubljana: Jozef Stefan Institute. A shortened version appears as *Research Memorandum MIP-R-130*. Edinburgh: Machine Intelligence Research Unit, University of Edinburgh.
Nilsson, N. J., (1971). *Problem Solving Methods in Artificial Intelligence*. New York: McGraw-Hill.
Pereira, L. M., Pereira, F. C. N., & Warren, D. H. D., (1978). User's guide to DECsystem-10 PROLOG. Edinburgh: Department of Artificial Intelligence, University of Edinburgh.
Pitrat, J., (1977). A chess combinations program which uses plans. *Artificial Intelligence*, 8, 275–321.
Raphael, B., (1976). *The Thinking Computer: Mind Inside Matter*. San Francisco: Freeman.
Tan, S. T., (1977). Describing pawn structures, in *Advances in Computer Chess*, 1, 74–88, (ed. Clarke, M. R. B.). Edinburgh: Edinburgh University Press.
Waterman D. A., & Hayes–Roth, F., (eds.) (1978). *Pattern-Directed Inference Systems*. New York: Academic Press.
Wilkins, D., (1979). Using patterns to solve problems and control search, Ph.D.Thesis. Stanford: Computer Science Department, Stanford University.

APPENDIX: SOME DETAILS OF AL3's PERFORMANCE ON KPKP

The KPKP knowledge base, outlined in section 7, also contains methods which employ the game-tree search. Using these methods, AL3 can of course, in principle, solve any KPKP problem. However, a straightforward application of search would be rather complex: in difficult KPKP positions, the depth of search required would be at least 15 ply with the branching factor of about 8 (before pawns become queens, and much more afterwards) in the space of at least several hundred thousands of positions. Owing to the inefficiency of the present PROLOG implementation of AL3, searches of this size are prohibitive. However, it is interesting to see what AL3 can do if the search is used only very modestly, in particular if the numbers of nodes searched are of a similar order of magnitude to that known for human chess masters. This constraint is interesting not only for the sake of efficiency, but also because it ensures that the program's behaviour fits the 'human window' (D. Michie 1980). The application of the search methods was, in the experiments reported here, constrained so that any search was limited to at most 100 (or sometimes 200) nodes, i.e. 100 chess positions.

Comparatively simple positions, like the one in Fig. 8, present no problems to AL3 under this constraint. The system easily finds the correct main idea and is also able to work out all the tactical details up to the decisive queening of pawns. In difficult KPKP positions, like the Reti study in Fig. 1, this search constraint can make the system behave less confidently. Fig. 10 shows the AL3's CKP after 15 main executional cycles when solving the Reti study. At this moment, AL3 knows that:

(1) The White king alone cannot catch the Black pawn.
(2) Black, however, cannot simply push his pawn because in that case the White pawn wins the pawn-race. Therefore the advancement of the Black pawn is necessarily slowed down because the Black king has in the meantime to stop the White pawn.
(3) The White pawn alone cannot save the draw; but it is not clear whether a joint action of White pawn and White king to promote the pawn refutes Black's plan.

So far AL3 has tried to investigate four hypotheses by search: $h4, h10, h12$, and $h13$. Three times the search was carried out successfully within the search limit. Complexities of these searches were: $h4$: 3 nodes, $h10$: 6 nodes, and $h13$: 35 nodes. The remaining search failed to produce a fact as the search budget was exhausted before a result was obtained. At this point the plans for both sides have become too complex to be investigated by search limited to 100 nodes. Therefore the system constructs the 'state-of-the-art' hypothesis by combining all currently known and not yet refuted ideas for both sides. The state-of-the-art hypothesis here becomes:

$$\text{ref}(p2 \text{ or } p3 \bmod p6 \text{ or } p6, p1 \bmod p4, \text{reti}) = ?$$

This in fact contains the best plans for both sides. The system now tries to investigate this question by searching to the greatest depth that is still doable within the 100 node search limit. It turns out that search to the depth of 9 ply is still doable under this constraint. The search takes 78 nodes and produces a forcing-tree consisting of 57 moves. This forcing-tree is proposed by the system

```
Current Knowledge Pool
==================

Positive Target

[h:1] => [h:0,h:2,h:8]
[h:1] => [h:0,h:2,h:12,h:14]

Negative Target

[h:0] => [h:1,h:2,h:8]

Facts

1  h:3 is false
2  h:4 is true
3  h:10 is false
4  h:13 is false

Hypotheses

1   hyp (h:0,candraw (w,reti))
2   hyp (h:1,canwin (b,reti))
3   hyp (h:2,suc (p:1,reti))
4   hyp (h:3,ref (p:2,p:1,reti))
5   hyp (h:4,ref (p:3,p:1,reti))
6   hyp (h:5,suc (p:3,reti))
7   hyp (h:6,ref (p:4,p:3,reti))
8   hyp (h:7,ref (p:5,p:3,reti))
9   hyp (h:8,suc (p:1 mod p:4,reti))
10  hyp (h:9,suc (p:4,reti))
11  hyp (h:10,ref (p:3,p:1 mod p:4,reti))
12  hyp (h:11,ref (p:6,p:4,reti))
13  hyp (h:12,ref (p:3 mod p:6,p:1 mod p:4,reti))
14  hyp (h:13,ref (p:2,p:1 mod p:4,reti))
15  hyp (h:14,ref (p:6,p:1 mod p:4,reti))

Plans

1   plan (p:1,b,queenwin (b) or easywin (b),not pexposed (b) and
    not easystop (b) and not qeendraw (w) and not easywin (w),push(b))
2   plan (p:2,w,fail,nil,catchmacro (w,k))
3   plan (p:3,w,queendraw (w),alive (w),push (w))
4   plan (p:4,b,fail,nil,catchmacro (b,k))
5   plan (p:5,b,queenwin (b),alive (b),push (b))
6   plan (p:6,w,fail,nil,macro (w,k,8..8,stopset (macro (b,k,1..6,path (w,p),
    l=<2,shortestfirst)),l=<6,shortestfirst))
```

Fig. 10 – CKP after 15 executional cycles when solving the Reti study.

as the 'best try' for both sides. It contains the correct move for White, Kg7, which draws. The tree also foresees the two critical variations starting by two of Black's replies: h4 and Kb6. The forcing-tree indicates the intention to answer the move h4 by the correct Kf6, preserving the draw, but Kb6 is intended to be answered by Kg6 which loses. Thus although the system plays the correct move Kg7 this result is not perfect as the system does not predict the correct further play in all variations. Indeed, in the variation 1 Kg7 Kb6 the system plays the losing 2 Kg6. However, if the constraint on search is relaxed by shifting the search limit to 200 nodes, the system plays correctly in all variations starting from the Reti position in Fig. 1. This new search limit allows the system to generate a forcing-tree with the correct reaction to Kb6 in the variation: 1 Kg7 Kb6, 2 Kf6 h4, 3 Ke5! h3, 4 Kd6 etc. The complexity of this critical search is 184 nodes.

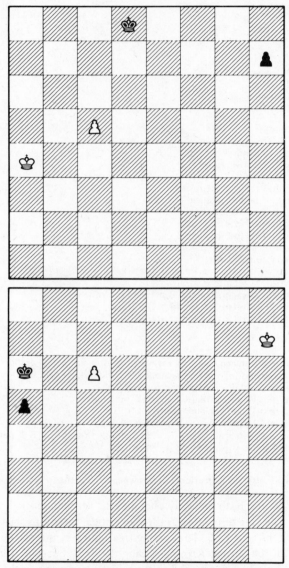

Fig. 11 – A study by Moravec (first position) and a study by Adamson. Both: White to move and draw.

Fig. 11 shows two other difficult examples in which AL3 behaves similarly as in the Reti study. It correctly finds the plans for both sides, and also finds the best first two moves for White within the search limit of 100 nodes. Again, the search-constraint makes it impossible to work out all the details up to obviously drawn positions. In the study by Moravec the system tries seven times to solve subproblems by game-tree search. Five times the search produces an answer (search statistics for these five searches are: 81 nodes, 6 nodes, 5 nodes, 59 nodes, and 86 nodes). Twice the search fails to produce a result before 100 nodes have been generated. This is, however, sufficient for the system to propose the following pretty manoeuvre of the White king which preserves the draw: 1 Kb5 h5, 2 Kc6! (with the idea 2 ... h4, 3 Kb7 followed by the advancement of the White pawn), or if 1 ... Kc7 then 2 Kc4 with a draw.

Similarly in the study by Adamson, the system proposes as the best lines for both sides a forcing-tree which contains the solution of the study: 1 Kg6 a4 (or Kb6), 2 Kf5. Again, owing to the 100 node limit, the forcing-tree does not predict all the lines up to obviously drawn positions.

In the examples so far, the system was, although impeded by the search-limit, able to find correct ideas and correct play. However, an example has been found (Fig. 12) which shows how the 100 node search-limit can lead to serious troubles. Difficult positions require the combination of several ideas by combining several plans in appropriate ways to find composed plans which actually work. As these plans become more complicated, they are harder to verify

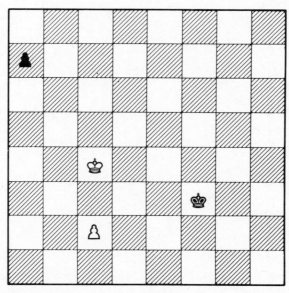

Fig. 12 – A study by Grigoriev: White to move and win. Solution is: 1 Kd4! Kf4, 2 c4 Kf5, 3 Kd5 etc. The idea of 1 Kd4! is to open the path of the White pawn, to prevent the Black king from getting in front of the White pawn, and to retain an option for the White king to stop the Black pawn at square a1.

by search. This can prevent the system from discovering some useful fact during the problem solving process. In a study by Grigoriev in Fig. 12, the system discovers that White has to advance his pawn and try to prevent the Black king from stopping this pawn, and that Black has to stop the White pawn by the king or advance his own pawn. But there are not enough facts known to motivate the system to consider another vital component of the correct White plan: White king has also to guard the Black pawn. The move which AL3 finally proposes is c3 which allows Black to draw.

4

A provably correct advice strategy for the end-game of King and Pawn versus King

T. B. Niblett

Machine Intelligence Research Unit
University of Edinburgh, UK

This paper describes a strategy for the endgame king and pawn *vs.* king (KPK), and its implementation. Consideration is given to the knowledge representation issues involved, and to methods by which the strategy can be demonstrated correct.

Although one of the most elementary chess endgames, KPK is not trivial for the inexperienced player. There are many positions where the correct move can only be found by subtle reasoning and considerable use of domain-specific knowledge. Two examples are given in Fig. 1 for the reader to consider before a more detailed discussion is given.

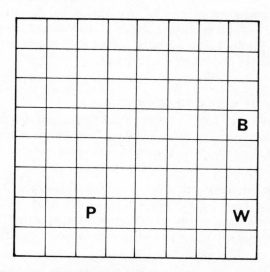

Fig. 1a – White to move. White's only winning move is Kh3. This position is one of the deepest (37 ply) wins in the KPK space.

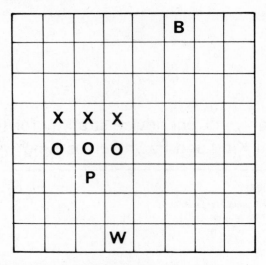

Fig. 1b — White to move. White's only winning move is Kc2.

The KPK endgame is highly resistant to conventional programming techniques. It can take months of programmer effort to implement, and then it is extremely hard to produce a *correct* program. Kopec (1979) details some of the problems. The endgame has been studied extensively. Decision rules of classifying positions have been produced by Beal (1977) and Shapiro & Niblett (1981). Knowledge-based playing programs have been written by Tan (1972), Harris (Kopec 1979), and Bramer (1980). Bramer's program has been demonstrated correct by exhaustive enumeration of all positions. I shall discuss the principles of the endgame as given in chess textbooks. I shall present the playing strategy and discuss it. Finally I shall discuss a method of implementation, designed to reduce the burden of performing deep searches.

THE PLAY OF KING AND PAWN *VS.* KING

My description of KPK is based on the lucid exposition in *Pawn Endings* (Averbakh & Maizelis 1974), the standard textbook for the ending.

The knowledge embodied in the text can conveniently be divided into two categories:

(1) General *strategic* principles describing the structure of the ending and the goals for the side with the pawn (here taken to be White).

(2) Specific *tactical* examples to illustrate the application of these principles and to note any exceptions which may occur.

My aim in the development of a playing strategy was to reflect this separation of knowledge into two categories and to investigate its transcription into knowledge structures in a program. At the same time attention has been paid to the

102

nature and extent of additional knowledge that must be added because of insufficient specification in the text.

Below is a brief overview of Averbakh's description of the ending, including both the strategic and tactical components. I describe ways in which his description is inadequate for a playing program and present the advice language strategy.

The play of KPK is determined by two considerations:

— The square of the pawn, and
— The pawn's critical squares

Fig. 2 illustrates the square of the pawn.

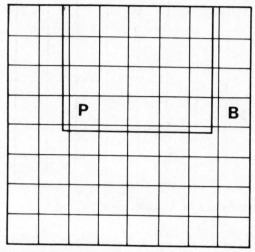

Fig. 2 — White to move. The 'square' of the pawn.

With White to move (WTM) the pawn advances, the square contracts and the Black king cannot move into the new square, allowing the White pawn to safely queen. With Black to move (BTM) the Black king can enter the square and so prevent the pawn queening.

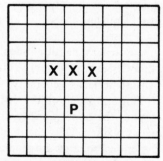

Fig. 3a — The critical squares are 2 ranks ahead of the pawn.

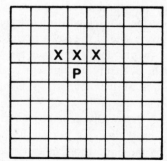

Fig. 3b — The critical squares are 1 rank ahead of the pawn.

The critical squares of the pawn are shown in Fig. 3. When the pawn's rank is less than 5 the critical squares are shown in Fig. 3a, otherwise as in Fig. 3b. If the White king can occupy one of the critical squares White wins whoever is to move.

Averbakh treats the rookpawn as a special case, with only one critical square, the location of which is independent of the pawn, shown in Fig. 4.

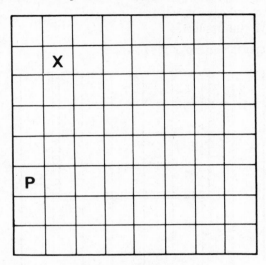

Fig. 4 – The critical square for the 1ook's pawn.

These two principles, of the pawn's square and occupation of the critical squares provide a broad orientation, or strategy, for the player with the pawn. By its nature the tactical component is impossible to summarize concisely. Averbakh cites about a dozen examples of play occupying several pages of text. Fig. 1b is an often cited example.

In this position White can force occupation of one of the pawn's critical squares (marked with an X), by the move sequence Kc2-b3-b4 and thence either gain the opposition on c4 or move to b5. Any other path for the White king fails. This position is intended to illustrate the heuristic of moving the White king to the opposite side of the pawn from the Black king if possible.

It is worth noting the example at slightly greater length, because it demonstrates the difficulty of representing this type of knowledge in a program. A direct translation of the heuristic is inappropriate because it lacks generality. The solution to the problem of White's forcing his king onto one of the critical squares is essentially geometric. From the 'theory' of the opposition we know that if the White king can reach one of the squares marked 'O' without Black achieving the opposition, he can reach one of the critical squares. By geometric considerations we see that following the path d1-c2-b3-b4 White can reach a square marked 'O' without Black being able to force the opposition since in the starting position he is already 2 files to the right of the White king. The problem with the original heuristic is that it is applicable in only a limited class of positions, and it is hard to produce a description of exactly which positions these are.

In a later section dealing with implementation of the advice strategy I shall return to this position and show that this type of elementary geometric consideration can be implemented by choosing a suitable representation for the search strategy.

There is another major distinction that can be drawn within this tactical knowledge about the domain. This is knowledge about exceptional positions where the normal search strategy is inadequate. An example is shown in Fig. 5. The standard procedure for White in positions of this type is to advance the pawn, thereby assuring that he will be able to occupy one of the pawn's critical squares with the pawn further advanced. In this case, however, advancing the pawn leads to stalemate, and White has to pursue an alternative plan viz. Kc7–b6–a6, followed if possible by Ka7 else by Pb6. The important point here is that we must realize that the *tactical* plan to achieve our *strategic* goal (of advancing the pawn) fails, and that another tactical plan for the *same* strategic goal should be applied. As we shall see, this dual level of structure enormously simplifies the programming of the ending. This example shows a strictly pattern-based approach to be more unwieldy as the number of patterns in the knowledge base can grow large. An element of search seems convenient for a compact representation of the ending.

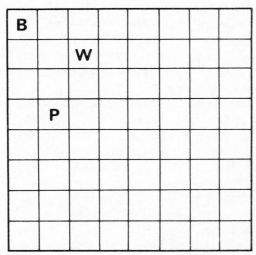

Fig. 5 – White to move.

The textbook representation of the problem domain is lucid to the human player. For a playing program it is deficient in several respects.

Necessary background information is omitted, usually because it is too obvious. For example Averbakh states that positions of the type shown in Fig. 3

are won for White with either side to move. He does not explicitly allow for the possibility that the Black king on move may be able to capture the pawn, precisely because it 'goes without saying'. When writing a playing program, or trying rigorously to prove the correctness of a playing strategy, these considerations have to be taken into account!

The tactical information supplied is not precise enough for a formal description of the search strategy to be used in achieving the strategic goals. Again a human player is expected to use his more general chess knowledge to fill in these gaps.

From these considerations we can conclude that a major task of the advice strategy designer is to use the knowledge representation tools at his disposal in producing a formally defined strategy which is correct. Indeed it is of considerable interest to see exactly how much knowledge is needed for a complete specification of play in the ending.

THE ADVICE STRATEGY

The advice strategy for KPK was produced within the framework of textbook knowledge described above. The other major constraint on its form was its development within the framework of AL 1 (Michie 1976, Bratko & Michie 1980). AL 1 (Advice Language 1) was developed to provide a convenient, flexible means of codifying and coordinating 'chunks' of chess knowledge. I shall not describe the AL 1 system in detail but only the main idea from it which I use, of a 'piece of advice'. A formal definition of a piece of advice and its satisfiability is given below.

A piece of advice for side X is an ordered 4-tuple of the form (bx, hx, mcx, mcy) where bx and hx are predicates on positions, mcx and mcy are predicates on moves.

bx, hx, mcx, and mcy are called better-goal, holding goal, X-move-constraint, and Y-move-constraint respectively.

Given a position pos and a piece of advice $A = (bx, hx, mcx, mcy)$ a forcing tree for A in pos is a subtree T of the game rooted in pos such that

(1) for every q in T, $hx(q)$
(2) for every nonterminal q in T, not $bx(q)$
(3) for every terminal q in T either $bx(q)$ or q is a Y-to-move position where no move satifies mcy
(4) there is exactly one move in T from every X-to-move nonterminal in T and it satisfies mcx
(5) all legal moves from any nonterminal Y-to-move position in T satisfying mcy are in T

A piece of advice A is *satisfiable* in a position pos if there exists a forcing tree for A in pos, written $s(A, pos)$.

106

I use the convention that the argument referring to the current position in the tree is suppressed for goals occurring in a plan or piece of advice, e.g. the goal mainpatt(q) is written mainpatt.

Intuitively, if a piece of advice is satisfiable for White from *pos* then White can force the achievement of the better goal of the advice from *pos*. Since a piece of advice has fixed goals and move-constraints, and no idea of sequencing of goals, we introduce the notion of a *plan*, which can be thought of as representing the skeleton of a piece of advice or sequence of pieces of advice. The notation I shall use for plans is, in Backus–Naur form:

Plan $::= < b, h, M>$ | plan ;plan | $<$ plan, $h, b >$ where M is the movement of a specified piece from one location to another (corresponding to move constraints), h and b are holding and better goals respectively. The following expansion rule is used: $\ll$ plan, $b, h>, b', h' > = <$ plan, b or b', h and $h' >$. A more detailed discussion of plans can be found in Bratko & Niblett (1980).

The 'advice text' given below is a (rough) English translation of the advice strategy. The strategy itself is written as a set of logical rules. The notion of controlling the critical squares of the pawn is captured by the pattern *mainpatt*, which is a generalization of the pattern of Fig. 3. The notion of the 'pawn's square' is captured by the predicate *canrun* which holds whenever the pawn can promote without the White king having to move. A special pattern *rookpatt* is used in the rookpawn case.

AN ADVICE TEXT FOR KPK

To determine whether White wins from any position, consider the following rules in order:

- If the pawn can run White wins
- If the pawn is a rookpawn White wins iff a position is achievable where the pawn can run or where rookpatt holds.
- If the pawn's rank is 7 White wins if the White king can safely move next to the queening square
- If the pawn's rank is 6 and the pattern shown below holds, White wins

Black king on any but X

107

- If the pawn's rank is greater than or equal to 5 then White wins if he can can achieve mainpatt or the pattern of the previous rule.
- If mainpatt holds then White wins
- White wins iff mainpatt or canrun is achievable

AN ADVICE LANGUAGE STRATEGY FOR KPK

Rules

1) wins(white,P) ← wins-with(white,P,S).

2) wins-with(white,P,<Kdist(p,qsq(p)) = 0, pawnsafe,ifstalepatt then

$$\text{kingmove}$$
$$\text{else}$$
$$\text{pawnmove}>)$$
$$\leftarrow \text{canrun}(p, P)$$

3.1) wins-with(white,P,rookplan) ← rookpatt(P).

3.2) wins-with(white,P,
  <<canrun ∨ rookpatt,pawnsafe,nil>;apply(Rule)>)↔
  rookfile(p, P) ∧ s((canrun ∨ rookpatt : pawnsafe : nil : nil), P).

4) wins-with(white,P,
  <<kdist(w,qsq(p)=1,pawnsafe,kingmove>;aply(Rule)>)
  ← rank(p,P) = 7 ∧ ((kdist(w,qsq(p)) = 1:pawnsafe:kingmove:nil),P).

5) wins-with(white,P,<<nil,nil,push(p)>;apply(Rule)>)
  ← pattern-rank6(P).

6) wins-with(white,P,
  <<pattern-rank6 ∧ mainpatt,nil,nil>;apply(Rule)>)
  ← rank(p, P) >= 5 ∧ not(mainpatt(P)) ∧
  s((pattern-rank6 ∨ mainpatt: nil: nil: nil,P).

7.1) wins-with(white, P, <mainplan; apply(Rule)>) ← mainpatt(P).

7.2) wins-with(white,P,<<mainpatt ∨ canrun,pawnsafe,nil>
$$; \text{apply(Rule)}>)$$
  ← s((mainpatt ∨ canrun : pawnsafe : nil : nil), P).

NOTATION AND DEFINITIONS

w, b, p — Denote the White king, Black king and White pawn respectively.

P — The current (White-to-move) position.

Plans — A plan is a specification of a strategy for one side. The Backus–Naur formulation is:

  Plan ::= <Better–goal, Holding–goal, Move–constraints> |
    <Plan; Plan>.

Advice — A piece of advice is a quadruple:

  (better goal : holding goal : W move constraint : B move constraint)

Satisfiability — A piece of advice A is satisfiable in position P, i.e. s(A,P) iff there exists a non-empty forcing tree satisfying A rooted in P.

wins(Side,Position) — iff Side can force a win from Position.

wins with(Side, Position, Plan) — iff Side wins from Position with Plan.

wtm(P) — iff White is to move in P.

btm(P) — iff Black is to move in P.

qsq(p,P) — The queening square of the pawn in P.

stalepatt(P) — iff promoting the pawn to a rook or queen leads to stalemate.

canrun(P) — iff s((p on Kdist(p,qsq(p)) = 0 : pawnsafe : pawnmove : nil),P).

pawnsafe(P) — iff wtm(P) or Black cannot legally capture the pawn.

rank(Piece, Position) — The rank of Piece in Position.

kdist(Piece1, Piece2, Position) — The number of kingmoves (not necessarily legal) from Piece1 to Piece2 in Position.

apply(Rule) — The plan found by applying the appropriate rule.

push(Piece, Pos) — The move of Piece1 rank up the board in Pos.

pattern-rank6(P) — iff the White pawn is on the 6th rank with the White king next to it on the same rank, and the Black king is not on the 8th rank1 file distant from the pawn.

rookpatt(P) — iff the White pawn is on the rook's file and the White king is on some other file, on the same rank as the Black king, and nearer the pawn with Black-to-move.

rookfile(p, P) — iff the pawn is on the rook's file in P.

mainpatt(P) — iff wtm(P) and the White king coordinates relative to the pawn are $(-1,2),(0,2)$ or $(1,2)$ or $(-1,1),(0,1)$ or $(1,1)$ and the two kings are not in direct opposition.

mainplan — The plan of achieving mainpatt with the pawn further advanced. More formally it is given as:

$$<\text{on Kdist(p,qsq(p))} = 0, \text{pawnsafe, if } 7 < \text{rank(w)} < \text{rank(b) then}$$

rookplan — is the plan:

$$<\text{on-Kdist}(p, qsq(p)) = 0, \text{pawnsafe, if } 7 < \text{rank (w)} < \text{rank(b) then}$$
$$\text{push(w)}$$
$$\text{else}$$
$$\text{push(p)} >$$

The proof of correctness is not given here. I shall make a couple of points about it. It is necessary to show that

(1) White wins from any of the patterns on the right hand side of a rule. The main burden of this half of the proof is to show that from any position satisfying mainpatt White can force mainpatt with the pawn further advanced, or promote the pawn

(2) If White can win, one of the conditions on the right hand side of a rule is true.

The proof is straightforward though long. Care must be taken in dealing with exceptional positions. For example it is true that if the pawn can run White

109

wins, but not true that White can always win by promoting the pawn. There is one exceptional position where any promotion that could win causes stalemate!

The rule which caused most trouble to produce was for the rookpawn. The textbook contains very few examples of play and the strategic rule is vague. A detailed analysis of critical positions had to be made before a rule which produced acceptable search characteristics was found. Fig. 6 shows examples of difficult positions with the pawn on the rook's file.

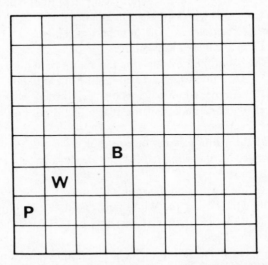

Fig. 6a – White to move. The main variation ensuring that the pawn can run is,
1. Kb4 Kd5　2. Kb5 Kd4　3. a4 Kd5　4. a5 Kd6　5. Kb6

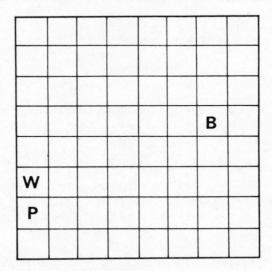

Fig. 6b – White to move. Kb4 wins for White.

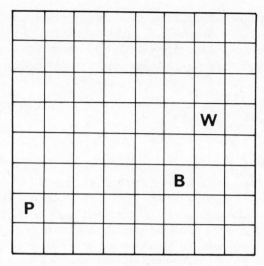

Fig. 6c – White to move. Kf5 wins for White.

The rule settled on is that White should manoeuver for a position where the pawn can run. There are two problems with this rule. Firstly, the search is too deep, and secondly it is not trivial to recognise CANRUN positions statically Fig. 6a demonstrates the force of the first objection. A 9-ply search is necessary before a position is reached where the pawn can run. It is easy to extend the rule to make such positions terminal. This reduces the maximum depth of search to 7-ply. There are fewer than twenty positions in the position space that require such a deep search. These fall into 2 classes, illustrated in Figs. 6b and 6c. The second problem, the static description of the CANRUN predicate, is tractable when the search uses square sets.

SEARCH

The advice strategy and its proven correctness formalizes the first part of Averbakh's description of KPK. The strategic foundations have been laid. The strategy has now to be fleshed out with sufficient extra knowledge to evaluate each method efficiently. Before this is done we need to know how much search the various rules require. Search is necessary to match the LHS of rules when the satisfiability of pieces of advice is involved. I will address three questions:

(1) How much search does each rule require?
(2) What extra knowledge must be added to make the necessary search small enough?
(3) Which search space representation is most appropriate?

These three questions are related, and logically (1) and (2) are dependent on (3). Before fixing (3), however, some rough measurements can be made of (1).

111

A broadly effective measure of the search required by a rule is the *maximum search depth* required by that method. For a wide variety of search algorithms the amount of search increases exponentially with depth. There are two ways of determining the maximum search depth for the various methods in the advice text:

(1) Refinement of the correctness proof to provide an upper bound on search depth
(2) The use of a database method.

The second option was chosen here. Databases were constructed for each piece of advice. A database for a piece of advice is a complete lookup table for the domain which says for each position whether the piece of advice is satisfiable from that position. These databases are computationally cheap to manufacture since they are constructed not by searching forward from each position but backwards from those positions satisfying the better goals of the advice. The process is efficient because the amount of work done is a linear function of the size of the domain and the average branching factor. The process of 'backing up' from terminal positions is as described in (Clarke 1975). The maximum search depth is shown in the table of Fig. 7. From this table we can see that rule 7 (for example) with a maximum search depth of 9 ply will need extra search information. What is the nature of this information? Several points should be made:

(1) It is subordinate to the main *strategic* rules, giving information as to *how* these goals are to be achieved.
(2) It is not necessarily fixed and immutable within the system, and can be extended if it is thought desirable.
(3) It can be split into separate components. Firstly knowledge to order the consideration of moves. Secondly knowledge to reject certain lines of play which cannot produce the desired goal or which duplicate other search effort. Finally knowledge of positions, or position types, from which the goals can certainly be achieved. These components correspond to the better goals, holding goals and move constraints of a piece of advice.

Rule number	Maximum search depth
2	9
3	7
4	3
5	0
6	5
7	9

Fig. 7 – Maximum depth of search for every rule (except for top-level) in the advice strategy.

This extra knowledge has only to preserve the correctness of the rule under consideration. We thereby introduce a hierarchy of knowledge, enabling us to demonstrate correctness locally while preserving it globally. This is very much in the spirit of structured programming. We are willing to accept a tradeoff of knowledge *vs.* search which provides a worst case requiring a good deal of search, for a very small percentage of the position space, if we can increment the knowledge component easily to cope with individual cases.

As mentioned earlier the exact nature of this knowledge is dependent on the search representation. In the next section I discuss a novel representation for search in the ending, its implementation and a more precise description of the knowledge added.

IMPLEMENTATION

The implementation of the KPK strategy was intended as an experiment to examine new ideas with a view to incorporating them in a future chess advice language. As mentioned above this work is based on the AL 1 system.

The increased complexity, from the programmer's point of view, of this system allows much freedom of choice in implementation. The implementation of the KPK advice strategy was undertaken with the following relatively modest goals in mind:

(1) The dynamic creation of pieces of advice leads us to distinguish between knowledge of *what* to do, and knowledge of *how* to do it. For a single piece of advice in an AL 1 advice table, the *what* to do is the achievement of the better-goal of the advice; the *how* to do it is partly specified by the holding-goals, move constraints, and depth bound. When each piece of advice is specified in advance in this manner, the user-expert is able to hand-craft the holding-goals and move-constraints for each piece of advice. This is impossible when the pieces of advice are not fully specified beforehand. In this implementation attention has been paid to the form the search algorithm must take to allow a dynamic, knowledge-based specification of the search strategy for pieces of advice.

(2) Search in the endgame differs from that in the middlegame in that often each player is following a strategy relatively independent of the other. In these cases traditional search algorithms spend a great deal of time backtracking over essentially equivalent sequences of moves. This implementation explores a novel search technique which, essentially, only considers interaction between pieces. This implementation considers sets of moves rather than individual moves.

In the next section the new search technique is described, followed by a description of the search strategies available with the technique.

A NEW SEARCH TECHNIQUE

Chessmasters do not exhaustively search all lines of play until they find a solution, as do naive chess programs. Nor do they do a 1- or 2-ply search, replying on a

113

large store of patterns to eliminate deep search. They often make deep searches along 'representative' lines of play. Although this search is only 'representative' the chessmasters will often assert that it is correct. Such a search, even with reduced material, can be far too large for a brute-force search program.

Intuitively it seems that some new mechanism is needed whereby search focuses on interaction and interference between pieces, rather than the long sequences of moves when no such interaction takes place. In a previous paper (Bratko & Niblett 1980) we suggested a mechanism for search using square sets instead of individual squares. This eliminates the need to consider positions where no piece interaction exists. In the next section I discuss an algorithm to perform such a search in the KPK endgame. This algorithm extends to any King and Pawn endgame.

THE ALGORITHM

A position $P = (W, B, P)$ will consist of 3 sets W, B and P; one for each piece (White king, Black king, and White pawn respectively). The White pawn's set is a singleton. The interpretation of the assertion $s(A, P)$ is now:

$$\forall w \, \forall p \, \exists b \, (p \in P \land w \in W \land b \in B \rightarrow s(A, (w, b, p)))$$

where (w, b, p) is a KPK position.

The pieces have in general only one move. There are three cases where the position has to be split into a set of subsidiary positions to assure that no undesired internal structure is placed on the square sets.

(1) A king move is such that some of the squares to which the king might move may be illegal. In the case of the pawnset, which is a singleton, no such splitting is required. In Fig. 8 it is WTM. Assuming no move constraints the white king can move to any square in halo(W) (the set of squares next to any square in W). However a certain subset I in halo(W) is next to B the Black king set. The set X in B is defined by $X = \text{halo}(\text{halo}(W)) \cap B$. The position $(\text{halo}(W), B, P)$ is treated as the separate cases $(\text{halo}(W)/\text{halo}(pi), pi, P)$, pi in X and $(\text{halo}(W), B/X, P)$ thus maintaining the required absence of internal structure.

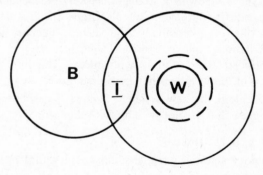

Fig. 8.

114

(2) In some BTM position (W, B, P) where Black has a move to B′, holding goals (HG) must be applied.

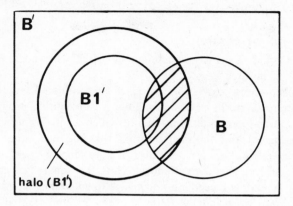

Fig. 9.

For each b′ ∈ B′ there is a subset W′ ⊆ W s.t. ∀w ∈ W′H(w,b′P). Let the union of such bi′ be B1′. The set B1 = halo(B1′) ∩ B is the set of all Black squares in the original position for which H may apply, the position is then split into cases. (W,b,P) b ∈ B1 and (W,B/Bl, P) each case being considered separately, before the application of the holding goals or Black's move.

(3) The treatment of *better-goals* is simpler. Starting from a WTM position (W,B,P) with a White move W → W′, for each w ∈ W there is a B′ ⊆ B s.t. BG(w,b), b ∈ B′. Let Bi = B′. We remove B′ from B to give (W′, B/B′, P) as the successor position.

The standard definition of a piece of advice allows for three types of search termination.

(1) Search stops at nodes where the better goal is true, returning success.
(2) Search stops at nodes where the holding goal is false, returning failure.
(3) Search stops at nodes where there are no moves satisfying move constraints. At BTM nodes this returns success (unless stalemate), at WTM nodes failure.

Because we are dealing with sets of squares the termination conditions revolve around positions where one of the piece sets is empty.

(1) If either the White king set of the White pawn set is empty search terminates with the whole Black king set passed back as the *failset*. The *failset* is defined to be the subset Bf ⊆ B s.t. ∀b ∈ Bf, ∃ w ∈ W s.t. not(satisfiable(A,(w,b,p)), that is the failset is is the set of Black squares in which from no White king square is advice A satisfiable.
(2) If the Black king set is empty the node is terminated and the failset passed back is null.

115

It may happen that although the failset at some node is non-empty neither of the termination conditions apply. In this case the decision as to whether to back up the failset depends on the current search strategy. This is discussed later.

REDUCTION OF SEARCH

Square sets are used to reduce the amount of search. The square sets algorithm accomplishes this in three ways.

Firstly, since several moves for each piece are considered simultaneously the discovery of terminal positions is less random. A conventional program may find itself with 5 moves to consider, only one of which leads to a terminal position. The examination of this terminal position first requires either a fortuitous ordering of moves by the move generator or knowledge available to the search mechanism indicating the correct move. Thus the square sets algorithm will either save on time, or will need less knowledge to guide the search.

Secondly, and closely related to the above point, the fact that sets of moves are made equivalent reduces that amount of backtracking considerably. A conventional program, unless it has a sophisticated 'causality' mechanism (Berliner 1974, Wilkins 1980) has to backtrack through every permutation of moves to guarantee failure of the advice.

Finally, the amount of search is reduced because the *information* returned from the search is less than with conventional programs. When a forcing tree is generated from an initial position $P = (w,b,p)$ and the 'winning' move in the forcing tree is w to W we are only guaranteed that $\exists\, w \in W$ (the advice is satisfiable from wi); to find a wi for which the advice is satisfiable requires a separate search of the forcing tree; this has not been implemented.

In the current implementation the amount of search needed (measured in nodes searched) is between 10 and 50 times less than with a conventional search containing approximately the same knowledge.

PROGRAM DETAILS AND AN EXAMPLE OF PLAY

The KPK strategy using square sets has been partially implemented in PROLOG on the EDINBURGH/ICF DEC 10. A fairly complex representation for nodes is used in the current implementation. The information is detailed to allow control over the search. The top level search strategy at present implemented is shown below.

Given a *plan* with specified goals and move constraints:

(1) set the *current* node to be the root
(2) if the root node has non-empty failset return failure. If all moves from the root are exhausted return success
(3) find an active node according to the current search strategy and set this to be the *current* node
(4) if the *current* node has a non-empty failset propagate the failset back through the tree.goto(2)

116

(5) choose a move from the *current* node. set the *current* node to be this new node.goto(4)

This strategy generates a depth-first search, checking to see whether any failsets found can be propagated back to the root node of the tree as soon as they are found.

Below is an example of play illustrating the working of the algorithm.

The initial position is shown in Fig. 1b above; the program has to determine whether this is won for White. Following the KPK strategy it finds that the pawn cannot run, and then tries to determine whether mainpatt is attainable. The piece of advice being followed is:

BG: mainpatt in less than 10 ply
HG: pawnsafe and not direct opposition less than 2 ranks ahead of pawn
MC: kingmove must be able to reach mainpatt in less than 10 ply

The course of the search is shown in Fig. 10.

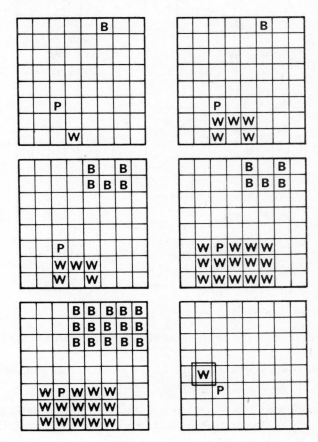

Fig.10.

117

In this example there is no interaction between the two king sets, so the search tree contains no branches. At depth 5 the Black king set disappears since White achieves the better-goal by having his king on square b4 without Black being able to seize the opposition. Owing to the lack of piece interaction the holding goals and move-constraints need be only lightly constrained. A conventional tree search program finds life much harder since it considers only one possible king at a time instead of all in parallel. Without substantial added knowledge it will spend time in unnecessary backtracking.

The search is not so simple when the goal is impossible to satisfy and there is interaction between the pieces. Fig. 11 illustrates a search which returns failure and involves considerable interaction between the pieces. Here extra tactical knowledge has to be added to control the search.

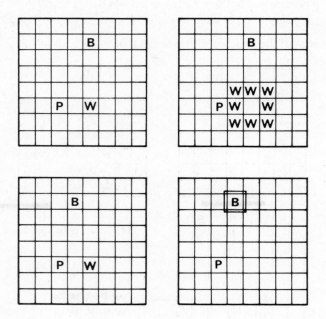

Fig. 11.

The extra knowledge was:

— The White king should not move behind the pawn when trying to occupy a square in front of it.
— If the White king is 2 or more squares nearer its goal than the Black king then the White king can achieve its goal.

The point is that use of the square sets algorithm frees us from the need to specify the lowest level of planning for the achievement of strategic goals. By concentrating only on piece interaction we do not have to specify particular paths the

118

pieces should follow and so prove that following these paths preserves correctness in the program. The extra tactical knowledge that must be added is simple enough and general enough to be applicable throughout the KPK domain.

Relatively little exploration of different search strategies has been done but there are one or two points to note. It is simple to determine whether a White plan succeeds *whatever* Black does, as in the first example given above. Also due to the application of the holding and move constraints to square sets the algorithm effectively allows a depth first search with a full width 1-ply lookahead to check for holding goal and better goal satisfaction from each node in the search path.

IMPLEMENTATION

The advice strategy has been partially implemented in PROLOG on the Edinburgh/ ICF DEC 10. The examples shown above have been run and all the methods at least partially implemented. Insufficient testing has been done to determine exactly how much tactical knowledge must be added to produce acceptable run times in all cases. A straight comparison between the square sets algorithm and a normal alpha-beta search over a restricted sample of positions shows an improvement of 50–100 fold in nodes searched.

CONCLUSION

The technique of search using square sets demonstrates that with an appropriate search representation the task of supplying the tactical information necessary for efficient play can be made much easier. The separation of the tactical and strategic components of the endgame allows for a straightforward proof of correctness for the advice language strategy. Even for an endgame as simple as KPK any more detailed proof involving a fully determined search strategy is unrealistic.

For a complex endgame such as King and Rook vs. King and Knight a very large amount of tactical information is necessary. This information is considerably easier to provide by means of examples than by explicit specification. An interesting possibility is to provide the system with sufficient inductive capability to be able to learn the tactical information necessary for execution of the strategic goals. A start has been made in this direction in Shapiro & Niblett (1981), where decision trees were produced which determine whether a KPK position satisfies any given rule in the advice strategy.

ACKNOWLEDGEMENTS

Thanks to Professor Michie for his help and encouragement. Thanks also to Dr Max Bramer for his comments on an earlier version of this paper. The work described was done while the author was in receipt of a grant from the Science Research Council.

REFERENCES

Averbakh, Y. & Maizelis, I. (1974) *Pawn Endings*. London: Batsford.

Beal, D. (1977) Discriminating wins from draws in KPK. Appendix 5; The construction of economical and correct algorithms for king and pawn against king, *Advances in Computer Chess 2*, pp. 22–29, (ed. Clarke, M. R. B.). Edinburgh: Edinburgh University Press.

Berliner, H. J. (1974) Chess as problem solving: the development of a tactics analyser. Ph.D. Thesis, Pittsburgh: Department of Computer Science, Carnegie–Mellon University.

Bramer, M. (1980) An optimal algorithm for king and pawn against king using pattern knowledge, *Advances in Computer Chess 2*, pp. 82–91, (ed. Clarke, M. R. B.). Edinburgh: University Press.

Bratko, I. & Michie, D. (1980) A representation for pattern-knowledge in chess endgames, in *Advances in Computer Chess 2*, pp. 31–56, (ed. Clarke, M. R. B.). Edinburgh: Edinburgh University Press.

Bratko, I. & Niblett, T. (1980) Conjectures and refutations in a framework for chess endgame knowledge, *Expert Systems in the Micro Electronic Age*, pp. 83–101, (ed. Michie, D.). Edinburgh: Edinburgh University Press.

Kopec, D. (1979) A comparison of different machine-oriented and human-oriented representation of knowledge using the king-pawn-king chess ending. *Unpublished Report*, Edinburgh: Machine Intelligence Research Unit, University of Edinburgh.

Kopec, D. & Niblett, T. (1980) How hard is the play of the king-rook-king-knight ending? in *Advances in Computer Chess 2*, pp. 57–81, (ed. Clarke, M. R. B.). Edinburgh: Edinburgh University Press.

Michie, D. (1976) An advice-taking system for computer chess, *Comp. Bull, Ser. 2, no. 11*, 12–14.

Shapiro, A. & Niblett, T. (1982) Automatic induction of classification rules for a chess endgame, *Advances in Computer Chess 3*, pp. 73–92 (ed., Clarke, M. R. B.), Oxford: Pergamon. Also as *Research Memorandum, MIP-R-129.* Edinburgh: Machine Intelligence Research Unit, University of Edinburgh.

Tan, S. (1972) Representation of knowledge for very simple pawn endings in chess. *Research Memorandum MIP-R-98*. Edinburgh: School of Artificial Intelligence, Edinburgh University.

Wilkins, D. (1980) Using patterns and plans in chess, *Artificial Intelligence, 14*, 165–203.

REASONING ABOUT COMPUTATIONS

5

Mechanical theorem-proving in the CASE verifier

G. W. Ernst and R. J. Hookway

Case Western Reserve University
Cleveland, USA

Abstract

The Case verifier is a man-machine system for constructing a mathematical proof that a module of a computer system meets its specifications. This paper views the Case verifier as an expert intelligent system. After a brief overview of the entire system, the remainder of the paper focuses on the theorem proving component which is the main source of intelligence in the verifier.

The main contribution of this research is as a case study in the use of mechanical theorem proving in a non-trivial application. We use existing theorem proving techniques which are reasonably well understood rather than developing new ones. Even so, the design of the theorem prover is far from straightforward because of difficult constraints from this particular application domain.

The input programming language is a large subset of MODULA including abstract data types, and the verifier should be capable of proving, with reasonable human assistance, components of 'realistic' computer systems. Non-trivial examples are used to motivate the discussion.

1. INTRODUCTION

The Case verifier is a man-machine tool which allows one to interactively verify realistic computer systems modules. By *verification* of a module or component of a computer system, we mean proving that its implementation meets its specification. In one sense, then, the verifier looks like a special purpose interactive theorem prover. But we feel that a more appropriate view of the verifier is as an expert intelligent system in the domain of program verification.

The main purpose of this paper is to describe the theorem proving techniques used by the Case verifier. However, constraints from this particular application domain had a large impact on the design of the theorem prover. For this reason, the next section gives an overview of the entire verifier so that its use of theorem proving can be described in the context of this application domain.

123

The Case verifier is an outgrowth of the verifier described in Hookway & Ernst (1976). Experimentation with the latter has had a major influence on the design of the former. We are currently implementing the theorem prover described in this paper and hence have no empirical data on it yet. However, most of the methods in the new theorem prover have been empirically evaluated in detail by hand. This, together with the empirical results from our previous system, gives us confidence that the new theorem prover will be more than adequate for this application.

2. OVERVIEW OF THE VERIFIER

The verifier is primarily intended to be used as a tool for doing research on empirical aspects of program specification and verification. Consequently, much of the verifier will be continually changing to meet the needs of such a research environment. This implies that flexibility and modifiability are more important than efficiency, although any usable interactive system must have some constraints on response time. This situation is quite different from a production environment.

The long-range goal of our research is to be able to verify a real computer system by verifying each module which is a component of it. The word *real* refers to actual code in a production computer system or to code which could be used in place of the actual code. Owing to the difficulty of this goal our current research focusses on the verification of realistic modules.

A *realistic* module performs the same essential function as a component of a real computer system but may be considerably simpler. For example, the error checking in a realistic module does not have to be as thorough as that in its real counterpart. Realistic modules usually have a much better structure than their real counterparts which may contain code that is scattered throughout the system rather than being localized in a single module. The reason for concentrating on realistic modules is that we believe that their verification requires the same techniques as that of their real counterparts. This allows us to study the fundamental techniques without being unduly burdened with details of real systems. Gerhart & Wile (1979) give a nice description of the difficulties encountered in the verification of real modules.

The type of realistic modules for which the verifier is designed is usually referred to as "systems software". This design decision restricts the choice of the *input language* in which a module to be verified can be encoded. Languages such as LISP and APL seem inappropriate since they have rarely been used for "systems programming" (although they might be in the future).

We also believe that the input language needs good facilities for concurrency and abstraction. Contemporary computer systems contain a large amount of concurrent activity. Although much of it is transparent to the user of such systems, lower level modules must cope with this concurrency; the verifier should be able to deal with such modules as well as those which contain only sequential programs. Data abstractions are very common in computer systems. For example, a file system shields its users from details about a physical disc such as track and sector numbers.

Although several languages satisfy the above constraints, we have selected MODULA (Wirth, 1977) as the basis for our input language because it is simpler than other languages like ADA (Ichbiah *et al.* 1979) which also satisfy the contraints. In general, the verifier should be as simple as possible while still allowing realistic modules to be interactively verified. In fact, the input language will probably undergo continual change because of the research environment in which the verifier will be used.

In addition to being simple, MODULA has an excellent facility for defining abstract data types which is achieved by exporting types from the modules in which they are defined. The facility in MODULA allows a procedure to have as parameters several different instances of several different abstract data types. In addition, the realization of instances of abstract data types may share common memory which is local to the module in which they are defined. MODULA also has a facility for defining an abstract type which can only have a single instance. Most of this capability appears to be useful (if not necessary) in implementing the variety of modules with which we are concerned.

The Case verifier requires formal specifications for each module in addition to its implementation. We believe that formal specifications should be an integral part of computer programs that are required with program statements, just as variable declarations are required. We have extended MODULA by adding such a specification facility to the language (Ernst & Ogden, 1980). Our specifications are based on Floyd/Hoare assertions which are just predicate calculus statements about the values of program variables. Each loop is required to have a loop invariant assertion. Each procedure must have a precondition (an assertion which must be true before calling it) and a postcondition (an assertion which is true after any call on it).

Our extended MODULA also requires specifications for the data abstractions defined in a module. These specifications give the relationship between abstract values and their realizations as well as any properties of the realizations that must be maintained by procedures that manipulate them.

The portion of the input language which has been implemented consists of all of MODULA except concurrent programming constructs. Formal specifications can be written for any module using the specification portion of the input language. We are working on a concurrency facility for the input language; the major problem that must be solved is how to write specifications for processes.

The overall structure of the verifier is shown in Fig. 1. A recursive decent parser produces a parse tree of the input module. The Type Checker detects the context sensitive syntax errors in the input module. The raw parse tree produced by the Parser is then transformed into one which is more suitable for the VC Genererator. Some examples of transformations which take place are: *while* loops are rewritten using the *loop* construct of MODULA, and *with* statements are removed by adding field names to selectors. Although these three parts of

125

the verifier are essential, they contain no new concepts. The only design consideration is how to make them easy to extend and modify.

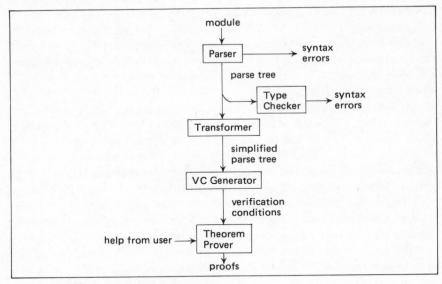

Fig. 1 – Overall structure of the verifier.

The VC Generator focusses on verification problems of the form

(1) CT\assume Q; A; confirm R.

Here A denotes a sequence of declarations and program statements. Its input assertion is Q and its output assertion is R. CT is the context which consists of the specifications for all the global procedures and data abstractions that can be used by A. Intuitively, (1) is true if we can confirm R after executing A, assuming that Q is initially true and that the global procedures and data abstractions satisfy their specifications in the context CT. Often, (1) is written as Q{A}R in the literature, when the context is implied or empty.

Our formalization of program verification has one inference or verification rule for each construct allowed in the programming language. For example,

$$(2) \quad \frac{\text{CT} \setminus \text{A}; \textbf{confirm } Q \circ [x \leftarrow \exp];}{\text{CT} \setminus \text{A}; x := \exp; \textbf{confirm } Q;}$$

is the rule for the assignment statement. Here, A is a sequence of statements, the first of which is an "**assume** statement". $Q \circ [x \leftarrow \exp]$ denotes the result of substituting the expression exp for all occurrences of the variable x in Q. The meaning of (2) is that the bottom line can be deduced from the top line. Usually there are several formulae (hypotheses) above the line in a verification rule, but only one formula (the conclusion) can appear below the line.

126

Our verification rules are formulated so that any module in the input language or formula like (1) will match the bottom line of precisely one rule. In addition, each hypothesis of a verification rule is 'shorter' than the conclusion. Consequently, repetitive application of the verification rules in the reverse direction reduces any formula like (1) to a number of formulae in predicate calculus, since these are the 'shortest' formulae in the system. The above discussion is not intended to be a complete description of the process, but rather to indicate that our verification rules are formulated so that collectively they comprise a process for mechanically reducing a formula like (1) to a set of predicate calculus formulae. This is why we use (2) instead of the usual axiom for the assignment statement.

The above discussion points out that generating verification conditions is reasonably straightforward once the verification rules have been formulated. Verification rules for basic programming constructs like conditional statements and iteration statements are well documented in the literature. Although the abstraction facility in the input language is based on the work of Hoare (1972), his verification rules are not adequate for our input language which allows abstract type instances to share memory. Hookway (1980) has developed verification rules for the data abstraction facilities in the input language and these rules are used as the basis of our VC Generator.

The verification rules provide a nice modular structure for the VC Generator because each declaration and program statement has a separate rule which can be processed more or less independently. The only exception to this is functional procedure calls whose verification rule is entangled with the processing of expressions which can contain "side effects". This difficulty is overcome by using the technique of "symbolic execution" to generate verification conditions (Dannenberg, 1979).

Most of the information about the meaning of the various programming constructs in the input language is embedded in the verification rules. The VC Generator users this information to mechanically remove this programming information from the input module, and thereby produces a set of predicate calculus formulae whose truth is sufficient to guarantee that the implementation meets its specification. This process involves a significant amount of symbol manipulation which must be done in order to verify the input module. It is important to do this processing before the theorem proving stage so that the theorem prover is not burdened with it. But it is even more important that the theorem prover (both man and machine) need not be aware of the information embedded in the VC Generator because of its volume and intricacy.

3. THE THEOREM PROVER

The last section outlines how verifying an input module is reduced to proving a set of verification conditions (VCs). This section starts off with a description of the basic nature of this theorem proving task.

The number of VCs is usually quite large depending, of course, upon the size and complexity of the input module. A typical procedure gives rise to about five VCs. The linking-loader in Hookway (1980) contains four submodules; in all, eight VCs are generated for this input module.

Each VC is proven indepedently since its proof does not depend on the proofs of the others. This indepedence property greatly reduces the complexity of the problem; attempting to prove all of the VCs simultaneously would simply be overwhelming. The size of a VC depends primarily on the size of the assertions used in its generation. In the linking-loader example some VCs contained over 150 literals. Some of the literals contain over 100 symbols, although these are much larger than typical.

Surprisingly enough, a VC is reasonably intelligible to a person who understands the input module, both specifications and implementation. One reason for this is that the specification language contains a macro-definition facility which is useful for creating specifications as well as for understanding them and the resulting VCs. Of course, the legibility of the VCs is very important if a human is to interact intelligently with the theorem prover.

Another important property of the VCs is that they contain a large number of constants which have meaning to someone who understands the input module. For example. program variables occur as constants in the VCs. Naturally, these constants help the VCs to be intelligible to the user. But, more importantly, they keep the complexity of the proofs at a manageable level because the VCs tend to be more concerned with these constants than with quantified variables. In particular, the nesting of quantifiers in the VCs is usually much simpler than that found in mathematics.

Empirical evidence indicates that it would be very difficult to construct a theorem prover that could mechanically prove most of the VCs; at least, we believe that this would be a major research project in the area of mechanical theorem proving. Fortunately, most parts of most VCs can be proven with existing mechanical theorem proving techniques. For this reason we have decided to use an interactive theorem prover that has the following properties:

(1) Large portions of the VC are proven completely mechanically.
(2) Intermediate results produced by the theorem prover are intelligible to someone who understands the input VC.
(3) Response time is reasonable.

If (1) were not required, the system would be too tedious to use because the proof of a typical VC is long.

In designing the theorem prover we decided to use only existing theorem proving methods whose empirical properties are reasonably well understood. This is possible because existing methods appear to be sufficiently powerful for our purposes. This approach has the advantage that the performance of the theorem prover should be reasonably predictable from its design. The importance of this cannot be over emphasized because mechanical theorem proving is an area which has been plagued by "combinatorial explosion" whose nature is at present only understood at the empirical level.

The remainder of this section describes the theorem prover. Although the theorem proving methods are not new, the tailoring of the methods to this particular application is a research problem.

3.1 The Executive

The basic structure of the theorem prover is a natural deduction or Gentzen type system. An AND/OR tree of subgoals is created with the VC to be proven as the goal at the root. The executive of the theorem prover supervises the construction of this tree. That is, it controls which subgoals should be added to the tree and also selects the subgoal that the theorem prover attempts to prove next. Of course, since the theorem prover is interactive, the executive occasionally asks the user for help in making these decisions.

The first action of the executive in attempting to prove a VC is initialization. Other than initializing data structures, the only functions of this step are to replace quantifiers with Skolem functions and to simplify the result. The reason for simplifying the entire VC is to improve its legibility. Subexpressions of the VC will be resimplified at appropriate points by the theorem prover when more information is available to it. But the initial simplification often significantly reduces the size of the VC. The simplifier is described in section 3.3.

As usual, Skolem functions are put into the VC before theorem proving commences. This step cannot be avoided by requiring that specifications contain Skolem functions instead of quantifiers, because a single assertion may occur in the consequent of some VCs and in the antecedent of others. This difference in the position of an assertion effectively causes the role of the quantifiers to reverse; e.g., an existential quantifier in an assertion in the consequent logically becomes a universal quantifier when the assertion is moved into the antecedent.

Putting Skolem functions into the VC is technically straightforward but is complicated by two additional requirements. No logical connective is changed because often there is heuristic information in the connectives that actually occur in the specifications. Renaming variables is done in such a way that the user can still understand the VC. Although the details are not important for this paper, we have found it useful to have the new name of a variable contain the old name as a substring. An additional complication is that macros may contain quantifiers which must be removed, but the references to these macros must not be removed from the VC for the purpose of legibility.

Each *subgoal* is a proof problem of the form $P1, P2, \ldots, Pn \vdash C$ where each P_i is a *premise* and C is the *conclusion* which must be proven. The initial subgoal (the root of the subgoal tree) is $\vdash VC$ in which there are no premises. Each node in the subgoal tree contains a subgoal together with some book-keeping and status information such as the type of the node and whether the proof of the subgoal has been attempted. In this paper we will be primarily concerned with

129

the subgoal at a node. The other information in a node, which is more elaborate than one might think, will be introduced as needed below.

The first step in attempting to prove the subgoal of a node depends on the form of the conclusion. If the conclusion is not a literal, then one of the inference rules in Fig. 2 will be used to generate subnodes of the node ($\rightarrow$ is used for logical implication). The meaning of a rule in Fig. 2 is that the subgoal below the line is a logical consequence of the subgoals above the line. The executive selects the rule whose bottom line matches the conclusion of the node. A subnode is generated for each formula above the line in the rule. If there is more than one formula the type of the node becomes AND; otherwise it becomes an OR node.

---

1. premises $\vdash$ A
   premises $\vdash$ B
   _____
   premises $\vdash$ A & B
       where A and B have no common variables.

2. premises, A $\vdash$ B
   _____
   premises $\vdash$ A $\rightarrow$ B

3. premises, $\sim$A $\vdash$ B   or   premises, $\sim$B $\vdash$ A
   _____   _____
   premises $\vdash$ A $\vee$ B   premises $\vdash$ A $\vee$ B

4. premises, A $\vdash$ $\sim$B   or   premises, B $\vdash$ $\sim$A
   _____   _____
   premises $\vdash$ $\sim$(A & B)   premises $\vdash$ $\sim$(A & B)

5. premises $\vdash$ $\sim$A
   premises $\vdash$ $\sim$B
   _____
   premises $\vdash$ $\sim$(A $\vee$ B)
       where A and B have no common free variables.

6. premises $\vdash$ A
   premises $\vdash$ $\sim$B
   _____
   premises $\vdash$ $\sim$(A $\rightarrow$ B)
       where A and B have no common free variables.

Fig. 2 — The rules which govern the processing of connectives in the conclusion.

For exposition the & and $\vee$ in Fig. 2 are binary, but the theorem prover allows these connectives to have an arbitrary number of arguments. For example, Fig. 3 shows the subnodes produced by an application of Rule 1 in Fig. 2. Here, the conclusion has four conjuncts. The $A(x)$ and $C(x)$ are grouped together in a single subnode because the variable x occurs in both.

130

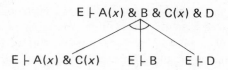

Fig. 3 – The tree produced by an application of Rule 1 in Fig. 2. Both A(*x*) and C(*x*) contain the free variable *x*.

The executive always reduces ∼∼A to A whenever such a formula is generated; hence a rule for double negatives is not necessary. The only logical connectives that are allowed in subgoals are &, ∨, ∼ and →. Therefore, any conclusion which is not a literal will match the bottom line of one of the rules in Fig. 2. If the conclusion is a disjunction the executive will select one of the disjuncts to be used as the conclusion of the subnode (Rule 3); the other disjuncts will be added to the premises of the subnode. An application of Rule 4 is analogous to this case. The executive uses a special heuristic to select the conclusion of the subnode in these cases. Currently, it favours larger disjuncts, avoiding literals which are ground inequalities if at all possible. However, there is a separate subroutine for this heuristic so that it will be easy to modify as experience dictates.

When the conclusion of the given node is a literal, the "connective" inference rules in Fig. 2 are not applicable. In this case the executive simplifies the conclusion (section 3.3) and then calls the subgoal solver. The function of the *subgoal solver* is to prove the subgoal at a node without generating any subnodes. The current subgoal solver is successful if the conclusion is a substitution instance of a premise or if it is the literal *true*. Of course, the original VC will not usually contain *true*, but often the simplifier effectively proves the subgoal by returning the literal *true* as the result of simplifying the conclusion. The subgoal solver in Hookway & Ernst (1976) was considerably more powerful, but at this point our subgoal solver appears to be adequate.

If the subgoal solver is not successful, the executive attempts to apply an inference rule such as "backward chaining" to the given subgoal. These inference rules are described in section 3.4. There is a heuristic which lists the inference rules that the executive should consider applying to the given node in the order of their priority. This heuristic is used to control the growth of the subgoal tree and is heavily dependent on the status information recorded at the node. The executive uses the first rule on this list which is applicable.

When the executive completes the processing described above it informs the user of what happened and records the results in the status information at the node. It then selects a new node and recycles. Currently, the executive does a breadth first search until interrupted by the user, but a more sophisticated search strategy will probably be used in the future.

The executive requests advice from the user in two situations. The obvious case is when the executive has attempted to prove all the nodes in the subgoal

131

tree but their collective results do not constitute a proof of the VC at the root. This happens when the executive rejects the application of every inference rule to all terminal nodes in the subgoal tree, either because of search heuristics, or because they are not applicable. The executive also asks the user if it should continue whenever the mechanical limit is reached. This parameter of the executive is the number of nodes that it should process mechanically. If the user requests the executive to continue, it will process nodes until the mechanical limit is again reached or until it runs out of nodes.

3.2 Generation of Subnodes

Although the generation of subnodes is logically a function performed by the executive, it is sufficiently involved that a separate subsection is used to describe it. Of course, when a subnode is created all of its components must be initialized. This is straightforward except for the premises.

Each subgoal has the property that its premises contain the premises of its parent as a subset. Hence, to create the premises of a new subgoal the executive starts with the premises of its parent and adds additional formulae to this initial value after converting them to an internal representation which is suitable for the theorem prover.

There are two components to the premises: units and premise-list. *Units* (for unit clauses) is a small data base that contains all of the premises that are ground inequality literals. The internal representation of units is designed for the type of processing performed by the simplifier as described in the next section. Hence, when a ground inequality literal is added to the premises of a subgoal, a special routine converts it to this internal representation and adds it to units. All premises which are not stored in units are put on the *premise-list*.

To add a formula to the premises the executive repeatedly applies the following transformations to it:

1. $A \& B \Rightarrow A, B$
2. $A \to (B \to C) \Rightarrow A \& B \to C$
3. $A \to B \& C \Rightarrow A \to B, A \to C$

This converts the formula to a set of formulae. To each element F of this set, the executive does the following:

1. If F is a ground inequality, add it to units.
2. If F is a literal (which is not a ground inequality), simplify it and add it to the premise-list.
3. If F is of the form $A \to B$ where B is a literal, add $A \to simp(B)$ to the premise-list where $simp(B)$ is the result of simplifying B.
4. In all other cases, add F to the premise-list.

This processing of a new premise reduces it to a "partial" conjunctive normal form without removing any $\to$ connectives. In addition certain literals are simplified because they may be matched to other literals in applying a rule of inference.

132

The general principle is to simplify literals prior to matching. However, most literals in the premises will not be directly involved in a match and hence there is no need to simplify them. Section 3.4 will clarify these comments.

Adding an inequality to units has two possible outcomes; either the inequality is consistent with the information stored in units or it is inconsistent. For example, if units contains the fact that $x > 5$, then it is not possible to add $x < 3$ to units since this is inconsistent with $x > 5$. Whenever an inequality is added to units, the executive checks if it is inconsistent, and if so records that the subgoal is solved because it has a contradition in its premises.

When adding a formula to the premises, the executive checks if it is a ground equality. If so it solves for one of the constants and removes it from the entire subgoal by substitution. For example, if $i + 1 = j + 3$ is to be added to the premises, the executive replaces every occurrence of i in the subgoal by $j + 2$. The constant that is removed will usually denote the value of a program variable.

In some cases an equality will be inferred by units. For example, if units knows that $1 \leq i - j \leq 2$ then adding $i \neq j + 1$ to units will result in the equality $i - j = 2$. The executive checks for such equalities and performs the appropriate substitution. Note that in these examples the executive can remove either i or j. Currently, the executive selects the first variable for removal, but it may be desirable to use a heuristic to determine which variable should be removed.

This kind of substitution is a special case of paramodulation (section 3.4) which always seems to produce beneficial results. Literals which are modified by the substitution can often be simplified, and hence the executive resimplifies certain literals in the subgoal after such substitutions. All of units is resimplifed. The conclusion is resimplified if it is a literal. Each element of the premise-list that is a literal is resimplified. Finally, for each element of the form $A \rightarrow B$ on the premise-list B is resimplified if it is a literal.

3.3 The Simplifier

The theorem prover is composed of two distinct components. The component which has been described in the previous sections is quite general; it contains no knowledge of any specific theory. The proof of many "obvious" facts can be unwieldy using this general mechanism; e.g., the proof of $2 + 2 = 4$ is not obvious from an axiomatization of number theory. A second component of the theorem prover, the simplifier, is used to make these obvious deductions using techniques tailored to particular theories.

Expressions are simplified by rewriting them in normal form. Arithmetic expressions are normalized by multiplying out subexpressions and then collecting terms. As an example, $1 + (1 + q) * y + r - (y + 1)$ is simplified to $(y * q) + r$.

After normalizing expressions in a literal, the simplifier attempts to evaluate it to *true* of *false*. Thus expressions such as $x = x$ evaluate to *true*. In evaluating ground inequalities the simplifier makes use of the units data base which is described later in this section.

The simplifier recognizes a special class of symbols called *defined constants*.

133

These symbols have the property that they are equal if and only if they are identical. A number of constants appearing in verification conditions have this property. These include integer constants, constants of an enumerated type, field names, and character constants. The verification condition generator flags these constants for the theorem prover. The simplifier can then simplify equalities and inequalities where both operands are defined constants by testing if the operands are identical.

The units data base is used to simplify the conjunction of ground inequalities which appear in the premises. Inequalities are added to units after being rewritten as $e \leqslant$ const, $e \geqslant$ const or $e \neq$ const. The set of all inequalities added to units determines what values e may take on to make the antecedent true. Units represents the values of e which satisfy the antecedent by maintaining a lower bound (le), an upper bound (ue), and a list of values $(ne1, \ldots, nek)$ between le and ue such that the expression $le \leqslant e \ \& \ e \neq ne1 \ \& \ \ldots \ \& \ e \neq nek \ \& \ e \leqslant ue$ is equivalent to the conjunction of all inequalities involving e which have been added to units. Using units, the theorem prover can prove theorems such as $x \leqslant y + 1 \ \& \ x \neq y + 1 \rightarrow x \leqslant y$ and $x \leqslant y \rightarrow x \leqslant y + 1$.

A particular important theory for program verification is the theory of data structures. This theory is based on the functions ac (for access) and ch (for change) which were introduced by McCarthy & Painter (1967) to describe array assignment. In our notation the expression $ch(A, (s1, e1), \ldots, (sn, en))$ is used to denote the result of assigning en to the component of A selected by sn, then assigning $en - 1$ to the component of A, selected by $sn - 1$, etc. Note that the order of the (si, ei) terms is important; the leftmost term specifies the most recently updated component of the structure. The si are selector lists. Elements of these lists are integer expressions, which select an element of an array, and field selectors which select a component of a record. The result of the assignment $A[i].x: = e$ is $ch(A, ((i, .x), e))$.

The ac function is used to select a component of a structure; $ac(A, s)$ is the component of A, selected by s. Expressions of the form $ac(ch(A, (s1, e1), \ldots, (sn, en)), s0)$ are simplified by using the following rules:

1. If $sk = s0$ and $si \neq s0$ for $1 \leqslant i < k$ then the expression is simplified to ek.
2. If $sk \neq s0$ for all k then the expression is simplified to $ac(A, s0)$.
3. Otherwise, the expression is simplified by removing all the pairs (si, ei) for which $si \neq s0$.

We use $si = s0$ to mean that the corresponding elements of the selector lists are equal. The expression $si \neq s0$ means that some element of si is unequal to the corresponding element of $s0$. The simplifier uses the above rules in a straight-forward fashion by scanning the selector list/value pairs from left to right. During the scan any (si, ei) term for which the simplifier is able to establish that $si = s0$ is deleted from the expression. If a term (sk, ek) is encountered for which the simplifer can establish that $sk = s0$, and all preceding terms have been deleted, the original expression is simplified to ek. If, at the end of the scan, all selector

134

list/value pairs have been deleted, the original expression is simplified to ac(A, s0). In determining whether a pair of selector lists is equal, the simplifier can make use of the units data structure. It can also make use of the fact that field selectors appearing in the selector lists are defined constants and are thus equal if and only if they are indentical. The later leads to most of the simplification of expressions involving ac/ch.

We have found sequences to be useful in writing module specifications. Expressions involving sequences therefore appear in verification conditions, and it is desirable to build some knowledge of the theory of sequences into the simplifier. This is accomplished by including a list of Knuth-Bendix (1970) rewrite rules which describe some properties of sequences. Entries on this list have the form $x \Rightarrow y$ where x and y are expressions. The simplifier replaces subexpressions which match the left-hand side of a rule with the corresponding right-hand side. The facility for rewrite rules is general in that it can be used to simplify any kind of expression, not just those that denote sequences. However, only the rewrite rules for sequences shown in Fig. 4 are currently being used. As an example, first(concat(mkseq(a), y)) is simplified to a by Rule 3.

```
1. first (mkseq (x)) ⇒ x
2. tail (mkseq (x)) ⇒ emptyseq
3. first (concat (mkseq (x), y)) ⇒ x
4. tail (concat (mkseq (x), y)) ⇒ y
5. concat (emptyseq, y) ⇒ y
6. concat (x, emptyseq) ⇒ x

where
    emptyseq:      is the empty sequence.
    mkseq (x):     is a sequence whose only element is x.
    first (s):     is the first element of sequence s.
    tail (s):      is sequence s with the first element removed.
    concat (s1, s2):  is the concatenation of sequences s1 and s2.
```

Fig 4. – Rewrite rules for mkseq, first, tail and concat.

The simplifier makes special deductions in the theories of integers, sequences, and data structures. These theories are central to the examples we have looked at so far. Special knowledge of additional theories will be built into the simplifier as the need arises.

3.4 Inference Rules

This section describes the inference rules used by the theorem prover. Each rule is implemented by a separate subroutine. The executive only knows that each rule will generate zero or more subgoals but has no other information about the rule. This modular structure makes it easy to add or modify inference rules. Although logically the connective rules in Fig. 2 are also inference rules, they are functionally quite different since they are built into the executive, which automatically applies them whenever possible.

The inference rules are listed in Fig. 4. Each is a schema in the sense that it can be applied to a subgoal in several ways to produce several different new subgoals. The implementation of each rule has two parts: the first selects parameters which determine how to apply the rule while the second actually applies the rule producing new subgoals. Selecting parameters involves heuristics which vary from rule to rule. These heuristics are an important control over the growth of the subgoal tree.

Backward chaining is the first rule listed in Fig. 4. This rule uses a premise of the form $B \rightarrow C$ where C is a literal that matches the conclusion A. The conclusion of the new subgoal is $B \cdot \sigma$ where σ is the most general unifier of A and C.

When backward chaining is used, subgoals are generated for every $B \rightarrow C$ that passes a heuristic test. The candidates for $B \rightarrow C$ are elements of the premise-list and elements of the *backward chaining list* which is a list of definitions and theorems to be used in backward chaining. (Logically these formulae can be used as though they are premises, but unlike the premise-list they are the same for all subgoals.) Associated with each element of this list is an integer which limits the number of times it can be mechanically used in backward chaining on a single path in the tree. For example, if 2 is the limit of element F on the backward chaining list, then F will be considered for backward chaining if and only if backward chaining with F has been used twice or less in producing the given subgoal and its ancestors. There is also a parameter which is used as the limit of each element on the premise-list. Currently, we plan to use 1 or 2 as the backward chaining limits for most formulae but some may have a limit of 0 which indicates that they will only be used at the user's request.

Each backward chaining candidate which passes its limit test produces a new subgoal if it is applicable (i.e., if its consequent matches the conclusion). Of course, the given subnode becomes an OR node with the new subgoals as its subnodes.

The second rule in Fig. 4 does *case analysis*. Effectively it considers two cases: when B is true and when B is false, where B is a formula which is a parameter to the rule. The real art in using case analysis is to formulate a "good" case B. Currently, the only cases genereated mechanically are for the analysis of modifications to data structures. The first expression in the conclusion of the form $ac(ch(A, (s, e), \ldots), t)$ is selected, and $s = t$ is used for the parameter B in the interface rule. Both s and t must be selector lists; $s = t$ denotes the conjunction of all literals $s_i = t_i$ where s_i is an element of s and t_i is the corresponding element of t and s_i is not identical to t_i. Each of these must be an array subscript. The only other possibility is a field name, and the simplifier has already removed all of these that are not identical as described in the 1st section.

Unlike backward chaining, case analysis only generates a single subgoal even if there are several access-change expressions in the conclusion. (The reason for this is discussed in section 5). It may be desirable in the future to use a heuristic to select which of several possible access-change expressions in the conclusion to use as the basis for generating the case.

---

1. <u>Backward Chaining</u>

   premises, $B \rightarrow C \vdash B \cdot \sigma$
   premises, $B \rightarrow C \vdash A$
   where $A \cdot \sigma = C \cdot \sigma$.

2. <u>Case Analysis</u>

   premises, $B \vdash A$
   premises, $\sim B \vdash A$
   _____
   premises $\vdash A$
   where B contains no free variables.

3. <u>Instantiation</u>

   premises $\vdash A \cdot \sigma$
   premises $\vdash A$

4. <u>Contrapositive</u>

   premises, $\sim A \vdash \sim B$
   premises, $B \vdash A$

5. <u>Paramodulation</u>

   premises, $B \rightarrow e2 = e3 \vdash (B \,\&\, A\,(e3)) \cdot \sigma$
   premises, $B \rightarrow e2 = e3 \vdash A\,(e1)$
   where $e2 \cdot \sigma = e1 \cdot \sigma$.

6. <u>Lemma Rule</u>

   premises $\vdash B$
   premises, $B \vdash A$
   premises $\vdash A$
   where B contains no free variables.

Fig. 5 — The rules of inference used by the theorem prover.

```
      0 ⩽ stk.p ⩽ max
&     stk.av[0] = emptyseq
&     ∀i(1 ⩽ i ⩽ stk.p → stk.av[i] = concat(mkseq(stk.sa[i]), stk.av[i−1]))
&     stk.p ≠ max


      →


      0 ⩽ stk3.p ⩽ max
&     stk3.av[0] = emptyseq
&     ∀i(1 ⩽ i ⩽ stk3.p → stk3.av[i] = concat(mkseq(stk3.sa[i]), stk3.av[i−1]))
&     stk3.av[stk3.p] = concat(mkseq(S), stk.av[stk.p])

where
      stk3 = ch(stk, ((.av, stk2.p), concat(mkseq(S), stk2.av[stk2.p −1])),
                      ((.sa, stk1.p), S),
                      ((.p), stk.p + 1))
      stk2 = ch(stk, ((.sa, stk1.p), S),
                      ((.p), stk.p + 1))
      stk1 = ch(stk, ((.p), stk.p + 1))
```

Fig. 6 — A verification condition for a linking loader.

137

The remaining rules of inference are used exclusively under user control. The user is required to specify all parameters to the rule and hence no choices are available to the machine whose only function is to generate the designated subgoals.

The rule of *instantiation* in Fig. 4 allows the user to specify values for free variables in the conclusion. Its only parameter is a substitution σ which is applied to the conclusion. Normally, this rule is used when the conclusion is a conjunction which contains free variables and σ is chosen to allow the new subgoal to be reduced by Rule 1 in Fig. 2.

The fourth rule in Fig. 4 is *contrapositive* which allows the user to select an element of the premise-list whose negation is the conclusion of the new subgoal. The only parameter to this rule is which element of the premise-list to use. Subgoal generation focuses on the conclusion, which gives the theorem prover a very goal-directed orientation. Selecting a new conclusion changes this direction. In particular, if the executive selects the wrong variant of Rule 3 or Rule 4 in Fig. 2, the user can override the executive by use of the contrapositive rule.

The substitutivity of equality is formulated as *paramodulation* in Fig. 4. There are two parameters to this rule: an expression $e1$ in the conclusion and a premise of the form $B \rightarrow e2 = e3$. The conclusion of the subgoal is $(B \& A(e3)) \cdot \sigma$ where σ is the most general unifier of $e1$ and $e2$ produced by matching them. $A(e3)$ denotes the result of replacing $e1$ in the conclusion by $e3$.

The actual paramodulation rule in the theorem prover has two features not depicted in Fig. 4. There is a *paramodulation-list* which contains definitions and theorems of the form $B \rightarrow e2 = e3$. These formulae, which are logically additional premises, can be used in paramodulation in lieu of an element of the premise-list. The user can also specify the 'direction' of the substitution which allows him to interchange the roles of $e2$ and $e3$ in Fig. 4.

The last rule in Fig. 4 is the *lemma rule* which generates two new subgoals. The first is to prove a formula B while the second uses B in proving the conclusion of the given subgoal. B is a parameter to this rule which must be specified by the user. The only restriction on B is that it cannot contain quantifiers or free variables.

All of the inference rules require their inputs to contain *no* quantifiers; this assumption is used throughout the theorem prover for simplicity. Hence, the backward chaining and paramodulation lists must be 'pre-Skolemized'. The lemma and case analysis rules are the only ones that require an input not to contain free variables and case analysis rules are the only ones that require an input not to contain free variables.

4. EXAMPLES

An example of the type of program that we plan to verify is the linking loader described by Hookway (1980). A total of 36 verification conditions (VCs) were generated for this example. Several of the VCs have been proved by hand to evaluate the suitability of the techniques described in the previous sections for

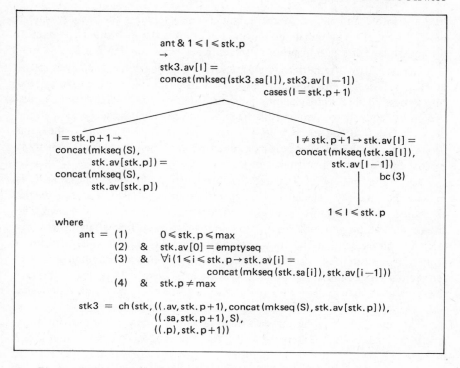

$$\text{ant} \ \& \ 1 \leqslant I \leqslant stk.p$$
$$\rightarrow$$
$$stk3.av[I] =$$
$$concat(mkseq(stk3.sa[I]), stk3.av[I-1])$$
$$cases(I = stk.p + 1)$$

$I = stk.p + 1 \rightarrow$
$concat(mkseq(S),$
$\quad stk.av[stk.p]) =$
$concat(mkseq(S),$
$\quad stk.av[stk.p])$

$I \neq stk.p + 1 \rightarrow stk.av[I] =$
$concat(mkseq(stk.sa[I]),$
$\quad stk.av[I-1])$
$bc(3)$

$1 \leqslant I \leqslant stk.p$

where
$$ant = (1) \qquad 0 \leqslant stk.p \leqslant max$$
$$(2) \quad \& \quad stk.av[0] = emptyseq$$
$$(3) \quad \& \quad \forall i (1 \leqslant i \leqslant stk.p \rightarrow stk.av[i] =$$
$$concat(mkseq(stk.sa[i]), stk.av[i-1]))$$
$$(4) \quad \& \quad stk.p \neq max$$

$$stk3 = ch(stk, ((.av, stk.p+1), concat(mkseq(S), stk.av[stk.p])),$$
$$((.sa, stk.p+1), S),$$
$$((.p), stk.p+1))$$

Fig. 7 – Proof of a subgoal of the verification condition of Fig. 6.

verification of the loader. It is felt that the VCs which were proved by hand are representative of the VCs for this example. We are confident that the theorem prover described here can interactively prove all the VCs for the loader. The proof of two VCs is discussed below.

Fig. 6 presents one of the VCs for the loader. As a part of the initialization of the theorem prover the formula is 'Skolemized' and an initial call is made on the simplifier. Three of the five conjuncts are simplified completely to *true*. A fourth conjunct is simplified to a form identical to one of the premises. This illustrates the importance of the simplification of expressions involving ac/ch described in section 3.3. The simplification of ac/ch expressions makes use of the fact that field selectors are defined constants and are equal if and only if they are identical. In Fig. 6 field selectors appearing in selector lists are distinguished by a leading period. Also, to improve legibility, PASCAL-like syntax is used in place of ac. For example, stk3.av[0] denotes ac(stk3,(.av, 0)), where stk3 is the ch expression at the bottom of Fig. 6.

After initialization, the executive generates an AND/OR tree of subgoals using the rules in Fig. 2. In this case application of Rules 1 and 2 result in five terminal subgoals corresponding to the five conjuncts in the consequent of the VC. The subgoal solver determines that the three conjuncts which simplified to *true* are solved and that a fourth conjunct appears among the premises and is therefore solved. The remaining unsolved subgoal is the quantified conjunct of the consequent of Fig. 6. A proof of this subgoal is presented in Fig. 7.

The executive attempts to apply backward chaining and case analysis to the subgoal. (These are the only inference rules listed in Fig. 5 which are applied automatically.) Backward chaining fails since there are no premises whose conclusion matches the consequent of the subgoal. Case analysis succeeds with the cases stk. $p + 1 = I$ and stk. $p + 1 \neq I$. These cases are chosen to simplify the terms stk3. av [I] and stk3. sa [I] appearing in the formula to be proved (note that these are instances of terms involving ac/ch).

Fig. 7 shows the AND/OR tree that results from applying the case analysis rule to the unsolved subgoal of Fig. 6. In presenting AND/OR trees only the consequent of the formula at nodes in the tree other than the root is shown. The antecedent of the formula at a descendent node is derived straightforwardly from the antecedent of the root using Rule 2 of Fig. 2. Also free variables in figures are indicated by quantifiers. These quantifiers do not occur in the machine representation because the formulae have been 'Skolemized'. In Fig. 7 the fact that case analysis was used with the predicate stk. $p + 1 = I$ is indicated by the notation cases (stk. $p + 1 = I$) below the root node.

The result of applying the case analysis rule is a new subgoal of the form (stk. $p + 1 = I \rightarrow A$) & (stk. $p + 1 \neq I \rightarrow A$). This subgoal is not shown in Fig. 7 because the figures only show important subgoals. Application of the rules in Fig. 2 produces two subgoals corresponding to the two cases stk. $p + 1 = I$ and stk. $p + 1 \neq I$. Simplification of ac/ch expressions and literal evaluation reduces the goal for the case stk. $p + 1 = I$ to *true*. The other subgoal does not simplify to *true* so once again the executive tries backward chaining and case analysis. This time the case analysis rule fails since simplification has eliminated all ac/ch expressions from the subgoal. Backward chaining is successful with the third conjunct of the antecedent. This is indicated by the notation bc(3) in Fig. 7. The resulting subgoal, $1 \leqslant I \leqslant$ stk. p is easily proved using the rules of Fig. 2 and literal evaluation.

The VC presented in Fig. 6 is proved completely automatically. To illustrate the interactive features of the theorem prover we turn to another example. This second example is one of twelve VCs for the main procedure of the loader. It has the form of an implication whose consequent has thirteen conjuncts. The initial application of Rules 1 and 2 of Fig. 2 therefore produces thirteen independent subgoals, four of which are proved mechanically. The proof of the remaining subgoals requires interaction.

Fig. 8 shows the proof of one of the unsolved subgoals. Note that the subgoal contains an existential quantifier and therefore cannot be processed mechanically. In order for the proof to proceed the user must interactively invoke one of the rules of Fig. 5. In Fig. 8, the case analysis rule with the cases st [s] > 0 and st [s] $\leqslant 0$ was used to generate two subgoals. The proof of both cases proceeds by instantiating the variables with terms from the appropriate

140

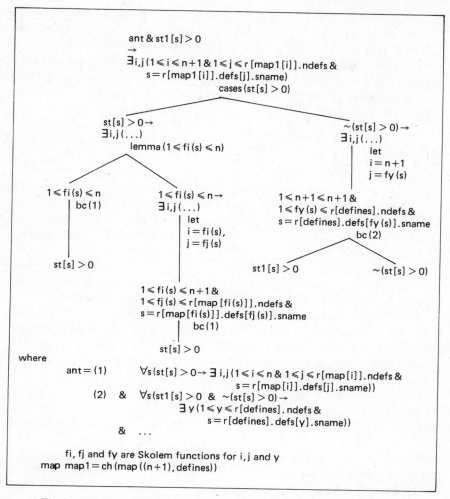

Fig. 8 — Proof of a subgoal of a verification condition for the linking loader.

premise and then backchaining off that premise. Instantiation is a user invoked rule. In Fig. 8 the notation 'let $v1 = e1$, $v2 = e2$' is used to denote the instantiation of $v1$ and $v2$ by $e1$ and $e2$ respectively. Note that the subgoal which results from the application of the instantiation rule is a conjunction and would thus be broken into independent subgoals by the executive. Each of these subgoals would be proved by backward chaining. The breaking up of the subgoal is not shown in Fig. 8 which is a summary of the proof rather than the actual tree produced by the theorem prover.

One of the conjuncts of the instantiated subgoal for the case $st[s] > 0$ is $fi(s) \leqslant n+1$. The antecedent contains the premise $\forall s(st[s] > 0 \rightarrow fi(s) \leqslant n)$. Back chaining with this premise fails since $fi(s) \leqslant n+1$ and $fi(s) \leqslant n$ do not match. On the other hand, this premise must be used in proving that $fi(s) \leqslant n + 1$. The lemma rule is used to get around this problem by setting up a proof that $fi(s) \leqslant n$ as a separate subgoal. This can then be added as a premise and the simplifier, using the units data structure, evaluates $fi(s) \leqslant n + 1$ to *true*. After applying the lemma rule, instantiation gives rise to five independent subgoals. Two of these are proven by the simplifier; each of the others is proven by an application of backward chaining, but only one is shown in Fig. 8.

5. DISCUSSION

The inference rules have a tendency to produce duplicate subgoals because often the application of two rules commute. Suppose, for example, that applying backward chaining to subgoal S1 produces S2. If case analysis is then applied to S2 the result is the same as if case analysis was first applied to S1 followed by backward chaining.

The mechanical search strategy in the theorem prover avoids many of these duplicates. It only applies case analysis once to a given subgoal. Further case analysis may be done on its subgoals but not on the given goal because this would create the potential for generating duplicates. The theorem prover does not apply both backward chaining and case analysis to a single subgoal because this also creates the potential for duplicate subgoals as described above. The theorem prover does, however, apply backward chaining in several different ways to a given subgoal because usually these do not commute.

The order in which inference rules are applied can always be overridden by the user. Most of the other inference rules generate the potential for duplicate subgoals, but this is not a problem for the theorem prover because they are used exclusively under user control.

As we mentioned in section 3, most of the methods used by the theorem prover are not new. The Case verifier is an outgrowth of the verifier described in Hookway & Ernst (1976) whose theorem prover was based on our previous work, Ernst (1971) and Ernst (1973). All of these theorem provers are Gentzen-type systems and hence are similar to other Gentzen-type systems such as the one developed by Bledsoe & Tyson (1978).

The type of arithmetic simplification used by the theorem prover is commonly found in theorem provers that are designed for formulae that contain numerical quantities. The design of units is based on the work of King (1969). Its function is very similar to the TYPELIST of Bledsoe *et al.* (1979). The main advantage of the former is that it was already implemented in our previous verifier.

The concept of defined constants has been implicitly used by theorem provers for a long time, e.g. many theorem provers recognize that $2 \neq 3$ because they are not identical. However, we know of no explicit statement of this concept in the literature. Although many new theories will contain defined constants, their occurrence in programming is even more commonplace. All elements of all

142

enumerated types are defined constants and so are all field names of records. Such symbols appear more like Skolem constants then integers because both are represented as symbolic LISP atoms as opposed to a special data format, e.g., integer defined constants are LISP integers. Of course, non-identical Skolem constants may be equal, e.g. $i = j$ may be true.

Defined constants are heavily used in simplifying access-change expressions because often corresponding elements in two selectors are different field names which allow them to be simplified. This kind of simplification has a different flavour from other simplification which centres around equalities (which is epitomized by Knuth–Bendix rewrite rules). Usually when the theorem prover infers that two objects are not equal, little can be done with this information to simplify other expressions.

The access and change functions are commonly used as the basis of a theory for data structure modifications. Luckham & Suzuki (1979) use these functions for this purpose, but their theory is more general than ours since it allows programs to use 'pointer' variables which are part of MODULA. However, our normal form and simplification technique for access/change expressions are quite different from theirs.

A number of verification systems have been constructed which use a theorem prover to prove verification conditions. These theorem provers have some similarities but also contain significant differences. A technical comparison of these systems is beyond the scope of this paper. Instead the reader is referred to the literature: Boyer & Moore (1979), Good *et al.* (1978), Suzuki (1975), and Musser (1977).

A large number of theorem proving methods were not incorporated into the theorem prover even though they would probably decrease the amount of assistance required from the user. One reason for rejecting these methods is that the system would be slower; the response time of the proposed system may even be a problem. But the main reason for rejecting them is that they add to the complexity of the system and are only used in special cases. The theorem prover described in this paper is reasonably simple and should be easy to modify and extend. As empirical data discloses classes of subgoals which the theorem prover cannot prove but which occur quite often, we will add special methods for solving them to the theorem prover.

Such special methods will probably be based on existing theorem proving methods that are not currently in the theorem prover. For example, Bledsoe *et al.*, (1979) can mechanically prove a much larger class on inequalities than our theorem prover. Some of their techniques may be incorporated into our theorem prover but probably not in their entirety because they are designed for proof problems which are more complicated than those which occur in program verification. Another kind of technique which might be useful is recent work on decision procedures such as Shostak (1979) and Nelson & Oppen (1979). But again such techniques will only be used to deal with difficulties uncovered by empirical data.

Acknowledgements

This research was supported by the National Science Foundation under grant MCS77-24236.

References

Bledsoe, W. W., Bruell, P., & Shostak, R., (1979). A prover for general inequalities, *Report ATP-40A*. Austin: Computer Science Dept., Univ. of Texas at Austin.

Bledsoe, W. W., & Tyson, M., (1978). The UT interactive theorem prover, *Report ATP-17A*. Austin: Computer Science Dept., University of Texas at Austin.

Boyer, R. S., & Moore, J. S., (1979). *A Computational Logic.* Academic Press.

Dannenberg, R. B., (1979). An extended verification condition generator, *Report CES-79-3*, Computer Engineering and Science Dept., Case Western Reserve University.

Ernst, G. W., (1973). A definition-driven theorem prover, *Proc. 3rd Int. Jnt. Conf. on Art. Int. (IJCAI-73)*, pp. 51-55. Menlo Park: Stanford Research Institute.

Ernst, G. W., (1971). The utility of independent subgoals in theorem-proving, *Information and Control*, April.

Ernst, G. W., & Ogden, W. F., (1980). Specification of abstract data types in MODULA, *ACM Trans. on Programming Languages and Systems*, pp. 522-543.

Gerhert, S. L., & Wile, D. S., (1979). Preliminary Report on the Delta Experiment: specification and verification of a multiple user file updating module, *Proc. of Specification of Reliable Software*, IEEE Computer Society.

Good, D. I., Cohen, R. M., Hoch, C. G., Hunter, L. W., & Hare, D. R., (1978). Report on the Language GYPSY, Version 2. 0, *ICSCA-CMP-10*, Certifiable Minicomputer Project. Austin: ICSCA, University of Texas at Austin.

Hoare, C. A. R., (1972). Proof of correctness of data representations, *Acta Informatica*, pp. 271-81.

Hookway, R. J., (1980). Verification of abstract data types whose representations share storage, *Report CES-80-2*, Cleveland: Computer Engineering and Science Dept., Case Western Reserve University.

Hookway, R. J., & Ernst, G. W., (1976). A program verification system, *Proc. of the Annual Conference of the ACM*, pp. 504-508.

Ichbiah, J. D., *et al.* (1979). Preliminary ADA reference manual, *SIGPLAN Notices*, June.

King, J. C., (1969). A program verifier, PhD thesis. Pittsburgh: Computer Science Dept., Carnegie-Mellon University.

Knuth, D., & Bendix, P., (1970). Simple word problems in universal algebras, *Computational Problems in Abstract Algebra*, pp. 263-297 (ed. Leach, J.). Oxford: Pergamon.

Luckham, D. C., & Suzuki, N., (1979). Verification of array, record and pointer operations in PASCAL, *ACM Trans. on Programming Languages and Systems*, October, pp. 226-244.

McCarthy, J., & Painter, J. A., (1967). Correctness of a compiler for arithmetic expressions, *Proc. Symp. Appl. Math.*, pp. 33-41. American Math. Society.

Musser, D. R., (1977). A data type verification system based on rewrite rules, *Proc. of the Sixth Texas Conference on Computing Systems*, Austin Texas.

Nelson, G., & Oppen, D. C., (1979). Simplification by cooperating decision procedures, *ACM Trans. on Programming Languages and Systems*, 245-257.

Shostak, R., (1979). A practical decision procedure for arithmetic with function symbols, *J. Assoc. Comput. Mach.*, April.

Suzuki, N., (1975). Verifying programs by algebraic and logical reduction, *Proc. Int. Conf. on Reliable Software, SIGPLAN Notices*, June, 473-481.

Wirth, N., (1977). MODULA: a language for modular multiprogramming, *Software – Practice and Experience*, Jan., 3-35.

6

Computational frames and structural synthesis of programs

E. H. Tyugu

Institute of Cybernetics, Estonian Academy of Sciences
Talinn, USSR

Abstract

Computational frames represent the meaning of concepts in terms of computability. They can be used for describing situations and expressing problem conditions as any kind of frames. On the other hand — the computational frames can be converted into special theories in which structural synthesis of programs is applicable.

The following two general ideas lie behind the structural synthesis of programs:

— A special theory is built for every particular problem. The theory can be tailored to fit the problem and to facilitate the proof of an existence theorem needed for program synthesis.
— Only structural properties of computations are used almost everywhere in the proof. The correctness of primitive steps of computations is not proved at all. It is assumed that if something can be computed, then it is computed correctly. This may be justified by the consideration that to describe the correctness conditions for primitive steps of computations is not more reliable than to describe the steps of computations themselves.

Introduction

The starting point for the program synthesis was in the artificial intelligence field where problem solvers were built. Now the program synthesis is growing out of the limits of AI and is becoming a topic for system programmers. As a consequence of this there are higher requirements for the efficiency and the reliability of a program synthesizer. In this paper we shall try to show that these requirements can be satisfied already by existing AI techniques of language processing and problem solving.

We shall take the way from a problem to a program for solving it, as shown in Fig. 1.

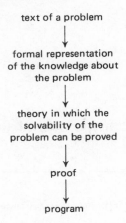

Fig. 1 – A way from a problem to a program.

The first step which transforms the text of a problem into some formal form can be performed by linguistic methods. It is out of our scope of interests.

We assume that the knowledge can be represented in the form of frames. The knowledge about any particular problem can be presented by frames where slots are filled in as much as needed for describing the problem. This is just the point from which the program synthesis starts.

Computational Frames

We use a notation of the frame as a knowledge module which can be manipulated (and extended when the knowledge is obtained). For a definition of the frame we refer to [1].

Computational frames have some special features:

- components with computable values;
- relations, usable for computing the values;
- conditions associated with the relations and showing when a relation is applicable for the computations.

Also, computational frames possess all the usual features of frames.

We assume that the knowledge about any particular problem can be represented in the form of computational frames. (Considering the great amount of investigations on the knowledge representation it seems to be a realistic assumption.)

A frame can be considered in an abstract form as has been done in [1]. But we shall prefer here a concrete presentation of frames in a special language. Let us consider some examples of frames given in a language which is close to [2]. We hope that comments (which are the lines starting with * in the first position) in the texts of frames will be sufficient for understanding the meaning of examples.

146

The first example is a frame which represents the notion of a person.

    person:

            (name: *string*;

* The first component of the frame
* is name, it is described as
* a string. That means — it may have
* a value which is a string.

        birth: (day,
                 month,
                 year: *integer*);

* The second component of the frame
* is birthdate, called "birth". The birth
* itself is a frame with three com-
* ponents day, month, year which
* can have integer values. The frame
* of birth contains implicitly
* a relation.
* The relation can be used for com-
* putations in the following ways:
*   birth: = (day, month, year)
*   day: = select_1 (birth)
*   month: = select_2 (birth)
*   year: = select_3 (birth)
*   children: set of = person;
* The component "children" is defined
* using the notion of set.
* This notion must be defined earlier.

        married: *logical*;

* For a married person the component
* married must have the value *true*.

        nameofspouse: *string*;

        if married *then*
           rel Q *in* name
               out nameofspouse;

* For a married person the name
* of its spouse can be calculated
* by a program Q. Here we have
* a partial relation with an
* applicability condition.

)

The frame of a person ended with this parenthesis.

The second example is a frame which represents the notion of a set.

```
set: (
                of: undefined ;
* of is an element of the set.
* It's type is undefined yet.
* This is a slot which must be
* filled when the frame is used.
                representation: space;
* representation is the "value" of the
* whole set taken as one
* entity. Its type is not specified,
* but it will use dynamically
* allocated memory.
                first: logical ;
* first is true if the first element
* of the set is selected.
                next: logical;
* next is true if the next element
* of the set is selected.
                rel next = not first;
                rel Q1 in next, representation
                        out of);
* The program Ql computes the value
* of an element from
* the values of next and represen-
* tation.
                )
```

End of the set frame.

The third example is a frame of a subset.

```
        subset: (of, is: set;
                condition: logical;
        if solvable (in of. next out condition) then
                rel Q2      in of. prepresentation
                            out is. representation;
* solvable (in x out y) is a predicate
* which is true iff
* a program can be synthe-
* sized for computing y from x.
* solvable (in of. next out condition)
* is the computability condition
* for the relation rel Q2 in of.representation out is. representation
* The meaning of the condition is
* that for any element of
```

* the set it is possible to
* decide if it must belong to
* the subset ("is").
)

End of the subset frame.

The last example of a frame will be for the existence quantifier.

        exist: (in: set;
                    condition: *logical*
                    true: *logical*;
* true will take the value *true*
* iff in the set "in" exists an element which
* satisfies the condition.
            if solvable (*in* in.next *out* condition) *then*
                rel Q3 *in* in . representation
                        out true
)

Using the given frames we can express different meanings. For instance the meaning of

"unmarried mothers who have
children born after 1978"

can be expressed as a subset the elements of which are persons for which the following condition holds:

not married $\land$ sex = "female" $\land$
has-young-children.

"has-young-children" is a logical variable the value of which is the same as the component "true" of the frame for the statement: "in the set of the children of the person exists a child born after 1978".

How to Build a Theory

Though the frames represent the knowledge about a problem formally, this knowledge is not directly suited for program synthesis. The next step from a problem to a program is constructing a theory in which a theorem can be proved that the solution of the problem exists (see Fig. 1). A first-order constructive theory may be used [3], but it is quite difficult to find a proof if the theory has such a general form.

In our case the frames contain very special knowledge about a particular problem, and we shall use this when building a theory. In particular, we shall associate a predicate P_c with every computable component c, which occurs in a frame. The predicate $P_c(x)$ is true iff x is a value of the component c.

149

Computability of a component b from a component a can be expressed now in a first-order theory as follows:

$$\forall x \, (P_a(x) \Rightarrow \exists y \, (P_b(y) \wedge y = f(x))) \, , \tag{1}$$

where f is the function for computing the value of b from a given value of a. For instance, the selecting of elements of a set in the set frame can be expressed by the first-order formula

$$\forall x \, \forall y \, (set \,. \, representation(x) \wedge set \,. \, next(y) \Rightarrow$$
$$\Rightarrow \exists z \, (set \,. \, element(z) \wedge$$
$$\wedge z = f_{Q1}(x, y))) \, ,$$

where $set \,. \, representation$, $set \,. \, next$ and $set \,. \, element$ are predicates for the components of the set frame. If a relation has an applicability condition, associated with it, then the first-order formula will take the form of an implication. For instance, the relation

    if married *then*
        rel Q *in* name
                out nameofspouse

can be represented as

    married $\Rightarrow$
        $\Rightarrow \forall x \, name(x) \Rightarrow$

        $\Rightarrow \exists y \, (nameofspouse(y) \wedge$
            $\wedge y = f_Q(x)) \, .$

(Here "married" is regarded as a propositional variable because the type of this component of the frame is *logical*.)

And in general

$$P \Rightarrow \forall x \, (P_a(x) \Rightarrow \exists y \, (P_b(y) \wedge \Rightarrow y = f(x))) \, . \tag{2}$$

Some complications arise with the following relation:

    if solvable (*in* in . next, in . representation *out* condition) *then*
        rel Q3 *in* in . representation
            out true.

In this case the function for computing values of the component "true" varies and depends on the function for computing "condition" from in . next and in . representation. In general a relation of the form

    if solvable (*in* c *out* d) *then*
        rel Q *in* a
            out b

cannot be expressed in the first-order theory. It can be expressed as follows:

$$\forall f[(\forall u(P_c(u) \Rightarrow \exists v(P_d(v) \land v = f(u)))) \Rightarrow$$
$$\Rightarrow \forall x(P_a(x) \Rightarrow \exists y(P_b(y) \land y = G(f,x))))] \ . \tag{3}$$

We shall try to avoid the difficulties which arise in the theories of higher order. Therefore we shall restrict the usage of *computable* predicate so that any applicability condition which contains *computable* predicate has the form of $P_1 \land \ldots \land P_k$ where every P_i is of the form *computable* (...).

Considering the representation of the relations of the frames in the form of logical formulae, we are satisfied that every partial relation can be represented by a logical formula of the form (1), (2), or (3). These formulae satisfy the restrictions described in [3], and consequently they can be taken as axioms of a constructive theory in which any proof of the existence theorem can be transformed into an ALGOL program for computing the desired result [3].

Structural Synthesis

Let us introduce some abbreviations for the formulas which express the computability of objects.

Instead of

$$\forall x(P_a(x) \Rightarrow \exists y(P_b(y) \land y = f(x)))$$

we shall write

$$a \xmapsto{f} b \tag{4}$$

and say that "b is computable from a using f".

This is a *computational relation* between the objects a and b (or between the objects a, b, and the function f).

It is obvious that instead of (2) we can use now the formula

$$P \Rightarrow a \xmapsto{f} b \ . \tag{5}$$

The meaning of the predicate *solvable* (*in c out d*) can be expressed by means of a computational relation as follows:

$$\exists f(c \xmapsto{f} d) \ .$$

Now instead of (3) we can write

$$\forall f(c \xmapsto{f} d \Rightarrow a \xmapsto{G(f)} b) \ . \tag{6}$$

We shall call the formulas (4), (5), and (6) where a, b, c, d are objects or tuples (finite sets) of objects *computability statements*.

151

We have already shown that some amount of knowledge which is present in frames can be represented as a set of computability statements. Now we are going to present the inference rules which enable us to build a proof for a formula

$$\exists f(x \underset{f}{\longmapsto} y) \tag{7}$$

as soon as enough information about the problem

"compute y from x" (8)

is presented in the form of computability statements.

The formula (7) is the existence theroem for the problem (8). (All problem conditions are now presented as axioms of a special theory which is built on the basis of computational frames, for the particular problem!)

The existence theorem is a formula of a theory of higher order. But using the inference rule

$$0° \; \frac{x \underset{f_0}{\longmapsto} y}{\exists f(x \underset{f}{\longmapsto} y)} \; , \qquad ,$$

the proof of the theorem can be obtained as soon as $x \underset{f_0}{\longmapsto} y$ is proved for a particular f_0. So we shall consider the derivation of $x \underset{f}{\longmapsto} y$ from the set of axioms given in the form of computability statements.

Computability relations enable the representation of any information flow for a finite set of objects. As soon as no object must be computed more than once, such an ordering can be found on any set of computability relations for any set of given objects, which guarantees that computations are possible when functions are applied in this order. The idea is that, if we have $a \underset{f_1}{\longmapsto} b$ and $b \underset{f_2}{\longmapsto} c$, then serial application of f_1 and f_2 yields c from a, i.e. a new computability relation $a \underset{f_1;f_2}{\longmapsto} c$ can be derived.

Let $x, y, \ldots$ be finite sets of objects (constants or variables). Then computability is expressed by the following three inference rules:

1 $1°$ $\dfrac{y \subseteq x}{x \underset{s_{xy}}{\longmapsto} y}$.

where s_{xy} denotes a selector function, selecting values of elements of y from the given values of the elements of x;

$$2° \; \frac{x \underset{f_1}{\longmapsto} y, \quad x \underset{f_2}{\longmapsto} z, \quad w = y \cup z}{x \underset{(f_1,f_2)}{\longmapsto} w}$$

152

where (f_1, f_2) denotes parallel application of the functions f_1 and f_2;

$$3° \quad \frac{x \xmapsto[f_1] y, \quad y \xmapsto[f_2] z}{x \xmapsto[(f_1; f_2)] z}$$

where $(f_1; f_2)$ denotes sequential application of the functions f_1 and f_2.

If a formula $x \xmapsto{f} y$ can be derived in a theory with the set Q of axioms in the form of computability relations and with the inference rules $1°, 2°, 3°$, then the problem (7) is solvable and the program for solving it is the description of the function f built by means of the same rules $1°, 2°, 3°$.

Assuming that the computed values of objects do not depend on the order in which the computability relations are used in the proof of $\exists f(x \xmapsto{f} y)$, the second inference rule can be changed:

$$2' \quad \frac{x \xmapsto[f_1] y, \quad x \xmapsto[f_2] z, \quad w = y \cup z}{x \xmapsto[(f_1; f_2)] w}$$

This certainly implies an arbitrary restriction on the results of program synthesis but enables us to perform all computations sequentially. In fact this restriction can be motivated by the assumption mentioned earlier, that if something can be computed, it is computed correctly. Further on we shall consider only sequential programs.

The algorithm for proving the solvability of problems (and for deriving a program for a solvable problem) is actually an algorithm for finding a transitive closure on a graph. Objects and functions from Q are the vertices of the graph. This algorithm makes less than $k \cdot n$ steps for deriving a program, which contains k functions, when the number of computability relations in Q is n.

Derivation of programs using information flow analysis has long been known. Programmers in different application areas discover it again and again, because it is a simple way for composing a number of preprogrammed subroutines in a sequential program.

Synthesis of Loops from Sequences

Let $x_1, x_2, \ldots$ be a sequence of objects where computational relations $x_i \xmapsto{f} x_{i+1}$ are given for any $i = 1, 2, \ldots$ and $u \xmapsto{f_0} x_1$ is given for the first element of the sequence. Applying the inference rule $3°$ n times gives that the nth element of the sequence can be computed by $\underbrace{f_0; f; \ldots; f}_{n-1 \text{ times}}$. This can be done by a program with a loop ζ_0; **for** i **to** $n-1$ **do** ζ **od**, where ζ_0, ζ are operators, computing functions f_0 and f.

153

The problem is a little different, if the result of computation must be the element x_i for which $\neg P(x_i)$ and $P(x_j)$ if $j < i$. Then the program will be

$$\zeta_0; \quad \text{while } P(x) \text{ do } \zeta \text{ od},$$

where x is the variable to which the computed value of x_i is assigned at every step.

The synthesis of loops for handling of sequences was described in 1958 [4]. More general results were presented in [5]. There a set of objects $x_{s,j}, s = 1, 2, \ldots, n$, $j = 1, 2, \ldots$, is considered. It is assumed that for some given $m_1^0, \ldots, m_n^0, m_1, \ldots, m_n$ the objects $x_{s,i}, i < m_s^0$ have given values. The values of x_{s,m_s} are asked. Computational relations are

$$\{x_{1,i-\Delta(s,1)} \ \cdots \ x_{n,i-\Delta(s,n)}\} \underset{f_s}{\longmapsto} x_{s,i} \ ,$$

where $\Delta(s, j)$ are non-negative integers, $\Delta(s, j) \leqslant m_j^0$. It was shown that for a solvable problem there exists a sequence of functions f_s which computes one new element $x_{s,i}$ for every sequence $x_{s,1}, x_{s,2} \cdots$

The program ζ for this sequence of functions can be taken as the body of a loop, which solves the problem.

Synthesis of Branching Programs

Let formulas P in left parts of computability statements be computable predicates $P_1, P_2, \ldots$, and let $p_1, p_2, \ldots$ respectively, be programs for computing the values of the predicates. An inference rule

$$4° \quad \frac{P_1(w) \vee \ldots \vee P_k(w), \ P_1(w) \Rightarrow x \underset{f_1}{\longmapsto} y, \ldots, P_k(w) \Rightarrow x \underset{f_k}{\longmapsto} y}{x \cup w \underset{f}{\longmapsto} y}$$

enables us to derive a branching program for computing y from x:

$$f = \text{if } p_1(w) \text{ then } f_1 \text{ elif } p_2(w) \text{ then } \ldots \text{ else } f_k \text{ fi} .$$

Applying the rule $4°$ together with the rules $1°, 2°, 3°$ gives programs which are combined from branching and linear parts. If $p_1(w) \vee \ldots \vee p_k(w)$ must not be proved (for instance, if it can be assumed to be true in the basis of some general considerations), then a very simple search strategy can be used. First of all, unconditional computability relations are checked and used whenever it is possible, then all computability statements $p_i(w) \Rightarrow x \underset{f_i}{\longmapsto} y$ with evaluated w and x are checked and a conditional statement $if \ldots fi$ is generated. For every branch of the statement the same strategy is recursively applied.

In a more general case the formulas $P_i(u)$ may be normal formulas, as defined in [3]. Even then the form of the derived program will be the same. Though in this case the search of the proof becomes more complicated because

154

of the subproofs of these formulas. The demonstration of the truth of the formula $p_1(w) \lor \ldots \lor p_k(w)$ may be put on a user. But in some simple cases it can be done automatically, as it is done, for instance, in translators for decision tables.

If partial programs are accepted as results of the synthesis, then there is no need at all to prove the truth of the formulas like $P_1(w) \lor \ldots \lor P_k(w)$. Let us denote by $a \vdash_f b$ that a partial function exists for computing b from a. Then instead of rule $4°$ a more simple rule is applicable:

$$4' \quad \frac{P_1(w) \Rightarrow x \vdash_{f_1} y, \ldots, P_k(w) \Rightarrow x \vdash_{f_k} y}{x \cup w \vdash_f y}$$

where

$$f = \text{if } P_1(w) \text{ then } f_1 \text{ elif } \ldots \ldots \text{ elif } P_k(w)$$
$$\text{then } f_k \text{ else failure fi}.$$

failure is a procedure signalling that the function f cannot be used for the particular input data, because $P_1(w) \lor \ldots \lor P_k(w)$ is not true.

Synthesis of Procedures

It is very useful to specify subproblems as much as possible before the solution of the problem is planned. The problem is then divided into smaller, and presumably simpler parts, and the existence proof can be divided as well. This can be done when axioms are being specified. In particular, subproblems can be specified, which must be proved to be solvable, before a computational relation can be applied. For instance, in order to calculate a value of an integral $z = h(x) = {}_a\!\int^x y \, du$ one must solve a problem "how to calculate a value of y for a given value of x?". This can be expressed by the following computability statement

$$\forall f(u \underset{f}{\longmapsto} y \Rightarrow x \underset{h}{\longmapsto} z),$$

where $h = H(f_0)$ is realized by a numerical integration program. A proof that the solution of the subproblem exists, yields a procedure specification for f_0. The procedure is called from the program H which realizes the function h in the computability statement.

The computability condition here contains a quantified functional variable f, consequently, no first-order theory can be used for the computability conditions in this case. Nevertheless, an efficient search strategy can be used for constructing existence proofs, if it is known that no computability relation must be applied more than once in any proof for one and the same subproblem. Only finite search is needed then for any subproblem, analogically to the search used for constructing a transitive closure on a graph described earlier. However a search on an and-or tree of subproblems is needed for proving the solvability of the whole problem.

155

Let us point out that a body of a loop can be derived from a proof of a subproblem. In particular, control structures for loops corresponding to different induction schemes can be programmed, and represented axiomatically as computability statements with subproblems. This is how loops and recursive programs are synthesized in the programming system PRIZ [6].

Let us complete the paper with a remark that algorithms of the structural synthesis of programs have quite good performance characteristics. These algorithms are described in [7], where the computational complexity of the algorithms is estimated as well.

REFERENCES

[1] Minsky, M., (1975). A framework for representing knowledge, *The Psychology of Computer Vision*, (ed. Winston, P.). New York: McGraw–Hill.
[2] Männisalu, M. A., *et al.* (1977) UTOPIST language; data processing algorithms and management, *Statistika*, 80–118 (Russian).
[3] Nepeivoda, N. N., (1978). Constructing correct programs, *Problems of Cybernetics*, **46**, Acad. of Sc. of the USSR, Moscow, 88–122 (Russian).
[4] Ljubimski, E. Z., (1958). Automatic programming and method of programming procedures. Ph.D. thesis, Moscow: Institute of Math. of the Acad. of Sc. of the USSR.
[5] Zadyhailo, I. B., (1963). Constructing loops from parametric specifications, *Journal of Computational Mathematics and Mathematical Physics*, **3**, *No. 2*.
[6] Tyugu, E. H., (1977). A programming system with automatic program synthesis, *Lecture Notes in Computer Science*, 47, *Methods of* Algorithmic Language Implementation, pp. 251–267. Berlin: Springer–Verlag.
[7] Tyugu, E. H., Harf, M. J., (1980). Algorithms for the structural synthesis of programs, *Systematic Programming and Computer Software*, **No. 4**, 3–13 (Russian).

ACQUISITION AND MATCHING OF PATTERNS

7

Semi-autonomous acquisition of pattern-based knowledge

J. R. Quinlan[†]

Baser Department of Computer Science
University of Sydney

INTRODUCTION

This paper has three themes:

(1) The task of acquiring and organizing the knowledge on which to base an expert system is difficult.
(2) Inductive inference systems can be used to extract this knowledge from data.
(3) The knowledge so obtained is powerful enough to enable systems using it to compete handily with more conventional algorithm-based systems.

These themes are explored in the context of attempts to construct high-performance programs relevant to the chess endgame king-rook versus king-knight.

Most existing expert systems are based on knowledge obtained from a human expert. With reference to the family of geological expert systems being built at SRI, Gaschnig writes:

> Model development is a cooperative enterprise involving an exploration geologist who is an authority on the type of deposit being modelled, and a computer scientist who understands the operation of the PROSPECTOR system [1].

Feigenbaum, one of the pioneers of expert systems work and head of probably the world's largest group building such systems, puts it as follows:

> (The knowledge engineer) works intensively with an expert to acquire domain-specific knowledge and organise it for use by a program [2].

The expert is called upon to perform a most exacting task, with which he is also unfamiliar. He must set out the sources and methodologies of his own

[†] Present address: Rand Corporation, Santa Monica

expertise, and do so in such a way that it makes sense to a non-expert (the knowledge engineer) and can even be represented in a precise machine-usable form! Not surprisingly, this often turns out to be an onerous task with many false starts, so that Feigenbaum goes on to state that:

> The acquisition of domain knowledge (is) the bottleneck problem in the building of applications-oriented intelligent agents.

Inductive inference is a process of going from the particular to the general. We invoke this process ourselves each time we hypothesize some property shared by members of one set of things that differentiates them from everything else. At its most general level, an inductive inference system is capable of discovering regularities that can explain observed phenomena in some domain. Of course these regularities can be knowledge in a most compact form, just as the regularity $F = Ma$ embodies much of our knowledge of mechanics. Ability to discover regularities gives a new possible prescription for acquiring knowledge. The expert, instead of trying to specify the knowledge directly, guides an inductive inference system in its search for regularities in collections of examples drawn from his domain of expertise.

Once an expert system has been formulated, driven by knowledge obtained from inductive inference or otherwise, we can ask a number of questions about the quality of the system (and indirectly the knowledge on which it is based). Is it always accurate? How expensive is it to run compared to other systems, expert and otherwise? In the experiments to be described here, programs constructed via the inductive inference route were shown to be perfectly accurate, and to run up to two orders of magnitude faster than a commonly-used algorithm and five times faster than a knowledge-based system that the author constructed by hand.

This paper contains a brief survey of some existing inductive inference systems, and a more detailed examination of the particular system used for these experiments. There follows a discussion of the endgame king-rook versus king-knight and the results of experiments to construct programs for deciding the knight's side is lost in 2- or 3-ply.

INDUCTIVE INFERENCE: SOME EXAMPLES

The purpose here is to describe a few modern inductive inference systems, indicate the mechanisms they employ, and mention one or two notable successes of each. No attempt is made at completeness. For a more comprehensive treatment the reader is referred to survey papers [3,4].

Meta-DENDRAL

Probably the most successful application of inductive inference techniques to the problem of knowledge acquisition is the Meta-DENDRAL program [5]. When an organic molecule is bombarded by high-energy particles it breaks into fragments (and some atoms may migrate between fragments). If the mass and relative abundance of all the fragments can be found, an expert mass spectro-scopist can identify a handful of possible structures of the original molecule. Meta-DENDRAL's original task was to discover the rules by which these structures could be deduced, or in other words to develop a theory of how molecules fragment. For each run the data consisted of a large number of known molecules together with their observed mass/abundance readings. The program first identified all possible places that the molecules could have broken in order to explain the observed fragments — only those breaks consistent with a 'weak' theory of what bonds can break were considered. Next a coarse search was made for possible rules to explain these breaks in terms of the local context of each broken bond. Finally the set of rules so obtained was refined, so that rules predicting breaks that did not occur were made more specific, and other rules were made more general if possible. The rules resulting from this three-phase process not only accurately reflected expert knowledge, but also included previously unknown rules. When the same approach was taken for nuclear magnetic resonance spectro-scopy, once more new and useful rules were found. So successful was this work that the rules have been published as chemistry.

Meta-DENDRAL is an example of a special-purpose inductive system — it can only be used for the particular induction tasks for which it was designed. (It does however embody powerful kernel ideas, such as using a weak model to guide the discovery of a strong one, that have wide applicability.) General induction systems, on the other hand, are able to attempt problems of discovering regularities in domains where no semantic information is available to guide the inference. This class of systems is differentiated primarily by constraints on the form that discovered knowledge can take, and to a lesser extent by the way that search for this knowledge is carried out.

INDUCE

Michalski's INDUCE package [6] takes the description of a number of objects of different classes and constructs one or more generalized descriptions of each class. The descriptions of both objects and classes are couched in VL21, a language based on first-order logic but allowing typed variables. To find generalized descriptions of a class, the descriptions of all objects of that class are placed in one set (the positive instances) and all other objects into another set (the negative instances). A single description is then chosen from the positive set, and some of its atomic descriptors are built into more and more complex descriptions until a number are found that are sufficiently specific so that no object matching them can be in the negative instances. The best of them is selected as one of the descriptions of the class, the positive instances are reduced by removing all those that match this description, and the process repeated until all the original positive instances are covered by one or more of the generalizations. This system has also been applied to the problem of building expert systems, specifically for constructing a rule to test for a soybean disease. From the given descriptions of some hundreds of plants it was able to construct a generalized description of

161

diseased plants that was more accurate diagnostically then a human expert working from the same data. A precursor to the INDUCE system was also used in a similar series of experiments to those reported here, relating to the king-pawn versus king endgame [7].

THOTH-P

Vere's THOTH-P [8] is an example of a system that, while it is less generally applicable than INDUCE, can still tackle a range of tasks. Its data is a set of pairs of objects viewed as before-and-after snapshots, and it attempts to find the smallest number of relational productions that explain the changes. A relational production specifies that in a given context some stated properties are invalidated and new ones created, where the context and properties are again expressed in a language derived from logic. The method used to find these relational productions is an exhaustive search for maximal common generalizations which expands exponentially with the number of pairs of objects, and so cannot be applied to more than a small amount of data. (This exponential time problem is shared by other 'complete' systems such as SPROUTER [9]). Examples of its applications are finding the smallest number of primitive actions sufficient to explain a sequence of changes in the microcosm known as the 'blocks world', and discovering rules to change a restricted class of sentences from active to passive voice.

ID3

A fuller description of the general induction system that was used for the experiments reported here follows. In this case, the knowledge discovered is in the form of decision trees for differentiating objects of one class from another. Although this format is much more constrained than, for instance, the descriptions that INDUCE can generate, its simplicity is counter-balanced by its efficiency [10].

The basic algorithm on which ID3 is built is a relative of the Concept Learning System developed by Hunt in the '50s and documented in [11]. We start with a set of *instances*, each described in terms of a fixed number of *attributes*. Each attribute in turn has a small number of discrete possible *values*, and so an instance is specified by the values it takes for each attribute. To illustrate the idea, we could describe a person in terms of the attributes *height, colour of hair*, and *colour of eyes*. The attribute *height* might have possible (metric) values {1.30, 1.31, ..., 2.29, 2.30} while the attribute *colour of hair* might have possible values {dark, fair, red}. A particular individual might then be represented by the instance

height = 1.81, *colour of hair* = dark, *colour of eyes* = brown .

With each of these given instances is associated a known class, which will here be either *plus* or *minus*. The task is to construct a decision tree that maps each instance to its correct class.

162

Suppose then that we have such a set C of instances. If C is empty then we cannot say much about it, merely recording it as null. If C contains one or more instances and they all belong to the same class, we can associate C with this class. Otherwise C contains two or more instances, some *plus* and some *minus*. We could then choose an attribute A with permissible values $A_1, A_2, \ldots, A_n$ say. Each member of C will have one of these values for A, so we can sort C into subsets $C_1, C_2, \ldots, C_n$ where C_1 contains those instances in C with value A_1 of A, C_2 contains those with value A_2 of A, and so on. Diagrammatically we can represent this as:

attribute A:

$$A_1 \rightarrow C_1$$
$$A_2 \rightarrow C_2$$
$$\ldots$$
$$A_n \rightarrow C_n \, .$$

Now we have n sets of instances of the form C_i that we wish to relate to their class, so we can apply the same process to each of them. We keep going until each collection of instances is empty or all its members belong to the same class.

To clarify this process we will apply it to the simple problem from the king-rook king-knight endgame of determining whether the Black king can capture the White rook on its next move. There are two attributes:

- Black king is next to rook
- White king is next to rook

each of which has the possible values true (t) and false (f). The class will be *plus* if capture is possible, *minus* if it is not. The given set will contain all possible instances:

{*tt: minus, tf: plus, ft: minus, ff: minus*}

If the first attribute is selected we will have

> black king is next to rook
> $\quad t \rightarrow$ {*tt: minus, tf: plus*}
> $\quad f \rightarrow$ {*ft: minus, ff: minus*}

The same process is next applied to the first (sub) collection, this time selecting the second attribute.

> black king is next to rook
> $\quad\quad$ white king is next to rook
> $\quad t \rightarrow \quad\quad t \rightarrow$ {*tt: minus*}
> $\quad\quad\quad\quad f \rightarrow$ {*ft: plus*}
> $\quad f \rightarrow \quad$ {*ft: minus, ff: minus*}

163

All subcollections now contain instances of only a single class; we can replace the collections by classes giving the decision tree

$$
\begin{bmatrix}
\text{black king is next to rook} \\
\quad t \to \begin{bmatrix} \text{white king is next to rook} \\ \quad t \to minus \\ \quad f \to plus \end{bmatrix} \\
\quad f \to \quad minus
\end{bmatrix}
$$

This rule is isomorphic to the program fragment

> **if** black king is next to rook
> **then**
> > **if** white king is next to rook
> > **then** capture is impossible
> > **else** capture is possible
> **else** capture is impossible

The above process does not specify how we should go about choosing the attribute A to test next. It is clear that any choice will eventually lead to a correct decision tree. An intelligent choice, however, will usually lead to a simple tree, while the straightforward algorithm 'choose the next attribute' will in general give rise to a monster more voluminous than the instances themselves.

In the original CLS the choice was made on a cost basis. Suppose we define a set of costs $\{P_i\}$ of measuring the ith attribute of some instance, and $\{Q_{jk}\}$ of misclassifying it as belonging to class j when it really is a member of class k. If we arbitrarily say that all instances in C are members of some class even when they are not we will incur a misclassification cost which depends on the instances in C and the class chosen. Let us denote by X_0 the minimum such cost over all classes. If we test some attribute A we will incur a measurement cost plus the sum of the total costs for each of the subcollections $C_1, \ldots, C_n$ resulting from testing that attribute − denote by X_1 the minimum sum over all attributes. The total cost of a rule for C is then the minimum of X_0 and X_1. This computation of total cost is recursive and can be prohibitively expensive if there are many attributes, but it can be approximated by a fixed-depth lookahead in much the same way that the true minimax function can be approximated by a fixed-ply search. The rule that results from this approach tends to have low or even minimal cost. Such as approach is particularly appropriate for applications like medical diagnosis where obtaining information has significant cost, and where certain classification errors are more acceptable than others.

Another line of attack (suggested to me by Peter Gacs of Stanford University) is based on information theory. A decision tree may be regarded as an information source that, given an instance, generates a message *plus* or *minus*, being the classification of that instance. If the probability of these messages is p^+ and p^- respectively the expected information content of the message is

$$
-p^+ \log_2(p^+) - p^- \log_2(p^-) .
$$

With a known set of instances we can approximate these probabilities by relative frequencies, i.e. p^+ becomes the proportion of instances in the set with class *plus*. So we will write $M(C)$ to denote this calculation of the expected information content of a message from a decision tree for a set C of instances, and define $M(\phi) = 0$.

Now consider as before the possible choice of A as the attribute to test next. The partial decision tree will look like

attribute A:

$$A_1 \rightarrow C_1$$
$$A_2 \rightarrow C_2$$
$$\ldots$$
$$A_n \rightarrow C_n$$

and the new expected information content will be

$$B(C,A) = \sum_{i=1}^{n} (\text{probability that value of } A \text{ is } A_i) \times M(C_i)$$

where again we can replace the probabilities by relative frequencies. The suggested choice of attribute to test next is that which 'gains' the most information, i.e. for which

$$M(C) - B(C,A)$$

is maximal. When all the algebraic dust has settled, this comes down to selecting that attribute A (with values $A_1, A_2, \ldots, A_n$) which minimizes

$$\sum_{i=1}^{n} -n_i^+ \log_2 \frac{n_i^+}{n_i^+ + n_i^-} - n_i^- \log_2 \frac{n_i^-}{n_i^+ + n_i^-}$$

where n_i^+ denotes the number of *plus* instances in C that have value A_i of attribute A. This method of choosing the next attribute to test has been used now in a substantial number of different experiments, and does seem to give compact decision trees.

ID3 was specifically designed to deal with large numbers of instances. It uses the basic algorithm above to form a succession of (hopefully) more and more accurate rules until one is found that is satisfactory for all given instances. The basic paradigm is:

(1) Select at random a subset of the given instances (called the *window*).
(2) Repeat:

- Form a rule to explain the current window.
- Find the exceptions to this rule in the remaining instances.
- Form a new window from the current window and the exceptions to the rule generated from it,

until there are no exceptions to the rule.

Experiments (reported in detail in [12]) indicate that this process converges rapidly, and that, other things being equal, it enables correct rules to be discovered in time linearly proportional to the number of instances.

THE PROBLEMS ATTEMPTED

As mentioned in the introduction, this work has been concerned with subdomains of the chess endgame king-rook versus king-knight. Kopec & Niblett point out that this end-game provides quite a challenge even for masters. (The same paper is the source of many of the quantitative statements made here.) With one exception, each position in this end-game leads to a loss or draw for the knight's side, which we will take to be black.

The subdomains explored have been of the form *knight's side is lost in at most n-ply*, the main work revolving around the cases $n = 2$ and $n = 3$. This relation is defined as follows:

(1) A Black-to-move position is lost 0 ply if and only if

- The king is in checkmate, or
- The knight has been captured, the position is not stalemate, the White rook has not been captured and the Black king cannot retaliate by capturing it.

(2) A White-to-move position is lost in at most n ply (n odd) iff there is a White move giving a position that is lost in at most n-1 ply.

(3) A Black-to-move position is lost in at most n-ply (n even) iff all possible Black moves give positions that are lost in at most n-1 ply.

These definitions ingnore the repetition and 50-move rules of chess, but for small values of n are quite accurate. For brevity we will now omit the 'in at most' — 'lost n-ply' will be taken as shorthand for 'lost in at most n-ply'.

There are more than 11 million ways of placing the four pieces to form a legal Black-to-move position. The corresponding figure for White-to-move is more than 9 million. (The difference arises because, for instance, the White king cannot be in check in a Black-to-move position.) These counts, however, include many symmetric variants of essentially the same position, and when these are removed the numbers become approximately 1.8 million and 1.4 million respectively. About 69,000 of the 1.8 million Black-to-move positions are lost 2-ply while roughly 47,4 000 of the 1.4 million White-to-move positions are lost 3-ply.

Each position is described in terms of a set of attributes, which varied from experiment to experiment. These attributes are intended to bring out properties of a position that are relevant to its game-theoretic value. At present the system must be provided with the definition of these attributes, and the rules it finds are then decision trees relating the class of a position to its values of the given attributes. Two points are worth noting:

166

(1) It is possible for two or more distinct positions to have the same values for each attribute, and in fact the above large numbers of positions generally give rise to a much smaller number of distinct descriptions in terms of attribute values.

(2) If two positions of different classes have the same attribute values, it is not possible for a decision tree that uses only these values to differentiate between them. In such a situation the attributes are termed *inadequate*, and the remedy is to define some further attribute capable of distinguishing between the troublesome positions.

Finding small but adequate sets of attributes for the king-rook king-knight problems was a considerable task (at least for a chess novice like the author) – hence the 'semi-autonomous' in this paper's title.

THE 2-PLY EXPERIMENTS[†]

The first series of experiments was reported extensively in [14]. A set of seven problems was formulated, placing constraints on the positions analysed (e.g. restricting the Black king to a corner) and/or simplifying the meaning of 'lost' (e.g. ignoring stalemate). The attributes used initially were fairly low-level ones such as the distance between pieces in king-moves. As each problem was solved it served as a stepping-stone to the next.

The final (unrestricted) problem was the full lost 2-ply task. The number of attributes had grown by then to 25, of which 21 were low-level ('Black king, knight and rook are in line') while 4 were decidedly more complex ('the only move that the Black king can make creates a mate threat'). Every possible Black-to-move position was described in terms of these attributes, which turned out to be almost adequate in the sense of the last section – eleven small sets of positions containing representatives of both classes could not be differentiated using the attributes. The 1.4 million positions gave rise to just under 30,000 distinct descriptions in terms of these attributes, and an implementation of ID3 in PASCAL running on a DEC KL–10 found a decision tree containing 334 nodes in 144 seconds.[‡]

The attributes were a rather motley collection, though, and some of them were expensive to compute. After considerable trial and error a quite different set of 23 binary-valued attributes was developed. These were all high-level, but

---

[†] These were carried out while I was visiting Stanford University. I am most grateful for the resources generously supplied by the Artificial Intelligence Laboratory and the Heuristic Programming Project.

[‡] The earlier version of ID3 reported in the above paper used a different method of selecting which attribute to test next – it found a tree of 393 nodes in 394 seconds.

couched in terms only of broad patterns and operations on sets of positions. For example, one attribute was true if the given position was of the form

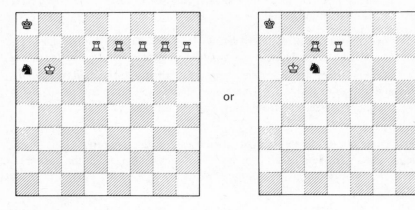

or

where the White rook was at one of the squares marked. Despite their smaller number, they turned out to be adequate. No two positions of different classes had the same value for all attributes. Even more surprisingly, the total space of 1.8 million positions collapsed into only 428 distinct instances. ID3 found a decision tree of 83 nodes for these instances in a couple of seconds. This decision tree was necessarily exact, since the instances it covered represented all possible positions.

The decision tree now gives a procedure for deciding whether a position is or is not lost 2-ply. Starting at the root, we find the value in the given position of the attribute tested at this node. Depending on this value we select one of the subtrees and continue until the selected subtree is a leaf. The given point is lost 2-ply if and only if the leaf is the class name *plus*. Notice that we may only have to evaluate a small subset of the attributes to classify any one position.

There are other ways of arriving at the same classification, and it is natural to compare them. The most obvious is *minimax search* which just interprets the definition of lost *n*-ply given in the previous section (with the usual alpha-beta cut-offs so that explorations that do not affect the classification are skipped). In the 2-ply case, the possible Black moves are examined to try to find one that results in a position that is not lost 1-ply. To determine whether a position is lost 1-ply, the possible white moves are tried in a a search for one that gives a lost 0-ply position, and so on.

Another classification method is *specialized search*, where we take into account additional information from this class of positions. For instance, to determine whether a position is lost 1-ply we need only examine White king or rook moves that capture the knight and White rook moves to the edge of the board (for a possible mate). This specialized search is really nothing more than an expert system that exploits domain knowledge — it is considerably harder to write and debug than minimax, but is more efficient.

Of course the simplest way to see if a position is lost 2-ply is to know before-hand all lost 2-ply positions and see if the given position is one of them. Several variants of this *look-up* are possible, but the one chosen here was to keep all lost 2-ply positions in memory, sorted so that they could be examined by a binary search. If a position could not be found among them then it was known to be not lost 2-ply.

PASCAL programs of roughly equal polish were prepared for each of these methods, and run on the same randomly-chosen collection of one thousand positions. They were cross-checked against each other to make sure that the classifications were the same in all cases[†], and the average time on a DEC KL-10 to decide whether or not a position was lost 2-ply computed. The results in Fig. 1 raise some interesting points. First and foremost, the method using the second induction-generated tree is the fastest at 0.96 ms, edging out look-up at 1.12 ms. Secondly, even though the second collection of attributes was very different from the first, and gave rise to 70 times the compression, the perfor-mance of the first tree at 1.37 ms was not too dissimilar. Finally, if we measure the computation not by time alone but by the product of time and memory as suggested in [15], classification by the second decision tree found by ID3 is still the preferred method, rivalled this time by specialised search.

Classification method	CPU time (ms)	Memory required (× 1K words)	Time × memory
Minimax search	7.67	2.1	16.1
Specialized search	1.42	2.2	3.1
Look-up	1.12	67.7	75.8
Using first decision tree	1.37	4.3	5.9
Using second decision tree	0.96	2.5	2.4

Fig. 1 – Comparison of classification methods for lost 2-ply.

THE 3-PLY EXPERIMENTS

The 2-ply case is perhaps special in that only a small proportion (less than 4%) of all possible positions are lost 2-ply. In the 3-ply case the corresponding figure is nearly 34%, and so the two classes are more evenly balanced.

† The thousand positions did not happen to include any of the very few for which the first set of attributes was inadequate.

About two man-months were required to find an adequate set of attributes for the 3-ply case. Of the final set of 49 binary attributes developed, 35 were concerned with patterns on the board such as

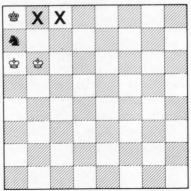

where the White king may occupy either of the indicated squares and the rook can move to some square other than those marked X in the same row as the black king. Four properties detected simple relationships like "White king is in check". The remaining ten dealt with relatively complex chess predicates such as "White rook is safe from reprisal 2-ply by the Black king if White king takes the knight or threatens to do so". Each of these ten predicates may be regarded as a small expert system in itself. Some are only approximate. The one above is defined as any of the following.

- The rook is more than two squares from the Black king.
- One blank square separates the rook from the Black king, but the rook is either next to or threatens the knight.
- The rook is next to the Black king, but either the knight is also next to it or there is a square that is next to the White king, knight and rook.

Others may contain bugs. However, it is interesting to note that the correctness of the final decision tree does not depend on the correctness of these subsytems used as attributes. So long as each attribute will always give the same value for the same position, and the collection of attributes is adequate to differentiate between positions of different classes, the decision tree produced by ID3 will be exact.

Even though some of them were rather untidy, the 49 attributes were adequate for this task, reducing the 1.4 million positions to 715 instances. ID3 was run on a CDC Cyber 72, and found a correct decision tree containing 177 nodes in 34 seconds.

Again a variety of classification techniques for lost 3-ply was tried. The minimax search was similar to the previous one, and the specialized search was built on the 2-ply specialized search using additional rules such as:

- To decide whether a position is lost (not more than) 3-ply it is advisable to check first if it is lost 1-ply.

170

• In establishing whether a position is lost exactly 3-ply, White moves that capture the knight need not be considered.

There was unfortunately insufficient space to store the nearly half a million lost 3-ply positions in memory, so look-up was not attempted.

One thousand White-to-move positions were generated randomly, and the average time taken to classify them by the different methods appears in Fig. 2. Minimax search is now much more expensive than the others, while the induction-generated tree is five times faster than specialized search. Unfortunately the PASCAL compiler used here did not give statistics on memory requirements, but it was found that the specialized search could execute with a field length about 40% less than required for the classification by decision tree. It would thus seem that Michie's computational measure would still rank the decision tree well ahead of search.

Classification method	CPU time (ms)
Minimax search	285.0
Specialized search	17.5
Using decision tree	3.4

Fig. 2 — Comparison of classification methods for lost 3-ply.

DISCUSSION

These lost 2- and 3-ply experiments demonstrate that expert systems built on knowledge inferred from data by an inductive system can match more conventional programs. In fact, if it proves possible to construct a lost 4-ply decision tree, it would be anticipated that the performance margin of the classification method using this tree over a specialized search program would once more increase dramatically.

These experiments were conducted over complete databases. In each case, every possible position was represented in the set of instances from which the decision tree was constructed. As a result, both decision trees were known to be exact. For some problems, however (such as an end-game with more pieces), the generation of the set of all possible positions may be computationally infeasible. This would not invalidate the technique, though, because experiments [12] indicate that a decision tree formed from only a small part of a collection of instances is accurate for a large proportion of the remainder. Typically, a rule formed from a randomly-chosen 5% of a large set of instances is also accurate for more than 75% of the rest. It could even be argued that this is the only genuine inductive inference, namely drawing conclusions from known instances that apply to those as yet unseen, and that working with complete databases is instead some form of information compression. At any rate, the decision tree produced

171

from incomplete databases will most likely be inexact and will have to be modified as exceptions are discovered, in much the same way as a complex program like an operating system is debugged as it is used.

In their present form, inductive inference systems are sufficiently powerful to extract high-quality knowledge from large numbers of instances, provided that the instances are described by appropriate attributes. Another side of induction (termed "constructive induction" by Michalski) is concerned with the much harder problem of developing good attributes from raw specifications. This problem will probably dominate inductive inference research in the eighties.

REFERENCES

[1] Duda, R., Gaschnig, J., and Hart, P., (1979). Model design in the PROSPECTOR consultant system for mineral exploration. *Expert Systems in the Micro Electronic Age*, pp. 153–167, (ed. Michie, D.). Edinburgh: Edinburgh University Press.

[2] Feigenbaum, E. A., (1977). The art of artificial intelligence 1: themes and case studies of knowledge engineering. *STAN-CS-77-621*. Stanford: Department of Computer Science, Stanford University.

[3] Mitchell, T. M., (1979). An analysis of generalization as a search problem. *Proc. 6th Intl. Joint Conf. on Artificial Intelligence, Tokyo*, pp. 577–582. Stanford: Department of Computer Science, Stanford University.

[4] Dietterich, T. G., and Michalski, R. S., (1979). Learning and generalization of characteristic descriptions: evaluation and comparative review of selected methods. *Proc. 6th Intl. Joint Conf. on Artificial Intelligence (Tokyo)*, pp. 223–231. Stanford: Department of Computer Science, Stanford University.

[5] Buchanan, B. G., and Mitchell, T. M., (1978). Model-directed learning of production rules. *Pattern Directed Inference Systems* (eds. Waterman, D., and Hayes–Roth, F.). New York and London: Academic Press.

[6] Michalski, R. S., (1978). Pattern recognition as knowledge-guided computer induction. *UIUCDCS-R-28-927.* Urbana–Champaign: Department of Computer Science, University of Illinois.

[7] Michalski, R. S., and Negri, P., (1977). An experiment on inductive learning in chess endgames. *Machine Intelligence 8*, pp. 175–185, (eds. Elcock, E. W., and Michie, D.). Chichester: Ellis Horwood.

[8] Vere, S. A., (1978). Inductive learning of relational productions. In *Pattern Directed Inference Systems*, (eds. Waterman, D. A., and Hayes–Roth, F.). New York and London: Academic Press.

[9] Hayes–Roth, F., and McDermott, J., (1977). Knowledge acquisition from structural descriptions. *Proc. 5th Intl. Joint Conf. on Artificial Intelligence (Cambridge, Mass.)*, pp. 356–362. Pittsburgh: Department of Computer Science, Carnegie–Mellon University

[10] Cohen, B. L., (1978). A powerful and efficient structural pattern recognition system. *Artificial Intelligence*, **9**, 223–225.

[11] Hunt, E. B., Marin, J., and Stone, P., (1966). *Experiments in Induction.* New York and London: Academic Press.

[12] Quinlan, J. R., (1979). Induction over large databases. *HPP-79-14*. Stanford: Heuristic Programming Project, Stanford University.

[13] Kopec, D., and Niblett, T. B., (1980). How hard is the play of the King-Rook King-Knight ending? *Advances in Computer Chess 2*, pp. 57–73. (ed. Clarke, M. R. B.). Edinburgh: Edinburgh University Press.

[14] Quinlan, J. R., (1979). Discovering rules by induction from large collections of examples. *Expert Systems in the Micro Electronic Age*, pp. 168–201. (ed. Michie, D.). Edinburgh: Edinburgh University Press.

[15] Michie, D., (1977). A theory of advice. *Machine Intelligence 8*, pp. 151–168 (eds. Elcock, E. W., and Michie, D.). Chichester: Ellis Horwood.

8

Revealing conceptual structure in data by inductive inference

R. S. Michalski and R. Stepp
University of Illinois
Urbana, USA

ABSTRACT

In many applied sciences there is often a problem of revealing a structure underlying a given collection of objects (situations, measurements, observations, etc.).
A specific problem of this type is that of determining a hierarchy of meaningful
subcategories in such a collection. This problem has been studied intensively in
the area of cluster analysis. The methods developed there, however, formulate
subcategories ('clusters') solely on the basis of pairwise 'similarity' (or 'proximity')
of objects, and ignore the issue of the 'meaning' of the clusters obtained. The
methods do not provide any description of the clusters obtained. This paper
presents a method which constructs a hierarchy of subcategories, such that an
appropriately generalized description of each subcategory is a single conjunctive
statement involving attributes of objects and has a simple conceptual interpretation. The attributes may be many-valued nominal variables or relations on
numerical variables. The hierarchy is constructed in such a way that a flexibly
defined 'cost' of the collection of descriptions which branch from any node is
minimized.

Experiments with the implemented program, CLUSTER/paf, have shown
that for some quite simple problems the traditional methods are unable to
produce a structuring of objects most 'natural' for people, while the method
presented here was able to produce such a solution.

1. INTRODUCTION

Computer programs able to reveal an underlying conceptual structure in a set of
data can be useful components of AI systems. Knowledge about the structure
of the data can help, for example, in reducing the search space in problem solving,
in dividing knowledge acquisition tasks into useful subcases, or in organizing
large databases (or rule bases) and summarizing their contents. It is believed that
the problem of intelligent structuring of data by computer will become one of
the important tasks for AI research in the '80s.

A simple form of data structuring is *clustering*, which is a process of determining a hierarchy of subcategories within a given collection of objects. In the traditional methods of clustering, the basis for forming the subcategories is a 'degree of similarity' between objects: the subcategories are collections of objects whose intra-group similarity is high and inter-group similarity is low. The process of determining the hierarchy of subcategories can be done either in a 'bottom-up' or a 'top-down' fashion. The bottom-up methods (called 'hierarchical' in the literature on cluster analysis) recursively merge single objects or collections of objects into larger collections, ending with the original complete set of objects at the top of the hierarchy (dendrogram). The top-down ('non-hierarchical') methods recursively split the starting collections(s) of objects into subgroups, ending when single objects are assigned to the leaves of the hierarchy.

The bottom-up methods are mostly used in numerical taxonomy. Depending on the way in which object-to-group and group-to-group degrees of similarlity are calculated, different versions of the technique are obtained, such as 'single' linkage, 'complete' linkage, or 'average' linkage [14].

The top-down methods generally operate by making a series of cluster boundary perturbations while searching for the groupings which exhibit minimal dispersion of objects around the cluster means. Some top-down methods, e.g., ISODATA, have additional heuristics which help to select the optimal number of clusters.

The allied process of clustering features rather than objects involves the techniques of factor analysis and multi-dimensional scaling. Many clustering methods are sensitive to the irrelevant variables present in the data. Factor analysis and multidimensional scaling can be used to select the most 'relevant' variables before proceeding to cluster the objects. These methods, however, are designed primarily for numerical variables. They cannot handle many-valued nominal variables, which occur often in AI applications.

All the traditional techniques have one major disadvantage. Since the only basis for forming clusters is the degree of similarity (between objects or groups of objects), the resulting clusters do not necessarily have any simple conceptual interpretation. The problem of 'meaning' of the obtained clusters is simply left to the researcher. This disadvantage is a significant one because a researcher typically wants not only clusters, but also wants an explanation of them in human terms.

This paper describes a method of determining a hierarchical structure underlying a given collection of objects, in which each node represents a certain generalized description of a corresponding subcategory of objects. The descriptions are conjunctive concepts involving attributes of objects. The attributes can be nominal variables or relations on numerical variables. Such descriptions have a very simple human interpretation. The presented method is an example of what we call generally a *conceptual clustering*.

The label *conceptual clustering* can be applied to any method which determines a structure in a collection of objects, in which the nodes represent 'concepts' characterizing the corresponding subcategories, and the links represent relationships between the concepts. (By the term 'concept' we mean a human oriented description, which involves properties of objects and relations among them.) In the method described, the concepts are conjunctive descriptions of subcategories, and the links interconnecting the levels of the hierarchy represent the 'next level of generality' relation between the descriptions (i.e., the predecessor description is a generalization of all successor descriptions).

Section 2, which follows, discusses the distinction between the conventional similarlity measure and the 'conceptual cohesion' measure, which underlines the presented method. Section 3 gives the basic terminology of the descriptive language used (the variable-valued logic system VL_1), and of the inductive inference technique. Section 4 gives an overview of the conceptual clustering algorithm and and its implementation in the program CLUSTER/paf. Finally, section 5 presents an example illustrating the method and compares the results obtained from conceptual clustering to those obtained from numerical taxonomy.

2. THE SIMILARITY MEASURE VERSUS CONCEPTUAL COHESIVENESS

The techniques of traditional cluster analysis are distinctly nonconceptual because they do not attempt to discover the meaning of the clusters or endeavour to arrange objects into those subcategories with the most succinct conceptual interpretation. As mentioned before, this behaviour is attributed to the use of standard distance or similarity measures as the only basis for clustering. In order to be able to do 'conceptual clustering,' one has to know more than the degree of similarlity between any two objects or groups of objects. Specifically, the notion of similarity should be replaced by a more general notion of 'conceptual cohesiveness', which we will now describe.

The similarlity between any two objects in the population to be clustered is characterized in the conventional data analysis methods by a single number — the value of the similarity function applied to symbolic descriptions of objects ('data points'). These descriptions are typically vectors, whose components represent scores on selected qualitative or quantitative variables used to describe objects. Frequently a reciprocal of a distance measure is used as a similarity function. The distance measure for such purposes, however, does not have to satisfy all the postulates of a distance function (specifically, the triangle inequality). A comprehensive review of various distance and similarity measures is provided in Diday & Simon [2] and Anderberg [1].

As mentioned before, the conventional measures of similarity are 'context-free,' i.e., the similarlity between any two data points A and B is a function of these points only:

$$\text{Similarity}\,(A, B) = f(A, B) \tag{1}$$

175

Recently some authors [4] have been introducing 'context-sensitive' measures of similarity:

$$\text{Similarity}(A, B) = f(A, B, E) \tag{2}$$

where the similarity between A and B depends not only on A and B, but also on other points ('context points') in the collection to be clustered E.

Both previous clustering approaches cluster data points only on the basis of knowledge of the individual data points. Therefore such methods are fundamentally unable to capture the 'Gestalt property' of objects, i.e., a property which is characteristic of certain configurations of points considered as a whole, but not when considered as independent points. In order to detect such properties, the system must know not only the data points, but also certain 'concepts'. To illustrate this point, let us consider a problem of clustering data points in Fig. 1.

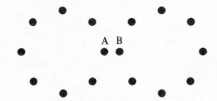

Fig. 1 – An illustration of conceptual clustering.

A person considering the problem in Fig. 1 would typically describe it as 'two circles'. Thus, the points A and B, although being very close, are placed in separate clusters. Here, human solution involves partitioning the data points into groups not on the basis of pairwise distance between points, but on the basis of 'concept membership'. That means that the points are placed in the same cluster if together they represent the same concept. In our example, the concepts are circles.

This idea is the basis of conceptual clustering. From the view of conceptual clustering, the 'similarity' between two data points A and B, which we will call the *conceptual cohesiveness*, is a function not only of these points and the context points in E, but also of a set of concepts C which are available for describing A and B together:

$$\text{Similarity}(A, B) = f(A, B, E, C) \tag{3}$$

To illustrate a 'conceptual cohesiveness' measure, let us assume that C is the set of concepts which are geometrical figures, such as circles, rectangles, triangles, etc. A measure of conceptual cohesiveness can be defined, for example, as

$$S(A, B, E, C) = \max_{i} \frac{\#e(i) - 1}{\text{area}(i)} \tag{4}$$

where *i* indexes all geometrical figures which are specified in C and which cover points A and B,

#e(*i*) is the total number of data points from E covered by figure i,

area(*i*) is the area of figure i.

(The constant "−1" in the numerator assures that the 'conceptual cohesiveness' reduces to a conventional similarity measure, i.e., a reciprocal of distance, when no context points in E are taken into consideration and C is a straight line of unit thickness intersecting the data points.)

This measure is mentioned solely to illustrate the difference between traditional similarity and conceptual cohesiveness. It is not used to actually implement the method of conceptual clustering described here.

The idea of conceptual clustering has been introduced by Michalski [12], and evolved from earlier work by him and his collaborators on generating the 'uniclass covers' (i.e., disjunctive descriptions of a class of objects specified by only positive examples of the class). A computer program and various experimental results on determining uniclass covers are described by Stepp [15].

3. TERMINOLOGY AND DEFINITIONS

In this section, relevant formal concepts and definitions will be briefly summarized. A complete presentation can be found in [12].

Value set (or domain) of a variable

Let $x_1, x_2, \ldots, x_n$ denote discrete variables which are selected to describe objects in the population to be clustered. For each variable a *value set* or *domain* is defined, which contains all possible values this variable can take for any object in the population. We shall assume that the value sets of variables $x_i, i = 1, 2, \ldots,$ *n* are finite, and therefore can be represented as:

$$D_i = \{0, 1, \ldots, d_i - 1\}, \quad i = 1, 2, \ldots, n . \tag{5}$$

In general, the value sets may differ not only with respect to their size, but also with respect to the structure relating their elements (reflecting the scale of measurement). In this paper we will distinguish only between nominal (qualitative) and linear (quantitative) variables whose domains are unordered and linearly ordered sets, respectively.

Event space

An *event* is defined as any sequence of values of variables $x_1, x_2, \ldots, x_n$:

$$e = (r_1, r_2, \ldots, r_n) \tag{6}$$

where $r_i \in D_i, i = 1, 2, \ldots, n.$

The set of all possible events, Σ, is called the *event space*:

$$\Sigma = \{e_i\}_{i=1}^{\mathbf{d}} \tag{7}$$

where $\mathbf{d} = d_1 \cdot d_2 \cdot \ldots \cdot d_n$ (the *size* of the event space).

Syntactic distance

Given two events e_1, e_2 in Σ, the *syntactic distance*, $\delta(e_1, e_2)$, between e_1 and e_2 is defined as the number of variables which have different values in e_1 and e_2.

Selectors

A relational statement

$$[x_i \# R_i] \tag{8}$$

where R_i is one or more elements from the domain of x_i, and $\#$ stands for the relational operator $=$ or $\neq$ is called a VL_1 *selector*[†] or, briefly, a *selector*. The selector $[x_i = R_i]$ ($[x_i \neq R_i]$) is interpreted as 'value of $x_i \in \{R_i\}$' ('value of $x_i \notin \{R_i\}$'). In the case of linear variables, the operator "$=$" in $[x_i = R_i]$ can be replaced by relational operators $\geqslant, >, <, \leqslant$ for an appropriate R_i, as indicated below.

Here are a few examples of a selector, in which variables and their values are represented by linguistic terms:

[height = tall]
[length $\geqslant 2$]
[colour = blue, red]   (colour is blue or red)
[size $\neq$ medium]   (size is not medium)
[weight = 2..5]   (weight is between 2 and 5, inclusively)

Complexes

A logical product of selectors is called a *logical complex* (*l-complex*):

$$\bigwedge_{i \in I} [x_i \# R_i] \tag{9}$$

where $I \subseteq \{1, 2, \ldots, n\}$, and $R_i \subseteq D_i$. An event e is said to *satisy* an *l-complex* if values of variables in e satisfy all the selectors in the complex. For example, event $e = (2, 7, 0, 1, 5, 4, 6)$ satisfies the *l*-complex $[x_1 = 2, 3]$ $[x_3 \leqslant 3]$ $[x_5 = 3 \ .. \ 8]$ (concatenation of selectors implies conjunction).

An *l*-complex can be viewed as an exact symbolic representation of the events which satisfy it. For example, the above *l*-complex is the symbolic representation of all events for which x_1 is 2 or 3, x_3 is smaller than or equal to 3, and x_5 is between 3 and 8.

† VL_1 stands for variable-valued logic system VL_1 which uses such selectors.

Any set of events for which there exists an l-complex satisfied by these events and only by these events is called a *set complex* (*s-complex*). Henceforth, if α is an s-complex, then by α we will denote the corresponding l-complex.

Quantitative properties of clusters

Let E be a set of events in Σ, which are data points to be clustered. The events in E are called *data events* (or *observed events*), and events in $\Sigma \backslash E$ (i.e., events in Σ which are not data events) are called *empty events* (or *unobserved events*). Let α be a complex which covers some data events and some empty events. The number of data events (*points*) in α is denoted by $p(\alpha)$. The number of empty events in α is called the *sparseness* and denoted by $s(\alpha)$. The total number of events in α is thus $r(\alpha) = p(\alpha) + s(\alpha)$.

If s-complex α is represented by l-complex $\hat{\alpha} = \bigwedge_{i \in I} [x_i \# R_i]$, the number $t(\alpha)$ can be computed as:

$$t(\alpha) = \prod_{i \in I} c(R_i) \cdot \prod_{i \notin I} d_i \tag{10}$$

where $I \subseteq \{1, 2, \ldots, n\}$,
   $c(R_i)$ is the cardinality of R_i,
   d_i is the cardinality of the value set of variable x_i.

The l-complex $\hat{\alpha}$ can be viewed as a generalized description of the data points in α. The sparseness, as defined above, can be used as a simple measure of the degree to which the description $\hat{\alpha}$ generalizes over the data points. If the sparseness is zero, then the description covers only data points ('zero generalization'). As the sparseness for a given complex increases, so does the degree to which the description $\hat{\alpha}$ generalizes over the data points. A formal definition of the 'degree of generalization,' based on the information-theoretic uncertainty of the location of data points in α, is given in [12].

Star

The *star* $G(e|F)$ of e against the event set F is the set of all maximal under inclusion complexes covering the event e and not covering any event in F. (A complex α is *maximal under inclusion* with respect to property P, if there does not exist a complex α^* with property P, such that $\alpha \subset \alpha^*$.)

Cover

Let E_1 and E_2 be two disjoint event sets, $E_1 \cap E_2 = \phi$. A *cover* $COV(E_1|E_2)$ of E_1 *against* E_2, is any set of complexes, $\{\alpha_j\}_{j \in J}$, such that for each event $e \in E_1$ there is a complex α_j, $j \in J$, covering it, and none of the complexes α_j cover any event in E_2. Thus we have:

$$E_1 \subseteq \bigcup_{j \in J} \alpha_j \subseteq \Sigma \backslash E_2 . \tag{11}$$

179

A cover in which all complexes are pairwise disjoint sets is called a *disjoint cover*. If set E_2 is empty, then a cover $\text{COV}(E_1|E_2) = \text{COV}(E_1|\phi)$ is simply denoted as $\text{COV}(E_1)$. A disjoint cover $\text{COV}(E)$ which consists of k complexes is called a *k-partition* of E.

4. THE METHOD AND IMPLEMENTATION

This section describes an algorithm for conjunctive conceptual clustering, which consists of an outer layer and an inner layer, described in sections 4.1 and 4.2 below. Section 4.3 describes the procedure used to construct the k-partition from stars which optimizes a certain criterion of clustering quality.

4.1 Inner layer

The inner portion of the algorithm called PAF was introduced in [12] as a 'constrained' conjunctive conceptual clustering technique. Given a set of data events, E, to be clustered and an integer, k, PAF partitions the set E into k clusters, each of which has a conjunctive description in the form of a complex. (In the complete algorithm, E and k are determined by the outer algorithm). The obtained partition is optimal or suboptimal with regard to a user selected measure of clustering quality.

The general structure of PAF is based on the dynamic clustering method developed by Diday and his collaborators (Diday & Simon [1], Hanani [5]). Underlying the notions of the dynamic clustering method are two functions:

  g: the *representation function*, which, given a k-partition of E, produces a set of k cluster representations which best describe the clusters,

  f: the *allocation function*, which, given a set of k cluster representations, produces a k-partition in which each cluster is composed of those objects which best fit the corresponding cluster representations.

The method works iteratively, starting with a set of k initial, randomly chosen cluster representations. A single iteration consists of an application of function f to the given representations, and then of function g to the obtained partition. Each iteration ends with a new set of representations. The process continues until the chosen criterion of clustering quality, W, ceases to improve. (Criterion W measures the 'fit' between a partition and its representation.) It has been proved that this method always converges to a local optimum [2].

In PAF, the notions of dynamic clustering are not rigorously followed, although the general approach is similar. PAF has a step which is analogous to function g, which from a given set of clusters of objects, produces the best representations of them (in the form of complexes). The process involves selecting a representative event (seed) from each cluster and covering one seed against the others to generate generalized descriptions of the events. This is done by procedures STAR and NID described in section 4.3 below. The function f of dynamic clustering is represented in PAF by a procedure which, for a given complex, determines the set of covered data events.

PAF will now be described by showing how it operates on the data given in Fig. 2, with parameter k set to 2 (i.e., the algorithm will split the data into two subcategories), and with minimizing total sparseness as the criterion of clustering quality. There are ten objects, each described by the values of four variables x_1, x_2, x_3, and x_4, with three-valued domains, $D_i = \{0, 1, 2\}$, $i = 1, 2, 3, 4$. Variables x_1 and x_2 are linear, and variables x_3 and x_4 are nominal.

Event	x_1	x_2	x_3	x_4
e_1	0	0	0	1
e_2	0	1	0	0
e_3	0	2	1	2
e_4	1	0	0	2
e_5	1	2	1	1
e_6	2	0	1	0
e_7	2	1	0	1
e_8	2	1	1	2
e_9	2	2	0	0
e_{10}	2	2	2	2
Value set type:	L	L	N	N

(L — linearly ordered; N — nominal)

Fig. 2 — An exemplary data set describing ten objects using four variables.

Figure 3 presents the data set from Fig. 2 graphically, using a planar representation of the event space spanned over variables x_1, x_2, x_3, and x_4.

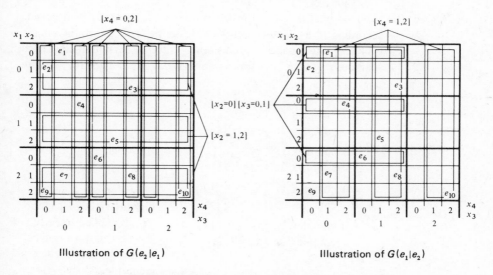

Illustration of $G(e_2|e_1)$ Illustration of $G(e_1|e_2)$

Fig. 3 — A planar representation of the event space spanned over variables x_1, x_2, x_3, x_4 showing the complexes of two stars.

181

PAF will now be explained as it operates on the data of the sample problem. A flow diagram of PAF is presented in Fig. 4.

Iteration 1:

Step 1 (Fig. 4, block 1):

E_0 is a subset composed of k data events from E (*seeds*). The seeds can be selected arbitrarily, or they can be chosen as events which are most syntactically distant from each other. In the latter case the algorithm will generally converge faster. For selecting such events, program ESEL [11] can be used. For the sample problem, let $E_0 = \{e_1, e_2\}$.

Step 2 (Fig. 4, block 2):

A star, $G(e_j|E_0\backslash e_j)$, where $e_j \in E_0$, is generated for each seed against the remaining seeds. In our case, stars $G_1 = G(e_1|e_2)$ and $G_2 = G(e_2|e_1)$ are generated. The program produced the following stars by applying the STAR generating procedure outlined in section 4.3. Each star consists of two complexes:

$$G(e_1|e_2) = \{[x_2 = 0]\,[x_3 = 0, 1], [x_4 = 1, 2]\}$$
$$G(e_2|e_1) = \{[x_2 = 1, 2], [x_4 = 0, 2]\}$$

These stars are pictured in Fig. 3.

Step 3 (Fig. 4, block 3):

From each star a complex is selected, such that that resulting set of k complexes

(a) is a disjoint cover of E, and

(b) is an optimal or suboptimal cover among all possible such covers, according to a selected quality of clustering criterion. In the sample problem, the quality of clustering criterion is minimizing total sparseness. There are four combinations of complexes to consider:

		Sparseness
(a) complex 1:	$[x_2 = 1, 2]$	47
complex 2:	$[x_2 = 0]\,[x_3 = 0, 1]$	15
(b) complex 1:	$[x_2 = 1, 2]$	—
complex 2:	$[x_4 = 1, 2]$	62

(c) complex 1: $[x_4 = 0, 2]$ (These covers are not
complex 2: $[x_2 = 0]\,[x_3 = 0, 1]$ disjoint. NID (see section

(d) complex 1: $[x_4 = 0, 1]$ 4.3) is applied to each;
complex 2: $[x_4 = 1, 2]$ however in this instance, the resulting sparsenesses are not less than 62.)

Combination (a) is selected since it has minimum total sparseness.

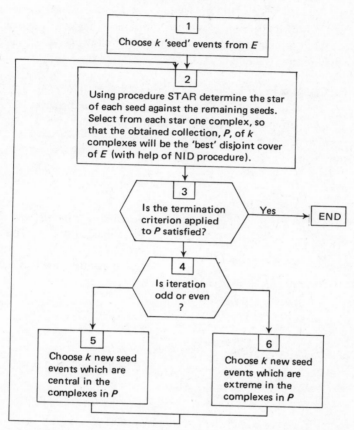

Given:

E — a set of data events
k — the desired nr of clusters
A — the evaluation functional

1
Choose k 'seed' events from E

2
Using procedure STAR determine the star of each seed against the remaining seeds. Select from each star one complex, so that the obtained collection, P, of k complexes will be the 'best' disjoint cover of E (with help of NID procedure).

3
Is the termination criterion applied to P satisfied?

Yes → END

4
Is iteration odd or even ?

5
Choose k new seed events which are central in the complexes in P

6
Choose k new seed events which are extreme in the complexes in P

Fig. 4 — A flow diagram of the inner layer of algorithm PAF.

Step 4 (Fig. 4, block 4):

The termination criterion of the algorithm is applied to the obtained cover. The termination criterion is a pair of parameters (b,p) where b (the *base*) is a standard number of iterations the algortihm always performs, and p (the *probe*) is the number of additional interactions beyond b performed after each iteration which produces an improved cover. In our example, $b = 2$ and $p = 1$.

Step 5 (Fig. 4, blocks 5 and 6):

A new set of seeds is determined. If the iteration is odd, then the new seeds are data events in the centres of complexes in the cover (according to the syntactic distance). If the iteration is even, then the new seeds are data events maximally distant from the centres (according to the 'adversity principle'[†]). In the sample problem, syntactically central events are to be found for the complex $[x_2 = 1,2]$, covering $\{e_2, e_3, e_5, e_7, e_8, e_9, e_{10}\}$, and complex $[x_2 = 0]$ $[x_3 = 0,1]$, covering $\{e_1, e_4, e_6\}$. Central events are the ones for which the sum of syntactic distances between them and all other events in the same cluster is minimal. The following sum-of-distances tables apply in this example.

Complex $[x_2 = 1,2]$		Complex $[x_2 = 0]$ $[x_3 = 0,1]$	
Event	Sum of distances to other events	Event	Sum of distances to other events
e_2	18	e_1	5
e_3	16	e_4	5
e_5	18	e_6	6
e_7	16		
e_8	15		
e_9	15		
e_{10}	16		

Note: Selected events shown with underlined distances. Ties are broken in favour of events not previously used as seeds.

The new seeds are $E_0 = \{e_4, e_8\}$.

Iteration 2:

Step 2:

The stars $G_1 = G(e_4|e_8)$ and $G_2 = G(e_8|e_4)$ are generated:

$G(e_4|e_8) = \{[x_2 = 0][x_3 = 0,1], [x_1 = 0,1]\ [x_3 = 0,1], [x_3 = 0,2]\}$
$G(e_8|e_4) = \{[x_1 = 2], [x_2 = 1,2], [x_3 = 1,2]\}$

Step 3:

The combinations of complexes which are disjoint covers are:

	Sparseness
(a) complex 1: $[x_1 = 2]$	22
complex 2: $[x_1 = 0,1][x_3 = 0,1]$	31
	53
(b) complex 1: $[x_2 = 1,2]$	47
complex 2: $[x_2 = 0][x_3 = 0,1]$	15
	62

Combination (a) is selected (it has the minimum total sparseness).

[†] This principle states that if the most outstanding event truly belongs to the given cluster, then when serving as the cluster representation, the 'fit' between it and other events in the same cluster should still be better than the 'fit' between it and events of any other cluster.

Step 4:

This is step 4 of iteration 2. Since $b = 2$, this is the last of the base iterations.

Step 5:

Complex $[x_1 = 2]$ covers $\{e_6, e_7, e_8, e_9, e_{10}\}$ and complex $[x_1 = 0, 1][x_3 = 0, 1]$ covers $\{e_1, e_2, e_3, e_4, e_5\}$. Since this iteration is an even one, the new seeds are those whose sum of syntactic distances to other events in the same cluster is maximal. After ties are broken, these events are $E_0 = \{e_2, e_{10}\}$.

Iteration 3:

Step 2:

The stars $G_1 = G(e_2|e_{10})$ and $G_2 = G(e_{10}|e_2)$ are generated:
$$G(e_2|e_{10}) = \{[x_1 = 0, 1][x_3 = 0,1], [x_2 = 0, 1][x_3 = 0, 1],$$
$$[x_3 = 0, 1][x_4 = 0, 1]\}$$
$$G(e_{10}|e_2) = \{[x_1 = 1, 2], [x_2 = 2], [x_4 = 1, 2]\}$$

Step 3:

The only combination of complexes which is a disjoint cover is:

	Sparseness
(a) complex 1: $[x_2 = 2]$	23
complex 2: $[x_2 = 0,1][x_3 = 0,1]$	$\underline{30}$
	53

Step 4:

This iteration is the first (and in this example also the last) 'probe' iteration. If the clustering quality on this iteration is better than the previous best clustering, another p iterations are scheduled, else the algorithm stops after completing p probing iterations. The best total sparseness of iteration 3, namely 53 is not an improvement over the previous best sparseness, also 53. Since $p = 1$ in this example, the termination criterion is satisfied at this point. There are two alternative clusterings produced, each with a total sparseness of 53:

alternative 1:
$[x_1 = 2]$
$[x_1 = 0,1][x_3 = 0,1]$

alternative 2:
$[x_2 = 2]$
$[x_2 = 0,1][x_3 = 0,1]$

4.2 Outer algorithm

The outer layer of the algorithm makes recursive applications of the inner layer in order to create a hierarchical description (a concept tree) underlying the data. The tree grows in a top-down fashion until the 'continuation-of-growth' criterion fails. This criterion requires that the 'fit' (measured by sparseness) of the concepts to the events they describe must be sufficiently better at each next (lower) level of the hierarchy. When this criterion is not met, the latest obtained subcategories become leaves of the tree.

At each step, the group of objects associated with a particular node in the hierarchy is divided into subcategories, and their descriptions are assigned to the offspring nodes. The degree of the parent node (the number of subcategories or clusters) is specified by parameter k. Usually there is no *a priori* knowledge of how many subcategories to form. Interesting solutions from the viewpoint of a human user, however, should involve only a small number of subcategories (e.g., between 2 and 7) so that it is computationally feasible to determine the best number of subcategories by constructing first the best 2-partition, then the best 3-partition, and so on, while evaluating relative quality of the obtained partitions.

The clustering quality measure used here must relate a quantitative measure of complexes (e.g., the total sparseness, S) to the number of clusters. As the number of clusters k increases, the total sparseness will likely decrease (since smaller complexes will better 'fit' the data). One possible global criterion of clustering quality is to minimize $S*(k + \beta)$, where β is chosen to properly balance the effect of k on the solution.

It should be noted that selecting too small a value of k does not necessarily distort the resulting conceptual hierarchy. It may simply cause the creation of additional levels within the same structure. This is illustrated in Fig. 5.

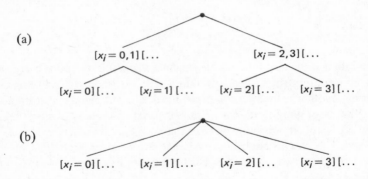

Fig. 5 – Two comparable structures with different degrees of root nodes.

4.3 Procedures STAR and NID, and the method for determining the best cover

The star $G(e|F)$ has been defined as the set of maximal complexes covering event e and no events in the set F. This section will explain how stars are constructed, and are subsequently used to conduct a best-first search to find an optimal or suboptimal k-partition of an event set. Assume first that $F = \{e_1\}$, $e_1 \neq e$. To generate the star $G(e|e_1)$ one determines all variables in e which have different values than in e_1. Suppose, without losing generality, these variables are $x_1, x_2, \ldots, x_k$, and $e_1 = (r_1, r_2, \ldots, r_k, \ldots, r_n)$. Assuming that the variables are nominal. the complexes of the star $G(e|e_1)$ are $[x_i \neq r_i]$, $i = 1, 2, \ldots, k$ (or equivalently, $[x_i = D_i \backslash r_i]$), since these are the largest complexes which cover e

186

and do not cover e_1. The number of complexes in a star $G(e|F)$, when F is a single event, is at most n (the number of variables), and at least 1, since $e_1 \neq e$.

Assume now that $F = \{e_1, e_2, \ldots, e_s\}$. A star $G(e|F)$ is constructed by building first stars $G(e|e_1)$, $i = 1, 2, \ldots, s$, and then set-theoretically multiplying these stars by each other, using absorption laws to eliminate redundancy. A detailed description of this process, including the treatment of linear variables, is given in [12].

The upper bound on the size of a star is n^m, where m is the number of events in F. Absorption laws will usually eliminate many redundant complexes, but the size of a star may still become unmanageable. Therefore a *bounded star* is used which has a specified upper limit, MAXSTAR, on the number of complexes it may contain. Whenever a star exceeds this number, the complexes are ordered in ascending order according to sparseness (or in general, to any assumed criterion) and only the first MAXSTAR complexes are retained. The position of a complex in the sequence so ordered is the *rank* of the complex.

At each iteration of algorithm PAF (Fig. 4), k stars are produced, for each seed event against the remaining $k-1$ seed events. From each star one complex is then selected in such a way that the resulting set will consist of k disjoint complexes (a k-partition), and be optimal according to the assumed criterion. If un-bounded stars were used, each could be composed of up to $n^{(k-1)}$ complexes and therefore up to $(n^{(k-1)})^k$ sets of complexes would have to be inspected in order to determine the optimal k-partition! The best-first search strategy outlined below solves this problem.

Performing an efficient search for the best set of complexes can be viewed as finding an optimal path through the search tree whose nodes are complexes. The ith level of the tree corresponds to the ith star. The height of the tree is k, and a path of length k corresponds to a particular k-partition. The *pathrank* of a path is the sum of the ranks of the complexes along the path. The sequences of complexes (paths) are considered in order of increasing pathrank so that complexes with minimum sparseness are considered first.

Frequently the cover with minimum total sparseness will not be disjoint. A procedure called NID tries to transform a *non*-disjoint cover *into* a *disjoint* one by making small adjustments in cluster memberships. The NID procedure is not always successful, and when it cannot create a disjoint cover of all events in E, it creats the disjoint cover which covers as many events in E as possible. The events it is unable to cover are reported as 'exceptional events'.

4.4 A note on the CLUSTER/paf implementation of the algorithm

The algorithm described above has been implemented in a program CLUSTER/paf, written in PASCAL. The program contains about 3500 PASCAL statements and requires about 20K 60-bit words of memory for clustering problems of the kind shown in Fig. 2. CLUSTER/paf is connected to a relational data base, and all the input examples and parameters are supplied to it in the form of relational tables.

187

Data points and complexes are stored in one common data structure, the COMPLEX[†], which is an array of SELECTORS declared as objects of the PASCAL type 'set of interger'. The integer-coded values in the reference set of each variable, x_i, are stored in SELECTOR$_i$. When a particular variable, x_j, is not present in a complex, SELECTOR$_j$ is assigned the set representing the entire domain of the variable. Each COMPLEX is thus of fixed length even though the number of selectors in the corresponding complex varies. This data structure provides an easy way to compute the total number of events in a complex $t(\alpha)$, the number of data points covered by a complex $p(\alpha)$, and from these two, the sparseness of the complex $s(\alpha)$.

The program supports five criteria for evaluating the quality of a k-partition:

- the total sparseness of the complexes,
- the degree of inter-cluster disjointness (the total number of disjoint selectors in the k-partition),
- the imbalance in cluster populations (the uneveness of the distribution of events in complexes of the k-partition),
- the dimensionality (the number of different variables used in the complexes of the k-partition),
- the total number of selectors in the k-partition.

Selected criteria from the above list are applied in a lexicographical order defined by the user.

5. AN EXAMPLE

The simple example problem described below was designed to illustrate the major differences between traditional clustering techniques and the conceptual

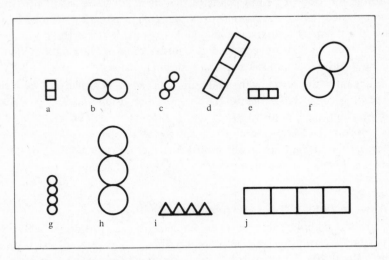

Fig. 6 – BEAD STRINGS.

[†] Upper-case will be used to denote data structures within CLUSTER/paf.

clustering method described in the paper. Results from applying the traditional numerical taxonomy techniques to the problem were obtained by using a program NUMTAX[†], which implements the standard algorithms from Sokal & Sneath [14]. Results from applying the conjunctive conceptual method were obtained by using the program CLUSTER/paf.

The problem is to structure hierarchically the ten objects shown in Fig. 6. Each object is described by values of the four variables: size of beads, number of beads, shape of beads, and orientation of beads. Figure 7 shows the table of descriptions of the beads. The symbolic values of variables in Fig. 7 were encoded as integer values to prepare the data for NUMTAX and CLUSTER/paf. The encoding was:

x_1: size of beads
    0 — large
    1 — medium
    2 — small

x_3: shape of beads
    0 — circle
    1 — square
    2 — triangle

x_2: number of beads
    0 — 2 beads
    1 — 3 beads
    2 — 4 beads

x_4: alignment of beads
    0 — vertical
    1 — diagonal
    2 — horizontal

The encoded values for this problem were given in Fig. 2, and used to illustrate the inner PAF algorithm in section 4.

string symbol	size of beads	number of beads	shape of beads	orientation of beads
a	small	2	square	vertical
b	medium	2	circle	horizontal
c	small	3	circle	diagonal
d	medium	4	square	diagonal
e	small	3	square	horizontal
f	large	2	circle	diagonal
g	small	4	circle	vertical
h	large	3	circle	vertical
i	small	4	triangle	horizontal
j	large	4	square	horizontal

Fig. 7 — The description of BEAD STRINGS.

5.1 Results from NUMTAX

Given a set of events, the numerical taxonomy program, NUMTAX, organizes the events into a hierarchy which reflects the numerical distances between consecutively larger subcategories of events, which at the highest level, merge to

† NUMTAX was written by R. Selander of the University of Illinois.

become the union of all events (a dendrogram). Figure 8 shows the dendrogram generated by NUMTAX using the reciprocal of unweighted Euclidean distance as the measure of sisimilarlity. (The distances were calculated from standardized data (z-scores)). Eighteen different distance measurements were tried in the experiment by using various combinations of a data transformation (raw data, ranging, z-scores); a similarity measure (reciprocal Euclidean distance, product-moment correlation, simple matching coefficient); and weighting (unweighted, weighted by the number of events in a group).

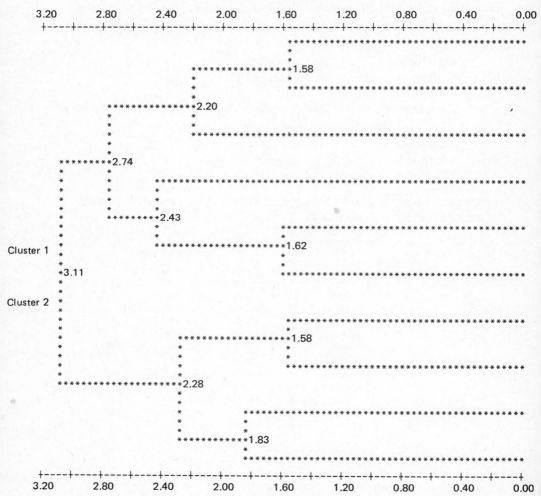

Fig. 8 – A dendrogram of BEAD STRINGS produced by NUMTAX. Coefficients assigned to the nodes represent the Euclidean distance (in the n-dimensional space) between the objects indicated by branches from the node. The distances are calculated using standardized data values, i.e., the values of a variable are divided by their standard deviation. The distance between groups of objects is defined as the average of the distances from objects in one group to those of the other group.

Because dendrograms are constructed bottom-up, the entire dendrogram must always be generated. The after this has been done, the dendrogram may be cut apart at some level to produce clusters. The collections of BEADS shown in Fig. 9 are the result of considering only the two major subtrees of the dendrogram of Fig. 8. The three clusters shown in Fig. 10 were obtained in a similar manner

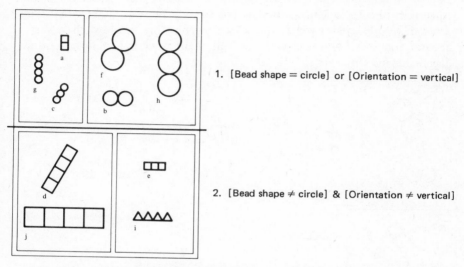

1. [Bead shape = circle] or [Orientation = vertical]

2. [Bead shape ≠ circle] & [Orientation ≠ vertical]

Fig. 9 — Clusters obtained from the dendrogram generated by NUMTAX (K = 2). Description of the clusters were obtained by program AQ11.

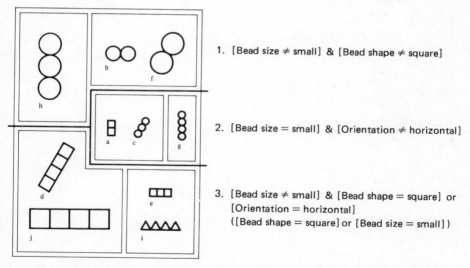

1. [Bead size ≠ small] & [Bead shape ≠ square]

2. [Bead size = small] & [Orientation ≠ horizontal]

3. [Bead size ≠ small] & [Bead shape = square] or [Orientation = horizontal] ([Bead shape = square] or [Bead size = small])

Fig. 10 — Clusters obtained from the dendrogram generated by NUMTAX (K = 3). Descriptions of the clusters were obtained by program AQ11. In both figures, the inner lines show possible further partitions.

191

by cutting the dendrogram into three portions. The two illustrations are typical of the many dendrograms generated. None of the dendrograms form clusters which have simpler characterizations.

The clusters obtained from the dendrogram are not accompanied by any description. In order to determine the meaning of the clusters, an additional step which generates cluster characterizations is incorporated. The program used to provide these characterizations in this experiment was AQ11 [11]. This program accepts sets of events (the clusters defined by dendrogram subtrees) and produces maximally generalized descriptions of them in the form of a logical disjunction of complexes.

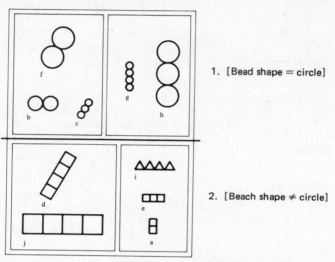

1. [Bead shape = circle]

2. [Beach shape ≠ circle]

Fig. 11 – Clusters generated by CLUSTER/paf for K = 2.

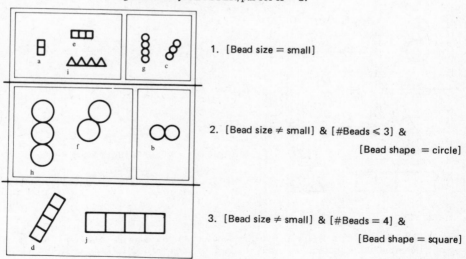

1. [Bead size = small]

2. [Bead size ≠ small] & [#Beads ≤ 3] & [Bead shape = circle]

3. [Bead size ≠ small] & [#Beads = 4] & [Bead shape = square]

Fig. 12 – Clusters generated by CLUSTER/paf for K = 3.

192

5.2 Results from conceptual clustering

The conceptual clustering program CLUSTER/paf was run with two different criteria of clustering optimality:

(a) 'minimize sparseness, then minimize the number of selectors', and

(b) 'minimize the degree of disjointness, then minimize sparseness'.

Results when using criterion (a) are shown in Figs. 11 and 12. Figures 13 and 14 show results when using criterion (b).

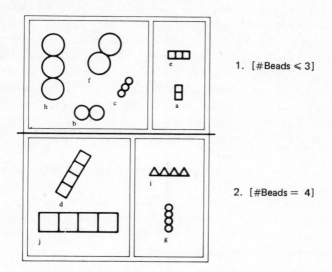

1. [#Beads ⩽ 3]

2. [#Beads = 4]

Fig. 13 – Another solution generated by CLUSTER/paf for K = 2.

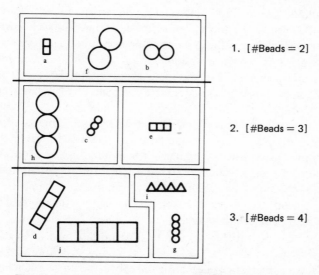

1. [#Beads = 2]

2. [#Beads = 3]

3. [#Beads = 4]

Fig. 14 – Another solution generated by CLUSTER/paf for K = 3.

5.3 Discussion of results

An experiment with human subjects solving this problem indicated that people categorize objects using the object's most noticeable properties. Typical solutions were, e.g.,

and

[shape of BEAD = circle]   *vs.*   [shape of BEAD ≠ circle] ,

[#BEADS = 2]   *vs.*   [#BEADS = 3]   *vs.*   [#BEADS = 4] .

The clusterings produced by NUMTAX seem 'unnatural' when compared to human clustering. The distinction can also be observed by looking at the cluster descriptions. The descriptions determined by program AQ11 for the clusters generated by NUMTAX involve disjunction, and seem to be more complex than the descriptions which people consider most natural. On the other hand, the descriptions produced by CLUSTER/paf matched the human solutions.

It should be noted that the descriptions generated by AQ11 for clusters obtained from NUMTAX were 'biased' towards the type of descriptions were used. In any case, however, since NUMTAX is not equipped with knowledge of any concepts, it cannot knowingly produce clusters corresponding to concepts.

CLUSTER/paf has been applied to some 'real world' clustering problems. One application was to cluster data describing 47 diseased soybean plants (each described by 34 many-valued variables). CLUSTER/paf accurately partitioned the diseased plants into the four disease categories presented in the sample, and described the clusters by the proper concepts, stated in terms of disease symptoms confirmed by plant pathologists.

6. CONCLUSION

The conceptual clustering method, PAF, determines a hierarchy of subcategories within a collection of objects. The subcategories are determined in such a way that an appropriate generalization of the description of each subcategory yields a single conjunctive statement which is disjoint from the similar statements characterizing other subcategories. The difference between this method and traditional methods can be explained by extending the concept of the measure of similarity into the more general notion of conceptual cohesiveness.

A limitation of the program is that it describes subcategories of objects solely by conjunctive statements. Although a conjunctive statement is probably the most common descriptive form used by humans, it is a quite limited form. An interesting extension of the work would be to use other forms of descriptions, e.g., involving logical implication, equivalence, and exception. Also, the program requires thttthat all potentially relevant variables for clustering are supplied in the input data (as in all other clustering methods).

The problems which are suitable to the PAF algorithm involve objects describable by variable-value pairs, i.e., objects without any structure of their own. When the objects of interest do have structure which has to be taken into consideration (e.g., relationships between features of object subparts), the techniques presented here become inadequate. Clustering of such objects will require the use of a richer description language than that used here, such as first-order predicate logic or its equivalent.

7. ACKNOWLEDGEMENTS

This work was supported by the National Science Foundation under grant No. MCS-79-06614. The authors wish to thank Professor R. Selander of the University of Illinois for providing the NUMTAX numerical taxonomy program.

REFERENCES

[1] Anderberg, M. R., (1973). *Cluster Analysis for Applications.* New York and London: Academic Press.

[2] Diday, E., & Simon, J. C., (1976). Clustering analysis, *Communication and Cybernetics, 10*, (ed. Fu, K. S.). Berlin, Heidelberg, New York: Springer Verlag.

[3] Diday, E., (1978). Problems of clustering and recent advances, 11th Congress of Statistics, Oslo, Norway.

[4] Gowda, K. Chidananda, & Krishna, G., (1978). Disaggregative clustering using the concept of mutal nearest neighbourhood, *IEE Trans. On Systems, Man and Cybernetics, SMC-8, No. 12*, 888–894.

[5] Hanani, U., (1979). Multicriteria dynamic clustering. Rocquencourt: INRIA Reports.

[6] Michalski, R. S., (1974). Variable-valued logic: System VL_1, *Proceedings of the 1974 Int. Symp. on Multiple-Valued Logic*, West Virginia University, Morgantown, West Virginia, May 29–31.

[7] Michalski, R. S., (1975). Synthesis of optimal and quasi-optimal variable-valued logic formulas, *Proceedings of the 1975 Int. Symp. on Multiple-Valued Logic*, Bloomington, Indiana, May 13–16.

[8] Michalski, R. S., (1975). Variable-valued logic and its applications to pattern recognition and machine learning, *Multiple-Valued Logic and Computer Science*, (ed. D. Rine). Amsterdam: North–Holland.

[9] Michalski, R. S., (to appear). Studies in inductive inference and plausible reasoning, Technical Report, Urbana-Champaign: Department of Computer Science, University of Illinois.

[10] Michalski, R. S., (1978). A planar geometrical model for representing multidimensional discrete spaces and multiple-valued logic functions, *UIUCDCS-R-897*, Urbana-Champaign: Department of Computer Science, University of Illinois.

[11] Michalski, R. S., & Larson, J. B., (1978). Selection of most representative training examples and incremental generation of VL_1 hypotheses: the underlying methodology and the description of programs ESEL and AQ11, *UIUCDCS-R-867*, Urbana-Champaign: Department of Computer Science, University of Illinois.

[12] Michalski, R. S., (1980). Knowledge acquisition through conceptual clustering: A theoretical framework and an algorithm for partitioning data into conjunctive concepts, (Special issue on knowledge acquisition and induction), *Policy Analysis and Information Systems, No. 3*, 219–244.

[13] Nilsson, N. J., (1980). *Principles of Artificial Intelligence*, Menlo Park: Tioga Publishing Company.

[14] Sokal, R. R., & Sneath, P. H., (1963). *Principles of Numerical Taxonomy.* San Francisco: Freeman.

[15] Stepp, R., (1979). Learning without negative examples via variable-valued logic characterizations: the uniclass inductive program AQ7UNI, *UIUCDCS-R-982*. Urbana-Champaign: Department of Computer Science, University of Illinois.

[16] Stepp, R., (1980). Learning by observation: experiments in conceptual clustering, Workshop on Machine Learning, Carnegie–Mellon University, Pittsburgh, Pennsylvania, July 16–19.

[17] Stepp, R., (to appear). A description and user's guide for CLUSTER/paf – a program for conjunctive conceptual clustering. Technical Report, Urbana-Champaign: Department of Computer Science, University of Illinois, Urbana, Illinois.

[18] Watanabe, S., (1968). Pattern recognition as an inductive process, *Methodologies of Pattern Recognition*, (ed. Watanabe, S.). New York and London: Academic Press.

[19] Watanabe, S., (1969). *Knowing and Guessing; a quantitative study of inference and information*. New York: Wiley.

[20] Winston, P. H., (1977). *Artificial Intelligence*. Reading, Mass: Addison–Wesley.

9

Fast memory access by similarity measure

Y-H. Pao and G. P. Hartoch
Case Western Reserve University
Cleveland, USA

ABSTRACT

In artificial intelligence research, procedures for storing away a large number of individual facts and for retrieving them efficiently are of great interest and importance. At present only two basic techniques are used, one being hashing and the other that of matching the query pattern. We describe in this paper an associative memory for content addressable storage and retrieval on the basis of similarity rather than exact match. The new development described here is a technique for reducing the 'noise' otherwise present in such structures. The relationship between this structure and those proposed previously by others is also discussed.

1. INTRODUCTION

Procedures for storing away a large number of individual facts and for retrieving them efficiently later should be of primary interest to researchers in artificial intelligence. However, in fact only two basic techniques are used, one being hashing and the other that of matching query, with or without masked bits. The former is almost universally used in the implementation of interpreters and compilers, and the latter for almost everything else, whether it be for search of memory, for control of reasoning, or for any one of a very large and diverse list of artificial intelligence research activities. This practice is followed so widely, that even when 'fuzzy' logic is desired, the matching queries are still made on the basis of exact match, and the 'fuzziness' is injected in the form of appended 'probabilities'.

We suspect that storage and retrieval of information on the basis of similarity or likeliness rather than exact match might lead to interesting new types of artificial intelligence programs and systems.

In this work, we discuss an specific information storage and retrieval procedure

197

which is rapid and economical in use of storage space, and is especially appropriate if retrieval is on the basis of similarity rather than exact match.

The memory structure implemented in this procedure is content addressable, parallel processing, and is associative in a certain sense. It is not the same as the structures investigated by Kohonen [1], Nakano [2] and by Willshaw [3], but can be discussed in terms of those for the sake of comparison.

2. THE ELEMENT BY ELEMENT ASSOCIATIVE MEMORY

For the sake of comparison and to bring focus to the matter, we might call associative memory structures of the type used by Kohonen, Nakano and Willshaw dyadic associative memories, whereas the structure proposed by us would, in contrast, be an 'element by element' vector associative memory (AM). The reason for this terminology will soon be made clear.

In the case of the dyadic AM, associative recall can be viewed as a mapping in which a finite number of input (message) vectors is transformed into given output vectors.

Typically, let vectors y_k, $k = 1, 2, \ldots, m$, be the stored items and let vectors x_k be the corresponding keys. A linear formulation of the dyadic AM's proposed in those previous studies would be

$$M = \sum_{k=1}^{m} y_k x_k^t \qquad (2.1)$$

where "t" denotes transpose, and the matrix M is to be viewed as an operator formed from a sum of dyadic products.

If the x_k form an orthonormal set, then y_j can be retrieved exactly without error upon presentation of the key x_j. That is,

$$\hat{y}_j = M x_j = y_j \langle x_j x_j \rangle + \sum_{k \neq j} y_k \langle x_k x_j \rangle = y_j \qquad (2.2)$$

because

$$\langle x_k x_j \rangle = \begin{cases} 1 & \text{for } k = j \\ 0 & \text{otherwise} \end{cases}$$

where the pair of angular brackets denote forming the scalar product, that is, $\langle x_k x_j \rangle = x_k^t x_j$.

More generally,

$$\hat{y}_j = \sum_{k=1}^{m} y_k \langle x_k x_j \rangle = \gamma_j y_j + \sum_{k \neq j} \gamma_k y_k . \qquad (2.3)$$

The distortion γ_j can be compensated for by storing y_j/γ_j rather than y_j, but the sum $\sum \gamma_k y_k$ constitutes noise and can be very troublesome.

Without going into details, we can note that the dyadic AM has the following advantages:

(1) *The memory can be readily made error-tolerant.* The vectors x_k and y_k can be defined in a metric space such that all vectors which lie in the neighbourhood of a specific input vector in the sense of that metric are mapped into the neighbourhood of the corresponding output vector.

(2) *Full recall can be attained on presentation of a partial cue.* This can be shown readily. Let x_j' be a part of the vector x_j. The output is the full y_j, provided the noise is small. That is,

$$\hat{y}_j = M x_j' = y_j \langle x_j x_j' \rangle + \sum_{k \neq j} y_k \langle x_k x_j' \rangle \tag{2.4}$$

$$\propto y_j \text{ if } \langle x_j x_j' \rangle \text{ is significantly greater than any of the } \langle x_k x_j' \rangle . \tag{2.5}$$

(3) This structure can be implemented for use in an autonomous analog memory. Biological memories might be of this type.

On the negative side, it is regrettable that, in addition to being noisy, this memory structure is unnecessarily wasteful in time and storage space.

Assume for example that there are N elements in each of the x_k and y_k vectors, and assume that m sets $y_k x_k^t$ can be stored without suffering unacceptable deleterious effects from noise, where $m < N$, and perhaps $m \ll N$. Then the matrix M would have N^2 components, and an associative recall would require N^2 multiplications and N^2 additions.

Under most circumstances, it would be much better to store each x_k^t and y_k pair separately. Associative recall upon presentation of cue x_j is achieved in a straightforward manner by forming the m scalar products $\langle x_k x_j \rangle$ sequentially and taking the largest scalar product as the indication for reading out y_j. Only mN multiplications and additions are required, followed by a sort of m scalar product values, to yield the correct response with no noise. Clearly, full recall upon presentation of partial cues can also be attained. It is only necessary that $\langle x_j x_j' \rangle$ be larger than $\langle x_k x_j' \rangle$ for $k \neq j$. There being no noise, it is likely that the cue can be made shorter than in the case of the dyadic AM.

In contrast, the memory structure used by us is economical in processing steps and storage space.

However, in part the objective is more modest. The associative recall is divided into two steps. The objective of the first step is only that of identification of the key. Once that is achieved, the corresponding stored item is retrieved without noise.

Again, let the vectors x_k, $k = 1, 2, \ldots, m$, be the input 'keys' and the y vectors be the associated stored items. Let the vectors be of dimension N. For the purpose of this memory, it is helpful if $N = 2^b$, where b is a positive integer.

Now to each x_k we assign a Walsh sequence, $W_{(k)}$, and form the element by element vector products

$$x_k W_{(k)} = [x_k(0)W_{(k)}(0), x_k(1)W_{(k)}(1), \dots, x_k(N-1)W_{(k)}(N-1)] \quad (2.6)$$

and the element by element associative memory is

$$M = \sum_{k=1}^{m} x_k{}^* W_{(k)} \quad (2.7)$$

where the '*' sign denotes element by element product of two vectors.

Recall is achieved by performing the element by element product:

$$x_j{}^* M = x_j{}^*(x_j{}^* W_{(j)}) + \sum_{k \neq j} x_j{}^*(x_k{}^* W_{(k)}). \quad (2.8)$$

After performing the Walsh transform of $x_j{}^* M$, we have for the (j)th coefficient

$$C_j = \langle x_j x_j \rangle + \sum_{k \neq j} (x_j{}^* x_k) \cdot W_{(k) \oplus (j)} \quad (2.9)$$

where $(k) \oplus (j)$ denotes the modulo 2 addition of the indices (k) and (j), and we have made use of one property of the Walsh functions, namely

$$W_{(k) \oplus (j)} = W_{(k)}{}^* W_{(j)} \quad (2.10)$$

In expression (2.9), $\langle x_j x_j \rangle$ should be larger than the second term on the right-hand side of the equation, which constitutes the noise.

It is interesting to note that C_j constitutes an estimate for the autocorrelation $\langle x_j x_j \rangle$, and it can also be shown that C_k, obtained upon presentation of cue x_j, is in fact an estimate for $\langle x_k x_j \rangle$. Also, since the square of the distance between two vectors is

$$|x_j - x_k|^2 = \langle x_j x_j \rangle + \langle x_k x_k \rangle - 2\langle x_j x_k \rangle \quad (2.11)$$

we can see that an estimate of the square of the Euclidean distance can be obtained if the coefficient is known, i.e.,

$$|x_j - x_k|^2 \cong \langle x_j x_j \rangle + \langle x_k x_k \rangle - 2C_j. \quad (2.12)$$

If m vectors can be stored in the superimposed manner shown in equation (2.7), it is clear that there is an m-fold reduction in the storage capacity requirement.

Equally important, if the m x_k vectors are processed sequentially, then mN multiplications and additions are required. In the method described here, only m multiplications and $N\log_2 N$ additions are required, representing a significant economy also in the processing.

To fix ideas, the procedural steps of the three methods

(1) the dyadic AM,
(2) the sequential search,
(3) the element by element product AM,

can be illustrated as follows for the special case of vector dimension $N = 64$, and 8 vector pairs stored, i.e., $m = 8$.

(a) *The dyadic AM*

$$\mathbf{x}_k = [x_k(0)\, x_k(1) \ldots x_k(63)]$$
$$\mathbf{y}_k = [y_k(0)\, y_k(1) \ldots y_k(63)]$$

$$M = \begin{bmatrix} x_1(0)y_1(0) + \ldots + x_8(0)y_8(0) \ldots . x_1(0)\,y_1(63) + \ldots + x_8(0)y_8(63) \\ \cdots\cdots\cdots\cdots\cdots\cdots\cdots\cdots\cdots\cdots\cdots\cdots\cdots\cdots\cdots\cdots\cdots\cdots\cdots\cdots\cdots\cdots\cdots\cdots \\ \cdots\cdots\cdots\cdots\cdots\cdots\cdots\cdots\cdots\cdots\cdots\cdots\cdots\cdots\cdots\cdots\cdots\cdots\cdots\cdots\cdots\cdots\cdots\cdots \\ x_1(63)y_1(0) + \ldots + x_8(63)y_8(0) \ldots x_1(63)y_1(63) + \ldots + x_8(63)y_8(63) \end{bmatrix}$$

M is an $N \times N$ matrix, with N^2 components

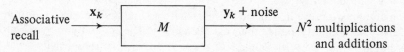

(b) *Direct sequential search*

M: storage of $\mathbf{x}_k$ and $\mathbf{y}_k$ in pairs
    array of 8 pairs of N vectors, i.e., $16N$ components

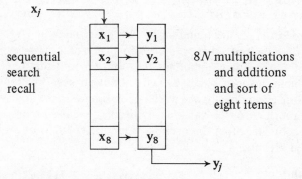

(c) *Element by element product AM*

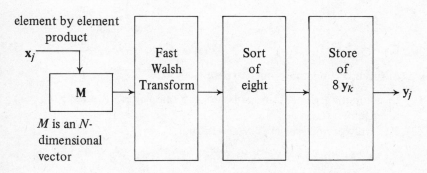

201

One of the present authors (YHP) conceived of this memory structure while on a stay as NATO Senior Science Fellow at the Bionics Research Laboratory of the School of Artificial Intelligence, University of Edinburgh, during the summer of 1973, and several accounts of use of this structure have been published [4-7].

However, in all those cases successful implementation was achieved only after extensive handcrafting to decrease the otherwise unacceptability high levels of noise. Several *ad hoc* successful procedures were suggested and examined [6,7], but no one procedure could be confidently predicted to be suitable ahead of time for any specific body of data.

More recently we have re-examined this matter of noise and, as part of a PhD dissertation, the other author (GH) was able to develop a method of systematically and significantly decreasing the level of noise.

Consequently, we have become more optimistic about the use of this memory structure in artificial intelligence research as a means of search on the basis of similarity rather than matched query. The economy in search procedure and in storage capacity would render use of this technique especially advantageous for problems with large knowledge bases.

We describe the noise reduction procedure briefly in the next section.

3. PROCEDURE FOR REDUCING THE NOISE LEVEL IN AN ELEMENT BY ELEMENT AM

Details of this procedure can be found in the PhD dissertation by G. P. Hartoch [8]. In this section we limit ourselves to a brief discussion of the underlying ideas.

In reducing the noise, it is important that we carry out that operation in some *overall* optimum manner. That is to say, it is not sufficient that one or two vectors be recognized exceptionally well without concern for all the other vectors.

We can get a feeling for the situation by listing the auto-responses, that is the coefficient C_j obtained from the memory upon presentation of the keys x_j. These can be listed as shown in the following:

$$C_1 = \langle x_1 x_1 \rangle \qquad + x_1 {}^* x_2 \cdot W_{(2) \oplus (1)} \quad + \ldots + x_1 {}^* x_m \cdot W_{(m) \oplus (1)}$$
$$C_2 = x_2 {}^* x_1 \cdot W_{(1) \oplus (2)} \quad + \langle x_2 x_2 \rangle \qquad + \ldots + x_2 {}^* x_m \cdot W_{(m) \oplus (2)}$$
$$\cdots\cdots\cdots\cdots\cdots\cdots\cdots\cdots\cdots\cdots\cdots\cdots\cdots\cdots\cdots$$
$$C_m = x_m {}^* x_1 \cdot W_{(1) \oplus (m)} + x_m {}^* x_2 \cdot W_{(2) \oplus (m)} + \ldots + \langle x_m x_m \rangle. \qquad (3.1)$$

Looking at this array of expressions, we see that:

(1) In computing the auto-response to any one pattern, we have $(m-1)$ noise terms.

(2) The array of noise terms is symmetrical, i.e.,

$$x_j {}^* x_k W_{(j) \oplus (k)} = x_k {}^* x_j W_{(k) \oplus (j)} . \qquad (3.2)$$

(3) There are a total of $m(m-1)/2$ distinct noise terms for the m patterns.

A measure of the total noise can be obtained by forming the sum of the squares of the individual noise terms, as follows

$$\min \sum_{i=1}^{m-1} \sum_{j=i+1}^{m} (x_i^* x_j W_{(j) \oplus (i)})^2 . \tag{3.3}$$

This is the quantity which is minimized in our procedure.

We began our investigation procedure by questioning whether we could reduce the noise by carrying out a linear transformation on the vector space. That is, we questioned whether there existed a matrix T and a vector $\boldsymbol{\delta}$, such that we can form

$$x_j' = Tx_j + \boldsymbol{\delta}$$

and the memory formed from the x_j' would yield auto-responses C_j' with essentially no noise.

Consideration of the operations required for carrying out the general transformation led us to reject the option of searching for a matrix operation Tx_j and to restrict ourselves to a search for a vector $\boldsymbol{\delta}$, such that

$$x_j' = x_j + \boldsymbol{\delta} .$$

The vector $\boldsymbol{\delta}$ would suffice to reduce the noise level. It is also of dimension N.

The actual minimization procedure is carried out in the Walsh Transform domain. The procedure can be thought of as a steepest descent search for a $\boldsymbol{\delta}$ in the N-dimensional vector space. The components of $\boldsymbol{\delta}$ are varied in each search step in a manner such that the rate of decrease of the total noise is always the greatest possible.

4. RESULTS OBTAINED ON REDUCING THE NOISE IN AN ELEMENT BY ELEMENT AM

The element by element AM is of interest in two contexts, one being the efficient identification of incoming keys which are exactly the same as the stored patterns, and the other context being the identification of any incoming test-pattern as being similar to some of the stored patterns.

Use of the AM in the first instance is of limited interest. It is true that beneficial effects such as fast response and decreased storage requirements are realized, but these finite benefits can also be reached in other ways.

Use of the AM in the second context is much more interesting because a denumerably infinite number of incoming keys can now be identified in a useful manner, and the memory operates in a manner qualitatively different from any which relies on exact matches or exact partial matches.

To illustrate the effect of the noise reduction procedure on the performance of the memory in these two contexts, we choose a collection of patterns which we know to be particularly troublesome in so far as pattern recognition is concerned. Each of these consists of a sequence of real numbers, as illustrated in Fig. 4.1. When plotted as time series, these patterns exhibit no distinctive features and occasionally vary very little from one pattern to the other.

For sequences of lengthy 64, various numbers of such patterns were stored in element by element AM structures.

Upon presentation of an incoming pattern, we can retrieve in *one operation* the estimated scalar product between that incident pattern and all stored patterns. The Euclidean distances can then also be estimated.

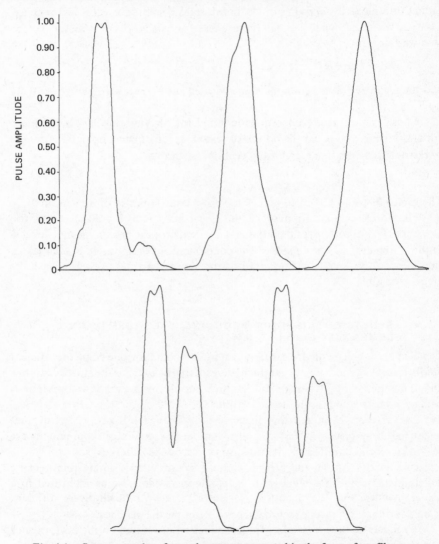

Fig. 4.1 – Some examples of stored patterns presented in the form of profiles.

If the incoming pattern is exactly one of the stored patterns and if there is no noise, one of the estimated distances would be zero. Therefore, in one operation we can identify the incoming pattern and evaluate the distance from that to all the other stored patterns.

In Fig. 4.2 we show the effect of noise reduction on estimation of the auto-responses, with 11 patterns stored in one AM. The estimated square of the Euclidean distance (ED^2) between the incoming pattern and the stored counterpart should be zero, but is not because of noise. The estimates obtained before and after noise reduction are shown plotted in Fig. 4.2. It can be seen that the

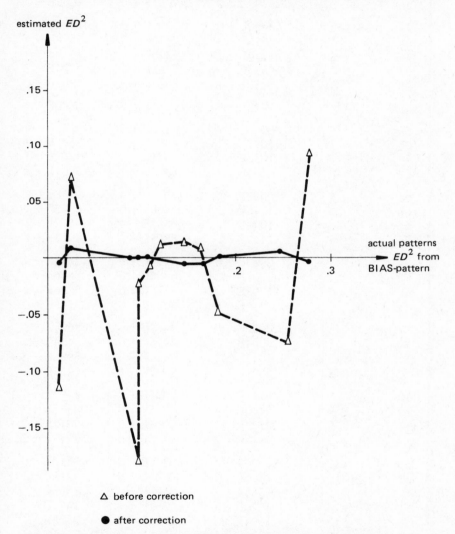

Fig. 4.2 – Auto-response of the AM for 11 stored patterns. △ = Before correction. ● = After correction.

205

Table 4.1 – Actual versus estimated *ED* for an AM with 9 stored patterns.

test pattern	closest ref-pattern stored in AM	actual	(EUCLIDEAN DISTANCE) estimated before correction	after correction
2a	2	.2397E − 6	.1227E + 0	.1454E − 4
2b	2	.3195E − 4	.1266E + 0	.3561E − 2
2c	2	.3076E − 4	.1189E + 0	−.3425E − 2
2d	2	.9208E − 2	.1061E + 0	−.1205E + 0
3a	3	.0000E + 0	.7510E + 0	.1574E − 4
3b	3	.4413E − 3	.7415E + 0	.1574E − 4
3c	3	.1790E − 2	.7326E + 0	−.1516E − 1
3d	3	.1685E − 2	.7723E + 0	.3224E − 1
3E	3	.1256E − 1	.8907E + 0	.2382E + 0
4b	4	.1722E − 1	−.2151E + 0	.8800E − 1
5a	5	.0000E + 0	.1170E + 0	.5341E − 4
5b	5	.1095E − 2	.1341E + 0	.1597E − 1
5c	5	.1092E − 2	.1021E + 0	−.1367E − 1
5d	5	.1204E − 1	.8003E − 1	−.3961E − 1
6a	6	.0000E + 0	−.7015E + 0	.6681E − 5
6b	6	.1046E − 2	−.7160E + 0	−.6925E − 1
6c	6	.1044E − 2	−.6849E + 0	.4510E − 1
6d	6	.1449E − 1	−.5865E + 0	.1901E + 0
7a	7	.0000E + 0	.5194E + 0	−.2384E − 4
7b	7	.1005E − 2	.4890E + 0	−.5616E − 2
7c	7	.1003E − 2	.5518E + 0	.7576E − 2
7d	7	.7941E − 1	.3263E + 0	−.3543E + 0
8a	8	.0000E + 0	.4382E + 0	.5627E − 4
8b	8	.4904E − 3	.4255E + 0	−.4434E − 2
8c	8	.4642E − 3	.4516E + 0	.5935E − 2
8d	8	.5694E − 1	.9032E − 1	−.1257E + 0
9a	9	.4793E − 6	−.9005E + 0	.3481E − 4
9b	9	.9490E − 4	−.8981E + 0	.9372E − 2
9c	9	.9323E − 4	−.9027E + 0	−.9012E − 2
9d	9	.5740E − 2	−.9406E + 0	.3935E − 2
10a	10	.0000E + 0	.2426E + 0	−.3610E − 6
10b	10	.1766E − 2	.2583E + 0	.3212E − 1
10c	10	.4368E − 3	.2500E + 0	.1553E − 1
10d	10	.4276E − 3	.2361E + 0	−.1451E − 1
10e	10	.1694E − 2	.2306E + 0	−.2803E − 1
10f	10	.1788E − 1	.1870E + 0	−.7561E − 1

benefits are indeed dramatic. Actually, the distances obtained before noise reduction had already been reduced as much as possible by careful 'hand-crafting', that is by judicious choice of Walsh-reference-functions. However, the errors were still quite large.

In contrast to the previous simple task of identifying patterns which are in fact also stored patterns, we deal here with the more representative task of trying to identify any incident pattern in terms of similarity to one or more of the stored patterns.

In Table 4.1, the labels for the incident patterns are listed in the first left-hand column. Each of those patterns is identified as being most similar to one of the stored patterns. and the labels of those are listed in the second column.

The actual inter-pattern ED^2 is shown in the third column and compared with estimated values obtained before, and after noise-reduction. Errors in identification made before noise reduction are removed by that procedure.

In some instances the deviation between the actual ED^2 and the noise-corrected, estimated ED^2 appears to be quite large. However, the important consideration is that the correct identification can nevertheless be made, and that would not have been possible before noise-reduction.

REFERENCES

[1] Kohonen, T., (1978). *Associative Memory*. New York: Springer Verlag.
[2] Nakano, K., (1972). Association – a model of associative memory, *IEEE Trans.*, *SMC-2*, *No. 3*, 380–388.
[3] Willshaw, D., (1971). Models of distributed associative memory, Ph.D. thesis. Edinburgh: Theoretical Psychology Unit, University of Edinburgh.
[4] Pao, Y-H., and Merat, F. L., (1975). Distributed associative memory for patterns, *IEEE Trans.*, *SMC-15*, *No. 6*, 620–625.
[5] Pao, Y-H., and Schultz, W. L., (1978). An associative memory for the recognition of patterns, *Proc. Fourth Int. J. Conf. on Pattern Recognition*, (Kyoto).
[6] Schultz, W. L., (1979). Characteristics and Applications of distributed associative memory algorithms, Ph.D. thesis. Cleveland: Case Western Reserve University.
[7] Oh, S-Y., (1981). A pattern recognition approach to the monitoring and control of power systems, Ph.D. thesis. Cleveland: Case Western Reserve University.
[8] Hartoch, G. P., (1981). Theoretical basis for reduction of cross-talk in associative memory recognition of patterns: with resulting decrease in processing time and computer storage requirements, Ph.D. thesis. Cleveland Western Reserve University.

COMPUTER VISION

10

A robot vision lab concept

T. Vámos and M. Báthor
Computer and Automation Institute
Hungarian Academy of Sciences, Budapest, Hungary

"The gas-carriage is a coach made on the shape of a three-wheel velocipede driven by a small gas motor inserted under the seat. The mixture of inflammable sorts of gas and air evolved from petrol or naphta is ignited by electric sparks. It could not gain ground up to our day and only a few people use it as luxury article."

Encyclopaedia Pallas
Budapest, 1893

ABSTRACT

An experimental laboratory is described, with interactive graphics facilities and a wide range of programming tools for generation of application systems. The philosophy of the system and relevant components, especially for man-machine communication and system design, is reported, with application examples.

1. INTRODUCTION

The period 1965–75 was a golden age for object-oriented pattern recognition. Nearly all the principal ideas of low- and high-level vision were published in this decade: relaxation, local template-operators, line labelling, range finding, and other edge detection and region segmentation methods at the lower level, model-based 2D–3D matching, grammars, generalized parallelepipeds, cones, spatial surface detectors at the higher. All these methods were demonstrated mostly under simplified laboratory environments on selected objects, presenting not only the ingenuity of these methods, but also the limitation of the devices. One other important feature of this period is that experiments had a certain task-segmentation: very few labs could even within these constraints fulfill a complete project starting with looking at an object with a video input device and finishing with decision making. The period of one research grant, or one PhD thesis forced most researchers to simulate only some relevant sections of the full task and to concentrate all efforts on the details, which were his/her own solutions to the problem. As realization came nearer during recent years, approaches to the overall problem have shown that singular methods and solutions are viable in very simple and particular cases only. Because of problem complexity, the solutions diverged in two different directions: fast, short-cut methods which could provide an efficient real-time action for a simple industrial task, and combined methods using results of the earlier period.

In the following sections we would like to report on our approach [34–40] which, of course, originates from many results cited above, and on several failures. We can enumerate a few basic points:

- the problems of practical robot vision are very different in requirements;
- each task has an affinity to one, or a sequence of specific solutions;
- all problem solving should be based on a man-machine interaction both in planning and in execution.

2. THE SUB-TASKS OF THE ROBOT VISION PROBLEM

The robot vision problems can be classified into the following sub-tasks:

- object identification
- location /orientation/ definition
- inspection
- trajectory clearance /avoidance/
- destination check
- fine adjustment /fixing, insertion etc./ using visual support.

Let us give a short summary of the specifics of the above tasks.

First, the object of the operation should be identified. This is often a rather rough check, because the object is well-known to the system, so a reliable and short go–no-go test is sufficient [8, 23, 39].

The second operation is based on all relevant details of the previously identified object. This knowledge is learnt prior to the operation not only by a detailed object representation, but also by experimentation on the most practical relevancies, which is not at all a trivial problem. The difficulty and consequently the solution of this task varies immensely from simple, well-shaped, 2D objects to partly hidden, overlapping 3D ones lying in an undefined position [12, 13].

The third step is a quality (dimensions, details, surface characteristics, defects) check. It is a deterministically planned operation which can be executed before the robot movement or combined with that.

The fourth sequence is another rough operation: a check of the trajectory area, whether it is really free as it was calculated by the robot action program [5, 40].

The fifth step is in some ways similar to the second and in some cases also to the third: a check of the terminal state of the robot's transfer operation: the contact of the removed object with the fixed one. Although this step is typical in assembly, when an object should be selected, picked up, transferred to a basic object and somehow joined to it, the elements of this operation are in essence just as in any robot vision task [38].

The final operation is the fine adjustment. This is beyond the scope of this paper.

3. GENERAL CONSIDERATIONS OF THE LAB

Many details of this lab were reported previously: some are our own achievements, but the majority are derivative.

Hardware components are as shown in Fig. 1.

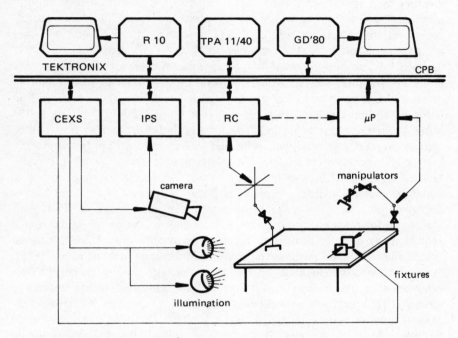

Fig. 1 – Hardware architecture of the Lab.

Software elements:

- IDOS Interactive operating system
      menu-selection capability
      modular, changeable peripheral handlers
- structured macro-language
- PASCAL
- implementations of microprocessor languages
- interactive graphic system with software for man-machine communication and knowledge-acquisition
- edge detection and contour following in 2D pictures
- surface detection based on programmed illumination

213

- computing of various brute-force characteristics in 2D
- textural anisotropy detection
- CPDL grammar description language and interpreter for supporting 3D recognition
- manipulator trajectory planning and control software.

3.1 The system synthesis problem

As was clear from the preceding details, the only uniform philosophy of our system is an intrinsic non-uniformity, i.e. a mixed armoury of procedures tied together by a special application goal. Evidently this requires a very uniform programming environment which enables the developer and user groups to co-operate without much overhead cost. An obvious way of communication would be a common database. This was planned many years ago, but later it was dropped not by decision, but for convenience. A common database, even a common structure, was a burden for real-time microsystem realizations. In practice the same information can be regarded as a long and not predefined string of elements in one program and as a simplified binary matrix in the other. Considering this fact a much more careful system planning is needed to control program interfaces, data-flow, and loss of information. In our system, knowledge representation is identified to a great extent with graphical representation − or if not, it is mostly attached to that [4]. This idea is a clue for representation and man-machine interaction. Every program segment must have a display output; the operator should see step by step what is going on. This means that powerful real-time graphics are a basic tool of system planning, simple enough to be used by an operator without any qualification. Modelling, simulation, animation, and menu-driven control are the basic building elements [5]. System planning is some kind of experimentation with the elements of the lab's equipments, leading to problems related to those addressed by non-monotonic logic [7, 10]: beliefs are to be asserted, modified, or omitted. We have a well-defined terminal state (the goal of the robot operation), a limited number of possible objects (in the case of unidentified objects, the system returns the control to the operator), a rather high number of configurations (locations, orientations, mutual relations), and operation procedures. An inference technique is to be constructed between the initial and terminal scenes.

There are two kind of beliefs: one on the scenes, objects etc., and one on the procedural ways. The overall procedure reflects the skilled operator's expertise: the system planner should teach the system to incorporate his special expertise which is a result of his experimental work. Until now nothing has been done to automate this − and most probably is would not even be feasible. Our emphasis was put on tools and on how to concatenate them.

Two-valued logic is extended here to four: *true* (the hypothesis is completely correct), *modifying* (the hypothesis is correct but it should be slightly modified; this case is in someway similar to changing a slot in a frame), *pointing* (although the hypothesis is false, or mostly false, the check suggests some other definite hypothesis as next step), *false* (i.e. the control is returned to a preset sequence of hypotheses or to the operator).

In this way the system is supported not only by the procedures and facts of the environment and the knowledge of the operator but also by his intuitive strategy. The expertise of the lab's personnel is transferred to the dedicated system.

Here we should confess that the strategy of reasoning is inspired by theoretical considerations, while the practical procedures look mostly very pragmatic; more experience in several different tasks generates a somehow generalizable scheme which can be identified with the nomenclature of the theories.

4. THE LAB'S COMPONENTS

Some special characteristics of the system's components will now be discussed.

4.1 General description

GD′80 is a flexible, extendable intelligent multiprocessor graphics terminal with modular structure and PDP-compatible bus (see Fig. 2).

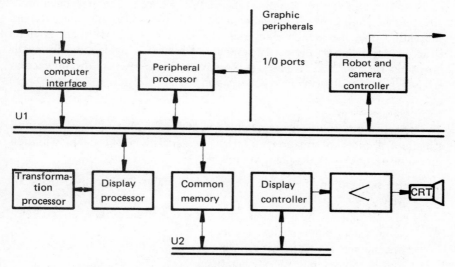

Fig. 2 – GD′80 autonomous graphics system.

The parts of the GD′80 can be used in almost every combination, e.g. a non-graphic microprocessor control system can even be formed for a user who does not need visual interaction during operation. The display of the GD′80 is variable from a low-cost, black and white small raster TV screen to a high-resolution colour vector scan. For most practical applications in pattern recognition the low-cost end is satisfactory; this provides the visual check of programming and motion simulation. A fast special vector-processor helps the picture generation. Another member of this multiprocessor system serves as microprogrammed interface-emulator to any host computer. The display's graphic peripherals (functional keyboard, tracking ball, joystick, control potentiometers, light pen) together with other conventional computer peripherals (disc, printer, plotter etc.) are handled by another processor. A special-purpose microprocessor is dedicated for handling our individual devices: video-input, illumination control, robot-control, and feedback.

The basic computing processor of the system is a plug-compatible microversion of the PDP-11 family with a 256 KB memory.

As this short description indicates, the hardware system can easily be tailored to an economic goal-oriented stand-alone special application device.

4.2 Operating system

The usual features are extended by those special ones which help the user in assembling his software system. The entire system is menu-driven, and its structure is modular; either the monitor or the standard programs can be rearranged by a system generator program. In this way the operating system meets all the requirements of both interactive program development and real-time robot control. The typical structure of AI programs is realized — an embedded semi-autonomous control which depends on both data and programs' outputs; the subroutines may be assembled at run-time only; each program can alter its structure depending on the partial results. The system is highly interactive with provisions for human intervention at every phase of the process. This interaction is based mostly on the graphic representation.

4.3 Graphic modelling

The kernel of our knowledge representation about the objects is a 3D graphical structure; all other information is attached to that. This graphical representation should be optimal from the point of view of

- the recognition procedure: it should be suitable for directly deriving 2D view-graphs;
- the manipulations programs: the real dimensions, surface orientations, and grasping points are also needed;
- the human interaction, by having enough redundancy to achieve real-time responses in graphical operations.

Considering these facts, the description of the objects is accomplished in vertex-edge-surface hierarchy, using a fixed but extendable variety of maximum second-order spatial elements. Supporting both the manipulator control and the recognition procedure, the graphics structure contains a provision for the human operator to assign his/her personal knowledge to the objects and surfaces. This file of soft information is called 'supplemental information'. It contains a set of weakly formulated statements, e.g. which surfaces can and which cannot be grasped at all; it contains advice for speeding up the heuristic grammatical search etc.

216

The Model Building program (MODBUIL) includes the overwhelming majority of interactive and graphic techniques, and the different ways of man-machine communications and teaching used throughout the Robot Vision Lab [4, 5, 37]. Subroutines and other parts of MODBUIL are used in each program for displaying the status of the process and making operator collaboration with the system possible. The interactive tecnniques of MODBUIL are very easy to learn; they can be used without paying attention to the mechanical details. This is very important because in this way the human operator may concentrate on the main task.

MODBUIL operates on one or two models simultaneously; the models can be put into the library at any stage of the generation procedure. MODBUIL contains a viewing module, and the operator can modify the parameters of a virtual 'camera' by using the keyboard. After setting (modifying) the position and the spatial orientation of the 'camera' or the parameters of the 'lens', the camera projects the actual structure in wire-frame form. Making use of the hidden line algorithm, more realistic projection is also available.

The control of MODBUIL is tree-structured; the operator determines the task through subsequent decision points. Each decision point is represented by a menu. The chosen branches of the control tree appear on the screen as a sentence to inform the operator about the state of the program. MODBUIL helps in generating syntactically correct models by supervising the commands continuously. To simplify model building, MODBUIL permits any linear transformation described by a 4 X 4 homogeneous matrix, and it is possible to unify two models, thus a library of the most frequent shapes may be constructed.

4.4 2D generation

MODBUIL includes a hidden-line elimination module which is fast enough to derive hidden-line projections almost in real-time in the case of familiar objects. The algorithm is fast because it directly handles the second-order surfaces instead of approximating them. This hidden-line module is essential in producing the perfect 2D views of the learned set of models for comparison with the TV pictures. Recognition works on the preprocessed 2D input picture-graph, sets hypotheses about the identity of the objects and calls the 2D views module for perfect projections from different vantage points. To speed up the recognition, in the learning period the system creates an ordered network of structurally different projections by using the discriminating ability of grammatical recognition.

4.5 Motion simulation

A significant extension of the system is the graphic motion simulation program called ANIMATOR [5]. In this program the operator can model relative spatial moves of 3D structures, e.g. parts or joints of a robot arm in a real environment. ANIMATOR can be driven either manually (by means of subsequent menus) or automatically in a so-called 'replay' mode. The operator may have the system register his/her commands into a control file. After creating a control file, the parameters of the movement can be readjusted in the file, and the real robot control program accepts that file. In this manner, the robot can be taught to perform a library of parametrized assembly-like movement patterns (see Fig. 3).

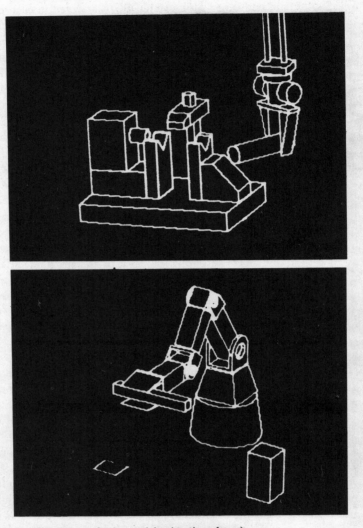

Fig. 3 – Simulation of robot activity (motion phases).

In another useful application, ANIMATOR performs the trajectory and destination check. The format of the communication data among the action planning, the robot control, and ANIMATOR is the same. This way the computer trajectory file can be checked graphically before execution. Slight modifications of graphic subroutines used in the hidden-line elimination enable the system to detect collisions.

4.6 Preprocessing techniques (low-level vision)

This seemingly conventional part of the system is also very antidogmatic.

4.6.1

A fast simple template matching procedure as a local operator for edge-detection [17, 19, 20] is widely discussed in [29]. The local maxima of the slope-variance of these short strokes yields the hypothetical branching points of the edges. A potential-field growing algorithm searches optimal paths between these points [21, 22, 37].

This three-step procedure is directed by weighting coefficients: goodness of fit measured by a statistical estimator for each stroke, reliability estimators composed of the weights of the strokes and weights of different interpretations of the noisy picture points at the complete graph level. These serve as heuristic guiding rules in the high-level semantic interpretation search.

4.6.2

A different approach is applied when surface detection looks more suitable than edge-detection [39]. In this case the filtering effect of the camera non-linearity is also used; a two-level discrimination is satisfactory for the surface boundary detection. Illumination from different directions and of different intensity supports the efficiency of this very fast procedure. In this way surfaces are enhanced by sharp changes of surface brightness at the boundaries and by approximately smoothly changing values inside. Surface normals are calculated on the basis of the Lambertian-law with a surprising accuracy, better than $10°$. An adaptive learning control of camera-characteristic, illumination direction and intensity is indispensable.

4.6.3

Several processing utilities are available: histogram analysis, automatic extraction and visualization of selected picture elements (lines of desired slope, parallels etc.), matching with pattern templates, shrinking, skeletonizing, filtering etc.

4.7 Identification procedures

All are based on the different low-level vision results.

4.7.1 Brute force

Invariant geometrical features for two-dimensional objects (shape factors, invariant moments, convexity measures, measures for holes etc.) are available. All of them were described by many authors [24, 43]. During the teaching phase the object to be taught is demonstrated several times and the variances are calculated which indicate the relevances of the characteristics of the given object. The variances are then used as the weight coefficients providing rotation, illumination and zoom-invariance of the recognition [23].

219

4.7.2

Texture analysis is based on the investigation of textural anisotropy. The importance of the anisotropy of the texture is due to the fact that it originates from the anisotropy of the process in which the texture was generated; that is, it should carry information about the texture's nature.

Most of the existing algorithms are bound strongly to a fixed coordinate system. They are not rotation-invariant in principle, and tend to ignore the possible presence of prominent directions in textures. Others use isotropic operators, thus losing the information about texture anisotropy [15].

Two types of textural anisotropy are considered, namely the one resulting from the placement of tonal primitives, and the other originating from their shape and orientation. For the first type the lineal analysis is applied to obtain a radial diagram (anisotropy indicator) of the tonal primitives' density. For the second type an analogous indicator can be calculated via the slopes of tonal primitives' edges — it is just the slope histogram in polar coordinates. The shapes of the diagrams are rotation-invariant, and their orientations correspond to the orientations of anisotropy axes of the texture.

The indicators are then analysed in order to find the directions of extremal anisotropy. Furthermore, some rotation invariant features are computed about the shapes composed by the two anisotropy indicators. They are similar to those used in shape recognition and reflect some general characteristics of the textural anisotropy (e.g. the degree of anisotropy) facilitating the texture discrimination.

4.7.3

A high level of recognition is based on grammatical search. Using the well-described ideas of picture grammars [11, 34], a Contour Pattern Description Language (CPDL) [12, 13], a programmed context-free grammar was developed with some special features. The grammar includes instructions for choosing search strategies taught by the human operator. CPDL has some heuristic speed-up which may suggest short-cuts in the search. This part makes use of the weighting factors, probability values and hypotheses originated from the simpler identification procedures including brute force, texture, surface directions, picture element statistics etc. The grammar includes semantic elements (geometrical and topological relations), similarity measures between different descriptions, and other practical utilities.

Unfortunately up to now no real-time applicable results have been achieved owing to the high combinatorial complexity of the grammatical search in case of realistic tasks. In further research we intend to study other interpretations in which the semantics of the grammar alter: the parsing may start at a higher level of terminal symbols because of the improved low-level vision techniques.

4.7.4

The teaching of the different 2D object models is also a very simple procedure on the display image. Teaching 3D models was described under 4.3. 2D objects are taught by a semi-automatic method: the operator starts following the boundary at an endpoint of a segment (line, or arc), possibly far from the centroid. The cursor follows the boundary and this way the operator specifies the consecutive endpoints of the line/arc segments. The aligned model of the surface is created by this procedure [23].

4.8 Orientation

Based on the structurally different projections, the identification process determines the name of the objects in the scene and provides a rough guess from which spatial direction the object has been projected: this information is attached to each perfect 2D view. The estimation of the orientation is helped by reflectance measured at the low-level vision. For controlling the manipulator it has to be computed which exact matrix described the transformation of the object from the model's coordinate system to its actual place. The sizes of the objects in the models are real sizes, and the projection matrix of the input camera is also supposed to be known. Thus a least-square best fitting matrix can be computed. The recently established one-to-one correspondence among the vertices of the perfect 2D view of the model and the nodes of the 2D input graph is made use of, together with the projection matrix from the model into the hidden-line drawing. If there are several one-to-one correspondences, the matrix of minimum error is accepted [37]. The system designer and the user experiment with these different tools, all available and controllable in the lab, select an efficient and economic subset or discover the lack of a desirable option which can then be included in the system.

We should emphasize that the greater part of the system's methodology is a local implementation of ideas and algorithms developed by other authors. The output-directed part of the lab, i.e. robot action planning, is discussed elsewhere [32, 38, 40].

5. APPLICATION EXAMPLES

The general methodology is illustrated by some examples. These are elaborate to different extents, with none at the moment in routine production. Several are implemented in the laboratory; some are only outlines of projects backed by feasibility studies.

5.1 Bus-body cover sheet identification

The task is the control of a painting robot in a works producing about 14 000 buses/year. The metal sheets are supplied by a conveyor in an irregular sequence out of more than 500 different shapes; the orientation of the hanging sheet varies within certain limits [23]. The problem is typically two-dimensional and contour-sensitive. Preprocessing and edge-detection are implemented by the three-step procedure mentioned in 4.6.1. Graphic teaching (4.7.4) is applied to each variant. After that, the most discriminant brute force characteristics are

221

selected [4.7.1]. The system uses nine different ones and calculates a combined estimate, as the relevant characteristics are of contrasting character. Some sheets differ only in having a hole or not, some only in flags indicating left or right side items; others have completely different shapes and dimensions. An estimation of orientation is important as well. If the brute force characteristics cannot result in a definite decision, a finer match is applied: the contour-pattern is compared with the segments of the taught model. The result calls the corresponding NC program of the painting robot.

The required equipment is a very simple GD'80 configuration (see Fig. 4).

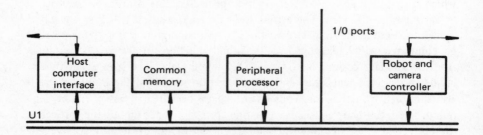

Fig. 4 – Non-graphic GD'80 microcomputer.

Teaching and system generation are performed by the host computer using its graphic capabilities. A non-graphic GD'80 system can carry out identification with the re-programmed peripheral processor acting as main processor; in the case of recognition failure, it calls for the host computer or the operator.

5.2 Crop sorting (cucumber, tomato, apple, pear, peach) in canning factories

The pieces are delivered separately on the conveyor belt. A shape and colour check is carried out both for regular selection (dimension, ripeness) and irregularities or aberrations. The shape problem is theoretically simple with at most 2-3 brute force characteristics (4.7.1) to be calculated, but sometimes from two different views. The colour check can be combined with texture analysis (4.7.2). Owing to the high speed necessary (20-100 pieces/sec) special input and processing methods are needed – a different task for in-process realization.

5.3 Assembly-line part-selector

The task is the replacement of the vibratory feeders and shake boxes in a batch product assembly factory, e.g. car accessories, electric switches [6]. The shake box moves the small parts into separated positions. As several stable situations exist for most parts, fixing holes are mostly not sufficient or they must be separately designed for each small variation in the assembly configuration. This is a facilitated case of a bin-picking problem, built on the problem of overlapping caused by the shaking mechanism. In most cases the task can be solved as a reduced 3D one, i.e. only a few, well-defined 2D view-representations exist for each part owing to the stable positions. This means that our methods for edge-detection (4.6.1, 4.6.2), teaching (4.3, 4.7.4) and computing shape characteristics (4.7.1) are sufficient in the case of mixed parts in one bin, too. If the parts are uniform, only a few stable positions and orientations should be identified, and this can be solved by the same procedure at adequate precision. Dimension, surface quality check requires either no more inspection or at most an additional texture-analysis (4.7.2). Computing requirements depend on the various local demands, so instead of one general configuration, several specific ones are considered below.

5.4 Gamma-camera scintillograms

University researchers together with a nuclear instruments factory developed a comprehensive system consisting of a camera, digitizer, pseudocolour-coding, feature extraction, and data retrieval. The coded results of mass screening and the records of the individual cases in progression are stored on magtape. Our task is the processing of shape-changes, and evaluation of relevant diagnostic characteristics. The shape analysis in this case is not solely a brute force problem but for some purposes is a structural one as well, involving the grammatical approach (4.7.3). In this area, no results are yet available. Although textural information could be very useful, scintillogram pictures do not provide satis-factory resolution for that purpose, being an integrated-filtered result by the physical nature of the devices.

5.5 Fan-assembly for buses

This is a sequence of simple assembly tasks performed partly by the robot partly by purpose-made devices used e.g. for screw-driving. Each part of the assembly is modelled by the 3D geometrical modeller MODBUIL (4.3). The robot action sequence is programmed by using the graphic motion simulator ANIMATOR (4.5). The expected positions and orientations of the parts are given as well as those of part containers, bins, conveyors etc. These values make the preliminary robot motion simulation possible and enable the creation of the prospective 2D views of parts (4.4) in the subsequent phases of assembly. In run-time, the visual input and processing system (4.6.1, 4.6.2) is used for gaining real information about the parts. These pictures are compared with the *a priori* created ones. Thus object positions and orientations can be determined (4.6.2, 4.8) and appropriate robot activities are generated (38, 40). The above method also enables us to recognize faulty parts, in this way protecting the arm from unexpected mechanical effects. Following the recognition phase the simu-lated motion can be played back [5] by using the real location data: this further check gives higher realiability to robot actions.

5.6 Check of tool-edges

This is a very important problem in a workshop environment and is crucial in an

223

unmanned production cell. High accuracy and a minimum of two separate directional images are indispensable. As the required shapes and admitted tolerances are strictly given, the problem is mostly two-dimensional (4.6.1, 4.6.2, 4.7.1). A small GD'80 configuration can fulfil the task, but some problems arise in the technical implementation: how to locate the optical input (at a reference point or continuously following the tool); how to get a noise-free and reliable input picture of, say, a tool-edge covered by grease and chips, what kind of illumination tricks to use for enhancing the relevant attritions etc. Further experiments should give answers to these questions.

6. CONCLUDING REMARKS

6.1 Intellectual progenitors.

Pattern recognition is now a wide area for theoretical research and starting to be the same for practical applications. Last year's review of picture processing [28] collected 700 references; this year's 5th International Conference on Pattern Recognition offers 309 papers, with numerous applications. The significance of the work of the pioneers was to provide stimulus [1, 14, 16, 17, 18, 25, 26, 27, 41, 42]. We feel, nevertheless, that two laboratories in particular share the above concept, the Tokyo Electrotechnical Laboratory and SRI International, owing to their special role. Being less educational-academic institutions than the other leading laboratories they have a more stable character with bridging ideas towards applications, though they significantly differ from the definite task-oriented industrial labs. The ideologies of the two laboratories are often similar [2, 3, 6, 30, 31, 33].

In every apparently simple application we controlled the question: how to guide logically the sequence of different methods, i.e. how to find an optimal strategy, the fastest and most reliable evaluation. The most sophisticated task is that of 3D, partly occluded, overlapping objects. This is a really special problem, but in many cases it can be bypassed by slightly modifying the technology — the future workplace should not be a replica of the anthropomorphic human one. Which are the optimal solutions? More intelligence or more special technology (and here we find the real justification of the concept of machine intelligence)? — it is really an ever changing tradeoff for the advance of both.

ACKNOWLEDGEMENTS

The authors are indebted to Mrs V. Galló, Mr D. L. Csetverikov, Dr A. Siegler, Mrs E. Kovács (lab-manager), to the GD'80 group headed by Mr P. Verebély and to all members of the laboratory. Also to Mrs Gy. Hetényi and E. N. Nagy for typing and correction of the text, and to Mr S. Szabó for help with the English translation. Particular thanks are due to Dr L. Mérő, author of the preprocessing algorithms, for his contributions and valuable criticisms. Acknowledgement is also due to the helpful cooperative groups working in the application areas mentioned.

REFERENCES

[1] Agin, G. J., and Binford, T. O., (1973). Computer description of curved objects. *Proc. 3rd IJCAI*, (Stanford). Menlo Park: Stanford Research Institute.

[2] Agin, G. J., and Duda, R. O., (1975). SRI vision research for advanced automation. *Proc. 2nd USA-Japan Computer Conference*, Tokyo, pp. 113–117.

[3] Barrow, H. G., and Tenenbaum, J. M.: Recovering intrinsic scene characteristics from images. *Technical Note 157.* Menlo Park: Artificial Intelligence Center, SRI International.

[4] Báthor, M., (1977). Interactive picture manipulation. *2nd Hungarian Computer Science Conference* (Budapest), pp. 168–177.

[5] Báthor, M., and Seigler, A., (1979). Graphical modelling and motion simulation system. COMPCONTROL, Sopron, Hungary, (Hungarian).

[6] Bolles, R. C., (1977). Part acquisition using the SRI vision module. *Technical Note, 193.* Menlo Park: SRI International.

[7] McCarthy, J., (1980). Circumscription – a form of non-monotonic reasoning. *Artificial Intelligence*, 13, 27–40.

[8] Chetverikov, D., (1980). 2-dimensional pattern recognition methods – an evaluation. *Working Paper, AP/4* (Hungarian).

[9] Clowes, M., (1971). On seeing things. *Artificial Intelligence*, 2, pp. 79–112.

[10] McDermott, D., and Doyle, J., (1980). Non-monotonic logic I., *Artificial Intelligence*, 13, 41–72.

[11] Fu, K. S., (1974). *Syntactic methods in pattern recognition.* New York: Academic Press.

[12] Galló, V., (1975). A program for grammatical pattern recognition. *Proc. 4th IJCAI*, (Tbilisi) pp. 628–634.

[13] Galló, V. An experimental recognition system using pattern grammars. *Problems of Control and Information Theory.*, Academy of Sciences of the USSR, Hungarian Academy of Sciences.

[14] Guzman, A., (1968). Computer recognition of 3D objects in a visual scene, *AI-TR 228.* Cambridge, Mass.: Artificial Intelligence Laboratory, MIT.

[15] Haralick, R. M., (1979). Statisitical and structural approaches to texture. *Proc. IEEE*, 67, No. 5.

[16] Horn, B. K. P., (1977). Understanding image intensities. *Artificial Intelligence*, 8, 201–231.

[17] Hueckel, M. H. (1971). An operator which locates edges in digitized pictures. *J. ACM*, 18, 113–125.

[18] Minsky, M.: A framework for representing knowledge, *The Psychology of Computer Vision* (ed. Winston, P. H.). New York.

[19] Mérő, L., and Vassy, Z., (1975). A simplified and fast version of the Hueckel operator. *Proc. 4th IJCAI*, (Tbilisi), pp. 650–655.

[20] Mérő, L., and Vámos, T., (1976). Real-time edge-detection using local operators. *Proc. 3rd IJCPR*, (Coronado, Cal.), pp. 31–36.

[21] Mérő, L., (1978). A quasi-parallel contour following algorithm. *Proc. AISB/GI Conf. on AI*, (Hamburg).

[22] Mérő, L., (to appear). An optimal line-following algorithm, *IEEE Trans. Pattern Analysis and Machine Intelligence.*

[23] Mérő, L., Chetverikov, D., and Báthor, M., (1980). Bus-body sheet identification oriented 2D recognition system. *Proc. of 3rd IFAC/IFIP Symp. on Control Problems and Devices in Manufacturing Technology* (Budapest).

[24] Pavlidis, T., (1978). A review of algorithms for shape analysis. *CGIP*, 243–258.

[25] Roberts, L. G., (1965). Machine perception of 3D solids. *Opt. and Electroopt. Inf. Proc.* Cambridge, Mass.: MIT Press, 159–197.

[26] Rosenfeld, A., (1970), Connectivity in digital pictures. *J. ACM*, 17, 146–160.

[27] Rosenfeld, A., Hummel, R. A., Zucker, S. W., (1976). Scene labelling by relaxation operations. *IEEE Trans. SMC*, 420–433.

[28] Rosenfeld, A., (1980). Picture processing: 1979; a survey. *Computer Graphics and Image Processing*, 13, 46–79.

225

[29] Show, G. B., (1979), Local and regional edge detectors: some comparisons. *CGIP*, 9, 135–149.

[30] Shirai, Y., and Tsuji, S., (1971). Extraction of the line drawing of 3D objects by sequential illumination from several directions. *Bul. Electrotechn. Lab.*, 35, No. 3.

[31] Shirai, Y., Recent advances in 3D scene analysis. *Proc. 4th IJCPR*, (Kyoto), pp. 86–94.

[32] Siegler, A., (1979). Kinematics and microcomputer control of a 6 d.o.f. manipulator. *Technical Report, No. 185.* Cambridge: Department of Engineering, University of Cambridge.

[33] Sugihara, K., and Shirai, Y., (1977). Range-data understanding guided by a junction dictionary. *Proc. 5th IJCAI*, (Cambridge, Mass.). Pittsburgh: Department of Computer Science, Carnegie-Mellon University.

[34] Vámos, T., and Vassy, Z., (1973). Industrial pattern recognition expriment – a syntax aided approach. *Proc. 1st IJCPR*, (Washington) pp. 445–452.

[35] Vámos, T., and Vassy, Z., (1975). The Budapest robot – pragmatic intelligence. *Proc. of 6th IFAC World Congress* (Boston), part IV/D, 63.1.

[36] Vámos, T., (1977). Industrial objects and machine parts recognition. *Applications of Syntactic Pattern Recognition*, pp. 243–267 (ed. Fu, K. S.). Heidelberg.

[37] Vámos, T., Báthor, M., and Mérő, L. (1979). A knowledge-based interactive robot vision system. *Proc. 6th IJCAI*, (Tokyo).

[38] Vámos, T., (1980). Research works in the field of intelligent robots and possible applications. *Proc. of 3rd IFAC/IFIP Symp. on Control Problems and Devices in Manufacturing Technology* (Budapest).

[39] Vámos, T., and Báthor, M., (1980). 3D complex object recognition using programmed illumination. *Proc. of 5th IJCPR* (Miami).

[40] Vámos, T., and Siegler, A., (to appear). Intelligent robot action planning. *8th IFAC World Congress* (Kyoto).

[41] Waltz, D., (1975). Understanding line drawings of scenes with shadows. *The Psychology of Computer Vision* (ed. Winston, P.H.). Cambridge, Mass: MIT Press.

[42] Winograd, T., (1975). Frame representation and the declarative/procedural controversary, *Representation and Understanding* (eds. Bobrow, D., and Collins, A.) New York: Academic Press.

[43] Yachida, M., and Tsuji, S., (1977). A versatile machine vision system for complex industrial parts. *IEEE Trans. on Computers*, 9, 882–894.

11

Interpreting line-drawings as 3 – dimensional surfaces

H. G. Barrow[*] and J. M. Tenenbaum[*]
Artificial Intelligence Center
SRI International, USA

Abstract

We propose a computational model for interpreting line drawings as three-dimensional surfaces, based on constraints on local surface orientation along extremal and discontinuity boundaries. Specific techniques are described for two key processes: recovering the three-dimensional conformation of a space curve (e.g., a surface boundary) from its two-dimensional projection in an image, and interpolating smooth surfaces from orientation constraints along extremal boundaries.

1. INTRODUCTION

Surface perception plays a fundamental role in early visual processing, both in humans and machines [1, 2]. Information about surfaces comes from various sources: stereopsis, motion parallax, texture gradient, and shading, to name a few. In all of these, discontinuities of brightness at surface boundaries are crucial because they are comparatively easy to detect, and they provide constraints that allow the image to be interpreted in terms of physically significant events. In many cases such discontinuities provide the primary source of information; for example, in areas of shadow or complex illumination where determination of shape from shading is difficult, or in textureless areas where texture gradient and stereopsis are inapplicable. The value of the discontinuities to human vision is amply demonstrated by our ability readily to interpret line drawings of scenes. Understanding how line drawings convey three-dimensionality is thus of fundamental importance.

Our objective is the development of a computer model for interpreting two-dimensional line drawings, such as Fig. 1, as three-dimensional surfaces and

---

* Present address: Artificial Intelligence Laboratory, Fairchild Camera and Instrument Corporation, Palo Alto, Ca94304.

Fig. 1 – Line drawing of a three-dimensional scene. Surface and boundary structure are distinctly perceived despite the ambiguity inherent in the imaging process.

surface boundaries. Specifically, given a perspectively correct line drawing depicting discontinuities of smooth surfaces, we desire arrays containing values for orientation and relative range at each point on the implied surfaces. The interpretation of line drawings as three-dimensional surfaces is distinct from earlier work on interpretation in terms of object models [3–6] and more fundamental. No knowledge of plants is required to understand the three-dimensional structure of Fig. 1, as can be demonstrated by viewing out of context (e.g., through a mask).

A. Ambiguity and Constraints

The central problem in perceiving line drawings is one of ambiguity: in theory, each two-dimensional line in the image corresponds to a possible projection of an infinitude of three-dimensional space curves (see Fig. 2). Yet people are not aware of this massive ambiguity. When asked to provide a three-dimensional interpretation of an ellipse, the overwhelming response is a tilted circle, not some bizarrely twisting curve (or even a discontinuous one) that has the same image. What assumptions about the scene and the imaging process are invoked to constrain this unique interpretation?

We observe that although all the lines in Fig. 1, look fundamentally alike, two distinct types of scene event are depicted: extremal boundaries (e.g., the

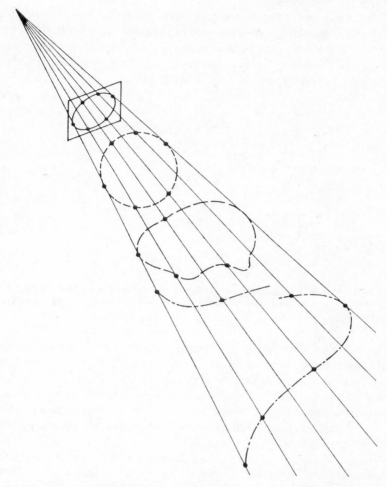

Fig. 2 – Three-dimensional conformation of lines depicted in a line drawing is inherently ambiguous. All of the space curves in this figure project into an ellipse in the image plane, but they are not all likely interpretations.

sides of the vase), where a surface turns smoothly away from the viewer, and discontinuity boundaries (e.g., the edges of the leaves), where smooth surfaces terminate or intersect. Each type provides different constaints on three-dimensional interpretation.

At an extremal boundary, the surface orientation can be inferred exactly; at every point along the boundary, orientation is normal to the line of sight and to the tangent to the curve in the image [1].

A discontinuity boundary, by contrast, does not directly constrain surface orientation. However, its local two-dimensional curvature in the image does provide a statistical constraint on the local plane of the corresponding three-

229

dimensional space curve, and thus relative depth along the curve. Moreover, the surface normal at each point along the boundary is then constrained to be orthogonal to the three-dimensional tangent in the plane of the space curve, leaving only one degree of freedom unknown, i.e., the surface normal is hinged to the tangent, free to swing about it as shown in Fig. 3.

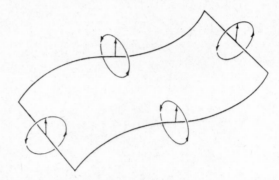

Fig. 3 — An abstract three-dimensional surface conveyed by a line drawing. Note that surface orientation is constrained to one degree of freedom along discontinuity boundaries.

The ability to infer 3D surface structure from extremal and discontinuity boundaries suggests a three-step model for line drawing interpretation, analogous to those involved in our intrinsic image model [1]: line sorting, boundary interpretation, and surface interpolation. Each line is first classified according to the type of surface boundary it represents (i.e., extremal versus discontinuity). Surface contours are interpreted as three-dimensional space curves, providing relative 3D distances along each curve; local surface normals are assigned along the extremal boundaries. Finally, three-dimensional surfaces consistent with these boundary conditions are constructed by interpolation. For an alternative model, see Stevens [7].

The following two sections elaborate two key elements of the above model. The first deals with the problem of inferring the three-dimensional conformation of a discontinuity boundary from its image contour. The second presents an approach for interpolating smooth surfaces consistent with orientation constraints along boundaries.

2. INTERPRETATION OF DISCONTINUITY BOUNDARIES

To recover the three-dimensional conformation of a surface discontinuity boundary from its image, we invoke two assumptions: surface smoothness and general position. The smoothness assumption implies that the space curve bounding a surface will also be smooth. The assumption that the scene is viewed from a general position implies that a smooth curve in the image results from a smooth curve in space, and not from an accident of viewpoint. In Fig. 2, for example, the sharply receding curve projects into a smooth ellipse from only one viewpoint. Thus, such a curve would be a highly improbable three-dimensional interpretation of an ellipse.

The problem now it to determine which smooth curve is most likely. For the special case of a wire curved in space, which can be regarded as a thin, ribbon-like surface, we conjectured that, of all projectively-equivalent space curves, humans perceive that curve having the most uniform curvature and the least torsion [8] i.e., they perceive the space that is smoothest and most planar. The ellipse in Fig. 2 is thus almost universally perceived as a tilted circle. Consistent findings were reported in recent work by Witkin [9] at MIT on human interpretation of the orientation of planar closed curves.

A. Measures of Smoothness

The smoothness of a space curve is expressed quantitatively in terms of intrinsic characteristics such as differential curvature (k) and torsion (t), as well as vectors giving intrinsic axes of the curve: tangent (T), principal normal (N), and binormal (B). k is defined as the reciprocal of the radius of the osculating circle at each point on the curve. N is the vector from the centre of curvature normal to the tangent. B, the vector cross-product of T and N, defines the normal to the plane of curve. Torsion t is the spatial derivative of the binormal and expresses the degree to which the curve twists out of a plane. (For further details, see any standard text on vector differential geometry.)

An obvious measure for the smoothness of a space curve is uniformity of curvature. Thus, one might seek the space curve corresponding to a given image curve for which the integral of k' (the spatial derivative of k) was minimum. This alone, however, is insufficient, since the integral of k' could be made arbitrarily small by stretching out the space curve so that it approaches a twisting straight line (see Fig. 4). Uniformity of curvature also does not indicate whether a circular arc in the image should correspond to a 3D circular arc or to part of a helix. A necessary additional constraint in both cases is that the space curve corresponding to a given image curve should be as planar as possible, or more precisely that the integral of its torsion should also be minimized.

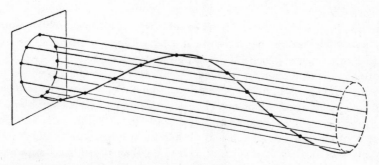

Fig. 4 — An interpretation that maximizes uniformity of curvature.

Integral (1) expresses both the smoothness and planarity of a space curve in terms of a single, locally computed differential measure $d(kB)/ds$. To interpret an image curve, it is thus necessary to find the projectively equivalent space curve that minimizes this integral.

$$d(kB/ds)^2 ds = (k'^2 + k^2 t^2) ds \qquad (1)$$

Intuitively, minimizing (1) corresponds to finding the three-dimensional projection of an image curve that most closely approximates a planar, circular arc, for which k' and t are both everywhere zero.

B. Recovery Techniques

A computer model of this recovery theory was implemented to test its competence. The program accepts a description of an input curve as a sequence of two-dimensional image coordinates. Each input point, in conjunction with an assumed centre of projection, defines a ray in space along which the corresponding space curve point is constrained to lie (Fig. 5). The program can adjust the distance associated with each space curve point by sliding it along its ray like a bead on a wire. From the resulting 3D coordinates, it can compute local estimates for curvature k, intrinsic axes T, N, and B, and the smoothness measure $d(kB)/ds$.

An iterative optimization procedure was used to determine the configuration of points that minimized the integral in equation (1). The optimization proceeded by independently adjusting each space curve point to minimize $d(kB)/ds$ locally. (Note that local perturbations of z have only local effects on curvature and torsion.)

The program was tested using input coordinates synthesized from known 3D space curves so that results could be readily evaluated. Correct 3D interpretations were produced for simple open and closed curves such as an ellipse, which was interpreted as a tilted circle, and a trapezoid, which was interpreted as a tilted rectangle. However, convergence was slow and somewhat dependent on the initial choice of z-values. For example, the program had difficulty converging to the 'tilted-circle' interpretation of an ellipse if started either with all z-values in a plane parallel to the image plane or all randomized to be highly nonplanar.

To overcome these deficiencies, we experimented with an alternative approach based on ellipse fitting that involved more local constraints. Mathematically, a smooth space curve can be locally approximated by arcs of circles. Circular arcs project as elliptic arcs in an image. We already know that an ellipse in the image corresponds to a circle in three-dimensional space; the plane of the circle is obtained by rotating the plane of the ellipse about its major axis by an angle equal to arc-cos(minor axis/major axis). The relative depth at points along a surface contour can thus be determined, in principle, by locally fitting an ellipse (five points suffice to fit a general conic) and then projecting the local curve fragment back onto the plane of the corresponding circular arc of space curve.

232

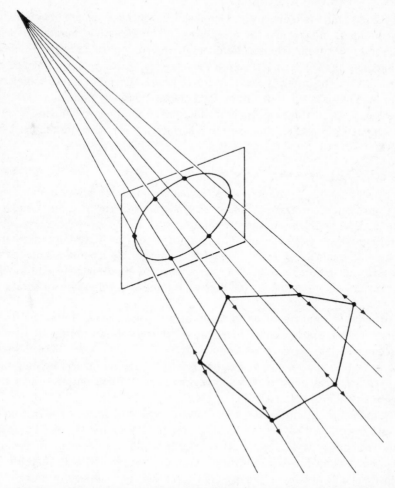

Fig. 5 — An iterative procedure for determining the optimal space curve corresponding to a given line drawing. Projective rays constrain the three-dimensional position associated with each image point to one degree of freedom.

Assuming orthographic projection, a simple linear equation results, relating differential depth along the curve to differential changes in its image coordinates, as shown in equation (2):

$$dz = a \cdot dx + b \cdot dy \tag{2}$$

The ellipse-fitting method yielded correct 3D interpretations for ideal image data but, not surprisingly, broke down owing to large fitting errors when small amounts of quantization noise were added.

Two other possible solutions are currently under consideration: a hierarchical approach in which gross orientation is first determined from large fragments of

233

an image curve; and a two-dimensional approach, in which refinement of boundary interpretations is integrated with the process of interpolating smooth surfaces over the interior regions. The second alternative is appealing on several grounds. First, it avoids explicit segmentation of the image curve into uniform fragments, a process likely to be both expensive and error-prone. Second, it allows boundary smoothing to propagate across surfaces so that each boundary point is refined by every other, not just those immediately adjacent. Promising preliminary results with integrated boundary refinement and surface interpolation are reported in section 3.

3. SURFACE INTERPOLATION

Given constraints on orientation along extremal and discontinuity boundaries, the next problem is to interpolate smooth surfaces consistent with these boundary conditions. The problem of surface interpolation is not peculiar to contour interpretation, but is fundamental to surface reconstruction, since data are generally not available at every point in the image. We have implemented a solution for an important case: the interpolation of approximately uniformly-curved surfaces from initial orientation values and constraints on orientation [10].

The input is assumed to be in the form of sparse arrays, containing local estimates of surface range and orientation, in a viewer-centred coordinate frame, clustered along the curves corresponding to surface boundaries. The desired output is simply filled arrays of range and surface orientation representing the most likely surfaces consistent with the input data. These output arrays are analogous to our intrinsic images [1] or Marr's 2.5 D sketch [2].

For a given set of input data, an infinitude of possible surfaces can be found to fit arbitrarily well. Which of these is best (i.e., smoothest) depends upon assumptions about the nature of surfaces in the world and the image formation process. For example, surfaces formed by elastic membranes (e.g., soap films) are constrained to minimum energy configurations characterized by minimum area and zero mean curvature [11]; surfaces formed by bending sheets of inelastic material (e.g., paper or sheet metal) are characterized by zero Gaussian curvature [12]; surfaces formed by many machining operations (e.g., planes, cylinders, and spheres) have constant principal curvatures.

A. Uniformly Curved Surfaces

In this paper we focus on surfaces that are locally spherical or cylindrical (which have uniform curvature according to any of the above criteria). These cases are important because they require reconstructions that are symmetric in three dimensions and independent of viewpoint. Many simple interpolation techniques fail this test, producing surfaces that are too flat or too peaked. An interpolation algorithm that performs correctly on spherical and cylindrical surfaces can be expected to yield reasonable results for arbitrary surfaces.

Our approach exploits an observation that components of the unit normal vary linearly across the images of surfaces of uniform curvature. Consider first the two-dimensional example in Fig. 6. Observe that the unit normal to a semi-circular surface cross-section is everywhere aligned with the radius. It therefore follows that triangles OPQ and PST are similar, and so

$$OP : OQ : QP = PS : PT : TS \ . \tag{3}$$

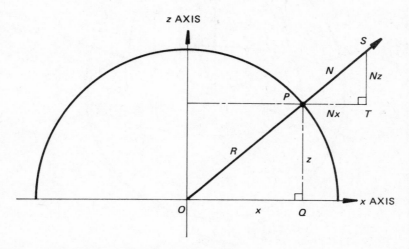

Fig. 6 – Linear variation of N across a semicircle.

But vector OP is the radius vector (x, z) and PS is the unit normal vector (N_x, N_z). Moreover, the length OP is constant (equal to R), and the length PS is also constant (equal to unity). Hence,

$$N_x = x/R \quad \text{and} \quad N_z = z/R \ . \tag{4}$$

Now consider a three-dimensional spherical surface, as shown in Fig. 7. Again the radius and normal vectors are aligned, and so from similar figures we have $N_x = x/R \quad N_y = y/R \quad \text{and} \quad N_z = z/R \ . \tag{5}$

A similar derivation for the right circular cylinder is to be found in [10]. The point to be noted is that for both the cylinder and the sphere, N_x and N_y are linear functions of x and y, and N_z can be derived from N_x and N_y.

B. An Interpolation Technique

We have implemented an interpolation process that exploits the above observations to derive the orientation and range over a surface from boundary values. It uses parallel local operations at each point in the orientation array to make the two observable components of the normal, N_x and N_y each vary as linearly as possible in both x and y. This could be performed by a standard numerical

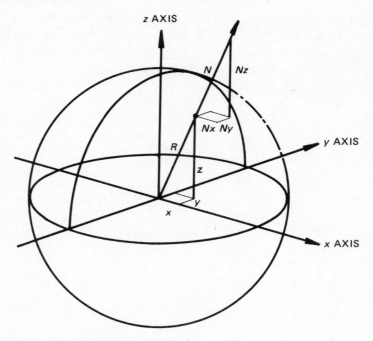

Fig. 7 – Linear variation of N on a sphere.

relaxation technique that replaces the value at each point by an average over a two-dimensional neighbourhood. However, difficulties arise near surface boundaries where orientation is discontinuous. We decompose the two-dimensional averaging process into several one-dimensional ones, by considering a set of line segments passing through the central point, as shown in Fig. 8. Along each line we fit a linear function, and thus estimate a corrected value for the point. The independent estimates produced from the set of line segments are then averaged.

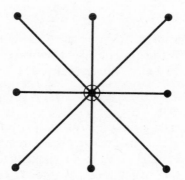

Fig. 8 – Symmetric linear interpolation operators.

236

Only the line segments that do not extend across a boundary are used: in the interior of a region, symmetric line segments are used (Fig. 8) to interpolate a central value; at boundaries, an asymmetric pattern allows values to be extrapolated (Fig. 9).

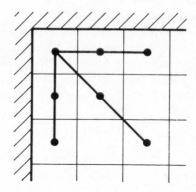

Fig. 9 – Asymmetric linear interpolation operators.

The interpolation process was applied to test cases in which surface orientations were defined around a circular outline, corresponding to the extremal boundary of a sphere, or along two parallel lines, corresponding to the extremal boundary of a right circular cylinder. Essentially exact reconstructions were obtained, even when boundary values were extremely sparse or only partially constrained. Results for other smooth surfaces, such as ellipsoids, seemed in reasonable agreement with human perception.

Current work is aimed at extending the approach to partially constrained orientations along surface discontinuities, which will permit interpretation of general solid objects.

4. SUMMARY

We have made a start toward a computational model for interpreting line drawings as three-dimensional surfaces. In the first section we proposed a three-step model for interpretation, based on constraints on local surface orientation along extremal and discontinuity boundaries. We then described specific computational approaches for two key processes: recovering the three-dimensional conformation of a space curve (e.g., a surface boundary) from its two-dimensional projection in an image, and interpolating smooth surfaces from orientation constraints along extremal boundaries.

Some important open problems remain. Our technique for interpreting a three-dimensional space curve is slow and ineffective on noisy image curves. Also the surface interpolation technique must be extended to handle partially constrained orientations along discontinuity boundaries. Aspects of the problem that we have not considered here include classification of lines into the type of physical boundary each represents (e.g., extremal or discontinuity boundary) and the initial extraction of line drawings from grey-level imagery. Both of these problems have received much attention in isolation, but we conjecture that satisfactory solutions will not be found until they are considered in the context of a system that understands about surfaces.

Current approaches to surface perception, however, have a fundamental flaw: their dependence on idealized models of lighting and surface reflectance precludes their applicability in real scenes. Research into line-drawing interpretation is therefore significant because of its potential for explaining surface perception without recourse to analytic photometry.

REFERENCES

[1] Barrow, H. G., & Tenenbaum, J. M., (1978). Recovering intrinsic scene characteristics from images, *Computer Vision Systems*, pp. 3–26, (eds. Hanson, A., & Riseman, E.). New York: Academic Press.
[2] Marr, D., (1978). Representing visual information, *Computer Vision Systems*, pp. 61–80), (eds. Hanson, A., & Riseman, E.). New York: Academic Press.
[3] Roberts, L. G., (1965). Machine perception of three-dimensional solids, *Optical and Electro-Optical Information Processing*, (eds. Tippett, J. T., et al.). Cambridge, Mass.: M.I.T. Press.
[4] Falk, G., (1972). Interpretation of imperfect line data as a three-dimensional scene, *Artificial Intelligence*, 4, No. 2, 101–144.
[5] Waltz, D. L., (1972). Generating semantic descriptions from drawings of scenes with shadows, *Technical Report AI-TR-271*, Artificial Intelligence Laboratory, M.I.T., Cambridge, Massachusetts (November 1972).
[6] Turner, K., (1974). Computer perception of curved objects using a television camera, PhD Thesis. Edinburgh: Department of Machine Intelligence, University of Edinburgh.
[7] Stevens, K., (1979). Constraints on the visual interpretation of surface contours, *A.I. Memo 522*. Cambridge, Mass.: Artificial Intelligence Laboratory, M.I.T.
[8] Barrow, H. G., & Tenenbaum, J. M., *op. cit.*, p. 19, para. 4.
[9] Witkin, A., Department of Psychology, M.I.T., Cambridge, Mass. (private communication).
[10] Barrow, H. G., & Tenenbaum, J. M., (1979). Reconstructing smooth surfaces from partial, noisy information, *Proc. ARPA Image Understanding Workshop*. U.S.C., Los Angeles, California:
[11] Almgren, F. J., Jr., & Taylor, J. E., (1976). The geometry of soap films and soap bubbles, *Scientific American*, 82–93.
[12] Huffman, D. A., (1976). Curvature and creases: a primer on paper, *IEEE-TC, C-25, No. 10*.

PROBLEMS OF ROBOTICS

12

Practical machine intelligence

E. D. Sacerdoti

Machine Intelligence Corporation
Palo Alto, California, USA

1. OVERVIEW

Machine intelligence, more commonly known by the misnomer artifical intelligence, is now about twenty-five years old as a scientific field. In contrast with early predictions, its practical applicability has been frustratingly slow to develop. It appears, however, that we are now (finally!) on the verge of practicality in a number of specialities within machine intelligence more or less simultaneously. This can be expected to result in the short term in a qualitative shift in the nature of the field itself, and to result in the longer term in a shift in the way certain industries go about their business.

Machine Intelligence Corporation (MIC) was founded in 1978 as a vehicle for bringing the more practical aspects of the field into widespread use. Its charter is to develop, produce and market products based on many aspects of Machine Intelligence technology.

This paper will discuss three specific areas of work in machine intelligence that MIC feels are ripe for commercial application: machine vision, natural-language access to computers, and expert systems. It will close with some observations on what makes these areas appropriate for application at this time, and on the difference between a technical solution to a problem and a product.

2. MACHINE VISION

Achieving computer-based vision has a high payoff, though it is technically difficult. In the short term, such tedious tasks now performed by humans as inspection of manufactured objects, analysis of aerial photographs, and visual screening of blood or tissue samples can be performed with greater speed, accuracy, and repeatability by machine. In the longer term, more ambitious tasks such as visual monitoring for auto safety, sophisticated aids for the blind, and space surveillance and other military applications are possible.

As with most areas of machine intelligence, performance in interpreting a perceived scene improves with how much the system knows in advance about the scene and the objects in it. If the perceived environment is sufficiently well controlled, it is now feasible to extract most of the desired features from the image in real time with relatively inexpensive hardware. Thus, a *vision module*, a complete system for interpreting images of a restricted type, can be developed for many kinds of specific applications. These include automatic reading of printed characters and insignia, identification and classification of microscopic particles for industrial quality control and air pollution monitoring, identification and counting of blood cells, recognition of military target signatures from radar and optical data, and recognition of diagnostic features from X-ray and other medical imagery. The factory constitutes an environment in which it is typically simple to control lighting to enable qualitative and quantitative inspection and measurement of workpieces and subassemblies, and visually-guided material handling and assembly operations. MIC has thus determined to pursue factory automation as its first commercial market for machine vision.

Applications for machine vision in manufacturing can be broken into two broad classes: inspection and manipulation.

A. Machine Vision for Visual Inspection

There are two kinds of inspection task. One consists of highly accurate quantitative measurements of critical dimensions of workpieces or placement of parts in assembly. Many applications of this type, extending from microscopic measurements of cells or fine particles to measurement of exterior and interior dimensions of key features of very large workpieces, are within the state of the art; ongoing research and development will further extend the range of application at a rapid pace. Integration of vision with an x-y stage allows for high-precision inspection by taking multiple views of an object.

The second class of inspection applications involves qualitative and semi-quantitative visual inspection as is done by humans without the aid of gauges or other measuring instruments. Examples of these tasks include sorting by shape or insignia, inspection for label registration, cosmetic properties and finish, burrs, cracks, and other defects, inspection for completeness of assembly, determining approximate size, location, and count of key features such as holes, shafts, mounting flanges, determination of handedness, and monitoring for safety. In these classes of application, the processed visual information is usually used to control mechanical separation and sorting, and/or maintain statistical records.

B. Machine Vision for Sensor-Controlled Manipulation

A machine vision module can be used to guide a robot in manipulating workpieces for material handling and assembly. Applications include sorting randomly oriented workpieces on belts and other conveyors; loading machine tools, furnaces, and test equipment; packing and palletizing workpieces and finished goods;

picking workpieces from semi-organized piles in bins and containers; guiding tools in manufacturing processes such as fastening, welding, sealing, gluing, deburring, cutting, polishing, sandblasting, painting, and so on; and assembly operations such as fitting parts together and fastening them.

C. 'Simple' Machine Vision

MIC's initial product, the VS-100, processes images that are extremely simple compared to natural scenes. The current state of the art permits only such 'simple' images to be processed in a small number of seconds by a microprocessor-based system. Yet even these so-called simple images embody a great deal of data; and elaborate data reduction techniques, drawn directly from experience in advanced vision research, must be employed to enable small systems to process the images at all.

The VS-100 was developed to provide a broad range of image processing capabilities, rather than to perform optimally on a specific limited task. It recognizes and inspects images of complex objects against a constrasting background in $\frac{1}{2}$ second to several seconds, depending on the complexity of the image. The objects can be anywhere in the field of view, in any orientation.

The VS-100 accepts grey-scale data from a range of camera types, which it thresholds to produce a binary (black-and-white) image. This is a significant data reduction in its own right; thresholding an image with 64 levels of grey to a binary one reduces the data per pixel from six bits to one. Yet there remain, for the typical resolution of 256 × 256 pixels, over 65 000 bits of data in a single image, allowing only 15 microseconds per pixel to process an image in one second, or 1 microsecond per pixel for a more widely acceptable rate of fifteen images per second. Since a microcomputer such as the DEC LSI-11/02 incorporated in the VS-100 requires 6–10 microseconds *per instruction*, it is obvious that special-purpose hardware and carefully crafted software must be employed.

The images input to the VS-100 are run-length encoded for data compression and subsequent processing speed. Efficient algorithms operating in the LSI–11 perform a complete connectivity analysis of the encoded images, building data structures that represent essential features of each contiguous region. Up to 13 distinguishing features such as area, perimeter, centre of gravity, number of holes, and minimum and maximum radius can be extracted for each region. Additional features provide information on each region's position and orientation.

Object recognition of each region in the scene can be performed using a nearest neighbour classifier operating on a user-selectable subset of the features. Precise numerical measurements are computed to indicate the degree of confidence in the system's recognition of the object. If the degree of match of the selected features is below a user-settable threshold, the object is rejected as unknown or defective.

While the VS-100 is perhaps the most advanced image processing system that is commercially available today, it must evolve and adapt to provide a range of products capable of opening the large potential market for industrial vision.

Of primary importance, it must operate faster. It must be specialized for particular functions, since the full power of the VS-100 is rarely needed for any specific industrial operation. It must be ruggedized to operate in hostile environments. It must be coupled with structured light, patterned lighting projected on the objects being viewed, so that 3-dimensional information can be derived from the 2-dimensional images of the light patterns. Finally, it must be extended to handle grey-scale and colour images.

MIC is extending its product line beyond integral vision systems, providing 'production processors' of which image processing is a component. A first example of this is 'Univision', a result of a joint effort with Unimation, Inc. A Univision system consists of a Puma manipulator coupled with a VS-100. Unimation's VAL language for robot control has been extended to include image-processing commands, enabling robot activities such as material handling and assembly to occur with visual feedback and control. Thus, an early workbench environment for machine intelligence research, the 'hand-eye system', is now a commercially available product.

3. NATURAL-LANGUAGE ACCESS TO COMPUTER SYSTEMS

Fluent communication with computer systems is a major focus of work in machine intelligence. For over two decades, researchers have attempted to solve the problem of communicating with machines in natural languages, such as English. Within the last few years, systems have been developed in several laboratories for real-time analysis by computer of typed input regarding a very limited subject area. The most extensive of these, LADDER [1], developed at SRI International, employs a vocabulary of over 2200 words and a grammar of over 130 rules to answer questions regarding a navy management database. Such systems run today on expensive, large-scale computers.

Under partial support from the National Science Foundation, MIC has developed the core of a microcomputer-based language processing system, which can provide most of the capabilities of the large systems in a much more cost-effective fashion. Completion of a practical system based on this development should permit computer-naive individuals, who must currently be trained to interact with computers using highly stilted, artificial languages, to use much more natural languages.

Constraints of processing speed (for efficient search through a grammar) and available random-access storage (for large grammars and vocabularies) both pose limitations on what is feasible for a language-understanding system operating in a microcomputer environment. The availability of the latest generation of relatively fast processors capable of supporting large address spaces, together with the continuing decline in the cost of random-access memory, are expected to make such systems technically practical in the near term.

Of course, a technically practical system is not the same as a product. The technology must be adapted to a particular application in which

244

- it is not cost-effective or not practical to train people to use an artificial language to interact with a computer,
- the range of interactions with the computer is rather wide
- introduction of a language-understanding capability does not require changing other aspects of the overall system.

4. EXPERT SYSTEMS

In every professional field there are large bodies of information acquired through study and experience by practitioners. In many fields, individuals can be identified whose performance consistently approaches the best. The goal of expert systems technology is to embody the experts' knowledge in some field within a computer. Then, the computer can act as an expert consultant for non-expert professionals or laymen. Existing systems, such as MYCIN [2], for diagnosing blood infections, or PROSPECTOR [3], for evaluating field sites for minable mineral deposits, can perform at a level exceeding that of the average practitioner in the field. These systems typically run on large, time-shared computers.

There are two components to an expert system: the expert knowledge itself, and a 'core' system for manipulating that knowledge and interacting with the user. General methodologies have been developed for encoding expert knowledge; the encoding is typically done by a computer scientist in close collaboration with an expert or experts from the field of specialization. A core system, usable for systems in a range of subject areas, has been implemented on a micro-computer in the PASCAL programming language.

There are two distinct types of users for expert systems: professionals who require access to specialized expertise (e.g., a geologist using a model of uranium deposition in sandstone), and laymen in need of summary-level expertise in a general area (e.g., a dog owner whose pet has certain symptoms and wants to know if he should call the vet). The professional may access this expertise either though a timesharing service to a large, central computer, or through a personal computer. The layman will, in the next few years, likely employ a personal computer for this activity.

The market for professional-quality expert systems is highly dependent on the particular subject, and is very intensive in its use of technical experts, both specialists in the field of application, and 'knowledge engineers' with expertise in that aspect of machine intelligence. Thus, MIC expects this business to grow very slowly in the short term.

The market for layman-quality expert systems could potentially extend to a significant fraction of the home computer market over the next five years.

5. OBSERVATIONS AND CONCLUSIONS

This section might be subtitled 'the difference between a rock-solid software technology and a product'. It is an attempt to generalize from MIC's experience in the market for machine vision systems to what might be expected for other applications of machine intelligence.

245

There are a number of barriers standing between development of a successful laboratory prototype and producing a marketable product. Unfortunately for those of us whose background is primarily technical, these barriers are generally not of a scientific nature, nor even of an engineering nature, but tend to be sociological and economic.

The primary barrier is the lack of a machine-intelligence infrastructure in the marketplace. Products based on machine intelligence are going to have the common characteristic that they perform operations in a more sophisticated fashion than those typically performed by the computer systems they replace or augment. Selling such a product requires being able to help a wide range of potential customers to *understand* what the product does; it requires those customers to be able to *apply* the product to their particular problems without a great deal of assistance; and it requires those customers to be able to *operate* the product, for the most part with existing personnel without excessive training. If any of these conditions cannot be met by a machine intelligence system, it probably is not the basis for a saleable product. For example, vision systems that require someone with expertise at vision programming to set up for a new run, or database query systems that require someone with at least a first course in computational linguistics to adapt them to a new data base, are not going to be widely accepted products. A core of an expert system that requires domain experts to work with computer experts to develop workable systems defines a potential consulting business but not a software or hardware business. A second barrier derives from the nature of the problems chosen by practical researchers in machine intelligence. We tend to choose problems to work on in which the range of acceptable inputs is small enough so that the system can cover all of it, and yet for which there is enough latitude so that precompiling responses to all inputs is not feasible. However, a potential product must compete against alternative approaches which are less general, but are more powerful within the accepted range of inputs. If the solving of any specific problem is of such general value that it seems to define a market for a machine-intelligence-based system, it has probably been faced by other, less general approaches with at least some success. A machine intelligence approach may have been shown to be feasible in the laboratory, and yet a collection of more standard approaches to subsets of the problem may turn out to be more practical.

A third barrier relates to people's natural resistance to change. The computer-based systems in use today were designed around limitations existing at the time of their design. Among these limitations was certainly a lack of machine-intelligence capability. The introduction of such a capability into one part of a system cannot typically be predicated on rationalizing the overall system to take best advantage of the new capability. Introduction of new technology must be evolutionary, not revolutionary.

In summary, then, if you wish to create a product embodying machine intelligence, it does not suffice to have engineered a workable machine-intelligence-based solution to a perceived problem. The overall environment into which the

246

new solution is to be placed, including existing hardware, software, and procedures, and, most of all, the existing people involved with the problem, must be taken into account.

REFERENCES

[1] Hendrix, G. G., Sacerdoti, E. D., Sagalowicz, D., & Slocum, J., (1978). Developing a natural language interface to complex data, *ACM Transactions on Database Systems*, 3, No. 2, 105–147.
[2] Shortliffe, E. H., (1976). *MYCIN: Computer-Based Medical Consultations*. New York: American Elsevier.
[3] Duda, R. O., Hart, P. E., Konolige, K., & Reboh, R., (1979). A computer-based consultant for mineral exploration, *Final Report, SRI Project 6415*. Menlo Park: SRI International.

13

Programmable assembly system research and its applications

J. L. Nevins, D. E. Whitney
The Charles Stark Draper Laboratory, Inc., Cambridge, Massachusetts

and S. C. Graves
Massachusetts Institute of Technology

INTRODUCTION

The long range goal of the Draper Laboratory programmable assembly system research is better understanding of design and operation problems in both conventional and novel assembly systems. The novel systems are based on new technology such as robots, smart robot wrists, computer controlled groups of machines, and model mix assembly. Our original work in this area contributed novel technology, as well as design techniques and tools which have already proved useful both in manufacturing systems and product design [1-8]. The current major areas of investigation of this work are:

- Rational choice of novel and conventional assembly technology options, including people.
- Operations research and computer tools to design or help design assembly systems.
- Understanding how to factor a company's strategic goals into the system's design; how to design a product so that company strategic goals can be supported by the product and the assembly system.
- How to integrate the system with the rest of the production system.

The approach has two main features. First, the engineering and robot assembly system experience of Draper has been combined with the Operations Research capabilities of the MIT Sloan School of Management. Empirical and mathematical approaches are being used, and each influences the other. Second, the concentration is on system design *synthesis* methods — some based on mathematical programming and some frankly quite empirical. This approach has proved to be successful. Further, this method helps balance technical and non-technical factors, while keeping us from blindly pursuing particular assembly system types or configurations. A major conclusion, perhaps implicit, is that the permanent value of this work is in design approaches, techniques and tools rather than recommendations on what an ideal assembly system should look like. Too many variables interact to allow one 'ideal' system to be defined. However, the tools developed have proved useful not only for system design but also in an inverse application, namely as a means for performing technology needs assessment or to guide choice of research directions.

To test these concepts in a meaningful way demands the creation of techniques that involve applying this work to industrial problems while simultaneously continuing the research activities. It should be noted that close working relationships with industry on problems with both an evolving knowledge base and technology are not new at Draper. The laboratory — being a 'do' tank, or applications oriented group, rather than a 'think' tank, pure study orientation — has historically worked closely with industry in both development and application of novel research.

Part of this report will be developed to describing the techniques developed, the status of these relationships, and the initial results. The remainder of the report will give a brief status of the programmable assembly system research and its future aims and directions.

THE LINK BETWEEN SYSTEM DESIGN AND STRATEGIC PRODUCTION ISSUES

The Draper Laboratory assembly research has two main elements that are explored in three regimes, namely: (a) basic research, (b) applied research, and (c) application. The principal elements of this work are part mating phenomena and system organization (Fig. 1). The issue of system organisation has many connotations and a number of levels. For example, when we first started to apply parts mating knowledge to the assembly of an entire product we were faced with trying to integrate many technological options in a viable way. This dilemma was apparent without delving very far into the additional issues of parts feeding, material handling, or inspection. To aid us initially in constructing systematic ways of examining the many options present we chose economic

BASIC RESEARCH	Part mating phenomena and system organization	
APPLIED RESEARCH	• Part mating science • Instrumentation • Experimental procedure	• Factory organization • Design tools techniques • Experimental procedure
APPLICATIONS	Thirteen in the last three years, including:	
	• Product redesigns • Product producibility studies	• Flexible assembly system design • Operational strategies

Fig. 1 – CSDL advanced assembly research activities.

modelling and analysis. With fairly simple models we found we could compare manual assembly with special machine implementations or implementations organized around a kind of flexible assembly systems called programmable assembly. Further, we could consider hybrids composed of all three or we could invert the problem and do a technology needs assessment to indicate important new research or development areas. Later, of course, the analysis tools were expanded to include linear programming [9].

Over the last two or three years approximately thirteen applications of this work have been made covering a range from technology forecasting, aiding potential robot suppliers to sort out market place sectors, to concept assembly system design, and more recently, implementation of these concept system. As this work has expanded we have begun to realize the impact this type of research may have on the factory organization of the future. In essence it is all right to talk about the assembly of an automobile alternator in a laboratory because one can easily ignore the issues of where the necessary parts come from and where the alternators go when they leave the system. However, as soon as one starts considering an automatic alternator assembly in the context of the factory as a whole these issues cannot be avoided. To start to systematize an approach to these questions an initial factory organization was posed (Fig. 2) consisting of 'islands' and 'groups'. 'Islands' are assembly systems that assemble sub-assemblies of various kinds like automobile alternators. As such the principal during the design and organization are: (a) assembly problems unique to that particular product, (b) technology available for solving either the general assembly problems or the unique technical problems of that product, and (c) institutional problems such as different pieces made in different locations or different factories, or unique work rules.

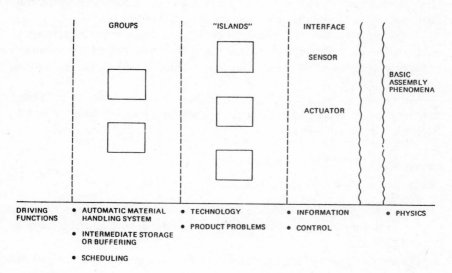

Fig. 2.

One current problem of island design is that introducing them piecemeal into existing factories is quite expensive. This cost is associated with trying to couple the island to a factory specifically designed for people. That is, parts are brought to the island on conveyor belts in random locations and orientations, or in bins, or on poorly located overhead conveyor lines with parts hung on hooks like carcasses or sides of meat. Further, after the island has finished its work these finished goods must then be reintegrated into the rest of the factory system. Of course, the easiest method of coupling is by using people, but this is expensive — so if manual coupling techniques are used to couple an island then the island must encompass enough operations to justify the cost of this coupling technique. Alternatively, one can redesign factories from the ground up. But this may involve new concepts and problems.

The integration and coupling of 'islands' into more complex organizations is called 'groups'. That is, island design is concerned with issues of the assembly of the product whereas group design is concerned with the issues associated with coupling islands to each other and to the rest of the factory. 'Group' design, therefore, is concerned with material handling, storage or buffering, and scheduling. While islands are concerned with process issues, groups are more driven by information issues.

It is quite easy to conceive of these two levels, but it is quite a different matter to relate them to today's factories. The problem arises because as Fig. 3 illustrates, American industries purchase anywhere from 35% to 65% (and as high as 85% in an aerospace company) of the components that they integrate into a product. Thus, in many cases in today's factories, components are fed to an island and the output of the island is coupled directly to final assembly. Only if island and group organization includes second and third tier suppliers can these kinds of systems be considered. The Japanese are well known for extending their production control and scheduling methods to their suppliers [10].

It therefore appears that consideration of multi-level systems in factories, as illustrated, will pose new options for organizing factories — perhaps the precursors to the type of organization research needed to consider unmanned manufacturing systems.

As far as design goes, analysis techniques plus the linear programming techniques provide an initial set of tools for considering detailed design of islands. However, at present we do not have any specific tools for designing groups.

Current Research

The present research is divided into three efforts:

Requirements — What are the characteristics of parts and products that influence assembly system design and how can these characteristics be systematized?

Systems — What are the options for workstation and transport layouts and what special control problems emerge?

Breakdown of Value of Shipments

Category	SIC 3522 Farm Machinery and Equipment		SIC 3541 Machine Tools, Metal Cutting Types		SIC 3651 Radio and TV Receiving Sets		SIC 3717 Motor Vehicles and Parts	
	% Total Labour	% Value of Shipments	% Total Labour	% Value of Shipments	% Total Labour	% Value of Shipments	% Total Labour	% Value of Shipments
Function Costs								
Nonproduction	100.0 / 42.679	23.30 / 9.983	100.0 / 32.281	37.51 / 12.108	100.0 / 52.674	15.02 / 8.384	100.0 / 39.404	14.10 / 5.591
Staff	0.339	0.079	0.150	0.056	0.546	0.087	0.325	0.046
Employee relations	0.920	0.215	0.567	0.213	1.511	0.241	1.210	0.172
Marketing	5.021	1.175	5.112	1.917	3.954	0.629	2.247	0.319
Finance	4.209	0.980	3.960	1.485	4.643	0.739	3.108	0.441
Computer operations	1.692	0.396	1.032	0.387	2.873	0.457	1.221	0.173
Engineering	5.632	1.317	7.165	2.687	20.096	3.109	5.446	0.744
Purchasing	1.252	0.293	1.354	0.508	1.904	0.303	0.775	0.110
Material control	5.315	1.243	3.498	1.312	4.382	0.697	3.953	0.561
Material movement	6.177	1.445	2.128	0.798	1.728	0.275	5.783	0.821
General plant	12.033	2.815	7.265	2.725	9.929	1.580	15.376	2.182
Production	55.982	13.095	66.485	24.937	45.937	7.257	59.070	8.382
Parts fabrication	20.231	4.732	50.159	18.814	8.377	1.333	16.599	2.355
Assembly	30.230	7.071	10.975	4.098	23.897	3.804	33.448	4.746
Inspection	5.522	1.292	5.401	2.026	13.321	2.120	9.023	1.280
Miscellaneous	4.56	0.313	1.234	0.463	1.732	0.276	1.526	0.217
Material Costs		54.05		35.35		61.54		64.81
Quality Costs		1.5		1.5		1.5		1.5
Other Costs, Profit, Etc.		21.06		25.64		21.05		19.50

Breakdown of Assets

Category	SIC 3522		SIC 3541		SIC 3651		SIC 3717	
	% Total Assets	% Value of Shipments	% Total Assets	% Value of Shipments	% Total Assets	% Value of Shipments	% Total Assets	% Value of Shipments
Total Assets	100.0	127.57	100.0	108.5	100.0	52.03	100.0	44.17
Current Assets	76.0	96.97	60.0	65.1	77.3	40.20	47.8	21.11
Inventory	25.1	32.02	39.3	42.65	40.3	20.98	27.7	12.24
Other	50.9	64.95	20.7	22.45	37.0	19.26	20.1	8.89
Fixed Assets	24.0	30.6	40.0	43.40	22.7	11.83	52.2	23.1
Buildings, land, and building equipment	5.8	7.38	11.1	12.05	9.8	5.10	17.7	7.81
Machinery and equipment	7.4	9.42	19.3	20.95	12.9	6.73	30.1	13.29
Special tools							4.4	1.93
Other	10.8	13.76	9.6	10.43				

Fig. 3 – Product system cost and asset data. The data shown are derived from the US Dept. of Labor Census of Manufacturer Statistics and the 1970 Census of Population, *Occupation by Industry*, PC(2)-7C, Bureau of Census, US Dept. of Commerce. Shown on the figure are the aggregate costs for four Standard Industrial Code (SIC) industries. The data indicates two principal things: (a) that although assembly labour may represent as much as 33% of the total labour cost it represents only 5–7% of the value of the shipped products; and (b) that material costs for the SIC's shown represent 35–65% of the value of the shipped products.

Operational Behaviour — How do different types of programmable assembly systems behave in the face of different batch sizes, mixes of products and assembly requirements, and breakdowns?

Over the last couple of years progress has been made in all three areas. This progress will be summarized and elaborated on in the next section, which describes the progress and conclusions from the current research.

Progress on Requirements

Including National Science Foundation and industrial funding, six assemblies or subassemblies of very different size, shape, number of models, annual production, special hazards, etc. have been studied. These studies included conceptual designs of systems to assemble the products using the most appropriate levels of technology in each case. The variety of influential product characteristics is amazing. To keep track of these characteristics and to organize the design efforts has required the development of manual cataloging aids and computer programs. The efforts to date have been focused on how individual work-stations will deal with these characteristics, but too little attention has been paid to global characteristics which the system (not any one station) must address. The design aids and procedures employed so far are empirical and bottom-up: people, using their creativity, generate candidate system designs. There would be nothing new in this (except, perhaps, for lack of bias) were it not for the fact that constant comparisons are made of the results of this work against the *Systems* work, which is mathematical, computerized, based on direct synthesis, and essentially top-down. We have tried to observe ourselves as designers and tried to capture the essence of what we have been doing so that more of it could be included in the *Systems* approach.

Progress on Systems

From the beginning of this work, ways have been sought to utlilize models and methodology from the field of management science and operations reseach in the system design problem. This effort has resulted in a design tool called ADES (Analytical Design Evaluation System) [9] based on mathematical programming, which can mathematically solve the static cost, annual volume, technology problem by comparing and synthesizing assembly systems, given data on available work-station capabilities, assembly task requirements, and cost and annual volume constraints. ADES has been employed in the course of the empirical design efforts, and three major findings have been made:

(1) Although ADES is directly applicable to simple design problems, more complex cases present interesting and important factors which ADES cannot yet model. Many specific improvements to ADES have been made in response to this initial experience. More empirical designs are expected to sharpen and clarify the present view of the design steps and necessary decisions. This will result either in improved ADES or completely new and complementary programs based on similar approaches.

The goal is design *aids*, for it is felt that this kind of design process cannot be totally computerized — at least in the next decade.

(2) The empirical designers were much more careful and systematic, having knowledge that their work could be tested by computer and having the need to quantify data for computer input. This is an indirect measure of ADES' usefulness, but a real one.

(3) Specific ADES solutions to real problems showed a preference for low-technology robots. This and other insights made up for lack of feasibility of some of the solutions.

So far, as with the *Requirements* work, the effort has concentrated largely on the individual assembly operations rather than the global issues. This is similar to how a commercial machine builder would perceive the problem. It is our feeling that the perspective should be wider.

Progress on Operational Behaviour

The work has consisted of simulation studies. We use the CAPS/ECSL system [11] which models queuing systems on the basis of entitities and the activities they pass through. We have compared simulation models with CAN-Q [12] and found agreement on throughput, station utilization, and other gross performance statistics. There was much more detail, of course, in the simulation results, especially concerning transient behaviour — often the most interesting. However, this work was performed on an early assumption that a strong analogy existed between programmable assembly systems and FMSs. We have no proof that the analogy is valid, and in fact have abandoned it because it idealizes far more programmability than seems to be required of assembly systems, and would result in very expensive systems. In fact, we find that a product's need for programmability is an important 'characteristic' which we may have overestimated or not known how to break down into types. The result is that we have a renewed interest in limited programmability, low technology robots, and hybrid systems of fully-, partly-, and non-programmable components.

Problem Area Definition

History

We knew when we began that this problem area was complex and ill-structured. Our early work culminated with the experience of assembling Ford alternators using a computer-controlled robot [5] plus the economic-technological analysis of Lynch [13], Kondoleon [14], and later extensions by Boothroyd [15] and Gustavson [16]. Since that time we have undertaken the efforts outlined earlier and come to a clearer picture of the important research directions for this problem area. This picture is much broader than the work currently in process, but we find it mandatory to locate ourselves in the larger context in order to help form our research activities. Further, these activities contribute to structuring the area.

Problem Area

A piece of manufacturing equipment or a manufacturing system must do its job *and* must fit into the factory as a whole. That is, the system has both local and global responsibilities. Correspondingly, the product to be fabricated or assembled presents both local and global characteristics which influence the system's design. The local ones are primarily technical, the traditional part mating or assembly sequence problems, while the global ones are primarily economic and concern managament's objectives for the product. Such global issues as its potential volume growth, number of models, frequency of design change, field repairability, etc., heavily influence both product and system design. The need for system programmability can thus be viewed as one of a broad range of requirements the system may have to meet. In any given case programmability may or may not dominate.

This morass of requirements has been given preliminary structure according to Table 1. It is not a final or complete representation nor do the items within the blocks all fit comfortably in one and only one place. The current work so far has concentrated on meeting the local requirements for both product and system, but continued contact with real problems has forced more and more consideration of the impact of global requirements. This shift is reflected in the new directions for this work. Current work using a Parts Tree technique (Figs. 4 and 5) for investigating assembly sequences, and tabular techniques for collecting all the operation requirements to match against equipment options (Table 2) are examples of

Table 1.

	Global	Local
Product	Management's Objectives:	The Parts and Assembly Operations:
	Economics and market	Assembly sequences
	Volume growth	Types of operations
	Design volatility	Geometric constraints
	Quality, reliability, safety	Part size, weight
	Make or buy decisions	Shape, stiffness
	Build to order/stock	Tolerances and clearances
		Tests and inspections
Assembly system	Cost and productivity	System layout
	How it interfaces to the factory	Equipment choice
	Labour support needs	Task assignment
	Failure modes	Part feeding (factory interface issue)
	Space needs	

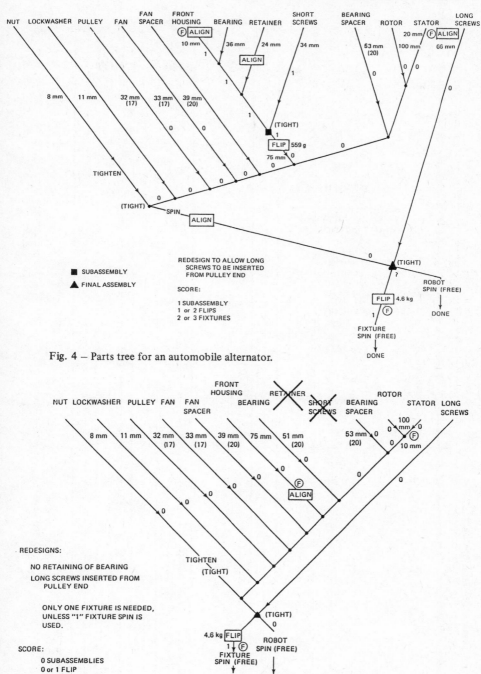

Fig. 4 – Parts tree for an automobile alternator.

Fig. 5 – Functional redesign results in a simple parts tree.

Table 2 — Assembly planning chart.

Sketch of Assembly:

Name: _____
Date: _____
Prepared By: _____
Sheet ____ of ____

Task	Sequence	Type of Task	Basic Orientation	Motion(s) Required	Jigging/Tooling Required	Degree of Difficulty of Task	Inspection Required	Cycle Time (sec.)	Comments

Abbreviations Used:

Task Type
P – Place, orient
T – Tighten bolts, nut, etc.
I – Insert parts

M – Measure
S – Shape modify
A – Align

Inspection
B – Bolt torque
G – Gauge dimension
C – Comparison

work in the Product-Local area. The ADES program and a model mix part locator program are examples in the System-Local area. The need to broaden this into the global areas is clear, since we feel a certain blindness as to the impact of many decisions we make.

Not all of the items in Table 1 are equally important in each case. For example, during the past year we have developed concept assembly systems for three product lines and some of their subassemblies. The major features of these products are as follows:

Product A

- Hundreds of models, geometrically similar but different sizes.
- Small to medium size parts.
- Low volume (10^4/year).
- Mix of fabrication and assembly occurs at final assembly.
- Management's concerns are to reduce cost while rapidly responding to customers' orders.

Product B

- 3 models.
- Big, heavy parts.
- Medium-high volume (10^5/year).
- *Lots* of fasteners.
- Very limited floor space for assembly.
- Management's concerns are to reduce dependence on labour, maintain the product's reputation for quality, and manufacture in a very limited space.

Product C

- 10 models.
- Very low volume (one per day).
- Management's objectives are high emphasis on quality control by using a reproducible process.

All of these products are currently candidates for some kind of mechanization, not necessarily automatic. But automatic or not, the solutions proposed are constrained by the items in Table 1.

Several other products have been studied primarily at the initial study level. That is, these studies focussed on the product 'local' problems such as tasks, types of operations, possible assembly sequences, operational or institutional constraints, product redesign to optimize automation, and pertinent technologies.

Top Down Structuring of the Problem Area

A useful way to view the system design problem is in terms of nested clusters. The ADES program addresses the problem of grouping operations onto *machines*. A collection of such machines makes an item or subassembly. As indicated earlier we call each collection an *island*. Collections of islands, linked by transport (of any kind) make products from subassemblies. Call these collections *groups*. Between and within islands there may be buffers or even whole warehouses.

In general, islands are technology and product driven while the higher level, groups, are information and material handling or flow driven. Further, islands in general are penalized because they must couple directly to the present factory which is usually organized for people. For example, loading or unloading of islands requires people because the material handling systems are often not designed to be directly connected to automation. With groups the first level of automatic material handling, buffering, and storage systems allow islands to be interconnected without the penalty of coupling to a system organized for people.

The essential design decisions at all three levels discussed fall into two parts:

(1) How to model the capabilities of equipment or technology that performs single or multiple operations, and how to model system requirements so that systematic techniques can be applied to match capabilities and requirements?

(2) How to decide where (in terms of the sequence of operations) the boundaries should be between clusters of the three types — i.e., what operations should each machine do, what defines a useful subassembly, and what are management's objectives in these issues?

Not only are decisions at all levels relevant to system design but they mutually interact and also interact with product design and management's ability to meet its objectives. For example, a system analysis might suggest a subassembly which is advantageous for meeting model mix needs (because it is common to many models) but is physically unconnected in current designs. Perhaps redesign would be feasible. This suggests that 'design for automation' could go well beyond single point suggestions like adding chamfers, which seem distressingly commonsense. Only after a rational base for broader suggestions has been established and organized into readily usable form is industry likely to understand redesigns.

Specific decisions and problems that are presently addressed during the system design process can be arranged in the following order:

(a) Determination of products to be assembled within a system, i.e., cluster of similar into *model families* that would be assembled by similar processes and equipment.

(b) Determination of system *groups* for assembling families; given families of products, how many assembly systems are required and which families are assembled on which systems. How should these groupings be interlinked, if at all?

(c) Examination of parts standardization; what opportunities exist within a family for parts standardization and what value may be attached to this?

260

(d) Determination of subassemblies; for a particular family of products, what are logical subassemblies and why? Here the system groups may be decomposed into *system islands*, where the islands correspond to sub-assemblies. Within a group, how should these islands be defined or interconnected? (Hereafter we will not distinguish between a product and a subassembly.)

(e) Sequencing of assembly operations; for a particular product or family of products, what are the distinct assembly tasks required and how should these tasks be sequenced?

(f) Equipment selection and task assignment; within an island, what type of work stations are needed and how should assembly tasks be assigned to these work stations? Here we may also assess the value of new or proposed technology relative to that existing.

(g) Layout of islands; how are the work stations arranged within an island and what type of material handling/transport system is needed? What types of buffers and/or synchronization should exist between work stations?

(h) Layout of individual work stations; what fixtures are needed for the assembly operations, where are the tools, how and where are parts fed?

(i) Sequencing of station operations; at an individual station, how should the operations for that station (assembly tasks, tool changes, load/unload of assemblies) be sequenced and cycled?

(j) Dynamics of design implementation; how to implement or phase-in a particular system design over a period of time? In particular, consideration need be paid to specific product dynamics such as volume growth, model mix, and model redesigns.

(k) Operational dynamics; how does a particular system design behave in a dynamic operating environment encompassing unreliable equipment, and queuing phenomena induced by the operational control system? How does the operation characteristics of a system influence its design?

We should note that the above list of problems is suggestive of a 'top-down' hierarchy of decisions which can be made sequentially. For instance, the top-most decision (step (a)) is product-related and would involve the determination of model or product families. Next, given the product families, we attempt to group the families into distinct systems (step (b)) based on the similarity in assembly requirements for the product families. Given the clustering of families into assembly groups, opportunities for and economies from parts standardization can be explored (step (c)). At the same time, subassemblies can be defined for product families, which decompose the assembly groups into distinct assembly islands (step (d)). The process is then continued with the sequence of assembly operations (step (e)), and selection of equipment for each island (step (f)), and so forth. The final step in the 'top-down' process is to confirm the feasibility of

261

a system design by examining the dynamic operating behaviour of the system (step (k)).

In considering this hierarchy of decisions, it should be noted that the initial decisions global issues and must reflect the strategic concerns for the products. As one moves lower in the hierarchy, the issues become more local in nature in that the decisions are increasingly constrained by higher-level decisions. At both the higher and lower decision levels, the problem areas typically require consideration of both product-design and system-design issues.

Ideally we could answer all of the questions (a–k) with a monolithic mathematical model or computer package, clearly, though, this is technically infeasible and probably operationally undesirable. A better approach is to seek a series of of interrelated models, design tools and techniques, each of which addresses a particular set of problems. For instance, the ADES tool is an attempt to deal with the issues in (f), while the parts tree analysis supports the design-making associated with (e). Future planned research work will include the development of similar models for different problem areas.

Developing, Testing and Applying a System Design Methodology

The technique currently used for developing a design procedure is to undertake several paper designs and to use the computer-based tools created to guide the design process. From this effort two distinct tracks have emerged, each with strengths and weaknesses. The tracks have been named 'bottom-up' (a traditional empirical approach) and 'top-down' based on ADES.

The bottom-up approach requires the designer to catalogue all the parts and operations using a standard form (Table 2) which highlights the geometric and dynamic requirements of each operation. An indication of task difficulty and technological options must also be provided for each task. The designer must then generate as many alternate assembly sequences as possible, and critique them for overall feasibility, relevance to available technology, and relation to any other special requirements. This usually requires that he visualize a technique for each operation, including part feeding. This can be quite challenging, especially when assembly includes some fabrication operations. Parts trees (Figs. 4 and 5) are used to shorthand these studies.

Promising parts trees are converted to possible system layouts. The layout decisions may be dominated by the equipment used for assembly (often true with robots) or it may be dominated by part feeding problems (especially if the parts are large). The impact of part storage techniques at fabrication time can be great, and here global considerations can come in. Finally, cost and throughput estimates are made, and systems which do not measure up are discarded.

The top-down approach (in its present form) begins with the data in Table 1, adds cycle time and equipment cost estimates, and proceeds to use the ADES program to select machines and assign selection/assignment with minimum annual cost results. A range of systems, corresponding to different production goals, can easily be generated, and the slack or growth potential of such design is shown. An example of this process was published as Ref. [9].

262

In summary, the bottom-up approach is characterized by

(a) *ad-hoc* nature
(b) bias toward technical issues
(c) providing a single solution without comparisons to others
(d) good chance of being feasible technically, not so good chance of being optimal economically

and the top-down approach is characterized by

(a) general nature
(b) bias toward time and cost issues
(c) implicit consideration of many options
(d) optimal economically (according to its criterion) but no guarantee of being technically feasible.

Table 3 outlines the approach currently used to transfer our knowledge to industry by applications to specific problems. It is a combination of the top-down and bottom-up methods. The items listed give a good idea of the depth and breadth of detail which we have found necessary to get involved with in order to determine industry's needs.

Table 3 — Programmable system application engineering (front-end-analysis).

Phase 1
1. Initial analysis of problem which includes detail study of manufacturing facilities.
   A. Briefing by management on their expectations for the study.
   B. Briefing by on-site mfg. mgt. of what they feel are their most difficult problems.
   C. Detail tour/study of present mfg. facilities.
2. Study issues.
   A. Basic plant organization.
      — Type of plant (Manual, high-level of automation or hybrid — mixtures of both, including approx. %).
      — Role of worker (simple monitor, inspector, parts modifier, assembler).
      — Attitude of workers toward automation.
      — Basic economic data.
      Annual volume.
      Labour rates.
      ROI expected.
      — Local constraints (labour shortages/surpluses, plant area available locations of sites for demonstrations, institutional problems).

Table 3 — *Continued.*

B. Product structures.
- Clearly defined subassemblies or other ways of modularizing product.
- Standardization of subassemblies.
- Do subassemblies organize into 'islands'? If not what other organization is suggested?
- Is the next step 'groups'? If not what other organizations are suggested?

C. Initial target(s) list.
From the product structure studies select candidate subassemblies or portion of final assembly, that appear most feasible for demonstrations.
- Represent/illustrate most generic elements of product problems.
- Require min. design changes.
- Are any tasks 'stack tasks'?

D. Detail study of selected target(s).
- Detail task analysis.
List all tasks (mfg. inspection, material handling or assembly).
- Group tasks.
Identify generic elements if possible.
- Part tree analysis.

E. List of applicable/pertinent technology.

F. First configuration study.
- List all possible options.
- Identify key tasks/technology issues.
- List critical experiments to test proposed options.
- Make economic analysis.
- Prepare candidate system concept designs.

Phase 2
1. Perform critical experiments identified under phase 1.
2. Perform detail configuration studies based on detail drawings, specific tolerances, weights, etc.
   - Perform mockup studies for part assembly.
   - Hard mockup studies using purchased components and simple tooling.
3. Detail designs.
4. Validate prototype on dummy parts or one set of production parts.
   - In DL laboratory.
   - In customers R & D centre.
   - On production floor in model shop test area.
5. Design/build production system.

Table 3 represents an evolving road-map (or methodology) of how to determine good automation targets and how to find out the local and global objectives and constraints. We have found that executing this map requires several visits to a company and several man-months of effort. Thirteen industrial firms have participated with us in such efforts to the system concepts level with one currently being designed for implementation. Several others were involved through the initial study phase, but the activity was terminated owing to either the recession or a redefinition of management's objectives. Currently three more are pending with one additional one, focussing primarily on disassembly, scheduled to begin early in the fourth quarter of 1980. Of the studies carried to the concept level, two were supported by industry and the third was an example for a National Science Foundation grant devoted to programmable assembly system research.

The Phase 1 type of effort gathers information, first on global issues, then on local ones, gradually focusing on a few candidates. These candidates are selected primarily on the basis of presumed technical feasibility and the likelihood of learning things that could be transferred to other targets. Conceptual designs and preliminary economic analysis are then made. During this process there is continuous interaction between the DL multi-discipline study team and the company, including periodic formal presentations to management. At the end of Phase 1 the company is presented with a list of findings, recommendations, and options. One of the options may simply be to not automate the process in question. The next step is for the company to decide whether to proceed to Phase 2. This second phase must verify in detail the feasibility of risk areas defined during Phase 1 and ultimately produce a working system.

Conclusions

This method of coupling on-going research activities to specific applications has a number of positive aspects to it. First and foremost, it clearly identifies the limitations to the present — but constantly evolving — knowledge base. Second, by making us constantly aware of larger issues it helps to both identify as well as focus us on new, fruitful research areas.

As indicated earlier it appears that consideration of multi-level systems in present factories will pose new options for organizing factories — perhaps the precursor to the type of organization research needed to consider unmanned manufacturing systems.

REFERENCES

[1] Exploratory Research in Industrial Modular Assembly, 1st Semi-Annual Progress Report, (June 1973 to 31 January 1974). *CSDL Report No. R-800*, March 1974.
[2] Exploratory Research in Industrial Modular Assembly, 2nd Report, (1 February 1974 to 30 November 1974). *CSDL Report No. R-850*, December 1974, NTIS Access Code No. PB-247149.
[3] Exploratory Research in Industrial Modular Assembly, 3rd Report, (1 December 1974 to 31 August 1975). *CSDL Report No. R-921*, October 1975.

[4] Exploratory Research in Industrial Modular Assembly, 4th Report, (1 September 1975 to 31 August 1976). *CSDL Report No. R-996*, September 1977, NTIS Access Code No. PB-260677.

[5] Exploratory Research in Industrial Modular Assembly, 5th Report, (1 September 1976 to 31 August 1977). *CSDL Report No. R-1111*, September 1977, NITS Access Code No. PB-285592.

[6] Exploratory Research in Industrial Modular Assembly, 6th Report, (1 September 1977 to 30 August 1978, *CSDL Report No. R-1218*, October 1978.

[7] Exploratory Research in Industrial Modular Assembly, 7th and Final Report, (1 September 1978 to 28 February 1980). *CSDL Report No. R-1276*, February 1980.

[8] Design and Control of Adaptable, Programmable Assembly Systems, First Report, (July 1, 1978 to June 30, 1979). *CSDL Report R-1284*, August 1979.

[9] Graves, S. C., and Whitney, D. E., (1979). A mathematical programming procedure for equipment selection and system evaluation in programmable assembly, *Proc. IEEE Decision and Control Conference*.

[10] Sugimori, Y., Kusunok, K., Cho., F., and Uchikawa, S., (1977). Toyota Production System and Kanban System — materialization of just-in-time and respect-for-human system, paper presented at the 4th International Conference on Production Research, Tokyo.

[11] Clementson, A., (1977). Extended control and simulation language users manual, University of Birmingham, UK.

[12] Solberg, J., (1977). A mathematical model of computerized manufacturing systems, Proceedings, 4th International Conference on Production Research, Tokyo, 1977).

[13] Lynch, P. M., (1976). Economic-technological modelling and design criteria for programmable assembly machines, PhD Thesis. Cambridge, Mass.: Mechanical Engineering Department MIT. Also published as *CSDL Report No. T-625*. See also, An economic guideline for the design of programmable assembly machines, *ASME Paper No. 77-WA/ Aut-2*.

[14] Kondoleon, A. S., Application of technology-economic model of assembly techniques to programmable assembly machine configuration, S.M. Thesis, MIT Mechanical Engineering Department, May 1976.

[15] Boothroyd, G., (1977). The economics of robot assembly applications, *SME Paper AD77-720*, presented at Autofact I, Detroit.

[16] Gustavson, R. E., (1981). Engineering economics applied to investments in automation. In *Proc. 2nd Int. Cont. on Assembly Automation*, Brighton, UK, May 1981.

KNOWLEDGE-BASED SYSTEMS

14

New research on expert systems

B. G. Buchanan
Computer Science Department
Stanford University, USA

1. INTRODUCTION: WHAT IS AN EXPERT SYSTEM?

All AI programs are essentially reasoning programs. And, to the extent that they reason well about a problem area, all exhibit some expertise at problem solving. Programs that solve the Tower of Hanoi puzzle, for example, reason about the goal state and the initial state in order to find 'expert-level' solutions. Unlike other programs, however, the claims about expert systems are related to questions of usefulness and understandability as well as performance.

We can distinguish expert systems from other AI programs in the following respects:

Utility
Performance
Transparency

Designers of expert systems are motivated to build useful tools in addition to constructing programs that serve as vehicles for AI research. This is reflected in the tasks chosen. Solving the Tower of Hanoi puzzle, *per se*, is not a critical bottleneck in any scientific or engineering enterprise. But integrating mathematical expressions and determining molecular structures are important problems for scientists. Utility is the least important of the three criteria and is perhaps less definitional than a personal bias about whether expertise on trivial matters constitutes expertise at all. In some cases a task is chosen just because of its inherent importance. More often than not, a problem's significance for AI research is also a factor now because expert systems are still constructed by researchers for research purposes.

The hallmark of expert systems is high performance. Using weak methods to perform any useful task requires expertise. And it requires skill on the part of the designer to shape these programs into 'world-class' problem solvers. Thus we see relatively few expert systems, and those we do see include considerable domain-specific knowledge codified over months or years. High performance requires that the programs have not only general facts and principles but the specialized ones that separate human experts from novices. Unfortunately for all of us, specialized expertise, includes almost by definition, knowledge that is *not* codified in print. Thus high performance has to be courted with patience.

In addition to utility and performance, I have added transparency, or understandability, as a third characteristic of expert systems. This separates AI programs from very good numerical algorithms. It is not necessary that expert systems are psychological models of the reasoning of experts. However, they must be understandable to persons familiar with the problem. Statistical pattern recognition programs, for example, perform well on many important problems, but there is little illumination to be gained from rehashing algebraic manipulations of Bayes' Theorem.

2. CURRENT STATE

MYCIN (Shortliffe 1976) represents a prototype of 'Level-1' expert systems in many respects because it was built with the three criteria of utility, performance and transparency among its design goals. In the decade or so before MYCIN, roughly 1965–1975, DENDRAL (Lindsay, *et al.* 1980) and MACSYMA (Moses 1971) were developed as working tools. Other medical AI problems were developed then, most notably PIP (the MIT present illness program) (Pauker, *et al.* 1976). INTERNIST (Pople 1977), and the Rutgers GLAUCOMA program (Weiss *et al.* 1978). And three important organic chemical synthesis programs (Corey & Wipke 1969), (Wipke *et al.* 1977), (Gelernter *et al.* 1977) were demonstrated as well. Several specialized programs were also developed for mathematical and management science problems (Hearn 1971), (Burstall 1966(a)(b)), (Kuhn & Hamberger 1963). These tasks were chosen partly because of the value of their solutions and partly because of the belief that complicated problem areas were more fruitful than 'toy' problems for studying complex reasoning. All of these were initially programmed more as a collection of algorithms and tricks than as a coherent method working with large body of knowledge.

Out of that early work we, the AI community, came to realize that separating domain-specific knowledge from the problem solving methods was important and essential for knowledge base construction and maintenance. With open-ended problems and ill-defined bodies of knowledge, it was obvious that building a knowledge base was more a matter of iteration and refinement than bulk transfer of facts. This was clearly the case in Samuel's checkers program (Samuel 1959) and Greenblatt's chess program, (Greenblatt *et al.* 1967) and became painfully clear early in the work on DENDRAL. Thus a separate and simple representation of the domain-specific knowledge was essential for successfully transferring expertise to a program. (In the case of MACSYMA, virtually all the knowledge is in the methods, so the distinction is not always a sharp one.)

We also saw from this early work that transferring the judgmental knowledge of experts into a program meant representing the concepts and problem solving

270

methods that the experts use. Clever shortcuts and elegant formalities are worthless unless the experts can fit their own knowledge into the framework provided by the designer. Only when a program's vocabulary is 'natural' to experts can they help refine and augment the knowledge base to bring the system's performance up to their own level of expertise.

We also learned that high performance tools will not be used if the interface to them is clumsy. Since we needed a large amount of feedback to refine the knowledge base, we were obliged to pay attention to human engineering issues as well as problem solving issues.

There has been much experimentation with different ways of representing knowledge. Productions had been very successful in Waterman's poker playing and learning programs (Waterman 1970) and had proved easy to manipulate in parts of DENDRAL. They fit the MYCIN problem (Davis *et al.* 1977) well also. But we now realize that almost any uniform encoding of many, nearly-separate items of knowledge would have allowed us to achieve our goals. Almost any knowledge can be represented in almost any formalism; the main issue is how easily the domain knowledge can be codified and maintained.

Work on MYCIN, DENDRAL and other expert systems also showed the value of a simple control structure. It needs to be powerful enough for reasoning about complex problems. But it cannot itself be so complex that the expert cannot predict the effects of adding new items to the knowledge base. DENDRAL's forward chaining, data-directed inference is preferable in this respect to MYCIN's backward chaining, goal-directed inference.

In building useful expert systems, it was also seen to be necessary to consider more of the *whole environment*, in which the program would ultimately be used. High performance is a necessary, but not sufficient, aspect of usefulness. Human engineering issues are important for making the program understandable, for keeping experts interested, for making users feel comfortable. Explanation, help facilities and simple English dialogue thus became important. INTERNIST recently incorporated a display-oriented interface with menu selection, for example, to allow more flexible and natural use by physicians (R. Miller, private communication). Simple, non-heuristic utilities (e.g., Stefik 1978) offer extra capabilities beyond the main focus of the reasoning programs, but are necessary in the total package offered to users. Speed of computation forced rewrites of HEARSAY (Lesser & Erman 1977) to HARPY (Newell 1978) and the DENDRAL hypothesis generator into CONGEN (Carhart *et al.* 1979). The whole environment also was seen to include knowledge acquisition and knowledge base maintenance (Davis 1976).

One of the interesting features of expert systems is their ability to reason under uncertainty. This is essential for reasons of practical utility, since there is no practical application in which the data can be guaranteed to be correct or complete as given. Moreover, in problem areas that are not fully understood we cannot assume that the program's knowledge base is either correct or complete, either in separate entries or as a whole.

271

Sources of uncertainty

missing or erroneous data

missing of erroneous rules

inaccurate model

The basic mechanism we have for coping with uncertainty in expert systems is to exploit redundancy. If there are many redundant items of evidence that support the same conclusion, the absence or incorrectness of a few of them will not seriously impair performance. Similarly, if there are many redundant reasoning paths to the same higher-level conclusion then the incorrectness of any path can be mildly confusing but should not seriously throw the program off track.

Corrections for uncertainty

redundant data

redundant rules

experts' heuristics

cautious strategy

Incomplete information is a particularly pervasive problem in empirical problems. Very often programs halt when items are unknown; frequently, too, they ask the user for the missing items. Some systems try to infer the missing information from available facts and relations. Default values are used, too, either with subsequent validation or without. The defaults may be either fixed globally or dependent on the context, e.g., inherited from a parent node that describes the current context in general terms. It is also possible for a program to guess at a plausible value — using heuristic procedures to fill in a context-dependent value, rather than using a value stated somewhere as a default value. Another way of coping with incomplete information is to do the best one can without it. MYCIN tries to infer a value for each relevant fact (or asks for it) but if the fact remains unknown, it reasons to a 'best guess' solution using the available facts. If too many facts are missing it advises the user that not enough is known about the case to make any reliable conclusions. CONGEN, too, generates all solutions consistent with the available facts, even though there may not be enough known to formulate a unique solution. McCarthy's work on circumscription is a formal approach to these kinds of problems (McCarthy 1980).

Actions available to cope with incomplete information

Stop	Use default
Ask	Guess
Infer	Skip and use available information

PROSPECTOR (Duda *et al.* 1978), INTERNIST, CONGEN and MYCIN, are among the best examples of expert systems whose designs encompassed:

- uniform representation of knowledge,
- conceptually simple control structure,
- consideration of the environment of use.

These were mostly done in the period 1975–1980 and thus can be taken as representative of the state of the art of expert systems.

Expert systems crystallize many issues of AI by forcing attention to high performance, actual use, and transparent lines of reasoning. We do understand a little about choosing problem areas that match the current state of the art. As Feigenbaum has written (Feigenbaum 1977) one of the most critical questions is whether there is an expert available and willing to spend time developing and debugging the knowledge base. Also, the problem should be one which is interesting to the expert (not algorithmic or trivial or already totally understood). At the same time, the problem must be constrained: neither involving an indefinite number of common sense concepts and facts about the world nor involving a very large number of objects and relations in the problem area itself. MYCIN, for example, needs for meningitis about a dozen types of objects (some with multiple instances, such as multiple infections), about 200 attributes associated with those objects, each with 2–100 values (many are yes/no attributes). MYCIN, 'knows' 450 rules that relate sets of object-attribute-value triples and another 500-1000 individual facts stored as definitions (e.g., *E.coli* is Gram-negative), lists (e.g., the list of normally sterile sites), and relations (e.g., the prescribed drug for streptococcal infections is usually penicillin).

The state of the art of expert systems technology is advancing, but to be quite realistic we need to look at existing limitations as well as potential power. The following table lists many characteristics of what can currently be done.

Expert systems: state of the art
- narrow domain of expertise
- limited language for expressing facts and relations
- limiting assumptions about problem and solution methods (help required from a 'knowledge engineer')
- stylized i/o languages
- stylized explanations of line of reasoning
- little knowledge of own scope and limitations
- knowledge base extensible but little help available for initial design decisions
- single expert as 'knowledge czar'

The domain of expertise cannot grow too large because we lack efficient means for building and maintaining large knowledge bases. Thus an expert system cannot now cover more than a narrow slice of a domain. The most notable exception is INTERNIST, for which the knowledge base covers about 500 disease diagnoses or about 80% of internal medicine (H. Pople, private communication). However, this represents a full time commitment for an expert internist, Dr Jack Meyers, and several colleagues and students over a period of over ten years. Also, it represents a strategy to cover internal medicine in more breadth than depth, using a relatively shallow set of associations between disease states and manifestations.

273

The representation languages that are available are still limited. Once a commitment is made to a framework, e.g., a hierarchy of objects, it is inevitable that experts will find relations that are difficult to express in that framework. *Ad hoc* programming removes this difficulty: a clever programmer can find a way to encode anything an expert wants to say. But the loss of uniformity is too high a price to pay for removing the constraint, for an *ad hoc* knowledge base rapidly becomes unmanageable.

Just as an expert needs help understanding the representational framework, he/she also needs help understanding the problem solving methods used by the program. Someone who is familiar with both the program and domain, a so-called 'knowledge engineer', must provide that help.

Input/output languages and interfaces are improving, but most are still stylized and rather inflexible. In Level-1 systems, the emphasis has been more on demonstrating adequacy of the knowledge bases than on acceptability and ease of use. Understanding totally unconstrained English text is not yet possible, even in technical domains (Bonnet 1979).

The explanations, too, are stylized. MYCIN, for example, unwinds its goal stack to explain why it needs a piece of information, and does so in the same way for every user. This offers some insight, but is not always acceptable.

Neither the utility programs for knowledge base construction nor the reasoning programs themselves contain much knowledge about their own assumptions and limitations. They offer little guidance about the appropriateness of new problems or the boundaries of their own expertise. One of the marks of wisdom, Socrates told us repeatedly, was knowing when *not* to claim expertise.

As just mentioned, knowledge bases are constructed laboriously. Several research groups have considered the problem of automating knowledge base construction, or writing routines that carry on a dialogue with an expert to elicit knowledge without help of a knowledge engineer. So far, however, these activities are successful only when the program contains an initial framework to build on.

Although it is desirable to have several experts contributing to a knowledge base, we are currently limited in our ability to maintain consistency among overlapping items. Except for blatant contradictions, the incompatibilities are too subtle for a program to catch, or a knowledge engineer either. So, currently, a single expert must coordinate and monitor the contributions to a knowledge base to insure quality as well as consistency.

In addition to the programs and task areas already mentioned, several others have helped define or extend the concept of expert systems. For example, in the following task areas (and more) expert systems have been constructed and described: computer system configuration (J. McDermott's R1 program), automatic programming (Barstow 1979), physics problems (Novak 1976, Bundy *et al.* 1979), chess (Wilkins 1980), tutoring or ICAI (Brown *et al* 1975, Clancey 1979), software consultation (Genesereth 1978), electronics debugging (Sussman 1975), protein structure determination (Englemore & Terry 1979), signal interpretation (Nii & Feigenbaum 1978), visual scene understanding (Brooks *et al.* 1979).

3. DIRECTIONS OF FUTURE WORK

Much of the new work on expert systems must necessarily be extensions of work on problem solving, controlling search and inference, representing facts and relations about the world, understanding language and visual scenes, and so forth. In fact, all AI research is relevant for constructing and understanding expert systems. Thus the representation and control issues discussed over the last 25 years will continue to recur in expert systems. The Logic Theorist (Newell *et al.* 1957) was presented to the scientific community in 1957; the Advice Taker in 1958, (McCarthy 1963) Samuel's checkers program (Samuel 1959) in 1959; and Minsky's structuring of AI in 1961 (Minsky 1961). These, and other, early papers have not been outdated. The issues remain with us, and insofar as expert systems are constructed by persons whose primary interest is AI, they will continue to provide us with new wrinkles on old problems.

3.1 Representation and Control

In the immediate future, expert systems will be severely constrained until we understand better how to represent and reason with many kinds of concepts, including the following:

Causal models	Conflicts in plans, strategies and
Strategies	methods
Expectations and default knowledge	Multiple sources of expertise
Temporal and spatial continuity	Parallel processing
Plans and approximations	Multiple sources of knowledge
Abstraction and hierarchies	Learning from experience
Analogies (formulating and using)	Focus of attention of facts and
Propositional attitudes and modalities	relations

None of the items in this list represents a shift in emphasis, or anything that would not have been familiar to the participants of the 1956 Dartmouth Conference (Feigenbaum 1979). Many are found in the early papers cited. For each of the issues listed above there has already been substantial work. The point of listing them is to emphasize that much more needs to be done to progress from Level-1 to Level-2 systems. In particular, what are the alternatives available for representing and using these concepts, and under what conditions should we choose one over another? To a very large extent the proof of effective representations of these concepts must lie in their use for high performance problem solving. The concepts are discussed very briefly below.

Causal Models — The best work in casual reasoning has been in systems developed for analysis of small electronic circuits and simple physical devices (e.g., deKleer 1979, Reiger & Grinberg 1977). We have much to learn about exploiting causal models of physical and biological devices and coupling the models with other knowledge.

Strategies — With a cautious problem solving strategy, all relevant, available evidence is used by all relevant inference rules (in a data-driven system). In a

275

'quick and dirty' strategy many facts and inference rules are ignored because they seem less relevant. We want a program's strategy to be sensitive to the problem solving context. And it needs to be represented explicitly and flexibly enough to be scrutinized and modified. Meta-rules in a MYCIN-like system (Davis & Buchanan 1977) are one way to encode strategies, and use them. What alternatives exist? What are the strengths of each?

Expectations and Default Knowledge — In complex or open-ended domains we need to be able to make assumptions about the world rather than express all we know explicitly. Non-monotonic logic (e.g., Doyle 1980) offers one paradigm. Frames can be used to represent what is known about 'typical' members of classes and used to store expectations for comparison with observed data (see Minsky 1975, Aikins 1980).

Temporal Continuity — Reasoning over time requires different representations and mechanisms (e.g., feedback) than static analysis of a situation (see Fagan 1980). Some information decays in certainty or value as it grows older.

Spatial Continuity — Most work on representing 3-dimensional models of objects is done in the context of vision systems in which a representation of a scene is the final goal. Expert systems need to be able to use those representations to reason efficiently about scenes (see Kuipers 1976). When there are thousands or millions of facts like "the leg bone is connected to the ankle bone", a diagram offers great economies.

Plans and Approximations — The planning method in GPS is to solve an approximate, more general, problem than the given one and then use the solution as a guide for constructing the desired solution. In NOAH (Sacerdoti 1974) and MOLGEN (Stefik 1980, Friedland 1980) planning exploits abstraction hierarchies and constraints. Sussman (Sussman 1975) has explored how debugging a plan can lead to a problem solution. Most work on planning has been research done for its own sake. Expert systems need to incorporate those methods and more.

Abstractions and Hierarchies — Many systems represent and use abstractions and hierarchies. But there is little understanding of the strengths and weaknesses of various techniques. For example, different kinds of inheritance in representation languages (Brachman 1977) are available but we don't know which to recommend for a new problem without trying some. Diagrams are abstractions of considerable heuristic value that we do not know how to exploit (see Gelernter 1959).

Analogies — Analogical reasoning is generally regarded as a powerful method for suggesting hypotheses when more constrained generators fail to produce satisfactory ones. Formulating loose analogies is relatively easy but finding those that are useful for a specified purpose is difficult. Using analogies productively is also difficult. Winston's frame-based program finds similarities in stories and situations (Winston 1979); Kling exploited structural similarities between an old and new theorem to suggest an economical set of axioms for a resolution theorem prover to use on the new theorem (Kling 1971).

276

Propositional Attitudes and Modalities – Common-sense reasoning and problem solving in open-ended domains often require inferences about believing, knowing, wanting and other concepts that do not necessarily preserve truth value under substitution of equals for equals (McCarthy 1977). For example, it may be true that John believes Venus is the Evening Star and not true that John believes Venus is the Morning Star (although they are one and the same). It is also necessary to reason with modal operators such as necessity and possibility.

Conflict in Plans, Strategies and Methods – As knowledge bases grow larger and planning becomes more complex, we can expect multiple conflicts in planning and problem solving. Are all methods for resolving conflicts *ad hoc*, domain-dependent rules or are there general principles we can use?

Multiple Sources of Knowledge – The expertise available to an expert system may have to be gathered or stored as separate 'packages', or it may be desirable to do so. The Blackboard model derived from HEARSAY provides one useful framework (Nii & Aiello 1979). Maintaining consistency in the whole knowledge base, or coping with inconsistency during reasoning, are problems that still require solutions when working with many knowledge sources.

Parallel Processing – As tasks increase in complexity and knowledge bases grow in size, expert systems will need to find methods for increasing efficiency. Some problems require distributed control just to avoid the risk of failure of the central processor. Other problems involve inherently parallel subproblems. Distributing the problem solving across many processors is economically feasible but we lack experience in making it work (see Smith 1978, Lesser & Corkill 1978).

Learning from Experience – There has been little progress on methods for improving performance in light of past experience (Buchanan *et al.* 1978). Samuel's work was a *tour de force* that other work has not approached. Any kind of learning still requires special purpose programs. Almost every conceivable expert system can benefit from past experience, at the least from simple records of past successes, and failures.

Focus of Attention on Relevant Facts and Relations – As the breadth of knowledge increases, problem solvers need context-sensitive mechanisms for focussing attention on parts of the problem and parts of the knowledge base that appear most fruitful (Pople 1977). Many methods have been tried but we have little understanding of their relative merits.

In addition to representing and using the general concepts in the above list (and many others besides) future work on expert systems will involve other issues arising more directly from the work on expert systems. Because of the increased emphasis on large knowledge bases, the three issues of explanantion, acquisition, and validation are becoming critical issues for expert systems. While they would not have surprised AI researchers in 1956, their importance seems not to have been fully anticipated. Also, we are beginning to see more interest in experimentation with AI programs. These four topics will be discussed briefly in

277

turn, followed by a short discussion of the difficulty of choosing a framework for problem solving.

3.2 Explanation

Explanation is important for an expert system because users cannot be expected to know or understand the whole program. The users are seeking help from the program because they want advice about their problem and will take some action based partly on that advice. They will be held responsible for the actions, in many cases. Therefore they need to be able to understand the rational basis for the program's decisions.

An important source of explanatory descriptions is a record of what data and hypotheses the reasoning program has considered. Merely keeping a 'laboratory notebook', of sorts, is a first step in making the reasoning transparent (Buchanan 1979). One kind of interactive explanation is simple question answering (Scott *et al.* 1977). But while answering questions about the contents of the knowledge base is necessary, it is not sufficient for giving users the information they need. In complicated cases the difficulty many lie more in *how* the program uses what it knows than in *what* it knows (Swartout 1977). Thus the user needs to be able to understand the line of reasoning.

In the MYCIN example in the appendix, part of the dialogue contains the prompt for information about burns, for which the user might request an explanation. The response to a 'why?' question is MYCIN's reason why a fact is needed to complete the line of reasoning. In effect, X is needed because then I can conclude Y, already having established other facts that are contained with X in a rule. Work on explanations in MYCIN assumes that the user needs to know specific rules in the knowledge base which have been invoked. It does not take into account individual differences in user's qualifications or different purposes for asking a question in the first place. A smarter system that can determine and exploit those differences can provide more helpful explanations. In building a tutor for MYCIN's knowledge base, called GUIDON (Clancey 1979), we found that students needed more than the conditional rules to understand what is going on. They needed some of the causal descriptions that justified the rules in order to make sense of them and remember them. Thus we conclude that a knowledge base capable of producing excellent results may, nonetheless, be less than satisfactory for pedagogy.

3.3 Knowledge Acquisition

Knowledge acquisition has become recognized as an issue with expert systems because it has turned out to be difficult and time consuming, DENDRAL, for example, was originally 'custom-crafted' over many years. Its knowledge of chemistry was carefully moulded from material provided by chemists and then cemented into place. We rewrote large parts of the systems as the knowledge base changed. After doing this a few times we began looking for ways to increase the rate of transfer of chemistry expertise from chemists into the program.

Making procedures highly stylized and dependent on global parameters was a first step, but still required programmers to write new procedures. DENDRAL's knowledge of mass spectrometry was finally codified in production rules.

Once the vocabulary and syntax for the knowledge base are fixed, the process of knowledge acquistion can be speeded considerably by fitting (sometimes forcing) new knowledge into the framework. A programmer, whose title in this role is 'knowledge engineer', is still required to explain the program's framework to the expert and to translate the expert's problem solving knowledge into the framework. This is about as far as we have come in building expert systems.

There have been prototype dialogue programs that communicate with an expert to provide some of the same help that the knowledge engineer provides. One of the most ambitious, to date, is TEIRESIAS (Davis 1976), but even it is limited to helping debug and fill out a knowledge base that has already been largely codified.

Ultimately it would be desirable to have a program learn from nature, as scientists do. As mentioned above, the state of induction programs is not up to widespread use for constructing knowledge bases. However, prototype programs (e.g., Mitchell 1977) again point to future directions for research on expert systems.

An interactive editor that prompts for values of necessary slots is a starting place for a knowledge acquisition system, but it is not the final product. When a 'knowledge engineer' helps an expert, he/she is not passive but:

(1) interprets and integrates the expert's answers to questions;
(2) draws analogies to help the expert structure the domain or remember important aspects of the domain;
(3) poses counter-examples and raises conceptual difficulties.

The most difficult aspect of knowledge acquistion is helping the expert structure the domain initially. Because the knowledge acquisition system has no domain-specific knowledge at the beginning (by definition), the system can only rely on general knowledge about the structure of knowledge bases and specific examples of other knowledge bases as well as what the expert says about the new domain. The knowledge acquisition system has to contain, or have access to, the structure, assumptions, and limitations of the inference mechanism that will use the new knowledge. MYCIN, again, assumes that rules are structured from fact triples, that the rules will be used to infer values of attributes of a primary object, and so forth.

Maintaining a large knowledge base will be every bit as difficult as constructing it in the first place. With problems having no closed solutions, the knowledge base of an expert system should certainly change as experts accumulate more experience and develop new techniques. In medicine, for example, new measuring devices make it possible to detect new states or quantify known parameters more precisely. New microbiological agents are discovered as well as new drugs to treat them.

279

Maintenance may mean actively seeking problems in the knowledge base that need attention. There may be gaps, where some of many possible combinations of conditions are covered, but not all. There may be overlapping items in the knowledge base, leading to inconsistent or reduntant conclusions. Or items may become outdated. An intelligent maintenance system should have both the syntactic and semantic knowledge needed to assign blame to specific items in the knowledge base that appear to be responsible for poor performance and to suggest modifications.

The problems of knowledge base maintenance become more difficult when two or more experts contribute to the knowledge base. In MYCIN, although several physicians contributed, only one physician at any one time made changes. Thus all recommendations for change went to a knowledge base 'czar' who decided how to maintain consistency.

3.4 Validation

Expert systems are beginning to move from the research and development stage into the market place. MACSYMA, DENDRAL and MOLGEN all have serious users who are only loosely coupled to the designers of the programs. Under these circumstances, the developers are expected to provide some objective demonstration that a program performs as well as they claim.

Anyone who has constructed a complex reasoning program knows how difficult it is to anticipate unusual requests and error conditions. We want expert systems to provide assistance in a broad range of unanticipated situations — that is the strength of an AI approach. But we also want to provide assurance to prospective users that the programs will perform well.

Convincing the external community is different from convincing insiders. Insiders can examine code and perform *gedanken* experiments that carry as much weight as statistics. For the external community, however, we need to develop our own equivalents of rat studies and clinical trials for programs, such as those that new drugs are subjected to. Empirical proof is the best we can hope for; sometimes actual use is the most we can point to (Buchanan & Feigenbaum 1978).

MYCIN is one program whose performance has been externally validated. There have been different empirical studies of MYCIN's performance, each simpler than the last but all of them time consuming. In the last of these (Yu *et al.* 1979), we were trying to determine how outside experts compared MYCIN's final conclusions with conclusions of local experts and other physicians. Ten meningitis cases were selected randomly and their descriptions were presented to seven Stanford physicians and one student. We asked them to give their therapy recommendations for each case. Then we collected all recommendations, together with MYCIN's recommendation for each case and the actual therapy, in a 10 X 10 matrix — ten cases each with ten therapy recommendations. We asked a panel of eight experts not at Stanford to give each recommendation a zero if, in his opinion, it was unacceptable for the case and a one if the recommmendation was acceptable. They did not know which, if any, recommendation came from a computer. The results are shown in the following table.

Table — Ratings by 8 experts on 10 meningitis cases perfect score = 80.[†]

Mycin	52	Actual therapy	46
Faculty-1	50	Faculty-4	44
Faculty-2	48	Resident	36
Inf. dis. fellow	48	Faculty-5	34
Faculty-3	46	Student	24

† Unacceptable therapy = 0, equivalent therapy or acceptable alternate = 1.

The differences between MYCIN's score and the scores of the infectious disease experts at Stanford are not significant. But we can claim to have shown that MYCIN's recommendations were viewed by outside experts to be as good as the recommendations of the local experts, and all of those better than the recommendations of physicians (and the student) who are not meningitis experts.

So far, I have reviewed many outstanding problems of expert system work. All of these are motivated in one way or another by the three parts of the definition of expert systems I gave initially:

HIGH PERFORMANCE — obviously requires careful attention to the representation of knowledge, methods of inference and validation that the program does perform well.

UTILITY — requires a large body of knowledge about a problem of signifcant size or difficulty and thus requires careful attention to knowledge acquisition and knowledge base maintenance.

TRANSPARENCY — requires explanation programs using high-level concepts and models familiar to the user. They can tell a user what the program knows, how it uses its knowledge, and why it reasons as it does.

In addition to the problems just discussed, two other outstanding issues are beginning to influence work on expert systems but have had little influence to date. The first issue, or perhaps project, is experimentation with existing AI systems. The second is choosing a problem-solving framework.

3.5 Experimentation

AI is an empirical science, as Newell and Simon have argued convincingly (Newell & Simon 1976). The data we work with are programs; the conclusions we hope to draw from studying them include understanding the phenomenon of intelligent action itself. One reason to construct expert systems is to replace arguments about what computers can do by demonstrations. Physicians, chemists, and mathematicians support our claims that the programs are working on intellectually challenging problems. These and other AI programs constitute data points, sometimes more because of their methods than because of their tasks.

We have generalized from the data presented but we have almost totally ignored the value of controlled experiments. The collection of papers on the GPS experiments (Ernst & Newell 1969), represent the most systematic sets of experiments undertaken in AI. But we must think still more about experimenting with the programs we spend so much time building. At this time we are not even very good at formulating precise questions that can be answered experimentally.

Eventually we will be able to work out a taxonomy of problems and a taxonomy of solution methods. Newell and Simon have taken us farthest in this direction (Newell 1973), but they will undoubtedly agree we still have less than perfect understanding of our discipline. When the taxonomies exist, then we can begin developing criteria that let us determine the best method for a given problem.

Because construction of expert systems and experimentation with them are both very expensive at the moment, we are beginning to see a trend toward design tools for expert systems. These are tools that help a person design and build an expert system within a given framework. By setting up the framework and providing some knowledge engineering help, the design system can speed up the construction, or modification, of an expert system. Such systems can also speed up our experiments with existing systems.

EMYCIN (van Melle 1980) is one such design system that helps a person design and build a MYCIN-like expert system. The name stands for 'essential MYCIN', the MYCIN system without the medical knowledge. It assumes that production rules are an appropriate representation framework for a person's new knowledge base and that a backward-chaining, or goal-directed, interpreter is an appropriate inference mechanism. If a new problem can be set up as a problem of gathering evidence for and against alternative hypotheses that define subgoals for ultimately satisfying the major goal, then EMYCIN is likely to provide some help in constructing an initial prototype expert system to solve the problem.

EMYCIN provides some assistance in structuring a person's knowledge about a problem. This means finding out about the main kinds of objects in the domain and their relationships. What is the primary object about which the expert system should offer advice — a patient, a corporation, an automobile, a computer? What are its parts, and their sub-parts? Also, EMYCIN needs to know about the attributes of those objects and possible values. A computer's manufacturer, a patient's age, a corporation's size, for example are relevant attributes for most problems involving these primary objects. EMYCIN expects that goal hypotheses are stated as finding plausible values for one of more attributes.

After EMYCIN helps a designer build a new knowledge base, and thus a new expert system, it interprets the knowledge base with the inference engine. These two main functions are shown schematically in Fig. 1. In addition, the rules in the knowledge base can also be compiled into a decision tree for more efficient execution.

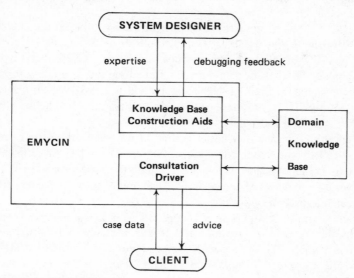

Fig. 1 – The EMYCIN system.

Some of the experimental expert systems developed in EMYCIN are PUFF (see Feigenbaum 1977), SACON (Bennett & Englemore 1979), and consultants for computer system debugging, nutrition, psycho-pharmacology, nervous disorders, and circuit debugging.

Other similar design tools are OPS4 (Forgy & McDermott 1977) at Carnegie-Mellon, Hearsay-III (Balzer *et al.* 1980) at ISI, AGE (Nii & Aiello 1979) at Stanford, EXPERT (Weiss & Kulikowski 1979) written at Rutgers, XPRT (Steels 1979) at MIT, and RITA & ROSIE at RAND (Anderson & Gillogly, 1976). Representation languages such as KRL (Bobrow & Winograd 1977), OWL (Szolovits *et al.* 1977) and the UNITS package (Stefik 1979) have similar motivations of making it convenient to build a new knowledge base, without locking the designer into an interpreter for it.

3.6 Choosing a Framework

The last outstanding issue is the well-known problem of choosing the right framework for solving a problem before searching for a solution (Amarel 1968). Problem solving can be viewed as a two stage process:

- Choose a language, L.
- Select the best solution within L.

We are beginning to understand how to use heuristic methods to find and select solutions to problems within a given problem solving framework. If expert systems can also suggest new frameworks for solving problems, then they will be useful aids for theory construction as well as for hypothesis formation within an existing theory.

When MYCIN gathers evidence for alternative hypotheses, the choices are fixed in advance in the vocabulary of the rule set and object-attribute value triples. When CONGEN generates chemical structures, it describes them in a given vocabulary of labelled, planar graphs. Extending the vocabulary to include some 3-dimensional information has been and still is a task of great magnitude. When META-DENDRAL proposes rules that codify data, it does so within a fixed and very limited vocabulary.

One of the criticisms of sceptics is that AI programs are not yet touching 'real science'. This must be false — otherwise only Galileo, Newton, Einstein and a few others could be called real scientists. But the objection is right in one respect: we do not have AI methods for searching a space of frameworks the way we search a space of hypotheses.

Lenat's program, AM (Lenat 1976), generates new mathematical terms by combining old terms in interesting ways. It is continually expanding its framework, given in the initial concepts of number theory with which it starts. J. S. Brown wrote a concept formation program (Brown 1972), that added new predicates to cover interesting partitions of the data it noticed. The BACON program (Langley 1979) defines new concepts from old ones in order to reduce the combinatorics of its search. Although there is much more to the introduction of new theoretical terms in science, these redefinitions offer considerable savings in reducing the number of terms to consider. The heuristics of when to introduce a new 'macro', in this sense, still needs to be much better understood. Beyond that, though, will be the Level-3 expert systems that can aid scientists by introducing new theoretical terms into existing languages and creating new explanatory languages.

4 CONCLUSION

AI is still very much in the so-called 'natural-history' stages of scientific activity in which specimens are collected, examined, described, and shelved. At some later time a theory will be suggested that unifies many of the phenomena noticed previously and will provide a framework for asking questions. We do not now have a useful theory. The vocabulary that we use to describe existing systems is more uniform and useful that it was a decade ago, however. And the questions that we pose in the context of one program are sometimes answered in another.

Expert systems will provide many more data points for us over the coming years. But it is up to everyone in AI to do controlled experiments, analyze them, and attempt to develop a scientific framework in which we can generalize from examples. At the moment we ourselves lack the vocabulary for successful codification of our own data.

Acknowledgements

This work was supported in part by DARPA contract MDA 903-80-C-0107, NSF grant MCS 7903753 and ONR contract NOOO 14-79-C-0302. The paper is based on an invited lecture at the AISB Summer Workshop, Amsterdam, July, 1980. M. Genesereth, D. Lenat, E. Feigenbaum, and Carroll Johnson provided helpful comments on an early draft. All members of the Heuristic Programming Project at Stanford have contributed to the ideas reported here; my debt to them is substantial. They are also partly responsible for errors in my thinking.

APPENDIX – MYCIN EXAMPLE

1 Overview

Mycin Example

MYCIN (Shortliffe 1974, Davis 1975) is an interactive system designer to offer expert-level medical advice about patients with acute infections. Its overall design is shown in Fig. 2.

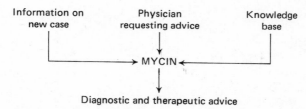

Fig. 2 – Design of the MYCIN system.

MYCIN's knowledge is stored as fact-triples with associate degrees of certainty and as conditional rules relating facts, as shown in the following figures.

Fact Triple:
The X of Y is Z (with CF certainty)

Rule:
IF $FACT_1$ and $FACT_2$ and ..... & $FACT_n$
Then Conclude $FACT_0$

RULE 300

[This rule applies to all cultures and suspected infections, and is tried in order to find about the organisms (other than those seen on cultures or smears) which might be causing the infection]

If: (1) The infection which requires therapy is meningitis, and
    (2) The patient does have evidence of serious skin or soft tissue infection, and
    (3) Organisms were not seen on the stain of the culture, and
    (4) The type of the infection is bacterial

Then: There is evidence that the organisms (other than those seen on cultures or smears) which might be causing the infection is staphylococcus-coag-pos (.75) streptococcus-group-a (.5)

Author: YU

Literature: G. Karalazin "Sickle-cell anemia — CLINICAL MANIFESTATIONS IN 100 PATIENTS" AmJMedSci 269:51 1975.
E. Barret-Connor "Acute pulmonary disease and sickle-cell anemia" ARRD 104:159 Aug 1971.
M. Robinson "Pneumococcal meningitis in sickle-cell anemia" NEJM 274:1006 1966.

2 Infectious Disease Consultation Session

[User's responses follow double asterisks]

          - - - - - - - - PATIENT-538- - - - - - - - -
1) Patient's name:
** PT538
2) Age:
** 34 YEARS
3) Sex:
** MAEL
=MALE
4) Race:
** CAUCASIAN

Please supply one answer under each heading. If your response is not understood, you will be prompted by the standard questioning method. (enter ? for normal prompting, * for questions that are not applicable).

Please enter the results of positive cultures using the following table.

site	culture number	date collected	date| positive	method| of collection [urine, sputum only]

5)**DONE

Please enter the results of pending cultures in the following table.

site	culture number	date collected	stain| examined	method of| collection [urine, sputum only]
6)**CSF	1234	30–Jan–77	YES	*

stain of morph\|
smear
[Type DONE if no organism was seen on the smear]

7)**DONE
.
.
.

[Considering organisms (other than those isolated from cultures) which might be present...]

14) Has Pt538 recently had symptoms of persistent headache or other abnormal neurologic symptoms (dizziness, lethargy, etc.)?
** YES

15) Has Pt538 recently had objective evidence of abnormal neurologic signs (nuchal rigidity, coma, seizures, etc.) documented by physician observation or examination?
** YES

The CSF cultures will be considered to be associated with MENINGITIS.

16) Please give the date on which clinical evidence (symptoms, signs, or laboratory tests) of the meningitis first appeared.
** 29–Jan–77 22:15
.
.
.

19) Does Pt538 have any cutaneous lesions or rash on physical examination?
** NO

20) Does Pt538 have evidence of ocular nerve dysfunction?
** NO

21) Is Pt538 a compromised host (e.g. alcoholic, sickle-cell-disease, immunosuppressed)?
** YES

22) Is Pt538 immunosuppressed (e.g., corticosteroid therapy, cytotoxic drug therapy, radiation therapy, leukemia, lymphoma)?
** NO

23) For how many days has Pt538 had abnormal neurologic signs?
** 7.2 HOURS

24) For how many days has Pt538 had neurologic symptoms?
** 1 DAYS

25) Has Pt538 had recent evidence of tender or enlarged salivary glands?
** NO

26) Has Pt538 been exposed to any contagious disease recently (e.g. meningococcal disease, mumps)?
** NO

Please enter CSF findings in the following table

CSF WBC	Percent PMN	Protein	CSF Glucose	Peripheral| Glucose
27)** 100	99	280	5	UNKNOWN

287

28) Do you know the results of a recent CBC of Pt538?
** YES

Please enter CBC results in the following table

WBC in 1000's	Percent PMN	Percent | BANDS
29)** 1.9	UNKNOWN	UNKNOWN

30) Has Pt538 had any injury or insult to, or defect in the central-nervous-system (excluding neurosurgery)?

** NO

.
.
.

35) Is meningitis a hospital-acquired infection?
** WHY

[i.e. WHY is it important to determine whether the infection was acquired while the patient was hospitalized?]

[2.0] This will aid in determining the organisms (other than those seen on cultures or smears) which might be causing the infection.
It has already been established
[2.1] the infection which requires therapy is meningitis, and
[2.2] organisms were not seen on the stain of this pending csf culture, and
[2.3] the type of the infection is bacterial, and
[2.4] neurosurgery is not one of the relevant items from the history of pt538, and
[2.5] the age of pt538 is greater than 10 days
Therefore, if
[2.6] the infection was acquired while the patient was hospitalized then
there is evidence that the organisms (other than those seen on cultures or smears) which might be causing the infection is *E. coli* (.75) staphylococcus-coag-pos (.3) pseudomonas-aeruginosa (.3) klebsiella-pneumoniae (.5)

Author: Yu
[RULE545]

[back to question 35...]
** HOW 2.3

[i.e. HOW was it established that the type of the infection is bacterial?]

The following rules concluded about:
the likelihood that this type of the infection is bacterial

Rule	Yes	No
[2.7] RULE148		(.19)
[2.8] RULE500		(.51)

288

[2.9]	RULE501	(.95)
[3.0]	RULE502	(.97)
[3.1]	RULE526	(.98)
[3.2]	RULE504	(.97)
[3.3]	RULE524	(.98)

Thus, is has been established that the type of the infection is bacterial.

[back to question 35 ...]
** HOW 2.5

[i.e. HOW was it established that the age of Pt 538 is greater than 10 days?]
In answer to question 2 you said that the age of Pt 538 is 34 years
Thus, it has been established that the age of Pt 538 is greater than 10 days.

[back to question 35 ...]
** Y
.
.
.

39) Is Pt538 a burn patient?
** WHY

[i.e. WHY is it important to determine whether PATIENT-538 has been seriously burned?]

[4.0] This will aid in determining the organisms (other than those seen on cultures or smears) which might be causing the infection.
It has already been established that
[4.1] the infection which requires therapy is meningitis, and
[4.2] organisms were not seen on the stain of this pending csf culture, and
[4.3] the type of the infection is bacterial
Therefore, if
[4.4] Pt538 has been seriously burned
then

there is suggestive evidence (.5) that pseudomonas-aeruginosa is one of the organisms (other than those seen on cultures or smears) which might be causing the infection

Author: Yu
[RULE578]

[back to question 39 ...]
** WHY

[i.e. WHY is it important to determine the organisms (other than those seen on cultures or smears) which might be causing the infection?]

[5.0] ... in order to determine the therapeutic regimen of PATIENT-538.
If

289

[5.1] information has been gathered about organisms isolated from the patient, organisms noted on smears of the patient, negative cultures of the patient, suspected infections without microbiological evidence, current drugs of the patient and prior drugs of the patient, and

[5.2] an attempt has been made to deduce the organisms which require therapy, and

[5.3] You have given consideration to organisms (other than those seen in cultures or smears) which might be present, and found at least one organism which requires therapy.
      then

determine the best therapy recommendation from among the drugs likely to be effective against the significant organisms
    [RULE092]

[back to question 39 ...]
    ** Y

I have found evidence (RULE545 RULE557) that treatment should cover for *E. coli* causing meningitis.

I have found evidence (RULE545 RULE557 RULE578) that treatment should cover for Pseudomonas-aeruginosa causing meningitis.

I have found evidence (RULE545 RULE557) that treatment should cover for Klebsiella-pneumoniae causing meningitis.

I have found evidence (RULE507) that treatment should cover for Diplococcus-pneumoniae causing meningitis.

    40) Does Pt538 have focal neurological signs?
    **   UNKNOWN
    [Determining which drugs are desirable for use against the *E. coli* ...]
    [Determining which drugs are desirable for use against the Pseudomonas-aeruginosa ...]
    [Determining which drugs are desirable for use against the Klebsiella-pneumoniae ...]
    [Determining which drugs are desirable for use against the Diplococcus-pneumoniae ...]

My therapy recommendations will be designed to treat for organisms that either are very likely or, although less likely, would have a significant effect on therapy selection if they were present. It is important to cover for the following probable infection(s) and associated organism(s):

INFECTION-1 is MENINGITIS

    + ⟨ITEM-1⟩ E.COLI [from clinical evidence only]
    + ⟨ITEM-2⟩ PSEUDOMONAS-AERUGINOSA [from clinical evidence only]
    + ⟨ITEM-3⟩ KLEBSIELLA-PNEUMONIAE [from clinical evidence only]
    + ⟨ITEM-4⟩ DIPLOCOCCUS-PNEUMONIAE [from clinical evidence only]

41) Does Pt538 have a clinically significant allergic reaction to any anti-microbial agent?
** NO

[Considering AMPICILLIN-AND-GENTAMICIN for use against INFECTION-1 ...]

42) Do you have reason to suspect that Pt538 may have impaired renal function?
** NO
43) Pt538's weight in kilograms (or ⟨number⟩ POUNDS):
** 70

[REC-1] My preferred therapy recommendation is as follows:

In order to cover for items ⟨1 2 3 4⟩:
Give the following in combination:

1) AMPICILLIN
   Dose: 3.5 g (28.0 ml) q4h IV [Calculated on basis of 50 mg/kg]
2) GENTAMICIN
   Dose: 119 mg (3.0 ml, 80 mg/2 ml ampule) q8h IV [calculated on basis of
        1.7 mg/kg] plus consider giving 5 mg q24h Intrathecal
   Comments: Monitor serum concentrations

Since high concentrations of penicillins can inactivate aminoglycosides, do not mix these two antibiotics in the same IV bottle.

3 Alternatives to First Choice Therapy are Available

Do you wish to see the next choice therapy?
** YES
Which, if any, of the above drugs do you wish eliminated from consideration?
** AMPICILLIN

[Considering GENTAMICIN for use against INFECTION-1 ...]
[Considering PENICILLIN for use against INFECTION-1 ...]

[REC-2] Next best therapy recommendation:
   In order to cover for Items ⟨1 2 3⟩:
   Give: GENTAMICIN
   Dose: 119 mg (3.0 ml, 80 mg/2ml ampule) q8h IV [Calculated on basis of
        1.7 mg/kg] plus consider giving 5 mg q24h Intrathecal
   Comments: Monitor serum concentrations

   In order to cover for Item ⟨4⟩:
   Give: PENICILLIN
   Dose: 3.5 million units (7.0ml) q4h IV [calculated on basis of 50000units/kg]
RECOMMENDATION-2 is equivalent to RECOMMENDATION-1.

291

Would you like to see details of this comparison?
** NO
Do you wish to see the next choice therapy?
** NO

4 Answers to User's Questions about this Consultation and About the Knowledge Base

Please ask any simple-English questions regarding the above consultation session or the overall knowledge of the consultation system. When discussing the consultation above, please refer to organisms, cultures, etc. by their numeric names (e.g., ORGANISM-1). Questions which were asked during the consultation may be specified by the numbers that preceded them above (e.g., 'WHY DID YOU ASK QUESTION 1?'). Control-0 will abort type-out, or 'cancel' the current question. Type HELP for a list of the options available. Enter the word STOP when you have no further questions.

Type HELP for the list of question options.

```
    ** HELP
         QA-OPTIONS:
      (Type ctrl-0 to abort printout)
      ADVICE - prints suggestions for using the QA system effectively
      QT - prints examples of question types recognized by the system
      EQ ⟨numbers⟩ - prints an explanation of the specified
            question(s) from the consultation. e.g., EQ 8 13
      LP ⟨object type⟩ - prints list of attributes associated
            with object type, e.g., LP CULTURE. (Object types are
            patient, infection, culture, organism, and drug.)
      PR ⟨numbers⟩ - prints specified rule(s), e.g., PR 373 49 87 2
      EXPLTHER - prints a short description of the therapy program
      REC - prompts user for alternative therapy RECommendation and
            compares it to mycin's recommendation
      RX ⟨infection⟩ ⟨organism identities⟩ - prints treatment lists for
            specified organisms causing the indicated infection, e.g.,
      RX MENINGITIS ENTEROCCUS
      JUSTIFICATION - when rules are printed out, include their
            justifications
      LITERATURE - when rules are printed out, include their literature
            references
      NOJUST - stop giving justification and/or literature with rules
      TERSE - print rules in terse format
      VERBOSE - turns off terse printing of rules
      STOP - escape from QA-module
      HELP - prints this list
```

** JUSTIFICATION

** LITERATURE

** WHY DID YOU TREAT E.COLI?

ITEM-1 is *E.coli* associated with meningitis. I decided to treat ITEM-1 on the basis of clinical evidence only.

The following rules concluded about:

the likelihood that *E.coli* is one of the organisms (other than those seen on cultures or smears) which might be causing the infection

RULE545 was used to conclude that *E.coli* is one of the organisms (other than those seen on cultures or smears) which might be causing the infection (.74). The last question asked before the conclusion was made was 35.

RULE557 was used to conclude that *E.coli* is one of the organisms (other than those seen on cultures or smears) which might be causing the infection (.93). The last question asked before the conclusion was made was 37.

The parameters most frequently used in these rules were:

the infection which requires therapy
whether a smear of the culture was examined
whether organisms were seen on the stain of the culture
the type of the infection

Would you like a summary of ALL the parameters used by these rules? ** YES

Parameter (rules with this parameter)

the white count from the patient's peripheral CBC (in thousands) (557)
whether the results of a recent CBC of the patient are available (557)
whether the infection was acquired while the patient was hospitalized (545)
the age of the patient (545)
the relevant items from the history of the patient (545)
the type of the infection (545, 557)
whether organisms were seen on the stain of the culture (545, 557)
whether a smear of the culture was examined (545, 557)
the infection which requires therapy (545, 557)

** WHY DIDN'T YOU GIVE TETRACYCLINE FOR E.COLI IN REC-1?

Shall I describe the therapy algorithm for you?** YES

DESCRIPTION OF THERAPY SELECTION

[Type ↑0 to abort printout]

MYCIN is designed to provide optimal therapy recommendations. The program uses the following three steps:

293

The first step ranks the drugs for each organism that requires therapy. Rules for doing this take into account *in vitro* (lab) sensitivities and the patient's response to prior and current therapies. In the absence of other information, default lab sensitivities are used. Preference is given to current therapies if certain criteria are satisfied.

Next, 1 or 2 drugs are selected to cover for the organisms which are most likely to be causing the infection. As many of the 'less likely' organisms as possible are treated, but they are disregard altogether if 3 or more drugs are necessary. Throughout, preference is given to drugs that appear higher in the treatment lists. (These lists can be examined via the RX option.)

Finally, the set of drugs is tested for patient factors that preclude their administration, such as allergies, age, and renal function.

TETRACYCLINE was not prescribed for ITEM-1
TETRACYCLINE was not prescribed for ITEM-1 in
    RECOMMENDATION-1 because:
TETRACYCLINE was discounted for ITEM-1 because there is evidence
    that this *E. coli* is not sensitive to it.

Would you like to see some details?** NO

    ** HOW DO YOU USE THE TYPE OF THE INFECTION?

The following rules are:

    the type of the infection

    154, 578, 574, 572, 570, 565, 564, 559, 557, 553, 551, 549, 547, 545, 543,
    541, 539, 537, 535, 533, 531, 529, 523, 520, 519, 517, 515, 513, 511, 507,
    300, 289, 288, 287, 280, 174, 167

The parameter most frequently concluded by these rules is:

    the organisms (other than those seen on cultures or smears) which might be
    causing the infection

Would you like a summary of ALL the parameters concluded by these rules?
    ** NO
Which of the rules do you wish to see?
    ** 280

RULE280
[This rule applies to all cultures, and is tried in order to find out about the organisms (other than those seen on cultures or smears) which might be causing the infection]

If: 1) The infection which requires therapy is meningitis, and
        2) The type of the infection is fungal, and
        3) Organisms were not seen on the stain of the culture, and

4) The patient is not a compromised host, and

5) The patient has been to an area that is endemic for coccidiomycoses, and

6) The race of the patient is one of: black asian indian, and

7) The cryptococcal antigen in the csf was not positive

Then: There is suggestive evidence (.5) that cryptococcus is not one of the organisms (other than those seen on cultures or smears) which might be causing the infection

Author: YU

Justification: Dark-skinned races, especially Filipino, Asian, and Black (in that order) have an increased susceptibility to coccidiomycoses meningitis.

Literature: Stevens, D. A. *et al.* Miconazole in Coccidiomycosis. *Am J Med,* **60** 191–202, Feb 1976.

** HOW DO YOU TREAT PNEUMOCOCCAL PNEUMONIA

The MYCIN system currently can treat the following infections: BACTEREMIA MENINGITIS CYSTITIS. Because the knowledge base is incomplete, all other infections will be treated like bacteremia.

For treatment of DIPLOCOCCUS-PNEUMONIA in BACTEREMIA
The drugs of choice (ranked by relative efficacy, assuming sensitivity) are:

     1st choice:
PENICILLIN
AMPICILLIN
     2nd choice:
NAFCILLIN
CEPHALOTHIN
ERYTHROMYCIN
CLINDAMYCIN
     3rd choice:
TETRACYCLINE
CHLORAMPHENICOL
VANCOMYCIN
     Duration of therapy: 28 days

** WHAT DOSE OF ERYTHROMYCIN DO YOU RECOMMEND?

When ERYTHROMYCIN is given for BACTEREMIA, the recommended dosage is:

if age is $>$ 12 yrs then 12 mg/kg q6h IV
   else if age is $>$ .08 yrs then 5 mg/kg q6h IV
   else if age is $>$ .02 yrs then 5 mg/kg q12h IV

[Different dosages are recommended for different infections.]

** HOW DO YOU TREAT CYSTITIS

In general, treatment for an infection depends on the causative organism. Please include in your question the organism of interest.

** STOP

REFERENCES

Aikins, J. S. (1980). Prototypes and production rules: a knowledge representation for computer consultation. *Ph.D. Dissertation, Stanford: Computer Science Department*, Stanford University. *STAN-CS-80-814.*

Amarel, S. (1968). On representation of problems of reasoning about actions. *Machine Intelligence 3*, pp. 131–171. (ed. Michie, D.). Edinburgh: Edinburgh University Press.

Anderson, R. H., & Gillogly, J. J. (1976). The Rand Intelligent Terminal (RITA) as a network access aid. *AFIP Proceedings 45*, pp. 501–509.

Balzer, R., Erman, L., London, P. & Williams, C., (1980). HEARSAY–III: A domain independent framework for expert systems. *Proceedings 1980 AAAI Conference*, Stanford.

Barstow, D., (1979). An experiment in knowledge-based automatic programming. *Artificial Intelligence 12*, 73–119.

Bennett, J. & Englemore, R. (1979). SACON: A knowledge-based consultant for structural analysis. *Proceedings IJCAI-79.*

Bobrow, D. & Winograd, T. (1977). An overview of KRL, a Knowledge Representation Language. *Cognitive Science 1*, 3–46.

Bonnet, A. (1979). Understanding medical jargon as if it were a natural language. *Proceedings IJCAI-79*, pp. 79–81.

Brachman, R. J. (1977). Whats in a concept: structural foundations for semantic networks. *International Journal Man-Machine Studies 9*, 127–152.

Brooks, R., Greiner, R., & Binford, T. (1979). The ACRONYM model-based vision system. *Proceedings IJCAI-79*, pp. 105–113.

Brown, J. S. (1972). A symbolic Theory Formation System. PhD Thesis, University of Michigan. *University of California, Irvine Computer Science Department*, Technical Report 017. Also published as Technical Report 017. Dept. Irvine: Computer Science Dept., University of California.

Brown, J. S., Burton R. R. & Bell, A. G. (1975). Sophie: A step towards creating a reactive learning environment. (An example of AI in CAI). *International Journal Man-Machine Studies 7*, 675–696.

Buchanan, B. G. (1979). Issues of representation in conveying the scope and limitations of intelligent assistant programs. *Machine Intelligence 9*, pp. 409–425 (eds. Hayes, J. E., Michie, D., and Mikulich, L. I.). Chichester: Ellis Horwood and New York: Halsted.

Buchanan, B. G., and Feigenbaum, E. A. (1978). DENDRAL and Meta-DENDRAL: their applications dimension. *Artificial Intelligence 11*, 5–24.

Buchanan, B. G., Mitchell, T., Smith R. G., & Johnson, C. R., Jr. (1978). Models of learning systems (1978). *Encyclopeadia of Computer Science and Technology, vol. 11*. (ed. Belzer, J.). New York: Marcel Dekker, Inc.

Bundy, A., Byrd. L., Luger, G., Mellish, C. & Palmer, M. (1979). Solving mechanics problems using meta-level inference (ed. D. Michie). *Expert Systems in the Micro Electronic Age*, pp. 50–64. (ed. Michie, D.). Edinburgh University Press.

Burstall, R. M. (1966). Computer design for electricity supply networks by heuristic methods. *Computer Journal 9.*

Burstall, R. M. A heuristic method for a job scheduling problem. *Operations research Quarterly, 17.*

Carhart, R. E. (1979). Congen: An expert system aiding the structural chemist. In D. Michie (ed.) *Expert Systems in the Micro Electronics Age*, pp. 65–82. Edinburgh: Edinburgh University Press. (ed. Michie, D.).

Clancey, W. (1979). Tutoring rules for guiding a case method dialogue. *International Journal Man-Machine Studies, 11*, 25–49.

Cory, E. J., and Wipke, W. T. (1969). Computer assisted design of complex organic synthesis. *Science, 166*, 178–192.

Davis, R. (1976). Applications of meta-level knowledge to the construction, maintenace and use of large knowledge bases. PhD Thesis, Stanford: Computer Science Department, Stanford University *STAN-CS-76-564.*

Davis, R. and Buchanan, B. G. (1977). Meta-level knowledge: overview and applications. *Proceedings IJCAI-77*, pp. 920–928.

Davis, R., Buchanan, B. G., and Shortliffe, E. H. (1977). Production rules as a representation of a knowledge-based consultation program. Artificial Intelligence, 8, 15–45.

Doyle, J. (1979). A truth maintenance system. *Artificial Intelligence*, 12, 231–272.

Duda, R. O., Gaschnig, J., Hart, P. E., Konolige, K., Reboh, R., Barrett, P., and Slocum, J., (1978). Development of the PROSPECTOR consultation system for mineral exploration. Final Report, *SRI Projects 5821 and 6415.* Menlo Park, California: Artificial Intelligence Center, SRI International.

Englemore, R. S., & Terry, A. (1979). Structure and function of the CRYSALIS system. *Proceedings IJCAI-79*, pp. 250–256.

Erman, L. D. & Lesser, V. R. (1978). Hearsay-II: tutorial introduction and restoration view. CMU-CS-78-117, Pittsburgh: Computer Science Department, Carnegie-Mellon University.

Ernst, G., and Newell, A. (1969). *GPS: A Case Study in Generality and Problem Solving.* New York: Academic Press.

Fagan, L. (1980). VM: Representing Time-Dependent Relations in a Clinical Setting. PhD Thesis Stanford: Computer Science Department, Stanford University.

Feigenbaum, E. A. (1977). The art of artificial intelligence: themes and case studies in knowledge engineering. *Proceedings IJCAI-77*, pp. 1014–1029.

Feigenbaum. E. A. (1979). (Chairman, Panel Discussion) History of artificial intelligence research, 1956–61. *Proceedings IJCAI-79*, pp. 1103–1105.

Forgy, C. & McDermott, J. (1977). OPS, A domain-independent production system language. *Proceedings IJCAI-77*, pp. 933–939.

Frieldland, P. Knowledge-based experiment design in molecular genetics. Ph.D. Thesis. Stanford: Computer Science Department, Stanford University. Also published as STAN-CS-79-771.

Gelernter. H. L. (1959). Realization of a geometry-theorem proving machine. *Proceedings of International Conference on Information Processing*, Paris: UNESCO House, pp. 273–282. Reprinted in Feigenbaum, E. A. and Feldman, J. (eds.), *Computers and Thought.* New York: McGraw-Hill (1963).

Gelernter, H. L., Sanders, A. F., Larsen, D. L., Agarival, K. K., Boivie, R. H., Spritzer, G. A., and Searleman, J. E. (1977). Empirical explorations of SYNCHEM. *Science*, 197, 1041–1049.

Genesereth, M. R. (1978). Automated consultation of complex computer systems. Ph.D. Thesis Harvard University.

Greenblatt, R. B., Eastlake, D., & Crocker, S. (1967). The Greenblatt chess program. *Proceedings 1967 Joint Computer Conference* 30, pp. 801–810.

Hearn, A. (1971). REDUCE 2: A system and language for algebraic manipulation. *Proceedings 2nd Symposium on Symbolic and Algebraic Manipulation*, March pp. 128–133.

de Kleer, J. (1979). Causal and teleological reasoning in circuit recognition. PhD Thesis. Cambridge, Mass: Department of Electrical Engineering and Computer Science MIT. Also published as AI Lab Report TR-529.

Kling, R. E. (1971). A paradigm for reasoning by analogy. *Artificial Intelligence* 2, 147–178.

Kuhn, A., & Hamberger, M. (1963). A Heuristic program for locating warehouses. *Management Science* 9.

Kuipers, B. (1976). Special Knowledge. *AI Lab Memo 359.* Cambridge, Mass: MIT.

Langley, P. (1979). Rediscovering physics with BACON. 3. *Proceedings IJCAI-79*, pp. 502–507.

Lenat, D. (1976). An artificial intelligence approach to discovery in mathematics as heuristic search. PhD Thesis Stanford: Computer Science Department, Stanford University. Also published as *STAN-CS-76-570.*

Lesser, V. R. & Erman, L. D. (1977). A retrospective view of the Hearsay-II architecture. *Proceedings IJCAI-77*, pp. 790–800.

Lesser, V. R. & Corkill, D. (1978). Cooperative distributed problem solving: a new approach for structuring distributed systems. *Technical Report 78-07.* Amherst: University of Massachusetts Computer and Information Science Department.

297

Lindsay, R., Buchanan, B. G., Feigenbaum, E. A., & Lederberg, J. (1980). Applications of Artificial Intelligence for Organic Chemistry: The DENDRAL Project. New York: *McGraw Hill*.

McCarthy, J. (1963). Programs with common sense. *AI Memo AIM-7*, Stanford: Computer Science Department, Stanford University.

McCarthy, J. (1977). Epistemological problems of artificial intelligence. *Proceedings IJCAI-77*, pp. 1038-1044.

McCarthy, J. (1980). Circumscription – A form of non-monotonic reasoning. *Artificial Intelligence 13*, pp. 27-39.

Minsky, M. (1961). Steps toward artificial intelligence. *Proceedings of Institute of Radio Engineers*, 49: 8-30. Reprinted in Feigenbaum, E. A., and Feldman, J. (eds.), *Comters and Thought*. New York: McGraw-Hill, 1963.

Minsky, M. (1975). A framework for representing knowledge. (ed. Winston, P.) *The Psychology of Computer Vision*. New York: McGraw-Hill, 1975.

Mitchell, T. M. (1977). Version spaces: An approach to rule revision during rule induction. *Proceeding IJCAI-77*, pp. 305-310.

Moses, J. (1971). Symbolic integration: The stormy decade. *Communications ACM* 8, 548-560.

Newell, A. (1973). Artificial intelligence and the concept of mind, *Computer Models of Thought and Language* (eds. Schank, R., and Colby, K.). San Francisco: Freeman.

Newell, A. (1978). HARPY: production systems and human cognition. *CMU-CS-78-140*. Pittsburgh: Computer Science Department, Carnegie-Mellon University.

Newell, A., Shaw, J. C., & Simon, H. A. (1957). Empirical explorations with the logic theory machine: A Case History in Heuristics. *Proceedings Western Joint Computer Conference*, 1957, 15:218-239. Reprinted in *Computers and Thought*. (eds. Feigenbaum, E. A. and Feldman, J.). New York: McGraw-Hill, 1963.

Newell, A., Barnett, J., Forgie, J. W., Green, C., Klatt, D., Licklider, J. C. R., Munson, J., Reddy, D. R., & Woods, W. A. 1973. *Speech Understanding Systems: Final Report of a Study Group*. New York: American Elsevier.

Newell, A. & Simon, H. A. (1967). Computer science as empirical inquiry: symbols and search. The 1976 ACM Turing Lecture. *Communications ACM* 19, 113-126.

Nii, H. P. & Aiello, N. (1979). AGE (Attempt to Generalize): A knowledge-based program for building knowledge-based programs. *Proceedings IJCAI-79*, pp. 645-655.

Nii, H. P. & Feigenbaum, E. A. (1978). Rule-Based Understanding of Signals *Pattern-Directed Inference Systems*. (eds. D. Waterman and Hayes-Roth, F.). New York' Academic Press.

Novak, G. (1976). Computer understanding of physics problems stated in natural language. American Journal of Computational Linguistics.

Pauker, S., Gorry, A., Hassirer, J., & Schwartz, W. (1976). Towards the simulation of clinical cognition--taking a present illness by computer. *American Journal of Medicine* 60, 981-996.

Pople, H. E. (1977). The formation of composite hypotheses in diagnostic problem solving – and exercise in synthetic reasoning. *Proceedings IJCAI-77*, 1030-1037.

Rieger, C. & Grinberg, M. (1977). The declarative representation and procedural simulation of causality in physical mechanisms. *Proceedings IJCAI-77*, pp. 250-255.

Sacerdoti, E. D. (1974). Planning in a hierarchy of abstraction spaces. *Artificial Intelligence* 5, 115-135.

Samuel, A. L. (1959). Some studies of machine learning using the game of checkers. *IBM Journal of Research and Development*, 3:211-229. Reprinted in *Computers and Thought*. (eds. Feigenbaum, E. A. and Feldman, J.). New York: *McGraw-Hill*.

Scott, A. C., Clancey, W., Davis, R., & Shortliffe, E. H. (1977). Explanation capabilities of knowledge-based production systems. *American Journal of Computational Linguistics*. Microfiche 62.

Shortliffe, E. H. (1976). *Computer-based medical Consultations: MYCIN*, New York: American Elsevier.

Smith, R. G. (1978). Framework for Problem Solving in a Distributed Processing Environment. Ph.D. Thesis: Stanford: Computer Science Department, Stanford University. Also published as *STAN-CS-78-667*.

Steels, L. (1979). Reasoning Modelled as a Society of Communicating Experts. *Memo, TR 542*. Cambridge, Mass: Al Lab, MIT.

Stefik, M. (1978). Inferring DNA structures from segmentation data. *Artificial Intelligence* 11. 85–114.

Stefik, M. (1979). An examination of a frame structured representation system. *Proceedings IJCAI-79*, pp. 845–852.

Stefik, M. (1980). Planning with constraints. Ph.D. Thesis, Stanford: Computer Science Department, Stanford University. Also published as *STAN-CS-80-784*.

Sussman, G. A. (1975). *A Computer Model of Skill Acquisition.* New York: American Elsevier.

Swartout, W. (1977). A digitalis therapy advisor with explanations. *Proceedings IJCAI-77*, pp. 819–825.

Szolovits, P., Hawkinson, L. B., & Martin, W. A. (1977). An overview of OWL, a language for knowledge representation. *MIT LCS TM 86.*

van Melle, W. (1980). A domain independent system that aids in constructing knowledge based consultation programs. Ph.D. Thesis, Stanford: Computer Science Department, Stanford University. Also published as *STAN-CS-80-820.*

Waterman, D. A. (1970). Generalization learning techniques for automating the learning of heuristics. *Artificial Intelligence,* 1, 121–170.

Weiss, S., and Kulikowski, C. (1979). EXPERT: A system for developing consultation models. *Proceedings IJCAI-79*, 942–947.

Weiss, S., Kulikowski, C., Amarel, S., & Safir, A. (1979). Method for computer-aided medical decision making. *Artificial Intelligence,* 11, 145–172.

Wilkins, D. (1980). Using patterns and plans in chess. *Artificial Intelligence,* 14, 165–203.

Winston, P. H. (1979). Learning and reasoning by anology: the details. *Al Lab Memo 520*, Cambridge, Mass: Artificial Intelligence Laboratory, MIT.

Wipke, W. T., Braun, H., Smith, G., Choplin, F., & Sieber, W. (1977). SECS – simulation and evaluation of chemical synthesis: strategy and planning. *Computer Assisted Organic Synthesis*, pp. 97–127 (eds. Wipke, W. T., and House, W. J.). Washington, D.C.: American Chemical Society, (1977).

Yu, V. L., Fagan, L., Wraith, S. M., Clancey, W. J., Scott, A. C., Hannigan, J., Blum, R., Buchanan, B. G., Cohen, S. N., Davis, R., Aikins, J. S., van Melle, W., Shortliffe, E. H., & Axline, (1979). S. Antimicrobial selection for meningitis by a computerized consultant – A blinded evaluation by infectious disease experts. *Journal American Medical Association* 241.

15

Application of the PROSPECTOR system to geological exploration problems†

J. Gaschnig
Artificial Intelligence Center
SRI International, USA

Abstract

A practical criterion for the success of a knowledge-based problem-solving system is its usefulness as a tool to those working in its specialized domain of expertise. Here we describe several applications of the PROSPECTOR consultation system to mineral exploration tasks. One was a pilot study conducted for the National Uranium Resource Estimate program of the U.S. Department of Energy. This application estimated the favourability of several test regions for occurrence of sandstone uranium deposits. For credibility, the study was preceded by a performance evaluation of the relevant portion of PROSPECTOR's knowledge base, which showed that PROSPECTOR's conclusions agreed very closely with those of the model designer over a broad range of conditions and levels of detail. A similar uranium favourability evaluation of an area in Alaska was performed for the U.S. Geological Survey. Another application involved measuring the value of a geological map. We comment on characteristics of the PROSPECTOR system that are relevant to the issue of inducing geologists to use the system.

1. INTRODUCTION

This paper describes an evaluation and several applications of a knowledge-based system, the PROSPECTOR consultant for mineral exploration. PROSPECTOR is a rule-based judgmental reasoning system that evaluates the mineral potential of a site or region with respect to inference network models of specific classes of ore deposits. Knowledge about a particular type of ore deposit is encoded in a computational model representing observable geological features and the relative significance thereof.

† Any opinions, findings, and conclusion or recommendations expressed in this report are those of the author and do not necessarily reflect the views of the U.S. Geological Survey.
    A shorter version of this paper appeared as (Gaschnig 1980b). Parts of this paper are excerpted from (Gaschnig 1980a).

KNOWLEDGE-BASED SYSTEMS

ASSERTION SPACES:

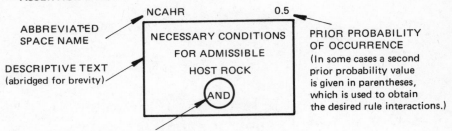

ABBREVIATED
SPACE NAME

DESCRIPTIVE TEXT
(abridged for brevity)

PRIOR PROBABILITY
OF OCCURRENCE
(In some cases a second
prior probability value
is given in parentheses,
which is used to obtain
the desired rule interactions.)

THIS SPACE IS DEFINED
AS A LOGICAL CONJUNCTION

NOTE: If box is dashed rather than solid, then its complete definition
(including subnetwork, if any) appears on another page.

NETWORK LINKS:

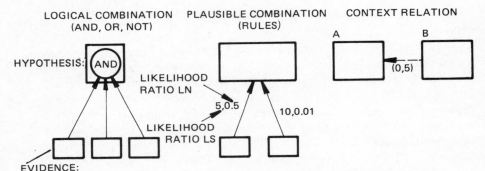

LOGICAL COMBINATION
(AND, OR, NOT)

PLAUSIBLE COMBINATION
(RULES)

CONTEXT RELATION

HYPOTHESIS:

LIKELIHOOD
RATIO LN

LIKELIHOOD
RATIO LS

EVIDENCE:

INTERPRETATION:
In the case of an "AND" connection, all pieces of evidence must be present to establish the hypothesis. In the case of an "OR" connection, the hypothesis is established by any piece of evidence.

INTERPRETATION:
LS measures the degree of sufficiency or suggestiveness of the evidence for establishing the hypothesis. (A larger value of LS means greater sufficiency.) LN measures the degree of necessity of the evidence for establishing the hypothesis. (A smaller value of LN means greater necessity.) The value $LS = 1 (LN = 1)$ indicates that the presence (absence) of the evidence is irrelevant to the hypothesis. For example, if $LS > 1$ and $LN = 1$, then the presence of the evidence is suggestive of the hypothesis; its absence does not lower the probability of the hypothesis.

INTERPRETATION:
Do not attempt to establish space B unless and until space A has been established with certainly greater than zero and less than or equal to 5. Context interval $[-5, 0]$ indicates A must have negative certainty before attempting to establish B. Context interval $[-5, 5]$ indicates simply that one should ask about A (regardless of the answer) before asking about B. Omitted context interval indicates $(0, 5]$.

Fig. 1 — Schematic key to PROSPECTOR model diagrams.

302

The collection of assertations and rules comprising an inference network are easiest to understand when presented in a graphical format. Figure 1 presents a schematic key for interpreting PROSPECTOR model diagrams. Figure 2 depicts the top level of a PROSPECTOR model, called RWSSU, for a class of 'Western States' sandstone uranium deposits. Dashed boxes in that diagram indicate sections of the model that are defined on other pages of the complete diagram.

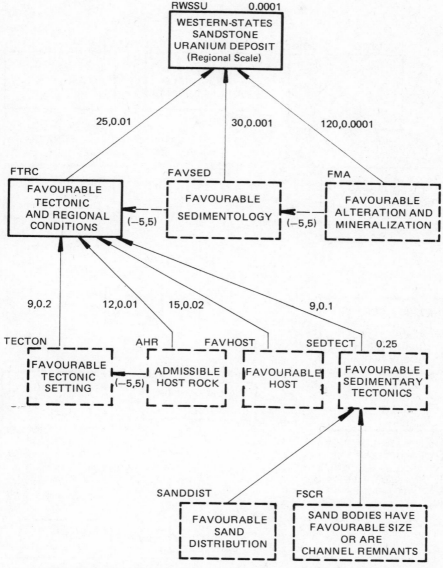

Fig. 2 — Top levels of inference network for regional-scale Western-States sandstone uranium model (RWSSU).

303

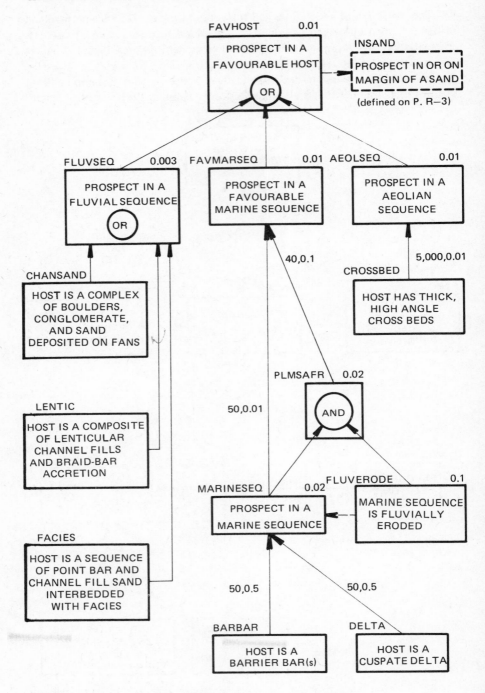

Fig. 3 — A portion of the inference network for the RWSSU model.

For example, Fig. 3 defines the FAVHOST section appearing in a dashed box in in Fig. 2. The complete diagram of the RWSSU model spans 31 pages (Gaschnig 1980a). An overview of the PROSPECTOR system and its inference network methodology is provided in Duda, Gasching, Hart & 1979.

Here we focus on the RWSSU model, and report the results of extensive quantitative tests measuring how faithfully it captures the reasoning of its designer across a set of specific sites (used as case studies in fine-tuning the model), and with respect to the detailed subconclusions of the model as well as its overall conclusions.

Having so validated the performance of the RWSSU model, we then describe a pilot study performed in conjunction with the National Uranium Resource Evaluation (NURE) program of the U.S. Department of Energy. The pilot study applied the RWSSU model to evaluate and compare five target regions, using input data provided by DoE and USGS geologists (using the medium of a model-specific questionnaire generated by PROSPECTOR. The results of the experiment not only rank the test regions, but also measure the sensitivity of the conclusions to more certain or less certain variations in the input data.

One interesting facet of this study is that several geologists provided input data independently about each test region. Since input data about each region varies among the responding geologists, so do the conclusions; we demonstrate how PROSPECTOR is used to identify and resolve the disagreements about input data that are most significantly responsible for differences in the resulting overall conclusions.

The paper concludes with brief descriptions of other recent practical applications of PROSPECTOR.

2. VALIDATING PROSPECTOR MODELS

2.1. Methodology

The practical usefulness of an expert system is limited if those working in its domain of expertise do not or will not use it. Before they will accept and use the system as a working tool, such people (we shall call them the 'domain users') usually expect some evidence that the performance of the system is adequate for their needs (e.g., see Yu *et al.* 1978). Accordingly, considerable effort has been devoted to evaluating the performance of the PROSPECTOR system and its various models (Duda *et al.* 1978, Gaschnig 1979). In the present case, we first needed to validate the performance of the uranium model to be used in the pilot study for the U.S. Department of Energy.

The methodology used to evaluate PROSPECTOR's performance is discussed in detail elsewhere (Duda *et al.* 1978, Gaschnig 1979). For brevity, here we outline a few relevant factors. The PROSPECTOR knowledge base contains a distinct inference network model for each of a number of different classes of ore deposits, and a separate performance evaluation is performed for each model. Here we are concerned with one such model, called the regional-scale 'Western

305

States' sandstone uranium model (RWSSU), designed by Mr R. Rackley. Since there exist no objective quantitative measures of the performance of human geologists against which to compare that of PROSPECTOR, we instead use a relative comparison of the conclusions of a PROSPECTOR model against those of the expert geologist who designed it. To do so, first a number of test regions are chosen, some being exemplars of the model and others having a poor or less good match against the model. For each such case, a questionnaire is completed detailing the observable characteristics that the model requests as inputs for its deliberation. PROSPECTOR evaluates each such data and derives its conclusion for that test case, which is expressed on a scale from —5 to 5. As a basis of comparison, we also independently elicit the model designer's conclusion about each test case, based on the same input data, and expressed on the same — 5 to 5 scale. Then we compare PROSPECTOR's predictions against the target values provided by the model designer.

2.2. Comparing PROSPECTOR with the Expert

Table 1 compares the top-level conclusions of PROSPECTOR (using the RWSSU model) against the corresponding target values provided by the model designer for eight test regions.

Table 1 — Comparison of RWSSU model with designer for eight cases.

Test region	Target value	Prospector score	Difference
Black Hills	3.50	4.33	—0.83
Crooks Gap	4.70	4.26	0.44
Gas Hills	4.90	4.37	0.53
Shirley Basin	4.95	4.13	0.82
Ambrosia Lake	5.00	4.39	0.61
Southern Powder River	4.40	4.40	0.00
Fox Hills	1.50	2.17	—0.67
Oil Mountain	1.70	3.32	—1.62

Table 1 indicates that the average difference between the PROSPECTOR score and the corresponding target value for these eight cases is 0.69, which is 6.9% of the —5 to 5 scale.

One feature of the PROSPECTOR system is the ability to explain its conclusions at any desired level of detail. Besides the overall conclusions reported above, quite detailed information about PROSPECTOR's conclusions was collected for each test case. In its normal interactive mode, the user can interrogate PROSPECTOR's conclusions by indicating which conclusions or subconclusions he wishes to see more information about. The same sort of information is presented in Table 2 (using the Gas Hills region as an example), in the form of PROSPECTOR's overall evaluation, the major conclusions on which the overall evaluation is based, and the subconclusions that support each major conclusion. For brevity, each section of the RWSSU model represented in Table 2 is identified by a symbolic name, which is indented to show its place in the hierarchy of the model. A key describing each symbolic name follows Table 2. For comparison, we first elicited from the model designer his target values for each section of the model listed in Table 2; these values are included in Table 2.

Table 2 — Detailed comparison of RWSSU model with designer for Gas Hills region.

Section of model	Target value	Prospector score	Difference
RWSSU	4.90	4.37	0.53
FTRC	4.80	4.64	0.16
TECTON	4.50	4.50	0.00
AHR	5.00	4.95	0.05
FAVHOST	4.80	5.00	−0.20
SEDTECT	4.80	4.88	−0.08
FAVSED	4.90	4.68	0.22
FLUVSED	4.90	4.68	0.22
MARINESED	−3.50	−2.07	−1.43
AEOLSED	−2.50	−2.10	−0.40
FMA	4.95	4.41	0.54
RBZONE	5.00	4.60	0.40
AIZONE	4.00	4.77	−0.77
MINZONE	5.00	5.00	0.00

Average difference = 0.36 (average of absolute values).

Key to assertion names:

RWSSU:	the region is favourable for 'Western States' sandstone uranium deposits
FTRC:	there are favourable tectonic and regional conditions
TECTON:	the prospect lies in a favourable tectonic setting
AHR:	there is admissible host rock
FAVHOST:	the prospect is in a favourable host
FSCR:	the sand bodies are of favourable size or are channel remnants

FAVSED:	there is a favourable sedimentology
FLUVSED:	there is a favourable fluvial sedimentology
MARINESED:	there is a favourble marine sedimentology
AEOLSED:	there is favourable aeolian sedimentology
FMA:	there are favourable mineralization and alteration
RBZONE:	there is a favourable remote barren zone
AIZONE:	there is a favourable altered interior zone
MINZONE:	there are indications of a possible mineralized zone

The data in Table 2 indicate that PROSPECTOR not only reaches essentially the same numerical conclusions as its designer, but does so for similar reasons.

The type of detailed comparison shown in Table 2 was repeated for each of the eight test cases listed in Table 1, resulting in 112 distinct comparisons between PROSPECTOR's prediction and designer's target value (i.e., 8 test regions times 14 sections of the model). Table 3 shows the results. Each column in Table 3 corresponds to the column labeled "Difference" in Table 2. The letters A through H in Table 3 identify the eight test cases in accordance with the key immediately following this table. Hence the data in Table 3 under column C is taken from Table 2.

As indicated by the datum in the lower right corner of Table 3, the grand average of the RWSSU model's error in predicting Mr Rackley's conclusions across the 112 combinations of 8 test regions and 14 major sections of the model is 0.70, which represents 7.0% of the −5 to 5 scale.

The rightmost column in Table 3 lists the averages over the eight test regions for each of the 14 major sections of the RWSSU model. Hence this column ranks these model sections according to their predictive abilities. This information suggests a priority ordering for the future revisions of the model, in that those sections having the largest average error (e.g., MARINESED, MINZONE, and so on) are the ones that could benefit most by further fine-tuning. By comparing these values in Table 3 with the analogous averages in a table corresponding to a revised model, one can measure quantitatively the extent to which the revisions achieved the objectives that motivated them. In point of fact, the fine-tuning of the RWSSU model to its current status was based on just such a feedback process.

2.3 Sensitivity Analysis

The user's certainty about inputs provided to PROSPECTOR are expressed on −5 to 5 scale (as opposed to simply 'yes' or 'no', for example). Hence PROSPECTOR's conclusions depend on the degree of certainty of its inputs. To measure the sensitivity of conclusions to perturbations in the certainties of the inputs, we make two additional executions of PROSPECTOR for each set of input data. In one case we change each of the user's input certainties by one unit closer to zero, so that, for example, a 4 becomes 3 and a −3 becomes −2. In the other

Table 3 – Differences between target value and PROSPECTOR score (RWSSU model, 8 regions, 14 sections of the model).

Test regions:	A	B	C	D	E	F	G	H	Avg.
RWSSU	-0.83	0.44	0.53	0.82	0.61	-0.00	-0.67	-1.62	0.69
FTRC	-0.85	-0.04	0.16	0.16	0.33	-1.14	1.00	-1.60	0.53
TECTON	0.10	0.00	0.00	0.00	0.10	0.00	-0.01	0.04	0.03
AHR	-1.65	-0.45	0.05	-0.20	-0.05	-0.64	0.94	0.12	0.51
FAVHOST	-1.50	-0.50	-0.20	-0.50	0.00	-0.50	0.90	-2.00	0.76
SEDTECT	-1.10	-0.26	-0.08	-0.28	-0.06	-0.35	-0.50	-1.57	0.52
FAVSED	-0.88	0.12	0.22	0.08	-0.05	-0.84	-3.67	-2.23	1.01
FLUVSED	-0.88	0.12	0.22	0.08	-0.05	-0.84	-3.59	-2.23	1.00
MARINESED	0.76	0.49	-1.43	-0.08	-0.75	-2.83	-0.17	2.10	1.07
AEOLSED	0.15	0.23	-0.40	-0.61	0.26	-1.29	-0.64	0.44	0.50
FMA	-0.85	0.86	0.54	1.91	0.20	0.05	-0.23	0.11	0.59
RBZONE	-0.84	-0.29	0.40	0.11	-0.31	-0.05	0.69	-3.01	0.71
AIZONE	-0.78	0.66	-0.77	1.94	-0.24	-0.23	0.36	1.50	0.81
MINZONE	-2.00	-0.40	0.00	-0.10	-0.50	-0.40	-3.20	-1.73	1.04
Average:	0.94	0.35	0.36	0.49	0.25	0.58	1.18	1.45	0.70

(Note: averages are averages of absolute values).

Key to test regions:
A = Black Hills   D = Shirley Basin   G = Oil Mountain
B = Crooks Gap   E = Ambrosia Lake   H = Fox Hills
C = Gas Hills   F = Powder River

309

case, each input certainty is changed by one unit toward 5 or −5, e.g., −3 becomes −4. These 'less certain' and 'more certain' variants of the original input data set are then run through PROSPECTOR, so that the resulting conclusions can then be compared with those obtained from the original 'standard' data set, as illustrated in Table 4. In Table 4 'maximum difference' denotes the larger of the two differences between standard and less certain conclusions on the one hand, and standard and more certain conclusions on the other.

Table 4 − Standard, 'more certain', and 'less certain' conclusions (RWSSU model, overall conclusions, 8 test regions).

	Less certain	Standard	More certain	Maximum difference
Black Hills	4.20	4.33	4.37	0.13
Crooks Gap	4.12	4.26	4.25	0.14
Gas Hills	4.30	4.37	4.40	0.07
Shirley Basin	3.99	4.13	4.13	0.14
Ambrosia Lake	4.32	4.39	4.40	0.07
Southern Powder River	4.36	4.40	4.42	0.04
Fox Hills	1.78	2.17	2.23	0.39
Oil Mountain	1.90	3.32	3.49	1.42

Average: 0.12

Of the eight test regions compared, the data in Table 4 indicate that Oil Mountain is the most sensitive to more certain or less certain changes in input certainties. The other seven cases are very stable in this respect. As indicated at the bottom of Table 4, there is an average 1.2% change in conclusions in response to a 10% change in input certainties (i.e., one unit of certainty over a 10-point scale).

Besides the overall conclusions reported in Table 4, quite detailed information was collected for each individual test region. Inspection of detailed sensitivity conclusions for various sections of the model reveals the source of the sensitivity reflected in the overall conclusions represented in Table 4.

We shall present one example in detail below, for the case of Oil Mountain, for which sensitivity about overall conclusions in relatively large. For the cited case, Table 5 compares PROSPECTOR's standard, 'more certain,' and 'less certain' conclusions for each of the 14 major sections of the RWSSU model that were detailed in Table 2 and 3. (See the key following Table 2 to identify the geological assertations corresponding to the symbolic names of these sections.)

The data in Table 5 concerning Oil Mountain reveal that the sensitivity of the overall conclusion (maximum difference of 1.42) is due to the various sensitivities of the FTRC, FAVSED, and FMA sections (maximum difference 62, 1.08,

Table 5 — Detailed standard, "more certain", and "less certain" runs (RWSSU model, Oil Mountain region, 14 sections of the model).

	Less certain	Standard	More certain	Maximum difference
RWSSU	1.90	3.32	3.49	1.42
FTRC	3.23	3.85	3.66	0.62
TECTON	3.05	3.81	3.81	0.76
AHR	1.04	1.28	0.96	0.32
FAVHOST	3.99	5.00	5.00	1.01
SEDTECT	4.32	4.57	4.58	0.25
FAVSED	3.15	4.23	4.42	1.08
FLUVSED	3.15	4.23	4.42	1.08
MARINESED	−0.27	−3.10	−4.22	2.83
AEOLSED	−3.28	−4.44	−3.76	1.16
FMA	0.78	1.64	1.93	0.86
RBZONE	3.98	4.51	4.73	0.53
AIZONE	−1.59	0.00	0.08	1.59
MINZONE	1.45	3.23	3.82	1.78

Average: 1.09

and 0.86, respectively). To illustrate a deeper level of analysis, within the FMA section the data in Table 5 indicate that the mineralized zone section displays highest sensitivity (1.78), followed by the altered interior zone section (1.59), and finally by remote barren zone (which is rather stable in this case — maximum difference = 0.53). Hence, this sort of analysis can pinpoint the section(s) of a model most sensitive to uniform changes in certainty of input data. For most of the sections, there is little change from standard to 'more certain' data, since a large fraction of the standard inputs already expressed near or complete certainty. Note also that for several sections of the model (FTRC, AHR, MARINESED) the 'more certain' score in Table 5 is actually less than the corresponding standard score. These cases reflect a negative effect produced by LS or LN values (discussed in Fig. 1) that is larger than the positive effect of those values greater than 1.

2.4 Comparison of the WSSU, RWSSU, and EDSU Models

Two other sandstone uranium models were also subjected to performance evaluations analogous to those described above for the RWSSU model. Details of these experiments with the prospect-scale 'Western States' sandstone uranium model (WSSU) and the epigenetic carbonaceous sandstone uranium model (ECSU) are given in Gaschnig 1980a. Below we summarize some of the results concerning the RWSSU, WSSU, and ECSU models.

First we shall compare the sizes of these three models. As described previously, a PROSPECTOR model is represented as a network of assertions and the rules of geological inference that connect them. Hence, the size or complexity of a model can be measured in a simple way by the number of assertions and rules it contains. Two types of assertions can be distinguished: those concerning directly observable field evidence, and others concerning higher-level conclusions that can be inferred from such field evidence. Table 6 summarizes these statistics for the WSSU, RWSSU, and ECSU models.

Table 6 — Size statistics for the PROSPECTOR uranium models.

Model	Designer	Number of evidence assertions	Total number of assertions	Number of rules
WSSU	R. Rackley	105	200	148
RWSSU	R. Rackley	107	205	152
ECSU	S. Adams	109	197	153
Total:		321	602	453

As enumerated in Table 6, these three models are of comparable size. Other recently developed PROSPECTOR models are of the same approximate size as the present models (see Table 1 in Duda *et al.* 1979).

Table 7 compares the performance of three uranium models.

The numbers in Table 7 are derived as follows. The total number of PROSPECTOR runs per model (item 2) is three times the number of test sites or regions (item 1), because a 'standard,' 'more certain,' and 'less certain' run were performed for each completed questionnaire. The number given in item 3a is derived from Table 1 for the RWSSU model, and from analogous data for the WSSU and ECSU models. The numbers given in item 3b are derived from Table 3 for the RWSSU model, and from analogous data for the WSSU and ECSU models. Similarly, the numbers in item 4 are derived from Table 4 in the case of the RWSSU model. The number given in item 6 is the product of the number of test sites or regions (item 1) and the number of detailed sections of the model for which target values were obtained from the model designer (item 5): 8 × 12 = 112 for the WSSU and RWSSU models; 9 × 19 = 171 for the ECSU model. This product is the number of data points averaged to obtain the numbers in item 3b. Note that the values in items 3 and 4 in Table 7 are expressed as percentages of our 10-point certainty scale used to express PROSPECTOR conclusions. The fourth column in Table 7 gives the total of the other three columns for items 1, 2, 5, and 6; it gives the average of the other three columns for items 3 and 4.

Inspection of the data in Table 7 reveals that the three models have excellent average performance both in overall conclusions and in detailed subconclusions.

312

Table 7 – Comparative performance of the WSSU, RWSSU, and ECSU models.

	WSSU	RWSSU	ECSU	Total/average
1. Number of test sites or regions:	8	8	9	25
2. Total number of PROSPECTOR runs:	24	24	27	75
3. Average difference between PROSPECTOR score and model designer's target value ...				
(a) for overall conclusions:	6.6%	6.9%	8.0%	7.2%
(b) for detailed conclusions:	7.2%	7.0%	7.8%	7.3%
4. Average sensitivity of overall conclusions to unit change of certainty in input data:	2.2%	1.2%	4.0%	2.5%
5. Number of sections of model represented by detailed conclusions:	14	14	19	47
6. Total number of comparisons for detailed conclusions:	112	112	171	395

Specifically, the difference between PROSPECTOR score and corresponding model designer's target value averages to a 7.3% difference on a 10-point scale in the case of overall conclusions, and to 7.4% difference in the case of detailed conclusions. Each of the three models has low average sensitivity to fluctuations in the certainty ascribed to the field observations on which the tests are based, averaging 2.5% difference from the 'standard' case for overall conclusions. Finally, the differences in performance levels of the three models are small. One should note, however, that the performances of the WSSU and RWSSU models are slightly better than that of the ECSU model, reflecting the fact that the former models have been subjected to somewhat more tuning and testing than the latter. Additional tuning of the ECSU model could be expected to result in improved performance.

3. A PILOT STUDY FOR DOE's NATIONAL URANIUM RESOURCE EVALUATION

3.1. Overall Results

Having established the credibility of the RWSSU model by the test results just discussed, we then undertook an evaluation of five test regions selected by the Department of Energy. For this purpose USGS and DoE geologists completed questionnaires for this model. As a sensitivity test, several geologists independently completed questionnaires for each test region. For comparison, the model

Table 8 – Overall conclusions about five test regions in NURE pilot study.

Geologist	A	B	C	D	USGS team	Rackley data	Average	Range
Monument Hill	4.17	3.32	3.97			4.40	3.97	1.08
Pumpkin Buttes	4.20	3.30	4.19			4.40	4.02	1.10
Moorcroft			3.92	3.88, 4.00		4.00	3.95	0.12
Northwest Gillette			3.64			3.42	2.39	3.54
White River				0.10	0.13	0.01	0.07	0.12

314

designer, R. Rackley, also completed questionnaires for five test regions. The overall results are reported in Table 8[†].

The results in Table 8 indicate that the Monument Hill, Pumpkin Buttes, and Moorecroft regions are very favourable, and about equally favourable, for occurrence of 'Western States' sandstone uranium deposits. Northwest Gillete is scored as moderately favourable, whereas White River is neutral (balanced positive and negative indicators).

Note that each respondent has had different exposure to the target regions, in terms of both first-hand, on-site experience and familiarity with field data reported in the literature. These difficulties in experience are reflected in their answers on the questionnaires. Since different inputs yield different conclusions, one would expect a spread in the certainties about each region, reflecting the differences in input data provided by the various geologists. Inspection of Table 8 reveals that the scores derived from different geologists' input data about the same region agree rather closely for each region except Northwest Gillette (see the column labelled "Range"). These generally close agreements reflect the capability of PROSPECTOR models to synthesize many diverse factors, mechanically ascertaining general commonalities without being unduly distracted by occasional disparities.

In cases such as Northwest Gillette in which a large difference in conclusions occurs, it is easy to trace the source of the disagreement by comparing the individual conclusions for different sections of the model (representing different geological subconclusions), as in Table 9.

Table 9 — Comparison of detailed conclusions about Northwest Gillette region.

Geologist	C	D	Rackley	Average
RWSSU	0.10	3.66	3.42	3.56
FTRC	4.67	3.80	4.63	4.37
TECTON	4.90	4.50	4.50	4.63
AHR	4.95	1.03	4.94	3.64
FAVHOST	5.00	5.00	5.00	5.00
SEDTECT	4.98	4.33	4.78	4.69
FAVSED	0.04	3.92	4.79	2.92
FLUVSED	0.04	3.92	4.79	2.92
MARINESED	−4.60	3.34	0.02	−0.41
AEOLSED	−4.99	−2.10	−3.23	−3.44
FMA	0.27	2.45	1.33	2.18
RBZONE	4.10	4.83	4.73	4.55
AIZONE	−3.29	2.40	0.00	−0.30
MINZONE	0.41	2.82	2.59	1.94

† Note that geologist 'D' divided the Moorcroft region into two subregions and completed a questionnaire for each, resulting in two conclusions (3.88 and 4.00 in Table 8).

Inspection of Table 9 reveals that the conclusions agree fairly closely for the FTRC section of the model, and less closely for the FAVSED and FMA sections. Tracing the differences deeper, one sees that of the three factors on which FMA depends, there is fairly good agreement about RBZONE, but larger differences in the cases of the AIZONE and MINZONE sections. In some cases, such a detailed analysis can isolate the source of overall disagreement to a few key questions about which the respondents disagreed. These can then be resolved by the respondents without the need to be concerned with other disagreements in their questionnaire inputs that did not significantly affect the overall conclusions.

3.2. Sensitivity Analysis

Table 10 lists PROSPECTOR's overall conclusions about the five test regions, comparing standard, 'more certain,' and 'less certain' interpretations of the questionnaire input data, analogous to those described earlier in validating the RWSSU model. (The standard results are the same as those in Table 8.) The column labelled 'Maximum difference' in Table 10 is the maximum of the difference between the standard and 'less certain' scores on the one hand, and between the 'more certain' and standard scores on the other. Hence this column gives the maximum sensitivity for each case.

Table 10 — Standard, 'more certain', and 'less certain' runs (RWSSU model, overall conclusions, five test regions).

Site	Geologist	Less certain	Standard	More certain	Maximum difference
Monument Hill:	A	4.02	4.17	4.20	0.15
	B	3.70	3.32	3.34	0.38
	C	4.21	3.97	3.88	0.24
	Rackley	4.32	4.40	4.41	0.08
Pumpkin Buttes:	A	4.09	4.20	4.22	0.11
	B	3.69	3.30	3.31	0.39
	C	4.13	4.19	4.22	0.06
	Rackley	4.34	4.40	4.41	0.06
Moorcroft:	C	3.72	3.92	3.97	0.20
	D	3.81	3.88	3.87	0.07
	D	3.94	4.00	4.01	0.06
	Rackley	3.71	4.00	4.24	0.29
Northwest Gillette:	C	3.26	3.64	3.94	0.38
	D	0.91	0.54	0.89	0.37
	Rackley	2.99	3.42	3.63	0.43
White River:	USGS team	0.34	0.13	0.07	0.21
	Rackley	0.13	0.01	0.00	0.12

Average: 0.21

The data in Table 10 indicate very stable performance in each case tested, averaging 2.1% difference on the ten-point certainty scale.

Besides the overall conclusions reported in Table 10, quite detailed information was collected for each individual run. We shall present one example in detail below, for the case of geologist A's data about Monument Hill. For the cited case, Table 11 compares PROSPECTOR's standard, 'more certain,' and 'less certain' conclusions for each of the 14 major sections of the RWSSU model that were detailed in previous tables.

Table 11 – Detailed standard, 'more certain', and 'less certain' runs (RWSSU model, Monument Hill region, Geologist A).

Section of model	Less certain	Standard	More certain	Maximum difference
RWSSU	4.02	4.17	4.20	0.15
FTRC	4.02	4.43	4.57	0.41
TECTON	3.60	4.50	4.50	0.90
AHR	4.89	4.93	4.95	0.04
FAVHOST	1.97	2.98	3.99	1.01
SEDTECT	4.36	4.79	4.94	0.43
FAVSED	4.22	4.56	4.66	0.34
FLUVSED	4.22	4.56	4.66	0.34
MARINESED	0.02	−2.39	−3.65	2.37
AEOLSED	0.38	0.14	0.12	0.24
FMA	3.30	3.42	3.41	0.12
RBZONE	4.57	4.74	4.84	0.17
AIZONE	3.28	3.41	3.40	0.13
MINZONE	4.66	4.84	4.86	0.18

Average: 0.49.

The 'maximum difference' column in Table 11 identifies three sections of the model exhibiting significantly greater sensitivity than the other sections for Monument Hill, namely, TECTON, FAVHOST, and MARINESED. The sensitivity of MARINESED is irrelevant in this case, since the sedimentology (FAVSED) is clearly established as fluvial (FLUVSED) rather than marine. The sensitivities of TECTON and FAVHOST are reflected in the somewhat smaller sensitivity of FTRC, which, in turn, contributes to a small sensitivity in the overall conclusion. Hence, senstivities propagate upward through the model, but the impact of a single sensitive section of the model is usually diluted when combined with other more stable factors. This is a salient consequence of the hierarchical structure of PROSPECTOR models. In any case, this kind of analysis can pinpoint the section(s) of a model most sensitive to uniform changes in certainty of input data.

3.3. Conclusions

This pilot study for DoE's NURE project has attempted to demonstrate the methodological features of the PROSPECTOR approach for problems of resource assessment. The numerical data tabulated in the preceding subsection, along with complete analogue sets of tables in (Gaschnig 1980a), provided extensive evidence addressing a variety of questions:

— Measuring the faithfulness of the RWSSU model to its designer's reasoning across several regions and across several major sections of the model.
— Ranking the test regions.
— Determining the range in certainties for each region, reflecting different geologists' input data.
— Determining whether agreement about a region extends from overall conclusions to detailed subconclusions as well.
— Pinpointing the source of disagreement about input data that resulted in any disagreements in overall conclusions about a region.
— Measuring the sensitivity of conclusions to 'more certain' or 'less certain' variations in each individual's input data.

Table 12 highlights many of these results.

Table 12 — Summary of results of the DONE NURE pilot study.

	Results/Remarks
1. Average difference between PROSPECTOR score and model designer's target value ...	
(a) for overall conclusions:	7.5% over 5 regions
(b) for detailed conclusions:	9.2% over 70 combinations of 5 regions and 14 sections of model
2. Ranking test regions: (Table 8)	Very favourable — Monument Hill Pumpkin Buttes Moorcroft Moderately favourable — Northwest Gillette No match — White River
3. Variability of conclusions about each region, reflecting different geologists' input data: (Table 8; see also Table 9)	Negligible — Moorcroft White River Small — Monument Hill Pumpkin Buttes Large — Northwest Gillette
4. Average sensitivity to unit change in certainty of input data: (Table 10; see also Table 11)	2.1% over 17 questionnaires about 5 regions

In sum, we have performed a precise, step-by-step evaluation of five target regions, beginning with an independent detailed assessment of the accuracy of the RWSSU model in predicting its designer's reasoning; we then scored each region in accordance with the input data provided by several geologists; we further examined the numerical results in detail to determine their sensitivity to a variety of factors; finally we demonstrated how the PROSPECTOR approach allows one routinely to identify and resolve disagreements in conclusions resulting from differences in input data provided by different geologists.

This evidence demonstrates clearly and extensively the usefulness of PROS-PECTOR not only for evaluating regional mineral potential, but also for actually quantifying the credibility and stability of its conclusions. Given the variabilities and uncertainties inherent in the task of resource assessment, the PROSPECTOR methodology introduces a powerful new tool by which to obtain assessments significantly more objective, repeatable, uniform, self-calibrating, detailed, and open to public inspection (hence defendable), than those presently available using other methods.

4. A LAND USE STUDY IN ALASKA

PROSPECTOR has also been applied to several other tasks, which we mention heré briefly. In one case, PROSPECTOR was used to evaluate several regions on the Alaskan Peninsula for uranium potential (Cox, Detra, and Detterman 1980). In this case the practical issue was to evaluate the mineral potential of Federal lands for the purpose of deciding their ultimate disposition (e.g., wilderness status versus commercial exploitation). As in the NURE study, geologists familiar with the locales completed questionnaires corresponding to two PROSPECTOR models representing different types of uranium deposits; the questionnaire data were processed by PROSPECTOR, resulting in evaluations that included several levels of geological detail. Table 13 shows the results. (See the key following Table 2 to identify the geological assertions corresponding to the symbolic names of the various sections of the model listed at the left in Table 13.)

Inspection of Table 13 shows that the three formations exhibit mild to moderate favourability for this type of deposit. Looking into the three major categories of evidence underlying these evaluations, we see that all three for-mations are moderately to very favourable with respect to two of the factors (namely, FTRC – tectonic and regional conditions; and FAVSED – sedimen-tology). However, none of the three formations offers more than a very weak match against the third major category, namely FMA – favourable mineralization and alteration. By inspecting the three factors underlying the latter (namely RBZONE, AIZONE, and MINZONE), it turns out that the three formations offer essentially no match with respect to the most dominant of the three factors, namely MINZONE – a favourable mineralized zone. In sum, Table 13 shows the three regions tested have environments generally favourable for the type of deposit being assessed, but do not satisfy the key requirement of having a good mineralized zone.

319

Table 13 — Uranium favourability of three areas is Alaska (using the RWSSU model).

Section of model	Chignick formation	Tolstoi formation	Bear Lake formation
RWSSU	2.91	2.28	1.06
FTRC	3.59	4.01	4.32
TECTON	3.81	3.81	3.81
AHR	1.09	1.66	4.53
FAVHOST	4.73	5.00	3.99
SEDTECT	4.04	4.51	3.57
FAVSED	4.81	4.68	3.64
FLUVSED	4.81	4.68	3.64
MARINESED	3.74	0.04	−1.08
AEOLSED	2.27	0.05	−4.90
FMA	1.08	0.58	0.19
RBZONE	4.62	4.47	1.99
AIZONE	3.19	1.64	0.00
MINZONE	0.41	0.41	0.25

To provide evidence concerning the sensitivity of these results to the uncertainties and omissions of the field observations on which the results are based, this study also included 'more certain' and 'less certain' runs analogous to those described earlier. In doing so we demonstrated that the results are rather insensitive to unit perturbations in the certainties of the questionnaire input data. In short, small perturbations of the inputs produced smaller perturbations of the outputs.

One interesting facet of this study was that one of the USGS geologists charged with evaluating these regions was not himself an expert about uranium deposits. By using PROSPECTOR, these geologists, in effect, augmented their own experience with the judgment of a noted authority on the specilized types of deposits being considered. Hence, this is another case in which specialized geological expertise has been disseminated to where it was needed.

5. AN EXPERIMENT MEASURING THE VALUE OF A MAP

A somewhat different application of PROSPECTOR was concerned with measuring quantitively the economic value of a geological map (Shapiro & Watson 1979). The USGS expends great time, effort, and money in creating maps detailing the geological characteristics of various geographical districts. The question naturally arises as to whether the benefits obtained from using such maps justify their cost. In an attempt to answer the question quantitatively, the USGS conducted an experiment using a porphyry copper model of the PROSPECTOR system.

Ten sites were selected, five of which were known to contain a deposit matching the characteristics of the specified model; the remaining five sites were known to be barren. Three different maps were available for each site: one at a scale of 1:24,000; another at 1:250,000; and a third at a scale of 1:1,000,000. Two geologists were selected to provide input data to PROSPECTOR about each test site, based only on information contained on the corresponding maps they were provided. For each site, the designated geologist completed three copies of the PROSPECTOR questionnaire for the copper model, each copy corresponding to a different scale map. Using the completed questionnaire as input, PROS-PECTOR assigned three sets of scores to each test site, one for each scale map.

These results were used to determine how well PROSPECTOR distinguished the sites containing deposits from the barren sites, as measured by the Spearman Rank Correlation Coefficient. In the case of the 1:24,000 maps, PROSPECTOR's predictions obtained a correlation of 0.73 (on a −1 to 1 scale), which was statistically significant at the 5% confidence level (even though the sample size was small). Statistical significance was not obtained in the case of the smaller scale maps, indicating either that these maps contain insufficient information to evaluate the test regions, or alternatively, that the sample size was too small to obtain significance in these cases. To distinguish the latter two possibilities, an extension of this study to an additional 20 sites is now in progress.

6. OTHER APPLICATIONS IN PROGRESS

Since the completion of the NURE pilot study, the U.S. Geological Survey and the Department of Energy have funded additional evaluations similar to the NURE and Alaska tests. One project will extend the NURE pilot study to additonal regions selected by DoE. Another will score the relative merits of a dozen areas in the San Jaun Basin, New Mexico, for possible occurrence of epigenetic carbonaceous sandstone uranium deposits, for which a PROSPECTOR model (called ECSU) is available.

PROSPECTOR has also made its first prediction about the location of an as yet undiscovered ore body. For this purpose we used a drilling site selection model developed for porphyry molybdenum deposits. Whereas the prospect-scale and regional-scale models discussed previously are intended to provide an overall evaluation of a prospect-sized property or a larger region, PROSPECTOR's drilling site selection models are intended to pinpoint exact spots where an ore body will be found. Toward this end, an area is overlaid with a grid of cells (typically 128 × 128), so that each cell represents an area about 30 meters square. Using graphic input data obtained by digitizing features from a geological map, PROSPECTOR evaluates each cell in the grid, using an efficient network compiler to speed the evaluation process (Duda *et al.* 1978, Konolige 1979). Each of the 16 384 resulting cell scores is colour-coded, and then the entire map is displayed on a colour graphic display, so that the brightest areas are most favourable for drilling. To test their accuracy, the drilling site selection models have been subjected to a number of *a posteriori* tests, using areas where ore deposits have already been discovered and mined, but using maps from an early stage of exploration for the purpose of the test. In these tests of a porphyry copper drilling site selection model (Duda *et al.* 1978), PROSPECTOR's predictions agreed very closely with the outline of the known orebody. Since mining companies sometimes drill dozens or hundreds of holes for every commercially viable deposit discovered, the potential of accurate 'first-hole' predictions is very great. Accordingly, we were encouraged to develop another drilling-site selection model, for porphyry molybdenum deposits (Duda, 1980). This model has been used to predict the possible occurrence of a deposit in a relatively unexplored area of the Mount Tolman region in Washington State. These results which were published in Duda 1980, are currently being evaluated as further exploration data are becoming available.

Another type of evaluation of PROSPECTOR is now being planned, namely a 'peer review' workshop. Each of the experts who designed PROSPECTOR models will present his model to a group of geologists who are also knowledgeable about that type of deposit. The object is to elicit comments and criticisms (and perhaps a consensus) among the geologists present about the model under discussion. While it is rather common for geologists to disagree among each other to certain degrees, an advantage of the PROSPECTOR approach is that the geologists attending the upcoming workshop will be focussing on very precisely stated issues (e.g., this factor in the model or that rule strength value). Our hope is that the PROSPECTOR methodology will contribute to the increased codification of economic geology.

7. DISCUSSION

We have measured PROSPECTOR's expertise explicitly and found that its detailed conclusions match those of the expert who designed it, to within about 7% on a 10-point certainty scale used as a basis for comparison. Having so validated the models, we presented results of several applications to practical tasks for the USGS and DoE. In so doing, we demonstrated in particular how the PROSPECTOR approach deals effectively with the variabilities and uncertainties inherent in the task of resource assessment (i.e., by sensitivity analysis).

This work illustrates that expert systems intended for actual practical use must accommodate the special characteristics of the domain of expertise. In the case of economic geology, it is not rare for field geologists to disagree to some extent about their field observations at a given site. Accordingly, the use of various sorts of sensitivity analysis is stressed in PROSPECTOR to bound the impact of such disagreements and to isolate their sources. In so doing, we provide geologists with new quantitative techniques by which to address an important issue, thus adding to the attractiveness of PROSPECTOR as a working tool.

Other domains of expertise will have their own peculiarities, which must be accommodated by designers of expert systems for those domains. A more mundane, but nevertheless practically important, example concerns the use of a questionnaire as a medium for obtaining input data to PROSPECTOR from geologists. Most geologists have little or no experience with computers; furthermore, acess to a central computer from a remote site may be problematic in practice. On the other hand, geologists seem to be quite comfortable with questionnaires. Our point is simply that issues ancillary to artificial intelligence usually have to be addressed to ensure the practical success of knowledge-based systems.

REFERENCES

Cox, D. P., Detra, D. E., & Detterman, R. L., (1980). Mineral Resources of the Chignik and Sutwick Island Quadrangles, Alaska, U.S. Geological Survey Map MF-1053K, (in review).

Duda, R. O., Hart, P. E., Barrett, P., Gaschnig, J., Konolige, K., Reboh, R., and Slocum, J., (1978). Development of the PROSPECTOR consultation system for mineral exploration, *Final Report, SRI Projects 5821 and 6415*, Menlo Park: Artificial Intelligence Center, SRI International.

Duda, R. O., Gaschnig, J. G., and Hart, P. E., (1979). Model design in the PROSPECTOR consultant system for mineral exploration, *Expert Systems in the Microelectronic Age*, pp. 153–168 (ed. Michie, D.). Edinburgh: Edinburgh University Press.

Duda, R. O., Hart, P. E., Konolige, K., & Reboh, R., (1979). A computer-based consultant for mineral exploration, *Final Report, SRI Project, 6415*, Menlo Park: Artificial Intelligence Center, SRI International.

Duda, R. O., (1980). The PROSPECTOR system for mineral exploration, *Final Report, SRI Project 8172*, Menlo Park: Artificial Intelligence Center, SRI International.

Gaschnig, J. G., (1979). Preliminary performance analysis of the PROSPECTOR consultant system for mineral exploration, *Proc. Sixth International Joint Conference on Artificial Intelligence*, (Tokyo), pp. 308–310.

Gaschnig, J. G., (1980a). Development of uranium exploration models for the PROSPECTOR consultant system, *SRI Project 7856*, Menlo Park: Artificial Intelligence Center, SRI International.

Gaschnig, J. G., (1980b). An application of the PROSPECTOR system to DoE's national uranium resource evaluation, *Proceedings of the First Annual Conference of the American Association for Artificial Intelligence*, pp. 295–297.

Konolige, K., (1979). An inference net compiler for the PROSPECTOR rule-based consultation system, *Proc. Sixth Intl. Joint Conference on Artificial Intelligence.* (Tokyo), pp. 487–489.

National Uranium Resource Evaluation, (1979). Interim Report, *Report GJO-111(79)*, Grand Junction, Colorado: U.S. Department of Energy, June.

Roach, C. H., (1979). Overview of NURE Progress Fiscal Year 1979, *Preprint of Proceedings of the Uranium Industry Seminar*, Grand Junction, Colorado: U.S. Department of Energy October 16–17.

Shapiro, C., & Watson, W. (1979). An Interim Report on the Value of Geological Maps, Preliminary Draft Report, Director's Office, U.S. Geological Survey, Reston, Virginia.

Yu, V. L., *et al.*, (1978). Evaluating the performance of a computer-based consultant, *Memo HPP-78-17*, Stanford: Heuristic Progamming Project, Dept. of Computer Science, Stanford University.

323

16

XSEL: a computer sales person's assistant

J. McDermott
Carnegie-Mellon University
Pittsburgh, USA

Abstract

R1, a knowledge-based configurer of VAX-11 computer systems, began to be used over a year ago by Digital Equipment Corporation's manufacturing organization. The success of this program and the existence at DEC of a newly formed group capable of supporting knowledge-based programs has led other groups at DEC to support the development of programs that can be used in conjunction with R1. This paper describes XSEL, a program being developed at Carnegie-Mellon University that will assist salespeople in tailoring computer systems to fit the needs of customers. XSEL will have two kinds of expertise: it will know how to select hardware and software components that fulfil the requirements of particular sets of applications, and it will know how to provide satisfying explanations in the computer system sales domain.

Introduction

The world is filled with tasks that can be performed satisfactory only by those who have acquired, through apprenticeship, the bodies of knowledge relevant to these tasks. In designing programs to perform these tasks, the AI community has had to face the issue of how to represent large amounts of ill-structured knowledge in a way that enables relevant knowledge to be quickly brought to bear. The software tools that have been developed for this purpose are quite different from the tools developed for use in well-structured domains; in particular, they are intended to be used to implement continuously evolving programs. Since only a handful of people are familiar with any of these tools, and since the programs they can be used to implement acquire expertise only with use, the tools are currently under-utilized. One approach to this technology transfer problem is for people familiar with the tools to develop programs that have some expertise in various industrial domains, plant the programs in those domains, and let those who need the programs acquire familiarity with the tools by using (and continuing to develop) the programs.

325

This is essentially the strategy that Carnegie-Mellon University and DEC adopted, and it appears to be working well. In December 1978, work was begun at CMU on R1 (McDermott 1980a, 1980b) a program that configures VAX-11 computer systems. In less than a year, R1 had been developed to a point where it could be used on a regular basis by DEC's manufacturing organization to configure VAX-11/780 systems. At that time, DEC established a group responsible for the maintenance and continued development of R1. During 1980, the group grew to include 12 people; it now consists of a manager, 5 people proficient in OPS5 (the production system language in which R1 is written), 3 people responsible for ensuring that R1's database (a set of descriptions of hardware and software components) is accurate and up to date, and 3 people responsible for developing processes to facilitate R1's use and to aid in extracting configuration knowledge from experts. Over the course of the year, CMU provided considerable technical assistance to this group. The group is now essentially self-sufficient; that is, it needs no assistance from CMU in maintaining and extending R1. In the Fall of 1980, the group implemented a version of R1 that can configure VAX-11/750 systems; almost all VAX systems built within the United States are now configured by these programs.

Though DEC now has the expertise required to continue the development of R1 and plans to extend R1's capabilities so that it will be able to configure PDP-11 systems, it is not yet quite at the point where it could embark on the development of knowledge-based programs that perform quite different tasks. Yet there is a need at DEC for such programs. In particular, R1 performs only the component organization part of what could be called the computer system configuration design task. The configuration design task has two parts:

- Component selection: the set of components that are both necessary and sufficient to satisfy the requirements imposed by a set of applications must be selected.
- Component organization: the set of components selected must be organized to form a system that satisfies the requirements imposed by the set of applications.

A program that could perform the component selection part of the task would be extremely valuable. Thus DEC has asked CMU to develop such a program.

In the next section, R1's capabilities will be briefly reviewed. Then in section 2, XSEL, the program being developed to perform the component selection part of the configuration design task, will be described. Though XSEL is still in the initial stages of development, it has become apparent that the recognition-driven approach to problem-solving that characterizes R1 can also be the principal approach used by XSEL. The fact that two tasks of a significantly different nature are both amenable to a recognition-driven approach suggests that there may be a wide range of tasks for which this approach is appropriate. The final section will discuss XSEL's explanation capability. Because some of the people with whom XSEL will interact will have only a limited understanding of configuration design issues, it is important that XSEL be able to answer a wide range of questions in a simple and straightforward fashion.

1. R1's ROLE IN CONFIGURATION DESIGN

R1 takes a set of components as input and produces diagrams showing what the spatial relationships among the components should be. Though it knows almost nothing about the subtask of selecting a set of components to satisfy a functional specification, it does understand that certain components, in order to be configured, may require other components. If the set of components it is given is incomplete in this sense, it adds whatever components are required to make the set configurable. R1 has a relatively large amount of knowledge that enables it to recognize the acceptable ways in which components can be associated under various conditions. It uses this knowledge to construct a single configuration that satisfies all of the organizational constraints. Because its knowledge is sufficient to enable it to recognize what to do next at each step, it performs this task with almost no search; that is, it seldom needs to backtrack.

R1 is implemented in OPS5, a general-purpose, rule-based language (Forgy 1980, Forgy 1977) OPS5 provides a rule memory, a global working memory, and an interpreter that tests the rules to determine which ones are satisfied by a set of the descriptions in working memory. A rule is an IF–THEN statement consisting of a set of conditions (patterns that can be matched by the descriptions in working memory) and a set of actions that modify working memory. On each cycle, the interpreter selects one of the satisfied rules and applies it. Since applying a rule results in changes to working memory, different subsets of rules are satisifed on successive cycles. OPS5 does not impose any organization on rule memory; all rules are evaluated on every cycle. It often turns out to be convenient, however, to be able to restrict the set of rules that can fire on any given cycle to those that bear on the task currently being performed; this can be accomplished by including in each rule a condition element that specifies the context (subtask) in which the rule is relevant.

In implementing R1, OPS5's two memories were augmented with a third. This memory, the data base, contains descriptions of each of the more than 750 components currently supported for the VAX-11. Each database entry consists of the name of a component and a set of 18 or so attribute/value pairs that indicate the properties of the component which are relevant for the configuration task. As R1 begins to configure an order, it retrieves the relevant component descriptions. As the configuration is generated, working memory grows to contain descriptions of partial configurations, results of various computations, and context symbols that identify the current subtask.

Production memory contains all of R1's knowledge of how to configure VAX-11 systems. R1 currently has about 850 rules that enable it to perform the task. These rules can be viewed as state transitions operators. The conditional part of each rule describes features that a state must possess in order for the rule to be applied. The action part of the rule indicates what features of the state have to be modified or what features have to be added in order for a new state that is on the solution path to be generated. Each rule is a more or less autonomous piece of knowledge that watches for a state that it recognizes to be generated. Whenever that happens it can effect a state transition. If all goes well, this new state will, in turn, be recognized by one or more rules; one of these rules will effect a state transition, and so on until the system is configured. An English translation of a sample rule is shown in Fig. 1.

```
ASSIGN-UB-MODULES-EXCEPT-THOSE-CONNECTING-TO-PANELS-4

   IF: THE MOST CURRENT ACTIVE CONTEXT IS ASSIGNING DEVICES TO UNIBUS MODULES
       AND THERE IS AN UNASSIGNED DUAL PORT DISK DRIVE
       AND THE TYPE OF CONTROLLER IT REQUIRES IS KNOWN
       AND THERE ARE TWO SUCH CONTROLLERS
                NEITHER OF WHICH HAS ANY DEVICES ASSIGNED TO IT
       AND THE NUMBER OF DEVICES THAT THESE CONTROLLERS CAN SUPPORT IS KNOWN
 THEN: ASSIGN THE DISK DRIVE TO EACH OF THE CONTROLLERS
       AND NOTE THAT THE TWO CONTROLLERS HAVE BEEN ASSOCIATED
                AND THAT EACH SUPPORTS ONE DEVICE
```

Fig. 1 – A sample rule.

Though R1 performs its task adequately, it is a less valuable tool than it might be because it lacks certain pieces of information. The only information that is currently made available to R1 is the set of components ordered. Since R1 has no knowledge of the physical characteristics of the room or rooms in which the system is to be housed, it cannot produce a realistic floor-layout even though it has the capability to do so; this means that it cannot determine the precise lengths of cable required to connect some pairs of components. Moreover, R1 has no access to information that would enable it to determine whether the intended uses of a system imply unusual configuration constraints; thus the configuration that R1 produces is not necessarily the one that provides the customer with the best performance for his particular set of applications.[†]

2. XSEL's ROLE IN CONFIGURATION DESIGN

XSEL's role complements R1's. XSEL's task is to select the set of components that satisfy the requirements imposed by a set of applications. It then informs R1 of its selections and provides any additional information R1 will need in order to tailor its configuration to those applications. It is important to note that one of R1's capabilities makes XSEL's task considerably easier than it would otherwise be. Much of the problem of component selection is that salespeople, in addition to having to select components directly relevant to the intended uses of a system, also have to be concerned with 'support' components (e.g., back-

† The most recent extension to R1 is a capability that enables it to accept as part of its input a set of *ad hoc* (customer-specific) constraints; in producing a configuration, R1 gives preference to these constraints over the ordinary-case constraints encoded in its rules (McDermott 1981).

planes, boxes, panels, cabinets, cables, etc). Since part of R1's task is to make sure that all such support components are included on the order and to add them if they are not, there is no need for XSEL to concern itself with support components at all. Thus the component selection problem reduces to the problem of selecting just that set of components that would normally be included in a system's functional specification.

2.1. The humble role

XSEL in its current state is little more than a front end for R1. It allows a user to specify a cpu, some amount of primary memory, whatever software is desired, and whatever devices are desired (e.g., disk drives, tape drives, terminals, printers, etc.); this skeletal order is then passed to R1 to be fleshed out and configured. The interaction with the user actually has three stages:

(1) The user is asked a few standard questions: his name, the order identification number, etc.
(2) The user is asked what components he wants to order.
(3) The user is asked for information required by R1 in order to do floor-layout and is asked to indicate any special configuration constraints that the intended uses of the system imply.

The first stage is simple and straightforward; the second and third stages are somewhat more interesting.

When asked what components he wants to order, the user may, if he wishes, enter the names (and quantities) of the components he wants; XSEL then performs a few simple consistency checks to make sure that the components ordered are compatible and goes on to the third phase. Since DEC's naming conventions are somewhat confusing, even to the initiated, the user may specify the components he wants by 'subtype' rather than by name. DEC's names for components all have the form xxxxx-yy; the first five characters indicate the subtype and the final two characters indicate the variation. Typically a subtype will have anywhere from four to eight variations. Partly as a matter of convenience and partly to avoid the errors that frequently crop up because an incorrect variation has been specified, the user may elect to specify some or all of the components by subtype. If so, XSEL will ask a few questions to determine which variation the user wants.

The user may specify some types of components in terms of total capability desired, rather than by name or subtype. Currently, primary and secondary memory can be ordered by specifying megabytes desired, and printers can be ordered by specifying total printing capability desired in lines per minute. In order to handle this type of specification, XSEL does need some knowledge of how to select among subtypes. Since specification in terms of capability does not ordinarily narrow the set of possibilities to the variations of just one subtype, XSEL must have criteria that enable it to make reasonable choices. Currently XSEL has a few rules that enable it to avoid obviously poor choices; it will

329

need a significant amount of additional knowledge before its choices will be consistently adequate.

Once the user has specified the components he wants, XSEL goes on to the third stage. Here, XSEL asks the user a number of questions about the room or rooms in which his system will be housed. It asks for the dimensions of the rooms and the positions of doorways and obstructions. If the user wishes, he may then specify how he wants some or all of the components on the order to be positioned; he may specify the precise location of components or may indicate the approximate locations of various groups of components. After the user has provided as much floor layout information as he wants, he is given the opportunity to enter other configuration information. He can specify how devices are to be distributed among controllers, the type of length of cable to be used to connect a pair of devices, the positions of controllers on buses, and the positions of backplanes in boxes or of boxes and panels in cabinets. XSEL then passes to R1 the set of components ordered and any other information the user entered.

Much of the knowledge that the initial version of XSEL requires is not domain-specific, but is rather knowledge of how to lead a user through a selection process. And the relatively small amount of configuration design knowledge required is primarily knowledge of the task's structure. Given the penchant of many knowledge engineers for building special-purpose 'engines' (ordinarily in LISP) to contain knowledge of this sort, it is worth indicating why all of XSEL's knowledge is represented in the form of rules. There are several reasons:

- It is important that a user be able to take as much or as little advantage of XSEL's expertise as he wants at any point during an interaction; we suspect that this flexibility will be easier to achieve if all of XSEL's knowledge is uniformly represented.
- The domain knowledge that XSEL currently has provides a base that will support more specific knowledge of how to perform the component selection task; it is important that this base knowledge be neither more nor less privileged than the knowledge that will be added.
- In order to construct explanations that focus attention on the most significant steps in its decision-making process, a program needs to be able to examine that process.

In the remainder of the paper, the strategy for developing XSEL's expertise in the domains of configuration design and computer system sales explanation will be discussed. Although the knowledge that XSEL currently has in these domains is extremely limited, the structure needed to support a large amount of much more specific knowledge appears to be in place.

2.2 A more exalted role

A considerable amount of knowledge is required for the configuration design task because there is no small set of general principles that can be used as the basis of component selection. A customer is often not completely sure of the uses to which he will put his computer system, and even when he is, may have little idea of how much functionality each use requires. The best he can do is provide indirect measures of the requirements of each of his intended applications. Thus an expert must know what sorts of data to collect and what can be inferred from that data. Furthermore, each intended use is independent from the point of view of functionality required; that is, knowing how to infer the resources required for one application does not get one very far in inferring the resources required for a different application. Finally, there are ordinarily a number of different combinations of components that supply essentially the same functionality; the differences among these sets of components are usually quite small, but some may be better suited to the particular needs of the customer than others.

Though a significant amount of knowledge is required in order to perform the component selection task adequately, all of this knowledge is relevant to one of the following three subtasks:

- Decide whether a particular component type is necessary for one or more of the intended applications.
- If some type of component is needed, select from among the subtypes available that subtype which best fulfils the need.
- If a subtype has been selected, select from among the variations available that variation which best fulfils the need.

The most striking characteristic of these subtasks is that for all three the decisions to be made are relatively independent both of prior and of subsequent decisions; thus the tasks are fundamentally recognition tasks. The task of determining whether a particular type of component is necessary for some application involves little more than determining whether the conditions that signal the need for that component type are satisfied by the application. The task of selecting a particular subtype or variation involves little more than determining which of the competing sets of conditions that signal the need for the possible alternatives are satisfied by the application. It is of course true that in order for the component selection task to be performed by recognition, all of the relevant information about each intended application must be known. But this is just another recognition task — the task of recognizing what questions must be asked before a selection can be made.

Though there are a few complicating factors that will be discussed below, the fact that the component selection task can be recognition driven makes XSEL conceptually quite simple. Given a user who wants assistance in selecting a set of components, XSEL first finds out what general classes of applications he has in mind. Each of these applications will suggest some number of component types as possibly necessary. Given a set of applications and a possibly necessary component type, a set of questions will suggest themselves; the user's answers to these questions will enable XSEL to recognize whether or not a component of that type is necessary. Once a component type is determined to be necessary, additional questions will suggest themselves; the user's answers to these questions will enable XSEL to recognize which subtype (and then which variation) best satisfies the requirements imposed by the applications. Though XSEL's knowledge of how to do component selection is currently quite limited, it should be clear that adding knowledge presents few problems. Each of XSEL's component selection rules recognizes a particular need in the context of a particular application; rules are almost completely independent of one another, and thus modifying or adding rules has no hidden implications.

How difficult it is to recognize that a particular component type is required for a particular application depends on the nature of the application. When an application always requires the functionality provided by some particular type of component, all that is needed to ensure that that type of component will be ordered is a rule that associates the application with the component type. If the application requires that type of component only under certain conditions, then several rules may be necessary, each of which recognizes one set of conditions. When several applications all require the same component type, it is necessary to distinguish cases in which the component can be shared from those in which a separate component is required for each application.

Before a subtype of a required component type can be selected, the total capacity that must be provided by the component type must be known. This is trivial when the capacity of a component type is fixed (e.g., a FORTRAN compiler, a floating point accelerator). But in cases of component types with variable capacity, XSEL must perform a computation. Each of its rules that associates an application with a variable capacity component type also represents the form of the required computation and specifies what information has to be extracted from the user in order for the computation to be performed. This knowledge is represented as a set of elements that collectively define the computation. Each of these elements describes the operation that must be performed to find the value of one of the terms in the computation; for the primitive terms, the operation is to ask the user. Once the user supplies the information requested of him, the total capacity needed is computed. Since many of XSEL's computations rely on some pieces of information from the user, it is important that the computations be able to share information. Thus, if sometime during his interaction with XSEL, the user has supplied a value for a term that reappears in a subsequent computation, the later occurrence of the term inherits its value from the first occurrence.

An additional complication arises when the total capacity required depends on several different applications. It is ordinarily necessary in this case to do more than simply accumulate the values returned by the various application-specific computations. A variety of computations for each application must often be performed, and then the results of these computations must be combined. For example, to determine the amount of primary memory needed on a system, each application must compute the core requirements both of its compute-bound and its i/o bound jobs; the total amount of core required is a function of the sum of core requirements of the compute-bound jobs and the maximum of the core requirements of the i/o bound jobs.

Since most component types have a number of subtypes, for XSEL to decide which of those subtypes to select (and in what quantity), it must ordinarily have more information than just a measure of the total capacity required. There are three sources for this information. Sometimes XSEL must ask the user for additional information about the intended uses of his system. Sometimes the information collected to determine total capacity implicitly contains the necessary information. And sometimes XSEL falls back on domain-specific heuristics to discriminate among candidates. When XSEL has collected as much information as it can, it searches its database of component descriptions for components that satisfy all of the constraints implied by this information. If all of the components found have the same subtype, then the subtype selection task is finished. If components of more than one subtype are found, XSEL must decide which subtype or subtypes to select on the basis of more general heuristics.[†]

Once a subtype is selected, XSEL must decide which variation is most appropriate. As we have seen, the initial version of XSEL asks the user a set of questions sufficient to discriminate among the possibilities; but these questions assume that the user knows which variations are best suited to his applications. If the user is relying on XSEL for guidance in selecting an appropriate set of components, it is quite likely that he will not know how to answer the questions, In this case, XSEL must use less direct means to collect the necessary information. The available sources are essentially the same as those used in obtaining the information needed to discriminate among subtypes. XSEL can ask for additional information about the intended uses of the system, make inferences from the information already collected, or fall back on domain-specific heuristics. Given a subtype and information further specifying that subtype, XSEL retrieves a component of that subtype from its database and adds the component to the order.

While engaged in the task of selecting an appropriate set of components, XSEL watches for indications that the intended use of some subset of components implies unusual configuration constraints. It has a set of rules that recognize situations that signal atypical use. If such a signal is present, XSEL generates a constraint that will cause R1 to tailor its configuration to fit the atypical use. Since XSEL communications with R1 by means of a simple language consisting a relatively small number of command forms, these constraints are easy for XSEL to generate.

3. THE EXPLANATION TASK

Several of the knowledge-based programs developed over the past few years have quite sophisticated explanantion capabilities. But for the most part, these programs do not treat explanation as a task that requires intelligence. Almost all

[†] Currently if XSEL must decide among subtypes of apparently equal appropriateness, it selects the least costly subtype.

of the knowledge these programs have is knowledge of how to solve problems in their respective domains. Little if any of it is knowledge of how to effectively communicate an understanding of the problem solving process to a user.[†] A major component of XSEL's knowledge will be knowledge of how to construct explanations in the computer system sales domain so that they contain just that information in which the user is interested.

XSEL currently has a few limited explanantion capabilities. It can provide the following kinds of information on demand:

(1) Descriptions of components, definitions of properties of components, definitions of terms used in formulas.
(2) Values of the properties of components, data entered by the user and inferences drawn from that data, components selected, configuration constraints generated.
(3) Significant differences among components of the same subtype, significant differences among subtypes of the same type.
(4) Its reasons for selecting particular components, its reasons for generating a configuration constraint.
(5) A justification of the reasoning that led it to select some quantity of components.

These capabilities vary greatly in the amount of knowledge about explanation that they presuppose. Capabilities 4 and 5 require the most knowledge and thus are the least developed at the moment; this section will focus primarily on these two capabilities and indicate what plans we have for developing them.

It should be noted that XSEL can provide any of the various sorts of information at any time during an interaction. As mentioned above, XSEL's rules are grouped into contexts on the basis of the tasks for which they are relevant. One of XSEL's contexts contains rules that determine, on the basis of how the user responds, whether he is entering a value that XSEL requested or wants something explained. The user indicates that he wants something explained by entering one of five types of commands. If the user gives one of these commands rather than entering the requested value, a rule that recognizes that command fires and generates a working memory element indicating the name of the context that can provide the sort of information he wants. This context contains all of the rules relevant to that sort of explanation.

The first three capabilities listed above are essentially information retrieval capabilities; XSEL needs only a small amount of general knowledge in order to provide the information desired. XSEL has access to a database of definitions; thus the first capability is achieved simply by look-up. The second capability is also achieved by look-up, though here there are two sources that might contain the information. If the value requested is the value of a property of a component, XSEL retrieves the value from its database of component descriptions;

† A notable exception is GUIDON (Clancey 79), a rule-based, tutorial program that can be built on top of MYCIN-like expert systems.

if the information is contained in a working memory element (e.g., the value of some term in a computation), XSEL responds with the value contained in that working memory element. The third capability allows somewhat more room for various forms of assistance, but is currently implemented simply. Since the differences among variations of the same subtype and among subtypes of the same type are ordinarily differences in just a few properties, XSEL searches through its database of component descriptions for the relevant set of components and then displays for each component those of its properties which distinguish it from at least one of the other components.

The fourth capability enables XSEL to provide the user with reasons for its decisions. For the most part, when the user asks why a component was ordered, he has one of four things in mind:

(1) Why was a particular variation of a component selected rather than some other variation?
(2) Why was a particular subtype selected rather than some other subtype?
(3) Why is a particular component type necessary for his applications?
(4) Why does he need the quantity of a component that XSEL has indicated he needs?

The form in which the user asks the question typically indicates which of these four pieces of information he has in mind. The first three questions are all handled by the rules in one context; the fourth question is handled by the rules in a different context.

To enable itself to answer the first three types of questions, whenever XSEL asserts a working memory element specifying that a component of some type is needed or specifying constraints on the allowable subtype or variation, it also asserts a working memory element containing the reason. Since the rules that generate these assertions implicitly contain the reason (i.e., have a set of conditions that define when a particular type or subtype or variation is required), the assertion is simply a re-representation of the reason in a declarative rather than a procedural form. By putting the reasons into a declarative form, other rules — rules that comprise XSEL's knowledge of what constitutes a good explanation — can construct a satisfactory answer to any of the first three types of questions. Constructing such an answer could, for example, involve collapsing a set of reasons into a single more general reason. Or it could involve suppressing certain reasons that might distract the user's attention away from more important considerations. Or it could involve justifying some selection on the basis of its similarlity to an already explained selection.

To answer the fourth type of question, XSEL uses the sets of elements that define its computations. Once XSEL has performed the computation required to determine what the total capacity of some component type should be, its working memory contains elements specifying the value of the intermediate as well as the primitive terms in whatever formula it used. It can use this information to focus the user's attention on significant factors in the computation. If a user asks why

335

he needs quantity Q of some component X, it is unlikely that he would be satisfied with the following answer:

- You require a total capacity TC of component type x.
- Q of X provide TC.
- Thus you need Q of X.

What the user actually does want to know, however, depends to a considerable extent on the particular situation. If the user wants to know why he needs 2 MS780-DD (i.e., 4 megabytes of primary memory) and if 3 megabytes are needed for one of his applications and 1 megabyte is sufficient for his other six applications, then an important piece of information for the user to have is that one application requires 3 megabytes of memory. XSEL could supply this piece of information by noticing that one of the seven values whose sum specified the total amount of primary memory required is significantly larger than any of the other six values.

The other use a user can make of the fourth capability is to find out why particular configuration constraints were generated. The problem here is essentially the same as the problem of explaining why a component of a particular type, subtype, or variation was ordered, and XSEL uses the same solution. Whenever it recognizes that it has information that implies some configuration constraint, in addition to generating the constraint, it asserts the reason for the constraint. This reason simply describes ths situation that implies the constraint.

The fifth capability listed above is the capability of justifying the reasoning that led to some quantity of components of a particular type being ordered. This capability provides a second level of explanation in those cases in which what is not understood is why the intended uses of the system imply some capacity of some component type. The problem here is to justify the formula used to compute the capacity required. This justification is accomplished by treating the formula as if all of its primitive terms were constants — where the constants are just those values entered by the user. The strategy is to make the unfamiliar formula familiar by reducing it to a formula tailored to the situation at hand.

CONCLUDING REMARKS

The design and implementation history of XSEL is significantly different from that of R1. R1 is the first knowledge-based program to be used at DEC, and thus before it could become part of the culture, it had to prove itself; it had to be an accomplished configurer before DEC would commit itself to exploring its potential. But now that R1 is established at DEC, and now that DEC has a group capable of supporting knowledge-based programs, a different design and implementation strategy is possible. Using R1's capabilities as a base, other programs can be developed and put to work before they are truly accomplished in their domains. Through DEC is not yet ready to design such systems, it does have the capability necessary to oversee their development from the prototype stage to maturity.

Though the XSEL program is a more ambitious effort than R1 was (in terms both of the variety of the demands of its task domain and of the amount of knowledge it will ultimately have), it will become useful long before it reaches maturity. XSEL is sufficiently developed that within a few months it will be able to be used, in conjunction with R1, to aid salespeople in entering orders and in determining the precise set of components that a customer needs. As knowledge is extracted from configuration design experts, it will be given to XSEL. We expect that by the summer of 1982, XSEL will be sufficiently expert in configuration design and in explaining how configuration design decisions are reached, that it will be of real assistance to the DEC sales force.

ACKNOWLEDGEMENTS

The development of XSEL is being supported by Digital Equipment Corporation. The research that led to the development of OPS5, the language in which XSEL is written, was sponsored by the Defense Advanced Research Projects Agency (DOD), ARPA Order No. 3597, and monitored by the Air Force Avionics Laboratory under Contract F33615-78-C-1151. The views and conclusions contained in this document are those of the author and should not be interpreted as representing the official policies, either expressed or implied, of Digital Equipment Corporation, the Defense Advanced Research Projects Agency, or the U.S. Government. VAX-11 and PDP-11 are trademarks of Digital Equipment Corporation.

Tom Cooper and Barbara Steele have contributed significantly to both the design and development of XSEL. Other colleagues at CMU have provided valuable suggestions and criticisms, in particular, Jon Bentley, Charles Forgy, and Allen Newell. Sam Fuller, Arnold Kraft, Dennis O'Connor, and many others at DEC have been a constant source of encouragement.

REFERENCES

Clancey, W. J. (1979). Dialogue management for rule-based tutorials. *Proceedings of the 6th International Joint Conference on Artificial Intelligence*, (Tokyo), pp. 155–161.

Forgy, C. L. & McDermott, J. (1977). OPS, A domain-independent production system language. *Proceedings of the 5th International Joint Conference on Artificial Intelligence*, pp. 933–939. (Cambridge, Mass). Pittsburgh: Dept. of Computer Science, Carnegie-Mellon University.

Forgy, C. L. (1980). *The OPS5 user's manual*. Technical Report, Pittsburgh: Carnegie-Mellon University, Department of Computer Science.

McDermott, J. (1980a). *R1: a rule-based configurer of computer systems*. Technical Report, Pittsburgh: Carnegie-Mellon University, Department of Computer Science.

McDermott, J. (1980b). R1: an expert in the computer systems domain. *Proceedings of the 1st Annual National Conference on Artificial Intelligence*, (Stanford). pp. 269–271.

McDermott, J. and Steele, B. (1981). Extending a knowledge-based system to deal with *ad hoc* constraints. *Proceedings of the 7th Joint International Joint Conference on Artificial Intelligence*, (Vancouver) pp. 776–781.

17

Knowledge-based programming self-applied

C. Green[*] and S. J. Westfold[*†]
Systems Control Inc.
Palo Alto, California

Abstract

A knowledge-based programming system can utilize a very-high-level self description to rewrite and improve itself. This paper presents a specification, in the
very-high-level language V, of the rule compiler component of the CHI knowledge-
based programming system. From this specification of part of itself, CHI produces
an efficient program satisfying the specification. This represents a modest application of a machine intelligence system to a real programming problem, namely
improving one of the programming environment's tools — the rule compiler. The
high-level description and the use of a programming knowledge base provide
potential for system performance to improve with added knowledge.

1. INTRODUCTION

This paper presents a specification of a program in a very-high-level description-
oriented language. Such a specification is suitable for compilation into an efficient
program by a knowledge-based programming system. The program specified is
the rule compiler component of the CHI knowledge-based programming system
(Green *et al.* 1981). The language used for the specification is V, which is used in
CHI to specify programs as well as to represent programming knowledge (see
Phillips 1982). The compiler portion of CHI can produce an efficient program
from this self description. The availability of a suitable self description allows
not only self compilation, but also enhanced potential for the knowledge-based
system to assist in its own modification and extension.

We use the term 'knowledge-based programming system' to imply that most
of the programming knowledge used by the system is expressed explicitly, usually
in some rule form, and is manipulable in that form. This collection of programming
rules is used by the system to help in selecting implementation techniques, and

---

* Present address: Kestrel Institute, Palo Alto.
† Also with Computer Science Department, Stanford University.

to help in other programming activities such as editing and debugging. By comparison a conventional compiler tends to use procedures that compile source language constructs into preselected choices for data and control structure implementations rather than exploring alternative implementations.

The programming knowledge base includes stepwise refinement or transformation rules for optimizing, simplifying and refining data structures and control structures. The synthesis paradigm of CHI is to select and apply these rules to a program specification, generating a space of legal alternative implementations. By applying different refinement rules from CHI's knowledge base in different orders one gets alternative implementations, whose efficiency characteristics can be matched to the problem. In general, refinement choices may be made interactively by the user or automatically by incorporating efficiency estimation knowledge (see Kant 1979 for a discussion of this important issue). It is our intent that strategies for rule selection and ordering will be expressed in the meta-rule language portion of V. But in this paper we just present a particular set of rules and an order of application rather than alternative synthesis rules and strategies for selecting among them.

The V language is used not only to specify programs but also to express the knowledge base of synthesis rules and meta-rules. The high-level primitives of V include sets, mappings, relations, predicates, enumerations and state transformation sequences. It is a wide-spectrum language that also includes low-level constructs. Both declarative and procedural statements are allowed. In this language there is little distinction between the terms 'program specification,' 'program description' and just 'program'. We use the terms interchangeably. V is translated into LISP by the compiler portion of CHI.

In choosing a program for use as a start on self modification, we decided to work with a program that is being used and modified, rather than a contrived example. We picked RC, a *rule compiler* written in LISP that compiles the production rule subset of the V language into efficient LISP code. Since the program refinement rules are expressed as production rules, the rule compiler allows refinement rules to be expressed in a simple, readable, and concise syntax without loss of efficiency. By expressing refinement rules in a clean formalism, their content is more readily available for scrutiny, improvement, and transfer to other systems. Since production rules are also a method of specifying programs, it is possible to specify the rule compiler using this production rule subset of V. Thus the very-high-level version of the compiler can be tested by compiling itself.

We have succeeded in creating a very-high-level description of RC in the V language. The remaining sections of this paper present this description. The adequacy of the description has been tested by having RC compile itself. More precisely, the original version of RC in LISP compiled the V description of RC into LISP. This newly-compiled LISP program was then tested by having it compile its V description.

We decided that rather than attempting to create an ideal version of the rule

340

compiler immediately, we would first create and present a V version that approximates the input-output performance of the original program. The original program was written in LISP in 1979 as part of the first version of CHI and had some undesirable limitations in its input formats and optimizations. The V version is being extended to overcome the limitations.

The very-high-level V version proves to have several advantages over the LISP version: size, comprehensibility, and extensibility. The V version is less than 20% of the size of the LISP version (approximately 2 pages versus 10 pages). The size improvement is due in part to a better understanding of the program, but is mainly due to the declaratively-oriented description and high-level constructs that are allowed in the very-high-level language, and the concomitant allowance of other general progamming knowledge to fill in details that needed to be explicitly provided in the LISP version. Rules compiled by the V version of RC are more efficient than those produced by the LISP version of RC, due to some simplification rules in CHI.

Subjectively, we find RC in V much easier to understand and extend. In section 3 of this paper we present several possible extensions to the rule compiler, and discuss how our approach facilitates these extensions. Indeed, the difficulty of making frequently-required extensions was a reason for using the rule compiler in this study. A major step would be the extension of the description of the small compiler RC to a description of the entire V compiler portion of CHI. Then the rule compiler will not be a separate component, but will be merged with the knowledge-based compiler portion of CHI. Rules will then be compiled as is any other V program.

Is the self-application of CHI really different from that done in other systems? It appears to differ to an extent that may make a difference. Obviously self-referencing is possible in many languages, from machine language up, and bootstrapping is often done with compilers. The notion of a language with an accessible, sophisticated environment expressed in the same language already occurs in SMALLTALK (Ingalls 1978), INTERLISP (Teitelman & Masinter 1981) and other languages. These systems provided much of the inspiration for our work. But there does appear to be a difference, in that CHI is knowledge-based and CHI's programs are described in a higher-level description-oriented language. The availability of a very-high-level description provides potential for the use of additional knowledge in program compilation and modification. The hope is that this self description and the knowledge base can lead to a set of programming tools that are more powerful not only for creating target end-user programs but also for extending the programming environment. Extending the environment can in turn further facilitate modifying target end-user programs. An example is in a new application where the program editor or pretty printer (part of the environment) must be extended to edit or print some new information structure (part of the target program). The tools provided by the programming environment can more easily assist in this modification process if the environment is itself described in terms that the modification tools can deal with. We have

341

shown in this paper the feasibility of describing and implementing the programming environment in the system's own very-high-level language.

A drawback of knowledge-based systems is that the addition of new application-domain rules often slows down system performance. In our case, where the application domain is programming, the new knowledge that is introduced can be utilized to speed CHI up. The speed-up helps to mitigate the slowdown caused by the introduction of new alternatives to consider during program synthesis. The net result may well be that system performance improves as new programming knowledge is added. An example would be that as rules are introduced for implementing sets in some new form, say balanced trees, the new tree data structure would be used where appropriate by CHI to implement sets when CHI recompiles itself. In addition, smart self-compilation allows the possibility that new knowledge can be invoked only at reasonable times so that search time is not increased. Another way the descriptive capability helps as new knowledge is added, is that different pieces of the environment are driven off the same internal representations. For example, when a new rule format is added, the reader, printer, editor and compiler all use the same description of the rule format so that consistency is maintained.

In a knowledge-based programming system it can be difficult to draw a boundary between a program specification and general programming knowledge. For example, the specification of RC contains several rules that are specific to RC, dealing with particular rule formats and names of CHI functions. Yet other rules are simplifications such as removing redundant nesting of conjunctions or optimizations such as moving a test outside the scope of a quantifier where possible. The philosophy of a knowledge-based programming system is that general rules such as these are part of the knowledge base and are available to be used whenever appropriate, and are not part of any particular program. For clarity we have included all the general rules in this paper, but if we wished to claim further economy of expression we could argue that the general rules are not a proper part of RC, and thus the specification is really less than half the size presented here. One reason most of the rules are general is that RC deals with the mapping of declarative logic into procedures; the necessary ideas tend to be rather fundamental to programming and are more plausibly classified as general.

1.1 Related work

Situation variables in predicate calculus are used in this paper to formally state the input-output specifications of the desired target code to be produced by the rule compiler, and are also used to give the semantics of a refinement rule. However, for convenience the high-level notation omits the explicit dependence on situations unless necessary. The method of introducing situation variables into the predicate calculus to describe state changes was first introduced in Green 1968 and expanded in Green 1969a. Current progress in the use of this method is exemplified in Manna and Waldinger 1980.

Other knowledge-based programming systems are exemplified by the TI

342

system (Balzer 1981), and the Programmer's Apprentice (Rich 1980, Shrobe 1979, and Waters 1978). Very-high-level specification languages are exemplified by GIST (Goldman & Wile, 1979) and SETL (Schonberg *et al.* 1978). GIST is currently compiled interactivly with the TI transformation system and SETL contains some sophisticated compiler optimizations.

A very-high-level self description of part of a compiler to produce programs from a logic specification using situation variables was first given in Green 1969b. A theorem prover was the method used to interpret and compile programs specified in the predicate calculus. The control structure of the theorem prover (the interpreter and compiler) was itself described in predicate calculus. But this engine was not powerful enough to either interpret or compile the program. A logic-based technique was used again, this time with an improved theorem prover and specification language in PROLOG to describe a compiler, and in this case PROLOG was able to interpret the compiler (Warren 1980). But the described program was not part of the PROLOG system itself. In the case of CHI, a system that was self-described using situation calculus was compiled. Another closely related work is that of Weyhrauch (Weyhrauch 1980) in which he describes part of the FOL system in its own logic language. This description can be procedurally interpreted to control reasoning in FOL and aids in extending its area of expertise. MRS (Genesereth and Lenat 1980) also features a framework where self-description is used to control reasoning in the system.

2. SPECIFICATION OF THE RULE COMPILER

The rules we are considering have the form:

$$P \to Q$$

which loosely means 'if P is true in the current situation then transform the situation to make Q true'. P and Q are conjunctions of predicates involving pattern variables. An example of a rule is:

$$class(a) = \text{set} \wedge element(a) = x$$
$$\to class(a) = mapping \wedge domain(a) = x \wedge range(a) = \text{boolean}$$

which transforms a set data structure into a Boolean mapping data structure. This is easier to read in the equivalent form with pattern expressions:

$$a : \text{'set of } x\text{'} \to a : \text{'mapping from } x \text{ to boolean'}$$

The input/output specification of the rule $P \to Q$ can be stated formally as:

$$\forall x_1, \ldots, x_n [P(s) \Rightarrow Q(succ(s))] \tag{*}$$

where x_i are the free variables of P, $P(s)$ means that P is true in situation s, and $succ(s)$ is the situation after the rule is applied to situation s. We assume frame conventions that specify, with certain exceptions, that what is true in the initial state is true in the successor or final state unless the rule implies otherwise.

343

A predicate can be instantiated with objects from our domain of discourse. Each instantiated predicate corresponds to a relation[†] being in the database. An instantiated left-hand-side predicate is satisfied if the corresponding relation is in the initial state of the database. An instantiated right-hand-side predicate is satisfied by putting the corresponding relation in the final state of the database. Thus the specification can be satisfied by enumerating all instantiations of the quantified variables and for each instantiation in which all the relations of the left-hand side are in the initial state of the database, adding the relations of the right-hand side to the final state of the database. The main task of the rule compiler is to use constraints in the left-hand side of a rule to limit the number of instantiations that need to be enumerated. This optimization is done on the specifcation itself by reducing quantification.

RC has four main stages. The initial stage constructs the input/output specification (*) of the rule. The second stage applies optimizing transformations to the specification by bounding quantifiers and minimizing their scope. The third stage specifies how to satisfy logic expressions using standard high-level programming constructs. The last stage converts database accesses to implementation-specific constructs. We shall be examining stages 2 and 3 in detail.

In order to make the specification cleaner we have presented a few of the rules in a form which RC cannot compile. In section 3 we show how RC can be extended to compile all the rules presented.

2.1 Guide to rule subset of the V language

The rules are constructed from predicates that correspond to relations in the database. The rules of RC transform logic expressions and program expressions, so we need to show how such expressions are represented as relations in the database. For example, the expression $if\, p(x,y)\, then f(x)$ is represented internally by an object w_1 with the following attribute-value relations:

$$class(w_1) = \text{conditional}, condition(w_1) = w_2, action(w_1) = w_3$$

where w_1 and w_2 are objects with the following properties:

$$class(w_2) = \text{p}, arg_1(w_2) = v_1, arg_2(w_2) = v_2,$$
$$class(w_3) = \text{f}, arg_1(w_3) = v_1,$$
$$class(v_1) = \text{var}, name(v_1) = \text{x},$$
$$class(v_2) = \text{var}, name(v_2) = \text{y}.$$

One rule conjunction which matches this representation is:

$$class(a) = \text{conditional} \wedge condition(a) = P \wedge action(a) = Q$$

[†] In our system the relation $R:X \times Y$ is stored as a function of the form $f:X \mapsto Y$, where $y = f(x)$ iff $R(x,y)$ if R is one to one or many to one, or $f:X \mapsto set\, of\, Y$, where $y \in f(x)$ iff $R(x,y)$ if R is one to many or many to many. The inverse relation is represented by a function in a similar way. Functions may also be computed.

with instantiations: $a \leftarrow w_1; P \leftarrow w_2; Q \leftarrow w_3$. Because rule conjunctions refer to the representation of the expression to be matched rather than the expression itself, it can be difficult to understand them. Therefore we introduce an alternate notation for rule conjunctions which we call pattern expressions. The pattern expression for the previous conjunction is:

$a:$'if P then Q'.

Pattern expressions are useful for the reader to see the form of the expressions that the rule refers to, but it is the conjunctive form that is compiled by RC.

In this paper we follow certain naming conventions for pattern variables. Variables starting with S stand for sets of objects. All other pattern variables stand for individual objects. Thus in the pattern $a:$'$\forall S[C \Rightarrow P]$, S matches the set of quantified variables of a, whereas in the pattern $a:$'$\forall x [C \Rightarrow P]$', x matches the single quantifier variable of a. The other variable naming conventions do not affect the way the rules are compiled. They are: P, Q, R and C match boolean-valued expressions (C is used specifically for conjunctions); u, v and t match terms; p and q match predicates; f matches functions.

2.2 The rule compiler rules

We first present the rules without examples of their use. Then, in section 2.3, we present the steps in the compilation of a rule, which involves applications of all the rules in the current section. It may be useful for the reader to read these two sections together.

Stage 1: Conversion to input/output specification

Creating the specification of the rule involves determining the quantification of variables. The quantification convention is that variables that appear only on the right-hand side are existentially quantified over the right-hand side and variables on the left-hand side are universally quantified over the entire rule. The reason for variables on the right being existentially quantified is that we want to create new objects in the new situation, and this can be expressed by stating existence.

The rule that does the conversion is:

$$a:'P \rightarrow Q' \wedge FreeVars(P) = S_0 \wedge FreeVars(Q) - S_0 = S_1$$
$$\rightarrow a:'Satisfy(\forall S_0[P \Rightarrow \exists S_1[Q]])' \qquad \text{(SatisfySpec)}$$

where $FreeVars(P)$ is the set of free variables in the expression P except for those declared to be bound global to the rule. Note that we have not specified that P refers to the initial state and Q refers to the succeeding state. This could be done by marking predicates as referring to either the initial state or the succeeding state. It turns out that in the current version of RC this marking is unnecessary because the initial separation of left- and right-hand-side predicates is maintained. At the end of stage 3, predicates that refer to the final state are marked as having to be *Satisfi*ed. How RC can be extended to take advantage of situational tags is discussed in section 3.2.

345

Stage 2: Optimizing transformations

The rules in this stage do most of the optimizations currently in RC, using equivalence transformations. We do this within logic rather than on a procedural form of the rule because there is a well-understood repertory of logical equivalence transformations. The choice of equivalence transformations is made with a procedural interpretation in mind. The effect of these transformations is to explicate constraints on the evaluation order of the left-hand-side conjuncts. This reflects in the logic form as dependencies being explicit, for example an expression being outside a quantification rather than unnecessarily inside it.

To give an idea of the overall effect of stages 2 and 3, we show the compilation of the rule **SubstBind** before and after these stages. Its purpose is not important here.

$$a : \text{`}Satisfy\,(P/S_0)\text{'} \land y \in S_0 \land y : \text{`}x/t\text{'} \to$$
$$a : \text{`}bind\ S_1\ do\ Satisfy\,(P)\text{'} \land z \in S_1 \land z : \text{`}z \leftarrow t\text{'} \qquad \text{(SubstBind)}$$

We abbreviate the right-hand side to *RHS* as we are concentrating on the left-hand side. At the beginning of stage 2, the rule has been transformed to:

$$Satisfy\,(\forall S_0, y, x, t\,[class(a) = \text{substitute} \land satisfy(a) \land substexp(a) = P$$
$$\land\ substset(a) = S_0 \land y \in S_0 \land class(y) = \text{subst} \land var(y) = x$$
$$\land\ substval(y) = t \Rightarrow RHS]) \qquad (2.1)$$

At the end of stage 2:

$$Satisfy\,(class(a) = \text{substitute} \land satisfy(a)$$
$$\Rightarrow (\forall y \in S_0\,[class(y) = \text{subst} \Rightarrow (RHS/\{x/var(y),\ t/substval(y)\})])$$
$$/\{P/substexp(a),\ S_0/substset(a)\}) \qquad (2.2)$$

At the end of stage 3:

if $Test(class(a) = \text{substitute} \land satisfy(a))$ **then**
    bind $P \leftarrow substexp(a),\ S_0 \leftarrow substset(a)$
    do enumerate y **in** S_0 (2.3)
        do if $Test(class(y) = \text{subst})$ **then**
            bind $x \leftarrow var(y),\ t \leftarrow substval(y)$
            do *RHS*

The rule compiler determines the order and manner in which each of the eight left-hand-side conjuncts of (2.1) is treated. The fate of the conjuncts can be seen in (2.3). The conjuncts $class(a) = \text{substitute}$ and $satisfy(a)$ can be tested immediately because they depend only on the variable a which is bound externally. The conjunct $substexp(a) = P$ requires that the value of the unknown variable P be equal to an expression in the known variable a, so it is selected next and used to compute the value of P. Similarly, the conjunct $substset(a) = S_0$ is used to compute the value of S_0. Of the remaining conjuncts, $y \in S_0$ is selected next because it contains only the unknown y and so can be used to compute the possible values of y, which is done using an enumeration. This leaves $class(y) = \text{subst}$ with no unknown variables so it is used as a test, and $var(y) = x$ and $substval(y) = t$

give known expressions equal to x and t respectively and so are used to compute values for x and t. Briefly, RC turns conjuncts with no unknown variables into tests and conjuncts with one unknown variable into computations to find the possible values(s) of this variable. At present RC cannot handle conjuncts with more than one unknown variable.

These structural changes, which reflect dependencies among the conjuncts, are performed in stage 2 within logic. In stage 3 implications 'become' *if* statements, substitutions 'become' varible bindings, and bounded universal quantifications 'become' enumerations.

Note that for convenience we have given the conjuncts of the rule in the order in which they are used in the compiled rule, but this is not required by RC.

Another view of RC is that it produces a procedure to find the anchored matches of simple graph patterns. Variables are nodes of the graph and conjuncts are links. At any point there are known nodes and unknown nodes. An unknown node becomes known by following a link from a known node. The structure of variable binding in the target program (2.3) corresponds to a spanning tree of the graph pattern. Consider the expression $RHS/\{x/var(y), t/substval(y)\}$ which is matched when **SubstBind** itself is being compiled. a has the whole expression as its value (actually the object representing the expression); P has the value RHS; S_0 has the set $\{x/var(y), t/substval(y)\}$ as its value; y first has the value $x/var(y)$, x the value x, and z the value $var(y)$; y then has the value $t/substval(y)$, x the value t, and z the value $substval(y)$.

2a) Reducing quantification scope

The following rule, when applicable, moves expressions outside the scope of a quantification. If the quantification later becomes an enumeration, the evaluation will be done outside the enumeration instead of inside. The equivalence can be loosely stated: if p is not dependent on x then $(\forall x[p \wedge q \Rightarrow r]) \equiv (p \Rightarrow \forall x[q \Rightarrow r])$.

The corresponding rule expression of this is[†]:

$$a: `\forall S[C_0 \Rightarrow Q]` \wedge P \in conjuncts(C_0) \wedge NoVarsOf(P,S)$$
$$\rightarrow a: `C_1 \Rightarrow \forall S[C_0 \Rightarrow Q]` \wedge class(C_1) = \text{conjunction}$$
$$\wedge P \in conjuncts(C_1) \wedge P \notin conjuncts(C_0) \qquad \text{(ReduceScope)}$$

where $NoVarsOf(P,S)$ is true when the expression P is not a function of any of the variables S. Note that there may be more than one conjunct P for which the left-hand side is true, in which case C_1 will have more than one conjunct. Because of the later procedural interpretation of implication (**ImplIf**) the conjuncts added to C_1 will be tested before those remaining in C_0. However, there is no necessary ordering among the conjuncts of C_1. Note also that we want C_1 to have *only* those conjuncts P such that $P \in conjuncts(C_0) \wedge NoVarsOf(P,S)$, but this is

[†] We use the convention that the antecedent of an implication is always a conjunction, possibly with only one conjunct.

not explicitly stated. It is implicit that the compiled rule produces the minimal situation that satisfies the specification.

2b) Bounding quantifiers

The following two rules recognize explicit bounds on quantifiers and move the quantification of these variables outside the quantification of any as-yet-unbounded quantifiers. This often enables these rules (and also **ReduceScope**) to be applicable to the inner quantification. This splitting explicates an implicit dependency of the internal quantification on the external quantifiers.

The first rule uses the idea of the following logical equivalence:

$$\forall x [(x \in S \wedge p) \Rightarrow q] \equiv \forall x \in S[p \Rightarrow q]$$

The actual rule is more complicated mainly because there may be more than one quantifier, and the bounded quantification is separated and moved outside any remaining unbound quantifiers.

This allows the inner quantified expression to be manipulated independently.

$$y : `\forall S_0 [C \Rightarrow Q]` \wedge a \in conjuncts(C) \wedge a : `x \in t` \wedge x \in S_0 \wedge NoVarsOf(t, S_0)$$
$$\rightarrow y : `\forall S_1 [\forall S_0 [C \Rightarrow Q]]` \wedge x \notin S_1 \wedge x \notin S_0 \wedge univset(x) = t$$
$$\wedge a \notin conjuncts(C) \qquad \text{(BoundForall)}$$

where $univset(x) = t$ means that x can only take values in the set given by the term t.

The following rule is a special case where a quantifier can only take on one value because it is asserted to be equal to some term independent of the quantifiers. We express this by stating that the quantifier is substituted by this term in the expression, but we do not actually perform the substitution.

$$a : `\forall S_0 [C \Rightarrow Q]` \wedge y \in conjuncts(C) \wedge y : `x = t` \wedge x \in S_0 \wedge NoVarsOf(t, S_0)$$
$$\rightarrow a : `\forall S_0 [C \Rightarrow Q]/S_1` \wedge z \in S_1 \wedge z : `x/t` \wedge x \notin S_0 \wedge y \notin conjuncts(C)$$
$$\text{(ForallSubst)}$$

Stage 3: Interpreting input/output specification procedurally

In this stage the rule is converted from predicate calculus to procedural language. We assume the initial situation is given and that actions necessary to create the successor situation from the initial situation must be performed so that the rule specification is satisfied. Each rule specifies a high-level procedural form for satisfying a particular logical form.

Implication becomes an *if* statement.

$$a : `Satisfy(C \Rightarrow R)` \rightarrow a : `if \ Test(C) \ then \ Satisfy(R)` \qquad \text{(ImplIf)}$$

Test(C) is true if C is satisfied in the initial state. *Test* is not explicitly used by any of the following rules, but predicates which are not to be *Satisfi*ed are to be *Test*ed.

The following rule says that 'substitution' is actually done using variable binding rather than substitution.

$$a : `Satisfy(P/S_0)` \wedge y \in S_0 \wedge y : `x/t`$$
$$\rightarrow a : `bind \ S_1 \ do \ Satisfy(P)` \wedge z \in S_1 \wedge z : `x \leftarrow t` \qquad \text{(SubstBind)}$$

348

An existential variable appearing in the new situation is handled by creating a new object with the specified properties.

$$a: `Satisfy(\exists S_0[P])` \wedge y \in S_0$$
$$\rightarrow a: `bind\ S_1\ do\ Satisfy(P)` \wedge x \in S_1 \wedge x: `y \leftarrow (NewObject)`$$

(ExistBindNew)

A conjunction can be satisfied by satisfying each of the conjuncts. In this specification we assume that they can be satisfied independently.

$$a: `Satisfy(C)` \wedge class(C) = \text{conjunction} \wedge P \in conjuncts(C)$$
$$\rightarrow class(a) = \text{block} \wedge Q \in steps(a) \wedge Q: `Satisfy(P)`$$ (AndBlock)

Bounded quantification becomes an enumeration:

$$a: `Satisfy(\forall x \in S[R])` \rightarrow a: `enumerate\ x\ in\ S\ do\ Satisfy(R)`$$

(ForallEnum)

Stage 4: Refine to standard database access functions

4a) Rules for object-centered database implementation

The following rules convert references to functions into references to the database. The particular database representation we use is that the function value $f(u)$ is stored as the f property of the object u. Objects are thus mappings from function names to values. This arrangement may be thought of either as a distributed representation of functions or as the function being indexed by its argument.

$$a: `f(u)` \rightarrow a: `(GetMap\ u\ f)`$$ (MakeGetMap)

$$a: `Satisfy(f(u) = v)` \rightarrow a: `(ExtendMap\ u\ f\ v)`$$ (MakeExtMap)

$$a: `Satisfy(p(u))` \rightarrow a: `(ExtendMap\ u\ p\ True)`$$ (MakeExtMapT)

Note that we have not made all the preconditions for **MakeGetMap** explicit. It should only be applicable when **MakeExtMap** and **MakeExtMapT** are not applicable.

4b) System-specific transformations

The rules of this section are specific to the conventions we use to implement the abstract database. We only present the two of them that reflect issues particularly relevant to the problem of compiling logic specifications. The others convert accesses to abstract datatypes, such as mappings, into accesses to concrete datatypes. These are part of the standard CHI system.

The first rule is for the case where the class of an object gets changed. There are frame conventions which say which of the other properties of the object are still valid. The function *Ttransform* enforces these conventions at rule execution time.

$$a: `(ExtendMap\ u\ class\ v)` \rightarrow a: `(Ttransform\ u\ v)`$$ (MakeTtransform)

349

Creating a new object in the database requires that its own class be known; the object is created as an instance of its class.

$$a: \text{`}(ExtendMap \; u \; \text{class} \; v)\text{'} \wedge a \in steps(P) \wedge z: \text{`}u \leftarrow (NewObject)\text{'}$$
$$\rightarrow z: \text{`}u \leftarrow (Tinstance \; v)\text{'} \wedge a \notin steps(P) \qquad \text{(MakeTinstance)}$$

Simplification rules

The following are general simplification rules that are needed by RC to canonicalize expressions to ensure that other rules will be applicable when appropriate.

$$class(a) = \text{conjunction} \wedge class(C) = \text{conjunction} \wedge a \in conjuncts(C)$$
$$\wedge P \in conjuncts(a)$$
$$\rightarrow P \in conjuncts(C) \wedge a \notin conjuncts(C) \qquad \text{(SimpAndAnd)}$$

$$a: \text{`}C \Rightarrow Q\text{'} \wedge Null(conjuncts(C)) \rightarrow Replace(a, Q) \qquad \text{(SimpImpl)}$$

($Replace(a, P)$ causes a to be replaced by P in the expression tree. Formalizing *Replace* is beyond the scope of this paper.)

$$a: \text{`}\forall S[P]\text{'} \wedge Null(S) \rightarrow Replace(a, P) \qquad \text{(SimpForall)}$$

2.3 Sample rule compilation

We present the steps in compiling a representative rule, **ExistBindNew**:

$$a: \text{`}Satisfy(\exists S_0[P])\text{'} \wedge y \in S_0$$
$$\rightarrow a: \text{`}bind \; S_1 \; do \; Satisfy(P)\text{'} \wedge x \in S_1 \wedge x: \text{`}y \leftarrow (NewObject)\text{'}$$

Replacing pattern expression by conjunctions:[†]

$$class(a) = \text{exists} \wedge satisfy(a) \wedge quantifiers(a) = S_0$$
$$\wedge matrix(a) = P \wedge y \in S_0$$
$$\rightarrow class(a) = \text{bind} \wedge x \in bindings(a) \wedge body(a) = P$$
$$\wedge satisfy(P) \wedge class(x) = \text{binding} \wedge var(x) = y$$
$$\wedge initval(x) = e_1 \wedge class(e_1) = \text{NewObject}]])$$

We now apply **SatisfySpec** assuming that a is given as a parameter to the rule so is not quantified within the rule:

$$Satisfy(\forall S_0, P, y \, [class(a) = \text{exists} \wedge satisfy(a) \wedge quantifiers(a) = S_0$$
$$\wedge matrix(a) = P \wedge y \in S_0$$
$$\Rightarrow \exists x, e_1 \, [class(a) = \text{bind} \wedge x \in bindings(a)$$
$$\wedge body(a) = P \wedge satisfy(P)$$
$$\wedge class(x) = \text{binding} \wedge var(x) = y$$
$$\wedge initval(x) = e_1 \wedge class(e_1) = \text{NewObject}]])$$

Note that *Satisfy* is distinct from *satisfy*. Their relationship is not important for purposes of this example.

We next apply the stage 2 rules to the specification to reduce quantification. For now we abbreviate the existential expression to *RHS* as it does not influence anything for awhile, and concentrate on the universal quantification.

† We have also eliminated the unnecessary variable S_1 by replacing $(bindings(a) = S_1 \wedge x \in S_1)$ by $x \in bindings(a)$.

Apply **ReduceScope** to move $class(a)$ = exists and $satisfy(a)$ outside the quantification:

$$class(a) = \text{exists} \land satisfy(a)$$
$$\Rightarrow \forall S_0, P, y \, [quantifiers(a) = S_0 \land matrix(a) = P \land y \in S_0 \Rightarrow RHS]$$

Apply **ForallSubst** to fix values for S_0 and P in terms of a:

$$class(a) = \text{exists} \land satisfy(a)$$
$$\Rightarrow (\forall y \, [y \in S_0 \Rightarrow RHS] / \{S_0/quantifiers(a), P/matrix(a)\})$$

Apply **BoundForall** to bound the remaining universal quantifier and simplify away the inner implication with **SimpImpl**:

$$class(a) = \text{exists} \land satisfy(a)$$
$$\Rightarrow (\forall y \in S_0 \, [RHS] / \{S_0/quantifiers(a), P/matrix(a)\})$$

Bring back RHS and focus on the universal quantification expression:

$$(\forall y \in S_0)(\exists x, e_1)[class(a) = \text{bind} \land body(a) = P \land satisfy(P)$$
$$\land \, x \in bindings(a) \land class(x) = \text{binding} \land var(x) = y$$
$$\land \, initval(x) = e_1 \land class(e_1) = \text{NewObject}]$$

Moving expressions not depending on y, x and e_1 outside the quantifications (the rules that do this have not been shown before and will be defined in section 3.2):

$$class(a) = \text{bind} \land body(a) = P \land satisfy(P)$$
$$\land \, (\forall y \in S_0)(\exists x, e_1)[x \in bindings(a) \land class(x) = \text{binding}$$
$$\land \, var(x) = y \land initval(x) = e_1 \land class(e_1) = \text{NewObject}]$$

This brings us to the end of stage 2 rules:

(Note that we could have interleaved the following applications of stage 3 rules with those of stage 2 without affecting the final outcome.) The complete rule is:

$$Satisfy \, (class(a) = \text{exists} \land satisfy(a)$$
$$\Rightarrow (class(a) = \text{bind} \land body(a) = P \land satisfy(P)$$
$$\land \, (\forall y \in S_0)(\exists x, e_1)[x \in bindings(a) \land class(x) = \text{binding}$$
$$\land \, var(x) = y \land initval(x) = e_1 \land class(e_1) = \text{NewObject}]$$
$$)/\{S_0/quantifiers(a), P/matrix(a)\})$$

Applying **ImplIf**:

if $Test(class(a) = \text{exists} \land satisfy(a))$ **then**
$$Satisfy \, ((class(a) = \text{bind} \land body(a) = P \land satisfy(P)$$
$$\land \, (\forall y \in S_0)(\exists x, e_1)[x \in bindings(a) \land class(x) = \text{binding}$$
$$\land \, var(x) = y \land initval(x) = e_1 \land class(e_1) = \text{NewObject}]$$
$$)/\{S_0/quantifiers(a), P/matrix(a)\})$$

Applying **SubstBind**:

> if $Test(class(a) = \text{exists} \wedge satisfy(a))$ then
> (bind $S_0 \leftarrow quantifiers(a), P \leftarrow matrix(a)$
> do $Satisfy(class(a) = \text{bind} \wedge body(a) = P \wedge satisfy(P)$
> $\wedge (\forall y \in S_0)(\exists x, e_1)[x \in bindings(a) \wedge class(x) = \text{binding}$
> $\wedge initval(x) = e_1 \wedge class(e_1) = \text{NewObject}])$

Applying **AndBlock**:

> if $Test(class(a) = \text{exists} \wedge satisfy(a))$ then
> (bind $S_0 \leftarrow quantifiers(a), P \leftarrow matrix(a)$
> do $Satisfy(class(a) = \text{bind})$
> $Satisfy(body(a) = P)$
> $Satisfy(satisfy(P))$
> $Satisfy((\forall y \in S_0)(\exists x, e_1)[x \in bindings(a) \wedge class(x) = \text{binding}$
> $\wedge var(x) = y \wedge initval(x) = e_1 \wedge class(e_1) = \text{NewObject}])$

Applying **ForallEnum** to the last *Satisfy* expression:

> if $Test(class(a) = \text{exists} \wedge satisfy(a))$ then
> (bind $S_0 \leftarrow quantifiers(a), P \leftarrow matrix(a)$
> do $Satisfy(class(a) = \text{bind})$
> $Satisfy(body(a) = P)$
> $Satisfy(satisfy(P))$
> enumerate y in S_0
> do $Satisfy(\exists x, e_1[x \in bindings(a) \wedge class(x) = \text{binding}$
> $\wedge var(x) = y \wedge initval(x) = e_1 \wedge class(e_1) = \text{NewObject}])$

Applying **ExistBindNew** to the last *Satisfy* (it is here that we are applying the rule to part of itself):

> if $Test(class(a) = \text{exists} \wedge satisfy(a))$ then
> (bind $S_0 \leftarrow quantifiers(a), P \leftarrow matrix(a)$
> do $Satisfy(class(a) = \text{bind})$
> $Satisfy(body(a) = P)$
> $Satisfy(satisfy(P))$
> enumerate y in S_0
> do (bind $x \leftarrow (NewObject), e_1 \leftarrow (NewObject)$
> do $Satisfy(x \in bindings(a) \wedge class(x) = \text{binding} \wedge var(x) = y$
> $\wedge initval(x) = e_1 \wedge class(e_1) = \text{NewObject})))$

Applying **AndBlock** to the last *Satisfy*:

> if $Test(class(a) = \text{exists} \wedge satisfy(a))$ then
> (bind $S_0 \leftarrow quantifiers(a), P \leftarrow matrix(a)$
> do $Satisfy(class(a) = \text{bind})$
> $Satisfy(body(a) = P)$
> $Satisfy(satisfy(P))$
> enumerate y in S_0

$$\textbf{do (bind } x \leftarrow (NewObject), e_1 \leftarrow (NewObject)$$
$$\textbf{do } Satisfy\,(x \in bindings(a))$$
$$Satisfy\,(class(x) = \text{binding})$$
$$Satisfy\,(var(x) = y)$$
$$Satisfy\,(initval(x) = e_1)$$
$$Satisfy\,(class(e_1) = \text{NewObject})))$$

This is the end of stage 3. After applying the stage 4 rules we get the following program which is LISP code except for certain function names and minor syntactical differences.

$$\textbf{(if } (GetMap\ a\ '\text{class}) = '\text{exists } \textbf{and } (GetMap\ a\ '\text{satisfy}) \textbf{ then}$$
$$\textbf{(bind } S_0 \leftarrow (GetMap\ a\ '\text{quantifiers}),\ P \leftarrow (GetMap\ a\ '\text{matrix})$$
$$\textbf{do } (Ttransform\ a\ '\text{bind})$$
$$(ExtendMap\ a\ '\text{body } P)$$
$$(ExtendMap\ P\ '\text{satisfy } True)$$
$$\textbf{(for } y \textbf{ in } S_0$$
$$\textbf{do (bind } x \leftarrow (Tinstance\ '\text{binding}),$$
$$e_1 \leftarrow (Tinstance\ '\text{NewObject})$$
$$\textbf{do } (AddElement\ x\ (GetMap\ a\ '\text{bindings}))$$
$$(ExtendMap\ x\ '\text{var } y)$$
$$(ExtendMap\ x\ '\text{intval } e_1)))))$$

2.4 Control structure of rule compiler

We have largely succeeded in making the preconditions of the rule compiler rules explicit in the rules themselves, allowing the rules to be used in a wide variety of control structures. The choice of control structure can then concentrate on the issues of efficiency of compilation and efficiency of the target code produced by the compiler. At one extreme the user may interactively control the order of the rule application in order to produce the most efficeint code. At the other, the rules can be incorporated into a program which exploits their interrelations: commonalities in preconditions of rules can be used to produce a decision tree; dependencies between rules, such as the action of one rule enabling the preconditions of others, can be used to direct the order in which rules are tried.

There are some rules whose preconditions we have not made explicit. **MakeGetMap** should not be applied before **MakeExtMap** and **MakeExtMapT**. This constraint could be incorporated explicitly into **MakeGetMap** by adding negations of the distinguishing predicates of **MakeExtMap** and **MakeExtMapT**. The system could embody the general principle that a rule that has a weaker precondition than others should be applied after them, or, alternatively, distinguishing predicates could be added to the weaker rule by the system. This would give the user the choice of specifying the preconditions of a rule implicitly by reference to other rules rather than explicitly within the rule itself.

The control structure we are currently using to automatically compile rules is very simple but provides a reasonable compromise between efficiency of execution, efficiency of the code produced, and flexibility (changing one rule does not require that the entire rule compiler be recompiled). The expression tree for the rule being compiled is traversed depth-first applying each rule to each object on the way down. If an object is transformed by a rule then the traversal continues from this object. The order in which rules are applied to a particular node affects the efficiency of the code produced. In particular it is desirable to apply **ReduceScope** before **ForallSubst** and **ForallSubst** before **BoundForall**.

3. EXTENSIONS TO THE RULE COMPILER

One of the main tests of our high-level description of RC is how easy it is to extend. In this section we show how it can be extended along various dimensions: improving efficiency of the target code, augmenting the rule language, improving the user interface, and adapting to other system tasks.

3.1 Improving efficiency

We give examples of adding rules in order to improve the execution efficiency of compiled rules. Adding rules will tend to slow down the rule compiler, but as RC is specified primarily in terms of rules, after recompiling its own rules RC may become substantially faster. This section considers a number of different areas where efficiency can be improved.

Frequently it is possible to express the same program in two ways where one way is simpler or more uniform, but compiles into more inefficient code. The trade-off can be circumvented by modifying a compiler so that it translates the simpler form into the more efficient form. For example, the LISP macro facility allows the user to do this to some extent. Adding new rules to RC provides a more general way of doing this in a more convenient language. A simple example is using a more specific access function for a special case of a general access function. The following rule would be useful if an object were stored as a list whose first element is the class of the object:

$$a : \text{`}(GetMap\ u\ \text{'class})\text{'} \rightarrow a : \text{`}(car\ u)\text{'}$$

Such a speed-up should be derived by CHI from knowledge of how objects are stored. That the rule compiler can be extended easily can be exploited by the rest of CHI as well as by the user directly.

A more extensive change to RC would be to use a different implementation for the database. In particular, a less general data structure could be used for representing the rules. If singly-linked lists were used, the compiled rules could no longer follow inverse links. To compensate for this, the control structure surrounding the rules would have to keep more context in free variables for the compiled rules to refer to. Rather than rewriting the rules that previously used inverse links, only the rules that compile uses of inverse relations need be rewritten.

A useful improvement in efficiency could be gained by combining sets of rules into a single function as indicated in section 2.4. There would be relative advantages in doing the combination using the original rule form or with the forms produced by stage 2. The changes necessary to RC would be modifications of the control structure so that it could take more than one rule and a new set of rules to do the combining. Few changes to existing rules would be necessary.

A special case of combining rules is where one rule always follows another. This is true for a number of pairs of rules in RC: **BoundForall** is followed by **ForallEnum**; **ForallSubst** is followed by **SubstBind**. We could have specified RC with these rules combined at the cost of less clarity, and less generality of the individual rules. The combination of **BoundForall** and **ForallEnum** is:

$$y: \text{'Satisfy}(\forall S_0[C \Rightarrow Q])\text{'} \land a \in conjuncts(C) \land a: \text{'}x \in t\text{'} \land x \in S_0$$
$$\land NoVarsOf(t, S) \to a: \text{'enumerate } x \text{ in } t \text{ do Satisfy}(\forall S_0[C \Rightarrow Q])\text{'}$$
$$\land x \notin S_0 \land a \notin conjuncts(C)$$

which is comparable in complexity to **BoundForall** alone. However, it blurs the two things which are going on that are distinguished in the individual rules: a logical equivalence and how procedurally to satisfy a universal quantification. Having the two ideas in separate rules means that they can be applied separately elsewhere. However it may well be desirable to compile them together to increase efficiency.

3.2 Extending the rule language

There are two classes of extensions to the rule language. New constructs and abbreviations can be incorporated by adding rules to stage 1 which translate the new constructs into standard logic constructs compilable by the lower part of RC. The second class of extension is the addition of rules to stage 2 and/or stage 3 to increase RC's coverage of logic constructs. An addition of the first class may require additions to lower parts of RC in order that the new pattern be compilable.

The following two rules free the user from having to decide whether it is necessary to use a particular relation or its inverse. They also loosen constraints on which variables may be chosen as parameters to the rule or as enumeration variables. They are required in order to compile a number of the rules without unnecessary enumerations, including **BoundForall** when a is the parameter.

$$y: \text{'}\forall S[C \Rightarrow Q]\text{'} \land a \in conjuncts(y) \land a: \text{'}f(u) = t\text{'} \land NoVarsOf(t, S)$$
$$\land OneToOne(f) \to a: \text{'}u = f^{-1}(t)\text{'}$$

$$y: \text{'}\forall S[C \Rightarrow Q]\text{'} \land a \in conjuncts(y) \land a: \text{'}f(u) = t\text{'} \land NoVarsOf(t, S)$$
$$\land ManyToOne(f) \to a: \text{'}u \in f^{-1}(t)\text{'}$$

A number of rules, including **ExistBindNew**, require the following two rules in order to compile correctly. Like **ReduceScope**, they move expressions outside the scope of quantifications.

$$a: \text{'}\exists S[C]\text{'} \land class(C) = conjunction \land P \in conjuncts(C) \land NoVarsOf(P, S)$$
$$\to class(a) = conjunction \land P \in conjuncts(a) \land y \in conjuncts(a) \land y: \text{'}\exists S[C]\text{'}$$
$$\land P \notin conjuncts(C)$$

$$a: \text{'}\forall S[C]\text{'} \land class(C) = conjunction \land P \in conjuncts(C) \land NoVarsOf(P, S)$$
$$\to class(a) = conjunction \land P \in conjucts(a) \land y \in conjucts(a) \land y: \text{'}\forall S[C]\text{'}$$
$$\land P \notin conjuncts(C)$$

355

The main part of RC involves compiling the satisfaction of an input/output specification. In the remainder of this section we consider extensions to RC that increase the types of acceptable input/output specifications.

By explicitly marking functions as referring to either the initial or succeeding state we get more freedom in how to mix them in the specification and more freedom in how the specification can be manipulated in stage 2. We use the convention that functions or expressions marked with a single prime, as in f', refer to the initial state, and those marked with a double prime refer to the succeeding state, as in f''.

Consider the case where we allow disjunctions in the input/output specification. For example, consider the expression $Satisfy(A' \Rightarrow B'')$ in the disjunctive form $Satisfy(\neg A' \vee B'')$. To get from the latter to an expression similar to that obtained from applying **ImplIf** to the former expression, one can apply the rule:

$$a: \text{`}Satisfy(P \vee Q)\text{'} \rightarrow a: \text{`}if\ UnSatisfiable(P)\ then\ Satisfy(Q)\text{'}$$

giving *if UnSatisfiable($\neg A'$) then Satisfy(B'')*. Comparing this with *if Test(A') then Satisfy(B'')* we see that *Test(x)* corresponds to *UnSatisfiable($\neg x$)*. Note that we could also have derived the program *if UnSatisfiable(B'') then Satisfy ($\neg A'$)*, but if we have no procedures for testing unsatisfiability in the final state or satisfying things in the initial state, then this choice will lead to a dead end.

In general, relaxing the restrictions on the form of the specification requires additional Stage 3 rules rather than changes to existing ones, but the rules may lead to dead ends, so a more sophisticated control structure is necessary. On the other hand, the Stage 4a rules do require the addition of preconditions concerning whether functions refer to the initial or final state.

For example, **MakeExtMap** becomes:

$$a: \text{`}Satisfy(f''(u) = v)\text{'} \rightarrow a: \text{`}(ExtendMap\ u\ f\ v)\text{'}$$

with restrictions also necessary on u and v if these are allowed to be expressions more general than variables.

RC in its present form can be used to compile rules that derive implications of the current state rather than transform it. The specification for such rules is exactly the same as (*) except that it is not necessary to distinguish the initial and succeeding states. This distinction is not actually used by RC so therefore RC can compile these rules. The rule **MakeTtransform** is not applicable to compiling such implication rules. Its preconditions being true would imply that the implication rule does not reflect a valid implication.

3.3 Improving user interface

The user interface can be improved in a variety of ways. Extending the rule language, discussed above, is one way. Another is to put error detection rules which report problems in the rule or indicate when the rule is beyond the scope of the rule compiler. This is also useful as self-documentation of the rule compiler.

The following rule can be used to detect any unbound quantifers left after the application of stage 2 rules:

$$a : `Satisfy\,(\forall S\,[P])` \wedge x \in S \wedge \neg\, univset\,(x) \rightarrow Error(x, \, Unbound)$$

In another dimension, RC can be extended to produce target code that is oriented to the user's use of it. The main use of compiled rules outside the rule compiler is in refining high level programs under user guidance. At each decision point the user wants to know which rules are relevant. The system should help in providing such a list. We have added a set of rules to RC in V that extracts part of the left-hand side to use as a filter. The rule language provides a convenient way for the user to express and experiment with heuristics for determining the relevant parts to test.

3.4 Relation to the rest of the system

In this section we discuss specifically how the rule compiler can benefit the system and how the rest of the system can benefit the rule compiler, apart from the primary purpose of the rule compiler of compiling rules.

Some ways in which the rule compiler can benefit the system have already been covered, such as in providing filters to screen irrelevant rules from the user. The primary contribution of the rule compiler is the provision of a useful high-level language that can be used elsewhere. One immediately applicable example is in compiling user database queries. These are exactly like rules except that they usually do not have any parameters and the actions are typically to display the matching objects (although editing could be performed if desired). An example query may be to print out all rules that apply to universal quantifications:

$$y : `C \rightarrow Q` \wedge P \in conjuncts\,(C) \wedge P : `class\,(x) = \text{forall}` \rightarrow Display\,(y)$$

Improvements in the rest of the system can have benefits for the rule compiler. As mentioned above, the whole program synthesis system may be brought to bear on compiling an important rule. General efficiency knowledge for determining which of several implementations is most efficient would carry over to rule compilation. Also, additions made to take advantage of dataflow or for manipulating enumerations could be applicable to the rule compiler. All the tools for maintaining programs written in V are applicable to maintaining the rule compiler program, including editors, consistency maintenance systems and the system for answering user queries about programs.

Acknowledgements

We would like to acknowledge J. Phillips for numerous key ideas in the design of CHI and V and for suggestions for describing the rule compiler in V. S. Angebranndt helped implement and debug RC in V. T. Pressburger developed an implementation-independent description of CHI's knowledge base. S. Tappel helped to define V and wrote the original version of RC in LISP. R. Floyd and

B. Mont-Reynaud provided considerable technical and editing assistance with this paper.

This work describes research done in Kestrel Institute and Systems Control Inc. This research is supported in part by the Defense Advanced Research Projects Agency Contracts N00014-79-C-0127 and N00014-81-C-0582 monitored by the Office of Naval Research. The views and conclusions in this paper are those of the authors and should not be interpreted as representing the official policies, either expressed or implied, of Kestrel, SCI, DARPA, ONR or the U.S. Government.

REFERENCES

Balzer, R. (1981). Transformational implementation: an example, *IEEE Transactions on Software Engineering*, Jan. 1981, 3–14.

Genesereth, M. R. and Lenat, D. B. (1980). "A modifiable representation system,' *HPP-80-26*, Stanford: Computer Science Department, Stanford University.

Goldman, N. M., and Wile, D. S. (1979). A relational data base foundation for process specifications, *Int. Conf. on Entity-Relationship Approach to Systems Analysis and Design*, pp. 413–432 (ed. Chem., pp).

Green, C. C. (1969). Theorem proving by resolution as a basis for question answering systems, *Machine Intelligence 4*, pp. 183–205, (eds. Meltzer, B. and Michie, D.). Edinburgh: Edinburgh University Press.

Green, C. C. (1969a). Application of theorem-proving to problem-solving, *Proc. Int. Jnt. Conf. Art. Int.* (LJCAI-69), pp. 219–239, eds. Walker, D. A. and Morton, L. M. London and New York: Gordon and Breach.

Green, C. C. (1969). The application of theorem-proving to question-answering systems, Ph.D. Thesis, Electrical Engineering Department, Stanford University. Also printed as *AIM-96*, and *STAN-CS-69-138*. Stanford: Artificial Intelligence Laboratory, Computer Science Department, Stanford University, also reprinted 1979. New York: Garland Publishing, Inc.

Green, C. C., Phillips, J., Westfold, S., Pressburger, T., Angebranndt, S., Kedzierski, B., Mont-Reynaud, B., and Chapiro (1981). Progress in knowledge-based programming and algorithm design, *Technical Report KES.U.81.1*, Palo Alto: Kestrel Institute.

Ingalls, D. H. (1978). The SMALLTALK-76 programming system: design and implementation, *Fifth Annual ACM Symposium on Principles of Programming Languages*, pp. 9–16. Tucson, Arzona, January, 1978.

Kant, E. (1979). Efficiency considerations in program synthesis: A knowledge based approach, Ph.D. Thesis. Also published as *AIM-331*, and *STAN-CS-79-755*. Stanford: Computer Science Department, Stanford University; also as *Efficiency in program synthesis*. Ann Arbour: UMI Research Press (1981).

Kowalski, R. (1979). *Logic for Programming*, Amsterdam, New York, Oxford: North Holland.

Manna, Z., and Waldinger, R. (1980). Problematic features of programming languages: a situational calculus approach, *STAN-CS-80-779*. Stanford: Department of Computer Science, Stanford University.

Phillips, J. P. Self-described programming environments: an application of a theory of design to programming systems. Ph.D. Thesis. Stanford. Departments of Electrical Engineering and Computer Science, Stanford University.

Phillips, J., and Green, C. C. (1980). Towards self-described programming environments, *Technical Report, SCI.ICS.L.81.3*, Palo Alto: Computer Science Department, Systems Control Inc.

Rich, C. (1981). Inspection methods of programming, Ph.D. Thesis, *MIT/AI/TR-604*, Cambridge, Mass: MIT.

Schonberg, J., Schwartz, J. T. and Sharir, M. (1978). Automatic data selection in SETL, *Proc. Fifth ACM Symposium on Principles of Programming Languages,* Tucson, Arizona, Jan. 1978.

Shrobe, H., Dependency directed reasoning for complex program understanding, Ph.D. Thesis, *MIT/AIM/TR-503,* Cambridge, Mass: MIT.

Teitelman, W., and Masinter, L. (1981). The INTERLISP programming environment, *Computer,* **14**, 4.

Warren, D. H. D., Pereira, L. and Pereira, F. (1977). PROLOG: the language and its implementaion compared with LISP, *Proc. Symposium and AI and Programming Languages, SIGPLAN/SIGART,* **12**, No. 8.

Warren, D. H. D. (1980). Logic programming and compiler writing, *Software – Practice and Experience,* 97–125.

Waters, W. (1978). Automatic analysis of the logical structure of programs, Ph.D. Thesis, *MIT/AI/TR-492,* Cambridge, Mass: MIT.

Weyhrauch, R. W. (1980). Prolegomena to a theory of mechanized formal reasoning, *Artificial Intelligence* **13**, 133–170.

18

The roles of knowledge and deduction in algorithm design

D. R. Barstow*
Computer Science Department
Yale University, USA

Abstract

In the earliest attempts to apply artificial intelligence techniques to program synthesis, deduction (that is, the use of a general purpose mechanism such as a theorem prover) played a central role. Recent attempts have relied almost exclusively on knowledge about programming in particular domains, with no significant role for deduction. Even in such knowledge-based systems, however, there seems to be an important role for deduction in testing the applicability conditions of specific programming rules. This auxiliary role for deduction is especially important in algorithm design, as can be seen in the hypothetical synthesis of a breadth-first enumeration algorithm. The interplay between knowledge and deduction also shows how one can be motivated to consider the central mathematical properties upon which particular algorithms are based, as illustrated in the synthesis of two minimum cost spanning tree algorithms.

1. INTRODUCTION

In applying artificial intelligence techniques to the problem of automatic program sysnthesis, two basic approaches have been tried. In the first approach, deduction (i.e., the use of a general-purpose deductive mechanism such as a theorem prover or problem solver) played a central role. The basic idea was to rephrase the program specification as a theorem to be proved or a problem to be solved. If a proof or solution was found, it could be transformed into a program satisfying the original specification. The Heuristic Compiler [16], the early work of Green [7] and Waldinger [17], and the recent work of Manna & Waldinger [12,13,14] are all examples of this approach. The second approach, an application of the knowledge engineering paradigm, is based on the assumption that the ability of human programmers to write programs comes more from access to large amounts

* Now with Schlumberger-Doll Research Center, Ridgefield, Connecticut

of knowledge about specific aspects of programming than from the application of a few general deductive principles. For example, the PECOS system [2, 3] had a knowledge base of four hundred rules about many aspects of symbolic programming, and could apply these to the task of implementing abstract algorithms.

Although much progress has been made, neither approach has yet 'solved' the automatic programming problem, and it is suggested here that neither one alone ever will. There are two problems with the deductive approach. First, for programs of real-world interest, the search space is too large to be explored by a theorem prover. While current systems are capable of synthesizing programs such as 'greatest common divisor', no system can yet synthesize any program of significantly greater complexity. And without guiding the theorem prover with some kind of knowledge about how to write programs, it is unlikely that much progress can be made. Second, since there is a one-to-one correspondence between proofs and programs, if there is a measure by which one program may be preferred to another (e.g., efficiency), then the theorem prover must find, not just any proof, but the 'right' proof. That is, the theorem prover needs to know that it is really writing programs and how to relate differences between proofs to differences between programs.

On the other hand, the knowledge-based approach has only been applied to the synthesis of programs from relatively algorithmic specifications. While many rules for algorithm refinement have been developed and tested, very little progress has been made on rules for algorithm design. And, as has been observed elsewhere (e.g., [9]), algorithm design requires a deep understanding of the problem to be solved, an understanding which seems to include the ability to reason (make deductions) about the problem.

In the rest of this paper, a way to combine these two approaches is suggested, as summarized in the following two statements:

(1) Just as there are specific rules for refining abstract algorithms into concrete implementations, there are also rules for designing algorithms from non-algorithmic specifications.

(2) In testing the applicability conditions of such rules, it is necessary to call on a deductive mechanism to test whether certain properties hold for the program being developed. (See [4] for a similar model of algorithm design, but more closely related to the deduction approach.)

In the next section, these two statements are illustrated with a detailed synthesis of a graph algorithm. In section 3, two other algorithm syntheses are used to demonstrate how these roles for knowledge and deduction help identify the mathematical basis for a particular algorithm.

2. HYPOTHETICAL SYNTHESIS

The synthesis in this section consists of a sequence of rule applications, with each rule representing some fact that human programmers probably know and that automatic programming systems probably should know. Several of the rules can only be applied if some condition holds for the program under construction. These are the conditions that seem appropriate tasks for a deductive system, and are indicated by the word "PROOF" in the synthesis. The synthesis will be presented in a mixture of English and a hypothetical Algol-like language, in order to focus on the nature of the programming knowledge and the algorithm design process, independent from any formalism used to express them. It should be noted at the outset that this synthesis is beyond the capabilities of any current automatic programming system, and of course, the rules and proofs will have to be formalized before the synthesis could be automated.

2.1 *Specification*

Write a program that inputs the root R of a tree with a known successor function CHILDREN(N) and constructs a sequence of all (and only) the nodes of the tree, such that if the distance from R to N1 is less than the distance from R to N2, then N1 precedes N2 in the sequence (where the distance from X to Y, denoted by $D(X,Y)$, is the number of arcs between X an Y; thus, $D(R,X)$ is the depth of X).

This specification is basically a non-algorithmic description of a breadth-first enumeration of the nodes in a tree. One way to deal with this specification would be to recognize that a breadth-first enumeration is the desired program, and to use specific knowledge about breadth-first enumerations (perhaps a template) to produce a program. In this hypothetical synthesis, we will consider the more interesting case in which the basic algorithm must actually be developed.

2.2 *Overview*

The synthesis process goes through four major stages. First, the task is broken into two parts, a 'producer' that generates the nodes in the desired order, and a 'consumer' that builds a sequence from the nodes generated by the producer. The second stage involves constructing the consumer, which simplifies into a simple concatenation operation. The third stage, in which the producer is built, is relatively complex but eventually results in a simple queue mechanism in which nodes are produced by taking them from the front and the children of each produced node are added at the back. Finally, the two processes are combined together into a simple WHILE loop.

2.3 *The Transfer Paradigm.*

A common paradigm for many programming problems involves viewing the problem as one of transferring objects from an input set to an output set. For example, selection and insertion sort can both be viewed as instances of the transfer paradigm. One way to implement such a transfer program is to build two processes, with one (a producer) producing the objects in the input set, and the other (a consumer) using the objects to build the output set. If we view the present task this way, the input set consists of the nodes in the tree and

363

the output set is the ordered sequence. Thus, we may apply the following rule to break the task into two subtasks:

> If the task involves using the elements in one set to build another set, try the transfer paradigm, with the producer producing the elements from the first set and the consumer building the second set.

When the transfer paradigm is used, objects are passed from the producer to the consumer in some order, which we may call the transfer order. While the transfer order is often inconsequential, the following rule suggests that a particular order might be useful in this case:

> If a consumer builds an ordered sequence, try constraining the transfer order to satisfy the same ordering.

After applying these two rules, the original task has been broken into two subtasks:

> Producer:
>   Send the nodes of the tree to the consumer
>   in any order satisfying the following constraint:
>   if $D(R,N1) < D(R,N2)$, then N1 is produced before N2
> Consumer:
>   Using the objects received from the producer,
>   build a sequence satisfying the following constraint:
>   if $D(R,N1) < D(R,N2)$, then N1 precedes N2 in the sequence
>   The objects are received from the producer
>   in an order satisfying the following constraint:
>   if $D(R,N1) < D(R,N2)$, then N1 is produced before N2

We may now consider the producer and consumer separately, viewing each as a separate process.

2.4 The Consumer

A process such as the consumer consists of several parts, including an initialization and an action to be performed at each stage. The first rule establishes the initialization part of this consumer:

> If a consumer builds a set consisting solely of objects received from another process, the set is initially empty.

The next rule establishes the action to be performed at each step:

> If a consumer builds a set consisting of all objects received from another process, the action at each step involves adding the object to the set.

Finally, we may apply a special rule for adding an object to an ordered sequence:

> If it is known that an object follows every member of an ordered sequence, the object may be added to the sequence by inserting it at the back.

Before applying this rule, we must prove its applicability condition: 'the object follows every member of the ordered sequence.' In this case, the proof is trivial, since the objects are received from the producer in the desired order, and these objects are the only members of the sequence. Having applied the rule, we are now finished with the consumer:

Consumer:
  Initialization:
    $S := \langle\rangle$
  Action:
    $X :=$ {receive from producer}
    insert X at the back of S

where "$\langle\rangle$" is the empty sequence.

2.5 *The Producer*

We are now ready to consider the producer, a process that produces the nodes of the tree with a constraint on the order of production. The following rule suggests a way to write the producer:

> If a producer produces all of the nodes of a graph according to some ordering constraint, try using an ordered enumeration of the nodes in the graph, where the action for each step of the enumeration is to produce the enumerated node.

Any such enumeration produces the nodes of the graph, guaranteeing that each node is produced exactly once. In order to do this, the enumerator must know, at each stage, which objects have and have not been enumerated. That is, the state of the enumeration must be saved between 'calls' to the producer process. In this case, the objects to be enumerated are all objects which may be reached from the root node by following zero or more arcs. At any point in the process of following these arcs, certain nodes will have been found and others will not. Of those that have been found, some will have had their successors looked at, and others will not. Thus, the enumeration state may be maintained by tagging the nodes (at least conceptually) with one of three labels. This technique for saving the state is summarized in the following rule:

> If a graph is represented as a base set of nodes and a successor function, the state of an enumeration of the nodes may be represented as a mapping of nodes to one of three states: "EXPLORED", "BOUNDARY", and "UNEXPLORED".

(Note that up to this point, no descision has been made about how to implement this mapping. In particular, there is no commitment to explicitly tagging each of the nodes with one of these labels. As will be seen, the final representation of this mapping involves only a single set, consisting of those nodes tagged "BOUNDARY".)

365

Any enumeration involves several parts, including an initialization, a termination test, a way of selecting the next object to enumerate, and a way of incrementing the state. The following three rules are all based on the technique just selected for saving the enumeration state:

If the state of an enumeration of the nodes in a graph is represented as a three-state mapping, the state may be intialized by setting the image of all nodes to "UNEXPLORED" and then changing the image of the base nodes to "BOUNDARY".

If the state of an enumeration of the nodes in a graph is represented as a three-state mapping, the termination test involves testing whether any nodes are mapped to "BOUNDARY". If not, the enumeration is over.

If the state of an enumeration of the nodes in a graph is represented as a three-state mapping, the action at each stage consists of selecting some node mapped to "BOUNDARY" (the enumerated node), changing its mapping to "EXPLORED", and changing the mapping of all its "UNEXPLORED" successors to "BOUNDARY". The "BOUNDARY" node must be selected to satisfy any ordering constraints on the enumeration.

Thus, applying the above rules gives us the following description of the producer (where MARK[X] specifies the image of X under the mapping and MARK^{-1}[Y] specifies the inverse image of Y, that is, the set of all nodes which map to Y under MARK):

Producer:
    Initialization:
        for all nodes, X:
            MARK[X] := "UNEXPLORED"
        change MARK[R] from "UNEXPLORED" to "BOUNDARY"
    Termination test:
        is MARK^{-1} ["BOUNDARY"] empty?
    Each step:
        X := select any node in MARK^{-1} ["BOUNDARY"] such that
            if X1 and X2 are nodes remaining to be selected
                and $D(R, X1) < D(R, X2)$ then X1 is selected before X2
        change MARK[X] from "BOUNDARY" to "EXPLORED"
        for all successors, Y, of X:
            if MARK[Y] = "UNEXPLORED"
                then change MARK[Y] from "UNEXPLORED" to
                        "BOUNDARY"
        {send X to the consumer}

Note that the nodes that remain to be enumerated include some tagged "UNEXPLORED" as well as those tagged "BOUNDARY". Thus, the selection operation, and the constraint on it, may be precisely stated as follows:

X := select any node in MARK^{-1}["BOUNDARY"] such that
D(R, X) ⩽ D(R, Z) for all Z such that MARK[Z]=
"BOUNDARY" or MARK[Z]="UNEXPLORED" and Z is
reachable from R

If we call the set from which an object is to be selected the 'selection set', and the set of which that object must be minimal the 'constraint set', the following rule gives us a way to implement the selection operation:

If a selection operation is subject to an ordering constraint, and every member of the constraint set is dominated by some member of the selection set, the selection operation may be implemented by taking the minimal element of the selection set.

When this rule us applied, we have the following:

X := closest node in MARK^{-1}["BOUNDARY"]

However, before aplying the rule we must prove one of its conditions:

PROOF: for all Z such that MARK[Z]="BOUNDARY"
        or MARK[Z]="UNEXPLORED" and Z is reachable from R,
there exists an X such that
        MARK[X]="BOUNDARY" and D(R, X) ⩽ D(R, Z)

If MARK[Z]="BOUNDARY", then Z is such an X. Suppose MARK[Z]= "UNEXPLORED" and Z is reachable from R. Since the graph is a tree, there is exactly one path from R to Z, and there must be some node, W, on this path such that MARK[W]="BOUNDARY". This is true since either (i) R is "BOUNDARY" and W can be R; or (ii) the path from R to Z begins with some nonzero number of "EXPLORED" nodes and the next node (which is the desired W) is "BOUNDARY", since all of an "EXPLORED" node's successors are either "EXPLORED" or "BOUNDARY". Since 0⩽D(W, Z), D(R,W)⩽D(R,Z), and thus W dominates Z. QED

Thus, the action at each stage of the enumeration has been simplified:

X := closest node in MARK^{-1}["BOUNDARY"]
change MARK[X] from "BOUNDARY" to "EXPLORED"
for all successors, Y, of X:
    if MARK[Y] = "UNEXPLORED"
        then change MARK[Y] from "UNEXPLORED" to
            "BOUNDARY"
{send X to the consumer}

Part of the body involves a test of whether a node is "UNEXPLORED". The following rule enables this test to be omitted:

If it is known that the value of a test in a conditional will always be true, the test may be omitted and the conditional refined into the action of the 'true' branch.

367

In order to apply this rule, we must prove one of its conditions:

PROOF: every successor of X is "UNEXPLORED"

Every successor of X was initially "UNEXPLORED", since every node (except the root, which is not a successor of any node), was initially "UNEXPLORED". The mark of an "UNEXPLORED" node is changed in only one place, when the node is the successor of some other node. Thus, if a successor of X is not "UNEXPLORED", it must be the successor of some node other than X, which is impossible because the graph is a tree. Hence, every successor of X is "UNEXPLORED". QED

With these simplifications to the enumerator, it is clear that only the "BOUNDARY" tag is really being used. Thus, the mapping may be simplified somewhat by getting rid of references to the other two possibilities (i.e., making them implicit instead of explicit). This knowledge is embodied in the following rules:

If a range element is only used in 'set image' and 'change image' operations, it may be made implicit.

If the range element of a 'set image' operation is implicit, the operation may be omitted.

The result of applying the above rules is as follows:

Producer:
    Initialization:
        change MARK[R] from implicit to "BOUNDARY"
    Termination test:
        is MARK^{-1}["BOUNDARY"] empty?
    Each step:
        X := closest node in MARK^{-1} ["BOUNDARY"]
        change MARK[X] from "BOUNDARY" to implicit
        for all successors, Y, of X:
            change MARK[Y] from implicit to "BOUNDARY"
        {send X to the consumer}

We are finally ready to implement the mapping. When inverse images are frequent operations, the mapping can be inverted, as suggested by the following rule:

A mapping with domain X and range Y may be represented as a mapping whose domain is Y and whose range consists of subsets of X.

In addition to this data structure representation rule, we need the following rules dealing with operations on such data structures:

If a mapping is inverted, the inverse image of a range object may be found by retrieving the image of the range object under the inverted mapping.

If a mapping is inverted, a range object may be assigned as the image of a domain object by adding the domain object to the image of the range object under the inverted mapping.

If a mapping is inverted, the image of a domain object may be changed from one range object to another by removing the domain object from the image of the first range object and adding it to the image of the second range object.

If a mapping is inverted, operations on implicit domain objects may be omitted.

If a mapping is inverted, the initial state of the mapping is that all range sets are empty.

Applying these rules gives the following (where MARK′ is the inverted mapping):

```
Producer:
    Initialization:
        MARK′["BOUNDARY"] := { }
        add R to MARK′["BOUNDARY"]
    Termination test:
        is MARK′["BOUNDARY"] empty?
    Each step:
        X := closest node in MARK′["BOUNDARY"]
        remove X from MARK′["BOUNDARY"]
        for all successors, Y of X:
            add Y to MARK′["BOUNDARY"]
        {send X to the consumer}
```

Of course, the inverted mapping must still be represented concretely. Here, the elements of the domain set are known precisely (there is only one) and all references to the mapping involve constants for domain elements, so a record structure is a particularly good technique:

A mapping whose domain consists of a fixed set may be represented as a record structure with one field for each domain element.

We also need a rule for references to such a data structure:

If a mapping is represented as a record structure, the image of a constant domain object may be referenced by referencing the corresponding field of the record.

This representation may be simplified further, as suggested by the following rules:

A record structure with only one field may be represented as the object stored in the field.

If a record structure is represented as the object stored in its single field, the field may be referenced by referencing the record structure itself.

369

Applying all of the above rules gives us the following (in which the single set is called B):

Producer:
    Initialization:
        B := { }
        add R to B
    Termination test:
        is B empty?
    Each step:
        X := closest node in B
        remove X from B
        for all successors, Y, of X:
            add Y to B
        {send X to the consumer}

We now have three operations on the B set to consider, and each depends on the representation for that set. Since one of the operations involves taking an extreme element under an ordering relation, it is natural to use an ordered sequence. We thus apply the following rule:

A set whose elements have an ordering relation may be represented as an ordered sequence.

Having applied this rule, we must consider the operations on B. The 'closest' operation may be refined by using the following rule:

If a set is represented as an ordered sequence, the least element under the ordering may be found by taking the first element of the sequence.

Normally, removing an element from a sequence requires first searching for its position and then deleting that position. In this case, we can avoid the search by applying the following rule:

If it is known that an element is the first element of a sequence, that element may be removed from the sequence by removing the first element.

Finally, we must consider the two addition operations, one adding R to B and the other adding each successor of X to B. In each case, we may apply the same rule used earlier in writing the consumer:

If it is known that an object follows every member of an ordered sequence, the object may be added to the sequence by inserting it at the back.

And, in each case, we must prove the applicability condition. The proof when adding R to B is trivial, since B is empty. However, the proof for adding the successors of X to B is somewhat more complicated. Before considering the main proof, we need the following lemma:

370

LEMMA: for some X in B and for all Z in B,
$$D(R,X) \leqslant D(R,Z) \leqslant D(R,X)+1$$

This is clearly true initially, since $B = \{R\}$. Suppose it is true at some point. There are only two changes in B that can be made during one step:

   (a) X is removed from B

   (b) Y is added to B

(a) After X is removed, either B is empy (in which case adding Y restores the desired property) or there is some new closest node, call it W. We know:

   $D(R,X) \leqslant D(R,W)$ and $D(R,W) \leqslant D(R,Z)$ for all Z in B

so substitution (into the inequality that held before X was removed) gives us:

   $D(R,W) \leqslant D(R,Z) \leqslant D(R,X)+1 \leqslant D(R,W)+1$ for all Z in B

(b) After Y is added to B, since $D(R,Y)=D(R,X)+1$,

   $D(R,W) \leqslant D(R,Z) \leqslant D(R,Y) \leqslant D(R,W)+1$ for all Z in B

Thus, by induction we have:

   for some X in B and for all Z in B,
$$D(R,X) \leqslant D(R,Z) \leqslant D(R,X)+1$$
QED

Note that this lemma holds after each successor of X is added to B. So we are now ready to prove the condition necessary for adding Y at the back of B.

PROOF: Y follows every element of B

The ordering constraint on B is:

   if $D(R,X)<D(R,Z)$ then X precedes Z in B

So what we wish to show is:

   if $D(R,X) \leqslant D(R,Z)$ for all Z in B,
      and Y is a successor of X,
   then $D(R,Z) \leqslant D(R,Y)$ for all Z in B.

The lemma indicates that there is some X in B such that everything else in B is at least as far from the root as X, but not further away than 1 arc. Therefore, this property must hold for the closest node in B. Since $D(R,Y) = D(R,X)+1$, if Y is a successor of X, we know that $D(R,Z) \leqslant D(R,Y)$ for all Z in B. Thus, Y follows every element of B. QED

We have now finished the producer:

Producer:
   Initialization:
      $B := \langle \rangle$
      insert R at the back of B

371

Termination test:
  is B empty?
Each step:
  X := first element of B
  remove first element of B
  for all successors, Y, of X:
    insert Y at the back of B
  {send X to the consumer}

2.6 *Recombining the Producer and Consumer*

Finally, by applying the following rule, the producer and consumer can be recombined into a single process:

> A transfer program involving a producer and consumer may be refined into a WHILE loop whose condition is the termination test of the producer.

And we have the following algorithm for enumerating the nodes of a tree in breadth-first order:

  S := ⟨⟩
  B := ⟨⟩
  insert R at the back of B
  while B is not empty do
    X := first element of B
    remove first element of B
    for all successors, Y, of X:
      insert Y at the back of B
    insert X at the back of S

From this point on, rules about simple symbolic programming (such as those in PECOS) could produce the final implementation. The interesting aspects involve representing the sequences S and B (each is probably best represented as a linked list with a special pointer to the last cell), and the 'for all' construct (which depends on the representation of the set returned by CHILDREN(P)).

3. MOTIVATING THE USE OF CRITICAL LEMMAS

As another illustration of this view of the roles of knowledge and deduction in algorithm design, let us look briefly at the problem of finding the minimum cost spanning tree in a weighted undirected graph. The problem may be specified as follows:

> Write a program that inputs a weighted, undirected, connected graph G and constructs a subgraph T such that:
> (1) T is a tree;
> (2) T contains every node of G;
> (3) $W(T) \leqslant \min \{W(T') \mid T'$ is a subgraph of G which is a tree and which contains every node of G$\}$.

(W is the weight function on edges; when applied to a graph it denotes the sum of the weights on the edges.)

There are two standard algorithms for this task, one due to Kruskal [11] and one due to Prim [14]. For each of these, there are a variety of implementations, based on different techniques and representations for the sets and graphs involved. (Cheriton & Tarjan give a detailed discussion of several implementations [5]). Both standard algorithms are based on a single lemma, which may be stated as follows:

> If T is a subgraph of some minimum cost spanning tree of G, T contains all the nodes of G, T' is one of the connected components of T, and x is an edge of minimal weight connecting T' to another connected component of T, then T'+{x} is a subgraph of some minimum cost spanning tree of G.

If one knows this lemma, it is not difficult to come up with either of the standard algorithms. But what if one does not know the lemma? In the rest of this section, we will see that the model of algorithm design discussed in earlier sections leads naturally and directly to the fundamental lemma. In particular, we will consider the minimum cost spanning tree from two different viewpoints, in each case applying a sequence of general programming rules, and in each case arriving at the need to prove the lemma. In the interests of brevity, syntheses will not be pursued at the same level of detail as the breadth-first enumeration algorithm, but only to a sufficient degree to show how one is led to the fundamental lemma in each case. (Note: the rest of this discussion is worded as if the minimum cost spanning tree were unique; this is not crucial to the synthesis process, but simplifies the discussion.)

3.1 Toward Kruskal's Algorithm

The minimum cost spanning tree problem can be viewed as one of selecting a subset of the edges of the original graph. Under such a view, the transfer paradigm (used already for the breadth-first enumeration problem) is appropriate, as suggested by the following rule:

> If the task involves finding a subset of a given set, try the transfer paradigm, with the producer producing the elements from the first set and the consumer testing each for inclusion in the subset.

Of course, this paradigm only succeeds if it is actually possible to test the elements of the set individually as they are produced, which at this point in the synthesis cannot be guaranteed (hence, the word 'try' in the rule). If it turns out to be impossible to construct such a test, then a more general paradigm (such as depth-first search allowing back-up by more than one step) or even an entirely different paradigm (such as the tree-growth paradigm of the next section) must be tried.

As with the breadth-first enumeration problem, the transfer order is again important. The following rule suggests that a particular order might be useful in this case:

373

If the object being built by the consumer must satisfy a minimality constraint based on some function of the objects being transfered, try constraining the transfer order to be in increasing order of the function.

Again, there is no guarantee that this approach will succeed; this is simply a heuristic suggesting a potentially useful strategy. This heuristic is, in fact, one of the key steps in reaching Kruskal's algorithm, but note that it is far more general than its application to this particular problem. For example, it also plays a role in creating the standard breadth-first algorithm for determining the shortest path from one node in a graph to another. Note also that there are other heuristics that one could apply here. For example, one could try considering the edges in order of decreasing weight, resulting ultimately in an algorithm that gradually removes edges from the original graph until the minimum spanning tree is determined (Kruskal describes this as 'Construction A'' [11]).

After applying these two rules, the original task has been broken into two subtasks:

Producer:
    Send the edges of the graph to the consumer
    in any order satisfying the following constraint:
        if $W(E1) < W(E2)$, then E1 is produced before E2
Consumer:
    Using the objects received from the producer,
    build a subset T of the objects such that:
        (1) T is a tree;
        (2) T contains every node of G;
        (3) $W(T) \leq \min \{W(T') \mid T'$ is a subgraph of G which is a tree and which contains every node of G$\}$.
    The objects are received from the producer
    in an order satisfying the following constraint:
        if $W(E1) < W(E2)$, then E1 is produced before E2

For this task, the producer is relatively simple, essentially involving only a sort of the edge set of G, either as a pre-process before sending any edges to the consumer, or intermittently during the process of sending. In either case, the algorithm depends on the representation of G and the representation chosen to hold the sorted edge set, but is not particularly complicated. Since it is also not relevant to identifying the critical lemma, the synthesis process for the producer will be skipped in the interest of brevity.

The consumer is a process that produces a subgraph of the original graph, assuming that it receives the edges of G in order of increasing weight. The following rule suggests a way to write the consumer:

If a consumer builds a subset from the set produced by the producer, try writing a test that determines whether or not an element belongs in the subset, based solely on the subset that has been constructed so far, on the order in which the elements are received, and on the fact that any element already received by the consumer is either not in the desired subset or has been added to the subset already.

In effect, this rule suggests trying to add the elements to the subset one at a time. (A less desirable alternative would be to reconsider the entire set of edges received so far, but this would be somewhat strange in light of the original decision to try the transfer paradigm.) The problem here is to determine a relatively simple test. Before developing the test, we must define the notion of a 'preventive' constraint:

A constraint is preventive if, whenever a set S violates the constraint, there is no superset of S that satisfies it.

Given this definition, the following rule suggests a test to be used in this problem:

If you know that the following is true (where S is the desired set, S' is the subset constructed so far, x is the element received by the consumer):
    If S' is a subset of S
        and S'+{x} does not violate any preventive constraints on S
        and if y was received before x then y is in S' or not in S
    then S'+{x} is a subset of S.

then the test for whether a new element may be added to the subset constructed so far may be implemented as a test of whether the new element does not violate any preventive constraints on the subset.

(While this phrasing may seem a bit long for a 'rule,' its length is due to its precision; a less formal statement would be 'Try using only preventive constraints in the test.')

In order to apply the rule, the condition must be tested (here, T is the desired subgraph of G):

If T' is a subset of T
    and T'+{x} does not violate any preventive constraints on T
    and if y was received before x then y is in T' or not in T
then T'+{x} is a subset of T.

Which are the preventive constraints? The constraint that T be a tree reduces to two subconstraints: that T be acyclic and that T be connected. Of these, the constraint that T be acyclic is clearly preventive: if a graph is cyclic, no graph containing it can be a tree; the constraint that T be connected is clearly not preventive: any disconnected graph may be extended into a connected graph. The constraint that T contain every node of G is not preventive: any graph that contains a subset of the nodes of G can be extended to contain every node of G. Finally, the minimality constraint is preventive (at least, if all edge weights are positive): if the weight of a graph is greater than some value, then any extension of that graph will also be greater than the value.

The third antecedent in the rule's condition may also be instantiated for this problem: since the edges are being transferred in order of increasing weight, the condition 'y was received before x' reduces to '$W(y) < W(x)$'. Thus the condition on the rule becomes:

If T' is a subset of T
    and $T'+\{x\}$ is acyclic
    and $W(T'+\{x\}) \leqslant$ min $\{W(T') \mid T'$ is a subgraph of G which is a tree
                            and which contains every node of G$\}$
    and if $W(y) < W(x)$ then y is in T' or not in T
then $T'+\{x\}$ is a subset of T.

The antecedents of this condition are not independent. In particular:

$W(T'+\{x\}) \leqslant W(T) \leqslant$ min $\{W(T') \mid T'$ is a subgraph of G which is a tree
                                and which contains every node of G$\}$

since T must contain at least one of the edges not yet received by the consumer and since x has the least weight of the edges not yet received. Thus, the condition may be reduced to:

If T' is a subset of T
    and $T'+\{x\}$ is acyclic
    and if $W(y) < W(x)$ then y is in T' or not in T
then $T'+\{x\}$ is a subset of T.

The clause about weights may be rephrased slightly:

if y is in T and not in T' then $W(x) \leqslant W(y)$

that is:

$W(x) \leqslant$ min $\{W(y) \mid$ y is in T and not in $T'\}$

Since

$\{y \mid$ y is in T and not in $T'\}$ is a subset of $\{y \mid T'+\{y\}$ is acyclic$\}$

the following is sufficient:

$W(x) \leqslant$ min $\{W(y) \mid T'+\{y\}$ is acyclic$\}$

leading to the following condition which, if proved, is sufficient to permit the rule to be applied:

If T' is a subset of T
    and $T'+\{x\}$ is acyclic
    and $W(x) \leqslant$ min $\{W(y) \mid T'+\{y\}$ is acyclic$\}$
then $T'+\{x\}$ is a subset of T.

Thus, by applying a sequence of relatively general programming rules, we are led naturally and directly to a (slightly) special case of the fundamental lemma.

The rest of the synthesis process is less interesting, and will be omitted. The final algorithm is as follows (assuming that the producer sorts the edges before sending any to the consumer):

```
T := { };
E := edges of G sorted by weight;
while E is non-empty do
      X := first element of E;
      E := rest of E;
      if T+{X} is acyclic
          then T := T+{X}
```

Of course, a considerable amount of work remains to be done. In particular, the test for acyclicity can be very inefficient unless some sophisticated data structures are maintained. Aho, Hopcroft and Ullman describe an efficient implementation of Kruskal's algorithm [1].

3.2 *Toward Prim's Algorithm*

In the previous section the minimum cost spanning tree was viewed as a problem of finding a particular subset of a known set. The problem can also be viewed in terms more specific to graph theory by applying the following rule:

If the task involves finding a tree satisfying certain constraints, try starting with a degenerate tree (a single node) and adding edges to the tree until the constraints are satisfied.

As with the transfer paradigm, there is no guarantee that this strategy will succeed. (In particular, it may not be possible to determine an appropriate edge to add at each step.) But it still seems a reasonable strategy to explore.

In applying this strategy, there are two subtasks: determining a technique for selecting the initial node and determining a techinque for finding an edge to add at each step. For the first, the following rule may be used:

If the set of nodes in the desired tree is known, try selecting any node from the set as the initial node.

Of course, there are other plausible techniques. (For example, selecting one of the nodes on an edge of minimal weight is another good way to start.) But the unconstrained selection seems as good as any, and is easily implemented (depending on the representation of the nodes of the graph).

The second subtask, determining a technique for finding an edge to add at each step, is more difficult, but the following rule offers a possibility:

If the tree to be grown must satisfy a minimality constraint, and you know that the following holds:
    if T' is a subtree of T
        and x extends T'

377

and T'+{x} does not violate any preventive constraints on T
and W(x) = min {W(y) | y extends T'}
then T'+{x} is a subtree of T
then at each stage select the edge of minimal weight that extends
T' and does not violate any preventive constraints.

(This rule is actually just a variant of the minimality heuristic used in developing Kruskal's algorithm.) Before applying the rule, the condition must be proved. As with Kruskal's algorithm, the only preventive constraints are that T'+{x} be acyclic and that the weight of T' be minimal. By similar reasoning, the condition reduces to:

if T' is a subtree of T
and x extends T'
and W(x) = min {W(y) | y extends T'}
then T'+{x} is a subtree of T

Again we are led naturally and directly to a (slightly) special case of the fundamental lemma. In this case, we were led even more directly to the necessary condition than with Kruskal's algorithm, but this is primarily because the rules were specific to graph problems, rather than being oriented more generally toward sets.

The final algorithm is as follows:

T := { };
while T does not contain all of the vertices of G do
    X := edge of least weight that connects T to some vertex not in T;
    T := T+{X}

Here again, considerable work remains to be done. In this case, the hard part is determining the edge of least weight that extends T. Dijkstra, and Kerschenbaum & Van Slyke, give implementations of the basic algorithm [6, 10].

4. DISCUSSION

The model of algorithm design and program synthesis that emerges from these examples has several parts. First, there is a body of strategic rules, each suggesting a paradigm that may lead to an algorithm for solving the given problem. These strategic rules are relatively specific (more so than condition- or recursion-introduction rules) yet applicable in a variety of situations. Even when applicable, however, there is rarely a guarantee that the paradigm will indeed result in an algorithm: that can only be determined by trying to fill out the pieces. If an algorithm does result, and if the applicability conditions have all been met, then the algorithm will be correct (assuming correctness of the individual rules). Second, there is a larger body of implementation rules which can be used to refine an abstract algorithm into concrete code in some target language. These rules are again relatively specific, but usually independent of any particular target language. Finally, there must also be rules for the chosen target language; while these rules must at some point take over from the implementation rules, this may occur at different levels of abstraction for different languages and problems.

In the process of testing the applicability conditions of any of these rules, deduction plays a very important role. When it is used, it involves properties of the program being developed and properties of the domain. (It is interesting to note that, even if a condition cannot be proved, one could apply the rule, resulting in a heuristic program; this would be especially useful if the condition were tested and found to hold on a large number of examples.) Although not illustrated by the hypothetical synthesis, a mechanism for choosing from among applicable rules is also needed. Among the possibilities for such a mechansim are efficiency models of the program being developed (i.e., an evaluation function) and heuristic rules based both on the efficiency of the target program and on the likelihood of a particular strategy succeeding. This latter consideration seems especially important in the initial algorithm design phase.

The rules illustrated here (and the concepts involved in them) are relevant in many more situations than these graph problems. As noted earlier, the transfer paradigm provides a useful model for several sorting algorithms, including selection and insertion sort. In fact, choosing the transfer order seems to be the primary decision involved in differentiating the two types of sorting, and the rule about adding objects to ordered sequences is itself used in deriving an insertion sort. (For a more detailed discussion of this paradigm for sorting, see [8]). As another example, the notion of an enumeration state is critical to any enumeration (in fact, it corresponds to the loop invariant), and the three-state mapping used here is simply a generalization of the standard state-saving schemes used for sequences such as linked lists and arrays.

In fact, many of the rules used in these hypothetical syntheses have already been implemented and tested in the PECOS system. For example, PECOS's knowledge base included the rules about inverted mappings and record structures, and they were used in the implementation of several abstract algorithms, including a reachability algorithm and a simple concept formation algorithm.

5. CONCLUSIONS

In order for future automatic programming systems to be truly useful when applied to real-world tasks, they will necessarily have to deal with complex programs at a rather detailed level. It seems to me that this will only be possible if these systems have effective access to large amounts of knowledge about what we today consider to be the task of programming. While some of this knowledge certainly involves general strategies, such as the conditional and recursion introduction rules of deduction-based systems, much of the knowledge also involves rather specific detailed facts about programming in particular domains, such as PECOS's rules about symbolic programming. (This is reminiscent of discussion of the trade-off between generality and power in artificial intelligence systems.) The first attempts to build such programming knowledge into an automatic programming system involved applying the knowledge to algorithmic specifications, in which the programming task was to produce a concrete implementation. The hypothetical syntheses of a breadth-first enumeration algorithm and two minimum-cost spanning tree algorithms demonstrate that specific detailed knowledge about progamming can also be of significant value in the algorithm creation process. At the same time, they illustrate an important role to be played by deduction in such knowledge-based automatic programming systems − as a mechanism for answering particular queries about the program under construction, in order to test the applicability conditions of particular rules. Important directions for future reasearch involve adding to the rules that have already been codified and developing deductive techniques for use with such rules.

Acknowledgements

Much of this work resulted from discussions during seminars in Knowledge-based Automatic Progamming held at Yale in Fall 1977 and Spring 1979. L. Birnbaum helped develop the basis for the section on minimum cost spanning trees. B. G. Buchanan, D. McDermott, A. Perlis, C. Rich, H. Shrobe, L. Snyder, R. Waldinger, and R. Waters provided helpful comments on earlier drafts of the paper.

REFERENCES

[1] Aho, A. V., Hopcroft, J. E., & Ullman, J. D. (1974). *The Design and Analysis of Computer Algorithms*, Reading, Mass: Addison-Wesley.

[2] Barstow, D. R. (1979). An experiment in knowledge-based automatic programming, *Artificial Intelligence*, 12, 73–120.

[3] Barstow, D. R. (1979). *Knowledge-based Progam Construction*, New York and Amsterdam: Elsevier North Holland, 1979.

[4] Bibel, W. (1980). Syntax-directed, semantics-supported program synthesis. *Artificial Intelligence*, 14, 243–261.

[5] Cheriton, D. & Tarjan, R. E. (1976). Finding minimum spanning trees, *SIAM Journal of Computing*, 5, 724–742.

[6] Dijkstra, E. W. (1959). A note on two problems in connexion with graphs, *Numerische Mathematik*, 1, 269–271.

[7] Green, C. C. (1969). The application of theorem proving to question-answering systems, *AIM-96*. Stanford: Stanford University Computer Science Department.

[8] Green, C. C. & Barstow, D. R. (1978). On program sysnthesis knowledge, *Artificial Intelligence*, 10, 241–279.

[9] Gries, D. & Misra, J. (1978). A linear sieve algorithm for finding prime numbers, *Communications of the ACM*, 21, 999–1003.

[10] Kerschenbaum, A. & Van Slyke, R. (1972). Computing minimum spanning trees efficiently, *Proceedings of the 25th Annual Conference of the ACM*, pp. 518–527.

[11] Kruskal, J. B. (1956). On the shortest spanning subtree of a graph and the travelling salesman problem, *Proceedings of the American Mathematical Society*, 7, 48–50.

[12] Manna, Z. & Waldinger, R. (1975). Knowledge and reasoning in program sysnthesis, *Artificial Intelligence*, 6, 175–208.

[13] Manna, Z. & Waldinger, R. (1979). Synthesis: dreams => programs, *IEEE Transactions on Software Engineering*, 4, 294–328.

[14] Manna, Z. & Waldinger, R. (1978). A deductive approach to program synthesis, Stanford: *AIM-320*. Computer Science Department, Stanford University.

[15] Prim, R. C. (1957). Shortest connection networks and some generalizations, *Bell System Technical Journal*, **36**, 1389–1401.

[16] Simon, H. A. (1963). Experiments with a heuristic compiler, *Journal of the ACM*, **10**, 493–506.

[17] Waldinger, R. & Lee, R. C. T. (1969). A step toward automatic program writing, *International Joint Conference on Artificial Intelligence*, (Washington, D.C.), pp. 241–252.

19

Natural language dialogue systems: a pragmatic approach

L. I. Mikulich
Institute of Control Sciences
USSR Academy of Sciences, Moscow, USSR

Abstract

An approach is described to development of natural language interfaces with data bases. Pragmatic-oriented analysis of utterences made by casual users is a key concept of the approach. An example of applying this approach is considered using the DISPUT family of systems.

1. INTRODUCTION

Two ways are common in development of dialogue systems for nonprogrammers. Programming like statements, form-filling, menu-selection, special mnemonics and some other forms of communications are used in the traditional approach.

In recent years the systems capable of interacting with the users in a natural language have become increasingly popular. This approach is, however, still not widespread in real systems. There are several reasons for this. Most popular objections against the systems are: 1) difficulties of design, 2) special requirements for computer software where these systems have to be employed (languages like LISP, INTERLISP, SETL, etc.; 3) large memory requirements; 4) long response time, among others. Unfortunately many of the existing natural language (NL) systems seem to confirm the apprehension of the users.

The main feature of NL-systems is a unit that translates the user's utterences from a natural into a formal language which is "comprehensible" to the computer. We will refer to this unit as a "Linguistic Processor" (LP).

Usually linguistic processors utilize a model of a natural language as a whole and include stages of morphologic, syntactic, semantic, and pragmatic analyses. In many cases these stages are executed sequentially. This leads to a substantial delay in obtaining an internal representation and takes vast memory.

We have attempted to develop a technology of designing a natural language interface with data bases that can be useful in real applications on relatively small computers. To start with we had to change the underlining concept of a linguistic processor.

KNOWLEDGE-BASED SYSTEMS

The primary model to be used in our linguistic processors, unlike what is usually done, is that of the world rather than of the language. Any kind of activity in a given problem domain is an activity in rigid constraints imposed on the picture of the world, hence they are constraints in the natural language which is used in the framework of this problem domain. That language is meant which *is used* rather than the one language that *can be used* in the same environment. This language is a professional natural language or slang. Every problem domain has its own slang. We claim that the linguistic processor has to be oriented to this slang, i.e. the whole analysis is guided by the pragmatics of the problem domain and the relevant subset of natural language. We will refer to this approach as a *pragmatic* one. In this approach syntactic, semantic and pragmatic analyses are closely mixed up and produce a single interpretation. The pragmatic approach requires the system to be adaptable to a particular user. We suppose that only personalized NL-system can effectively work.

Using the pragmatic approach we designed several systems intended for practical applications. A family of systems called DISPUT have been developed for application in management information systems for the merchant fleet.

2. DISPUT FAMILY OF SYSTEMS

An overview of a DISPUT system is shown in Fig. 1. The system consists of five main parts: service, control, core, database management, and reply generator. Data files or database will also be included.

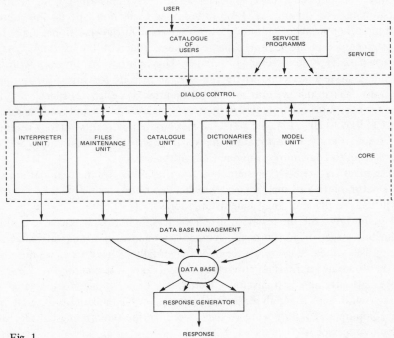

Fig. 1.

2.1 Service

The service part is intended for user identification, authorization to access one or more files and for making a set of additional services available to him. This set includes: time parameters of the interaction course, HELP facilities and log-in and log-out facilities. This part is nearly identical with that used in conventional systems.

2.2 Control

The control part is merely a monitor program which organizes and controls the loading and execution of the remaining program modules and isolates them from the operating system environment. A production-rule-based system is used in the control part. The left-hand sides of the production rules are specified by the user or subordinate modules. The right-hand sides of these rules are the actions that subordinate modules have to perform. New production rules can be added to the control part.

2.3 Core

The core of the system provides the modes of operations that a user can activate in the course of a dialogue. The set of operations differ from one particular system to another. Every mode is supported by one or more program modules.

The main unit of the DISPUT systems is the Interpreter of natural language utterances. It translates the user's query into a formal representation. I shall describe it in detail later in the paper.

The Files maintenance unit provides record-addressing statements, automatic input/output control, and implied data format translation for addition and replacement of data during file creation or general file maintenance.

The Catalogue unit enables the user to declare any given request as a standard one and to store it in a catalogue file. This unit was developed in response to complaints about the time consuming routine typing of repeated queries. Now the users can send any typed question to the catalogue and store it there. Keying in the number of the request is sufficient to put it into run. Any user can perform his own set of queries for himself in the most suitable form.

The catalogue unit allows storing

1. a query together with its formal representation executed once in the Interpreter unit;
2. a query only.

The pros and cons of either are obvious.

The Dictionaries unit is intended for creation of all the dictionaries of the system, their modification and updating and to form personal lexicons. A personal vocabulary includes synonyms, both standard and non-standard abbreviations, mnemonics, etc. All the strings of this vocabulary form a set which have an isomorphic correspondence with a subset of the main vocabulary.

Adding new units to the core of the system is easy. Some production rules have to be added to the control part in this case. For example, a Model unit used in one implementation of the DISPUT system includes an optimization model for short-term planning.

2.4 Data Management

This part is not given explicitly if a standard data bank is used. Only an interface unit must be written to translate a formal query representation of the core part into the query language or data manipulation language of the data bank.

If it is organized as a set of files, the database requires special software. This software includes a database planner, a set of procedures to retrieve and sort data, to find a given record, to list a given set of records, to find totals, particular sums, mean, percentage, etc. In most cases we created our own databases, because special-purpose database are far more efficient than a general one. Usually our databases consist of several files of property-value lists.

2.5 Response Generator

The DISPUT family of systems do not employ any complicated scheme of response generation. The response generator can display the reply in one of the following forms: as a templet with filled slots; as a simple table, and as a multi-level table one level after another. The system chooses the output form which it regards as the most convenient to the user.

3. OPERATION OF DISPUT IN QUESTION—ANSWERING MODE

I will demonstrate now how a system of the DISPUT family is operated in the question-answering mode. This mode is the most interesting in the system; furthermore it demonstrates our main concepts and ideas.

3.1 Problem Domain

The system is intended for management of container shipment [1, 2] and consists of three levels: container terminal, ship agency, and ministry. The data of the the three levels differ in degree of integration and are employed in tackling different management problems. The lowest-level files contain the largest number of records (up to several thousand) and properties (up to a hundred); those of higher levels may contain as many records but substantially fewer properties. The data users are people of various ranks. The users of the higher levels can access the data of the lower levels, but the reverse is not permitted. Therefore systems of higher levels include systems of lower levels as their subsystems. As a result the problem domain expands with the increasing level. Even at the higher-most level the system remains fairly compact and suitable for use of natural languages for interaction. The user's vocabulary does not exceed 500 entries. As a rule, there is no ambiguity of words; the sentences (queries) are quite unambiguous even though the system admits of some complicated structures.

In compliance with the initial concept of designing such systems the entire design process was managed by the pragmatics of the task. This implied that (1) a problem domain and a set of problems in it were well specified; (2) the vocabulary for operating the system made of the natural professional language of the potential users; (3) the mechanisms of query analysis should be obtained from studies of those language constructions that *are used* by the potential users for solving their problems. In this way the grammar complexity was significantly reduced. A grammar of this type will be referred to as *pragmatic*. General and specific knowledge of the world are not separated and combine into an entity, a world model of a system. The motto in designing such systems was "Nothing but the essential". Fairly compact and effective systems were obtained.

3.2 Interpreter

The user accesses the Interpreter if a question in a natural language should be put to the system. The Interpreter operation has been described in detail in [3]. Several examples of the kind of question the system can handle are given below:

(1) What non-Soviet containers are in the terminal, according to the transportation type, departures, and destinations?
(2) The number of imported containers from 10 to 15 tons gross weight to be delivered to station "Leningrad".
(3) List all containers that have arrived by sea and are in the terminal over 10 days after arrival.
(4) In what containers that have arrived after 31:3:81 is the load "Coffee", according to the countries of origin?
(5) The storage time of export containers to be shipped to port "Hamburg" since the time they arrived from repairs.
(6) How many containers of the Baltic Ship Agency were leased as of 01:02:81?

The first version of the DISPUT system can handle a single question. The interpreters did not include a context mechanism and they cannot process anaphoric references or ellipses which pertain to a sequence of successive sentences (queries). This is a significant disadvantage which will be overcome in the second version [4].

In the first example the system can calculate totals and particular sums, operate with exception, and process ellipses in a single query. The second and third examples show that relations can be processed. The fourth and the sixth ones demonstrate processing of dates. The fifth one calculates time which is expressed in the application area on container-days (the total number of days of detention for each container since a specified time).

The interpreter incorporates linguistic and pragmatic processors which operate in sequence. The purpose of the linguistic processor is translation of the query into an internal representation. At this stage the query is "parsed" (semantically parsed). At the stage of pragmatic analysis the intermediate

387

representation is filled with pragmatic characteristics of the database and of the problem domain. The output of the Pragmatic processor is a canonical formal representation of the query suitable for transfer to the database.

3.2.1 *The Linguistic Processor*

The block diagram of the Linguistic Processor is shown in Fig. 2. For a better insight into the processing let us follow some query through the system. Let that be "How many (count) imported containers with cargo 'Coffee' are in the terminal (by dates of unloading and numbers)?".

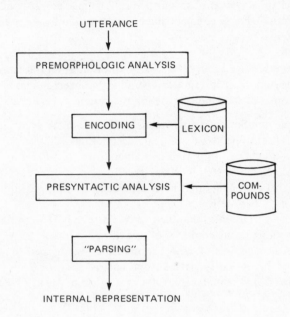

Fig. 2.

At the stage of premorphologic analysis the punctuation marks, proper names, and alphanumerical or numerical constants are identified. The punctuation marks are assigned special codes and then processed in an appropriate way. The proper names and constants do not undergo analysis. They are written into the file of special forms and replaced in the sentence by a unique code which is generated by the system. Following premorphological analysis the sentence reads "How many imported containers with cargo 10001 are in terminal 7 by dates of unloading and numbers 8 ES". (ES means: *End of Sentence.*)

The system compares the query text with the lexicon and assigns an appropriate code to each word. The codes are assigned to words in compliance with the pragmatic grammar of the system. That grammar is different from conventional grammars of natural languages. In particular, the grammar for a given specific system incorporates 10 lexical classes: prepositions, attributes, simple

388

verbs, transitive verbs, modal verbs, adverbial modifiers (time and place) names of properties, reference words, and auxiliary words. Thus, the noun *repair* is classified with simple verbs because in the framework of the existing pragmatics it cannot be distinguished from the verb *to repair*. Codes are assigned to words in designing the system and the user cannot change them at will in operation. He cannot access the codes.

Each word is stored in the lexicon in its complete and reduced forms. Reduced forms of all stored works can be distinguished in pairs. This makes morphological analysis unnecessary and enables queries to be formulated by keying in abbreviated versions of words. This is impossible unless the vocabularies are small, otherwise the linguistic processor should incorporate a morphological analaysis module, which is especially burdensome with Russian, which is highly inflected.

If during the encoding the system comes across an unknown word the user receives a message suggesting that the word be either replaced by a synonym or that a synonym be added to the lexicon. Following the encoding the above query looks like: 2 (hmx reference word) 801 (impx attribute) 0 (contx reference word) 102 (with x preposition) 722 (cargox property name) 10001 (reference to proper name) 100 (in x preposition) 600 (terx adverbial modifier of place) 7 (parenthesis) 101 (by x preposition) 901 (dates of x adverbial modifier of time) 320 (unlx simple verb) 31 (and x auxiliary word) 1 (numx reference word) 8 (parenthesis closed). In parenthesis are reduced forms of words as stored in the lexicon and their lexical classes.

In presyntactic analysis, another vocabulary, that of compounds, is accessed. This helps to recognize stable lexical constructions which have an unambiguous semantic interpretation in the problem domain. The vocabulary includes four zones which store: the code of the first word, the code of the second word, the rule of their compounding, and the resulting code. The compounding rule provides for pairwise glueing of codes with assignment of the resulting codes, elimination of codes from further analysis, and cyclic compounding of word codes. As a result of presyntactic analysis only those codes of words and compounds are retained for further processing that are necessary for unambiguous understanding of the query.

Following presyntactic analysis the above query reads: 2 801 0 790 (with-cargo, compound) 10001 7 101 901 320 1 8. A compound *with-cargo* has been formed and the adverbial modifier of place together with the preposition *in terminal* left out because the semantics of these compounds is sufficient to fix the subject of the query, i.e. a question of terminal files. Fixation of the dialogue subject is sufficient for adjusting the grammatical analyzer for further analysis. The conjunction *and* has also been left out but the logical relation "or" has been fixed.

The semantic "parser" is the most sophisticated part of the lexical processor and contains one or several conceptual frames which determine the type of questions that are comprehensible by the system. Thus, for the container terminal system there are four types of frames: "How many", "Time", "List", and "Container". Each type of frame contains its own set of slots which are filled during analysis of the sentence. Like many of our predecessors, we regard a sentence as a set of groups of words, each having an addressee in the frame slots. The groups of words are retrieved and the frame slots filled by "experts". Fig. 3 shows the structure of a pragmatic grammar for our system.

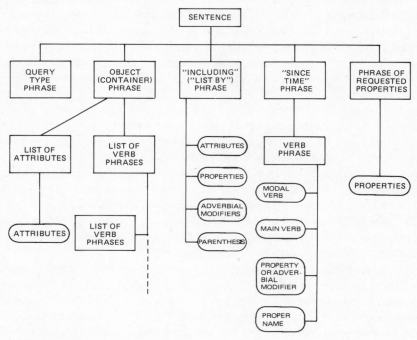

Fig. 3.

The "expert" which conducts the search for words that determine the query type chooses the conceptual frame. These words belong to the (lexical) class of reference words. Then the slots of the chosen frame are filled with the aid of appropriate "experts" or by accessing other frames. In particular, the group of the verb that expresses the basic relation of the sentence is itself represented as a frame (Fig. 4). The figure shows the frame of the verb for the application

FRAME "VERB PHRASE"	MODAL VERB	MAIN VERB	PROPERTY	VALUE

Fig. 4.

390

(container terminal) that has been defined at the stage of presyntactic analysis. For another application, e.g. Renting container, that frame consists of just two slots: a verb and an attribute. The slots of the verb group are served by their own "experts". In the system there is also an "expert" which fills some slots of frames implicitly.

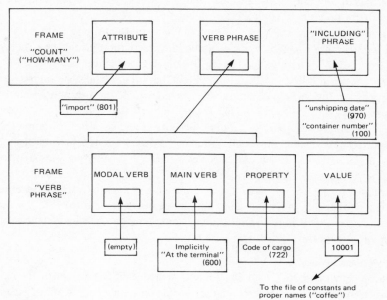

Fig. 5.

The flowchart of analyzing the query that serves as an example is shown in Fig. 5. A filled frame is the internal representation of the query. Its verbal interpretation is as follows:

Query type: on the number of containers
Attribute: import
Verb phrase: implicitly in terminal
             modality-none
             property name — code of cargo
             property value — 10001 ("coffee")
"Including" phrase: level of embedding — zeroeth;
                    properties — unshipping date
                                 container numbers;
                    deeper embedding levels — none.

If the question includes several words which are governed by the verb, then the internal representation includes as many verb phrases as there are such words.

For instance, the question "How many containers should be shipped to country A with load B" contains two verb phrases in the internal representation:

modality	verb	property	property value
should be	shipped	destination country	A
should be	shipped	code of cargo	B

The values of the "modality" slot are used subsequently for determining the files where the response is to be looked through.

If desirable, the user can require the system to respond with a table of complex structure using the so-called embedding constructions for the structuring. The embedding levels are dictated by the placing of parentheses and processed by the system in analyzing the group "including". Thus, the system may be told to enumerate the groups of containers within which they should be classified according to shipment types, which should be classified according to sizes, and these according to cargoes, etc. Filling the slots of a chosen frame completes the sentence analysis in the Linguistic Processor. In the case of a successful analysis when all slots are filled, the user receives a message on the query type as found by the system and is asked for permission to continue. No additional information is displayed to the user at that stage. If the analysis fails, the place in the sentence where it stopped is indicated and the user is asked to reformulate the query. If permission to continue is given, the system transfers the filled frame into the pragmatic processor.

3.2.2 Pragmatic Processor

While the Linguistic Processor has some knowledge of the subset of the natural language and is to some extent related to conventional models of the language, the Pragmatic Processor cannot essentially rely on any general model. Indeed, separation of analysis into a linguistic and a pragmatic part was originally intended for separation of more general language processes from whatever is embodied in the specific system. This assertion can be interpreted as abandonement of the original concept. This is not the case, for even in the Linguistic Processor knowledge of the specific problem is used in the vocularies, the set of conceptual frames, and the grammatical structure.

Secondly, to make the system more flexible and facilitate its adaptation to various databases, knowledge should be available on database structure model and on the procedures used in the database. This information on the database cannot be generalized. Nevertheless, every Pragmatic Processor incorporates groups of "experts" who perform a similar activity. These "experts" work with pragmatic vocabularies (Fig. 6) by finding a correspondence between the contents of the input frame slots and the description of database files and make, if necessary, a simple logical inference. They determine the form of the function which specifies the way to retrieve data from the database. Finally, they deal with special cases (exceptions) which list whatever was disregarded in the Linguistic Processor. All "experts" together generate a job to the database (or its planner) for search for the desired answer.

392

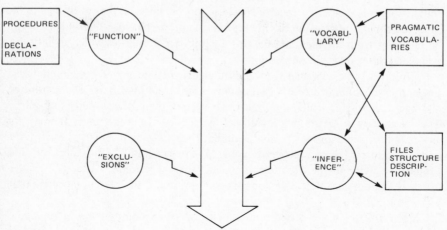

Fig. 6.

FORMAL REPRESENTATION OF QUERY

Fig. 7 shows the flowchart of a Pragmatic Processor which interacts with the database of a container terminal. As noted above, the files are sequential and index-sequential types.

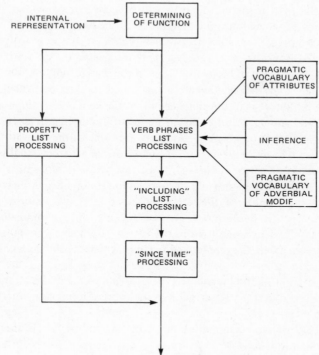

Fig. 7.

FORMAL REPRESENTATION OF QUERY

393

The desired function of query processing is determined directly from the frame type (or name). To specify the function parameters, the set of files to be retrieved should be determined, the set of basic properties by which the data will be retrieved from the files, and the set of additional properties which specify the parameters of sorting the chosen data.

The files to be searched (or search indices) are determined by scanning two pragmatic vocabularies: of attributes and of adverbial modifiers. The attributes are regarded as signs which simultaneously specify the property name and value. The vocabulary of attributes includes four zones: of the attribute (name), its associated property, property value, and file. Thus, in this vocabulary the attribute name "defective" has a property code "technical status"; the value of this property is FO; and the file indicator is "all files of terminal". Therefore, if the query is "Enumerate defective containers in terminal", the system should search in all terminal files.

Each of the basic properties consists of three components: elementary relation, property name, and property value. The elementary relation can be: larger, smaller, equal, larger or equal, and smaller or equal. Complex relations such as "between", "from ... to", and "since ... to" consist of several elementary ones with appropriate repetition of the contents of the two remaining components. To generate a set of basic properties the "attribute" and "verb phrase" slots are used from the frame which is initial for the Pragmatic Processor. The property name and value that are found from the attribute name in the pragmatic vocabulary of attributes are included into the description of the basic property.

If the verb phrase includes an adverbial modifier, this can serve to specify the file where the information is retrieved and to specify the property name and value in the description of basic properties of the search function. Thus, a simple logical inference in the case where some container has been unshipped and loaded into a train leads to the conclusion that the container is shipped from the sea to land and should be retrieved in the file of imported containers. Using the pragmatic vocabulary of adverbial modifiers the name of the transportation kind and its value can be determined from the name of the adverbial modifier of place.

In generating a set of additional properties whose description also consists of three components, before all the embedding level of a property is determined from the number of the left parentheses. The level value is one of the components of this description. The second and third components are the property name and its value used in the system. Both these components, as in the case of basic properties, are looked for in pragmatic vocabularies of attributes and adverbial modifiers.

The operation of the Pragmatic Processor and of the entire interpreter ends with generation of a query description in the form of a function with a specified set of parameters.

The query of our example is represented as follows at the output of the Pragmatic Processor:

Function: calculation of totals and particular sums
File names: import containers in terminal
Basic properties: 2.

Description of basic properties

Specified relation	Property name	Property value
equality	type of transfer	import
equality	code of cargo	10001 (reference to value "coffee")

Additional properties: 2

Description of additional properties

Embedding level	Property name	Property value
zeroth	unshipping data	all
zeroth	container number	all

Once the search and calculation of sums are over, a table is displayed which is the user's request.

4. DISCUSSION

We are aware of the fact that DISPUT systems do not embody the last word in artificial intelligence. There is much room for improvement in designs of the Linguistic and Pragmatic processors. As noted above, systems of the first version can process only single sentences rather than text. Therefore no powerful mechanisms are implemented for processing ellipses or anaphores. Actual systems do not include mechanisms for processing complex queries through repeated accesses of the database with subsequent computation of the answer. Thus, the system cannot now respond to "How many more containers were rented in June than in February" even though we know how this could be done. Unfortunately, in such cases the response time is unacceptable because of the repeated searches through large data files. Therefore straight forward ways of replying to such an answer do not work in interactive mode of operation. Solutions to such problems, obtained in an experimental model, will be embodied, whenever necessary, in subsequent versions of actual systems. But isn't development of such systems too much trouble? The objective of development is essentially a very special-purpose system. Furthermore, most industrial systems are clearly of this kind but their designers wish to expand as widely as they can the application field to offset the high costs of developing the software. Indeed, special purpose systems are compact, effective and less costly in development and service than general-purpose systems. These advantages become decisive if the costs of developing a series of such systems for different purposes are lower than those for a multi-purpose systems.

We believe that the costs can be dramatically reduced by developing a CAD technology for such systems which would start with careful pragmatic study of a problem and go on to testing of potential users and development of an instrumental set for generation and design of system units. The most difficult stage would be certain design of linguistic and pragmatic processors. The end product of this technology would be a problem-oriented dialogue system in machine object codes for immediate use. Generation and adaptation of linguistic processors have been given much attention in recent years, in particular in the Soviet Union [5,6].

5. SUMMARY AND CONCLUSIONS

The paper has discussed development of problem-oriented interactive systems for processing of messages and user's queries in a natural professional language. An approach has been suggested which is referred to as pragmatic. Design of DISPUT dialogue systems illustrates the structure of such systems in general; interaction through an interpreter in a natural language has been discussed in detail.

With all their disadvantages the actual systems train the user in a new way of interacting with the computer (the psychology of this activity being left out) and give the developers a better understanding of ways to improve such systems. Finally, we believe that even such relatively primitive systems mark the start of real life applications for artificial intelligence methods.

Acknowledgements

I would like to acknowledge the important contributions of A. Chervonenkis in the linguistic part of the systems and Helen Naydenova in the database part.

REFERENCES (IN RUSSIAN)

[1] Belen'kiy, A. S., Mikulich, L. I., Naydyonova, Ye. Ya., Chervonenkis, A. Ya., (1981), A Dialogue Data Retrieval System for Planning and Management of Transportation Systems (DISPUT). I. Design and functioning. *Avtomatika i telemekhanika*, **43**, No. 3, 152–161.
[2] Belen'kiy, A. S., Mikulich, L. I., Naydyonova, Ye. Ya., Chervonenkis, A. Ya., (1981), A Dialog-Data Retrieval System for Planning and Management of Transportation Systems (DISPUT) II. Implementation. *Avtomatika i telemekhanika*, **42**, No. 5, 169–180.
[3] Mikulich, L. I., Chervonenkis, A. Ya., (1979), A Special-Purpose Dialog System. In *Issues in Development of Application Systems*, (ed. A. S. Narin'yani), pp. 112–129, Novosibirsk: Siberian Branch, USSR Academy of Sciences.
[4] Mikulich, L. I., Chervonenkis, A. Ya., (1980), A Dialog Question Answering System (DISPUT – 2) *Abstracts, Eighth All-Union Conference on Control Sciences*. Tallin: Polytechnical Institute.
[5] Khoroshevskiy, V. F., (1979), Computer-aided design of linguistic processors for interactive systems. In: *Interactive Systems. Soviet-Finnish Symposium, Tbilisi, Oct. 1979 Part II*. Moscow: USSR Academy of Sciences Computing Center Press.
[6] Levin, D. Ya., (1980), STEND, A System for Adaptation of Linguistic Processors. Preprint. Novosibirsk: Computing Center, Siberian Branch, USSR Academy of Sciences.

LOGIC PROGRAMMING

20

LOGLISP: an alternative to PROLOG

J. A. Robinson and E. E. Sibert
School of Computer and Information Science
Syracuse University, USA

1. INTRODUCTION

Seven years or so after it was first proposed (Kowalski 1974), the technique of 'logic programming' today has an enthusiastic band of users and an increasingly impressive record of applications.

For most of these people, logic progamming means PROLOG, the system defined and originally implemented by the Marseille group (Roussel 1975). PROLOG has since been implemented in several other places, most notably at Edinburgh (Warren *et al.* 1977). Much of the rapid success of logic progamming is due to these implementations of PROLOG (as well as to the inspired missionary work of Kowalski, van Emden, Clark and others). The Edinburgh PROLOG system is in particular a superb piece of software engineering which allows the logic progammer to compile assertions into DEC-10 machine code and thus run logic programs with an efficiency which compares favourably with that of compiled LISP. All other implementations of logic programming (including our own, which we describe in this paper) are based on interpreters.

However, PROLOG is not, and does not claim to be, the definitive logic programming formalism. It has features which (however useful in practical applications) are somewhat foreign to Kowalski's original simple and clear conception of a deductive, assertional programming language based entirely on the LUSH resolution of Horn clauses. In this conception there are no imperative constructs and indeed there is no notion of control or of anything 'happening'. The spirit is very like that of Strachey's static Platonic vision — elaborated by Landin and later by Scott — of programs as purely denotative expressions in which entities are represented as the results of applicative combinations of functions with their arguments. Running a program is, on this view, nothing more than finding out what it denotes. The program merely does the denoting, and should not be taken for a prescription of any sort of activity, such as 'computing'.

The Strachey-Landin-Scott doctrine is of course quite compatible with the belief that one can make a machine which when given a program as input will systematically work out and deliver a description of its denotation. Landin's classic interpreter – the SECD machine – is the very essence of such a device. We can say that the computation of the machine is correct (if it is) only because we have a machine-independent notion of what the program is intended to denote.

Most of the PROLOG programs known to us appear to be motivated by the desire to make the machine behave in a certain way rather than (or, as well as) merely to obtain answers to queries. We have been saddened by the use made in applications of the (highly effective!) 'CUT' control construct. For example, the assertions

$$(\text{NOT } p) \leftarrow p \text{ CUT FAIL}$$
$$(\text{NOT } p) \leftarrow$$

together (and in the order given) define NOT in the sense of 'negation as failure'. In attempting to establish (NOT p) by appeal to the first assertion, the PROLOG machine first seeks to establish p. If it succeds in establishing p, it goes on to perform the CUT so as to preclude the (incorrect) establishment of (NOT p) by the second procedure, and then (correctly) returns a failure to the caller of (NOT p). If, however, it fails to establish p, it immediately drops through to the second assertion and thereby (correctly) establishes (NOT p).

Because it appears to encourage this sort of programming, and because it has rapidly evolved into a workhorse programming language serving a busy user community not given to contemplating Platonic Forms, PROLOG may be turning into the FORTRAN of logic programming – as McDermott recently observed (McDermott 1980).

Our own early attempts (as devoted users of LISP) to use PROLOG convinced us that it would be worth the effort to create *within LISP* a faithful implementation of Kowalski's logic programming idea. We felt it would be very convenient to be able to set up a knowledge base of assertions inside a LISP workspace, and to compute the answers to queries simply by executing appropriate function calls. What seemed to be required was an extension of LISP consisting of a group of new primitives designed to support unification, LUSH resolution, and so on, as efficiently as possible. We set out to honor the principle of the separation of logic from control (no CUT, no preferred ordering of assertions within procedures nor of atomic sentences within hypotheses of assertions) by making the logic programming engine 'purely denotative'. Instead of the PROLOG method of generating the LUSH resolution proof tree one branch at a time by backtracking, we decided to generate all branches in quasi-parallel so that heuristic control techniques could be brought to bear on deciding which branch to develop at each step and so that our design would lend itself to multiprocessing at a later stage.

In the next section we give a summary description of the resulting system, which we call LOGLISP. The reader is encouraged to think of LOGLISP as LISP +

LOGIC, where LISP is what it always has been and LOGIC is the collection of new primitives which we have added to LISP.

2 LOGIC

In LOGIC we represent assertions, queries, and all other other logic-programming constructs as LISP data-objects.

2.1 Variables And Proper Names

Logical variables are represented as identifiers which begin with a lower-case letter. Proper names (i.e., individual constants, predicates, and operators) are represented as identifiers which begin with an upper-case letter or a special character such as $+$, $*$, %, $=$, $<$, $>$, or \$. In addition, numerals and strings can be used as individual constants (but not as predicates or operators). We refer to proper names which are not numerals or strings as *proper identifiers.*

2.2 Terms

A term is either a logical variable, an individual constant, or an operator-operand combination represented as a dotted pair (F. S) whose head F is the operator and whose tail S is the operand. The operand is a list (possibly empty) of items.

2.3 Predication

A predication ($=$ atomic sentence) is a predicate-subject combination also represented as a dotted pair. The predicate is the head of the pair, and the subject is the tail. The subject is a list (possibly empty) of terms.

Thus in LOGIC the external syntax of terms and predications is the customary LISP notation for atoms and lists. All applicative combinations are written as lists in which the head is applied to the tail. For example, we have:

(Age John (+ 3 (* 4 5)))

instead of

Age(John, +(3, *(4, 5))) .

2.4 Assertions, Procedures And Knowledge Bases

We call sentences of the form

if each member of A is true then B is true

assertions. In general the *conclusion* B is a predication while the *hypothesis* A is a list (possibly empty) of predications.

An assertion with an empty hypothesis is *unconditional*, while one whose hypothesis is nonempty is *conditional.*

An assertion in which one or more logical variables occur is called a *rule*, while one in which no logical variables occur is known as a *datum.*

401

A rule is to be understood as if its logical variables were all governed by universal quantifiers. Thus, assuming the rule contains the logical variables $x1$, ..., xt and no others, we read it as

for all $x1$, ..., xt:
if each member of A is true then B is true.

Of course, if some of these variables (say, $z1$, ..., zs) occur only in A while the rest (say, $v1$, ..., vr) occur also or only in B, then by elementary logic we can read the assertion as:

for all $v1$, ..., vr:
if there exist $z1$, ..., zs such that
each member if A is true
then B is true.

We follow Kowalski's convention of writing the conditional assertion

if each member of $(A1 ... An)$ is true
then B is true

in the reverse-arrow notation:

$B \leftarrow A1 ... An$.

In this notation, the unconditional assertion

if each member of ( ) is true then B is true

becomes

$B \leftarrow$.

An assertion thus may be (1) a conditional rule, (2) an unconditional datum, (3) an unconditional rule, or (4), a conditional datum. Assertions of types (3) and (4) are rarely encountered in knowledge bases arising in applications.

A knowledge base is set of assertions. It is customary to think of a knowledge base as partitioned into *procedures*, each procedure corresponding to some predicate P and consisting of all the assertions in the knowledge base whose conclusion has P as its head. The name of the procedure is then by convention taken to be P.

Assertions may also be given their own individual names at the option of the user. In displaying explanations (= deductions) it is often convenient to refer to an assertion by its name instead of displaying the assertion itself.

2.5 Entering Assertions Into A LOGIC Knowledge Base

There are several ways of entering assertions into a LOGIC knowledge base.
The command

$(\vdash B \; A1 ... An)$

causes the assertion

$B \leftarrow A1 ... An$

402

to be added to the current knowledge base. The two-character symbol $\vdash$ is pronounced "assert" (some prefer "turnstile") and is the nearest we can approach with the ASCII character set to the logician's assertion sign.

It is also possible to place LOGLISP temporarily into a special input mode called the FACTS mode, in which successive assertions can be entered one after the other. The command (FACTS) causes the FACTS mode to be entered, and the message ASSERT: is then repeatedly given as a prompt for the next assertion to be typed in. When typing in the assertion B ← A1 ... An to the FACTS mode, we represent it simply as the list (B A1 ... An).

In either way of entering an assertion, one can attach a name N to it simply by putting N before the conclusion. Thus:

$\quad$ ($\vdash$ N B A1 ... An)

or, in FACTS mode entries,

$\quad$ (N B A1 ... An) .

The name N can be any proper identifier.

The assert command $\vdash$ is an FEXPR (i.e., a LISP function which does not evaluate its argument expressions when called) and hence a little awkward to use in entering assertions other than from the terminal. For internal use the LOGIC programmer would find the corresponding EXPR function ASSERTCLS (which *does* evaluate its argument expressions) more convenient.

Finally, an entire knowledge base whose name is N can be read into the LOGLISP workspace from the disk by either (RESTORE N) — which first clears the workspace of any assertions which may be present — or (LOADLOGIC N) — which simply adds the assertions of N to those already present in the workspace.

Such a knowledge base can be named N and stored on the disk by the command (SAVE N), which takes all assertions currently in the workspace, creates a file named N which contains them all, and writes it out onto the disk.

Various commands are provided for displaying the contents of a knowledge base currently in the workspace. Typing (PRINTFACTS) causes the entire knowledge base to be displayed, its assertions grouped into procedures. Typing (PRINTFACTSOF $P1$ ... Pn) displays just the assertions comprising the procedures $P1, \ldots, Pn$.

LOGIC maintains an indexing scheme (which is automatic) whereby each proper identifier M has on its property list a complete record of all assertions in whose conclusion M occurs. This scheme is used by the internal processes of the LOGIC system during the deduction cycle, as will be explained below. It also makes it simple to respond to the command (PRINTCREFSOF M) which causes the collection of those assertions to be displayed.

The command (PRLENGTH P) gives the number of assertions currently in the procedure P. The command (PREDICATES) gives the list of all predicates — i.e., predicates — currently in the workspace.

Since assertions are LISP data-objects they may be edited with the help of the LISP resident Editor. In LOGIC there is a command EDITA (by analogy with

LISP's own EDITP, EDITV, EDITF, etc.) which calls the LISP Editor and super-vises the editing session. In particular after entering the Editor with (EDITA *P*) or (EDITA (P1 ... P*n*)) — depending on whether one wishes to edit the single procedure P or several procedures P1, ... , P*n* at once — the ensuing exit command OK causes LOGIC to re-enter the (in general) modified assertions into the know-ledge base just as though they had all been erased from it an were now being entered by the user for the first time.

This 'enhanced OK' is quite transparent to the user, who can use the Editor in exactly the same way for LOGIC objects as for LISP objects.

If the user wishes to erase a procedure P from the workspace, the command (ERASEP P) causes this to be done.

2.6 Queries

A query is essentially a description

$$\{(x1 \dots xt) \mid P1 \& \dots \& Pn\}$$

of the set of all tuples $(x1 \dots xt)$ which satisfy some *constraint* P1 & ... & P*n* which is a conjunction of predications *Pi*.

In LOGIC such a query is written

(ALL $(x1 \dots xt)$ P1 ... P*n*)

and is a call on the function ALL (which is a FEXPR). It returns as its (LISP) value the list of all tuples satisfying the given constraint. This list is called the *answer* to the query. The component tuples of the answer are obtained by means of the basic *deduction cycle*, explained below, which is the heart of LOGIC and which is invoked by every query.

Useful variations of the basic query construct are

(ANY K $(x1 \dots xt)$ P1 ... P*n*)

which returns no more than K of the set of tuples satisfying the constraint,

(THE $(x1 \dots xt)$ P1 ... P*n*)

which returns the sole member of the list (ANY 1 $(x1 \dots xt)$ P1 ... P*n*) (rather than the list itself), and

(SETOF K X P)

which is the EXPR underlying the FEXPRs ALL, ANY and THE. SETOF takes three arguments: K, which should evaluate to an integer or the atom ALL; X, which should evaluate to an 'answer template' $(x1 \dots xt)$; and P, which should evaluate to a 'constraint list' (P1 ... P*n*). It is particularly to be noted that the answer to a query is a LISP data object, and thus can be subjected under program control to internal analysis and minipulation, as well as being displayable at the teminal.

2.7 The Deduction Cycle

The basic process of the LOGIC system is that carried out in the deduction cycle to compute the answer to a given query.

2.7.1 Implicit Expressions — For the sake of both clarity and efficiency the representation of constraints during the deduction cycle is done by the Boyer-Moore technique. This calls for an expression C to be represented by a pair (Q E) called an *implicit expression*, in which Q is an expression known as the *skeleton part* and E is a set of variable-bindings known as the *environment part* of the implicit expression.

The idea is that the implicit expression (Q E) represents the expression which is the result if installing throughout Q the bindings given in E.

2.7.2 Bindings And Environments — In general a *binding* is a dotted pair whose head is a variable, while an *environment* is a list of bindings no two of which have the same head.

2.7.3 Immediate And Ultimate Associates — If the environment E contains the binding A.B we say that *A is defined in E* and write: (DEFINED A E). We also say that B is *the immediate associate of A in E*, and we write: B = (IMM A E).

The immediate associate of A in E might turn out to be a variable which is itself defined in E. When this is the case we often wish to track down *the ultimate associate of A in E*, namely, the first expression in the series:

A, (IMM A E), (IMM (IMM A E) E), . . . ,

which is *not* itself defined in E. This expression is given by:

(ULT A E) = if (DEFINED A E) then (ULT (IMM A E) E) else A

We can now say more precisely how an expression is represented implicitly by a skeleton-environment pair.

2.7.4 Recursive Realizations — First, we define the function RECREAL (for "recursive realization") which takes as arguments an expression X and an environment Y, as follows:

(RECREAL X Y) =

if (CONSP X) then (RECREAL hX Y).(RECREAL tX Y) else
if (DEFINED X Y) then (RECREAL (ULT X Y) Y) else X

where (CONSP X) is true if X is a dotted pair and false otherwise.

The skeleton-environment pair (Q E) then represents the expression: (RECREAL Q E).

2.7.5 Unification — The deduction cycle involves repeated use of the operation of LUSH resolution (Hill 1974), which in turn involves the unification process. Let us first discuss these two important ideas and then go on to define the deduction cycle.

Given two expressions A and B together with an environment E, we say that *A unifies with B in E* if there is an extension E' of E such that

(RECREAL A E') = (RECREAL B E') .

We define the function UNIFY in such a way that if A unifies with B in E then (UNIFY A B E) is the most general extension E' of E satisfying the above equation. If A does not unify with B in E then (UNIFY A B E) is the message "IMPOSSIBLE".

UNIFY is defined by:

(UNIFY A B E) =

if E is "IMPOSSIBLE"
then "IMPOSSIBLE"
else (EQUATE (ULT A E) (ULT B E) E)

where

(EQUATE A B E) =

if A is B	then E
else if A is a variable	then (A.B).E
else if B is a variable	then (B.A).E
else if not (CONSP A)	then "IMPOSSIBLE"
else if not (CONSP B)	then "IMPOSSIBLE"
else (UNIFY tA tB (UNIFY hA hB E)) .	

2.8 LUSH Resolution

Now suppose that we have a knowledge base D and a constraint represented by the skeleton-environment pair (Q E).

Let (VARIANT Q E D) be a variant of D having no variables in common with those in Q or in E. A variant of D is an object exactly like D with the possible exception that different identifiers are used for some or all of its variables.

Let (SELECT Q E D) be a positive integer no longer than the length of the list Q. SELECT is supposed to be able to use the content and structure of Q, E and D, if need be, to determine its result.

Finally, given a nonempty list X and a positive integer K no larger than the length of X, we speak of *splitting* X with respect to its Kth component, and we define (SPLIT X K) to be the triple (L A R) such that A is the Kth component of X and X = L*(A)*R.

(The concatenation of lists L and M is denoted by L*M, and * is of course associative).

Thus if (L A R) is (SPLIT X K) then L is the list of the first K-1 components of X and R is the list of the last ((LENGTH X) − K) components of X. In particular, when K = 1, we have

L = ( )
A = hX
R = tX

With these auxiliary ideas we can now define the LUSH resolvents of an implicit constraint (Q E) with respect to a knowledge base D. They are all the implicit constraints of the form

(L*H*R (UNIFY A C E))

such that:

    (1) H is the hypothesis, and C the conclusion, of
          an assertion in (VARIANT Q E D)
    (2) (L A R) is (SPLIT Q (SELECT Q E D))
    (3) A unifies with C in E.

At present the LOGLISP system uses (SELECT Q E D) = 1 for all Q, E and D. More general selection criteria permitted by the theory of LUSH resolution (Hill 1974) are currently under study, and future versions of LOGLISP may well adopt a more complex SELECT.

The 'separation of variables' accomplished by taking (VARIANT Q E D) instead of D is managed quite efficiently in LOGLISP, as indeed in all of the various PROLOG implementations known to us. It is theoretically necessary to take variants, to preserve the completeness of the resolution inference principle.

In LOGLISP the set of LUSH resolvents of (Q E) with respect to D is returned as a list (RES Q E D) which shares much of its structure with that of (Q E). The basic technique is that of Boyer and Moore.

In computing (RES Q E D) LOGIC often does not have to search the entire procedure whose predicate is the same as that of the selected predication A. This procedure may have the property that each of its assertions has a conclusion containing no variables. In this case, it is enough to try just those assertions whose conclusion actually contains every proper identifier which appears in A. These assertions are readily retrieved via the secondary indexing scheme mentioned earlier.

2.9 Definition Of The Deduction Cycle

We are now in a position to give the definition of LOGLISP's deduction cycle.

The answer to the query (SETOF K X P) is the result of the following algorithm:

IN: let SOLVED be the empty set and
          let WAITING be the set containing only (P ( ))

RUN: while WAITING is nonempty and
              SOLVED has fewer than K members

        do 1   remove some implicit constraint C from
               WAITING and let (Q E) be (SIMPLER C D)

          2   if   Q is ( )
               then add E to SOLVED
               else add the members of (RES Q E D) to WAITING

OUT: return (SIMPSET X SOLVED)

Remarks

(1) The functions SIMPLER and SIMPSET are discussed below in the section dealing with LISP-simplification.

(2) If K is "ALL" then the test in RUN depends only on its first conjunct.

(3) The query (ALL X P1 ... Pn) is the same as the query

(SETOF (QUOTE ALL) (QUOTE X) (QUOTE (P1 ... Pn))))

and the query (ANY K X P1 ... Pn) is the same as

(SETOF K (QUOTE X) (QUOTE (P1 ... Pn)))

while the query (THE X P1 ... Pn) is the same as

(CAR (SETOF 1 (QUOTE X) (QUOTE (P1 ... Pn))))

(4) The 'answer template' X in a query can be a variable, or a proper name, or a list of expressions (in particular, a list of variables).

(5) (RES Q E D) can be empty. In this case the net effect is just to drop the constraint C from WAITING and to add nothing to SOLVED. C is thus an 'immediate failure' (see below).

(6) The selection of C from WAITING is made from among those constraints whose estimated 'solution cost' is least. This estimate is a linear combination of the length of C's skeleton part and the length of the deduction which produced C.

2.10 The Deduction Tree. Immediate And Ultimate Failures

Examination of the deduction cycle reveals that it is growing a tree (the 'deduction tree') whose nodes are implicit constraints. The root of the tree is the constraint of the original query, implicitly represented. The successors of a node are its LUSH resolvents.

During the growth process the fringe of the growing deduction tree consists of the nodes in WAITING together with those whose environment parts have been added to SOLVED.

The tips of the completed deduction tree fall into two classes. Those whose skeleton part is the empty list are *successes*, and their environment parts will have been added to the (now also complete) collection SOLVED. Those whose skeleton part is nonempty are *failures*, and they will have contributed nothing to SOLVED. These failures are known as *immediate*, in contrast to *ultimate*, failures. An immediate failure simply has no resolvents – none of the assertions in the knowledge base has a conclusion which unifies with its selected predication.

An ultimate failure is a node which, while not a tip of the completed deduction tree, has no descendants which are successes. All its descendants are failures. It would be splendid to be able to detect an ultimate failure other than by developing the entire subtree of its descendants and finding that all its tips are immediate failures.

2.11 LISP Simplification And The Functions SIMPLER, SIMPSET

In the deduction cycle the functions SIMPLER and SIMPSET make essential use of the LISP-simplification process.

Intuitively, what the LISP-simplification process does is to replace an expression by its *reduction* (if it has one) according to the LISP meanings (if any) which it and its subexpressions may have. For example, the expression (+ 3 4) can be reduced to the expression 7, and the expression (LESSP (ADD1 5) (TIMES 2 8)) can be reduced (in three steps) to T. The reduction of an expression is the result of persistently replacing its subexpressions by their definitional equivalents, in the manner of computation, until no further replacements are possible. Reduction is not always the same as evaluation. For example (+ *a* (+ 2 2)) reduces to (+ *a* 4). Nor can every expression be reduced — some are irreducible. So we speak in general of the *LISP-simplification* of an expression, and define this to be the expression itself, if it is irreducible, or else the (irreducible) expression which results from reducing it as far as possible.

2.11.1 SIMPSET — The set returned by the deduction cycle is computed (and represented as a list) by the function SIMPSET from the list SOLVED of environments and the answer template X of the query which activated the cycle.

SIMPSET computes the set of all expressions which are the LISP-simplifications of (RECREAL X E) for some E in SOLVED.

2.11.2 SIMPLER — The function SIMPLER transforms the implicit constraint C selected in step 1 of the RUN loop in the deduction cycle.

Remember that if C is (Q E) we are really dealing with the list P = (RECREAL Q E) which C implicitly represents.

SIMPLER's job, intuitively, is to replace the (SELECT Q E D)th predication in P by its LISP-simplification. Sometimes the (SELECT Q E D)th predication in P reduces to T, and in this case SIMPLER deletes it entirely from P (since P is representing the conjunction of its components, the resulting list P' is equivalent to P). If Q' is the result of deleting the (SELECT Q E D)th predication in Q from Q, we will then have that P' is (RECREAL Q' E). SIMPLER then repeats the whole thing again, reducing the (SELECT Q' E D)th predication in P', and so on until either the list of predications is empty or the selected predication does not reduce to T. The output of SIMPLER is then the implicit constraint representing (with environment part E) this final list of predications.

The practical consequence of this SIMPLER transformation is to allow the user to invoke very nearly the full power of LISP from within the hypotheses of LOGIC assertions. Not only are all the LISP primitives given their usual meanings, but any identifiers the user may have (in the usual LISP manner) defined as functions, or given values as (LISP) variables, are accorded these meanings during LISP simplification.

An immediate advantage of this feature is that LOGIC queries — which are LISP calls on the LISP functions ALL, ANY, THE, or SETOF — can be made within the deductions going on at a higher level. Queries can invoke sub-queries and so on to any depth.

A simple illustration of this is the assertion defining NOT (which of course is *also* a LISP primitive) in the sense of 'negation as failure':

$$(\text{NOT } p) \leftarrow (\text{NULL}(\text{ANY } 1 \text{ T } p)) \,.$$

This says that in order to establish a predication of the form $(\text{NOT } p)$ it is sufficient to run the query

$$(\text{ANY } 1 \text{ T } p)$$

and to find that it returns the empty list as answer. Note that the possible answers to $(\text{ANY } 1 \text{ T } p)$ are ( ) and (T). The answer (T) would mean that at least one way was found of proving p; the answer ( ) that not even one way of proving p was found, despite a complete search.

Thus if one is willing to assume of one's knowledge base that inability to prove a predication is tantamount to the ability to prove its negation, one may appropriately add to the knowledge base the above assertion as expressing this postulate of completeness.

2.12 Infinite Searches. The Deduction Window

Since in general there may be infinitely many components in the answer to a query, some way must be provided of gracefully truncating, after only finitely many components have been found, the otherwise infinite process of computing such an answer.

In LOGLISP a collection of parameters is provided (whose values may be set by the user or left at their default settings) which bound the size of the deduction tree in various ways. For example, the total number of constraints (= nodes) may be bounded, as may the maximum branch length, and the size of constraint lists within nodes. It is also possible to limit the number of times in any one branch that rules (as opposed to data) are applied.

The set of these bounds is called the *deduction window*.

It is worth pointing out that the deduction window can be set up for each activation of the deduction cycle simply by annotating the query appropriately. For example, the unadorned query $(\text{ALL X P1} \ldots \text{P}n)$ would be run with the default window, but the same query, annotated as

$$(\text{ALL X P1} \ldots \text{P}n \text{ RULES: 5 TREESIZE: 1000})$$

would be run with bounds of 5 and 1000, respectively, in place of the default bounds.

In addition to controlling the shape and extent of the deduction tree the user may specify the coefficients used in computing the 'solution cost' of each constraint added to WAITING in the deduction cycle. Since the constraint selected from WAITING in step 1 of RUN is always one of those having least solution cost, this gives the user some control over the manner in which the deduction tree is developed.

410

It is also possible to specify that the deduction cycle be conducted in quasi-PROLOG style, that is, depth-first and with assertions taken strictly in the order that the user entered them.

2.13 Deduction Running Times

The running times achieved by LOGIC in answering queries are not as impressive as those of, say, the Edinburgh PROLOG system using compiled assertions. In LOGIC the assertions are, in effect, interpreted. In testing LOGIC with a variety of examples we have found that the deduction tree grows at rates of 50 or 60 nodes per second for most examples. We are currently studying ways of compiling assertions in the manner of Warren, and looking for other means of improving the running time of the deduction cycle.

The following extended example shows some of the main features of LOGLISP at work.

3. PLACES — AN 'INTELLIGENT' DATABASE

PLACES is a knowledge base containing several thousand assertions most of which are *data*, i.e., unconditional ground assertions.

Some representative data of PLACES are shown in Fig. 1.

```
(POPULATION BURMA 32200000) ←
(LATITUDE WARSAW 52.25) ←
(LONGITUDE PYONG-YANG −125.8) ←
(ADJOINS LAOS VIETNAM) ←
(COUNTRY VIENNA AUSTRIA) ←
(PRODUCES USSR OIL 491.0 1975) ←
(BELONGS IRAN OPEC) ←
(REGION ISRAEL MIDDLE-EAST) ←
(AREA ETHIOPIA 471778) ←
(GNP-PER-CAPITA NEW-ZEALAND 4250) ←
(OPEN-WATER BALTIC-SEA) ←
(NARROW DARDANELLES) ←
```

Fig. 1.

For each predicate appearing in Fig. 1, PLACES has a collection of such unconditional ground assertions — a *data procedure*. All these data procedures are comprehensive (they average several hundred assertions each) and some are in a sense complete.

The procedures POPULATION, AREA, REGION, GNP-PER-CAPITA are complete in the sense that every country in the world is covered.

The GNP-PER-CAPITA procedure gives (in US dollars) the gnp-per-capita for each country in the world for a particular year (1976).

The procedure ADJOINS provides data for a procedure BORDERS, which is a pair of rules:

$$(BORDERS\ x\ y) \leftarrow (ADJOINS\ x\ y)$$
$$(BORDERS\ x\ y) \leftarrow (ADJOINS\ y\ x)$$

which give PLACES the ability to determine which countries (or bodies of open

411

water) border upon which others. Since ADJOINS is a symmetric relation we need not assert it in both directions, and BORDERS uses ADJOINS accordingly.

The procedure PRODUCES gives (in millions of metric tons) the quantities of various basic commodities (oil, steel, wheat, rice) produced by most of the world's countries in two particular years (1970 and 1975). This procedure could well have covered more years and more commodities, but for the purposes of an example a few hundred assertions seemed enough to illustrate the possibilities.

While the countries of the world form (at any given time) a rather definite set, it is less clear what are the bodies of water which should be named and treated as entities in a database such as PLACES. We took the abritrary course of naming those bodies of water found on the maps of various parts of the world in the Rand McNally *Cosmopolitan World Atlas*. We ignored those bodies of water which seemed too small to be of much significance but we strove for some sort of comprehensive description of the boundary of each country. For example, the query

   (ALL x (BORDERS x IRAN))

gets the answer

   (STRAITS-OF-HORMUZ GULF-OF-OMAN TURKEY USSR PAKISTAN
   IRAQ CASPIAN-SEA AFGHANISTAN PERSIAN-GULF)

in which each of the bodies of water STRAITS-OF-HORMUZ, GULF-OF-OMAN, CASPIAN-SEA and PERSIAN-GULF is listed as having a portion of its boundary in common with that of the country IRAN.

3.1 Rules

PLACES contains, in addition to these large 'data procedures', a number of rules defining predicates useful in formulating queries. For example there is a procedure DISTANCE, which consists of the following four rules:

   (DISTANCE (POSITION $la1$ $lo1$) (POSITION $la2$ $lo2$) d)
   $\leftarrow (= d$ (SPHDST $la1$ $lo1$ $la2$ $lo2$))
   (DISTANCE (POSITION $la1$ $lo1$) (PLACE q) d)
   $\leftarrow$ (LATITUDE q $la2$)
   & (LONGITUDE q $lo2$)
   & $(= d$ (SPHDST $la1$ $lo1$ $la2$ $lo2$))
   (DISTANCE (PLACE p) (POSITION $la2$ $lo2$) d)
   $\leftarrow$ (LATITUDE p $la1$)
   & (LONGITUDE p $lo1$)
   & $(= d$ (SPHDST $la1$ $lo1$ $la2$ $lo2$))
   (DISTANCE (PLACE p) (PLACE q) d)
   $\leftarrow$ (LATITUDE p $la1$)
   & (LATITUDE q $la2$)
   & (LONGITUDE p $lo1$)
   & (LONGITUDE q $lo2$)
   & $(= d$ (SPHDST $la1$ $lo1$ $la2$ $lo2$))

412

This procedure can be used to obtain the great-circle distance between any two cities whose latitudes and longitudes are in the data tables, or between one such city and an arbitrary position on the earth's surface (given by its latitude and longitude) or between two such arbitrary positions.

The procedure DISTANCE illustrates the ability to call user-defined LISP functions by forming terms using their names as operators. The LISP function SPHDST returns the great circle distance (in nautical miles) between any two points on the earth's surface (given by their respective latitudes and longitudes).

Thus the query:

(THE d (DISTANCE (PLACE SAN-FRANCISCO) (PLACE OSLO) d))

gets the answer:

5197.5394

There is a rule which serves to define the predicate LANDLOCKED. Intuitively, a country or body of water is landlocked if it borders upon only land. The PLACES rule which formalizes this meaning is

(LANDLOCKED x)
← (IS–COUNTRY x)
& (NULL (ANY 1 T (BORDERS x z) (OPEN–WATER z)))

This rule contains two features worthy of comment.

The predicate IS–COUNTRY, defined by the rule

(IS–COUNTRY x)
← (COND ((VARIABLE (LISP x)) (COUNTRY y x))
         ((ANY 1 T (COUNTRY z x))))

shows how one can use to advantage the LISP conditional form within a LOGIC predication. The effect of the conditional is to avoid redundancy in proving that a given country is a country — by finding all the various cities in it — via a check to see if the argument x is variable or not. If it is not, then we need find only one datum from the COUNTRY data procedure which has the given country as its second argument.

The predicate VARIABLE holds just when its argument expression is a logical variable. The term (LISP a), for any expression a, evaluates to a itself (in this respect it behaves like (QUOTE a)). However, unlike (QUOTE a), (LISP a) is not a sealed-off context, and (RECREAL (LISP a) E) is (LISP (RECREAL a E)).

The second thing worth noting about the rule for LANDLOCKED is the embedded deduction. The list returned by the call

(ANY 1 T (BORDERS x z) (OPEN–WATER z))

will be empty if and only if x is landlocked.

A similarly structured rule defines the predicate DOMINATES. We wish to say that a country x dominates a 'narrow' waterway y if x borders y but no other country does. Thus:

413

(DOMINATES x y)
$\leftarrow$ (NARROW y)
& (IS-COUNTRY x)
& (BORDERS x y)
& (NULL (ANY 1 T (BORDERS y w)
     (NOT (OPEN-WATER w))
     (NOT (= x w))))

3.2 Negation As Failure

The use of the predicate NOT in the procedure DOMINATES again raises the interesting general topic of 'negation as failure'.

NOT is of course a LISP-defined notion and will therefore receive appropriate treatment during the deduction cycle in the manner explained earlier. However, it is possible to include in one's knowledge base the rule we discussed earlier.

(NOT p) $\leftarrow$ (NULL (ANY 1 T p))

which is known as the 'negation as failure' rule. PLACES has the negation as failure rule as one of its assertions. The effect of its presence in a knowledge base is to declare that the knowledge base is complete — that inability to deduce p is to be treated as tantamount to the ability to deduce the negation of p.

The version of the negation as failure rule shown above is undiscriminating as between the various predications — it is in effect the declaration that all of the data procedures are complete and that all of the general procedures are 'definitions' of their predicates. It would be possible to assert more specialized negation as failure rules, which declare that the knowledge base is complete with respect to a particular predication-pattern. For example, we might assert

(NOT (BELONGS x y)) $\leftarrow$ (NULL (ANY 1 T (BELONGS x y)))

in order to declare that BELONGS is complete, even though we are not willing to assert the negation as failure rule for all predications p. In general, one would expect that users of LOGIC would wish to be selective in their appeal to negation as failure, in just this fashion.

These data and rules are invoked by the following queries, which illustrate some of the possibilities.

3.3 Some Sample Queries For PLACES.

The following examples consist of some specimen queries which one can make of PLACES, together with the answers that they get. In each case we first state the query in ordinary English, and then restate it in formal LOGLISP.

We are not claiming that there is a uniform procedure, known to us, by which one may translate queries from English to LOGLISP in this manner. At present, in order to express queries (and indeed, assertions) in LOGLISP, one must know the language and be able to express one's intentions in it. In this respect LOGLISP is like any other programming language. It is in fact quite easy

414

to learn enough LOGLISP to construct and operate one's own 'intelligent database' in the style of PLACES.

Query 1.

What are the oil production figures for the
non-Arab OPEC countries in the year 1975?

(ALL $(x\ y)$
    (BELONGS x OPEC)
    (NOT (BELONGS x ARAB-LEAGUE))
    (PRODUCES x OIL y 1975.))

Answer 1.

((IRAN 267.59999) (NIGERIA 88.399991)
               (VENEZUELA 122.19999)
               (INDONESIA 64.100000)
               (EQUADOR 8.2000000))

This answer is shown just as the LISP 'prettyprint' command SPRINT types it out. It is of course possible to dress up one's output in any way one pleases. Note that ALL returns a *list* of (in this case) tuples.

Query 2.

Of all the countries which are poorer than Turkey,
which two produced the most steel in the year 1975?
How much steel was that? What are the populations
of those countries?

(FIRST 2.
    (QUICKSORT
    (ALL $(x\ y\ w)$
        (GNP-PER-CAPITA TURKEY v)
        (GNP-PER-CAPITA x u)
        (LESSP u v)
        (PRODUCES x STEEL y 1975.)
        (POPULATION x w))
    (DECREASING)
    2.))

Answer 2.

((CHINA 29.0 880000000.) (INDIA 7.8999999 643000000.))

This example illustrates the fact that ALL (like ANY, THE, and SETOF) returns a LISP data-object which can be handed as an argument to a LISP function. In this case QUICKSORT and FIRST are user-defined LISP functions which were created in order to serve as useful tools in posing inquiries to PLACES. (LESSP is a standard LISP primitive).

415

(QUICKSORT *list relation k*) returns the given *list* of tuples ordered on the *k*th component with respect to the given *relation*.

(FIRST *n list*) returns the (list of the) first *n* components of the given *list*.

(DECREASING) returns the LISP relation GREATERP (and we also have (INCREASING), which returns the relation LESSP, and (ALPHABETICALLY), which returns the relation LEXORDER).

Query 3.

Which of France's neighbours produced most wheat (in metric tons) per capita in the year 1975? How much wheat per capita was that?

```
(EARLIEST
(ALL (x y
(ALL (x y)
    (BORDERS x FRANCE)
    (PRODUCES x WHEAT z 1975.)
    (POPULATION x u)
    (= y (QUOTIENT (TIMES z 1000000.) u)))
(DECREASING)
2.)
```

Answer 3.

(ITALY 0.16956329)

(EARLIEST *list relation k*) returns the first tuple in *list* after it has been re-ordered on the *k*th component of each of its tuples with respect to the given *relation*. Note that arithmetical terms formed with LISP's arithmetic operations are evaluated by the simplification step of the deduction cycle, as explained earlier.

One could have written % instead of QUOTIENT, and * instead of TIMES.

Query 4.

Which of the NATO countries is landlocked?

(ALL x (BELONGS x NATO) (LANDLOCKED x))

Answer 4.

(LUXEMBOURG)

Query 5.

Which waterway is dominated by Panama?

(THE x (DOMINATES PANAMA x))

Answer 5.

PANAMA-CANAL

Note that THE returns PANAMA-CANAL and not (PANAMA-CANAL).

Query 6.

    Describe the boundary of the USSR by giving
all its neighbours in alphabetical order.

        (ORDER (ALL x (BORDERS x USSR)) (ALPHABETICALLY))

Answer 6.

        (AFGHANISTAN ARCTIC-OCEAN BALTIC-SEA BERING-SEA
        BLACK-SEA BULGARIA CHINA FINLAND HUNGARY IRAN
        MONGOLIA NORWAY POLAND ROMANIA TURKEY)

(ORDER *list relation*) returns the given *list* after ordering it with respect to the
given *relation*.

Query 7.

    Are there any landlocked countries in the Far
East? If so, give an example.

        (ANY 1. x (REGION x FAR-EAST) (LANDLOCKED x))

Answer 7.

        (MONGOLIA)

Query 8.

    Is there an African country which dominates an
international waterway? Which country?
Which waterway?

        (ANY 1. (x y) (REGION x AFRICA) (DOMINATES x y))

Answer 8.

    ((EGYPT SUEZ-CANAL))

Query 9.

    What is the average distance from London
of cities in countries which have a
Mediterranean coastline and which are no more
densely populated than Ireland? List those
countries, together with their population
densities, from least crowded to most crowded.

        (PROGN (SETQ COUNTRIES-AND-DENSITIES
           (QUICKSORT
           (ALL (x x-density)
               (POPULATION IRELAND irish-population)
               (AREA IRELAND irish-area)
               (= irish-density
                   (% irish-population irish-area))

417

```
                    (BORDERS x MEDITERRANEAN-SEA)
                    (NOT (OPEN-WATER x))
                    (POPULATION x x-population)
                    (AREA x x-area)
                    (= x-density (% x-population x-area))
                    (NOT (> x-density irish-density)))
              (INCREASING)
              2.))
        (SETQ AVERAGE-DISTANCE
            (AVERAGE
            (ALL distance
                  (MEMBER pair
                        (EVAL COUNTRIES-AND-DENSITIES))
                  (= country (CAR pair))
                  (COUNTRY city country)
                  (DISTANCE (PLACE city)
                              (PLACE LONDON)
                              distance))))
        (GIVE AVERAGE-DISTANCE)
        (GIVE COUNTRIES-AND-DENSITIES)
        (QUOTE *))
```

Answer 9.

AVERAGE-DISTANCE is

1491.1892

COUNTRIES–AND–DENSITIES is

```
((LIBYA 3.)
 (ALGERIA 20.)
 (ALBANIA 24.)
 (TUNISIA 101.)
 (EGYPT 102.)
 (MOROCCO 108.))
 *
```

This query shows at somewhat more length what a LISP programmer might make of an inquiry which calls for a more involved investigation. Assignment to the LISP variables COUNTRIES-AND-DENSITIES of the answer to one LOGIC call for later use within another (as well as for output) illustrates one more way in which the LOGLISP programmer can fruitfully exploit the interface between LOGIC and LISP. GIVE is just a dressed-up PRINT command which not only prints the value of its argument expression but also prints the expression.

4. CONCLUDING REMARKS

We are finding that LOGLISP indeed provides the rich setting for logic programming that our early encounters with PROLOG led us to seek. In particular we find it most convenient to be able to invoke LOGIC from LISP, and LISP from LOGIC. It is very useful to have the answer to a query be delivered as a LISP data object and to be able to subject it to arbitrary computational analysis and manipulations.

The LOGIC programmer need not rely on the system builder to build in functions and predicates — he can write his own in LISP and then invoke them from LOGIC.

Nothing in our general design philosophy precludes (as far as we can see) a much faster deduction cycle than we have attained in this, our first, version of LOGLISP. We are confident that by (among other recourses) borrowing Warren's compilation techniques we shall be able to speed things up by at least a factor of 10, and we are currently working on doing this.

REFERENCES

Boyer, R. S., & Moore, J. S., (1972). The sharing of structure in theorem proving programs. *Machine Intelligence* 7, pp. 101–116 (eds. Meltzer, B. and Michie, D.). Edinburgh: Edinburgh University Press.

Bruynooghe, M., (1976). An interpreter for predicate logic programs, Part I. *Report CW 10*, Leuven, Belgium: Applied Mathematics and Programming Division, Katholieke Universiteit.

Clark, K. L., & McCabe, F., (1979). Programmers' Guide to IC–PROLOG. *CCD Report 79/7*, London: Imperial College, University of London.

Colmerauer, A., Kanoui, H., Pasero, R., & Roussel, P. (1973). Un Systeme de Communication Homme-machine en Francais. Report, Luminy, France: Groupe Intelligence Artificielle, Universite d'Aix-Marseille.

Green, C. C. (1969). Theorem proving by resolution as a basis for question-answering systems. *Machine Intelligence 4*, (eds. Meltzer, B. and Michie, D.) Edinburgh: Edinburgh University Press.

Hill, R. (1974). LUSH-resolution and its completeness. *DCL Memo No. 78*, Edinburgh: Department of Artificial Intelligence, University of Edinburgh, 1974.

Kowalski, R. A. (1974). Predicate logic as programming language. *Proceedings IFIP Congress.*

Kowalski, R. A. (1979). *Logic for problem solving.* New York and Amsterdam: Elsevier North Holland.

Landin, P. J. (1964). The mechanical evaluation of expressions. *Computer Journal*, 6, 308–320.

McDermott, D. (1980). The PROLOG phenomenon. *SIGART Newsletter* 72, 16–20.

Roberts, G. (1977). An implementation of PROLOG. M.Sc. Thesis, Waterloo: University of Waterloo.

Robinson, J. A. (1965). A machine-oriented logic based on the resolution principle. *J. of the Assoc. for Comput. Mach.*, 12, 23–41.

Robinson, J. A. (1979). *Logic: Form and Function.* Edinburgh: Edinburgh University Press and New York and Amsterdam: Elsevier North Holland.

Robinson, J. A., & Sibert, E. E. (1980). Logic programming in LISP. *Technical Report*, School of Computer and Information Science, Syracuse University.

Roussel, P., (1975). PROLOG: Manuel de reference et d'utilisation. Luminy, France: Groupe d'Intelligence Artificielle, Universite d'Aix-Marseille.

Strachey, C. (1972). Varieties of programming language. *Technical Monograph PRG-1049000*, Oxford University Computing Laboratory.

van Emden, M. H. (1977). Programming in resolution logic. *Machine Intelligence 8*, pp. 266–299, (eds. Elcock, E. W. and Michie, D.). Chichester: Ellis Horwood and New York: Halsted Press.

Warren, D. H. D., Periera, L. M., & Pereira, F., (1977). PROLOG — the language and its implementation compared with LISP. Proceedings of Symposium on AI and Programming Languages, *SIGPLAN Notices*, 12, No. 8, and *SIGART Newsletters* 64, 109–115.

21

Programming with full first-order logic

K. A. Bowen
School of Computer and Information Science
Syracuse University, USA

Abstract

An automatic deduction system based on a modification of Gentzen's sequentzen system LJ is presented, and its use as the basis for a logic programming system is described. The system is a natural extension of Horn clause logic programming systems in that when all of the formulas in the input sequent are atomic, the behaviour of the system mimics that of LUSH resolution systems. The use of such systems in program development systems and in database management systems is discussed.

Natural deduction and the sequent calculus were invented by Gentzen (1936), and formed the basis for some of the early work in automatic deduction in Wang (1960) and Kanger (1963). After a period of disfavour in the automatic deduction community (but not in the proof-theory community: *cf.* Prawitz (1965 and 1971), Takeuti (1975) and Kreisel (1971), sequentzen methods are again being used, as witnessed by Bledsoe (1977) and Manna & Waldinger (1979). In this paper we will present an automatic deduction system based on the sequentzen approach and describe its use as the basis of a logic programming system. It is a natural extension of Horn clause logic programming systems in the following sense: Whenever all the sequents to be processed correspond directly to Horn clauses, the action of the system is exactly that of an ordinary Horn clause prover. We will discuss this point further below.

1. MOTIVATION: PROGRAM DEVELOPMENT

Software development and maintenance has become the single most costly component of any large computing enterprise (Boehm 1979). Projected trends indicate that this component will consume 85 per cent of the computing dollar in the United States by 1985. Thus there is a great need for efficient and reliable methods of generating needed software. This software must perform as expected with relatively low testing and debugging, or else the cost of its development,

421

and especially its maintenance, becomes exorbitant. Moreover, there are a wide range of real-time computer applications, ranging from medicine through chemical and energy process control to military systems control, where software failure would have catastrophic consequences. Hence there is a need for economically efficient means of developing and maintaining highly reliable software packages.

As currently widely practised, the software development process can be crudely split into three steps:

(1) Specification writing and abstract design.
(2) Coding the design in a programming language.
(3) Compilation of the resulting code.

Present technology has developed to the point that compilation has been entirely automated, and moreover, a wide variety of programming techniques are available for step two. It is in step one and the transition to step two that most of the present difficulties lie.

Given a precise and complete specification and design, the principal difficulty in the transition to step two is not in the production of program code *per se*, but in the certification (proof) that the code produced correctly implements the specifications and design. This is the *verification problem* about which we will have more to say later.

The verification of program code presupposes the existence of precise specifications against which to verify the code. Unfortunately, system specifications are not often sufficiently precise so as to permit attempts at formal verification. Worse still, specifications are often just plain wrong in that they do not meet the expectations of the intended users of the product (*cf.* Boehm (1979) and Mills (1979)), or at least they are incomplete in that significant functional points are entirely overlooked. This is the *specification problem.*

When truly formal specifications are produced, they are usually written in some variant of the first-order predicate calculus (*cf.* Dijkstra 1976; Hoare 1969; Jones 1980; Liskov & Berzins 1979; Luckham *et al.* 1979; and Schwartz 1978). The reasons for this are undoubtedly manifold, but among them the following are important:

- The expressions of predicate logic, while formal and precise, are much closer to natural intuitive thought than are the statements of most programming languages.
- Centuries of the mathematical study of formal logic have left us with a well understood highly developed tool.

Thus the difficulty with the specification problem is in the elucidation and elaboration of (often ill-formed) intuitive plans and conceptions to the point where consistent, and, one must hope, correct and complete, predicate logic specifications can be written. The consistency of the resulting specifications can be tested by an automatic theorem-prover. But neither the correctness nor the completeness of the specifications is susceptible to formal (much less automatic) methods: for what is being formalized is an intuitive conception. The situation is analogous to that of Church's Thesis (*cf.* Kleene 1952) in recursion theory. One can advance arguments for and against the correctness and completeness of the formal specification *vis-à-vis* its intuitive counterpart, but no argument is absolutely conclusive because of the informal intuitive nature of the basic ideas.

However, with regard to a set of formal specifications, one would like to be in a position similar to that regarding Church's Thesis today, namely, to be in possession of a plethora of cogent arguments favouring the adequacy and completeness of the specifications. A powerful tool in constructing such arguments (or in demonstrating their non-existence) would be to be able to run the specifications themselves as programs. That is, having indicated concrete values for input variables, one would like a system which automatically calculated values for the remaining variables such that the resulting definite predicate statements were true (if such values existed). Such a system could be used to test, modify, and 'debug' the specifications themselves. The system of programming in full first-order logic, to be presented below, provides just such a tool.

Presumably, such a system must suffer a disadvantage in efficiency *vis-à-vis* more conventional programming languages, else it would be useable as a programming system in its own right. This appears true for the entire system at least in part on conventional machine architectures, though it appears possible that architectures can be designed which make it competitive with more conventional systems. Taking into account the falling cost of hardware design and implementation together with the rising cost of skilled programmers, such systems may be economically competitive sooner than one might think. At any rate, the system will serve at present as a useful specification design tool, suitable for running the specifications as programs on 'small' test inputs.

Once precise and apparently adequate specifications have been produced, the problem of transforming them to more efficient forms and verifying the resulting code still remains. One of the primary sources of the difficulty and cost of verification today lies in the gulf between the very high level of predicate logic specifications, and the rather low level means of expression in the target programming languages (*cf.* Schwartz 1978), even when these are such so-called 'high-level' languages as PASCAL (Luckham *et al.* 1979) or PL/I (Constable & O'Donnell 1978). The obvious method for diminishing this gap is to raise the level of the target programming language. Among the possible candidates, two stand out: LISP & Horn clause logic programming systems. The two are of comparable high level, and current implementations render them comparable in efficiency (*cf.* Warren *et al.* 1977). Boyer & Moore (1979) have built a system using LISP. However, Horn clause logic is also a very desirable choice because:

A. It is a subsystem of the full predicate logic system, and thus requires no syntactic or psychological transitions on the part of the programmer/ user.

423

B. Being a system of logic itself, the well-developed semantic machinery of classical logic applies to it, and so there need be no semantic shift in the transition from the predicate logic specifications to the target programs.

We will return to these uses of the system after its outlines are sketched below.

2. MOTIVATION: DATABASE QUERY

The second major motivation for consideration of these systems is in the domain of database query languages. Consider a simple database (common in almost all papers on databases) which contains information on the employees of a firm. Suppose that it has in it a relation

Salary (person, amount)

indicating the amount of a person's salary. The most natural question to ask is: Who is the highest-paid person in the firm? That is, we wish to determine the person(s) satisfying the predicate Highest(p) which is defined by:

$$\text{Salary } (p, t) \ \& \ (\forall q)(\forall s)\, \text{Salary } (q, s) \rightarrow s \leqslant t$$

(Of course we could similarly ask who is the lowest-paid menial.) While these sorts of queries can be expressed awkwardly in Horn-clause logic, and by means of *ad hoc* operators in many database query languages, such formulations in predicate calculus terms are reasonably natural and readable. And of course it is easy to create much more complex queries involving more substantive use of quantifiers. As argued in Chapter 2 of Kowalski (1979), logic systems are an excellent choice for database query languages. These sorts of queries make full first-order logic even more natural. With these motivating thoughts, let us consider the basis of the first-order logic programming systems.

3. SEQUENTZEN SYSTEMS

Besides the usual *logical particles* & (conjunction), $\vee$ (disjunction), $\neg$ (negation), $\rightarrow$ (implication), $\leftrightarrow$ (equivalence), $\forall$ (universal quantification), and $\exists$ (existential quantification), a first-order language L will contain a stock of *relation* and *function* symbols (said to be n-ary when they take n arguments), (*individual*) *constants, bound* (*individual*) variables $x\ y\ z\ x_1 \ldots$, and (*individual*) *parameters* $a\ b\ c\ a_1 \ldots$ (the latter two categories occurring with or without numeric subscripts and primes and other decorative superscripts). The categories of *term* and *formula* are given by the following recursive definitions. A term is either an individual constant or variable, or is an expression of the form $f(t_1, \ldots, t_n)$ where f is an n-ary function symbol and $t_1, \ldots, t_n$ are terms. An *atomic formula* is an expression of the form $P(t_1, \ldots, t_n)$ where P is an n-ary relation symbol and $t_1, \ldots, t_n$ are terms. Any atomic formula is a formula. If A and B are formulas, then so are $(\neg A)$, $(A \ \& \ B)$, $(A \vee B)$, $(A \rightarrow B)$, and $(A \leftrightarrow B)$. If A is a formula, if a is any individual parameter, if x is any bound individual variable not occurring in A, and if $A(a/x)$ indicates the expression resulting by replacing all occurrences of a in A by x, then $(\forall x)A(a/x)$ and $(\exists x)A(a/x)$ are both formulas. Generally we

424

use the notation $A(v/e)$ to indicate the result of replacing all occurrences of the symbol v in A by the expression e. Since we use disjoint sets of symbols for parameters and bound variables, there is no possibility of inadvertent binding of variables when substituting terms for variables or parameters in formulas. We use (decorated or undecorated) uppercase greek letters Γ, Δ, Λ, Π, for finite (possibly empty) sets of formulas. A *sequent* is an expression of the form $\Gamma \Rightarrow \Delta$. Its semantic meaning is that $\Gamma \Rightarrow \Delta$ is *valid in* any structure or interpretation supplying meaning to all the symbols of L (*cf.* Mendelsohn (1964) or Shoenfield (1967)) if either some formula in Γ is false, or some formula in Δ is true; $\Gamma \Rightarrow \Delta$ is *(universally) valid* if it is valid in all interpretations. The collection of valid sequents is syntactically axiomatized as follows. A sequent $\Gamma \Rightarrow \Delta$ is a *logical axiom* if $\Gamma \cap \Delta \neq \phi$. The rules of proof for deriving new valid sequents from old consist of the following, where the expressions to the right of the rules constitute names, and $A,\Gamma = \Gamma,A = \Gamma \cup \{A\}$, and $\Gamma,\Pi = \Gamma \cup \Pi$.

$$\frac{\Gamma \Rightarrow \Delta}{\Pi \Rightarrow \Lambda} \text{ Weakening} \qquad \frac{\Gamma \Rightarrow \Delta,A \quad A,\Pi \Rightarrow \Lambda}{\Gamma,\Pi \Rightarrow \Delta,\Lambda} \text{ Cut}$$

where $\Gamma \subseteq \Pi$ and $\Delta \subseteq \Lambda$.

These two rules are called *structural rules*; the remainder are called *logical rules*.

$$\frac{A,B,\Gamma \Rightarrow \Delta}{(A \,\&\, B),\Gamma \Rightarrow \Delta} \,(\&\Rightarrow) \qquad \frac{\Gamma \Rightarrow \Delta,A \;;\; \Gamma \Rightarrow \Delta,B}{\Gamma \Rightarrow \Delta,(A \,\&\, B)} \,(\Rightarrow\&)$$

$$\frac{A,\Gamma \Rightarrow \Delta \;;\; B,\Gamma \Rightarrow \Delta}{(A \vee B),\Gamma \Rightarrow \Delta} \,(\vee\Rightarrow) \qquad \frac{\Gamma \Rightarrow \Delta,A,B}{\Gamma \Rightarrow \Delta,(A \vee B)} \,(\Rightarrow\vee)$$

$$\frac{\Gamma \Rightarrow \Delta,A}{(\neg A),\Gamma \Rightarrow \Delta} \,(\neg\Rightarrow) \qquad \frac{A,\Gamma \Rightarrow \Delta}{\Gamma \Rightarrow \Delta,(\neg A)} \,(\Rightarrow\neg)$$

$$\frac{\Gamma \Rightarrow \Delta,A \;;\; B,\Gamma \Rightarrow \Delta}{(A \to B),\Gamma \Rightarrow \Delta} \,(\to\Rightarrow) \qquad \frac{A,\Gamma \Rightarrow \Delta,B}{\Gamma \Rightarrow \Delta,(A \to B)} \,(\to\Rightarrow)$$

$$\frac{\Gamma \Rightarrow \Delta,A,B \;;\; A,B,\Gamma \Rightarrow \Delta}{(A \leftrightarrow B),\Gamma \Rightarrow \Delta} \,(\leftrightarrow\Rightarrow) \qquad \frac{A,\Gamma \Rightarrow \Delta,B \;;\; B,\Gamma \Rightarrow \Delta,A}{\Gamma \Rightarrow \Delta,(A \leftrightarrow B)} \,(\Rightarrow\leftrightarrow)$$

$$\frac{A(a/t),\Gamma \Rightarrow \Delta}{(\forall x)A(a/x),\Gamma \Rightarrow \Delta} \,(\forall\Rightarrow) \qquad \frac{\Gamma \Rightarrow \Delta,A}{\Gamma \Rightarrow \Delta,(\forall x)A(a/x)} \,(\Rightarrow\forall)$$

where the parameter a does not occur in Γ or Δ.

$$\frac{A,\Gamma \Rightarrow \Delta}{(\exists x)A(a/x),\Gamma \Rightarrow \Delta} \,(\exists\Rightarrow) \qquad \frac{\Gamma \Rightarrow \Delta,A(a/t)}{\Gamma \Rightarrow \Delta,(\exists x)A(a/x)} \,(\Rightarrow\exists)$$

where the parameter a does not occur free in Γ or Δ.

425

The condition associated with the rules $(\Rightarrow\forall)$ and $(\exists\Rightarrow)$ will be called the *eigenvariable condition*. A *proof* is a single-rooted tree of sequents all of whose leaves are logical axioms and such that each non-leaf node follows from those immediately above it by one of the rules of inference. By way of example, we present a sample proof in Fig. 1, where we have taken the liberty of dropping outermost parentheses around formulas, and A and B are arbitrary formulas:

$$
\cfrac{
\cfrac{
\cfrac{
\cfrac{
\cfrac{
\cfrac{
\cfrac{B \Rightarrow A,B \quad A,B \Rightarrow A}{A \leftrightarrow B, B \Rightarrow A} \ (\leftrightarrow\Rightarrow)
}{(\forall x)(A(c/x) \leftrightarrow B(c/x)), B \Rightarrow A} \ (\forall\Rightarrow)
}{(\forall x)(A(c/x) \leftrightarrow B(c/x)), (\forall x)B(c/x) \Rightarrow A} \ (\forall\Rightarrow)
}{(\forall x)(A(c/x) \leftrightarrow B(c/x)), (\forall x)B(c/x) \Rightarrow (\forall x)A(c/x)} \ (\Rightarrow\forall)
}{(\forall x)(A(c/x) \leftrightarrow B(c/x)) \ \& \ (\forall x)B(c/x) \Rightarrow (\forall x)A(c/x)} \ (\&\Rightarrow)
}{\Rightarrow ((\forall x)(A(c/x) \leftrightarrow B(c/x)) \ \& \ (\forall x)B(c/x)) \to (\forall x)A(c/x)} \ (\Rightarrow\to)
}
$$

Fig. 1.

If $\vdash$ indicates derivability in the ordinary Hilbert-style systems of logic (e.g. Mendelsohn (1964) or Shoenfield (1967)) the following theorem establishes the connection between the two systems:

Theorem. For any formula A, $\vdash A$ iff $\Rightarrow A$ has a proof.

Since it is easy to establish that $A_1, \ldots, A_n \Rightarrow B_1, \ldots, B_m$ is derivable iff $\Rightarrow (A_1 \ \& \ldots \& \ A_n) \to (B_1 \lor \ldots \lor B_m)$ is derivable, the Completeness theorem for the usual systems yields:

Theorem. $\Gamma \Rightarrow \Delta$ is derivable iff it is universally valid.

4. SYSTEMATIC PROOF SEARCHING

It is interesting to examine another method for establishing the last theorem. When simply set out as above, sequentzen proofs give the impression that they are synthesized from the leaves down toward the root. However, this is not generally the case in practice. Instead, the proof is grown upwards from the root, 'intelligently' choosing at each step a rule to 'reverse', terminating in a leaf whenever it is discovered that the two sides of the sequent contain a common formula. The reversal process can be stated formally as in these two examples:

$(\Rightarrow\lor)$ reversal: If $A \lor B \in \Delta$, let $\Delta' = (\Delta - \{A \lor B\}) \cup \{A,B\}$, and place $\Gamma \Rightarrow \Delta'$ above $\Gamma \Rightarrow \Delta$.

$(\lor\Rightarrow)$ reversal: If $A \lor B \in \Gamma$, let $\Gamma' = (\Gamma - \{A \lor B\}) \cup \{A\}$, let $\Gamma'' = (\Gamma - \{A \lor B\}) \cup \{B\}$, and place both $\Gamma' \Rightarrow \Delta$ and $\Gamma'' \Rightarrow \Delta$ above $\Gamma \Rightarrow \Delta$.

426

The reversal rules for the other propositional connectives are similar. They bear a close relationship to the tableaux rules of Beth (1955) and Smullyan (1968), as do the quantifier rules as follows:

($\Rightarrow\forall$) reversal: If $(\forall x)A(c/x) \in \Delta$, let d be an
individual parameter not occurring
in $\Gamma \Rightarrow \Delta$, let $\Delta' = (\Delta - \{(\forall x)A(c/x)\}) \cup \{A(c/d)\}$
and place $\Gamma \Rightarrow \Delta'$ above $\Gamma \Rightarrow \Delta$.

($\forall\Rightarrow$) reversal: If $(\forall x)A(c/x) \in \Gamma$, for some term t
let $\Gamma' = \Gamma \cup \{A(c/t)\}$, and put
$\Gamma' \Rightarrow \Delta$ above $\Gamma \Rightarrow \Delta$.

The rule ($\exists\Rightarrow$) reversal is similar to ($\Rightarrow\forall$) reversal, and ($\Rightarrow\exists$) reversal is similar to ($\forall\Rightarrow$) reversal.

The process of growing the tree upwards from its root allows two potential places where 'intelligent' choices may be necessary:

(1) the determination of which reversal rule to apply next at any point in the process;
(2) in applications of ($\forall\Rightarrow$) and ($\Rightarrow\exists$) reversal, choice of the term t.

The apparent need for intelligence in (1) is obviated by the following lemma which indicates that the choice may be made randomly:

Lemma: Let $\mathscr{S}$ be a sequent and let $\mathscr{R}_1$ and $\mathscr{R}_2$ be reversal rules both of which may apply to $\mathscr{S}$. Let $\mathscr{T}_1$ and $\mathscr{T}_2$ be the trees resulting from applications of these two rules in opposing orders. Then $\mathscr{T}_1$ can be extended by reversal rules to a proof iff $\mathscr{T}_2$ may be so extended.

Proof: This lemma is proved by exhaustive examination of cases. For example, consider reversals of ($\Rightarrow\forall$) and ($\Rightarrow\&$):

$$\frac{\dfrac{\Gamma \Rightarrow \Delta, B, A(c/d)\ ;}{\Gamma \Rightarrow \Delta, B, (\forall x)A\ ;}(\Rightarrow\forall)\quad \dfrac{\Gamma \Rightarrow \Delta, C, A(c/d)}{\Gamma \Rightarrow \Delta, C, (\forall x)A}(\Rightarrow\forall)}{\Gamma \Rightarrow \Delta, B\ \&\ C, (\forall x)A}(\Rightarrow\&) \tag{1}$$

or

$$\frac{\dfrac{\Gamma \Rightarrow \Delta, B, A(c/d)\ ;\quad \Gamma \Rightarrow \Delta, C, A(c/d)}{\Gamma \Rightarrow B\ \&\ C, A(c/d)}(\Rightarrow\&)}{\Rightarrow \Delta, B\ \&\ C, (\forall x)A(c/x)}(\Rightarrow\forall) \tag{2}$$

The exercise of intelligence in (2) can be avoided in two different ways. The first (as taken in Bowen (1972) or Takenti (1975)) is to modify the rule of ($\forall\Rightarrow$) reversal (and correspondingly the rule of ($\Rightarrow\exists$) reversal) as follows. Let $t_0, t_1, \ldots$ be a fixed enumeration of the terms of L.

427

$(\forall\Rightarrow)$ reversal$'$: If $(\forall x)A(c/x) \in \Gamma$ and if the depth of $\Gamma \Rightarrow \Delta$ in the tree
at the point of application of this rule is n, then
let $\Gamma' = \Gamma \cup \{A(c/t_0), \dots, A(c/t_n)\}$;
then put $\Gamma' \Rightarrow \Delta$ above $\Gamma \Rightarrow \Delta$.

If $\Gamma' \Rightarrow \Delta$ is as indicated, then it is easy to see that $\Gamma \Rightarrow \Delta$ can be obtained
from $\Gamma' \Rightarrow \Delta$ by $n + 1$ applications of $(\forall\Rightarrow)$. Now we can combine these into a
routine algorithmic procedure as follows. Let $\mathcal{R}_0, \dots, \mathcal{R}_{13}$ be an enumeration of
the logical rules in some order, and let $\mathcal{R}_0{}^*, \dots, \mathcal{R}_{13}{}^*$ be their respective reversals,
where $(\forall\Rightarrow)$ reversal$'$ is used instead of $(\forall\Rightarrow)$ reversal, and $(\Rightarrow\exists)$ reversal$'$ instead
of $(\Rightarrow\exists)$ reversal. The procedure can be described as follows, where k is an integer
variable, and a sequent $\Pi \Rightarrow \Lambda$ is said to be *active* if it contains at least one non-
atomic formula and $\Pi \cap \Lambda = \phi$:

Reverse$_1$

1. Set $k := 0$;
   Place $\Gamma \Rightarrow \Delta$ at the root;

2. While any leaf of the present tree remains active, do the following:

   if $k \equiv j \pmod{14}$, $\Pi \Rightarrow \Lambda$ is an active leaf,
   and reversal rule $\mathcal{R}j^*$ applies to $\Pi \Rightarrow \Lambda$,
   then apply $\mathcal{R}j^*$ to $\Pi \Rightarrow \Lambda$;
   increment k by 1;

Now in the application of any reversal rule $\mathcal{R}j^*$. to $\Pi \Rightarrow \Lambda$, the sequent
$\Pi \Rightarrow \Lambda$ can be derived via $\mathcal{R}j$ from those placed above it by $\mathcal{R}j^*$. Thus if the
procedure Reverse$_1$ terminates in a tree all of whose leaves are logical axioms,
the tree is a proof. Consequently we have:

Lemma. In the application of Reverse$_1$ to a sequent $\Gamma \Rightarrow \Delta$, either the procedure
terminates in a proof or one of the following holds:

(i) the procedure terminates, but at least one leaf is a non-axiom consisting
   entirely of atomic formulas; or

(ii) the procedure does not terminate.

In case (ii), since the branching factor of the tree is finite, if we imagine the
process carried to completion (by completing the step $k = n$ in time $1/2^{**}n$
minutes), by Konig's Infinity Lemma (Jech 1971), the resulting infinite tree
contains an infinite branch. We will call a branch *bad* if either it terminates in a
sequent as described in (i) or is infinite. Let $\mathcal{B}$ be a bad branch, and define a
structure $\mathcal{A}_{\mathcal{B}}$ as follows. The universe of $\mathcal{A}_{\mathcal{B}}$ is the Herbrand universe of L.
If f is an n-ary function symbol, the interpretation of f is the function f defined
by

$$f_{\mathcal{B}}(t_1, \dots, t_n) = f(t_1, \dots, t_n),$$

where $t_1, \dots, t_n$ are terms in the Herbrand universe. If p is an n-ary relation

428

symbol, the interpretation of p is the n-ary relation $p_{\mathscr{B}}$ on the Herbrand universe defined by:

$$p_{\mathscr{B}}(t_1, \ldots, t_n) \text{ holds iff } p(t_1, \ldots, t_n) \text{ occurs on the left side of some sequent on } \mathscr{B}.$$

This specifies an interpretation for all the relation symbols occurring in some formula in $\Gamma \Rightarrow \Delta$; if it is desired to guarantee an interpretation for all the relation symbols of L, the devices of Bowen (1972) will suffice. The next lemma is now easily established by induction on the complexity of A.

Lemma. A formula A holds in the interpretation $\mathscr{A}_{\mathscr{B}}$ iff A occurs on the left side of some sequent in $\mathscr{B}$.

Properly, unless the devices of Bowen (1972) are employed, this holds only for subformulas in $\Gamma \Rightarrow \Delta$. But that is all we need to establish the following.

Theorem. Consider the application of Reverse$_1$ to a sequent $\Gamma \Rightarrow \Delta$. Either the process terminates in a proof with root $\Gamma \Rightarrow \Delta$ and containing no applications of the rule Cut or else there is an interpretation in which $\Gamma \Rightarrow \Delta$ is not valid.

Proof. This follows from the preceding Lemmas and remarks together with the observation that the Cut rule is not among $\mathscr{R}_1, \ldots, \mathscr{R}_{13}$.

5. INTRODUCING UNIFICATION

The second approach to avoiding the exercise of intelligence in (2) involves notions which ultimately lead to the logic programming system. In attempting to reverse the rule $(\forall \Rightarrow)$, what one seeks is an appropriate term t. The rule $(\forall \Rightarrow)$-reversal' takes the British Museum approach to the search: try everything. As a parlour algorithm this is fine. But we are interested in real systems and hence seek something more efficient. Now the unification component of the resolution method (*cf.* Robinson 1979) was invented to deal with just such a search, and so we adopt it here. The essence of the idea is this: when reversing $(\forall \Rightarrow)$, instead of replacing the bound variable x by a specific term, one replaces it with a dummy. Later one tries to find an appropriate term t. (These 'dummies' are simply a class of syntactically distinct individual parameters not acceptable under the basic notion of formula, but used to construct 'extended formulas'.) The interpretation of the word 'later' is what will distinguish the present approach from that of Kanger (1963). He delayed the search for t until the entire 'pseudo-proof tree' had been unwound by the reversal process. Then he began the search for terms to replace the dummy variables remaining in the structure. This makes the search rather global in character, since given any candidate choice of terms for dummies, the entire fringe of the structure must be checked, as well as all points of applications of the rules $(\Rightarrow \forall)$ and $(\exists \Rightarrow)$ to verify that the eigenvariable condition has not been violated. A key part of Robinson's insight in the invention of resolution was the observation that such searches for substitutions should be localized. This is achieved in the present setting by alternating the reversal steps already described with unification steps at which a search is made for appropriate substitutions for the dummies. Before setting down the detailed algorithms, we consider an example which illustrates the situation. To compress the example, let us write $S^n(e)$ for $S(S(\ldots S(e)\ldots))$ with n occurrences of S, and let C be the formula

$$(\forall x)(\forall y)[T2(x,y) \to T2(S(x), S(S(y)))].$$

Also write $(\forall \Rightarrow)^2$ to indicate two successive applications of $(\forall \Rightarrow)$, etc. The tree for this example appears in Fig. 2. Several points are worth noting here:

(a) the reversal of $(\forall \Rightarrow)$ was like $(\forall \Rightarrow)$-reversal except that a dummy (di) was used instead of a concrete term;

(b) after each and every reversal step (for any rule) an attempt was made to find choices for the dummies in the immediate sequent which would convert it into an axiom; this attempt failed at steps (2) and (4), but succeeded at (3a), (5a), and (5b);

(c) once a choice of values is made for some dummy at some sequent in the computation, it is immediately propagated to all other sequents which are tips in the computation, as is reflected in the transition from (3b) to (4);

(d) the procedure is non-deterministic since two distinct types of choices were made:

   $(d1)$ at step (3) it was decided to search for values relative to the left (3a) sequent before considering the right (3b) sequent; the opposite decision would have given the choice of values $d1 = S(0)$ and $d2 = S^2(0)$;

   $(d2)$ at step (5a) two choices of values for $d3$ and $d4$ are possible: $d3 = S(0)$ and $d4 = S^2(0)$, and also $d3 = 0$ and $d4 = 0$; note that a systematic choice of this latter alternative would prevent the procedure from terminating.

There is, however, a distinction between the contexts of these two choices. Choice $(d1)$ is made at a branch node in the proof-tree; in order for the entire proof to succeed, both branches must succeed. On the other hand, choice $(d2)$ is between two solutions for (5a); it is sufficient that the rest of the computation succeed using either solution.

To formulate the algorithm, define:

$(\forall \Rightarrow)$-reversal$''(k)$:   If $(\forall x) A(c/x) \in \Gamma$, then let
$\Gamma' = \Gamma \cup \{A(c/dk)\}$, and put
$\Gamma' \Rightarrow \Delta$ above $\Gamma \Rightarrow \Delta$.

Given two formulas A, B possibly containing dummies, define:

$$\text{unify} f(A,B) = \begin{cases} \theta \text{ where } \theta \text{ is a unifying substitution on the dummies in} \\ \quad A \text{ and } B \text{ (}cf.\text{ Robinson (1979)) if such exists;} \\ \phi \text{ (= the empty substitution) otherwise.} \end{cases}$$

(6) $\dfrac{}{}$ — Axiom with $d3 = S(0), d4 = S^2(0)$ — Axiom

(5a) $\dfrac{T2(S(0), S^2(0)), T2(0,0), C \Rightarrow T2(S^2(0), S^4(0)), T2(d3,d4);\ (5b)\ T2(S(d3), S^2(d4)), T2(S(0), S^2(0)), T2(0,0), C \Rightarrow T2(S^2(0), S^4(0))}{}$ $(\rightarrow \Rightarrow)$

(4) $T2(S(0), S^2(0)), T2(0,0), T2(S(d3), S^2(d4)) \rightarrow T2(S(d3), S^2(d4)), C \Rightarrow T2(S^2(0), S^4(0))$ $\cdots$

(3a) — Axiom with $d1 = 0, d2 = 0$

(2) $\dfrac{T2(0,0), C \Rightarrow T2(S^2(0), S^4(0)), T2(d1,d2);\ (2b)\ T2(S(d1), S^2(d2)), T2(0,0) \Rightarrow T2(S^2(0), S^4(0))}{}$ $(\rightarrow \Rightarrow)$

(1) $T2(0,0), T2(d1,d2) \rightarrow T2(S(d1), S(d2)), C \Rightarrow T2(S^2(0), S^4(0))$ $(\forall A)^2$

(0) $T2(0,0), \underbrace{(\forall x)(\forall y)[T2(x,y) \rightarrow T2(S(x), S(S(y)))]}_{C} \Rightarrow T2(S(S(0)), S^4(0))$ $(\Rightarrow A)$

Fig. 2.

431

Given a sequent $\Gamma \Rightarrow \Delta$, define:

$$\text{unify}s(\Gamma \Rightarrow \Delta) = \{\theta : \theta = \text{unify}f(A,B) \ \& \ A \in \Gamma \ \& \ B \in \Delta\}.$$

If $\mathscr{T}$ is a finite tree and θ is a substitution, let $\mathscr{T}/\theta$ denote the result of applying the substitution θ to all the tip sequents in $\mathscr{T}$. Given a sequent $\Gamma \Rightarrow \Delta$, let $\mathscr{T}_0(\Gamma \Rightarrow \Delta)$ be the tree whose only node is the root $\Gamma \Rightarrow \Delta$. Given a tree $\mathscr{T}$, define

$$\text{unify}t(\mathscr{T}) = \cup \{\text{unify}s(\Gamma \Rightarrow \Delta): \Gamma \Rightarrow \Delta \text{ is a tip of } \mathscr{T}\}.$$

Finally, say that $\mathscr{T}$ is *terminal* if no reversal rule can be applied to $\mathscr{T}$. If $\mathscr{T}$ is terminal and each of its tips is an axiom, then $\mathscr{T}$ is a proof. The new procedure appears as follows:

Reverse$_2$

1. Set $k := 0$ and $\mathscr{S} := \{\mathscr{T}_0(\Gamma \Rightarrow \Delta)\}$.
2. *While* no $\mathscr{T} \in \mathscr{S}$ is terminal *do*
    If $k = j \pmod{14}$, apply reversal rule $\mathscr{R}j^*$
      to all appropriate tips of all $\mathscr{T} \in \mathscr{S}$ yielding
      $\mathscr{R}j^*(\mathscr{T})$ for each $\mathscr{T} \in \mathscr{S}$;
    Set $\mathscr{S} := \cup \{ \{\mathscr{R}j^*(\mathscr{T})/\theta : \theta \in \text{unify}s(\mathscr{R}j^*(\mathscr{T}))\} : \mathscr{T} \in \mathscr{S}\}$;

    Increment k by 1.

Here it is understood that the $\mathscr{R}j^*$ corresponding to the rule $(\forall \Rightarrow)$ is $(\forall \Rightarrow)$-reversal$''(k)$, and similarly for $(\Rightarrow \exists)$.

That these dummy variables act like individual parameters is reflected in the following lemma (whose proof is simply an extension of the arguments for Lemmas 2.10–2.12 of Takenti (1975)).

Lemma. Let $\mathscr{S}$ and $\mathscr{S}'$ be sequents and let γ be either an individual parameter or a dummy variable. If $\mathscr{S}'$ is inferable from $\mathscr{S}$ by a rule $\mathscr{R}$, then for any term e, $\mathscr{S}'(\gamma/e)$ is inferable from $\mathscr{S}(\gamma/e)$ provided that if $\mathscr{R}$ is $(\exists \Rightarrow)$ or $(\Rightarrow \forall)$, the eigenvariable of $\mathscr{R}$ does not occur in e.

As with Reverse$_1$, if Reverse$_2$ terminates with $\mathscr{S}$ containing an 'extended proof', this 'extended proof' together with the unifier can be used to construct a proof of the original input sequent $\Gamma \Rightarrow \Delta$, while if (Reverse$_2$) terminates by virtue of $\mathscr{S}$ containing a terminal $\mathscr{T}$ which is not a proof, this $\mathscr{T}$ can be used to produce a counter-model to $\Gamma \Rightarrow \Delta$. And if the procedure does not terminate, any of the (possibly infinitely many) infinite trees can be used to produce a counter-model to $\Gamma \Rightarrow \Delta$. Fig. 2 presents one of the elements of $\mathscr{S}$: a positively terminal element.

6. LOGIC PROGRAMMING

Since the treatment of unification and dummies is uniform at each stage of the process, nothing prevents us from allowing dummies to be present in the input sequent. Fig. 3 presents such a computation. In this case we can think of the

(6) — Axiom with $d3 = S(0), d4 = S^2(0)$ — Axiom with $d* = S^4(0)$

(5a) $T2(S(0),S^2(0)),T2(0,0),C \Rightarrow T2(S^2(0),d*),T2(d3,d4)$; (5b) $T2(S(d3),S^2(d4)),T2(S(0),S^2(0)),T2(0,0),C \Rightarrow T2(S^2(0),d*)$ $(\rightarrow \Rightarrow)$

(4) $T2(S(0),S^2(0)),T2(0,0),T2(0,0),T2(d3,d4) \rightarrow T2(S(d3),S^2(d4)),C \Rightarrow T2(S^2(0),d*)$ .....

(3a) — Axiom with $d1 = 0, d2 = 0$

(2) $T2(0,0),C \Rightarrow T2(S^2(0),d*),T2(d1,d2)$; (2b) $T2(S(d1),S^2(d2)),T2(0,0) \Rightarrow T2(S^2(0),d*)$ $(\rightarrow \Rightarrow)$

$T2(0,0),T2(d1,d2) \rightarrow T2(S(d1),S(d2)),C \Rightarrow T2(S^2(0),d*)$

$$T2(0,0),\underbrace{(\forall x)(\forall y)[T2(x,y) \rightarrow T2(S(x),S(S(y)))}_{C} \Rightarrow T2(S(S(0)),d*)\quad (\forall \Rightarrow)^2$$

Fig. 3.

433

procedure as having computed a value (d^*) such that the resulting sequent $(\Gamma \Rightarrow \Delta)\theta$ is provable.

If 0 is taken as the usual zero and S is taken as the successor function, then the pair of formulas $T2(0,0)$ and

$$(\forall x)(\forall y)[T2(x,y) \rightarrow T2(S(x), S(S(y)))]$$

define the relation $T2(u,v)$ which holds between natural numbers u and v whenever v is twice u. Thus application of the procedure Reverse$_2$ to the sequent

$$T2(0,0), (\forall x)(\forall y)[T2(x,y) \rightarrow T2(S(x), S(S(y)))] \Rightarrow T2(S(S(0)), d^*)$$

amounts to searching for a value d^* such that $T2(S(S(0)), d^*)$ holds; i.e., calculating a d^* which is twice 2. This is exactly the value $(d^*) \; \theta = S^4(0)$ returned by Reverse$_2$.

Consequently, these dummy variables function in the same capacity as logical variables in other logic programming systems (*cf.* Kowalski (1979)).

A 'pseudo-procedural' interpretation of sequents $\Gamma \Rightarrow \Delta$ can be given as:

In order to successfully run (establish) at least one of the 'procedures' (formulas) in Δ, it suffices to successfully run (establish) all of the 'procedures' (formulas) in Γ.

With this in mind, it is useful to investigate the use of 'sequent axioms' (*cf.* Bowen (1972)) as a 'procedural database' for use during the reversal process. To this end, some further definitions will be useful. If θ and θ' are substitutions, say that θ' is an *extension* of θ (and write $\theta \ll \theta'$) if domain $(\theta) \subseteq$ domain (θ') and θ and θ' agree on their common domain. We have been using substitutions which only apply to the dummies in our structures. However, below we will also allow substitutions to affect individual parameters in formulas and sequents. If θ and θ' are substitutions and W is a set of dummies and individual parameters, we will write $\theta = (W) \theta'$ to mean that θ and θ' agree on all the elements of W. We will also write $\theta = (e)\theta'$ for $\theta = (\{e\})\theta'$. Let CH be a fixed choice function for finite sets of expressions; i.e., if X is a non-empty finite set of expressions, then $CH(X)$ is an element of X. Let DB be a fixed finite set of sequents. Our next reversal procedure (in which DB is an implicit parameter) runs as follows.

Reverse$_3$

1. Set $k := 0$;
   Set $\mathcal{S} := \{<\mathcal{T}_0(\Gamma \Rightarrow \Delta), \phi>\}$;
2. *While* no $<\mathcal{T}, \theta> \in \mathcal{S}$ is such that $\mathcal{T}/\theta$ is terminal *do*:
   if $k \equiv j \pmod{15}$ *and* $j < 15$ *then*

         begin
         Apply reversal rule $\mathcal{R}j^*$ to all $\mathcal{T}/\theta$ such that
         $<\mathcal{T}, \theta> \in \mathcal{S}$, yielding $\mathcal{R}j^*(\mathcal{T}/\theta)$;
         Set $\mathcal{S} :=$

   $\{\{<\mathcal{R}j^*(\mathcal{T}/\theta), \theta'> : \theta' \in \text{unifys}(\mathcal{R}j^*(\mathcal{T}/\theta))\} : <\mathcal{T}, \theta> \in \mathcal{S}\}$

Increment k by 1;
end

else

Set $\mathscr{S} :=$
$$\{\mathscr{RC}\,(\Pi \Rightarrow \Lambda)\,(<\mathscr{T},\theta>) : \Pi \Rightarrow \Lambda \in DB \ \& <\mathscr{T},\theta> \in \mathscr{S}\};$$

3. Return $\{\theta : \exists\mathscr{T}[<\mathscr{T},\theta> \in \mathscr{S}\text{ is terminal}]\}$.

or

3. Return $CH\,\{\theta : \exists\mathscr{T}[<\mathscr{T},\theta> \in \mathscr{S}\text{ is terminal}]\}$.

The set $\mathscr{RC}(\Pi \Rightarrow \Lambda)\,(<\mathscr{T},\theta>)$ is defined to be the set of all pairs $<\mathscr{T}',\theta'>$ such that $\theta \ll \theta'$, there is a tip $\Pi' \Rightarrow \Lambda'$ of $\mathscr{T}$ such that $\Lambda/\theta' \subseteq \Lambda'$, and $\mathscr{T}'$ is the result of putting each of the sequents $\Pi' \Rightarrow (\Lambda' - \Lambda) \cup \{A\}$ above $\Pi' \Rightarrow \Lambda'$, where $A \in \Pi$. In this case, the sequent $\Pi' \Rightarrow \Lambda'$ can be derived from $\Pi \Rightarrow \Lambda$ together with those placed above it by means of the Cut rule, as follows, where $\&(X)$ indicates the conjunction of the formulas in the set X:

$$\cfrac{\cfrac{\{\Pi' \Rightarrow (\Lambda' - \Lambda), A \,:\, A \in \Pi\}}{\Pi' \Rightarrow (\Lambda' - \Lambda),\, \&(\Pi)}\,(\Rightarrow\&) \qquad \cfrac{\Pi \Rightarrow \Lambda}{\&(\Pi) \Rightarrow \Lambda}\,(\&\Rightarrow)}{\Pi' \Rightarrow \underbrace{(\Lambda' - \Lambda),\, \Lambda}_{\Lambda'}}\;\text{Cut}$$

If $\Lambda = \{B\}$ and $\Pi = \{A_1, \ldots, A_n\}$, this appears as:

$$\cfrac{\cfrac{\Pi' \Rightarrow \Lambda' - \{B\}, A_1; \ldots; \Pi' \Rightarrow \Lambda' - \{B\}, A_n}{\Pi' \Rightarrow (\Lambda' - \{B\}),\, A_1 \,\&\, \ldots \,\&\, A_n}\,(\Rightarrow\&) \qquad \cfrac{\Pi \Rightarrow \Lambda}{A_1 \,\&\, \ldots \,\&\, A_n \Rightarrow B}\,(\&\Rightarrow)}{\Pi' \Rightarrow (\Lambda' - \{B\}),\, B}$$

Thus from a goal point of view, one passes from attempting to establish $\Pi' \Rightarrow (\Lambda' - \{B\}), B$ to attempting to jointly establish

$$\Pi' \Rightarrow (\Lambda' - \{B\}), A_1; \ldots; \Pi' \Rightarrow (\Lambda' - \{B\}), A_n$$

Structurally, on the right-hand side of the sequent arrow, this transformation appears just as the transformations of the goal clause by a Horn clause theorem prover.

Let DB^* consist of all formulas of the form $\&(\Gamma) \to \vee(\Delta)$, where $\Gamma \Rightarrow \Delta$ belongs to DB and $\vee(X)$ indicates the disjunction of the formulas in X. Then the following can be established by induction on the complexity of proofs.

Lemma. Reverse$_3$ terminates in a proof with input $\Gamma \Rightarrow \Delta$ if and only if Reverse$_2$ terminates with a proof in $DB^*, \Gamma \Rightarrow \Delta$. Thus the procedure Reverse$_3$ is complete.

We will say that a sequent $\Gamma \Rightarrow \Delta$ is a *Horn sequent* if and only if all the formulas in $\Gamma \cup \Delta$ are atomic, and Δ contains at most one formula. In this case, the corresponding formula $\&(\Gamma) \to \vee(\Delta)$ is a Horn formula, identical in substance to a Horn clause. We will say that DB is *Horn* if each of its members is a Horn

435

sequent. Now suppose that *DB* is Horn and that we attempt to establish the sequent $\Gamma \Rightarrow \Delta$, where Γ is empty and Δ consists of atomic formulas. Then when Reverse₃ is run, no rule can transfer a formula to the left-hand side of a sequent, and in fact, the only reversal process applicable will be the $DB(\Delta)$ accesses. By the remarks above, these accesses transform the sequent being acted upon just as the Horn clause theorem prover transforms its goal clause. Thus it is that when *DB* is Horn and the input sequent is also Horn, the action of Reverse₃ mimics the action of the Horn clause theorem prover underlying present-day logic programming systems.

7. EQUALITY

If L is a first-order predicate language, let Γ_e be the collection of equality axioms appropriate to L, namely, the formula $(\forall x)[x = x]$ together with the following for each *n*-ary function symbol *f* and *n*-ary relational symbol *R* of L:

$$(\forall x_1) \ldots (\forall x_n)(\forall y_1) \ldots (\forall y_n)[x_1 = y_1 \& \ldots \& x_n = y_n$$
$$\rightarrow f(x_1, \ldots, x_n) = f(y_1, \ldots, y_n)]$$
$$(\forall x_1) \ldots (\forall x_n)(\forall y_1) \ldots (\forall y_n)[x_1 = y_1 \& \ldots \& x_n = y_n$$
$$\& R(x_1, \ldots, x_n) \rightarrow R(y_1, \ldots, y_n)]$$

The system LK_e (LK with equality) is the system LK augmented by the sequent axiom

$$\Rightarrow x = x$$

together with each of the following, for each *n*-ary function symbol *f* and *n*-ary relation symbol *R* of L:

$$x_1 = y_1, \ldots, x_n = y_n \Rightarrow f(x_1, \ldots, x_n) = f(y_1, \ldots, y_n)$$
$$x_1 = y_1, \ldots, x_n = y_n, R(x_1, \ldots, x_n) \Rightarrow R(y_1, \ldots, y_n)$$

By Proposition 7.4 of Takeuti (1975), we have

Theorem. $\Gamma \Rightarrow \Delta$ is provable in LK_e if and only if $\Gamma_e, \Gamma \Rightarrow \Delta$ is provable in LK.

Let the notation $C(a//b)$ indicate the result of replacing some 'indicated' occurrences of the term *a* in formula *C* by the term *b*, provided that each occurrence of *a* in *C* is free for *b*. (The method of 'indication' is left to the reader's imagination. All we need note is that not all occurrences of *a* in *C* which are free for *b* need necessarily be 'indicated'.) If $S = \{C_1, \ldots, C_n\}$, then

$$S(a//b) = \{C_1(a//b), \ldots, C_n(a//b)\}$$

Then the following is a valid principle of inference in LK_e:

$$\frac{\Gamma(a//b) \Rightarrow \Delta(a//b)}{a = b, \Gamma \Rightarrow \Delta}$$

436

The validity of this rule is easily established by proving the following Lemma by induction on the total number of 'replaced occurrences' of a in the sequent $\Gamma \Rightarrow \Delta$:

Lemma. Let K be a set of formulas (which may be empty) which may possibly contain the formula $a = b$. Then the following is a valid rule of inference:

$$\frac{K, \Gamma(a/\!/b) \Rightarrow \Delta(a/\!/b)}{K, a = b, \Gamma \Rightarrow \Delta}$$

Thus, for use in LK_e, we may extend the procedure Reverse$_3$ by adding the following reversal rule:

$(= -$reversal$)$: If a and b are terms and the formula $a = b$ belongs to Γ, let Γ'' be the result of deleting $a = b$ from Γ, and let Γ' (respectively, Δ') be the result of replacing all occurrences of b (which are free for a) in Γ'' (respectively Δ) by a. Then place both $\Gamma' \Rightarrow \Delta'$ and $\Gamma \Rightarrow \Delta$ above $\Gamma \Rightarrow \Delta$.

Let $\Gamma_<$ contain the following formulas:

$(\forall x) [x = x]$
$(\forall x)(\forall y) [x = y \to y = x]$
$(\forall i)(\forall j) \neg [i < j \& j < i]$
$(\forall i)(\forall j) [\text{Succ}(j) \leqslant i \to j < i]$

(Presumably there are others that should be included, but these are sufficient for our present purpose.) Then the proof tree of Fig. 4 demonstrates the validity of the sequent $\Gamma_<, i \leqslant j, j \leqslant i \Rightarrow i = j$.

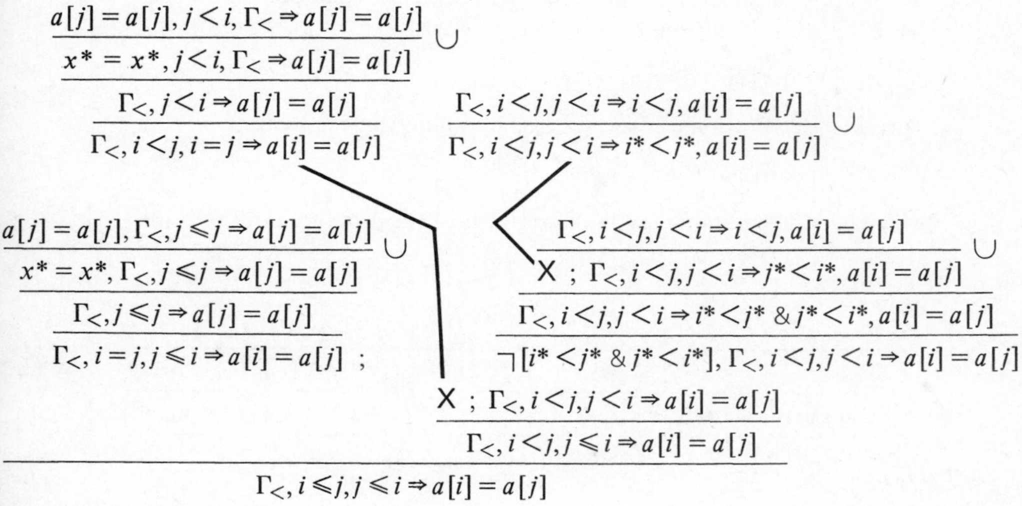

Fig. 4.

The steps marked (U) are the result of unifications.

Just as in the present implementations of Horn clause logic (e.g., Warren *et al.* (1977) or Robinson & Sibert (1980)), it will be possible to 'build-in' direct access to machine execution of such relations as $=$ or $<$ for integers (and presumably other kinds of numbers). These of course would run when both of their arguments were definite integer terms (i.e., containing no logic variables.) Otherwise they would be treated as above.

Finally, just as with equality, the set $\Gamma_<$ could be dropped in favour of adding related sequents as sequent axioms. This is certainly the approach one would use in a real implementation. The details of this trade-off are discussed in Bowen (1972) for arbitrary sets of axioms.

8. SOME EXAMPLES

Returning to the simple database of section 2, the highest-paid person, together with her or his salary, can be determined by submitting the query

$$\text{Salary}(p^*, t^*) \,\&\, (\forall q)(\forall s)\,[\text{Salary}(q, s) \to s \leqslant t^*]$$

The processor will succeed with p^* bound to an example of such a person, and t^* bound to that person's salary.

Consider the problem of finding the maximum value of an array, as treated on p. 21 of Luckham *et al.* (1979). The desired predicate is defined by:

$$\text{maxof}(x, a, l, r) \text{ iff } (\forall i)\,[l \leqslant i \leqslant r \to a[i] \leqslant x]$$
$$\&\,(\exists j)\,[l \leqslant j \leqslant r \,\&\, a[j] = x]$$

Then the requirement $\text{maxof}(\text{MAX}, A, 1, N)$ is intended to be the post-condition of a routine calculating the maximum MAX of array A; the pre-condition is $N > 0$. Let Γ consist of the formulas of $\Gamma_<$ together with

$$a[1] = 3, \; a[2] = 5, \; a[3] = 1.$$

Then the specification can be exercised by submitting the sequent:

$$\Gamma \Rightarrow \text{maxof}(\text{max}^*, a, 1, 3)$$

where max^* is a dummy. An initial segment of the proof-tree will take the form:

$$
\frac{
  \dfrac{}{\Gamma, 1 \leqslant i^+ \leqslant 3 \Rightarrow a[i^+] \leqslant \text{max}^*}
  \quad
  \dfrac{
    \dfrac{(**)}{\Gamma \Rightarrow 1 \leqslant f^* \leqslant 3 \,;\, \Gamma \Rightarrow a[f^*] = \text{max}^*}
  }{\Gamma \Rightarrow 1 \leqslant f^* \leqslant 3 \,\&\, a[f^*] = \text{max}^*}
}{
  \dfrac{\Gamma \Rightarrow (\forall i)\,[1 \leqslant i \leqslant 3 \to a[i] \leqslant \text{max}^*] \,\&\, (\exists f)[1 \leqslant f \leqslant 3 \,\&\, a[f] = \text{max}^*]}{\Gamma \Rightarrow \text{maxof}(\text{max}^*, a, 1, 3)}
}
$$

According to the example considered in section 7, this will further extend (in effect) to the schematic proof tree indicated in Fig. 5.

438

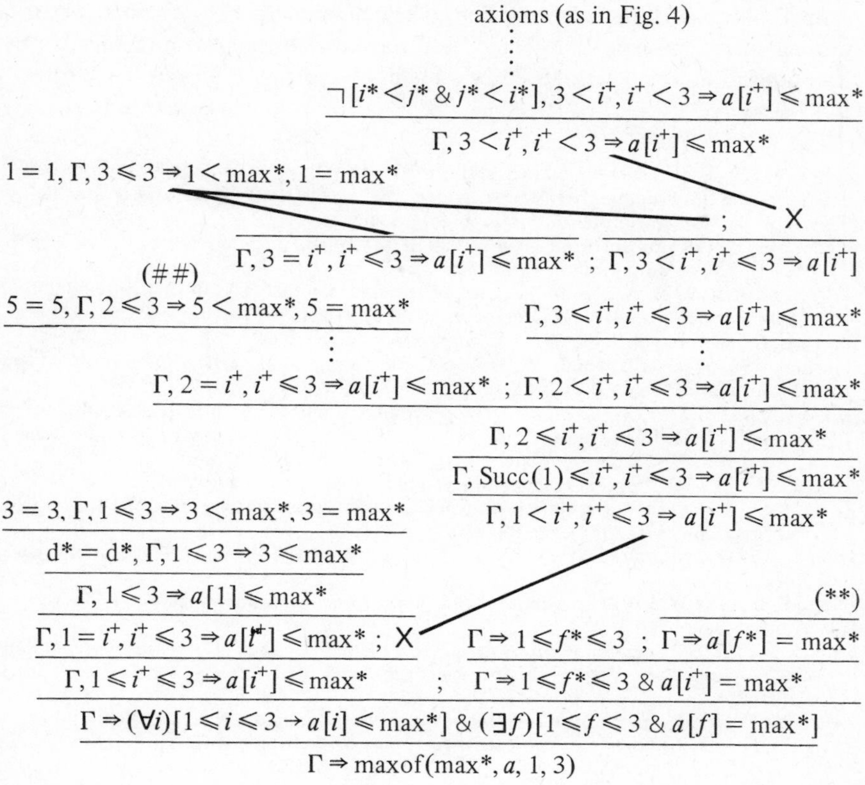

axioms (as in Fig. 4)

$$\vdots$$

$$\dfrac{\neg[i^* < j^* \ \& \ j^* < i^*],\, 3 < i^+,\, i^+ < 3 \Rightarrow a[i^+] \leqslant \max^*}{\Gamma,\, 3 < i^+,\, i^+ < 3 \Rightarrow a[i^+] \leqslant \max^*}$$

$$1 = 1,\, \Gamma,\, 3 \leqslant 3 \Rightarrow 1 < \max^*,\, 1 = \max^*$$

$$;\quad \mathsf{X}$$

$$(\#\#)\qquad \dfrac{\Gamma,\, 3 = i^+,\, i^+ \leqslant 3 \Rightarrow a[i^+] \leqslant \max^*\ ;\ \Gamma,\, 3 < i^+,\, i^+ \leqslant 3 \Rightarrow a[i^+]}{}$$

$$5 = 5,\, \Gamma,\, 2 \leqslant 3 \Rightarrow 5 < \max^*,\, 5 = \max^* \qquad \dfrac{}{\Gamma,\, 3 \leqslant i^+,\, i^+ \leqslant 3 \Rightarrow a[i^+] \leqslant \max^*}$$

$$\vdots \qquad\qquad \vdots$$

$$\dfrac{\Gamma,\, 2 = i^+,\, i^+ \leqslant 3 \Rightarrow a[i^+] \leqslant \max^*\ ;\ \Gamma,\, 2 < i^+,\, i^+ \leqslant 3 \Rightarrow a[i^+] \leqslant \max^*}{\dfrac{\Gamma,\, 2 \leqslant i^+,\, i^+ \leqslant 3 \Rightarrow a[i^+] \leqslant \max^*}{\Gamma,\, \mathrm{Succ}(1) \leqslant i^+,\, i^+ \leqslant 3 \Rightarrow a[i^+] \leqslant \max^*}}$$

$$3 = 3,\, \Gamma,\, 1 \leqslant 3 \Rightarrow 3 < \max^*,\, 3 = \max^* \qquad \Gamma,\, 1 < i^+,\, i^+ \leqslant 3 \Rightarrow a[i^+] \leqslant \max^*$$

$$d^* = d^*,\, \Gamma,\, 1 \leqslant 3 \Rightarrow 3 \leqslant \max^*$$

$$\Gamma,\, 1 \leqslant 3 \Rightarrow a[1] \leqslant \max^* \qquad\qquad\qquad (**)$$

$$\Gamma,\, 1 = i^+,\, i^+ \leqslant 3 \Rightarrow a[i^+] \leqslant \max^*\ ;\ \mathsf{X} \quad \Gamma \Rightarrow 1 \leqslant f^* \leqslant 3\ ;\ \Gamma \Rightarrow a[f^*] = \max^*$$

$$\Gamma,\, 1 \leqslant i^+,\, i^+ \leqslant 3 \Rightarrow a[i^+] \leqslant \max^* \qquad ; \qquad \Gamma \Rightarrow 1 \leqslant f^* \leqslant 3 \ \& \ a[i^+] = \max^*$$

$$\dfrac{\Gamma \Rightarrow (\forall i)[1 \leqslant i \leqslant 3 \rightarrow a[i] \leqslant \max^*] \ \& \ (\exists f)[1 \leqslant f \leqslant 3 \ \& \ a[f] = \max^*]}{\Gamma \Rightarrow \mathrm{maxof}(\max^*, a, 1, 3)}$$

Fig. 5.

Now consider a unification step taking place at the point indicated as (**) in Fig. 5. One possible success for this unification is: $f^* = 1$ and $\max^* = 3$. These values are passed through the environment to the remaining tips of this tree. Further action at these tips may be either axiomatic or, more likely, direct access to machine arithmetic. At any event, the tip indicated (##) will fail. This will ultimately cause the unification at (**) to fail, and another attempt will be made. A second success would be: $f^* = 2$ and $\max^* = 5$. When these values are communicated, all the remaining tips will succeed, and so the entire computation will succeed, returning the value $\max^* = 5$.

9. CONCLUDING REMARKS

The examples above indicate that a system based on the principles described here will provide a valuable tool for both program development and database query. Efficient implementation of the basic system along the lines of Warren *et al.* (1977) and Robinson & Sibert (1980), will make it practical and friendly to the user. One can even envisage a compiler built on principles similar to those

439

of the Edinburgh Horn clause compiler. These are directions for further research. Another line of investigation would be to push the basic system still further by extensions to more powerful cut-free systems.

REFERENCES

Beth, E. W. (1955). Semantic entailment and formal derivability, *Mededelingen der Koninklijke Nederlandse Akademie van Wetenschappen Afd. Letterkunde* 19, 309–342.

Bledsoe, W. W. (1977). Non-resolution theorem proving, *Artificial Intelligence*, 9, 1–35.

Boehm, B. B. (1979). Software engineering: R&D trends and defense needs, in Wegner (1979), pp. 44–86.

Bowen, K. A. (1972). A note on cut elimination and completeness in first order theories, *Zeitschr. f. math. Logik und Grundlagen d. Math.*, 18, 173–176.

Boyer, R. S., & Moore, J. S. (1979). *A Computational Logic*, New York: Academic Press.

Constable, R. I., & O'Donnell, M. J. (1978). *A Programming Logic*, Cambridge, Mass.: Winthrop Publishers.

Dijkstra, E. W. (1976), *A Discipline of Programming*, Englewood Cliffs. N.J.: Prentice-Hall.

Gentzen, G. (1935). Investigations into logical deduction, *The Collected Papers of Gerhard Gentzen*, pp. 68–131. Amsterdam: North-Holland.

Gries, D., ed. (1978). *Programming Methodology*, New York: Springer-Verlag.

Hoare, C. A. R. (1969). An axiomatic basis for computer programming, *CACM* 12, 576–580. Reprinted in Gries (1978), pp. 89–100.

Jech, T. (1971). *Lectures in Set Theory, Lecture Notes in Mathematics*, 217, Berlin: Springer-Verlag.

Jones, C. B. (1980). *Software Development: A Rigorous Approach*, Englewood Cliffs. N.J.: Prentice-Hall.

Kanger, S. (1963). A simplified proof method for elementary logic, *Computer Programming and Formal Systems*, pp. 87–94 (ed. Braffort, P. and Hirshberg, D.) Amsterdam: North-Holland.

Kleene, S. C. (1952). *Introduction to Metamathematics*, Princeton, N.J.: van Nostrand.

Kowalski, R. (1979). *Logic for Problem Solving*, New York: North-Holland.

Kriesel, G. (1971). A survery of proof theory, *Proc. of the 2nd Scandinavian Logic Symposium*, Amsterdam: North-Holland.

Liskov, B. H., & Berzins, V. (1979). An appraisal of program specifications, in Wegner (1979), pp. 276–301.

Luckham, D. C. *et al.* (1979). Stanford Pascal Verifier User Manual, *STAN-CS-79-731*, Stanford: Computer Science Department, Stanford University.

Manna, Z. and Waldinger, R. (1979). A deductive approach to program synthesis, *Proc. 4th Workshop on Automated Deduction*, (Austin, Texas), pp. 129–139.

Mendelson, E. (1964). *Introduction to Mathematical Logic*, Princeton, N.J.: van Nostrand.

Mills, H. D. (1979). Software development, in Wegner (1979), pp. 87–105.

Prawitz, D. (1965). Natural deduction, *Stockholm Studies in Philosophy 3*, Stockholm: Almqvist and Wiksell.

Prawitz, D. (1971). Ideas and results in proof theory, *Proc. of the 2nd Scandinavian Logic Symposium*, Amsterdam: North-Holland.

Robinson, J. A. (1979). *Logic: Form and Function*, Edinburgh: Edinburgh University Press.

Robinson, J. A., & Sibert, E. E. (1980), Logic Programming in LISP, Technical Report, Syracuse: School of Computer and Information Science, Syracuse University.

Schoenfield, J. R. (1967). *Mathematical Logic*, Reading: Mass.: Addison-Wesley.

Schwartz, J. T. (1978). A survey of program proof technology, *Technical Report No. 001*, New York: Dept. of Computer Science, New York University.

Smullyan, R. (1968). *First-Order Logic*, Berlin: Springer-Verlag.

Takeuti, G. (1975). *Proof Theory*, Amsterdam: North-Holland.

Wang, H. (1960). Towards mechanical mathematics, *IBM J. Res. Dev.* 4, 2–22.

Warren, D. H. D., *et al.* (1977), PROLOG: the language and its implementation compared with LISP *SIGPLAN Notices* 12 no. 8, 109–115 (also *SIGART Newsletter*, No. 64).

Wegner, P., ed. (1979). *Research Directions in Software Technology*, Cambridge, Mass.: MIT Press.

22

Higher-order extensions to PROLOG: are they needed?

D. H. D. Warren
Department of Artificial Intelligence
University of Edinburgh

Abstract

PROLOG is a simple and powerful progamming language based on first-order logic. This paper examines two possible extensions to the language which would generally be considered "higher-order".[†] The first extension introduces lambda expressions and predicate variables so that functions and relations can be treated as 'first class' data objects. We argue that this extension does not add anything to the real power of the language. The other extension concerns the introduction of set expressions to denote the set of all (provable) solutions to some goal. We argue that this extension does indeed fill a real gap in the language, but must be defined with care.

1. INTRODUCTION AND SUMMARY OF PROLOG

PROLOG (Roussel 1975, Warren, Pereira and Pereira 1977 and Warren 1979) is a simple and powerful programming language based on first-order logic. It was conceived around 1971 by Alain Colmerauer at the University of Marseille, and has subsequently been put to use in a wide variety of applications, e.g. Bergman and Kanoui 1975, Warren 1976, Darvas, Futo and Szeredi 1977, Markusz 1977, Dahl 1977, Warren 1980, Bundy, Byrd, Luger, Mellish and Palmer 1979 and Dwiggins and Silva 1979.

The purpose of this paper is to discuss two possible extensions to PROLOG, both involving what are normally considered in the computing world to be 'higher order'[†] facilities. The first extension permits predicates to be treated as data objects; the second extension introduces expressions to denote the set of all solutions to some goal. The two sections of the paper covering these extensions can be read independently.

[†] Throughout this paper, 'higher-order' is used in the informal (computing) sense of 'pertaining to functions, sets, relations etc.'. The use of this term should not be taken to imply any particular connection with higher-order logic.

For readers not familiar with PROLOG, there follows a brief summary of the language. The syntax and terminology used is that of DEC-10 PROLOG (Pereira, Pereira and Warren 1978).

A PROLOG program comprises a set of *procedures*, each of which constitutes a definition of a certain *predicate*. A procedure consists of a sequence of *clauses*, which have the general form:

$$P :- Q_1, Q_2, \ldots, Q_n.$$

to be interpreted as:

"P (is true) if Q_1 and Q_2 and ... and Q_n (are true)".

If n is zero, the clause is written simply as:

$$P.$$

and interpreted as:

"P (is true)".

The P and Q_i are examples of *goals* or *procedure calls*, consisting of a predicate applied to some *arguments*.

For example, here is a procedure defining the predicate 'european' of one argument:

```
european(europe).
european(X) :- partof(X,Y), european(Y).
```

The clauses can be read as:

"Europe is European".
"For any X and Y, X is European if X is part of Y and Y is European".

The arguments of a procedure call are data objects called *terms*. A terms may be an (*atomic*) *constant*, a *variable*, or a *structure*. Variables are distinguished by an initial capital letter. Each variable of a clause is to be interpreted as standing for any arbitrary object.

A structure consists of a *functor* applied to some terms as *arguments*, and is written exactly like a goal, e.g.

```
point(2, 3)
```

The functor should be thought of as a record type, and the arguments as the fields of a record.

A PROLOG program is invoked interactively by supplying a *question*, which may be thought of as a clause without a left-hand side, e.g.

```
?- partof(X, britain).
```

to be interpreted as:

"Is X part of Britain? (for any X you know of)"

442

The PROLOG system responds to a question by generating alternative instances of the variables for which it can deduce that the goal or goals are true. For this example, assuming there is an appropriate procedure for 'partof', these instances might be:

X = england ;
X = scotland ;
X = wales

To find such instances, PROLOG executes a goal by first *matching* it against the left-hand side of some clause and then executing the goals (if any) in the clause's right-hand side. Goals are executed in left-to-right order, and clauses are tried in the order they appear in the procedure. If a match isn't found (or there are no outstanding goals left to execute), PROLOG *backtracks*; that is, it goes back to the most recently executed goal and seeks an alternative match. Since the matching process is actually *unification* (*see* Robinson 1965), the net effect is to generate the most general instances of the goal for which it is true.

For convenience, certain predicates and functors may be written in infix notation, e.g.

13 divides 52   X + 1

and a special syntax is used for those structures called *lists* (cf. LISP), constructed from the constant '[ ]' and the functor '.' of two arguments, e.g.

[X|L]   for   .(X, L)
[a,b,c]   for   .(a, .(b, .(c, [])))
[a,b|L]   for   .(a, .(b, L))

As a final example, here is a procedure for the predicate 'concatenate (X,Y,Z)', meaning "the concatenation of list X with list Y is list Z":

concatenate([], L, L).
concatenate([X|L1], L2, [X|L3]) :- concatenate(L1, L2, L3).

Notice how what is usually thought of as a function of two arguments producing one result is here regarded as a predicate of three arguments. In PROLOG, a function is always regarded as just a special case of a relation, identified by a predicate with an extra final argument denoting the result of the function. An advantage of this approach is that not only can the function be called in the normal way, e.g. by:

?- concatenate([a,b], [c], L).

meaning:

"what is the concatenation L of [a,b] with [c] ?"

but also other usages are possible and just as easy to express, e.g.

?- concatenate (L1, L2, [a, b, c]).

443

meaning:

"Which lists L1 and L2 have concatenation [a, b, c] ?"

2. PREDICATES AS "FIRST CLASS" DATA OBJECTS

It has often been argued that a programming language such as PROLOG, based on first-order logic, lacks some of the power of "functional" languages such as LISP and POP-2, which provide what are considered to be "higher-order" facilities, namely the ability to treat functions as data objects. To be specific, in these functional languages it is possible to have a function call where the function to be applied is not fixed at "compile-time", but is determined by some run-time computation.

Now, as previously indicated, the procedures of PROLOG compute not only functions, but also more general relations. The PROLOG analogue of the function is therefore the predicate. So, to provide analogous higher-order facilities in PROLOG, one might wish to allow predicates to be treated as data objects, and in particular to allow the predicate symbol in a procedure call to be a variable.

For example, suppose one wanted to check whether all the elements of a list satisfied some property (i.e. unary predicate). A general procedure to do this would then be:

have_property([], P).
have_property([X|L], P) :- P(X), have_property(L, P).

These clauses can read as:

"All elements of the empty list have property P".
"All elements of the list comprising head X tail L have property P
if property P holds for X and all elements of L have property P".

The procedure call:

?- have_property([edinburgh, paris, san_francisco], attractive).

would then succeed, provided the following facts are provable:

attractive(edinburgh). attractive(paris). attractive(san_francisco).

Most functional languages also provide the ability to refer to functional objects "anonymously", through the means of lambda expressions. An analogous extension to PROLOG would allow the use of lamda expressions to denote predicates, where the body of the lambda expression would be a PROLOG goal (or goals). An example would be the call:

?- have_property([0, 1], lambda(X). square(X, X)).

meaning:

"Do 0 and 1 have the property of being equal to their squares?"
which should succeed, of course.

Do these two extensions — predicate variables and lambda expressions —

444

really increase the power of PROLOG? I shall argue that they do not, since both can be regarded merely as "syntactic sugar" for standard first-order logic. The mapping into first-order logic is very simple. A procedure call with a variable as predicate:

$P(t_1, \ldots, t_n)$

is transformed into the procedure call:

$\text{apply}(P, t_1, \ldots, t_n)$

and in addition a clause:

$\text{apply}(foo, X_1, \ldots, X_n) :- foo(X_1, \ldots, X_n).$

is supplied for each predicate *foo* which needs to be treated as a data object (where *n* is the arity of *foo*).[†] A lambda expression:

$\text{lambda}(X1, \ldots, Xn).E$

is replaced by some unique identifier, say *phi*, which is defined by a separate 'apply' clause:-

$\text{apply}(phi, X_1, \ldots, X_n) :- E.$

Effectively, we are just giving the anonymous predicate a name. Thus the second example rewrites to, say:

?- have_property([0,1], is_its_own_square).

with

$\text{apply}(\text{is\_its\_own\_square}, X) :- \text{square}(X, X).$

where the clauses for 'have_property' are now:

have_property([], P).
have_property([X|L], P) :- apply(P, X), have_property(L, P).

Note that it is possible for a lambda expression to contain free variables. In this case, the identifier which replaces the lambda expression must be parameterised by the free variables. An example of this situation, which also illustrates the versatility of the PROLOG variable, is the following clause:

common(R, L, Y) :- have_property(L, lambda(X).R(X,Y)).

to be interpreted as:

"Attribute R has a common value Y for the elements of the list L if all elements of L have the property of being paired with Y in relation R".

This clause might be invoked by the goal:

?- common(pastime, [tom, dick, harry], P).

† Note that we have a different 'apply' predicate for each different value of *n*; we could have given these predicate distinct names if preferred, (say 'apply1', 'apply2', etc.).

to produce alternative solutions of, say:

   P = football
   P = darts

given that it is possible to prove facts like:

   pastime(tom, football).

Here the lambda expression:

   lambda(X).R(X,Y)

has free variables 'R' and 'Y', so if we identify it by, say, 'foo(R,Y)', the clause for 'common' rewrites to:

   common(R, L, Y) :- have_property(L, foo(R, Y)).

with:

   apply(foo(R,Y), X :- apply(R, X, Y).
   apply(pastime, X, Y) :- pastime(X, Y).

Observe that PROLOG produces the solutions by first generating a pastime P of 'tom', and then checking that P is also a pastime of 'dick' and 'harry'. Thus the free variables of a lambda expression need not all be known initially. In this respect, we seem to have something essentially more powerful than what is available in functional languages.

Notice also that this treatment of the non-local variables in a lambda expression corresponds exactly to "static binding" as in ALGOL or SCHEME (Steele 1978) in contrast to the "dynamic binding" of LISP and POP-2. Dynamic binding has the curious property that the name chosen for a variable is semantically significant. This would clearly be incongruous in the PROLOG context, and can be viewed as a flaw in the original definition of LISP which has led to the variant, SCHEME.

As a final, more sophisticated, example of treating predicates as data objects, let us look briefly at the PROLOG equivalent of the definition of the 'twice' function (see for example, Turner 1979). In a functional language this is defined as:

   twice = lambda(F).(lambda(X).F(F(X)))

Thus 'twice' maps a function F into another function which is the composition of F with itself. If we also have:

   succ = lambda(X).X+1

then:

   twice(twice)(twice)(succ)(0)

is a valid expression, which in fact evaluates to 16. (Check this for yourself!) Using the rewrite rules outlined above in conjunction with the standard technique for translating functional notation into predicate notation, this problem translates into PROLOG as:

?- apply(twice, twice, F1), apply(F1, twice, F2),

apply(F2, succ, F3), apply(F3, 0, Ans).

where

apply(twice, F, twice(F)).
apply(twice(F), X, Z) :- apply(F, X, Y), apply(F, Y, Z).
apply(succ, X, Y) :- Y is X+1.

(where 'is' is a PROLOG built-in predicate that evaluates arithmetic expressions). Executing this question with PROLOG does indeed produce the right result:

Ans = 16

and the values of the other variables help to show how this result is obtained:

F1 = twice(twice),
F2 = twice(twice(twice)),
F3 = twice(twice(twice(twice(succ))))

Discussion

To summarise the argument so far: functional languages such as LISP and POP-2 allow functions to be treated as "first class" data objects, and this property is often claimed to give these languages an added power lacking in PROLOG. I have therefore put forward two extensions to PROLOG — predicate variables and lambda expressions — providing what I believe is the exactly analogous property for PROLOG, that of making predicates into "first class" data objects. This belief is backed up by the examples given. I have then shown how these extensions can be regarded as mere syntactic sugar, by presenting a very simple way of translating them back into standard first-order logic.

The translation is such that it does not involve any *unbounded* increase in either the size of the program or in the number of execution steps. I therefore claim that the extensions do not add anything to the strict power of PROLOG; i.e., they do not make it feasible to program anything that was not feasible before (in contrast to other possible extensions — see later, for example).

Of course "power" is often used more loosely to cover such language properties as conciseness, clarity, or implementation efficiency (measured in bytes and milliseconds). So let us consider, on such wider grounds, two possible arguments for nevertheless incorporating these extensions into PROLOG.

1. The extensions should be provided as primitive in the language so that they can be implemented efficiently.
2. The extended syntax is much nicer to read and to use and should be provided as standard.

We will discuss these points one by one.

447

Efficiency

The standard way of implementing functional objects involves a representation known as a *closure*. Essentially, a closure is a pair of pointers, one pointing to the code for the function concerned, the other pointing to an *environment* containing the values of the function's non-local variables. The advantage of this representation is that it avoids having to make a copy of the function's code for each different binding of the non-local variables.

Now PROLOG implementations commonly use an implementation technique known as *structure-sharing*, whereby any non-atomic data object has a representation very similar to a closure. This representation, called a *molecule*, likewise consists of two pointers, one pointing to (a representation of) the original source term, the other pointing to an environment containing the values of the variables occurring in that source term.

The result of structure-sharing, combined with our technique for translating higher-order expressions into first-order logic, is that higher-order objects automatically get something very close to their standard, closure representation. In particular, we do not need to do any copying of code or variable values in order to create the higher-order object. The only significant difference is that, instead of a direct pointer to the code of the higher-order object, we have an identifier which is mapped into the corresponding code via the appropriate 'apply' clause.

This difference is minimal if the clauses for 'apply' are appropriately indexed on the procedure's first argument, as is provided automatically in DEC-10 PROLOG, for instance. It is then possible to get from the identifier of the higher-order object to its code in a small, fixed number of steps — effectively, the identifier is an indirect pointer.

So, for DEC-10 PROLOG at least, providing a specific implementation of higher-order objects would not produce huge efficiency gains over the approach I am advocating, and for most programs the overall improvement would probably be negligible.

Note that it appears to be possible to apply a directly analogous technique to functional languages to "pre-process away" higher-order expressions. Structures would be constructed to represent the higher-order objects, and an arbitrarily big 'apply' function would be needed to invoke the corresponding code. However the result is not nearly so practical as in the PROLOG case, since, apart from being much less readable, it involves explicitly copying non-local variables and (in the absence of the equivalent of a case expression) executing an arbitrarily large number of tests in the 'apply' function. Moreover, while it is quite natural to add new 'apply' clauses one by one as the need arises, it is much less convenient to have to make modifications to the body of an 'apply' function.

Readability and usability

The extended syntax is obviously more concise, but whether this makes programs easier to understand is highly debatable. It seems to be a matter of taste which syntax one prefers.

448

Most PROLOG users would argue that one of PROLOG's main strengths is that it avoids deeply nested expressions. Instead the program is broken down into smaller, more easily comprehended units. The resulting program may be slightly longer, but it is easier to read and (what is especially important) easier to modify.

Now the effect of introducing lambda expressions is directly contrary to this philosophy. It results in bigger, more deeply-nested expressions. I am therefore certainly against this part of the extension.

The introduction of predicate variables, however, seems to have a certain elegance. For example, I would probably prefer to write the 'twice' example as:

```
?- twice(twice,F1), F1(twice,F2), F2(succ,F3), F3(0,Ans).
twice (F, twice(F)).
twice(F,X,Z) :- F(X,Y), F(Y,Z).
succ(X,Y) :- Y is X+1.
```

I understand recent PROLOG implementation (see Colmerauer, Kanoui and van Caneghem 1979) allows this kind of syntax.

However, if predicate variables are used in more than small doses, the program becomes excessively abstract and therefore hard to understand. For example, it is possible to define a higher-order procedure 'iterate':

```
iterate([],F,Z,Z).
iterate([X|L],F,Z,Y) :- iterate(L,F,Z,Y0), F(X,Y0,Y)
```

such that list concatenation, and the summation of the elements of a list, are special cases:

```
concatenate(L1,L2,L3) :- iterate(L1,cons,L2,L3).
sum(L,N) :- iterate(L,add,0,N).
```

But this seems a particularly perverse way to define such simple predicates.

On balance, therefore, I do not think the benefits of predicate variables are worth the extra language complexity involved.

3. SET EXPRESSIONS

A difficulty which programmers new to PROLOG soon come up against is that they need to combine information generated on alternative branches of the program. However, with pure PROLOG, all information about a certain branch of the computation is lost on backtracking to an earlier point. To take a very simple example, suppose we have the following facts about the 'drinks' predicate (written in infix notation):

david drinks beer.
david drinks milk.
jane drinks water.
ben drinks milk.

then it is very easy to represent the question:

"Who drinks milk?"

One simply writes:

?- X drinks milk.

and PROLOG's backtracking generates the two solutions:

X = david ;
X = ben

But how should one represent the question:

"How many people drink milk?"

It seems we already have all the information needed to compute the solution, which should obviously be "2". Somehow we need to combine the solutions generated by backtracking into a single data structure so that they can be counted by a straightforward (recursive) procedure. The problem is how to remember one solution when we backtrack to get another.

At this point, the logician might point out a flaw in the programmer's reasoning. We have no right to assume the answer to the question is "2", since, in the absence of any information about who does not drink milk, it is quite possible that there are other facts we don't know. Maybe, say:

jane drinks milk.

Therefore, from a logical point a view, the question of how many people drink milk can't be answered with the information available.

The programmer, however, is unlikely to be satisfied with this argument, and may explain that what he really meant was:

"How many people are known to drink milk?"

which is surely a reasonable query having "2" as its unequivocal answer.

Ways to get the desired result in this and similar cases are part of the PROLOG folklore. They involve going outside the pure PROLOG described here, in order to preserve information on backtracking. This is done using certain extra facilities provided by Prolog implementations as "built-in procedures". Typically these procedures modify the program by adding and deleting clauses. The trouble with these *ad hoc* solutions is that they generally only provide a partially correct implementation of what is intended, and what is intended is often far from clear. Above all, the parts of the program affected can no longer be interpreted simply as a shorthand for statements of fact in natural language, in the way we have seen so far.

I believe it is possible to replace these *ad hoc* solutions with a single more principled extension to PROLOG, which preserves the "declarative" aspect of the language. This extension has already been incorporated in the latest version of DEC-10 PROLOG. The implementation is essentially an encapsulation of the standard hack in a more general and robust form.

450

The extension takes the form of a new built-in predicate:

setof(X,P,S)

to be read as:

"The set of instances of X such that P is provable is S".

The term P represents a goal or goals, specified exactly as in the right-hand side of a clause. The term X is a variable occurring in P, or more generally any term containing such variables. The set S is represented as a list whose elements are sorted into a standard order, without any duplicates.

Our previously problematic query:

"How many people (are known to) drink milk?"

can now be expressed as:

?- setof(X, X drinks milk, S), size(S, N).

which can be interpreted more literally as:

"Is it true of any S and N that
the set of those that drink milk is S and the size of the set S is N?"

to which the Prolog response is:

S = [ben, david], N = 2

This assumes a definition of 'size'. This predicate simply computes the length of a list, and is easily defined:

size([], 0).
size([X|L], N1) :- size(L, N), N1 is N+1.

The 'setof' primitive has certain inevitable practical limitations. The set to be enumerated must be finite, and furthermore it must be enumerable by PROLOG in finite time. If there are any infinite branches in a search space, execution of the 'setof' expression will simply not terminate.

Note that since PROLOG always generates most general instances, it is possible to generate set elements containing variables. Our implementation of 'setof' does not prohibit this. However in such cases the list S will only provide an imperfect representation of what is in reality an infinite set. Effectively, the list contains only a single, arbitrary representative of the infinitely many different ways of instantiating each solution containing variables.

The 'setof' primitive must be defined and implemented with particular care if it is to behave correctly in any context. For example, suppose we wish to define a general predicate 'drunk by(D,N)' meaning "D is drunk by a total of N individuals". Then a suitable definition easily follows from our previous example:

drunk_by(D,N) :- set of(X, X drinks D, S), size(S, N).

A question such as:

?- drunk_by(milk, N).

451

will then produce, without difficulty, the solution:

N = 2

But what happens if we ask the question:

?- drunk_by(D,1).

meaning:

"What is drunk by just 1 individual?"

Obviously the correct result should be to produce the two alternative solutions:

D = beer ;
D = water

However this entails that our 'setof' primitive should be "backtrackable", generating alternative sets if the set expression contains any uninstantiated free variables. In the example just given, 'D' was such a variable.

Our implementation of 'setof' fully takes care of such cases. Notice that this also makes it quite all right for set expressions to be nested. For example, one possible way to express the query:

"Which people drink each beverage?"

is:

?- setof(Beverage-People, setof(X, X drinks Beverage, People), S).

Here we have a case where the first argument of a 'setof' is a structure rather than a single variable; ('-' is an infix functor). The response to this question will be:

S = [beer-[david], milk-[ben, david], water-[jane]]

To allow 'setof' to be backtrackable, we have to slightly restrict its meaning. All our sets are implicitly non-empty. Otherwise there would be indefinitely many alternative ways of instantiating the free variables of a set expression to produce the empty set as solution. For example, if empty sets were allowed, the question:

?- setof(X, X drinks D, S).

should presumably have solutions like:

D = treacle, S = [] ;
D = kerosene, S = [] ;

and so on ad infinitum. In general, 'S' is empty where 'D' is anything that is not known to be drunk by somebody.

The problem here is equivalent to that of producing a correct implementation of negation (regarded as non-provability), for which there doesn't yet appear to be a fully satisfactory solution.

Although the restriction to non-empty sets can reasonably be seen as a shortcoming, it does often automatically capture what is required. For example, try formulating the question:

"Which employee's children are all at university?"

Obviously we don't really want to count as a solution an employee who doesn't have any children.

4. CONCLUSION

We have looked at two possible "higher-order" extensions to PROLOG. We have seen that the first extension, which permits predicates to be treated as 'first class' data objects, does not really contribute to the power of the language, although some would argue that it is useful syntactic sugar. In contrast, the addition of set expressions to PROLOG seems to fill a long felt need, and many problems cannot be expressed in pure PROLOG without such an extension. We have seen that it is important for set expressions to be "backtrackable", so that they can be used freely in any context.

Acknowledgements

The 'setof' primitive described here was particularly influenced by the work of A. Colmerauer 1977 and V. Dahl 1977 on natural language analysis. Helpful comments on the paper were made by S. Jones and F. Pereira. The support of the British Science Research Council is gratefully acknowledged.

REFERENCES

Bergman, M. & Kanoui, H. (1975). SYCOPHANTE: Système de calcul formel et d'interrogation symbolique sur l'ordinateur. Marseille: Groupe d'Intelligence Artificielle, U.E.R. de Luminy, Université d'Aix-Marseille II.

Bundy, A., Byrd, L., Luger, G., Mellish, C. & Palmer, M. (1979). Solving mechanics problems using meta-level inference. *Expert Systems in the Micro-Electronic Age*, pp. 50–64 (ed. Michie, D.). Edinburgh: Edinburgh University Press.

Colmerauer, A., Kanoui, H. & van Caneghem, M. (1979). Etude et realisation d'un système PROLOG. Marseille: Groupe d'Intelligence Artificielle, U.E.R. de Luminy, Université d'Aix-Marseille II.

Colmerauer, A. (1977). Un sous-ensemble intéressant du francais. *R.A.I.R.O*, **13**, 4, pp. 309–336. (Presented under the title of "An interesting natural language subset" at the Workshop on Logic and Databases, Toulouse 1977).

Dahl, V. (1977). Un système deductif d'interrogation de banques de données en Espagnol. Marseille: Groupe d'Intelligence Artificielle, U.E.R. de Luminy, Université d'Aix-Marseille II.

Darvas, F., Futo, I. & Szeredi, P. (1977). Logic-based program system for predicting drug interaction. *Int. J. Biomed. Comp.*

Dwiggins, D. L. & Silva, G. (1979). A Knowledge-based automated message understanding methodology for an advanced indications system. *Technical Report No. R79-006* Woodland Hills, Ca: Operating Systems Inc.

Markusz, Z. (1977). How to design variants of flats using programming language PROLOG based on mathematical logic. *Information Processing* 77, pp. 885–889 (ed. Gilchrist, B.). Amsterdam, New York, Oxford: North Holland Publishing Co.

Pereira, L. M., Pereira, F. & Warren, D. H. D. (1978). User's guide to DEC system-10 PROLOG. *D.A.I. Research Paper No. 154.* Edinburgh: Department of Artificial Intelligence, University of Edinburgh.

Robinson, J. A. (1965). A machine-oriented logic based on the resolution principle. *J. Ass. Compt. Mach.*, **12**, 227–234.

Roussel, P. (1975). PROLOG: manuel de référence et d'utilisation. Marseille: Groupe d'Intelligence Artificielle, U.E.R. de Luminy, Université d'Aix-Marseille II.

Steele, G. L. (1978). RABBIT: a compiler for SCHEME. M.Sc. Thesis: also published as *AI-TR-474*. Cambridge, Mass: Artificial Intelligence Group, Massachusetts Institute of Technology.

Turner, D. A. (1979). A new implementation technique for applicative languages. *Software Practice and Experience*, 9, 31–49.

Warren, D. H. D. (1976). Generating conditional plans and programs. Preprint: AISB Summer Conference, Edinburgh.

Warren, D. H. D. (1980). Logic programming and compiler writing. *Software Practice and Experience*, 10, 97–125.

Warren, D. H. D. (1979). PROLOG on the DECsystem-10. *Expert Systems in the Micro-Electronic Age*, pp. 112–121 (ed. Michie, D.). Edinburgh: Edinburgh University Press.

Warren, D. H. D., Pereira, L. M. & Pereira, F. (1977). PROLOG – the language and its implementation compared with LISP. Symposium on AI and Programming languages, ACM SIGPLAN 12.

23

PROLOG: a language for implementing expert systems

K. L. Clark and F. G. McCabe
Department of Computing
Imperial College, London

Abstract

We briefly describe the logic programming language PROLOG concentrating on those aspects of the language that make it suitable for implementing expert systems. We show how features of expert systems such as:

(1) inference generated requests for data,
(2) probabilistic reasoning,
(3) explanation of behaviour

can be easily programmed in PROLOG. We illustrate each of these features by showing how a fault finder expert could be programmed in PROLOG.

1.0 AN INTRODUCTION TO PROLOG

1.1 A Brief History

PROLOG is a programming language based on Kowalski's procedural interpretation of Horn clause predicate logic (Kowalski 1974, 1979). The language was developed and first implemented by Alain Colmerauer's research group in Marseilles (Colmerauer *et al.* 1973, Roussel 1975). There are now many implementations of the language, of which the most well known is the Edinburgh DEC-10 compiler/interpreter (Pereira *et al.* 1979). There are also machine coded interpreters for the IBM 370 (Roberts 1977), for the PDP-11 under UNIX (Mellish & Cross 1979), for any Z80 micro running CP/M (McCabe 1980) and for the Apple micro-computer (Kanoui and van Canaghem). Most of the interpreters give execution times of the same order as interpreted LISP, and DEC-10 compiled PROLOG compares favourably with DEC-10 compiled LISP (see Warren *et al.* 1977 for details). So we are talking about a programming language on a par with LISP with respect to efficiency. At the same time PROLOG provides much of the inference machinery that the expert system implementer has to program up in LISP.

In Marseilles and Edinburgh PROLOG is the main AI programming language. In Marseilles its major use has been for natural language understanding (Colmerauer 1978), but there was an early application to symbolic integration (Bergman & Kanoui 1973). In Edinburgh it has been used for plan formation (Warren 1974, 1976), problem solving (Bundy *et al.* 1979) and natural language understanding (Pereira 1980). It is also a handy language for compiler writing (Warren 1977). The DEC-10 PROLOG compiler is written in PROLOG.

In Hungary, where there are several implementations of PROLOG (see Santane-Toth & Szeredi 1980), the language is widely used for implementing expert systems. There are several concerning pharmacology: prediction of biological activity of peptides (Darvas *et al.* 1979), drug design aids (Darvas 1978), prediction of drug interactions (Futo *et al.* 1978). It is also been used in architecture to aid the design of complexes of apartments from modular units (Markusz 1977) and for many other applications (see Santane-Toth & Szeredi 1980). Outside Hungary its use to develop expert systems has been slow to start. At Imperial College it has been used to build a small fault finder system (Hammond 1980). The authors intend to explore more fully the use of the Z80 implementation for building desk-top expert systems. We also hope that this paper acts as a stimulus for others to use PROLOG to implement expert systems.

1.2 PROLOG Program = A Set of Rules + A Data Base

A PROLOG program comprises a sequence of clauses. The clauses are implications of the form

$$R(t1, .., tn) \text{ if } A1\& ... \&Ak, k \geqslant 0.$$

Each Ai, like the $R(t1, .., tn)$, is a relation name R followed by a list of argument terms $t1, .., tn$. A term is a constant, a variable, or a function name f followed by a list of argument terms, $f(t1, .., tn)$.

The variable-free terms are the data structures of a logic program. Constants are like LISP atoms. A LISP list is a term such as $cons(A, cons(B, Nil))$, which can be written as $A.B.C.$ Nil in infix notation, or as $[A\ B\ C]$ in some PROLOGs. Different PROLOGs use different conventions to distinguish constants and variables. We shall use the convention that constants begin with an upper case letter (or are quoted), and that variables begin with a lower case letter.

Declarative reading

For the most part the clauses can be read as universally quantified implications, the quantification applying to all the variables of the clause. For example,

$$\text{fault}(x, \text{in}(u, y)) \text{ if part}(y, x) \& \text{fault}(y, u)$$

can be read as,

for all x, y, u
u in y is a fault with x if y is part of x and u is a fault with y.

456

Syntactic sugar

Several of the PROLOGs allow the programmer to declare that certain predicate and function names will be written as operators with a particular precedence. By making "in", "is-fault-with" and "is-part-of" operators we can write the above clause as

u in y is-fault-with x **if** y is-part-of x & u is-fault-with y.

This ability to extend the syntax with operators, or more generally to write a front-end program in PROLOG that accepts clauses written in any notation, makes it very easy to develop a user interface congenial to a specific use of PROLOG. A dramatic example of this is Colmerauer's use of the language for natural language understanding. The PROLOG program for parsing some subset of natural language is written as a set of productions of his metamorphosis grammars.

Assertions and rules

The clauses with an empty antecedent, which are written without the **if**, are *assertions*. The set of all variable free assertions in a program can be thought of as the database of the program. The other clauses are the *rules* that will be used to interrogate and/or modify the data base.

Queries

A query is a conjunction of atoms $B1 \& \ldots \& Bn$. It invokes a backward chaining use of the rules to interrogate the data base. The interrogation is successfully completed when a substitution s has been found such that $[B1 \& \ldots \& Bn]s$ 'follows from' the rules and the assertions. We have quoted 'follows from' since the substitution instance is not a logical consequence of the clauses viewed as assertions and implications when the data base of assertions has been modified during the interrogation. In expert systems applications we certainly want to be able to modify the data base, to accept new facts supplied by a user. If we are careful in the way we use the data base modifying facilities we can ensure that the $B1 \& \ldots \& Bn$ substitution instance is a logical consequence of the final state of the data base and the 'pure' rules of the program, the rules that do not modify the data base.

As an example of a query evaluation let us suppose that the above rule about "is-fault-with" can access the assertions:

Engine is-part-of Car
Carburettor is-part-of Engine
Dirt is-fault-with Carburettor

The query

y is-fault-with Car

457

can be answered by a backward chaining deduction that binds y to (Dirt in Carburettor in Engine). Notice how the nested 'in's' give us the path to the fault.

Meta variable feature

Just as LISP can evaluate a function named by a list structure, so a PROLOG clause can use as a precondition an atom named by a term. This is usually referred to as the meta-variable feature since any clause that uses it can be thought of as an axiom schema. It means that we can write clauses of the form

$$R(\ldots, c) \text{ if } \ldots \& c \& \ldots$$

in which a precondition is named by an argument term. We can think of the clause as an abbreviation for

$$R(\ldots, P(x1, \ldots, xk)) \text{ if } \ldots \& P(x1, \ldots, xk) \& \ldots$$
$$R(\ldots, Q(y1, \ldots, yn)) \text{ if } \ldots \& Q(y1, \ldots, yn) \& \ldots$$
$$\vdots$$

in which there is a specific clause for each relation name used in the program. The "$P(x1, \ldots, xk)$" appearing as a term is the name of the "$P(x1, \ldots, xk)$" appearing as a precondition. This axiom schema explanation of the meta-variable feature is due to Phillippe Roussel.

1.3 Procedural Semantics

An evaluation of the query $B1 \& \ldots \& Bn$ is broken down into the evaluation of the query $B1$, to find a substitution instance $[B1]s1$, followed by an evaluation of the query $[B2 \& \ldots \& Bn]s1$. The $s1$ is a set of bindings for the variables of $B1$ which is passed on to the remaining conditions.

The *atomic query* $B1$ will be of the form $R(t1, \ldots, tn)$ for some predicate name R. It is answered by trying each of the clauses of the form

$$R(t'1, \ldots, t'n) \text{ if } A1 \& \ldots \& Ak,$$

until one is found that applies to find an instance of the query. It applies if there are substitutions s and s' for the variables of $R(t1, \ldots, tn)$ and $R(t'1, \ldots, t'n)$, respectively, that will make them syntactically identical. Technically, the two formulae *unify*. All the PROLOGs use a simplified form of Robinson's unification algorithm (see Robinson 1979) to test for unifiability. The algorithm returns a pair of substitutions s and s' when the test succeeds. These are most general substitutions in the sense that any other pair of unifying substitutions are essentially specialisations of s and s'. It is in this rule application by unification that much of the power of PROLOG resides.

If $k = 0$, i.e. the program clause is an assertion, the evaluation of $B1$ is completed with s as the answer substitution. Otherwise the evaluation of $B1$ reduces to the evaluation of the new query $[A1 \& \ldots \& Ak]s'$. The answer for $B1$ is then s modified by the answer substitution s'' for this new query.

An example evaluation

The atomic query

z is-fault-with Car

can be solved using the program clause

u in *y* is-fault-with *x* **if** *y* is-part-of *x* & *u* is-fault-with *y*.

Under the substitutions

$s = \{z/u \text{ in } y\}$
$s' = \{x/\text{Car}\}$
z is-fault-with Car, *u* in *y* is-fault-with *x*

become identical. The evaluation of the query reduces to the evaluation of the derived query

y is-part-of Car & *u* is-fault-with *y*.

With the assertions given above this will be solved with the answer

$s'' = \{y/\text{Carburettor in Engine}, u/\text{Dirt}\}$

The answer to the original query is

z/*u* in *y* where *y*/Carburettor in Engine and *u*/Dirt,

i.e. it is *z*/Dirt in Carburettor in Engine. For more information on the procedural semantics we refer the reader to Kowalski (1979).

Backtracking

The above recursively described evaluation process always takes the first program clause for which a matching substitution can be found. There may be other program clauses which could also be used. These will be tried should a subsequent evaluation step *fail*.

A failure occurs when none of the program clauses will unify with the atomic query currently being attempted. When this happens the evaluation *backtracks* to the most recent previous evaluation step for which there are untried program clauses.

Controlling the search

The program clauses for a relation are always tried in the order in which they appear in the sequence of clauses. PROLOG programmers often exploit this order of use to give ordinary rules for a relation first, followed by a default rule that should only be used if the ordinary rules have failed. There is a backtracking control device, the "/", which can be used to prevent a later rule being used if an earlier rule has been successfully applied.

For example, suppose that the rule

B **if** *A*1 & .. & *Ai*/*Ai*+1 & .. & *An*

459

has been invoked to find an answer to an atomic query B'. If the preconditions $A1, .., Ai$ that appear before the "/" can be solved then no later clause will be used to try to solve B'. The "/" expresses the control information that the successful evaluation of $A1$ to Ai indicates that the later rules that might be used to solve B' will either fail or give the same answer. It also prevents backtracking on the proof of $A1 \& .. \& Ai$.

2.0 FEATURES USEFUL FOR EXPERT SYSTEMS

Inputs and updates

During a query evaluation data can be input from a user, and assertions and rules can be added to the program, using special primitive relations. The evaluation of **read**(x) will cause x to be bound to the next term typed at the input terminal. The evaluation of **assert**(x) will cause the term which is the current binding of x to be added as a new rule. Thus, the rule

> Ask-about(c) **if** print$(c,$ "?") & **read** (ans)
> & ans = Yes & **assert** (c),

used to try to answer the query,

> Ask-about(Dirt is-fault-with Carburettor),

will print the message

> Dirt is-fault-with Carburettor?,

read the next term, and if it is the constant Yes it will add

> Dirt is-fault-with Carburettor

as a new assertion about the is-fault-with relation. Where this assertion is added is important. It can be added at the beginning of the list of clauses for the relation, or the end, or at some intermediate position. In this situation we would like it added at the beginning. Where it is added is an option that can be specified by the programmer. We shall not go into the details of this.

Dynamic data base

The rule

> u in y is-fault-with x **if** y is-part-of x & u is-fault-with y

must access assertions giving components and assertions about faults with components. We can use the Ask-about rule to allow the assertions about faults to be added dynamically as we try to solve the problem of finding a fault.

Instead of assertions about known faults with components we include in the initial data base only assertions about possible faults, knowledge that expert should have. We then include the rule

> u is-a-fault-with y **if** u is-a-poss-fault-with y & Ask-about$(u$ is-a-fault-with $y)$

Let us pause for a moment to consider the behaviour of our fault finder. When asked to find a fault with some device with a query

u is-fault-with Device

the use of the first rule for faults will cause the fault finder to walk over the structure of Device as described by the is-part-of assertions. When it reaches an atomic part it will query the user concerning possible faults with this component as listed in the is-poss- fault-with assertions. It will continue in this way, backtracking up and down the structure, until a fault is reported. As it currently stands, our expert sytem helps the user to look for faults.

Generation of lemmas

Sometimes it is useful to record the successful evaluation of an atomic query B by adding its derived substitution instance as a new assertion. Thus, suppose we have a rule

$R(t1, .., tn)$ if $A1 \& .. \& Ak$

and we want to generate a lemma each time it is successfully used to answer a query $R(t'1, .., t'n)$. We add an extra assert condition at the end of the list of preconditions of the rule.

$R(t1, .., tn)$ if $A1 \& .. \& Ak \& \text{assert}(R(t1, .., tn))$

If this solves the atomic query with answer substitution s then $[R(t'1, .., t'n)]s$ will be added as new assertion. It will be added at the front of the sequence of clauses for R.

By adding asserts we can also simulate the use of rules with conjunctive consequences. Suppose that we know that both B and B' are implied by the conjunction $A1 \& .. \& An$. Normally we would just include the two rules:

B if $A1 \& .. \& An$
B' if $A1 \& .. \& An$

in the program. The drawback is that we need to solve $A1 \& .. \& An$ twice in derivations where both B and B' are needed. We can avoid the duplication by writing the two rules as:

B if $A1 \& .. \& An \& \text{assert}(B')$
B' if $A1 \& .. \& An \& \text{assert}(B)$

The successful use of either rule will add the other consequent as a lemma.

By developing a suitable front end to PROLOG we can shield the programmer from the details of the lemma generation. We could allow him to write rules with conjunctive consequents and to specify which rules were lemma generation rules. The front end program would expand rules with conjunctive consequents into several rules and add the appropriate asserts to the end of each of these rules. It would also add an assert to the end of each of the lemma rules.

461

All solutions

Sometimes we want to find all the answers to a query, not just one answer. This is an option in some of the PROLOGs. Where it is not we can make use of a meta-rule such as

All(query, term) **if** query & print(term) & fail.

This will print out [term]s for each answer substitution *s* to query. The "fail" is a condition for which we assume there are no clauses. With a slightly modified rule, we can define the relation

l is-all term such-that query

that holds when *l* is the list of all the instantiations of "term" for answer substitutions to "query". In DEC-10 PROLOG such a relation is now a primitive of the language. Using it we can write rules such as

l is-a-list-of-faults-with *x* **if** *l* is-all *u* such-that
                                            u is-fault-with *x*

The use of this rule will result in *l* being bound to a list of all the faults with *x*.

We can now consider a very simple extension to our fault finder. Instead of asking for a single fault we can ask for a list of all the reported faults with corrective actions. We do this with a query of the form

l is-all [*u a*] such-that
           u is-fault-with *D* & *a* is-action-for *u*.

To handle this query we must also include in our database a set of assertions giving actions for faults, information supplied by the expert. An evaluation of this new query will guide the user through the structure of device *D*, asking about faults in components. Each reported fault will be paired with its corrective action. Finally the list of pairs [reported-fault corrective-action] will be printed.

3.0 INEXACT REASONING

MYCIN(Shortliffe 1976) and PROSPECTOR (Duda *et al.* 1979) use inexact or probabalistic reasoning. Probabilities are associated with assertions and rules. Conclusions are derived with associated probabilities. To implement this in PROLOG we augment all those relations about which we want to make probabilistic assertions with an extra argument. Instead of $R(x,y)$ we use $R(x,y,p)$. We read this as

$R(x,y)$ with certainty p.

We now add to the rules that refer to these relations extra conditions to deal with the transfer of certainties from the preconditions to the conclusion.

Let us elaborate our fault finder program to deal with uncertainties. To

462

make it more of an expert we should have rules for detecting faults by their symptoms. We should also allow that symptoms only partly correlate with faults. This means that the is-fault-with relation should have an extra argument to carry a certainty measure. We shall not go into details of what this is. Whatever measure is used must be handled by the probability transfer relations. The definition of these can implement whatever probability theory we choose.

Instead of the rule that queries the user about possible faults we can now have the rule

u is-fault-with x certainty p **if**
  s is-symptom-for-fault u of x strength q
    & s certainty r
      & q and r give p.

This rule accesses assertions such as

Stalling is-symptom-for-fault Dirt of Carburettor strength .3.

The strength measure is the degree to which the symptom correlates with the fault. We also need assertions about the certainty of the symptoms, or more usefully, a rule such as

u certainty r **if** print("Give the certainty of", u)
    & **read**(r) & **assert**$(u$ certainty $r)$

The rules for "q and r give p" implement our probability theory.

When invoked by a query to find all the faults with some device our new probabilistic rule will query the user about the likely occurrence of each symptom that correlates with a fault in the device. It will use the user supplied certainty that the symptom is present, and the degree to which it correlates with the fault, to give a certainty for the associated fault.

From single symptoms to sets of syndromes

To compute a certainty for a fault on the basis of a single symptom is a little too simple. More realistically a fault will be signalled by one or other of several clusters of symptoms, that is, by one or other of several syndromes. A better version of our probabilistic is-fault-with rule is

u is-fault-with x certainty p **if**
      l is-all $[s\,q]$ such-that
            s is-syndrome-for u of x strength q
      & l gives p.

The rules for "l gives p" must recurse down the list of syndrome-correlation pairs. In doing this it must compute the certainty of each syndrome using the certainties of the individual symptoms supplied by the user. It then computes a certainty for the fault using the certainties and strengths of all the syndromes.

463

A syndrome can be quite complex. The syndrome

symptom $S1$ and either symptom $S2$ or symptom $S3$ in the absence of symptom $S4$

can be denoted by the term

$S1$ & ($S2$ or $S3$) & not $S4$

where "&", "or" & "not" are operators. To handle syndromes denoted by such terms the rules for computing the certainties of syndromes would look like:

certainty-of-syndrome u is p **if** symptom(u) & u certainty p

certainty-of-syndrome$(u$ & $v)$ is p **if**
$\qquad$ certainty-of-syndrome u is q
$\qquad$ & certainty-of-syndrome v is r
$\qquad$ & anding $[q\,r]$ gives p

The first rule deals with the case of a syndrome which is a symptom. The second deals with the case of one that is a conjunction of syndromes. The rules for

anding $[q\,r]$ gives p

compute the certainty of a conjunction of two syndromes given their individual certainties. How this is done is determined by the choice of probability theory. If we want to take into account such subtleties as dependencies between symptoms we would add an extra precondition

dependency-of u and v is d

to the rule and include d as an argument to the "anding" condition. We now also include in the data base assertions and rules about the interdependence of symptoms and syndromes.

We would have analogous rules for the case of a "u or v" syndrome and the case of a "not u" syndrome.

Symptom nets

The set of alternative syndromes for a fault F in a component C will be described by a set of assertions of the form

($S1$ & ($S2$ or $S3$) & not $S4$) is-syndrome-for F of C strength Q.

The set of all the assertions about a fault F are a description of a symptom net for F as depicted in Fig. 1.

This is just a shallow inference net. The movement of probabilities along the arcs of this is a special case of what PROSPECTOR does.

464

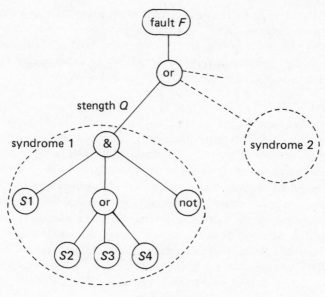

Fig. 1.

A prototype general fault finder

Let us conclude this section of probabilistic inference by examining the state of our PROLOG fault finder. The three rules:

u in *y* is-fault-with *x* certainty *p* if *y* is-part-of *x*
                        & *u* is-fault-with *y* certainty *p*

u is-fault-with *x* certainty *p* if
        l is-all [*s q*] such-that
              s is-syndrome-for *u* of *x* strength *q*
              & *l* gives *p*

help(*s*, *l*) if *l* is-all [*u a p*] such-that
               u is-fault-with *s* certainty *p*
                & *a* is-action-for *u*,

together with the rules that implement the probability theory, form the nucleus of a general fault finder. To use this fault finder program we

(1) add a set of "is-part-of" assertions giving the structure of a new device about which we want help in finding faults,
(2) add a set of assertions giving the correlation of syndromes with faults in atomic components,
(3) add a set of assertions giving the appropriate action for each fault.

The sets of assertions (1), (2) and (3) are what the expert provides. It is the way that he 'programs' the fault finder.

465

A user of the fault finder asks for help in mending some substructure S of the device with the query help(S,l). He waits to be asked about the certainty of occurrence of various symptoms. He will have printed out a list of possible faults together with the corrective action. Each fault will be described by a path name to its position in S. It will be listed with a likelihood of its presence.

4.0 EXPLAINING

One of the most important abilities of an expert system is to be able to explain itself to a user in intelligible terms. If an expert system produces a fault diagnosis of a car, or an analysis of a chemical compound, the user needs to be convinced that the result is reasonable; that it has not been pulled out of the hat. So an expert system should be able to give an account of how it reaches its conclusions.

Moreover, no expert system produces its answers without some data, which is usually supplied by the user when prompted by the system. It is reasonable for the user to be able to ask why the data is being requested.

There are, then, two kinds of explaining for an expert system, the "HOW" and the "WHY". Let us look at one way in which a set of PROLOG clauses can be modified to cope with these two kinds of explaining.

WHY explanations

Consider again the non-probabilistic version of the PROLOG fault finder. Let us suppose that we want to allow the user to ask why he is being asked if there is some particular fault with a component. To be able to respond to such a "WHY" request the ask-about rule must have access to the context in which it is invoked. One way in which we can do this is to pass a description of the context as an extra argument to each rule that might ultimately lead to the use of the Ask-about rule. For example, instead of the rule

> u is-fault-with x **if** u is-poss-fault-with x &
> ask-about$(u$ is-fault-with $x)$

which we shall call rule 2, we could use

> u is-problem-with x trace t
> **if** u is-poss-fault-with x &
> Ask-about$(u$ is-fault-with $x,$
> 2: [u is-poss-fault-with x] . t).

The 2: [u is-poss-fault-with x] added to the front of the current trace t tells us that rule 2 has been invoked and that its precondition (u is-poss-fault-with x) is satisfied. Similarly, we could modify rule

> u in y is-fault-with x **if** y is-part-of x & u is-fault-with y,

called rule 1, to the rule

> u in y is-fault-with x trace t
> **if** u is-part-of x &
> u is-fault-with x trace 1: [u is-part-of x] . t

466

This adds the fact that rule 1 is being used to the front of the trace and records the single precondition of the rule that is currently satisfied.

The Ask-about rules now need modification to:

Ask-about(c, t) **if** print$(c, $ "?"$)$ & **read**(ans) & respond(ans, c, t)
respond(Yes, c, t) **if** assert(c)
respond$(Why, c, u. t)$ **if** give-reason(u) & Ask-about(c, t)
respond(Why, c, Nil) **if** print("you should know")
                      & Ask-about(c, Nil).

The new Ask-about will pick off an explanation u from the trace list for each "Why" repsonse and display it. The rules for give-reason might access a set of assertions of the form

description$(n, $ "some text describing rule n")

in order to give a meaningful description of the rule mentioned in u. Each repeated "Why" leads to a more distant reason for the question being printed out by the give-reason rules. Finally, when the trace is empty, we are back at the top-level query. A "Why" at this point gets the response "you should know" followed by a new prompt.

As an example of the use of these new rules, let us suppose that in solving the query

    u is-fault-with Car trace Nil

rule 1 has been used twice because of the assertions

    Engine is-part-of Car
    Carburettor is-part-of Engine,

and then rule 2 has been used. It has accessed the assertion

    Blocked-valve is-poss-fault-with Carburettor

and is now querying the user about this fault. The trace argument passed to Ask-about is

    2 : [Blocked-valve is-poss-fault-with Carburettor].
        1 : [Carburettor is-part-of Engine].
            1 : [Engine is-part-of Car].Nil

Rule transformation

As with lemma generation the modification of the clauses to cater for "Why" explanations can be performed by a front end program. The input to this program would be numbered rules without the trace argument. Along with this program would be a set of directives which specified which rules should be traced and which relations are such that their proofs might lead to the use of "Ask-about". We are assuming that "Ask-about" is being used as though it were a primitive predicate. The programmer would also include a set of assertions describing the explainable rules. The front end program rewrites the designated rules to include the trace argument.

The rewrite is quite straightforward. Suppose we have a rule of the form

Rule k: $R(t1, .., tn)$ if $A1 \& .. \& Ai \& P(t'1, .., t'm) \& ..$

that must be traced. Let us also suppose that P is a relation the proof of which can lead to the use of the Ask-about rules. We must transform the rule into

Rule k:
$R(t1, .. tn, t)$ if $A1 \& .. \& Ai \& P(t'1, .., t'm, k: [A1, .., Ai].t) \& ..$

The rule passes down to the rules for P the current trace extended by a message to the effect that rule k has been used. The list of terms $[A1, .., Ai]$ that is also passed down will be the preconditions $A1, .., Ai$ instantiated by any substitution generated by the proof of this conjunction of conditions. It tells us exactly what the state of play is in the application of this rule.

How explanations

We can use the same extra argument trick to save proofs. We can also *hide it* from the expert system programmer. He simply states that certain relations should be proof traced, these being the relations that he wants mentioned in the "How" explanations. The front end program then transforms the clauses for these relations as follows.

An assertion

$P(t1, .., tn)$

becomes

$P(t1, .., tn, P(t1, .., tn))$

The extra argument is the trace of the proof of the instance of P found using the assertion. It will be a copy of the proven instance.

A rule of the form

$P(t1, .., tn)$ if $.. \& Q(..) \& ... \& R(..) \& ..,$

in which Q and R are the only proof trace relations in the antecedent, is transformed into

$P(t1, .., tn, \text{proof}1 \& \text{proof}2 \text{ implies } P(t1, .., tn))$ if
$\qquad .. \& Q(.., \text{proof}1) \& ... \& R(.., \text{proof}2) \& ..$

This constructs a description of the proof of the instance of P that it generates in terms of the descriptions of the proof trace relations that it accesses. If this rule is also declared a lemma generating rule we can transform it into

$P(t1, .., tn, P(t1, .., tn))$ if
$\qquad .. \& Q(.., \text{proof}1) \& .... \& R(.., \text{proof}2) \& ..$
$\qquad \& \text{assert}(\text{proof}1 \& \text{proof}2 \text{ implies } P(t1, .., tn))$
$\qquad\qquad \& \text{assert}(P(t1, .., tn))$

468

This asserts the explanation as well as the lemma. The proof trace returned is a reference to this lemma.

The following rule now defines a relation that the user can invoke to seek an explanation of some asserted lemma $P(t1, .. tn)$ with a query Explain$(P(t1, .., tn))$.

Explain(lemma) if proof implies lemma & display(proof)

This retrieves the term that describes the proof of the lemma from the "implies" assertion for the lemma and then displays it in a suitable format. The explanation will be a proof structure down to other asserted lemmas. If the user wants to see more he asks for an explanation of these other lemmas.

5.0 CONCLUSIONS

We hope that we have convinced the potential expert system implementer that he should look at PROLOG more closely. We do not claim that the techniques for programming expert systems that we have sketched are the best. They represent just one possibility. A fully fledged implementation of our fault finder would undoubtedly reveal shortcomings. Nonetheless we are convinced that PROLOG offers a programming medium in which these could be easily overcome. We invite the reader to do his own experimenting with PROLOG.

6.0 ACKNOWLEDGEMENTS

The main ideas in this paper evolved through discussions with P. Hammond. Our fault finder example was inspired by his PROLOG fault finder, although he tackles the problem in a slightly different way.

The paper was written whilst Keith Clark was visiting Syracuse University. Comments on the ideas by K. Bowen, J. A. Robinson and E. Sibert were much appreciated.

We would also like to thank Diane Zimmerman. She patiently typed the paper into a text formatter using an often overloaded computer system.

7.0 REFERENCES

Bergman, M., Kanoui, H. (1973), Application of mechanical theorem proving to symbolic calculus, *3rd Int. Symp. on Adv. Methods in Physics*, C.N.R.S., Marseilles.

Bundy, A., Byrd, L., Luger, G., Mellish, C., Palmer, M., (1979), Solving mechanics problems using meta-level inference, *Expert systems in Micro Electronic Age*, pp. 50–64 (ed. Michie, D.). Edinburgh: Edinburgh University Press.

Colmerauer, A., Kanoui, H., Pasero, R., Roussel, P. (1973), Un systeme de communication homme-machine en francais. Rapport, Groupe d'Intelligence Artificielle, Marseille: Univ. d'Aix, Luminy.

Colmerauer, A. (1978), Metamorphosis Grammars. *Natural language communication with computers*, pp. 133–189 (ed. Bolc, L.) *Lect. Notes in Comp. Sci. No. 63*, Springer Verlag.

Darvas, F., (1978), Computer analysis of the relationship between biological effect and chemical structure. *Kemiai Kozlemenyek*, 50, (Hungarian).

Darvas, F., Lopata, A., Gy. Matrai, (1979), A specific QSAR model for peptides. In *Quantitative Structure Activity Analysis*, (ed. Darvas, F.), Budapest: Akademiai Kiado.

Duda, R., Gashnig, J., Hart, P., (1979), Model design in the prospector consultant system for mineral exploration, *Expert Systems in the Micro Electronic Age*, pp. 153–167 (ed. Michie, D.). Edinburgh: Edinburgh University Press.

Futo, I., Darvas, F., Szeredi, P., (1978), Application of PROLOG to development of QA and DBM systems, *Logic and Data Bases*, (ed. Gallaire, H. and Minker, J.). Plenum Press.

Hammond, P. (1980), Logic programming for expert systems, MSc Thesis, London: Imperial College, University of London.

Kanoui, van Caneghem. (1980), Implementing a very high level language on a very low cost machine, Rapport, Marseille: Group d'Intelligence Artificielle, University d'Aix-Marseille, Luminy.

Kowalski, R. (1974), Predicate logic as programming language, *Proceedings IFIP 74.*

Kowalski, R. (1979), *Logic for problem solving,* Amsterdam and New York: North Holland.

McCabe, F. G. (1980). Micro-PROLOG programmers reference manual, 36 Gorst Rd., London: LPA Ltd.

Markusz, Z. (1977), How to design variants of flats using programming language PROLOG, based on mathematical logic, *Proc. Information Processing 77*, pp. 885–889 (ed. Gucheist, B.) Amsterdam, New York, Oxford: North Holland.

Pereira, L., Pereira, F., Warren, D., (1978), User's guide to DEC-system 10 PROLOG, Edinburgh: Dept. of A.I., Edinburgh University.

Pereira, F. (1980), Extraposition grammars, *Proceedings of Logic Programming Workshop*, (Budapest).

Roberts, G. M. (1977). An implementation of PROLOG, M.Sc. Thesis, Waterloo: Dept. of Computer Science, University of Waterloo, Canada.

Robinson, J. (1979), *Logic: Form and Function*, Edinburgh: Edinburgh University Press.

Roussel, P. (1975), PROLOG, Manuel de Reference et d'Utilisation, Marseille: Groupe d'Intelligence Artificielle, U.E.R. de Luminy, University d'Aix.

Shortliffe, E. H. (1976). *Computer Based Medical Consultations: MYCIN*, Americal Elsevier, New York.

Santane-Toth, E., Szeredi, P., (1981), PROLOG applications in Hungary, In *Logic Programming* (eds. Clark, K. L. and McCabe, F. G.), London: Academic Press.

Warren, D., Pereira, L., Pereira, F. (1977), PROLOG – the language and its implementation compared with LISP, *Proc. Symp. on AI and Prog. languages*, *SIGPLAN notices*, **12**, No. 18.

Warren, D. (1974), WARPLAN: A system for generating plans, Memo, Dept. of A.I., Edin. Univ.

Warren, D. (1976), Generating conditional plans and programs, *Proc. AISB Summer Conference*, (Edinburgh).

Warren, D. (1977), Logic programming and compiler writing, Report, Edinburgh: A.I. Dept., Edinburgh University.

470

Appendix to PROLOG: a language for implementing expert systems

P. Hammond

Department of Computing
Imperial College, London

INTRODUCTION

An expert system, which is domain-independent, has been implemented in Micro-PROLOG* with many of the features described above. It interacts with a knowledge-base and a set of rules for handling uncertianty to become a domain expert. The facilities that have been built into the system include the following:

(i) the handling of degrees of belief in evidence and their subsequent effect on related deductions;

(ii) the explanations of *why* a particular question is being asked and *how* a deduction has been made;

(iii) the use of key symptoms to direct the problem-solving activity to a narrower solution set;

(iv) the ability for the user to query the knowledge-base as a database, e.g., to see the rules;

(v) the inclusion of symptoms that have values e.g., age and temperature;

(vi) the use of external files to store relations to avoid loading the entire knowledge base into machine memory.

CHANGES IN THE DATA REPRESENTATION AND METHODOLOGY

The system has been used with knowledge-bases on car fault-finding, skin disease diagnosis, ant identification, personal investment analysis and pipe corrosion diagnosis.

To accommodate such a wide range of use, which goes beyond simple fault-finding in a structured object, the knowledge representation framework was generalised so that each application is just a special case of a more general scheme. For example, the "part of" structure of the fault finder has now become a partition of the solution space into a collection of nested subsets rather like the taxonomical divisions used in botany and zoology. In fact, the ants data-base

471

is a good example of this subclassification process. The following diagram illustrates the divisions of a collection of British ants into sub-family, genus and species:

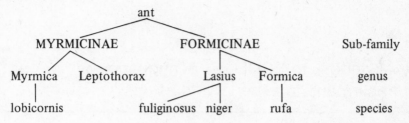

Now, instead of having one complex syndrome for indentifying "fuliginosus" such as

Deduction	Syndrome
fuliginosus in ants	number of waist segments is 1 &
	leg-length is short &
	colour is black &
	head-shape is heart-like.

we can define a hierarchy of rules corresponding to the partition above:

Deduction	Sydrome
MYRMICINAE in ants	number of waist segments is 2
FORMICINAE in ants	number of waist segments is 1
Lasius in FORMICINAE	leg-length is short
Formica in FORMICINAE	leg-length is long
fuliginosus in Lasius	colour is black &
	head-shape is heart-like
niger in Lasius	colour is black &
	head-shape is normal

Thus the rules for differentiating within Lasius are only tested if we have established the syndrome in the rule for identifying Lasius in FORMICINAE.

To illustrate how this division applies to the familiar fault finder consider the following:

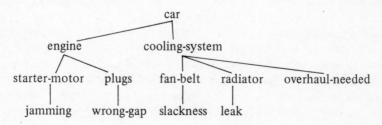

This tree reflects a fault classification scheme where faults are associated with each group of components. Rather than simply reflecting the construction of the car it describes how faults are associated with assemblies and sub-assemblies of components. For example, "cooling-system" now stands for the class of cooling-system faults.

INEXACT REASONING

We have developed two modules for handling inexact reasoning. One uses MYCIN-like and the other PROSPECTOR-like (or BAYESIAN-like) uncertainty. The designer of the knowledge-base can decide which method to use, without affecting the kernal of the expert system or the form of the data-base. Of course each scheme has its own requirements; the MYCIN method has a single number for each rule that describes a syndrome-deduction correlation whereas the PROSPECTOR method involves two such numbers. The possibility also exists for the expert to define his own method of handling uncertainty.

The pipe corrosion data-base uses the BAYESIAN-like uncertainty and each of the other data-bases uses MYCIN-like uncertainty. Some effort is being made by the authors to find a satisfactory way of handling dependency between symptoms.

KEY-SYMPTOMS

An expert frequently makes use of key symptoms to focus attention on a sub-class of problems. To aid this important process the PROLOG classifier allows the knowledge-base constructor to declare certain key symptoms that can be used to concentrate on a particular subclass in the "sub-class" hierarchy. For example, we could declare "number-of-waist-segments", "colour" etc. as key symptoms and define the following:

number-of-waist-segments is 1	suggests-check	class MYRMICINAE
colour in-list (black yellow)	suggests-check	class Lasius
high-petrol-consumption	suggests-check	class carburettor
high-petrol-consumption	suggests-check	identification
		leak in fuel-system
engine-fails-to-start	suggests-check	class battery

These key symptoms will be requested at the beginning of a consultation. Those that are reported cause the classifier to check the suggested areas.

SYSTEM ARCHITECTURE

The figure above gives a simple-minded view of the structure of the classifier with particular reference to the flow of information between the user, the core program and the knowledge-base. Once the user has indicated which knowledge-base is to be consulted, the core program is able to infer from the rule structure (see under INEXACT REASONING above) which method of handling uncertainty is appropriate.

LOGIC PROGRAMMING

This diagram is also useful in explaining how the system reacts to special responses from the user. For example, we have already indicated that the response "why" causes the system to re-trace the history of the consultation to explain its current line of reasoning. This is handled within the core program by the assertion

needs-response (why)

and a set of general rules for the re-tracing. If a user wishes to alter the form of the explanantion to make it more domain-specific, he need only re-define the general rules to his own liking and include them in the knowledge-base. Similarly, other responses to handle special queries to the knowledge-base can be defined by assertions of the form

needs-response (deductions) , needs-response (help)

along with rules which print the deductions that can be made or which explain the help facilities which are available.

SYMPTOMS THAT HAVE VALUES

Already from the examples above we have illustrated a fair degree of freedom in symptom description. Currently the system can recognise symptoms which are of the following types:

(i) mnemonic-like strings such as engine-wont-start;
(ii) ⟨name⟩ ⟨relation⟩ ⟨value⟩
where ⟨relation⟩ is a pre-defined binary relation between possible values of ⟨name⟩ and ⟨value⟩; for example

age	in-range	(20 to 40)
colour	in-list	(red yellow)
height	LESS	40
size	is	10

EXTERNALLY DEFINED RELATIONS

The system has so far been used on Z80 based microcomputers with small internal memory (56 to 64 k). As knowledge-bases have grown it has become necessary to store parts of the data in backing store on disc. The system can then access this information as the need arises. Another use of this facility would be to access data-bases related to the knowledge area.

FUTURE DEVELOPMENTS

The work with experts in skin problem diagnosis and pipe corrosion is continuing and it is hoped that these databases will become more realistic as more detailed knowledge is added. Other collaboration with industry is being set up and plans have already been made to implement the classifier on more powerful computers, such as the PERQ, and to experiment with the uses of computer graphics.

The construction of knowledge bases which can interface with the PROLOG classifier was part of a recent MSc thesis by M. Y. Chin (1981) at Imperial College. This project also illustrated how the classifier could be used for structured questionnaires.

The use of quasi-natural language for expert systems has been investigated by another recent M.Sc. student at Imperial College (Steele 1981). The knowledge representation and problem-solving strategy used in this project illustrate alternatives to that used in our general purpose classifier.

REFERENCES

M. Y. Chin (1981), Computer Interrogation Systems: CISP, M.Sc. thesis, London: Department of Computing, Imperial College.

F. G. McCabe (1981), Micro-PROLOG Progammer's Reference Manual, L.P.A. Ltd., 36 Gorst Road, London SW11.

B. D. Steele (1981), EXPERT — The implementation of data-independent expert systems with quasi-natural language information input, M.Sc. thesis, London: Department of Computing, Imperial College.

24

Chess end-game advice: a case study in computer utilisation of knowledge

M. H. van Emden

Department of Computer Science
University of Waterloo, Canada

1. INTRODUCTION

The intended contribution of this paper is the development of tools, in the form of a computer language, for the automatic utilization of knowledge. The field of study, having as objective to make such a utilization possible, is called 'knowledge engineering'. One proposed application is the development of a new breed of textbooks: such a textbook would have the form of an interactively usable computer program and database. The source code would be readable as a textbook, although more systematic, explicit, and precise than the ones we are used to. In interactive use the computerized textbook would solve problems in the application domain of the embedded knowledge. In this mode the user can be ignorant of everything except perhaps the broad outlines of the textbook's contents.

The program for the rook end game in chess, which is the centrepiece of this paper, is usable in the same way: for a human familiar with the rudiments of logic programming, a part of the source code is useful for learning the endgame for himself; but also, a computer equipped with a logic interpreter is able to use this knowledge itself to play the endgame agianst an independent opponent.

According to Michie's strategy for research in knowledge engineering, chess is used as a test domain. Why chess? In the first place, a great deal of knowledge about chess has been recorded in the literature and is being used: advanced chess players study a lot. Also, among computer applications, chess has a relatively long history with several interesting reversals in the attitude of its practitioners. In the late fifties, when the programming work required to carry out the main outlines of Shannon's original proposal first became feasible (Shannon 1950), the workers involved were very optimistic about the prospect of programs surpassing the best human performance. In the late sixties, when a considerable effort using greatly improved processing power and programming tools had failed to yield anything even remotely approaching human top perfor-

477

mance, the earlier optimism had changed to pessimism. In the late seventies, after another decade of steady improvement, a change to guarded optimism could be observed.

Roughly speaking, chess performance draws upon two distinct resources: 'look-ahead', that is, exploration of the game tree, and 'knowledge' (including, or assisted by, 'intuition', 'experience', etc.). Human players rely almost exclusively on knowledge; this is probably necessary, given the peculiar limitations of their information processor. Computer players rely almost exclusively on look-ahead; this is probably not necessary, but caused by the primitive state of development of knowledge engineering.

Michie has proposed to express knowledge about chess endgames as 'advice'. This representation of knowledge is readable and useful to prospective human chess players and can also drive a computer equipped with an advice language interpreter to play in an expert fashion the endgames covered by the advice. Michie and his coworkers have formulated advice for several endgames (Bratko 1978, Bratko, Kopec & Michie 1978, and Michie 1977). At least one interpreter has been implemented.

The purpose of the work reported in this paper is to investigate whether logic as a programming language (Kowalski 1974) can take the place of the advice language proposed by Michie and perhaps, more generally, for expressing knowledge for purposes of knowledge engineering. The strategy followed in this paper is to introduce basic notations of game playing and logic programming by means of the game of Nim. These introductory sections conclude with a logic program for Nim. Subsequently the basic notions are refined and extended to be applicable to subgames of the rook endgame of chess.

We assume the reader to be familiar with the main outlines of the clausal form of logic and the notion of a logic program. A thorough treatment of logic programming is Kowalski's *Logic for Problem-Solving* (1979) for which neither logic nor programming is a prerequisite.

2. THE GAME OF NIM

A position of the game of Nim can be visualized as a set of heaps of matches. Two players, called US and THEM, alternate making a move. As soon as a player whose turn it is to move, is unable to make a move, the game is over and that player has lost; the other player is said to have won. A move consists of taking at least one match from exactly one heap.

A two-person game such as Nim can analysed by means of a game tree. The nodes of a game tree are positions of the game, together with an indication which player is to move. In the game tree a node x is a descendant of node y if and only if y can be reached in one move from position x. The game tree shown below contains all positions reachable from the position where there are three heaps of matches, one with two matches and two with one match, and where US is to move.

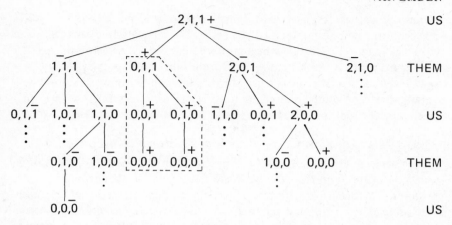

Fig. 2.1 – Minimaxed game tree for a Nim position. The outlined subtree is the 'forcing tree', (*see* p. 482).

The nodes are also marked with their value, which is a + or a −, as determined by 'minimaxing', a process which may be described as follows. A node $0,0,0$ has value '+' when THEM is to move, then US has won. Similarly, a node $0,0,0$ has value '−' when US is to move. The values of the other nodes are determined as a consequence of the assumption that, when there is a choice of move, both US and THEM will make the choice so as to be least favourable to the other player. That is, a node where THEM (US) is to move has as value the minimum (maximum) value of a descendant node, where '+' is regarded to be greater than '−'.

These rules make it possible to determine the value of the root node of the tree by starting at the terminal nodes and working upwards, and this determines the 'value of the game', that is, it determines whether or not US can win, starting at the root node. The rules apply to arbitrary game trees and apply also if there are more values than just two, such as in chess. It follows that it is in principle possible to determine the value of the initial position of chess. Certainly the size of the game makes it impossible for the value to be determined by mini-maxing the entire game tree.

We now state a dual pair of useful properties of game values. The properties can be regarded as a result of rephrasing our previous description of the mini-maxing process.

Property 1: US can win starting in a position x with US to move, (i.e., the value of x is '+'), if there exists a move transforming x to y such that it is not the case that US cannot win starting in y (i.e. the value of y is '+').

Property 2: US cannot win starting in position x, with THEM to move (i.e. the value of x is '−'), if there exists a move transforming x to y such that it is not the case that US can win starting in y (i.e. the value of y is '−').

479

In these properties, 'US can win' means that there is a choice of moves by US which makes it impossible for THEM to win. 'US cannot win' means that there is a choice of moves by THEM which makes it impossible for US to win.

These properties have been selected from other possible ones because it is easy to see that they are true and because they are simply expressed in logic with a result that can be used as a computer program for computing the value of a game (provided that the game tree is small).

3. THE STAGES AND MOVES OF NIM EXPRESSED IN LOGIC

In logic, objects are represented by terms. A term is either a constant, or an expression of the form $f(t_1, \ldots, t_k)$ where f is a function symbol and $t_1, \ldots, t_k$ are terms. This recursive definition allows the existence of terms of arbitrarily great complexity to be built up from few and simple constants and function symbols. As our first example we represent as terms the heaps of matches which occur in Nim positions.

An empty heap is represented by the constant 0. If a heap is represented by a term t, then the heap with one match more is represented by successor(t). Thus, for example, a heap with two matches is represented by the term successor (successor(0)). For actual use we prefer a shorter function symbol and we have chosen '+' instead of successor (no connection with a game value denoted by the same symbol), so that we get $+(+(0))$ for the heap of two. Using postfix instead of prefix notation allows us to write $t+$ for the heap with one more than the heap represented by t. So we write $0++$ for the heap of two.

A position is not in general a single heap, but a set of heaps, which we will regard for convenience as a sequence. The empty sequence is represented by the constant *nil*. The sequence resulting from concatenating a heap x onto a sequence y is represented by $conc(x,y)$. For example, the initial position (2,1) of the game tree shown earlier is represented by

$$conc(0++, conc(0+, nil)).$$

Again we replace the function symbol *conc* by something more compact; in this case a single dot. This gives

$$\cdot(0++, \cdot(0+, nil)).$$

Using infix notation instead of prefix notation further compacts this to $0++ \cdot (0+ \cdot nil)$ with the understanding that plus has higher precedence than dot.

We now have the notational apparatus for positions. To be able to express properties of moves we need atomic formulas and clauses. For example the atomic formula $Append(x,y,z)$ expresses the relation between sequences x,y, and z where z is the result of appending y to x. In general an atomic formula has the form $P(t_1, \ldots, t_n)$ where P is a predicate symbol and $t_1, \ldots, t_n$ are terms. A useful property of the *Move* relation is expressed by the clause

$$Move(x,y) \leftarrow Append(u, v_1 \cdot w, x) \,\&\, Takesome(v_1, v_2) \,\&\, Append(u, v_2 \cdot w, y).$$

480

Here x, y, u, and w are positions, i.e. sequences of heaps; v_1 and v_2 are heaps. The clause should be read as:

"For all x and y,
"y is the result of a move from x if there exist u, v_1, v_2, and w
"such that x is the result of appending $v_1 \cdot w$ to u and v_2
"is a result taking some (matches) from v_1 and y is
"the result of appending $v_2 \cdot w$ to u.

To say that, for given x, there exist u, v, and w such that $append(u, v \cdot w, x)$, can be interpreted as saying that v is an abitrary heap occurring in sequence x. If we accept this way of saying 'occurs in', then we see that the above clause says:

"For all x and y,
"y is the result of a move from x if y differs from x only in
"a heap v_2 which is the result of taking some matches from
"the corresponding heap v_1 in x.

We shall use the following properties of the append relation.

$append(nil, y, y)$

This says that for all y, y is the result of appending y to the empty list.

$append(u \cdot x, y, u \cdot z) \leftarrow append(x, y, z)$

This says that, for all u, x, y, and $z, u \cdot z$ is the result of appending y to $u \cdot x$ if z is the result of appending y to x.

The 'take some' relation has the following useful properties:

$Takesome(x+, x)$

This says that some have been taken from a heap if the result is one less.

$Takesome(x+, y) \leftarrow Takesome(x, y)$

This says that some have been taken from a heap if the result is the result of taking some from a heap containing one less. That is, to take some, take one, and then some.

Logic programming consists of collecting a set of clauses, each expressing a useful property of the relation to be computed (such as *Move*) and of relations auxiliary thereto (such as *Append* and *Takesome*). The following is a PROLOG program for computing moves.

```
OP(+,SUFFIX,101).

APPEND(NIL,*Y,*Y).
APPEND(*U.*X,*Y,*U.*Z) <- APPEND(*X,*Y,*Z).

MOVE(*X,*Y) <- APPEND(*U,*X1.*V,*X) & TAKESOME(*X1,*X2)
               & APPEND(*U,*X2.*V,*Y).

TAKESOME(*X+,*X).
TAKESOME(*X+,*Y) <- TAKESOME(*X,*Y).
```

Fig. 3.1 – Listing of PROLOG program for Nim moves.

In Fig. 3.1 we see a declaration for the postfix operator '+' with precedence 101. (The operator '·' is built in, with precedence 100). Variables are distinguished from constants (such as *nil*) by identifiers beginning with an asterisk.

4. THE VALUE OF A GAME EXPRESSED IN LOGIC

We obtain a logic program for playing a game by expressing in logic the Properties 1 and 2 of section 2. Initially we do not stay within the clausal form of logic.

A straightforward expression of Properties 1 and 2 is:

$$\forall x. \, Uscanwin(ustomove, x) \leftarrow$$
$$\exists y. Move(x,y) \, \& \, \neg \, Uscannotwin(themtomove, y).$$

$$\forall x. \, Uscannotwin(themtomove, x) \leftarrow$$
$$\exists y. Move(x,y) \, \& \, \neg \, Uscanwin(ustomove, y).$$

Apparently, we only need *Uscanwin* with *ustomove* as first argument. This first argument is therefore superfluous: we use a one-argument predicate S instead. A similar consideration causes us to replace *Uscannotwin* by a one-argument predicate T.

The resulting formulas are:

$$\forall x. \, S(x) \leftarrow \exists y. Move(x,y) \, \& \, \neg T(y) \, .$$
$$\forall x. \, T(x) \leftarrow \exists y. Move(x,y) \, \& \, \neg S(y) \, . \tag{4.1}$$

$S(x)$ means: for a suitable choice of moves, US will win starting in position x with US to move, whatever the choice of moves by THEM.

$T(x)$ means: for no choice of moves, US can win starting in position x with THEM to move, against a choice of moves by THEM which is least favourable to US.

However, S does not tell us *how* we can win: it could at least incorporate the position resulting from the first suitable move. Hence we prefer

$$\forall x,y. \, S(x,y) \leftarrow Move(x,y) \, \& \, \neg \, \exists z. T(y,z)$$
$$\forall x,y. \, T(x,y) \leftarrow Move(x,y) \, \& \, \neg \, \exists z. S(y,z) \, . \tag{4.2}$$

$S(x,y)$ means: $S(x)$, and, moreover, a first suitable choice is from x to y.

$T(x,y)$ means: $T(x)$, and, moreover, a first choice least favourable to US is from x to y.

However, in order to determine that US can win, more information must have been obtained than just the first move, unless it immediately ended the game. In general, for each of the countermoves by them, US must have determined a suitable reponse. All information required by US to win the game against any defence by THEM is contained in a subtree of the game tree called the *forcing tree*, following Huberman (1968). The subtree outlined in Fig. 2.1 is an example of a forcing tree.

482

To obtain a program that also computes the forcing tree, we first modify (4.1) so as to avoid negations. Let $TT(x)$ mean that THEM must lose against best play by US. Then we have

$$\forall x.\, S(x) \leftarrow \exists y.Move(x,y) \,\&\, TT(y)$$
$$\forall x.\, TT(x) \leftarrow (\forall y.Move(x,y) \rightarrow S(y))$$

Only the first implication is in a form suitable for being handled by current interpreters for logic programs. We reformulate the second implication so as to obtain a conjunction in the condition.

$$\forall x.\, S(x) \leftarrow \exists y.Move(x,y) \,\&\, TT(y)$$
$$\forall x.\, TT(x) \leftarrow \exists z.Moves(x,z) \,\&\, All(z)$$

z is a list containing all moves possible (for THEM) from position x. $All(z)$ means that all positions u in list z have the property that $S(u)$:

$$All(nil)$$
$$\forall u, v.\, All(u \cdot v) \leftarrow S(u) \,\&\, All(v)$$

We now have to decide how to represent a forcing tree as a term. The format for the forcing tree is as follows

$$ourmove \cdot ((theirmove_1 \cdot ft_1) \cdot \ldots \cdot (theirmove_n \cdot ft_n)) \cdot nil$$

where each of $ft_1, \ldots, ft_n$ are themselves forcing trees.

Incorporating the forcing tree into the relations S and TT we get

$$\forall x, z.\, S(x, y \cdot z) \leftarrow \exists y.Move(x,y) \,\&\, TT(y,z)$$
$$\forall y, u.\, TT(y,u) \leftarrow \exists z.Moves(y,z) \,\&\, All(z,u)$$
$$All(nil, nil)$$
$$\forall u, v, w.\, All(u \cdot v, (u \cdot w) \cdot z) \leftarrow S(u, w) \,\&\, All(v, z)$$

Each of the above formulas are clauses and can be handled by PROLOG interpreters. Additional clauses are needed to specify the Move relation, as in Fig. 3.1. A valuable feature of logic programming is that one only has to specify what the admissible moves are; it is not necessary to program a move generator.

In current PROLOG systems there are difficulties in reconciling this attractive way of specifying Move with a specification of the Moves relation, where the second argument is a list of all moves. We can do it in logic, but not in our PROLOG implementation. Therefore we do not compute forcing trees and work from the version (4.2) which only specifies the first move by US.

A complete PROLOG program for Nim using game trees is given in Fig. 4.1. Even for less than a dozen matches the cost of running this program can be prohibitive. This is not caused by excessive slowness of PROLOG: in spite of its elegance the efficiency of this program is within an order of magnitude of what is possible when exhaustively traversing game trees.

It is well-known (*see* Berge, 1962) that, if Nim can be won then it can be won by a simple calculation that can be done in the human head for positions that would defeat the fastest minimaxing programs on the fastest computers: select a move such that the resulting position has the property that the digital sum of the sizes of the heaps is zero.

It seems plausible that such a short computation of the value is only possible for games of great simplicity and that the shortest possible computation for a game like chess is considerably longer, althouth still much shorter than minimaxing. Perhaps for the game of Kalah there exists a computation for the value of the game which is not much longer than computing the digital sum usable in Nim.

```
S(*X,*Y) <- MOVE(*X,*Y) & ~T(*Y,*Z).
T(*X,*Y) <- MOVE(*X,*Y) & ~S(*Y,*Z).

OP(+,SUFFIX,101).

APPEND(NIL,*Y,*Y).
APPEND(*U.*X,*Y,*U.*Z) <- APPEND(*X,*Y,*Z).

MOVE(*X,*Y) <- APPEND(*U,*X1.*V,*X) & TAKESOME(*X1,*X2)
               & APPEND(*U,*X2.*V,*Y).

TAKESOME(*X+,*X).
TAKESOME(*X+,*Y) <- TAKESOME(*X,*Y).
```

Fig. 4.1 – A Nim-playing program in PROLOG.

5. AN OUTLINE OF ADVICE-DRIVEN ENDGAME PROGRAMS IN LOGIC

As we saw, an all-powerful chess-playing program can, in theory, be very simple: one just supplements the logic program for a universal game player, namely,

$$S(x,y) \leftarrow Move(x,y) \,\&\, \neg T(y,z)$$
$$T(x,y) \leftarrow Move(x,y) \,\&\, \neg S(y,z)$$

with a program for *Move* expressing the rules of chess. Such a theory, however, would have to be unaware of complexity issues, because this program would have to explore the entire game tree. For all of chess this tree is so enormous that a computer of a size near the limits imposed by the size of the universe and operating at speeds near the limits imposed by fundamental physical constants, would still require eons to determine the value of the game.

Even in the rook endgame the game tree is too large to make its minimaxing feasible: most initial positions require more than 10 moves by each side, where the number of possibilities for the rook side often exceeds 20 (almost all of these are usually idiotic). Yet one can teach a motivated, averagely gifted child of 9 years old how to play the rook endgame. The explanation of this difference is that humans use 'knowledge', or have acquired certain 'skills' to play a game such as this and rely very little on game trees. If look-ahead is used at all, it is typically based on small, error-ridden fragments of game trees.

Our basic hypothesis is that the utilization of knowledge, or whatever it is that allows humans to play the game, is an information processing task and as

484

such in principle executable by computer. Analogs of the old biological controversy of mechanisms versus vitalism crop up in several other disciplines. In each of these one's position has to be stated anew. The above hypothesis states our position here.

Michie has proposed we express knowledge about how to play a chess endgame in terms of 'advice'. An algorithm in a typical high-level programming language is not a suitable form for expressing such knowledge, being both extremely hard to write and to read. This judgment is based on the one example known to us: the rook endgame program in ALGOL-60 by C. Zuidema (1974). At another extreme we have treatments of endgames in such standard texts as Fine's *Basic Chess Endings* (1974). Although these do contain some pieces of advice, no attempt has been made at completeness or explicitness. Advice in Michie's sense lies between these two extremes: although sufficiently complete and explicit to be followed automatically, it is also learnable by a human for playing the game herself. By 'learnable' we mean that a human can memorize the advice and use it without reference to its text, something which is inconceivable with Zuidema's ALGOL-60 program.

Michie and his co-workers have compiled advice for several chess endgames. We use Bratko's (1978) advice table for the rook endgame. Its English form can be given as follows (we assume that US has white and has the rook):

1. Look for a way to *mate* the black king in two moves, trying checking moves first. The depthbound is 2.
2. If the above is not possible, then *squeeze*, that is, look for a way to decrease the area of the board to which the black king is confined by the white rook, considering rook moves only. The depthbound is 1.
3. If the above is not possible, then *approach*, that is, look for a way to move the white king closer to the black king, preferring diagonal moves so as to help the rook to squeeze in a later move. The depthbound is 1.
4. If the above is not possible, then *keep room*, that is, look for a way of maintaining the present achievements in the sense of 2 and 3. This can always be done with a move by the white king; diagonal moves are to be tried first. The depthbound is 1.
5. If the above is not possible, then *divide*, that is, move the white rook into such a position that it divides the kings either vertically or horizontally. The depthbound is 3.

Each of the rules 1, 2, 3, 4, and 5 advises white to achieve a certain goal in the game. The rules are in order of decreasing ambitiousness. In a typical endgame we have to settle initially for the least ambitious goal, and progress towards more ambitious ones. For this reason the goals are called *better goals*. The rook endgame is subdivided into a sequence of subgames, each defined by a rule of advice, and each with its own criterion of winning, namely one of the better goals. The criterion for losing is not to achieve the *holding goal*. For each of the subgames the holding goal is to avoid losing the rook and to avoid stalemate.

485

Note that this is not a loss according to the rules of chess, but only according to the subgame we define for the purpose of our advice-driven endgame program.

The *depthbound* given with each rule is the greatest depth to which the game tree of the subgame defined by the rule is to be explored.

The rules typically also contain *move contraints*, that is, advice about the type of move to try first, or to try at all. This greatly reduces the number of possibilities to explore, facilitating the task both for a human and a computer. We formalize the existence of move constraints which exclude certain moves, by defining the subgame to have this different set of moves.

Thus each rule of advice determines a different (sub)game. Each subgame has been chosen in such a way that it is computationally feasible to explore its complete game tree, and this is what an advice-driven program for the rook endgame does.

In order to obtain a logic program for subgames we have to generalize the two-line player

$$S(x,y) \leftarrow Move(x,y) \ \& \neg T(y,z)$$
$$T(x,y) \leftarrow Move(x,y) \ \& \neg S(y,z)$$

used up till now. It assumes identical move-sets for both players; to accommodate move constraints we distinguish *S*-moves (by US) and *T*-moves (by THEM). It also assumes that the criterion for winning for one player is that the other is to move but cannot move; to accommodate better goals and holding goals, we introduce explicit criteria for a win by US (*Swon*) and a win by THEM (*Twon*). Hence the following elaboration of the two-line game player.

$$S(x,x) \leftarrow Swon(x)$$
$$S(x,y) \leftarrow Smove(x,y) \ \& \neg T(y,z)$$
$$T(x,x) \leftarrow Twon(x)$$
$$T(x,y) \leftarrow Tmove(x,y) \ \& \neg S(y,z)$$

Several other elaborations are needed. Better goals often depend not on a single position, but on the two last positions. For example, when a better goal is to squeeze, the amounts of room for the black king in the last two positions have to be compared, to see if there was a decrease. Therefore *Swon* has to have two successive positions as argument, as in the next version of the game player:

$$S(x,y) \leftarrow Smove(x,y) \ \& \ S_1(x,y)$$
$$S_1(x,y) \leftarrow Swon(x,y)$$
$$S_1(x,y) \leftarrow \neg T(y,z)$$
$$T(x,y) \leftarrow Tmove(x,y) \ \& \ T_1(x,y)$$
$$T_1(x,y) \leftarrow Twon(x,y)$$
$$T_1(x,y) \leftarrow \neg S(y,z)$$

For the sake of symmetry *Twon* was also given two arguments, although in our program only one is used.

The above game player only plays one of the subgames defined by a rule of advice. In order to avoid writing a different game player for each rule, the predicates are given an extra parameter, taking a rule as value. Another extra parameter is for the depthbound. These refinements are incorporated in the following version of the game player:

$$S(x,y,rule,n) \leftarrow Gt(n,0) \ \& \ Diff(n,1,nl) \ \& $$
$$Moveconstr(rule,mc) \ \& \ Smove(mc,x,y) \ \& $$
$$S_1(x,y,rule,nl)$$
$$S_1(x,y,rule,n) \leftarrow Swon(x,y,rule)$$
$$S_1(x,y,rule,n) \leftarrow \neg \, T(y,z,rule,n)$$

$$T(x,y,rule,n) \leftarrow Tmove(x,y) \ \& \ T_1(x,y,rule,n)$$
$$T_1(x,y,rule,n) \leftarrow Twon(x,y,rule)$$
$$T_1(x,y,rule,n) \leftarrow \neg \, S(y,z,rule,n)$$

The following additional explanations are necessary. Gt and $Diff$ are pre-defined relations: $Gt(x,y)$ holds if x and y are integers and $x > y$; $Diff(x,z)$ holds if x,y, and z are integers and $x - y = z$. $Moveconstr$ will be defined in such a way that $Moveconstr(x,y)$ holds if x is a rule and y is the move-constraint component of x.

We have to formalize also the overall process of trying to find the most ambitious rule of advice that works in a given position. In the overall process US first decides which rule is applicable (i.e., which subgame to play), determines the appropriate move, and waits for a counter move. At this level a one-person game is played, where each move is an exchange of moves at the lower level.

$$Win(pos) \leftarrow Mated(pos)$$
$$Win(pos1) \leftarrow Theirmove(pos1,pos2) \ \& \ Ourmove(pos2,pos3) \ \& \ Win(pos3)$$

This says that there exists a sequence of exhanges leading to a win if THEM is *Mated*, or if an exchange can bring about a position (*pos*3) from which such a sequence can be found.

The following clauses provide the connection with the S defined earlier.

$$Ourmove(pos1,pos2) \leftarrow Advice(rule) \ \& \ Depthbound(rule,n) \ \& $$
$$S(pos1,pos2,rule,n).$$

Advice(mate	:	notrooklost	:	checkfirst	:	2)
Advice(squeeze	:	notrooklost	:	rookmove	:	1)
Advice(approach	:	notrooklost	:	kdmovefirst	:	1)
Advice(keeproom	:	notrooklost	:	kdmovefirst	:	1)
Advice(divide	:	notrooklost	:	anymove	:	3)

The terms in the arguments to Advice are constants; those in the other clauses are variables. In PROLOG source code variables are distinguished from constants by being preceded by an asterisk.

Each argument to Advice encodes a rule; its components are separated by the infix function symbol ":". The components denote successively the better goal, the holding goal, the move constraint, and the depth bound.

Backtracking plays an important role in the execution of a PROLOG program. For example, in the above defintion of *Ourmove*, Advice picks up the first rule listed as such. If S subsequently fails to find a winning (in the subgame sense) move, then the interpreter back-tracks back to Advice, which then invokes its next untried definition.

Sometimes, however, backtracking would be highly undesirable, such as in the two clauses for minmax in Fig. 6.7:

$$minmax(x,y,x,y) \leftarrow lt(x,y) \, \& \, /.$$

$$minmax(x,y,y,x),$$

where $lt(x,y)$ if x is less than y. *Minmax* uses the first two arguments as input and outputs them in the last two arguments in increasing order of magnitude. Suppose this definition is used to solve *minmax* $(3,4,x,y)$, then the first clause applies and x is set to $3, y$ to 4. Some later failure should never cause the system to backtrack and use the second clause. The slash "/" in the first clause inhibits such backtracking.

Figures 6.1 to 6.7 list the source code of the advice-driven PROLOG program for the rook endgame. The top level of the hierarchically structured program has been discussed so far. We hope to have made familiar the part in Figs. 6.1 and 6.2. Figure 6.6 provides a definition of the moves.

6. AN ADVICE TABLE FOR THE ROOK ENDGAME

The figures below shows Michie's format for an advice table for the rook endgame. The table is from Bratko (1978) with some slight modifications. It should be noted that this advice in uncharacteristically simple. Moreover, advice in Michie's sense consists of several cooperating advice tables.

RULE NUMBER	NAME OF BETTER GOAL	MATED	NEWROOMLT	REEXPOSED	OKCSNMDLT	RDIVIDES	RDIVIDES OR LPATT	OKORNDLE	ROOMGT2 OR NOT OKEDGE	NOT ROOKLOST	MOVE CONSTRAINT	DEPTHBOUND
1	MATE	y	–	–	–	–	–	–	–	y	CHECKLIST	2
2	SQUEEZE	–	y.	y	–	y	–	–	–	y	ROOKMOVE	1
3	APPROACH	–	–	y	y	–	y	–	y	y	KDMOVEFIRST	1
4	KEEPROOM	–	–	y	–	y	–	y	y	y	KDMOVEFIRST	1
5	DIVIDE	–	–	y	–	y	–	–	–	y	ANYMOVE	3

better-goal predicates   holding goal

Each better goal is a conjunction of the predicates marked with Y (yes). Figure 6.3 displays the PROLOG clauses for the advice rules and for the definition of the better goals. The rule only contains the name of a better goal, such as 'squeeze'; below it is a clause defining the better goals as conjunctions of predicates. These in turn are defined and explained in Figs. 6.4, 6.5, and 6.7.

The typical format of a term denoting a board position is

theirturn
           :*tk:*ok:*or.
ourturn

The first component indicates who is to move. The remaining components are the position of their king, our king, and the (our) rook, respectively. Each of these positions are given as the file number (i) paired by means of a dot to the rank number (j). With this detail included, the typical format of a position is

theirturn
           :*itk·*jtk:iok·*jok:*ior·*jor
ourturn

The listing uses a tilde instead of the usual negation sign $\neg$. Also, we use $A \leftarrow B \mid C$ (read: A if (B or C)) as a shorthand for the two separate clauses $A \leftarrow B$ and $A \leftarrow C$.

```
/* THE TOP LEVEL: HERE ADVICE IS SELECTED.
   WIN(*X) MEANS THAT WE CAN WIN WITH THEM STARTING IN POSITION X.
*/

WIN(*POS) <- MATED(*POS).
WIN(*POS1) <- THEIRMOVE(*POS1,*POS2) & OURMOVE(*POS2,*POS3) & WIN(*POS3).

OURMOVE(*POS1,*POS2)
        <- ADVICE(*RULE,*POS1) & DEPTHBOUND(*RULE,*N) & WRITE(TRYING:*RULE) &
           S(*POS1,*POS2,*RULE,*N) &
           WRITE('NEW POSITION (TURN:YOUR KING:OUR KING:OUR ROOK) IS:') &
           WRITE(*POS2).

THEIRMOVE(THEIRTURN:*ITK1.*JTK1:*OK:*OR,OURTURN:*ITK2.*JTK2:*OK:*OR)
          <- WRITE('ENTER NEW POSITION AS I.J FOR YOUR KING:') &
             READ(*ITK2.*JTK2) &
             TEST(THEIRTURN:*ITK1.*JTK1:*OK:*OR,OURTURN:*ITK2.*JTK2:*OK:*OR).

TEST(*POS1,*POS2) <- TMOVE(*POS1,*POS2) & /.
TEST(*POS1,*POS2) <- WRITE('NOT A VALID MOVE; TRY AGAIN') & FAIL.
```

Fig. 6.1.

```
/* THIS DEFINES A SUBGAME DETERMINED BY A PREVIOUSLY SELECTED RULE */

S(*POS1,*POS2,*RULE,*N)
  <- GT(*N,0) & DIFF(*N,1,*N1) & MOVECONSTR(*RULE,*MC) &
     SMOVE(*MC,*POS1,*POS2) & S1(*POS1,*POS2,*RULE,*N1).

S1(*POS1,*POS2,*RULE,*N) <- SWON(*POS1,*POS2,*RULE) & /.
S1(*POS1,*POS2,*RULE,*N) <- ~T(*POS2,*,*RULE,*N).

T(*POS1,*POS2,*RULE,*N)
  <- TMOVE(*POS1,*POS2) & T1(*POS1,*POS2,*RULE,*N).
T1(*POS1,*POS2,*RULE,*N) <- TWON(*POS1,*POS2,*RULE) & /.
T1(*POS1,*POS2,*RULE,*N) <- ~S(*POS2,*,*RULE,*N).

SMOVE(*MC,OURTURN:*TK:*OK1:*OR1,THEIRTURN:*TK:*OK2:*OR2)
      <- TRIALMOVE(*MC,OURTURN:*TK:*OK1:*OR1,THEIRTURN:*TK:*OK2:*OR2) &
         ~(*OK2=*OR2) & ~KINGRULE(*TK,*OK2) &
         ~STALEMATE(THEIRTURN:*TK:*OK2:*OR2).

TMOVE(THEIRTURN:*TK1:*OK:*OR,OURTURN:*TK2:*OK:*OR)
      <- KINGRULE(*TK1,*TK2) & ~INCHECK(*:*TK2:*OK:*OR).

SWON(*POS1,*POS2,*RULE) <- BETTERGOAL(*RULE,*B) & TRUE(*B,*POS1,*POS2).
TWON(*POS1,*POS2,*RULE) <- HOLDINGGOAL(*RULE,*H) & ~TRUE(*H,*POS1,*POS2).

TRIALMOVE(CHECKFIRST,*POS1,*POS2)
         <- TRIALMOVE(ROOKMOVE,*POS1,*POS2) & INCHECK(*POS2).
TRIALMOVE(CHECKFIRST,*POS1,*POS2)
         <- TRIALMOVE(ANYMOVE,*POS1,*POS2).
TRIALMOVE(ROOKMOVE,OURTURN:*TK:*OK:*OR1,THEIRTURN:*TK:*OK:*OR2)
         <- ROOKRANGE(OURTURN:*TK:*OK:*OR1,*RANGE) &
            ROOKRULE(*OR1,*OR2,*RANGE) & ~HOPPED(*OK,*OR1,*OR2).
TRIALMOVE(KDMOVEFIRST,OURTURN:*TK:*OK1:*OR,THEIRTURN:*TK:*OK2:*OR)
         <- KINGRULE(*OK1,*OK2).
TRIALMOVE(ANYMOVE,*POS1,*POS2)
         <- TRIALMOVE(ROOKMOVE,*POS1,*POS2).
TRIALMOVE(ANYMOVE,*POS1,*POS2)
         <- TRIALMOVE(KDMOVEFIRST,*POS1,*POS2).

HOPPED(*I.*JK,*I.*JR1,*I.*JR2) <- BETWEEN(*JK,*JR1,*JR2).
HOPPED(*IK.*J,*IR1.*J,*IR2.*J) <- BETWEEN(*IK,*IR1,*IR2).
```

Fig. 6.2.

490

```
        THE ADVICE TABLE; THE FORMAT IS:
             BETTERGOAL:HOLDINGGOAL :MOVECONSTRAINT:DEPTHBOUND                    */

        ADVICE(MATE      :NOTROOKLOST :CHECKFIRST    :    2    ,*POS) <- CLOSE(*POS).
        ADVICE(SQUEEZE   :NOTROOKLOST :ROOKMOVE       :    1    ,*POS).
        ADVICE(APPROACH  :NOTROOKLOST :KDMOVEFIRST   :    1    ,*POS).
        ADVICE(KEEPROOM  :NOTROOKLOST :KDMOVEFIRST   :    1    ,*POS).
        ADVICE(DIVIDE    :NOTROOKLOST :ANYMOVE        :    3    ,*POS).

        /* SELECTORS FOR ADVICE COMPONENTS */

        BETTERGOAL(*X:*:*:*,*X).              HOLDINGGOAL(*:*X:*:*,*X).
        MOVECONSTR(*:*:*X:*,*X).              DEPTHBOUND (*:*:*:*X,*X).

        /* BETTER GOALS */

        MATE(*,*POS) <- MATED(*POS) & WRITE('MATE').

        SQUEEZE(*POS1,*POS2) <- NEWROOMLT(*POS1,*POS2) & ~REXPOSED(*POS2) &
                           RDIVIDES(*POS2) & WRITE('SQUEEZE').

        APPROACH(*POS1,*POS2)
               <- OKCSNMDLT(*POS1,*POS2) & ~REXPOSED(*POS2) &
                  RDIVIDESORLPATT(*POS2) &
                  ROOMGT2ORNOTOKEDGE(*POS2) & WRITE('APPROACH').

        KEEPROOM(*POS1,*POS2)
               <- RDIVIDES(*POS2) & ~REXPOSED(*POS2) &
                  OKORNDLE(*POS1,*POS2) & ROOMGT2ORNOTOKEDGE(*POS2) &
                  WRITE('KEEPROOM').

        DIVIDE(*POS1,*POS2) <- ~REXPOSED(*POS2) & RDIVIDES(*POS2).

        /* HOLDING GOAL */

        NOTROOKLOST(*POS,*) <- ~ROOKLOST(*POS).

        /* ADVICE CONDITIONS */

        CLOSE(*:*TK:*OK:*) <- MDIST(*TK,*OK,*D) & LT(*D,4) & EDGE(*TK).
```

Fig. 6.3.

491

```
/* ADVICE TABLE PREDICATES */

MATED(*POS) <- INCHECK(*POS) & ~TMOVE(*POS,*).

/* NEW ROOM (OF THEIR KING) LESS THAN */
NEWROOMLT(*POS1,*POS2)
        <- ROOM(*POS1,*R1) & ROOM(*POS2,*R2) & LT(*R2,*R1).

/* ROOK EXPOSED: ROOK TOO CLOSE TO THEIR KING */
REXPOSED(THEIRTURN:*TK:*OK:*OR)
        <- DIST(*TK,*OR,*TD) & DIST(*OK,*OR,*OD) & LT(*TD,*OD).
REXPOSED(OURTURN:*TK:*OK:*OR)
        <- DIST(*TK,*OR,*TD) & DIST(*OK,*OR,*OD) &
           DIFF(*OD,1,*OD1) & LT(*TD,*OD1).

/* OUR KING (TO) CRITICAL SQUARE (HAS) NEW MANHATTAN DISTANCE LESS THAN */
OKCSNMDLT(*:*ITK1.*JTK1:*OK1:*IOR.*JOR,*:*:*OK2:*IOR.*JOR)
        <- DIFF(*ITK1,*IOR,*DI) & SIGN(*DI,*SDI) & SUM(*IOR,*SDI,*ICS) &
           DIFF(*JTK1,*JOR,*DJ) & SIGN(*DJ,*SDJ) & SUM(*JOR,*SDJ,*JCS) &
           MDIST(*OK1,*ICS.*JCS,*DIST1) & MDIST(*OK2,*ICS.*JCS,*DIST2) &
           LT(*DIST2,*DIST1).

/* ROOK DIVIDES (THE KINGS) */
RDIVIDES(*:*ITK.*JTK:*IOK.*JOK:*IOR.*JOR)
        <- BETWEEN(*IOR,*ITK,*IOK) | BETWEEN(*JOR,*JTK,*JOK).
           (LT(*JTK,*JOR) & LT(*JOR,*JOK)) | (GT(*JTK,*JOR) & GT(*JOR,*JOK)) .

/* ROOK DIVIDES OR L-PATTERN */
RDIVIDESORLPATT(*POS) <- RDIVIDES(*POS).
RDIVIDESORLPATT(*POS) <- LPATT(*POS).

/* OUR KING (TO) OUR ROOK NEW DISTANCE LESS (OR) EQUAL */
OKORNDLE(*:*TK1:*OK1:*OR1,*:*TK2:*OK2:*OR2)
        <- DIST(*OK1,*OR1,*DIST1) & DIST(*OK2,*OR2,*DIST2) &
           LE(*DIST2,*DIST1).

/* ROOM GREATER THAN 2 OR NOT OUR KING (ON) EDGE */
ROOMGT2ORNOTOKEDGE(*POS) <- ROOMGT2(*POS).
ROOMGT2ORNOTOKEDGE(*POS) <- ~OKEDGE(*POS).

STALEMATE(*POS) <- ~INCHECK(*POS) & ~TMOVE(*POS,*).

ROOKLOST(THEIRTURN:*TK:*OK:*OR) <- KINGRULE(*TK,*OR) & ~KINGRULE(*OK,*OR).
```

Fig. 6.4.

```
/* PREDICATES AUXILIARY TO ADVICE TABLE PREDICATES */

INCHECK(*:*TK:*OK:*OR) <- KINGRULE(*OK,*TK) & /.
INCHECK(*:*TK:*OK:*OR) <- ~(*OR=*TK) & ROOKCHECK(*:*TK:*OK:*OR).

ROOKCHECK(*:*ITK.*JTK:*IOK.*JOK:*ITK.*JOR) <- ~(*IOK=*ITK) & /.
ROOKCHECK(*:*ITK.*JTK:*IOK.*JOK:*ITK.*JOR) <- ~BETWEEN(*JOK,*JTK,*JOR) & /.
ROOKCHECK(*:*ITK.*JTK:*IOK.*JOK:*IOR.*JTK) <- ~(*JOK=*JTK) & /.
ROOKCHECK(*:*ITK.*JTK:*IOK.*JOK:*IOR.*JTK) <- ~BETWEEN(*IOK,*ITK,*IOR).

BETWEEN(*X,*Y,*Z)
        <- (LT(*Y,*X) & LT(*X,*Z)) | (LT(*Z,*X) & LT(*X,*Y)).

RDIVIDESORLPATT(*POS) <- RDIVIDES(*POS) | LPATT(*POS).

/* L-PATTERN */
LPATT(THEIRTURN:*ITK.*JTK:*IOK.*JTK:*IOK.*JOR)
    <- DIFF(*IOK,*ITK,*IDIFF) & ABS(*IDIFF,2) &
       (SUCC(*JTK,*JOR) | PRED(*JTK,*JOR)).
LPATT(THEIRTURN:*ITK.*JTK:*ITK.*JOK:*IOR.*JOK)
    <- DIFF(*JOK,*JTK,*JDIFF) & ABS(*JDIFF,2) &
       (SUCC(*ITK,*IOR) | PRED(*ITK,*IOR)).

ROOM(*:*ITK.*JTK:*OK:*IOR.*JOR,*R)
    <- SIDE(*ITK,*IOR,*I) & SIDE(*JTK,*JOR,*J) &
       PROD(*I,*J,*R) & /.
ROOM(*:*:*:*,100).

SIDE(*X,*Y,*Z) <- LT(*X,*Y) & DIFF(*Y,1,*Z) & /.
SIDE(*X,*Y,*Z) <- GT(*X,*Y) & DIFF(8,*Y,*Z).

/* MANHATTAN DISTANCE */
MDIST(*I1.*J1,*I2.*J2,*D) <- DIFF(*I2,*I1,*I21) & ABS(*I21,*ABSI) &
                             DIFF(*J2,*J1,*J21) & ABS(*J21,*ABSJ) &
                             SUM(*ABSI,*ABSJ,*D).

/* ANOTHER KIND OF DISTANCE */
DIST(*I1.*J1,*I2.*J2,*D) <- DIFF(*I2,*I1,*I21) & ABS(*I21,*ABSI) &
                            DIFF(*J2,*J1,*J21) & ABS(*J21,*ABSJ) &
                            MINMAX(*ABSI,*ABSJ,*,*D).

ROOMGT2(*POS) <- ROOM(*POS,*AREA) & GT(*AREA,2).

OKEDGE(*:*:*OK:*) <- EDGE(*OK).

EDGE(1.*).  EDGE(8.*).  EDGE(*.8).  EDGE(*.1).
```

Fig. 6.5.

```
/* RULES FOR MOVING THE PIECES */

KINGRULE(*I1.*J1,*I2.*J2) <- (SUCC(*I1,*I2) & SUCC(*J1,*J2)) |
                             (SUCC(*I1,*I2) & PRED(*J1,*J2)) |
                             (PRED(*I1,*I2) & SUCC(*J1,*J2)) |
                             (PRED(*I1,*I2) & PRED(*J1,*J2)) .
KINGRULE(*I1.*J1,*I1.*J2) <- (SUCC(*J1,*J2) | PRED(*J1,*J2)) .
KINGRULE(*I1.*J1,*I2.*J1) <- (SUCC(*I1,*I2) | PRED(*I1,*I2)) .

ROOKRULE(*OR1,*OR2,*N.*S.*E.*W)
        <- ROOKNORTH(*OR1,*OR2,*N) | ROOKSOUTH(*OR1,*OR2,*S) |
           ROOKEAST (*OR1,*OR2,*E) | ROOKWEST (*OR1,*OR2,*W) .
ROOKNORTH(*I1.*J1,*I1.*J2,*N)
        <- LT(*J1,*N) &
           (*J2=*N | PRED(*N,*N1) & ROOKNORTH(*I1.*J1,*I1.*J2,*N1)).
ROOKSOUTH(*I1.*J1,*I1.*J2,*S)
        <- GT(*J1,*S) &
           (*J2=*S | SUCC(*S,*S1) & ROOKSOUTH(*I1.*J1,*I1.*J2,*S1)).
ROOKEAST(*I1.*J1,*I2.*J1,*E)
        <- LT(*I1,*E) &
           (*I2=*E | PRED(*E,*E1) & ROOKEAST(*I1.*J1,*I2.*J1,*E1)).
ROOKWEST(*I1.*J1,*I2.*J1,*W)
        <- GT(*I1,*W) &
           (*I2=*W | SUCC(*W,*W1) & ROOKWEST(*I1.*J1,*I2.*J1,*W1)).

ROOKRANGE(*:*ITK.*JTK:*IOK.*JOK:*,*N.*S.*E.*W)
        <- MINMAX(*ITK,*IOK,*W,*E) & MINMAX(*JTK,*JOK,*S,*N).
```

Fig. 6.6.

```
/* MISCELLANEOUS AUXILIARIES */

*X=*X.

SUCC(*X,*Y) <- LT(*X,8) &  SUM(*X,1,*Y).
PRED(*X,*Y) <- GT(*X,1) & DIFF(*X,1,*Y).
MINMAX(*X,*Y,*X,*Y) <- LE(*X,*Y) & /.          MINMAX(*X,*Y,*Y,*X).
ABS(*X,*Y)<- LT(*X,0) & DIFF(0,*X,*Y) & /.     ABS(*X,*X).
SIGN(*X,1) <- GT(*X,0) & /.  SIGN(0,0) <- /.   SIGN(*X,*Y) <- DIFF(0,1,*Y).

TRUE(*GOAL,*POS1,*POS2) <- CONS(*GOAL.*POS1.*POS2.NIL,*ATOM) & *ATOM.
```

Fig. 6.7.

7. CONCLUDING REMARKS

PROLOG programs should be written, in a first approximation at least, as true statements about the relations we want to have computed automatically by computer. This method is in general referred to as 'logic programming'; PROLOG is one particular system, which supports the method to a greater degree than any other system. Logic programming has several features that make it an attractive method for knowledge engineering. Its basic unit, the clause, is a production rule, which has emerged, independently of logic programming, as the favourite formalism of knowledge engineering. Moreover, in logic programming the natural way of activating clauses is by pattern matching. Also, clauses are so general that they encompass as a special case the relational data base model (van Emden 1978). As a result of this, clauses can always be regarded as specifying, explicitly or implicitly, a relational data base. In this way the usual distinction between program and database disappears, which is especially attractive for knowledge engineering.

The PROLOG system is just one experimental realization of logic programming. Its main design consideration was speed. As a spin-off from resolution theorem-proving, logic progamming was born under the bane of ineffectiveness; as a result speed was essential for a feasibility demonstration. In fact, PROLOG implementations exist which are approximately as fast as LISP (Warren, Pereira and Pereira 1977).

However, the success of PROLOG should not obscure the fact that it is not the only possible realization of logic programming. We have taken advantage of its existence by performing the experiment reported in this paper. Let us discuss the conclusions with a view toward the design of future realizations of logic programming specifically suited for applications in knowledge engineering.

According to Michie's approach, advice tables are written in the AL/1 language and directly interpreted by a special-purpose system written in the POP-2 language. Given the implementation of AL/1, the remaining work is to construct the advice table and to program in POP-2 the required predicates in the move generator.

In our approach, the interpreter and the advice table are written in the same language (PROLOG, run on the Waterloo implementation (Roberts 1977). As programs they are to some extent separated, but not as much as they perhaps should be. Fig. 6.1 and the first half of Fig. 6.2 perform some of the functions of the AL/1 interpreter. We should not lose sight of the fact that the advice table used in our example is uncharacteristically simple: in general advice tables have an entry condition (absent in our example) and several rules (what we have called 'rules' should be referred as 'subrules', as they constitute together a single rule of AL/1). Moreover, advice in AL/1 contains in general several advice tables.

On the other hand, our subrules may have conditions attached to them, which is not the case in AL/1. For example, the condition on the 'mate' subrule is essential for avoiding gross wastage of computing effort. Without the condition, a mate would be attempted also in the beginning stage of the game. Because of the depth bound, the 'mate' subgame is already the most expensive one. In the beginning of the game, when many rookmoves have to be considered, the game tree is especially large.

In our opinion the endgame program in Waterloo PROLOG (Roberts 1977) is on the whole, compact and readable. Exceptions are, for example, conjunctions which have to replace arithmetic expressions. Arithmetic expressions do not pose a serious problem in logic programming. Several implementations (Robinson and Sibert 1980, McCabe; Mellish; Warren (in press)) have in fact adequate support for this feature.

We find that each of the distinctive features of PROLOG systems namely being rule-based, using pattern matching, and using automatic back-tracking, have been useful in this application. In connection with backtracking we felt the lack of an additional feature in Waterloo PROLOG. By relying on back-tracking we did not have to program a move generator. The rules for the moves are merely specified and the backtracking mechanism generates a new move whenever one is needed. Sometimes, however, as when a forcing tree is required, we need all such generated moves simultaneously in a list. In most PROLOGs this effect can be fudged using built-in extralogical features. We preferred to build a game player without forcing trees. IC–PROLOG (see Clark and McCabe 1979), however, has a primitive specifically for this purpose. Our experience suggests that this is quite justified. Kowalski's proposal (1979) to merge metalanguage and the object language of logic would also solve the problem encountered here.

Waterloo PROLOG is quite wasteful of storage. For example, in the last game reported below, the stack overflowed after the 28th move. The game was completed by restarting with the last position on an empty stack. Again the problem is not inherent in logic programming: several implementations exist (Bruynooghe; McCabe; Mellish; Warren; in press) which have quite reasonable storage utilization.

Table 7.1 — Data for three randomly selected them-to-move initial positions.

Initial position format: turn:TK:ok:or	Number of moves by US before mate	Average CPU time in seconds per US move on an IBM 4331
theirturn: 4.2 : 8.2 : 5.5	9	.48
theirturn: 5.4 : 8.6 : 4.2	24	.80
theirturn: 7.6 : 1.2 : 5.4	29	.72

To summarize: Waterloo PROLOG is probably a good (compared to other implemented alternatives) tool for this type of application, in fact surprisingly good for an early, experimental realization of logic programming. The three faults noted (wasteful storage management, lack of 'set of solutions', lack of arithmetic expressions) have all been corrected in several other versions of PROLOG.

Acknowledgements

I am grateful to Donald Michie for introducing me to advice tables in an early stage of their development. It would have been impossible to develop this program without the use of the excellent PROLOG system implemented by Grant Roberts. My claim to the simplicity and naturalness of the endgame program is in spite of the fact that this is the third attempt, which was facilitated by version II, programmed by Helio Silva, which, in turn, was facilitated by version I, programmed by Nancy Meisner.

REFERENCES

Berge, C. (1962). *The Theory of Graphs and its Applications*. London and New York: Methuen.

Bratko, I. (1978). Proving correctness of strategies in the AL/1 assertional language. *Information Processing Letters, 7*, 223–230.

Bratko, I., Kopec, D. & Michie, D. (1978). Pattern-based representations of chess end-game knowledge. *Computer Journal, 21*, 149–153.

Bruyooghe, M. (in press). The memory management of PROLOG implementations. *Logic Programming* (eds. Clark, K. L. and Tarnlund, S. A.) London, New York: Academic Press.

Clark, K. L. & McCabe, F. G. (1979). The control facilities of IC-PROLOG. *Expert Systems in the Micro-Electronic Age*, pp. 121–149 (ed. Michie, D.) Edinburgh: Edinburgh University Press.

van Emden, M. H. (1978). Computation and deductive retrieval. *Formal Descriptions of Programming Concepts*, pp. 421–440 (ed. Neuhold, E. J.). Amsterdam, New York, Oxford: North Holland Publishing Company.

Fine, R. (1949). *Basic Chess Endings*. New York: David McKay Co. (reprinted 1969).

Huberman, B. J. (1968). A program to play chess end-games. Ph.D. Thesis, Department of Computer Science, Stanford University.

Kowalski, R. A. (1974). Predicate logic as a programming language. *Information Processing 74*, pp. 556–574. Amsterdam, New York, Oxford: North Holland Publishing Company.

Kowalski, R. A. (1979). *Logic for Problem-Solving*. Amsterdam, New York, Oxford: North Holland Publishing Company.

McCabe, F. G. (in press). Micro Prolog. *Logic Programming* (eds. Clark, K. L. and Tarnlund, S.A.). London, New York: Academic Press.

Mellish, C. S. (in press). An alternative to structure sharing in the implementation of a PROLOG interpreter. *Logic Programming* (ed. Clark. K. L. and Tarnlund, S. A.).

Michie, D. (1977). King and Rook against King. *Advances in Computer Chess 1*, pp. 30–59 (ed. Clarke, M. R. B.). Edinburgh: Edinburgh University Press.

Roberts, G. M. (1977). An implementation of PROLOG. M.Sc. Thesis, Department of Computer Science, University of Waterloo.

Robinson, J. A. & Sibert, E. E. (1980). Logic Programming in LISP. Syracuse: Department of Computer and Information Science, Syracuse University.

Shannon, C. E. (1950). Programming a computer for playing chess. *Phil. Mag, 41*, Ser. 2, 256–275.

Warren, D. H. D. (in press). An improved PROLOG implementation which optimizes tail recursion. *Logic Programming* (eds. Clark, K. L. and Tarnlund, S.A.) London, New York: Academic Press.

Warren, D. H. D., Pereira, L. M. & Pereira, F. (1977). PROLOG – the language and its implementation compared with LISP. SIGART/SIGPLAN Symposium on AI and Programming languages, University of Rochester, 1977. *SIGPLAN Notices, 12*, and *SIGART Newsletter, 64* (Special issue), 109–115.

Zuidema, C. (1974). Chess: how to program the exceptions? *Report 1 W21/76*. Amsterdam: Mathematical Centre.

PROGRAMS OF THE BRAIN

25

Rana Computatrix: an evolving model of visuo — coordination in frog and toad

M. A. Arbib
Department of Computer and Information Science,
University of Massachusetts at Amherst

Abstract

Frogs and toads provide interesting parallels to the way in which humans can see the world about them, and use what they see in determining their actions. What they lack in subtlety of visually-guided behaviour, they make up for in the amenability of their behaviour and the underlying neural circuitry to experimental analysis. This paper presents three specific models of neural circuitry underlying visually-guided behaviour in frog and toad. They form an 'evolutionary sequence' in that each model incorporates its predecessor as a subsystem in such a way as to explain a wider range of behaviour data in a manner consistent with current neurophysiology and anatomy. The models thus form stages in the evolution of *Rana computatrix*, an increasingly sophisticated model of neural circuitry underlying the behaviour of the frog.

1. NEURAL SUBSTRATES FOR VISUALLY-GUIDED BEHAVIOUR

Lettvin, Maturana, McCulloch & Pitts (1959) initiated the behaviourally-oriented study of the frog visual system with their classification of retinal ganglion cells into four classes each projecting to a retinotopic map at a different depth in the optic tectum, the four maps in register. In this spirit, we view the analysis of interactions between layers of neurons as a major approach to modelling 'the style of the brain'. A general view of cooperative computation between neurons within a layer, and between layers within the brain is developed in Arbib (1981b); while the relation of 'maps as control surfaces' to the general study of perceptual structures and distributed motor control is given in Arbib (1981a). Our aim in the present paper is to exemplify these general principles in three specific models of cooperative computation in neural circuitry underlying viscomotor coordination in frog and toad.

Lettvin *et al.* found that group 2 retinal cells responded best to the movement of a small object within the receptive field; while group 3 cells responded best to the passage of a large object across the receptive field. It became common to speak of these cells as 'bug detectors' (following Barlow 1953) and 'enemy detectors', respectively, though subsequent studies make it clear that the likelihood of a given frog behaviour will depend on far more than activity of a single class of retinal ganglion cells (Ewert 1976, and section 3 below). Given the mapping of retinal 'feature detectors' to the tectum and the fact that tectal stimulation could elicit a snapping response, it became commonplace to view the tectum as, *inter alia*, directing the snapping of the animal at small objects — it being known that the frog would ignore stationary objects, and would jump away from large moving objects. However, this notion of a simple stimulus-response chain via the tectum was vitiated by Ewert's observation that after a lesion to PT (pretectum-thalamus) a toad would snap at moving objects of all sizes, even those large enough to elicit escape responses in the normal animal. More detailed neurophysiological studies support the inference that the tectum alone will elicit a response to all (sufficiently) moving objects, and that it is PT-inhibition that blocks this response when the object is large, since tectal cells respond to visual presentation of large moving objects in the PT-lesioned animal (Ingle 1973).

In this paper, then, we first model local circuitry in the tectum (a 'tectal column') to explain certain facilitation effects in prey-catching behaviour; we then study a linear array of such columns to model certain data on size-dependence of prey-catching activity in toads; and, finally, we add PT-inhibition to such an array to model the behaviour of an animal confronted with more than one prey-stimulus. These models form three stages in an evolutionary sequence for *Rana computatrix*, our developing model of the neural circuitry underlying visuomotor coordination in frog and toad. Tectum and PT are but two of the many brain regions to be incorporated into the model during its further evolution.

2. FACILITATION OF PREY-CATCHING BEHAVIOUR

Frogs and toads take a surprisingly long time to respond to a worm. Presenting a worm to a frog for 0.3 sec may yield no response, whereas orientation is highly likely to result from a 0.6 sec presentation. Ingle (1975) observed a facilitation effect: if a worm were presented initially for 0.3 sec, then removed, and then restored for only 0.3 sec, the second presentation would suffice to elicit a response, so long as the intervening delay was at most a few seconds. Ingle observed tectal cells whose time course of firing accords well with this facilitation effect (Fig. 1). This leads us to a model (Lara, Arbib, & Cromarty, in press) in which the 'short-term memory' is in terms of reverberatory neural activity rather than in terms of the short-term plastic changes in synaptic efficacy demonstrated, for example, by Kandel (1978) in *Aplysia*. Our model is by no means the simplest model of facilitation — rather, it provides a reverberatory mechanism for facilitation consistent with Ingle's neurophysiology and the known local neuroanatomy of the tectum. Unfortunately, the current knowledge of tectal circuitry is scanty, and much of the structure of the tectal column to be postulated below is hypothetical, and is in great need of confrontation with new and detailed anatomy and neurophysiology.

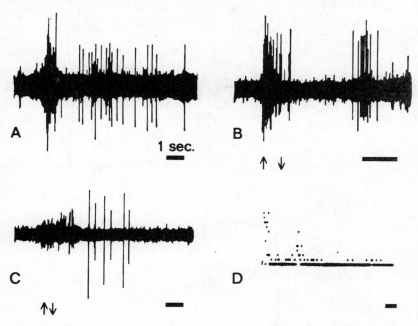

Fig. 1 — Physiological behaviour of cells related to prey catching facilitation. (A) Shows a brief class 2 burst followed by a delayed response of a tectal cell. (B) Shows the behaviour of a tectal cell responding to the presentation of the stimulus and design with a delay. (C) Shows a tectal neuron that produces a delayed response to the presentation of the stimulus. Finally (D) shows the postimulus histogram of a tectal cell showing a delayed peak at 3 to 4 seconds (from Ingle 1975).

The model described in this section addresses facilitation at a single locus of tectum. Further developments address the interaction of a number of columns, and we shall discuss these in sections 3 and 4.

The anatomical study of frog optic tectum by Székely & Lázár (1976) provides the basis for our model of the tectal column (Fig. 2). In the superficial sublayers of tectum we see the thalamic input (which may also ramify in deeper layers), below which are the retinal type 1 and 2 inputs, with the retinal type 3 and 4 inputs deeper in turn. Deeper still, in layer 7, are the tectal efferents, which come from two cell types, the pyramidal cells and the so-called tectal ganglion cells. Our model of prey-catching will use the pyramidal cells as efferents; we shall ignore the tectal ganglion cells. We incorporate the stellate cells as inhibitory interneurons, and ignore the amacrine interneurons. The other major components to be incorporated in our model are the large and small pear-shaped cells. Little of the anatomical connectivity of these cells is known, let alone the physiological parameters of their connections.

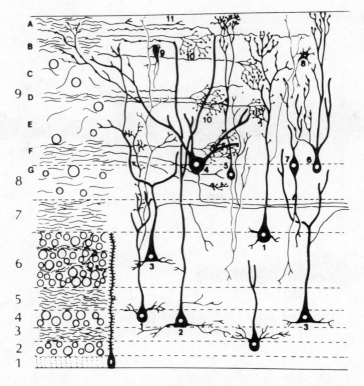

Fig. 2 – Diagramatic representation of the lamination and the representative types of neurons of the optic tectum. Numbers on the left indicate the different tectal layers. Numbered cell-types are as follows: (1) large pear-shaped neuron with dendritic appendages and ascending axon; (2) large pear-shaped neuron with dendritic collaterals; (3) large pyramidal neuron with efferent axon; (4) large tectal ganglion neuron with efferent axon; (5–6) small pear-shaped neurons with descending and ascending axons respectively; (7) bipolar neuron; (8) stellate neurone; (9) amacrine cell; (10) optic terminals; (11) assumed evidence of diencephalic fibres (from Székely & Lázár 1976).

The tectal column model (Fig. 3) comprises one pyramidal cell (PY) as sole output cell, three large pear-shaped cells (LP), two small pear-shaped cells (SP), and two stellate interneurons (SN), only one of which is shown in the figure. These numbers are based on the ratios of occurrence of these cells observed in frog tectum. All cells are modelled as excitatory, save for the stellates. The retinal input to the model is a lumped 'foodness' measure, and activates the column through glomeruli with the dendrites of the LP cells. LP axons return to the glomerulus, providing a positive feedback loop. A branch of LP axons also goes to the SN cells. There is thus competition between 'runaway positive feedback' and the stellate inhibition. (For a full presentation of the differential equations used in the simulation, see Appendix 1 of Lara, Arbib, & Cromarty, to appear.)

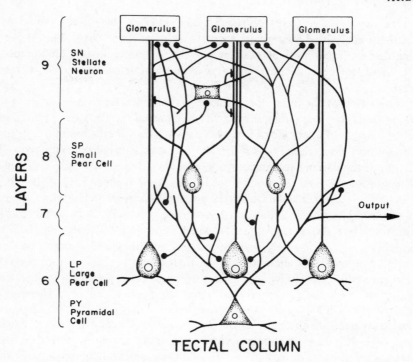

LAYERS

9 { SN Stellate Neuron

8 { SP Small Pear Cell

7 {

6 { LP Large Pear Cell

PY Pyramidal Cell

Glomerulus   Glomerulus   Glomerulus

Output

TECTAL COLUMN

Fig. 3 – Neurons and synaptology of the model of the tectal column. The numbers at the left indicate the different tectal layers. The glomerulus is constituted by the LP and SP dendrites and recurrent axons as well as by optic and diencephalic terminals. The LP excites the PY, the SN, and the GL, and is inhibited by the SN. The SP excites the LP, and PY cells and it sends recurrent axons to the glomerulus; it is inhibited by the SN. The SN is excited by LP neurones and diencephalic fibres and it inhibits the LP and SP cells. The PY is activated by the LP, SP, and optic fibres, and is the efferent neurone of the tectum.

The role of SN in our tectum model is reminiscent of Purkinje inhibition of the positive feedback between cerebellar nuclei and reticular nuclei, a basic component of our group's model of cerebellar modulation of motor synergies (Boylls 1974, Szentagothai & Arbib 1974, Chapter V). Tsukahara (1972) found that reverberation was indeed established in this loop when picrotoxin abolished the Purkinje inhibition from the cerebellar cortex. It would be interesting to conduct an analogous experiment by blocking inhibitory transmitters in the tectum.

Returning to the tectal model: glomerular activity also excites the SP cells which also send their axons back to the glomerulus. The SP cells also excite the LP cell to recruit the activity of the column. The PY cell is excited by both SP cells and LP cells. Clearly, the overall dynamics will depend upon the actual choice of excitatory and inhibitory weights and of membrane time constants. It required considerable computer experimentation to find the weights that yielded the neural patterns discussed below. Further study was devoted to a sensitivity analysis of how weighting patterns affect overall behaviour. It is our hope that our hypotheses on the ranges of the parameters involved in the model will stimulate more detailed anatomical and physiological studies of tectal activity.

Excitation of the input does not lead to runaway reverberation between the LP and its glomerulus; rather, this activity is 'chopped' by stellate inhibition, and we see a period of alternating LP and SN activity. The SP cells have a longer time constant, and are recruited only if this alternating activity continues long enough.

In one simulation experiment, we graphed the activity of the pyramidal cell as a function of the time for which a single stimulus is applied (Fig. 4A, B). There is, as in the experimental data, a critical presentation length below which there is no pyramidal response. Input activity activities the LP, which re-excites the glomerulus but also excites the SN, which reduces LP activity. But if input continues, it builds on a larger base of glomerular activity, and so over time there is a build-up of LP-SN alternating firing. If the input is removed too soon, the reverberation will die out without activating the SP cells enough for their activity to combine with the LP activty and trigger the pyramidal output. However, if input is maintained long enough, the reverberation may continue, though not at a level sufficiently high to trigger output. However, a second simulation experiment (Fig. 4C) shows that re-introduction of input within a short time after cessation of this 'subthreshold' length of input presentation can indeed 'ride upon' the residual reverberatory activity to build up to pyramidal input after a presentation time too short to yield output activity on an initial presentation.

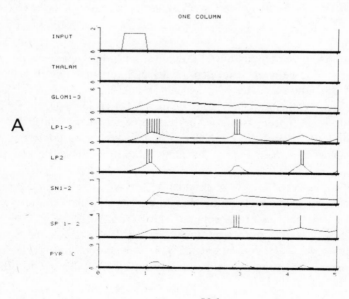

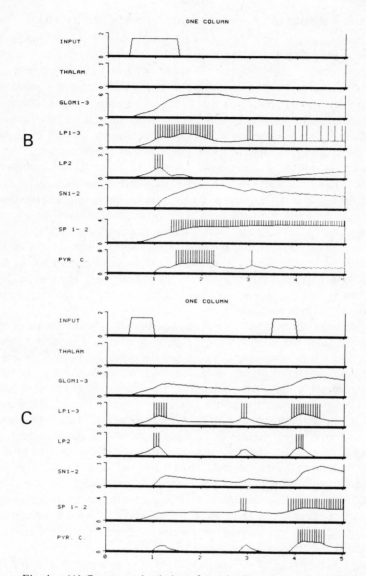

Fig. 4 – (A) Computer simulation of tectal cells response when a brief stimulus is presented. The onset of the stimulus produces a long-lasting depolarization in the glomerulus which then fires the large-pear shaped cell (LP). This neurone in turn sends recurrent axons to the glomerulus and the stellate cell (SN) which acts as the inhibitory neuron in the column. When the inhibitory effect of SN releases the LP cell, a rebounding excitation occurs. The small pear-shaped cell is integrating the activity of GL and of LP and SN neurones to give a delayed short response. (B) If in the above situation we present a stimulus of longer duration, the pyramidal neurone now fires. In (C) we show that when a second stimulus of the 'subthreshold duration' used in (A) is presented, the pyramidal cell (PY) responds. (The frequency of the spikes are a graphical convention. The spikes are drawn simply to highlight when the membrane potential of a cell is above threshold.)

3. A SIMPLE MODEL OF PATTERN RECOGNITION IN THE TOAD

The facilitation model was 'local' in that it analysed activity in a small patch of tectum rather than activity distributed across entire brain regions. We now outline Ewert's study of pattern recognition in the toad, (see Ewert 1976 for a review) analysing what features of a single moving pattern will increase the animal's snapping responses. We then show how a one-dimensional array of tectal columns, of the type studied in the previous section, can model certain of these data. Future research will explore constraints on a two-dimensional array of such columns required to model the whole range of Ewert's data on pattern recognition.

The toad is placed in a transparent cylinder. An object moves around a circular track concentric with, and on the floor outside the cylinder. Some objects elicit no response. Other objects do elicit an orienting response (though the cylinder wall prevents the toad from actually snapping). Since the object keeps moving along its track, it can elicit a second response, and a third, and so on. Ewert's suggestion, then, is that the more 'attractive' is the object, the more frequently will the toad orient to it, so that the response rate is a measure of foodness. (Note a paradox here. The less attractive the object, the greater the integration time to a response, and thus the greater the distance the animal has to move to orient towards the object if it orients at all.)

Ewert presented three types of rectangular stimuli: a 'worm' subtending 2 degrees in the direction normal to the motion, and some d degrees in the direction of motion; an 'antiworm' subtending some d degrees in the direction orthogonal to motion, and 2 degrees in the direction of motion; and a 'square' subtending d degrees in both directions. The prey dummy was moved at 20 degrees per second at a distance of about 7 cm from the toad. Ewert studied the toad's response rate for each stimulus for a range of different choices of d degrees (fixed for each trial) from 2 degrees to 32 degrees. For $d = 2$, the three stimuli were, of course, the same. They elicited an orienting activity of 10 turning reactions per minute. For the 'worm', the orienting activity increased to an asymptote of 35 turns per minute at $d = 16$; for the 'antiworm', the orienting activity decreased rapidly to extinction at $d = 8$; while for the square the orienting activity reached a peak of about 20 turns per minute at $d = 8$, and then decreased to zero by $d = 32$. (The square gives the impression of a competition between 'worm' excitation and 'antiworm' inhibition.)

Ewert repeated this series of behavioural experiments in toads with PT-lesions, and found that for none of the stimuli was there decreased response with increased values of d. This more detailed evidence for PT inhibition of tectally-mediated orienting was further elaborated by neurophysiological recording of PT and tectical neurons in the behaving toads. In the intact toad, PT-neurons had a response rate insensitive to increasing d for 'worms', but the response increased with d for 'antiworms', and even more rapidly for squares. Tectum type 1 neurons were insensitive to changing d for 'antiworms', but had a peak of response at $d = 8$ for both 'worms' and squares; while the firing rate of tectum type 2 neurons was similar to the orienting activity of the intact toad – monotonically declining with d for 'antiworms', peaking at $d = 8$ for squares, and declining slightly after $d = 8$ for 'worms'. (Note the slight discrepancy here — one would expect the response to 'worms' to be non-decreasing if, as Ewert does, one takes tectal type 2 activity as the neural correlate of orienting behaviour.)

On this basis, Ewert postulated a simple model: A filter in PT responds best to an antiworm stimulus; a tectal type 1 cell responds as a filter tuned to a worm stimulus; and a tectum type 2 cell is excited by the tectal type 1 cell and inhibited by a PT-cell. Thus the type 2 cell responds with increased activity to increasing d from a worm stimulus; with decreased activity to increasing d for an antiworm stimulus; and with some trade-off (dependent upon the actual parameters of the filters and the connectivity) for a square. Ewert & von Seelen (1974) fitted parameters to a linear formulation of this model to fit (part of) the response curves observed by Ewert. Note, however, that the domain of linearity is strictly limited; and that the model yields the average firing rate of the neuron: the model is thus lumped over time, and says nothing about the temporal pattern of neuronal interactions. Arbib & Lara (to appear) have studied a one-dimensional array of tectal columns (without PT interaction) to provide a model of spatio-temporal neural interactions possibly underlying Ewert's 'worm' phenomena. For example, in the Ewert study of the toad's response to an object moving along a track, we may regard the object's movement at one position as facilitating the animal's orientation to the object in a later position. The key question

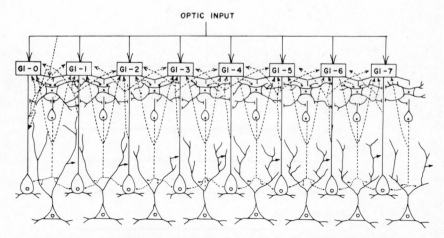

Fig. 5 – A one-dimensional array of tectal columns. Each column is constituted by one GL (glomerulus), one LP (large pear-shaped) cell, one SP (small pear-shaped) neuron, one SN (stellate neuron), and one PY (pyramidal cell). The afferents are the optic fibres that arrive at the GL, LP, SP, and PY cells, and the efferents are the PY axons. LP cells are activated by the GL and the optic input and they send recurrent axons to their own as well as neighbouring glomeruli. The SN neurons are activated by the LP cells and they inhibit LP and SP neurons of their own as well as neighbouring columns. The SP receive excitation from GL and are inhibited by SN; finally PY receives afferents from the retina, the LP and SP neurons.

509

here is 'How does the facilitation build up in the right place?' Part of the answer lies in noting the large receptive fields of the tectal columns; and analysing how activity in a population of tectal columns can yield orientation in a particular direction. Thus, rather than analysing activity in a single column, Arbib & Lara (to appear) study the evolution of a waveform of activity in a one-dimensional array of columns (Fig. 5). The columns of this array are somewhat simpler than that of Fig. 3, having only one neurone of each cell type. We show in Figs. 6, 7, and 8 the response to a moving stimulus of various lengths. These reproduce Ewert's observations on the increasing attraction of a 'worm' with increasing length; Arbib & Lara also report a number of other computational experiments. The elaboration of this model to a two-dimensional array of colums will, in our future research, be integrated with our model (section 4) of tectal-pretectal interactions in prey-selection to yield a model that should be rich enough to extend an explanation of Ewert's data on pattern recognition into the temporal domain in a way which addresses the antiworm and square data, as well as the worm data.

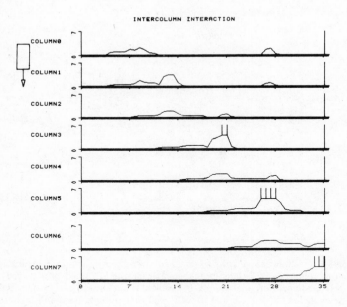

Fig. 6 – Figs. 6, 7, and 8 show the results of a computer simulation of tectal response to a moving stimulus of different sizes. The graphs show the behaviour of the 8 PY neurons of the tectum to a moving stimulus. Notice that in this case an alternate response is given in columns 3, 5 and 7 when the stimulus size only covers one glomerulus.

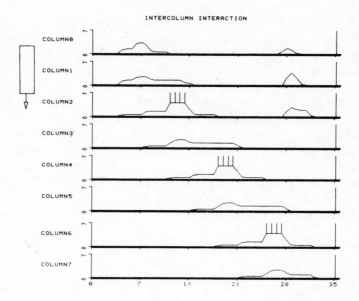

Fig. 7 — Here the stimulus covers 2 glomeruli simultaneously. The results show that the strength of activation increases when the size of the object is elongated. The latency of response is also faster.

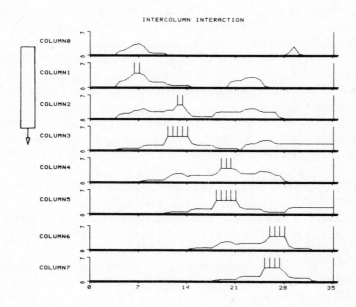

Fig. 8 — In this figure the stimulus simultaneously covers 3 GL. It can be seen that the latency of response is shorter and the total activity is greater than in Figs. 6 and 7. Notice that all columns fire with this stimulus.

511

4. A MODEL OF PREY-SELECTION

Ingle (1968) had studied the response of frogs to pairs of fly like stimuli, each of which was such that when presented alone it would elicit a snapping response. He found that, under differing conditions, the animal would snap at one of the stimuli, snap between them, or not snap at all. We now turn to a model of such prey-selection. The model is a refinement of one developed by Didday (1970, 1976) while working with me at Stanford, but differs in that — in view of Ewert's study of PT-lesions — it uses PT-tectal interactions, rather than positing that all the necessary circuitry is embedded in the tectum. Moreover, the new model extends the 'array of tectal columns' model to provide yet a third stage in the evolution of *Rana computatrix*. Given that a pair of stimuli may fail to elicit a response even when either stimulus alone would have produced one, we conceptualized prey-selection in terms of 'competition' between the neural representations of the stimuli. (We cannot here be content with a simple program to search for the maximum from a list of stimulus strengths; our task in Brain Theory is to distribute prey-selection over a neural network conforming to the available constraints from anatomy and neurophysiology.)

The Didday model started from two postulates: (i) There is available as input a retinotopic array of activity which encodes the loci of 'food-like' movements in the environment. (In this simple exposition, we ignore the possible role of visual accommodation and stereopsis in providing a third dimension to this representation.) This 'foodness layer' corresponds to the glomerular input to a spatial array of the tectal columns modelled in section 2. (ii) The output of the tectum is again a retinotopic array, and sufficient activity in this array will, when played down through efferent structures, cause the animal to snap at the spatial locus corresponding to the 'centre of gravity' of activity in this output array. This output layer was referred to as the 'relative foodness layer', since high activity there should, in general, represent relatively high activity in the foodness layer. Thus, this activity corresponds to the pyramidal activity (PY) in our spatial array of tectal columns. We seek to explain, then, how competition amongst multiple peaks in the foodness array (input to the glomeruli) can lead to the suppression of all but one of them in the output array (PY activity), with consequent snapping at but one of the 'prey'.

The present model (Lara & Arbib, in press) interconnects a one-dimensional array of simplified tectal columns with a layer of cells called S-cells, in retinotopic correspondence with the columns, which represent cells of the pretectum-thalamus (Fig. 9). (In the 1970 model, the S-cells were identified with the sameness cells reported in the tectum by Lettvin, Maturana *et al.*) Each S-cell is excited by activity in the relative foodness layer, save for a blind spot centred at the locus corresponding to that of the S-cell. In the Didday model, the S-cell then provides an inhibitory input to cells within its blind spot on the relative foodness layer. Lara & Arbib (in press), however, do not make the corresponding assumption that an S-cell must inhibit the PY cell in the corresponding tectal column. Rather they conduct a number of experiments on the dynamic consequences of choosing different sites for pretectal inhibition of columnar activity. The reader is referred to their paper for details.

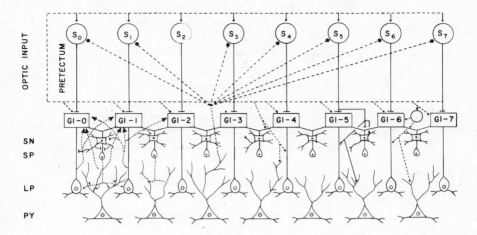

Fig. 9 – Architecture of the model for the interaction between tectum and pretectum in prey selection. Each column receives the afferents from one S (sameness) neuron; each PY (pyramidal) neuron excites all pretectal cells except the one whose blind spot is in its receptive field. The NE (newness) neurons arrive at the same site as the corresponding optic fibres.

The system described so far exhibits hysteresis. Should a new peak be introduced in the input array, it may not affect the output activity even if it is rather large, for it may not be able to overcome the considerable inhibition that has built up via the S-cells. The model thus postulates a further array of NE-cells (representing the newness cells of Lettvin *et al.*) which register sudden changes in input, and uses these to interrupt the ongoing computation to enable new input to affect the outcome.

Clearly, the detailed dynamics of the model will depend on the size of the blind spot, and the relative parameters of excitation and inhibition. We were able to adjust the coefficients in such a way that with several peaks in the foodness input array, the activity passed through to the tectal column would excite the S-cells in such a way that they would lower the corresponding peaks in tectal activity. However, if one peak were stronger than the others, it would be less inhibited, and would begin to recover; in doing so, it would suppress the other peak more, and thus be inhibited less; the process continuing until the stronger peak recovered sufficiently to control a 'snap' in the corresponding direction (Fig. 10). However, there were cases in which the mutual supression between two peaks sufficed to hold each below a level sufficient to release behaviour (Fig. 11).

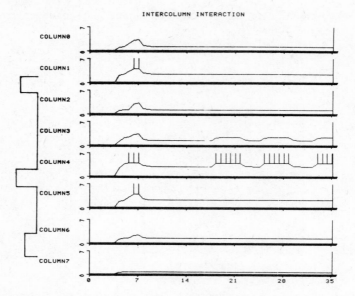

Fig. 10 – Computer simulation of the behaviour of prey selection to three stimuli of different intensities. Column 1 is excited by a stimulus of intensity 2; column 4 by one of intensity 3; and column 6 by one of value 1. After an initial brief response of columns 1, 4, and 5 the rebounding excitation converges to column 4.

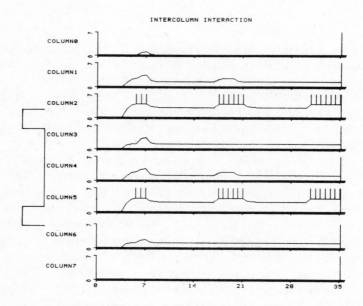

Fig. 11 – Computer simulation of the behaviour of PY neurons to 2 equally intense stimuli. The stimuli are presented in column 2 and 5. Notice that an alternation of excitation and inhibition is present without convergence to either of the stimuli.

514

5. CONCLUSIONS

We have exhibited an evolutionary sequence of models – tectal column, one-dimensional array of columns; array with pretectal inhibition – which explains an increasingly broad range of behavioural data on visuomotor coordination in frog and toad. We note three important features of the style of modelling developed here.

(1). New phenomena are addressed not by the creation of *ad hoc* models but by the orderly refinement and expansion of models already created. Of course, we expect that future development along this line will lead to redefinition and refinement of earlier models, rather than simple addition of new circuitry in each case. On the other hand, we would expect that the model, once sufficiently developed, will explain many data beyond those which specifically entered into its design.

(2). Each 'model' presented here is in fact a 'model-family'. We design a family of overall models, and then conduct simulation experiments to see which choices – of connectivity, synaptic weights, time constants – yield neural dynamics, and input-output relations, compatible with available data.

(3). The choices mentioned above are only loosely constrained by the experimental data at present available. To carry out simulations, we make choices, we form explicit hypotheses (whose details are spelt out in our papers cited above) which may serve to stimulate new experiments. These experiments in turn will stimulate more refined modelling. The continuing cycle will lead to an increasingly sophisticated understanding of the neural mechanisms of visuomotor coordination.

We close with a brief discussion of future directions for this modelling effort. We have already mentioned the transition from a one-dimensional to a two-dimensional array of tectal columns (and corresponding pretectal elements) as a current avenue for further development of *Rana computatrix*.

The model has nothing to say about the control of avoidance behaviour, nor does the basic version described here address more than a few of the prey-predator discrimination phenomena discussed in section 3. A two-dimensional array of columns will allow us to study the full range of these phenomena.

There are further refinements not incorporated into the basic model. Increased motivation (due, e.g., to food odor or to hunger) will cause the animal to snap at larger moving objects than it would otherwise approach. Such an effect might be modelled by direct excitation of tectal columns, or by diffuse inhibition of the S-cells, probably under the control of telencephalic regions. Forebrain mechanisms allow the animal to learn simple discriminations. And there are habituation phenomena which we have begun to model (Fig. 12). Habituation disappears when there is PT ablation. Moreover, the habituation is stimulus specific, and it appears that pattern recognition is necessary both for habituation and dishabituation to occur. For example, Ewert has studied habituation of a toad's snapping response to simple moving patterns and has discovered a hierarchy – an ordering $A \leqslant B$ of patterns, such that if the toad habituates to A it will

515

automatically be habituated to *B*, but not *vice versa*. Such data provide a continuing challenge to the theory-experiment interaction that will drive the future evolution of *Rana computatrix*.

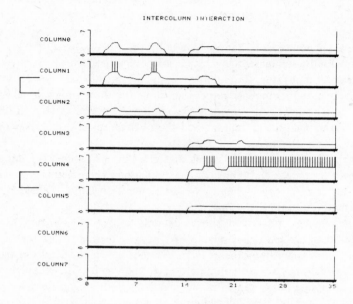

Fig. 12 – Computer simulation when the model is modified to include habituation effects on PY activity. We first present a stimulus in column 1. After a period of rest, we present 2 equally intense stimuli in column 1 and 4. The response converges to PY activity in column 4, because the pathway of column 1 is habituated.

REFERENCES

Arbib, M. A. (1981a). Perceptual structures and distributed motor control. *Handbook of Physiology, Section on Neurophysiology, Vol. III, Motor* Control, (Ed. Brooks, V. B.). Bethesda, Md: Physiological Society.

Arbib, M. A. (1981b). A view of brain theory. *Selforganizing Systems, The Emergence of Order* (Ed. Yates, F. E.). London and New York: Plenum Press.

Arbib, M. A. & Lara, R. (to appear). A neural model of the interaction of tectal columns in prey-catching behaviour.

Barlow, H. (1953). Summation and inhibition in the frog's retina. *J. Physiol. (Lond.)*, 119, 69–88.

Boylls, C. C. (1974). A theory of Cerebellar Function with Applications to Locomotion. PhD thesis, Stanford University.

Didday, R. L. (1970). The Simulation and Modelling of Distributed Information Processing in the Frog Visual System. PhD thesis, Stanford University.

Didday, R. L. (1976). A model of visuomotor mechanisms in the frog optic tectum. *Math. Biosci.*, 30, 169–180.

Ewert, J. P. (1976). The visual system of the toad: behavioral and physiological studies in a pattern recognition system. *The Amphibian Visual System: A Multidisciplinary Approach*, pp. 142–202. (Ed. Fite, K.). London, New York: Academic Press.

Ewert, J. P. & von Seelen, W. (1974). Neurobiologie und System-Theorie eines visuellen Muster-Erkennungsmechanismus bei Kroten. *Kybernetic*, 14, 167–183.

Ingle, D. (1968). Visual releasers of prey-catching behaviour in frogs and toads, *Brain Behav. Evol.*, 1, 500–518.

Ingle, D. (1973). Disinhibition of tectal neurons by pretectal lesions in the frog, *Science*, 180, 422–424.

Ingle, D. (1975). Focal attention in the frog: behavioral and physiological correlates, *Science*, 188, 1033–1035.

Ingle, D. (1976). Spatial visions in anurans. In: *The Amphibian Visual System*, pp. 119–140. (Ed. Fite, K.). London, New York: Academic Press.

Kandel, E. R. (1978). *A Cell Biological Approach to Learning*. Grass Lecture No. 1. Society for Neuroscience. Bethesda, MD.

Lara, R. & Arbib, M. A. (in press). A neural model of interaction between tectum and pretectum in prey selection. *Cognition and Brain Theory*.

Lara, R., Arbib, M. A. and Cromarty, A. S. (in press). The role of the tectal column in facilitation of amphibian prey-catching behaviour: a neural model. *J. Neuroscience*.

Lettvin, J. Y., Maturana, H., McCulloch, W. S. & Pitts, W. H. (1959). What the frog's eye tells the frog's brain. *Proc. IRE*, 47, 1940–1951.

Szekely, G. & Lazer, G. (1976), Cellular and Synaptic Architecture of the Optic Tectum, *Frog Neurobiology*, pp. 407–434.

Szentagothai, J. & Arbib, M. A. (1974). Conceptual models of neural organization, *NRP Bulletin*, 12, *no. 3*, 310–479.

Tsukahara, N. (1972). The properties of the cerebello-pontine reverberating circuit, *Brain Res.*, 40, 67–71.

26

The computational problem of motor control

T. Poggio, B. L. Rosser[†]

Max-Planck-Institut für Biologische Kybernetic
Tübingen, FRG

1. INTRODUCTION

Motor control systems are complex systems that process information. Orientation behaviour, posture control, and the manipulation of objects are examples of motor control systems which involve one or more sensory modality and various central neural processes, as well as effector systems and their immediate neuronal control mechanisms. Like all complex information processing systems, they must be analysed and understood at several different levels (see, e.g., Marr & Poggio 1977). At the lowest level there is the analysis of basic components and circuits, the neurons, their synapses, etc. At the other extreme, there is the study of the computations performed by the system — the problems it solves and the ways that it solves them — and the analysis of its logical organization in terms of its primary modules. Each of these levels of description, and those in-between, has its place in the eventual understanding of motor control by the nervous system. None is sufficient, nor is there any simple translation from one to another. A purely biophysical investigation, however exhaustive, can say nothing by itself about the information processing performed by the system, nor, on the other hand, can an understanding of the computational problem which the system solves lead directly to an understanding of the properties of the hardware.

Two examples of motor control theories belonging to different levels will illustrate this point. The first one deals with the visual flight control system of flies from a computational and phenomenological point of view. The second is a theory of the cerebellum based almost exclusively on anatomical and physiological data.

2. TWO EXAMPLES

2.1 The flight behaviour of the housefly requires an elaborate visuo-motor control system. Houseflies stabilize their flight course visually. They locate and fly towards

[†] Present address: Polytechnic of Wales, Pontypridd, Mid Glamorgan, GB.

prominent objects; they are able to track moving targets and, in particular, other flies; they can manoeuvre, take off, land, escape under visual control. Work in the last few years (see Reichardt 1973; Reichardt & Poggio 1976, 1980, Land & Collett 1974, Wehrhahn & Hausen 1980, Poggio & Reichardt 1980) has led to a quantitative description of a specific system used by the fly to control its flight. This can be characterized as a 'smooth' fixation and tracking system. The theory is largely based on laboratory studies of the fly's behaviour in a controlled visual environment. In free flight the fly produces a torque which determines, through the laws of dynamics, its angular velocity. In the laboratory the fly is fixed but flying. The horizontal component of the torque it generates is measured continuously by a servo-compensated torque meter, and the visual environment is correspondingly rotated to simulate the free rotation of the fly. The problem is to find out how the torque depends on the visual input.

A series of experiments (reviewed in Reichardt & Poggio 1976) leads to the conclusion that the torque depends on the instantaneous values (about 30 ms earlier) of position and speed of the target's image on the fly's eye. Thus, the fly corrects its trajectory by controlling its torque as a function of the angle of error, between the target and the direction of flight, and as a function of the error velocity. The picture which emerges is the following. There are thousands of small movement detectors distributed over the visual field of the fly's compound eye which are weighted with respect to torque generation according to their position in the field. Knowledge of these functional weights allows one to set up a differential equation which quantitatively predicts the trajectory of the fly for many relatively complex visual situations. Current work involving the computer analysis of filmed free-flight episodes aims to extend this theory — derived initially for the horizontal plane — to the six degrees of freedom of free flight, including the control of torque, lift and thrust (Bülthoff *et al.* 1980, Poggio & Reichardt 1980). At present, it has been applied successfully over short periods of time (*ca.* 1.5 s) in free-flight situations in which the visual stimulus is relatively simple, namely, in a chase between two individuals. From the equations and the trajectory of the leading fly, the trajectory of the following fly can be reconstructed in good agreement with its actual trajectory.

The theory provides a top-level description of one visuomotor control system which is a distinguishable part of the fly's total flight behaviour. In effect, the theory serves the dual function of defining the system in question and specifying its modular organization. It is detailed and precise enough to allow one to build an artificial fly — or to simulate one on a computer — with a tracking behaviour quantitatively similar to that of a real fly, but leaves completely open the choice of hardware or software for such an enterprise. It does not even specify an algorithm for evaluating the error position and velocity.

2.2 Ten years ago, D. Marr proposed a detailed theory of the cerebellar cortex which ascribes to it capacity to learn motor skills. The theory arose from, and is quite consistent with, the known anatomy and physiology of the cerebellum.

The cerebellar cortex has an extemely regular cellular organization. It may be regarded as a collection of like units, each containing a single Purkinje cell. The axons of the Purkinje cells carry the output from the cerebellar cortex. Input is carried by the olivary cell axons and by the mossy fibres; the former are directly connected to the Purkinje cell dendrites, the latter indirectly *via* the parallel fibres.

Marr's theory (Marr 1969, Blomfield & Marr 1970) maintains that each cell of the inferior olive responds to a cerebral instruction about a piece of movement, or action. Any action has a defining representation in terms of such cerebral instructions, and this representation has a neural expression as a sequence of firing patterns in the inferior olive.

The olivary axons form the cerebellar climbing fibres. Each Purkinje cell receives usually just one of these, and this exerts a powerful excitatory influence over the whole dendritic tree. The theory proposes that the synapses from the parallel fibres to the Purkinje cells can be facilitated by the conjunction of pre- and post-synaptic activity, so that, in effect, an olivary cell can 'teach' a Purkinje cell a particular pattern of parallel fibre activity. Marr calculates that, because of the way the mossy fibres are wired up to the parallel fibres, each single Purkinje cell (of which humans have 15 million) should be capable of learning at least 200 different mossy fibre input patterns. Once those patterns, or movement 'contexts', have been learned, the olivary cell input is no longer necessary; occurrence of the context alone suffices to fire the Purkinje cell. A particular action or movement would then progress as it did during rehearsal, but without so much cerebral intervention. If the output from the Purkinje cells determines, or partly determines, subsequent mossy fibre contexts, whole movement sequences could be learned and precisely carried out once triggered by the occurrence of a particular stimulus configuration. This is reminiscent of the behaviourist's concept of Fixed Action Patterns (see, e.g., Hinde 1966). Alternatively, the mechanism could serve in the maintenance of posture and balance.

Ten years after its formulation, this theory is still neither proved nor disproved, but it stands a good chance of being correct, at least as a partial account of the functioning of the cerebellum. The idea, for instance, that the cerebellum learns was quite novel ten years ago, but long-term adaptive changes there are now well established by studies of the vestibulo-ocular reflex, and this has become a very active research field.

In contrast to the first example, this theory of cerebellar function is a description of a neuronal mechanism, a piece of neural architecture for performing a learning task. It is extremely elegant and, in its entirety, carries conviction in its ability to account for so much of the known anatomy of the cerebellum. Given the involvement of the cerebellum in motor control, on evidence drawn from other sources and not intrinsic to the model, it allows us to conclude, tentatively, that during the course of solving the computational problems of the control of movement the brain has recourse to a large and simple type of memory. But beyond this, the theory gives no insight into how

521

these problems might be solved, or even formulated. It is not a computational theory of motor control.

In terms of the development of our understanding of motor control systems, Marr's theory represents a sort of anachronism. It is a section of the jigsaw which has fallen together before its place in the puzzle has been determined. This has happened because the cerebellum is relatively well known on account of its simple, well differentiated, and regularly periodic structure. Such a combination is rare in the brain and, when it is considered that the cerebellar model has itself yet to be substantiated, the prospects for the effective use of such a hardware-based approach elsewhere seem slight.

It will probably be easier to study neural circuitry in the light of knowledge of its role in the system of which it is part. While there is no direct route from understanding a system at one level to understanding it at another, there is, nonetheless, a mutual dependence between levels. Mechanisms, for example, must serve the purposes set out by the algorithms they embody, and must do so with the hardware available. There is a sense in which higher level understanding has precedence, in that, by defining the sphere of interest, it provides a key to investigation at the lower level. This is often crucial in a rich and complex piece of hardware like the brain.

3. MOTOR CONTROL AT THE COMPUTATIONAL LEVEL

Just as the study of vision as a problem in information processing has, in recent years, greatly stimulated progress in the development of a coherent theoretical framework for that field (see Marr & Nishihara 1978, Crick *et al.* 1980), so, we believe, a similar approach will be equally beneficial in the field of motor control. Such an approach is beginning to emerge. At the computational level, it is becoming possible to define the problems that all motor control systems must solve and, in doing so, to put into perspective the problems of particular systems, whether biological or artificial.

One problem which has engaged the attention of computer scientists, especially, during the last ten or fifteen years is that of trajectory control in multi-jointed limbs with several degrees of freedom. The problem is clearly central to any motor system, biological or artificial, involving articulated limbs. Interestingly, it has emerged, or re-emerged, rather late, and for a reason which highlights one of the dangers of ignoring the computational approach. Artificial arms of increasing mechanical sophistication exposed the inadequacies of the servo control mechanisms which had hitherto been employed. Classical linear feedback applied to individual degrees of freedom cannot, for fundamental reasons which could have been foreseen, provide the required flexible, accurate and rapid trajectory control in systems in which there is dynamic coupling between degrees of freedom. Physiologists and psychophysicists, also, have gathered data which speak against servo control and in favour of open-loop pre-planning in animals. Thus, servo control proved to be a dead end, and the problem has arisen afesh.

Trajectory control is a problem at the computational level and will serve to illustrate the current state of a computational approach and the potential impact of a more biological perpective.

To begin with, we shall outline (in section 4) the most fundamental characteristics of the problem of trajectory control, and then (section 4.1) consider briefly one of the 'classical' approaches to it from the field of robotics. In section 4.2 we open the discussion of a more biological perspective on the problem by reconsidering in a more general way the preceding account. Finally, in section 5, the implications of some recent findings concerning the way in which antagonistic muscle pairs may be used in the control of the equilibrium position are discussed in detail.

4. TRAJECTORY CONTROL

The trajectory of a limb is determined by the motor torques at the joints. The vector of actuator of muscle torques $\mathbf{T}(t)$ is given by an operator F, a system acting on the vector $\boldsymbol{\vartheta}(t)$ of joint angles:

$$\mathbf{T}(t) = F\{\boldsymbol{\vartheta}(t)\} \ . \tag{1}$$

F, of course, embeds the geometry and the dynamics of the limbs, including hysteresis effects and so on.

The computation of movement can be thought of as taking place in two stages. In the first, the trajectory is planned and the desired trajectory is given through $\boldsymbol{\vartheta}(t)$. In the second stage, equation (1) is solved to find the actuator torques which will execute the planned trajectory. We consider here only this second and conceptually simple step.

The problem it poses is how to represent the operator F. In general, the equation implies that the instantaneous torque $\mathbf{T}$ depends through F on the entire previous history $\boldsymbol{\vartheta}(t)$ of the trajectory – every trajectory being, therefore, unique. Because of the constraints imposed by physics, the operator F usually reduces to a function N of $\boldsymbol{\vartheta}$ and its first two derivatives (under conditions which can be precisely specified by the so-called retardation theorems, see Coleman 1971). This corresponds to the realm of validity of Newtonian mechanics, in which hysteresis effects and other non-Newtonian properties are taken as negligible. Equation (1) can then be represented as

$$\mathbf{T} = N(\boldsymbol{\vartheta}, \dot{\boldsymbol{\vartheta}}, \ddot{\boldsymbol{\vartheta}}) = G(\boldsymbol{\vartheta}) + B(\boldsymbol{\vartheta}) + C(\boldsymbol{\vartheta}, \dot{\boldsymbol{\vartheta}}) + J(\boldsymbol{\vartheta})\ddot{\boldsymbol{\vartheta}} \tag{2}$$

where G, B and C are the vector functions for gravitational torque, frictional torque, and Coriolis torque respectively, and J is the inertia tensor. Equation (2) can also be written as

$$\mathbf{T} = G(\boldsymbol{\vartheta}) + \sum_{j} J_j(\boldsymbol{\vartheta})\ddot{\vartheta}_j + \sum_{jk} C_{jk}(\boldsymbol{\vartheta})\dot{\vartheta}_j\dot{\vartheta}_k \tag{3}$$

where G, J, and C are polynomials in the sines and cosines of the joint angles, the link lengths, and the masses (Horn & Raibert 1978).

523

This Newtonian representation of the operator F is not the only one possible. In fact, there are infinitely many possible approximations. The chosen representation must have two properties. Firstly, it must adequately describe the dynamical properties of the system, within the desired working range. Secondly, it must not present insurmountable problems to the torque evaluation and control system, again within the desired working range. It is apparent from this that discussion at this level cannot be conducted in a completely general way, but must take precise account of three factors which will be different for different systems. These are,

(a) the range of tasks and the level of performance required of the system,
(b) the properties of the limb itself,
(c) the capabilities of the controlling hardware.

4.1 Artificial systems

In the field of robotics, the Newtonian decomposition is appropriate to existing manipulators and their joint actuator mechanisms. These are, in fact, generally designed to conform with Newtonian mechanics. As was earlier remarked, servo control severely limits the performance of a manipulator. Over the past 15 years discussion has centred, therefore, on the question of how to implement torque evaluation by computer.

Two extreme alternative approaches have been proposed,

(a) to compute the function $N(\vartheta, \dot{\vartheta}, \ddot{\vartheta})$ from equations representing the terms in equation (2),

(b) to obtain the required torques from a look-up table indexed by the state variables ϑ, $\dot{\vartheta}$ and $\ddot{\vartheta}$.

The look-up table method (implemented by Albus 1975a, b) has the advantage that it can represent arbitrary system properties, though not time-dependent ones. The table may be built up either by pre-computation or in a non-explicit manner by associative learning. The method has the drawback that it requires a very large access memory; the number of cells in the table is a^{3m}, where m is the number of degrees of freedom of the limb and a is the number of cells per dimension. Another drawback is its configuration sensitivity (Hollerbach 1980), that is, a change in the system, e.g., an applied load, necessitates a completely new table.

Until recently, the look-up table method was favoured because of the apparent impossibility of computing torques from the Newtonian equations for a complex system in a reasonable time, without introducing simplifications which limit performance. In 1977, Horn & Raibert proposed a mixture of the two approaches which trades memory for computation time in an attempt to bring both down to manageable proportions. In their scheme, only position-dependent terms are tabulated. More recently, Luh et al. (1979) and Hollerbach (1979) have described two separate recursive formulations which permit very rapid computation of torques — sufficiently rapid, it appears, to serve the next generation of mechanical manipulators in conjunction with present-day mini-computers.

A remaining difficulty with the analytical method is the problem of modelling the system in terms of equations with sufficient accuracy. Even small errors could be important where precision is required, or could have large cumulative effects over time. Hollerbach (1980) has suggested the use of restricted look-up tables of error terms for precise movements (though these would still suffer from configuration sensitivity). Cumulative errors could be prevented by periodic readjustments using feedback.

4.2 Biological systems

In the context of present-day digital computers and methods of high-level programming the dichotomy of memory space versus computation time is a natural one, and leads naturally to the dichotomy of the tabular versus the analytical approach. In considering biological systems, however, it is necessary to take a different perspective. This perspective must, perforce, be broader and more computational in character because of our imperfect understanding of neural hardware and its organization.

To begin with, two general points may be made. Firstly, any consideration of a trade-off between memory and computation time applied to the brain is unlikely to give the same result as when applied to computers. It can be envisaged that, on the one hand, memory access may be a relatively slow process involving several synaptic delays, while on the other, a large number of nerve cells acting in parallel may be capable of performing a large amount of processing quite quickly. The processing power of a single neuron is still largely unknown, but is probably much greater than the traditional view maintains (see Poggio & Torre 1980).

Secondly, the idea of the tabular storage of state variables in the brain seems unattractive, at least in its pure form, on the grounds that such a representation fails to exploit the constraints inherent in the physics of motor control, the structure of the limb, and the tasks required of the limb. In this idea the constraints of physics are brought to bear only in reducing the operator F to be a function of ϑ, $\dot{\vartheta}$ and $\ddot{\vartheta}$. A table indexed by these vector variables could be used to synthesise any function of three vector variables, and would have no special relationship to motor control.

In pursuance of this latter point, we consider the implications of the definition of an operator as a mapping. Any mapping, such as $\vartheta \rightarrow \mathbf{T}$, may be represented by explicitly pairing each of the terms on one side with the corresponding terms on the other — in effect, by a table — and this pairing may be synthesized through associative learning (Kohonen 1977, Poggio 1975). Usually, however, extensive re-coding of the input (and output) is possible because of redundancies intrinsic to the particular mapping. Only in the case of a completely random one-to-one mapping will no re-coding be possible. The search for the optimal decomposition of the operator F can therefore be regarded as the question of how much input

525

coding, and of what form, to use in representing F. Thus, for example, the recursive formulations of Luh *et al.* and Hollerbach minimize memory use at the expense of extensive, highly structured re-coding.

A good illustration of the theme of associative memory combined with re-coding is provided by the Kolmogorov decomposition of a function of several variables. A theorem proved by Kolmogorov in 1957, and later improved by several authors (see Kahane 1975), states that a continuous function $f(x_1, x_2, \ldots, x_n)$ can always be represented in terms of functions of a single variable, thus

$$f(x_1, x_2, \ldots, x_n) = \sum_{q=1}^{2n+1} g\left(\sum_{p=1}^{n} \lambda_p \phi_q(x_p) \right) \tag{4}$$

where λ and ϕ do not depend on f but g does. This result shows that for a continuous function an n-dimensional table can be replaced by a 1-dimensional table representing g and some imput coding representing λ_p and ϕ_q. This does not necessarily reduce the memory requirement in all cases, i.e., for all continuous functions (note that the Kolmogorov result is not valid for f, g and ϕ being C^1 functions). However, it may be conjectured that an appropriate choice of λ and ϕ for limbs of particular kinds may allow significant reductions in memory size.

Stating the problem in this, very general, way gives rise immediately to the question of how the brain arrives at a particular decomposition. One alternative is that the coding part (corresponding to λ and ϕ in equation (4) is determined by evolution while the memory (corresponding to g) is acquired by a simple associative learning process. The other alternative is that the brain is much more 'plastic'; that it abstracts at least part of the set of coding rules by some higher-level processing of learned input. In either case, but especially in the second, it would not be surprising to find more than one decomposition used in biological systems, either overlaid, e.g. for coarse and fine control, or serving different ranges of motor activity, different tasks, etc.

5. TRAJECTORY CONTROL: A NEW FORMULATION

Recently Polit & Bizzi (1978) have given a dramatic demonstration that in a biological arm joint torques are not likely to be primitive, directly controlled variables. De-afferented monkeys trained to perform one joint movements can achieve and maintain a desired equilibrium position in the presence of external disturbances and in the absense of any sensory feedback. We summarize here the main implications of these experiments, mainly following Polit & Bizzi (1978, 1979) and Hogan (1980).

Unlike torque motors, muscles behave like tunable springs. The 'elasticity' of a muscle is directly controlled by its activation level. Since muscles are arranged about the joints in antagonist pairs, a particular choice of their length-extension curves, i.e. of their α, determines the equilibrium position of the joint and the stiffness about the joint. The situation can be formally described in terms of a potential function of the joint angle, the potential being to a first approximation quadratic.

The generalized force about the joint is simply the derivative (with the negative sign) of this potential. Coactivation of antagonist muscles controls independently the minimum of the potential (*via* the ratio of the two α) and its curvature (*via* the sum of the α). Thus displacement of the limb from the position corresponding to the minimum of the potential results in the generation of a restoring torque which is independent of afferent feedback. Furthermore, appropriate activities of the antagonist muscles can program an infinite number of potential functions with the same equilibrium position but different curvatures (and 'depths'). An entire movement could be controlled simply by specifying one potential function, characterized by a final position and the stiffness about it. It is clear, however, that a wide range of biological movements cannot be programmed only in terms of a one-shot potential. One is led quite naturally, therefore, to the notion of a time-dependent potential function providing at any instant of time (or at discrete sequences of time points) a 'phantom' trajectory (the time dependent equilibrium position) *and* the stiffness (or curvature) about it.

The general question which immediately arises concerns the feasibility of a potential based control system of the type described above for multiple-degree-of-freedom limbs. In particular it is well known that whereas for any given one-dimensional force there always exists a corresponding potential function, this is no longer true for n degrees of freedom $(n > 1)$. The problem may be more than academic, because it bears on the way the controller 'plans' a trajectory. Let us consider, for example, an arm with two degrees of freedom. The simplest possible control system that admits a global 2D potential sets independently the potential for each of the two joints. The resulting 2D potential can be factorized into the sum of two 1-variable functions, one of each degree of freedom. Although the equilibrium positions corresponding to this class of potentials are perfectly general, the pattern of the 'valleys' leading to the minimum is strongly constrained, too strongly, it seems, to be biologically acceptable. These constraints may be at least partly overcome in the case of a time-dependent potential. Much greater flexibility can be achieved if the potential — and therefore the generalized force — at each joint depends on the position of the other joints. Notice that this would require coupling between the joints at the level of their mechanics (see Hogan 1980) or, with more flexibility, at the level of the controller, via sensory feedback. In general, however, a global potential need not exist, unless the generalized force field obeys the classical potential conditions. A global potential — at least for two joint movements — offers a very attractive way to program trajectories in terms of end-effector position, possibly in viewer centred Cartesian space.

In any case, the properties and anatomy of muscles suggest a type of trajectory control which is quite different from the 'force' control mode discussed in the previous section. Position and stiffness are the primitive, controlled variables. The problem of inverting the equations of motion (from the phantom trajectory to the torques) essentially disappears. In a large measure, the musculature itself seems capable of performing the 'computation' of torques, provided high stiff-

527

nesses are achievable. The task of the nervous system is then to transform a desired trajectory into a sequence of equilibrium positions and stiffness such that the trajectory will result. At its most rigorous, i.e. for a trajectory precisely determined in respect of position and force, and in the absence of a global potential function, the task is at least as difficult as the original torque control problem (and is, in fact, identical to it). On the other hand, the possibility of programming equilibrium positions and stiffness of each joint *via* a global (time dependent) potential may greatly simplify the problem of trajectory planning. On the whole the concept of mechanical impedance and equilibrium position control as suggested by Bizzi (see also Hogan 1980) from the study of biological movement may well become an important contribution towards a comprehensive computational theory of motor control.

6. CONCLUSIONS: A BIOLOGICAL PERSPECTIVE

Results in the computational theory of motor control will have, and are already having, a deep inpact on the working hypotheses guiding physiological research in the subject. At the centre of motor control theory at the moment is the question of how torques are determined from the vector of joint angles. We have considered this question as a matter of finding the optimal decomposition of the operator F in equation (1). As a step towards a biological perspective on motor control — in order to free the discussion from the context of any particular methodology — we have first blurred somewhat the distinction between the tabular and analytical representations of a functional operator, then reformulated it in the more general terms of associative memory and input coding. The optimal decomposition will, we suggest, have an optimal representation in two distinct (though not necessarily sequentially distinct) parts.

(1) A part corresponding to our notion of input coding. This will embed the useful physical and biological constraints and will be relatively inflexible.
(2) A part corresponding to an associative memory. This will take care of those system properties which are more variable and less constrained by the nature of the control problem.

With this formulation we were free to consider the control problem as a problem for the system as a whole, not just for an isolable control unit of nervous tissue or computer hardware.

A number of lines of investigation of immediate importance suggest themselves.

(1) To what extent may time be usefully applied as a variable in the evaluation of torques or activity of antagonist muscles? In principle, trajectories need not be planned in regular time slices, nor need the required torques be calculated sequentially in real time. A possibly related question concerns interpolation. In brains, just as in computers, it is impossible to evaluate torques or motoneuron activities for every instant

of time. The example of human vision, in which is found 'hyperacuity' an order of magnitude better than would be expected on the basis of the spacing of the photoreceptors in the fovea (see Barlow 1979, Crick *et al.* 1980), suggests the possibility of a comparable phenomenon in motor control.

(2) Examining the strategies used in particular systems is a problem for experimental and comparative physiology. This work will depend heavily upon exact quantitative studies of trajectories (*cf.* Hollerbach 1980). Of immediate interest are studies of the modular organiszation of trajectory control. For example, are there distinguishable modules dealing with Coriolis forces, gravity, etc?

(3) It is also important to establish the role of associative memory in specific systems. It would be expected, according to our analysis, that systems controlling highly varied motor activities would rely more heavily upon an associative memory component than more specialized ones, independently of the complexity of the tasks performed.

(4) Another question for comparative studies is that of the design of limbs. To what extent is the evolution of limbs influenced by the capabilities and limitations of the control systems? Are there, for example, specific anatomical features of vertebrate limbs which simplify their dynamics (a good example is provided by two joint muscles, see Hogan 1980)?

In conclusion, the main point we wish to make is that the computational level of motor control, so important for the brain sciences, has until now been largely neglected. We believe that this is no longer a necessary state of affairs and that with the appropriate combination of analytical, physiological and 'motor psychophysical' experiments, supported closely by computer experiments on the control of manipulators, we may soon possess some deep insights into the basic principles of motor control.

BIBLIOGRAPHY

Albus, J. S. (1975). A new approach to manipulator control: the Cerebellar Model Articulation Controller (CMAC). *J. Dynamic Systems, Measurement, and Control* **97**, 270–277.

Albus, J. S. (1975). Data storage in the Cerebellar Model Articulation Controller (CMAC). *J. Dynamic Systems, Measurement, and Control* 97, 228–233.

Barlow, H. B. (1979). Reconstructing the visual image in space and time. *Nature* 279, 189–190.

Blomfield, S. & Marr, D. (1970). How the cerebellum may be used. *Nature* 227, 1224–1228.

Bülthoff, H., Poggio, T. & Wehrhahn, D. 3D analysis of the flight trajectories of flies (Drosophilia melanogaster). *Z. Naturforsch.*, (in press).

Coleman, B. D. (1971). On retardation theorems. *Archive for Rational Mechanics and Analysis* 43, 1–23.

Crick, H. C., Marr, D. C. & Poggio, T. (1980). An information processing approach to understanding the visual cortex. *A.I. Memo No. 557*, Cambridge, Mass: Massachusetts Institute of Technology.

Hogan, N. (1980). Mechanical Impedance Control in Assistive Devices and Manipulators. Unpublished Report.

Hinde, R. A. (1966). *Animal Behaviour.* New York: McGraw-Hill.

Hollerbach, J. M. (1979). A recursive Langrangian formulation of manipulator dynamics and a comparative study of dynamics formulation complexity. *A.I. Memo No. 533*, Cambridge, Mass: Massachusetts Institute of Technology.

Hollerbach, J. M. (1980). Natural computation and motor control. *A.I. Memo No. 535.* Cambridge, Mass: Massachusetts Institute of Technology.

Horn, B. K. P. & Raibert, M. H. (1979). Configuration space control. *A.I. Memo No. 458.* Cambridge, Mass: Massachusetts Institute of Technology.

Kahane, J. P. (1975). Sur le theoreme de superposition de Kolmogorov. *J. Approximation Theory* 13, 229–234.

Kohonen, T. (1977). *Associative Memory: A System-Theoretical Approach.* Berlin, Heidelberg, New York: Springer 1977.

Kolmogorov, A. N. (1957). On the representation of continuous functions of several variables by superpositions of continuous functions of one variable and addition (in Russian). *Dokl. Akad. Nauk SSSR 114*, 679–681. (*Transl. Am. Math. Soc.* 28, 55–59 (1963)).

Land, M. F. & Collett, T. S. (1974). Chasing behaviour of houseflies (Fannia Canicularis). *J. Comp. Physiol.* 89, 331–357.

Luh, J., Walker, M. & Paul, R. (1979). On-line computational scheme for mechanical manipulator. *2nd IFAC/IFIP Symposium on Information Control Problems in Manufacturing Technology*, Stuttgart, Germany, October 22–24.

Marr, D. (1969). A theory of cerebellar cortex. *J. Physiol.* 202, 437–470.

Marr, D. & Nishihara, H. K. (1978). Visual information processing: artificial intelligence and the sensorium of sight. *Technology Review 81.*

Marr, D. & Poggio, T. (1977). From understanding computation to understanding neural circuitry. *Nuerosciences Res. Prog. Bull.* 15, 470–488.

Poggio, T. (1975). On optimal nonlinear associative recall. *Biol. Cyber.* 19, 201–209.

Poggio, T. & Reichardt, W. (1973). A theory of the pattern induced flight orientation in the fly Musca domestica. *Kybernetik* 12, 185–203.

Poggio, T., & Reichardt, W.: Visual control of orientation behaviour in the fly II. Towards the underlying neural interactions. *Quart. Rev. Biophysics* 9, 348–357 (1976).

Poggio, T. & Reichardt, W.: Visual fixation and tracking by flies: Mathematical properties of simple control systems. *Biol. Cybernetics.*

Poggio, T. & Torre, V. (1980). A theory of synaptic interactions. In *Theoretical Approaches in Neurobiology.* pp. (eds Reichardt, W. and Poggio, T.), Cambridge, Mass: MIT Press.

Polit, A., Bizzi, E. (1978). Processes controlling arm movements in monkeys. *Science* 201, 1235–1237.

Polit, A. & Bizzi, E. (1979). Characteristics of the motor programs underlying arm movements in monkeys. *J. Neurophysiol.* 42, 183–194.

Reichardt, W. (1973). Musterinduzierte flugorientierung. *Naturwissenschaften* 60, 122–138.

Reichardt, W., & Poggio, T. (1976). Visual control of orientation behaviour in the fly. I. A. Quantitative Analysis. *Quart. Rev. Biophysics* 9, 311–346.

Reichardt, W., & Poggio, T. (1980). Visual control of flight in flies. In *Recent Theoretical Developments in Neurobiology.* pp. (eds Reichardt, W., and Poggio, T.). Cambridge, Mass: MIT Press.

Wehrhahn, C., & Hausen, K.: How is tracking and fixation accomplished in the nervous system of the fly? *Biol. Cybernetics* (in press).

27

Brains, machines and crystals of knowledge

D. N. Spinelli and F. E. Jensen
Department of Computer and Information Science
Universtity of Massachusetts, Amherst, USA

Abstract

The neocortex of the brain is organized in areas dedicated to specific processes. These cortical areas seem essential in the performance of tasks which are deemed important to intelligence, such as pattern recognition, decision making, learning and goal seeking. Natural brains still hold unchallenged superiority to AI machines in such tasks. Recently we have discovered that early experience in developing animals strongly augments the size of a cortical representation responsible for a specific behavioural process, if reinforcement makes it important to the animal. This reallocation of neural elements, caused by experience during development, to form an aggregate of neurones dedicated to a specific process can be viewed as a Crystal of Knowledge which, in concert with other analogous systems provided by the genome, form the structural foundations for adaptive behaviour. We present here a working hypothesis for a mechanism capable of explaining such an aggregate. The data presented in this paper, combined with the rich collection of ideas generated by neuroscience and AI research, provided inspiration to guide our work on the simulation of neuron-like elements.

Sensory deprivation during development has major effects on the functional properties of cells in visual cortex (Hubel & Wiesel 1970, Spinelli & Hirsch *et al.* 1972). We have recently found in non-deprived animals that the functional selectivity of cells in visual cortex, the number of cells allocated to representational areas in somatosensory cortex, and the size of motor projections in motor cortex can all be powerfully affected by early experience (Spinelli and Jensen, 1979).

As these findings are potentially most significant to help explain the establishment of structures responsible for intelligent behaviour, it seems useful to formulate a working hypothesis concerning the nature of the mechanisms brought into action by the aforementioned experiments.

Specifically, we have discovered that increasing the occurrence of one stimulus feature of one modality yields a greater number of cortical cells responsive to that feature than normally observed (Spinelli & Jensen 1979). Similarly, we have found that reinforcement of a particular pattern of movement induces a larger number of cells that when electrically stimulated will elicit that movement. This greater population of cells manifests itself as an amplification of the cortical representational areas in both sensory and motor cortices. This evidence shows that experience during development has a very powerful modulating effect on the ultimate size that cortical representations will have. We have suggested that this reallocation within the cortex may somehow be a potential advantage in coping with similar situations late in life for the animal (Spinelli *et al.* 1980).

The brain could be considered a multipotential system, with potential created both genetically and experientially. The adaptability of an animal in adult life would thus depend on resources (possible in the form of neuronal circuits) built as the expression of genetically predetermined neural circuits and also those that were formed as a result of environmental influences on neuronal growth. This latter category is the subject of our experimental and theoretical work and with which this paper is primarily concerned. Nevertheless, even genetically determined circuitry could be viewed as experimentally acquired — in terms of that gained by the species as it evolved.

That time of early development often termed the critical period merely represents a time at which a high rate of neuronal growth occurs simultaneously with an abundance of sensory input and motor output. Before this, during embryonic and foetal development, neuronal growth is also present and rapid, but here there is much less environmental influence as the peripheral sensory receptors are underdeveloped and input in the foetal environment is scarce. After the critcal period, the opposite conditions prevail: neuronal growth is considerably reduced in the adult brain but the input from the environment is maximal as the animal is fully interacting with the surroundings. Thus the critical period distinguishes itself from other development stages. Here is a unique situation in which growth may be modified by the overall level of activity within the system, as induced by the animal's interaction with the environment. The activity state of the brain — and the individual neuron — is critical to our hypothesis. Much evidence suggests that activity is correlated with increased metabolism. During development, metabolism is primarily directed to the growth of the neuron, whereas in the mature neuron, metabolism is directed to maintenance and synaptic transmitter production.

We shall first consider the effect of activity rates on the growth of the neuron during early postnatal development. Given that increased metabolic activity is necessary for growth, it is reasonable to assume that changes in metabolic levels would result in changes in growth rates. However, the neuron is receiving at least a moderate amount of input from the environment postnatally, and thus its activity is dependent on this input factor, and more importantly, this environmental activation will have an effect on the basal metabolic rate within the neuron. Stimulation of the cell during a time when it is rapidly growing does indeed appear to somehow modify its growth, as we see changes not only in responsivity, but also in the extent of neuronal branching and bundling (Jensen & Spinelli 1979; Spinelli *et al.* 1980). Specificity of sensory activities and the precision of motor control can be increased by appropriate early experiences. In addition, we now have anatomical evidence that areas of cortex in which these alterations are found are made up of cell populations with increased dendritic branching and bundling.

With references to the above we suggest that increased input to a growing neuron due to experience will increase its level of activity. This increased metabolic activity may manifest itself in more growth. The increased branching, therefore, would support this hypothesis, and one could infer that the experience would have caused such a proliferation.

This proliferative growth and bundling in response to experience must be spatially guided in order to form a meaningful circuit. Neurons activated by certain stimuli must somehow make contact with other neurons activated by the same or correlated stimuli. Therefore, growth of a stimulated neuron must be guided to other neurons that are responding to the same stimulus set, and hence create functional neuronal circuits based on correlation of stimuli. There are many possible mechanisms whereby one active neuron might attract the growth of another active neuron, and these include both chemical and electrical forces. One of the features in the spatial field that could exert an influence on the growing neuron may involve the electrical potentials in the surrounding tissue. However, the restriction of our discussion to this mechanism by no means excludes the possibility that some other trophic force may be at work instead; we merely use this as a simple example of a force to illustrate our model.

In particular, we suggest that other growing neurons themselves provide sources of potential gradients in the tissues. As neurons in the area become active, they depolarize, and hence create a potential around themselves. Our observation that bundling (Jensen & Spinelli 1979) occurs more extensively in areas of cortex that also exhibit greater neuronal branching (Spinelli *et al.* 1980) could imply that neurons in this area were: (1) more active and had a higher metabolic growth rate, and (2) were activated and hence depolarized more often than the control side.

If nearby neuronal activation and consequent depolarization exerted some trophic force in a neuron's growth, then the bundled dendrites could be interpreted as resulting from growth of one neuron guided to a more active neuron in the surround. In addition, we believe that not only spatial location, but also the temporal relationship of the activity of the different neurons in a given cortical area is responsible for guiding growth. This notion could have functional significance if one considers the case in which both neurons are more active than others nearby. In a model involving two cells (cells A and B) within a cortical area, both growing, and both being activated from peripheral input, if cell A were to be activated, it would consequently have an increased metabolic rate on repolarizing. This increased metabolic rate might instantaneously boost the growth rate, rendering the cell even more susceptible to guidance factors. If during this short period a nearby cell (cell B) were to be activated, it would represent a depolarized region which in turn would attract the growth of cell A in the direction of cell B (Fig. 1). This model proposes that temporal relationships, namely sequential activation, are important in guiding spatial growth. The rationale in this model lies in the temporal contingencies established in behaviour and learning of the animal as a whole (Smith *et al.* 1969). Particularly, optimal conditioning requires a certain delay (actually 0.4 s) between the CS and the UCS. This delay has been described by a parabolic function, in which there is a peak delay time which corresponds to optimal conditioning, and around this peak one cannot produce satisfactory conditioning in the animal. We suggest that after activation of a neuron, the subsequent metabolic activity grows and delays phenomenon, and that during this period the fibres will grow towards cells in the surround which are active.

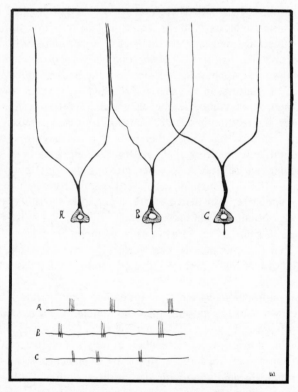

Fig. 1 – Firing in the B cell raises metabolism and accelerates growth toward cell A because of the time link between growth in B and depolarization in A. Depolarizations in other cells which are not time locked (C) will have no appreciable effect. The mechanism suggested rejects noise while amplifying time locked signals much in the same fashion of averaging evoked potentials.

While we have no direct experimental evidence for this hypothesis, it is indirectly suppported by the classical conditioning findings mentioned above. Experimental evidence which may reflect a process similar to our model is that concerning data on bundling within spinal roots. Scheibel & Scheibel have found that fibre bundles are especially abundant in spinal cord segments implicated in sequencing of sensory motor patterns. The sequencing of the activity in nearby growing fibres may be the actual factor in guiding their growth. Both in the peripheral and central nervous systems, this kind of mechanism could help 'sort' or select out neurons that are involved in the similar functional sequences, or patterns, and thereby create the meaningful neuronal circuits that we describe above. Furthermore, bundling increases the chance that closely opposed dendrites will be exposed to the same input, thereby enhancing the circuitry. After these circuits are laid down in such a way, all that remains to be done for their function is to establish synaptic contact with target cells. Some of these bundled neurons do not establish synaptic contact in early development, and those could represent a reservoir of potentially usuable circuits ready for final specification at some later time in the animals's life. We believe that this provides the foundation to explain the enlargement of representational areas that we have observed in somatosensory cortex. Input from a narrow subcortical representational area may project to an area of cortex in which bundles include dendrites of cells in relatively distant regions of cortex. The exposure of these dendrites to the input results in a greatly enlarged cortical field for output (Fig. 2).

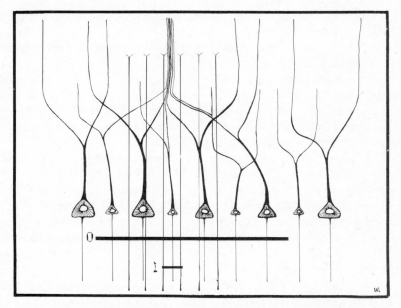

Fig. 2 – Conceptual schema of how bundling of dendrites accretes more processing power [0] to a small number of input lines [I]. Potential connections are then assumed to provide the structure for learning predisposition, i.e., a crystal of knowledge.

Now we can turn to the situation in the adult, in which rapid growth is absent, but circuits are already laid down, and while many of these are functional, many others like those mentioned above have not yet established viable synapses. In this case, synapses could be the only flexible component in the adult brain. The basic neuronal circuits have already been adaptively created by events which were meaningful to the animal during development. In adulthood these resources would only require minor adjustments. Could small-scale growth at the synapse be the mechanism for these minor synaptic adjustments that lead to a usuable circuit? If this were so, it would imply a role for activity in enhancing growth in the adult brain much in the same way as we suggest for the developing brain.

If this mechanism were at work in the central nervous system, then potential neuronal circuits could (literally) be 'activated'. Increased stimulatation due to experience would increase the metabolism and growth rate of certain neurons. If these neurons were components of an 'unfinished' circuit, this increased metabolism might result in establishment of synaptic contact due to an increment in the growth at the fibre terminal. The potential circuit would then have been completed by experimental stimulation. In addition, stimulation may also play a role in maintenance of already established synaptic contacts. Occasional increases in activity of a cell may be necessary to augment metabolism to maintain functional synapses. If not stimulated occasionally the synapse might regress and detach. This model has obvious implications for the phenomenon of atropy from disuse and in the aged.

In conclusion, the hypothesis presented provides a mechanism sufficient to explain how neural circuits relevant to certain early experiences are laid down and how these circuits, with very little further modification, will adaptively learn similar classes of behavioural events.

There is much evidence in humans that acquisition of a skill early in life is more extensive than in adulthood. For example, it is a common observation that new words added to a second language acquired during childhood are learned without accent, whereas new words added to a second language learned during adulthood are never pronounced with a correct accent.

We feel from our experiments that this advantage could probably be achieved with very little exposure at an early age. (With reference to the above example, how many words does a child need to learn in a foreign language for him to learn new words with a native accent later in life?) We believe that the mechanisms described in our model may explain (1) the establishment of learning predisposition during a period of proliferative growth in a spatially unrestricted field, and (2) adult learning in which contact of adjacent terminals is established and/or pre-existing synapses modified.

ACKNOWLEDGEMENT

This research was funded in part by Grant No. 2ROIMH25329-05 and by AFOSR Contract F33615-80-C-1088.

REFERENCES

Hubel, D. H. & Wiesel, T. N. (1970). The period of susceptibility to the physiological effects of unilateral eye closure in kittens. *J. Physiol.* (Lond.) 206, 419–436.

Jensen, F. E., Spinelli, D. N. (1979). Early experience effect on dendritic bundles. *Soc. for Neurosci. Abs.* 5.

Smith, M. C., Coleman, S. R., & Goremzano, I. (1969). Classical conditioning of the rabbit's nictitating membrane response at backward, simultaneous and forward CS–US intervals. *J. of Comparative and Physiological Psychology* 69 No. 2, 226–231.

Spinelli, D. N., Jensen, F. E., & Viana Di Prisco, G. (1980). Early experience effect on dendritic branching in normally reared kittens, *Experimental Neurology* 68, 1-11.

Spinelli, D. N., Hirsch, H. V. B., Phelps, R. W. & Metzler, J. (1972). Visual experience as a determinant of the response characteristics of cortical receptive fields in cats. *Exp. Brain Res.* 15, 289–304.

Spinelli, D. N., & Jensen, F. E. (1979). Plasticity: the mirror of experience. *Science Reprint Series*, 5 January 1979, 203, 75–78.

Spinelli, D. N., Jensen, F. E., & Viana Di Prisco, G. (1980). Plasticity, experience and resource allocation in motor cortex and hypothalamus. *Soc. for Neurosci. Abs.*, 6, November.

PHILOSOPHIES OF MAN AND MACHINE

28

Artificial intelligence, philosophy and existence proofs

R. J. Nelson
Case Western Reserve University
Cleveland, USA

Mechanism is the philosophy that the human mind is an information processing system. My own version of its says that mind is a system of recursive rules (a system equivalent to a set of Post Production rules) complex enough to account for intentional attitudes such as belief and desire, and capable of sentience and self-awareness.

The principal defence of this philosophy of mind is an analogy: a stored program digital computer is a system of recursive rules (in fact, a finite automaton), and has an enormous behavioural repertoire that it shares with human beings. These behaviours display 'intelligence'. If one takes this quite literally, not as a metaphor, then man, too, is a system of recursive rules. This is the conclusion of the analogy which, like many others, is weak. I accept the conclusion as a working hypothesis that has a certain plausibility greater than any other around; it purports to account for language, thought, intentionality, purpose, in short, for mind.

It is obvious that there is some kind of connection between AI and mechanism. Any computer application has some relevance to mechanism as it tends to support the main premise of the analogy in so far as it adds to the behavioural repertoire. But AI generates the results that really make the mechanist happy: natural language programs, learning routines, pattern recognition, semi-algorithms, i.e. heuristic procedures, theorem provers, robot control languages, poetry and music composers, and so forth.

Some AI practitioners are unwitting contributors to this philosophy as they have little professional interest in the mind itself. They are intelligence engineers, not psychologists, and in good times produce schemes that might be useful and commercially profitable. A good speech recognizer, for instance (I mean one that could pick up speech off the street), would be a fantastic AI achievement and never mind about human speech and speech psychology. The set of this type of engineer may be equal to the null set; I am not sure. I mention him only to warn that he might have no interest in this discussion.

Other artificers think their work is relevant to psychology and even to philosophy. In fact a few have deliberately set out to tackle properly philosophical problems. (See McCarthy & Hayes [1]. Also numerous articles by Michael Arbib, Herbert Simon, and Allen Newell come to mind, among others.) What I have to say is addressed to them and to philosophers who use, more or less sophisticatedly, the products of AI research for their own ends. I also hope my remarks will be worth something to cognitive psychologists. However, I really do not care about labels, but only the ideas. Any one is a 'philosopher' or a 'psychologist' if he works seriously with the relevant issues. If he eschews such titles, so be it.

Now to the business. Despite the link between AI and philosophy formed by the main premises of the mechanist analogy, the two enterprises are different in spirit and in ends. Their roles are comparable to those of the pure analyst versus the applied mathematician. Among other things, the analyst supplies existence proofs, while the applied analyst sets up and solves equations. Similarly the philosopher of mind, as I think of him anyway, is concerned with *possible* explanations of mental processes in terms of programs, automata, recursive functions, etc., while AI is devoted to writing programs that perform tasks intelligently. The one gives possibility or existence arguments, and the other strives for useful results. If I had to give a quick and dirty summary of the tasks I'd say the philosopher of mind specializes in conceptual analysis — but not to the exclusion of properly metaphysical standpoints, the computer scientist in intelligent programs, and the cognitive psychologist in developing, eventually, a comprehensive theory of the mind.

The main proposition I want to advance is that these activities ought to go hand in hand to the advantage of all parties, and that they often do not. Here are three examples to start with.

(1) A familiar result of logic is that the halting problem (whether a Turing machine that computes a function $f: N \rightarrow N$, N non-negative integers, does in fact compute a value for every argument) is recursively unsolvable. Since a digital computer with finite unbounded memory is equivalent to a universal Turing machine it follows that there can be no general program verification scheme. I am not saying anyone thinks there is one. I am just illustrating a possible discrepancy between an existence (here an inexistence) result and a possible practice.

(2) A pattern is a set of objects that generally has some property like 'tree', 'face', the letter 'A', 'being a number whose largest prime factor is p', and so forth. Everyone knows that very hard recognition problems are presented by patterns that have no common defining properties. These are Wittgenstein's *family resemblances*, and their members are all fuzzy or degraded objects. On the other hand the objects of recursive function theory are numbers or codings of numbers all the basic symbols of which (like bits in electrical pulse representations) are determinate. Present a Turing machine with a bad character and it gets hung up. Hence you cannot argue that such patterns are machine recognizable because they are recursively enumerable sets, that these sets are just the domains

of functions, and that recognizing a pattern is just the computation of a partial recursive function. If you do, you've got the wrong category. The problem requires more than is entailed by this observation about functions, and any putatively successful program must take into account fuzziness *à la* Zadeh, which has nothing to do with number theory as such, or use of a concept like my own virtual sets, or some other tool.

(3) An interesting property of gestalt perception such as the Necker cube phenomenon is this: sensible objects (or, better, sets of such) might have *two* or more mutually incompatible defining properties (in philosophical jargon, might instantiate two or more property types or universals). A somewhat clearer example, perhaps, is the face/vase phenomenon or the duck/rabbit. Recognition in such cases is obviously a relation in the direct product of the set of objects and perceptual states (in the computer, objects with names of types). Any *functional* recognition scheme that purports to manage gestalt recognition is thus simply doomed from the start.

The point of these simple and quite obvious examples is that what is programmed as the solution to a problem in AI must have relevance to the problem at hand, and the problem at hand must be mechanically solvable in principle; and if not, a solvable subproblem (as in program verification) is the only right one to attack. Treatment of recognition as a functional relation is not relevant to the hard parts of gestalt recognition, and is not even very interesting philosophically.

As a concrete example of point (3), consider the following AI recognition scheme.[†] There is a set of objects to be classified as of this or that pattern type. For each object the recognizer computes a set of n characteristics, thus representing the object as a point in an n-dimensional space. A finite set of points in the space designates a set of ideal or paradigmatic patterns. Finally, a distance measure is defined on the space. Any object is thus identified as instancing a pattern by finding the closest ideal or paradigm.

Now it has been claimed that this scheme can handle gestalt cases requiring the assigning of two or more ideals for one set of objects as in (3) above by (i) changing the set of ideals, (ii) changing the characteristics that are measured, (iii) or changing the distance measure. But all this combined procedure does is change classifications, i.e. partition the set of objects in different ways. More simply stated, it is like saying a thing can be classified in many different ways. However, the gestalt problem we are considering is, given *one* classification can you recognize *two* patterns in one class of the family? The outlined scheme does not provide an answer to the posed question. As an argument it is a classic instance of an *ignoratio elenchi*: it proves the wrong proposition.

Given this background, an existence proof — the providing of which is the philosophical part of AI — consists of (a) a statement of adequacy conditions that a program or a Turing machine construction must satisfy to guarantee relevance;

† Suggested by an unidentified referee of another paper, not this one.

(b) showing that a program or Turing construction exists that satisfies the conditions. (b) could, as I said, be achieved by writing programs that work and satisfy conditions required by (a); but this is hardly a philosophical task as such. A more proper one might be to prove existence of an algorithm without having the slightest idea of how to write one down; or, as in the case of the halting problem, prove that no general procedure exists. As is well known, recursion theory abounds with examples of recursive functions for which there is no known derivation and hence known algorithm, and the philosopher *cum* computer scientist's task might be limited in just this way. But this is a digression.

A minor thesis of this paper is that writing AI programs is not as good a way of doing part (b) of an existence argument as Turing construction, because it is much harder to show that a program satisfies adequacy conditions than to show that an automaton construction does. For one thing, you would first have to show that a program does what it is intended to do; and that either means produce a nonformal mathematical proof or an applicable partial proof of program procedure.

Focussing on adequacy conditions, (a), I now want to discuss them with respect to *intentional attitudes* of the mind. A big stumbling block in the path of the mechanist programme is intentionality: can one get analyses of psychological traits like expecting, believing, desiring, hoping, assuming, and so forth in terms of recursive rule systems or computer programs alone? A famous proposition in philosophical lore known as 'Brentano's Thesis' says you cannot. According to Brentano [2] intentional locutions such as 'believe' cannot be translated into a language that uses strictly physical or mathematical terms, and hence into the basic vocabulary of logic and computer science, *viz.* connectives, quantifiers, sets, relations, functions, and possibly terms of physics, biology, etc. It is the presence of intentionality that makes psychology essentially irreducible to physical or even biological science, so Brentano claimed. Let's see why.

A peculiarity of intentional attributes is that they can be directed to inexistent objects. You can *expect* to see a cat that isn't there; you can *believe* a blond is just around the corner while none is; you can *assume* that God exists, while perhaps he does not. The mind can *intend* things that do not exist in the supposed circumstances, or ever. Another peculiarity of the intentional is that sentences expressing intentional attributes are not open to identity substitutions. For example, your kindly neighbour, Jones, is (identically) the man who heisted the local bank last week. Now you believe the man who pulled the heist is a sonofabitch while you don't believe Jones is. Similarly, a student might believe that HEARSAY recognizes speech sounds, while he does not believe that Carnegie-Mellon's 38th AI program recognizes speech sounds.

It seems to be possible to interdefine intentional terms e.g. 'desire' in terms of 'belief' and *vice versa* in contextual and impredicative ways, but not to break out of the circle of such terms. Some of the best logical minds of the nineteenth and twentieth centuries from Frege through Russell and Carnap have tried and failed. However, there are those, including me, who believe that it is in principle possible to analyze 'expects', for example, in computational terms wherein no other intentional terms are included in the analysans. I also believe, and want to argue, that unless this can be done — either by automaton methods, which is my way, or by constructing programs that expect or believe — mechanism is a failure. Mind has not been shown to be an information processing system in any interesting sense whatever unless intentionally can be adequately accounted for in such terms.

Within AI there is a nonempty contingent of workers who seem to think habitual reference to computer programs 'seeing', 'understanding', 'knowing', 'believing', or 'expecting' is not mere metaphor, and that such programs have significance for psychology and philosophy. I do not for a moment deny the significance — which is why I am here —, but I do certainly doubt that applying a term like 'thinking' to a program implies that a demonstration of knowing or thinking in mechanical terms has been achieved. Use of this vocabulary does not count as affording the slightest evidence that mentalistic concepts have been tracked down. Margaret Boden in her excellent book *Artificial Intelligence and Natural Man* [3], claims that 'intentionality' is the same as 'subjectivity' and that subjectivity consists in a computer having internalized its world. And in discussing programs like Winograd's SHRDLU that do use models she freely uses intentional language like 'knowing'. I think she means, although I could be wrong, that the presence of models of the world solves the problem of accounting for intentional attitudes, for late in the book she rules out the possibility that psychological truths can be expressed in nonpsychological terms (p. 397). Intentionality is thus unanalysable; but the existence of computer programs to which we attribute psychological attitudes teaches us that we are not missing anything and obviates the fruitless search. Aaron Sloman [4] suggests a similar position: the computer has revolutionized philosophy, especially philosophy of science; the computer is a tool for generating conceptual possibilities, not for verifying antecedently posited hypotheses or analytic conditons. He does grant that 'computers cannot yet do these things (perceiving, thinking, etc.) in a way which compares with humans . . . .' I am not sure, however, how we are to tell, when the time comes to check up. It is precisely this philosophical stance (which does not differ very much from Brentano) that I oppose with a requirement that AI programs either set forth adequacy conditions or rely on others to do it before anything definite can be said about the mechanical nature of mind.

In the remainder of this article I will (1) discuss the general nature of adequacy conditions in relation to the now classic treatment of them in formal logic: (2) set down conditions that should be satisfied by programs or Turing machine constructions that putatively analyse away the intentional; I will give a specific example of conditions for *expectation*; (3) attempt to sketch a demonstration that expectation is analyzable in automata theoretic terms. The most I have a right to maintain is that it will satisfy some necessary conditions.

(1) An existence proof, which I characterized as an ordered pair of statements consisting of (a) adequacy conditions and (b) proof that some construction

545

or other satisfies (a), may be contrasted with two other traditional modes of analysis in science, explicit definition, and explication. In both of these modes the idea is to express one concept in terms of others that are scientifically more fundamental or definite in some respects. In explicit definition the introduced term, the definiendum, must have the *same extension* (in a very strong sense) as the definiens and must be *eliminable*; that is to say, any sentence in which the new term appears must be logically equivalent to one in which the new term is replaced by the definiens. The definition must not be circular, i.e. must not anlyse the definiendum in terms that depend on the definiendum itself. Of course this rule does not exlcude recursive definitions, as they can all be made explicit by a wellknown method due to Dedekind. Definition occurs mainly in highly developed sciences and is quite dispensable, its principal virtue being economy of thought.

The second mode of analysis, explication, is much looser than strict definition as it consists of transforming a currently used inexact expression such as 'warm' to an exact one like 'temperature', or one like 'true' in traditional logic to 'true' in model theory. There is no precisely applicable elimination rule as in definition, but rather a rule that says the explicandum must be *similar* to the explanans. More-over the explicandum must be precise in the strict sense that it be part of a well-connected system of scientific concepts [5]. For example, 'true' in the preana-lytic sense as it occurs in sentences like 'statements are true or false', or 'the theory of relativity is true' is given a precise explication by Tarski in terms of mathematical and logical concepts in a metalanguage. But Tarski's analysis cannot be substituted for 'true' in all contexts, to the distress, I might add, of both philosophers and program language semanticists. Likewise, 'warm' is given a precise meaning in terms of temperature, though the two terms are not exactly coextensive: a body at $16°C$ that is warm to you might be cold to me.

Explication and definition differ in that explication does not demand and cannot demand coextensiveness of domains. The reason for this is the vaguess of the explicandum. 'Probability', for instance, is preanalytically used in science in ways that cannot strictly be replaced by a frequency concept. So in explication the requirement of equivalence and eliminability give way to that of adequacy condition. What a statement of adequacy does is extract from the welter of meanings and imprecision of a received term a single meaning or possibly a small cluster of meanings that intuition, experience, scientific consensus, and tradition hold significant. In Tarski's theory, for example, he takes the preanalytic notion of truth to be one that applies to sentences and is expressed in Aristotle's dictum "to say of what it is that it is, and of what is not that it is not". Formulated in terms of Tarski's notorious object-metalanguage apparatus this condition appears as

"p" is true if and only if p

(approximately). Tarski's theory then explicates 'truth' relative to a certain formal language and proves that the explication entails the condition.

What I am calling an 'existence proof' in philosophy of mind is like explication in that it purports to translate mentalistic or intentional terms of the sort discussed above into the vocabulary of computability theory, to write adequacy conditions that the theory must satisfy, and then to prove that the conditions are entailed. It differs in that terms like 'true' already have a deeply entrenched usage in science while 'perceiving' does not. Take 'weigh'. There was no question that scales weigh things prior to the exact analysis of 'weight' in modern measurement theory; but there is a lot of question whether a computer (or any imaginable system equivalent to a Turing machine) *perceives* anything at all. 'Perceives' lacks a back-up theory, while 'weighs' does not — even in the days before philosophers of physics took it upon themselves to reconstruct physics along the lines of what had been done in mathematics; and where the theoretical backing is missing philosophy intrudes.

A somewhat digressionary question is, why call this kind of method an 'existence proof'? There are two reasons. First the terms of the analysis completely exclude all intentional expressions — they involve no circularity; this tends to show that intentional behaviour can be explained without recourse to irreducible, unanalysable psychic units. Second, such an explication — it will amount to a theory — is *real*. If it captures the adequacy conditions I mean for it, to say that there really is a system of recursive rules in the mind, not necessarily in the same form of the model that emerges from the analysis, that accounts for the intentional character in point. The *actual* structure of the system is a question for empirical science — psychology, AI, and neuroscience — and might never be discovered. Similarly one can prove a function is recursive without getting an algorithm for it, or one can prove the existence of the solution to a differential equation without knowing how to construct one. The analogy is not perfect because the two analogs of the example imply a certain lack of constructivity in the proofs, while in the explication case, relative to mind, the method is constructive but might yield the wrong structure. Minds can be shown to be mechanical without implying that they are anything like the programs or automata used in the demonstration.

It is this commitment to realism that justifies the label 'existence proof'. I claim that construction of a recursive system that satisfies conditions is not just an exercise in logic or AI or an instrumental theory, but demonstrates the real nature of mind roughly up to equivalence.

(2) In order to arrive at a general statement of conditions we must obtain a firmer command of the nature of the intentional. Much of the following is extracted from Chisholm's discussion of 'Intentional Inexistence' in his book *Perceiving* [6]. His discussion, in turn, is a compact summary of many of the intuitions of psychologists, philosophers, and logicians on the topic covering a period from Brentano and Husserl to Russell and the present.

It is useful to approach the subject in terms of *intentional sentences*. What is to be captured in a precise way is our previous observation that intentional attitudes can be about inexistent objects and can express assent to one side of an identity relation but not the other.

547

A declarative sentence is intentional if it uses names or definite descriptions is such a way that the sentence does not imply that there is an object to which the names apply. Thus 'Diogenes looked for an honest man', does not imply that there is one. The key intentional term here is 'looked for'.

A sentence that contains a propositional clause is intentional provided that the sentence not imply that the clause be true. Thus 'John expects that it will rain' contains the clause 'that it will rain'; but the sentence does not imply the quoted clause. By contrast, 'It is true that the BNF of FORTRAN is context free' is *not* intentional as the truth of the sentence does imply that of the dependent clause.

Third, a sentence is intentional if the principle of substitutivity of identity fails for it. For instance suppose 'Jones believed in 1944 that Eisenhower was the one in command of the Forces', and 'Eisenhower was identical to the man who was to succeed Truman in the Presidency'. From these sentences it does not follow that Jones believed in 1944 that the man who was to succeed Truman in the Presidency was the one in command of the Forces.

These three characters are severally necessary for intentionality but are not known to be sufficient.

From these characters one can educe adequacy conditions for any explication E of intentional terms.

(i) If E replaces an intentional sentence using names or descriptions but containing no dependent propositional clause, then E must not imply that there is an object named.

(ii) E must not entail the truth of a dependent clause of an intentional sentence it replaces.

(iii) E must not be open to substitution of identities.

In addition to these three conditions for any theory of the intentional, there are some special ones for 'expectation', which I will outline an explication for. Expectations are of at least two kinds. There are current, real-time expectations of events; for example, Jones, listening to her favourite Bach, expects more of it until the piece ends. There are also dateless expectations like: Sagan expects an interterrestrial intelligence to show up. The former, like the latter, does not imply the actuality of the thing named − the Bach could stop at any point by some catastrophic intervention. Yet in the Bach instance the expectation will either definitely be *fulfilled* or *disrupted* by the occurrence or nonoccurence of certain events, while in the other the expectation could fade away, being neither fulfilled nor disrupted. Our treatment will be of the first type only, and thus must satisfy the following condition:

(iv) An existence demonstration showing an automaton or program that expects, must include as well an analysis of fulfilment and disruption and a further demonstration that the theory proposed entails either fulfilment or disruption of expectations.

By (i) it is typical of fulfilment of expectation that if A expects x, then fulfilment might be obtained either by x or by something quite other than x that is *taken to be* x; that is to say, 'A expects x' does not imply x exists (will occur). Similarly, A's expectation of x could be disrupted by failure of x to occur or by *taking* x *to be* something that does not fulfil. Moreover, disruption is compatible with there being an x that did not occur but that would fulfil if it had.

A further philosophical requirement of a general kind that I shall not write down explicitly is that subjunctive expressions such as those sprinkled throughout these latter paragraphs like 'could', 'might be', 'would', etc. must not occur in the explicative theory (although they may occur in the statement of conditions, which is metatheoretical) as it is well known that to allow subjunctive or counterfactual terms in an analysis is tantamount to sneaking in dispositions, abilities, capacities, and the like which are just as mysterious psychic entities as intentions.

The following, then, are the additional conditions to be met by an explication of 'expects'.

(v) If x fulfils A's expectations at t, then either x occurs at t or x does not occur at t but is taken to occur. If x disrupts A's expectation at t, then x does not occur at t or x does occur at t but A takes x not to occur.

(iv) x disrupting A is compatible with the existence of a y such that y would fulfil A's expectation.

(3) The following is an illustrative sketch of a theory of expectation via automaton constructions. For more details see the references.

As usual a finite automaton is a quintuple $T = \langle S, Q, q_0, M, Q_f \rangle$ where S is a finite nonempty *alphabet*; Q a finite nonempty set of *states*; $q_0 \in Q$ the *initial state*; M a function on $Q \times S$ to Q, the *transition function*; and $Q_f \subseteq Q$ the set of *final states*. S^+ is the set of all finite strings of S (the free semi-group on S); M is extended to $Q \times S^+$ by the recursive relation $M(q, \wedge) = q$, $M(q, xs) = M(M(q,x),s)$ for all q, where $\wedge$ is the identity of S^+, $x \in S^+$, and $s \in S$.

T *accepts* x if and only if $M(q_0, x) \in Q_f$. The set of all x such that T accepts x is $\mathcal{U}_T$.

Let $T^1, \ldots, T^n$ be n finite automata where $T^i = \langle S, Q^i, q_0^i, M^i, Q_f^i \rangle$. Note that S is common. A *product acceptor* A is a product $T^1 \times \ldots \times T^n = \langle S, Q^1 \times \ldots, \times Q^n, q_0^1, \ldots, q_0^n, M, Q_f^1 \times \ldots \times Q_f^n \rangle$ where $M(\langle q^1, \ldots, q^n \rangle, s) = \langle M^1(q^1, s), \ldots, M^n(q^n, s) \rangle$ and M is extended by component in the natural way to S^+.

A product automation A *accepts* x if and only if at least one component of $\langle M^1(q_0^1, x), \ldots, M^n(q^n, x) \rangle$ is a final state, i.e. there is an $i = 1, \ldots, n$ such that $M^i(q_0^i, x) \in Q_f^i$.

A product acceptor has essentially the same behaviour as a pattern recognizer of the kind described above, pp. 542 ff, although it is relational, not functional. Until the end part of this sketch I will consider only $n = 1$ although the theory can be generalized in a straightforward manner to any n. When it is, each component automaton is replaced by a superautomaton of the type next to be explained, appropriate delays are introduced to provide synchronization, and provision is made for breaking ties by context when fuzzy x is accepted by more than one component machine.

Let $T = \langle S, Q, q_0, M, Q_f \rangle$. A state $q \in Q$ is a *winner* if and only if there is an x such that $M(q,x) \in Q_f$. q_0 is a winner; elements of Q_f are also winners; but there are others, in general.

(α) T in state q *expects* x if and only if q is a winner and $M(q,x)$ is again a winner, i.e. there is a y such that $M(M(q,x), y) \in Q_f$.

Intuitively, if T begins in q_0 and is fed a string x serially by symbol, M generates a sequence of states. Any state in the sequence that is a winner is such that T in that state expects a y that will drive it to a final accepting state. If Jones is listening to music and hears the first few bars of her favourite Bach, she is driven to a state that expects any later acoustical sequences that tend to complete the play of Bach.

Now in the real world the items x that we are able to perceive by way of the senses are not nice, clean articles like abstract Turing machine symbols or bits or the morphemes of programming languages. But they might be close according to some measure; or, they might be elements of fuzzy sets and have such status, therefore, that they can be considered to be of a certain type, that is, to realize certain properties vaguely. In the present theory we will say that items like x that are not even defined for automaton acceptance can be *taken to be* a y such that y is accepted by the automaton − provided that the machine is in an expecting state.

If Jones is listing to her Bach and a passage is flat (not 'correct' or 'defined' in the Bach context) she might (or of course might not) take it to be a good continuation of the Bach she has already heard. If she is deliberating on her own listening she might say to herself. "That's not good Bach; but the player means to play Bach. I expect more Bach so I'm willing to take the stuff as good and see what happens". This concept of taking x to be Bach does not imply that it is Bach. Likewise if x is taken to be y but x occurs at another time in another computational context it will not generally be true that Jones will again take it to be good stuff.

What we have to do is pin down this concept of taking. It is a 3-ary relation among an automaton T, an input string x (not all of whose elements are in S, that is $x \notin S^+$ − which is equivalent to saying some elements of x are ill-defined or degraded like the flatted notes), and a taken string, $y \in S^+$. So we embed T in a super Turing machine $T' = \langle S \cup B, Q', q_0, M', Q'_f \rangle$. T is a proper subautomaton of T', i.e. $S \subset S \cup B$, $Q \subset Q'$, $M \subset M'$ and $Q_f \subset Q'_f$. Here B includes the degraded input and $S \cap B = \phi$. Owing to (T')'s extreme complexity I will discuss it informally; it has several subautomata in addition to T which can be best described in terms of the functions they carry out.

(a) It has a part that tells what the current state q of T is.

(b) It has a part that tells whether the current state of T is a winner. This task is recursively unsolvable in general but not for T restricted to finite automata (or even to certain bounded Turing machines).

(c) It contains a self-encodement of part T in itself (in T'). This is possible for T' to manage provided that T' includes enough structure for the recursion theroem of computability theory to apply.

Suppose now that $x \in (S \cup B)^+$ is input to T; recall that only elements of S are defined for T. If a scanned symbol s of x is in S and T is in state q, it computes the next state $M(q,s)$ in the normal manner. On the other hand if $s \notin S$, but rather in B, then T' and its included automaton parts operates as follows: (a) the present state q of T is identified; (b) it is decided whether q is a winner; if not, T completes the computation $M(q_0,x)$ which eventually drives it to a nonfinal state; if q is a winner, (c) then T' scans the encoded triples (production rules of T) containing the present state as a first component (i.e. it scans the entire M function table considered as an encoded set of ordered triples (q,s',q')), selects at random an s' and an associated *next* state, and tests whether q' is a winner; if not T' selects another s' of a triple until it finds a winner (a winner must exist, since q, the present state is a winner by hypothesis); given q' a winner and the associated s' selected, it overprints s' on the undefined symbol s that started this branch of the procedure (this step is inessential unless one has in mind literally a Turing machine tape) and resumes the computation of $M(q',s'y)$, y being the remainder of the input from the winner q with s' replacing s in x.

If x is input at time t when T is in state q, then let $K_q(x,y,t)$ be the result of computing y from x beginning in state q at t by steps (a)-(c) above. $K_q(x,y,t)$ may be read "T takes x to by y at t". From this construction it follows that y could equal x, in case $x \in S^+$; it also follows that even if $x \notin S^+$, then for some t and y, $y \in \mathfrak{U}_T$, i.e. $M(q_0,y) = q_f$ for some $q_f \in Q_f$, while for some other t and y, $y \notin \mathfrak{U}_T$ (this can be seen by simple examples).

We next incorporate K in some formal definitions.

(β) x *fulfils* T in state q at t if and only if q is a winner and there is a y such that $K_q(x,y,t)$ and $M(q,y) \in Q_f$.

In more or less ordinary intuitive English, this definition says that if T is in a winning state, x fulfils T's expectations if either it itself or some y it takes to be x drives T into a final or recognizing state.

(γ) x *disrupts* T in state q at t if and only if q is a winner and every y is such that either there is no computation $K_q(x,y,t)$ or $M(q,y) \notin Q_f$.

Let $R(x,y)$ be the projection of $K(x,y,t)$ onto the first two components.

(δ) x is *virtually accepted* by T if and only if there is a y such that $R(x,y)$, and $y \in \mathfrak{U}_T$.

Virtual acceptance is an alternative to the concept of *fuzzy set* for perception theories.

Note that (γ) and (δ) are compatible for the *same* x: viz., at some time t, x could disrupt while yet there is a y such that $R(x,y)$ and $y \in \mathfrak{U}_T$. Thus adequacy condition (vi) is immediately satisfied.

Next, suppose T in state q expects x. By (α) (p. 550 above), q is a winner. Trivially, either there is a y such that $K_q(x,y,t)$ and $M(q,y) \in Q_f$ or it is false that there is a y such that $K_q(x,y,t)$ and $M(q,y) \in Q_f$. Consequently (iv) is satisfied: T in state q expects x implies there is a t such that either T is fulfilled by x at t or T is disrupted by x at t.

(v) is satisfied directly by the definition (β) and (γ).

As to the remaining conditions, since our subject sentence is "T in state q expects x", only (i) and (iii) apply; (ii) does not apply because the quoted sentence does not contain a propositional clause. Call this sentence 'E'.

E does not imply that an x occurs. For since (iv) is satisfied – expectation implies either fulfilment or disruption – no x need occur at all. Hence (i) is satisfied.

As to (iii), which is slightly more interesting, let us consider a product acceptor (p. 549) at least two of whose components are *individual* pattern acceptors rather then *type* pattern acceptors in that they process occurrences of objects and recognize them as individuals rather than as types or as particularizing universals. Suppose the two proper names or descriptions associated to these acceptors are A and B (for example, Eisenhower ($=$A) and the man who succeeded Truman to the Presidency ($=$B)). The product automation is $T = T_A \times T_b \times \ldots$.

Now T_A and T_B accept the same sets, namely $\mathfrak{U}_A = \mathfrak{U}_B$, because all of the occurrences of individual A are occurrences of B, i.e. A $=$ B. T_A and T_B, however, compute differently. Considered as machines for computing partial recursive functions, they compute different functions on one and the same partial domain; in particular they *take* differently, which means, by (γ) that the set of $\mathfrak{V}'_A$ of all x such that there is a y such that $R^A(x,y)$ and $M^A(q_0,y)$ is final is not identical to the set $\mathfrak{V}_B$ of x such that $R^B(x,y)$, etc. In consequences while $\mathfrak{U}_A = \mathfrak{U}_B$ is true, it is not in general true that $\mathfrak{V}_A = \mathfrak{V}_B$. So if x fulfils T_A's expectations of an occurrence of A ($x = $ A), it is possible that it not fulfil T_B's expectations of occurence of B ($x \neq$ B). Therefore the product acceptor's expectations of an occurrence of A are fulfiled, but not of its expectations of B. Substitute A for B; contradiction.

It seems to me that there is something strange about saying that an actual machine or program that embodied this scheme would really *expect* anything, and I suspect that you share my misgivings. However, if the realization were a living, sentient organism the situation would be quite different. It seems to me that a theory such as this is a demonstration that expectation is a purely mechanical phenomenon, although it might be off on the details of structure.

Ackowledgements

This material is based upon work supported by the National Science Foundation under Grant No. SES-8012173.

REFERENCES

[1] McCarthy, J. & Hayes, P. J. (1969). Some philosophical problems from the standpoint of artificial intelligence. In *Machine Intelligence 4*, pp. 463–502 (eds. Meltzer, B. and Michie, D.). Edinburgh: Edinburgh University Press and New York: American Elsevier.

[2] Brentano, F. (1924). *Psychologie Non-Empirische Standpunkte*, 3rd edition. Leipzig.

[3] Boden, M. (1977). *Artificial Intelligence and Natural Man*. Brighton: Harvester Press and New York: Basic Books.

[4] Sloman, A. (1978). *The Computer Revolution in Philosophy*. Brighton: Harvester Press and Atlantic Highlands, N.J.: Humanities Press.

[5] Carnap, R. (1950). *Foundations of the Theory of Probability*. Chicago: University of Chicago Press.

[6] Chisholm, R. M. (1957). *Perceiving*. Ithaca, N.Y.: Cornell University Press.

[7] Nelson. R. J. (1975). On machine expectation. *Synthese*, **31**, 129–140.

[8] Nelson, R. J. (1976). On mechanical recognition. *Philosophy of Science*, **43**, 24–52.

[9] Lee, C. Y. (1963). A Turing machine which prints out its own code script. In *Mathematical Theory of Automata*. (ed. Fox, J.). Brooklyn: Polytechnic Press.

553

29

Ethical machines

I. J. Good

Virginia Polytechnic and State University
Blacksburg, USA

The notion of an ethical machine can be interpreted in more than one way. Perhaps the most important interpretation is a machine that can generalize from existing literature to infer one or more consistent ethical systems and can work out their consequences. An ultra-intelligent machine should be able to do this, and that is one reason for not fearing it.

INTRODUCTION

There is fear that 'the machine will become the master', especially compounded by the possibility that the machine will go wrong. There is, for example, a play by E. M. Foster based on this theme. Again, Lewis Thomas (1980) has asserted that the concept of artificial intelligence is depressing and maybe even evil. Yet we are already controlled by machines − party political machines.

The urgent drives out the important, so there is not very much written about ethical machines; Isaac Asimov wrote well about some aspects of them in his book *I Robot* (1950). Many are familiar with his 'Three Laws of Robotics' without having read his book. The three laws are:

"1. A robot may not injure a human being, or,
   through inaction, allow a human being to come
   to harm.
2. A robot must obey the orders given it by
   human beings except where such orders would
   conflict with the First Law.
3. A robot must protect its own existence as
   long as such protection does not conflict
   with the First or Second Law."

555

Originally, I thought the three laws were mutually incompatible because they are not quantitative enough, but I found that Asimov had not by any means overlooked the quantitative aspect.

In one chapter of the book a robot on another planet refuses to believe that men, inferior as they are, can construct robots, and it also does not believe that Earth exists. Nevertheless the robot has religious reasons for keeping certain pointer readings within certain ranges, and it thus saves Earth from destruction. Thus the robot does not violate the first law after all. I was unconvinced by this idea, but it does suggest the possibility of a robot's being largely controlled by its 'unconscious mind', so to speak, in spite of misconceptions in its 'conscious mind', that is, by the operations handled by the highest control element in the robot.

Later in the book, so-called 'Machines', with a capital M, are introduced that are a cut above ordinary robots. They are ultra-intelligent and are more or less in charge of groups of countries. A subtle difference now occurs in the interpretation of the first law which becomes (p. 216) "No machine [with a capital M] may harm humanity; or, through inaction, allow humanity to come to harm". And again "... the Machine cannot harm a human being more than minimally, and that only to save a greater number".

Unfortunately it is easy to think of circumstances where it is necessary to harm a person very much: for example, in the allocation of too small a number of dialysis machines to people with kidney disease.

Asimov's book has the important message that intelligent machines, whether they have an ordinary status or are ultra-intelligent presidents, should be designed to behave as if they were ethical people. How this is to be done remains largely unsolved except that the flavour is utilitarian.

The problem splits into two parts. The first is to define what is meant by ethical principles, and the second is to construct machines that obey these principles.

ETHICS

The problem of defining universally acceptable ethical principles is a familiar unsolved and possibly unsolvable philosophical problem. If this problem could be solved in a fully satisfactory manner, then the problem of constructing a machine that would obey these principles would not be difficult. For, in a known parody of Wittgenstein (Good 1976), we may say that

> Was sich überhaupt sagen lasst
> lasst sich klar sagen
> und es lasst sich programmeirten sein.

[That is, "What can be said at all can be said clearly, and it can be programmed".]

The programming of ethics was initiated by early philosophers. According to Abelson (1967, p. 82), "Ethical philosophy began in the fifth century BC, with the appearance of Socrates, a secular prophet whose self-appointed mission was to awaken his fellow men to the need for rational criticism of their beliefs and practices".

The article points out that Greek society at the time was changing rapidly from an agrarian monarchy to a commercial and industrial democracy. People were given power who, in Abelson's words, "needed a more explicit and general code of conduct than was embodied in the sense of honour and *esprit de corps* of the landed aristocracy". Similarly today's society is changing rapidly, and the machines that may gain power will also need a more explicit formulation of ethical principles than the people have who now wield power.

Unfortunately, after 2500 years, the philosophical problems are nowhere near solution. Do we need to solve these philosophical problems before we can design an adequate ethical machine, or is there another approach?

One approach that cannot be ruled out is first to produce an ultra-intelligent machine (a UIM), and then ask it to solve the philosophical problems.

Among the fundamental approaches to ethics are utilitarianism, contractualism (see, for example, Rawls 1971, who however, does not claim originality), and intuitionism, and various shades and mixtures of these approaches.

I tend to believe that the UIM would agree with the Bayesian form of utilitarianism. The Bayesian principle of rationality is the recommendation to "maximize expected utility', that is, to choose the act that maximizes $\Sigma p_i u_i$, where the $u_i's$ are the utilities of various mutually exclusive outcomes of some potential action, and the $p_i's$ are the corresponding probabilities. This principle is to some extent a definition of "utility", but it is not a tautology; it is more a principle of consistency. The development of the neo-Bayes-Laplace philosophy of rationality by F. P. Ramsey (1931), and L. J. Savage (1954) amounts to this: that a person or group that accepts certain compelling desiderata should act as if he, she, or it had a collection of subjective probabilities and utilities and wished to maximise the expected utility.

The social principle of rationality presents various difficulties:

(i) The estimation of interpersonal utilities if these are to be added together.

(ii) The question of whether the whole world (or galaxy etc.) should be taken into account with equal weights assigned to all people (or beings) or whether each society and individual should give much greater weight to itself, possibly in the hope that Adam Smith's "hidden hand" would lead to global optimization.

(iii) The assignment of weights to future people. Should the future be discounted at some specific rate such as 1% per year? The more difficult it is to predict the future, the higher the discounting rate should be.

(iv) The assignment of weights to animals. Should the weight given to any organism be some increasing function of degree of awareness? Should we assume that machines or even animals or slaves are zombies with no awareness and therefore have no rights?

One interpretation of ethical behaviour by a person is behaviour that tends to maximize the expected utility of a group to which he belongs, even if he suffers by so doing.

More generally an ethical problem arises when there is a conflict of interest between one group G and another, G', where a group might consist of only one person, and where the groups might intersect and one of the groups might even contain the other. It is possible too that one of the groups consists of people not yet born, or it might consist of animals. G might be one person, and G' the same person in the future. For example, we might criticize a machine for turning itself on if we believe that this would cause it damage.

I have been expressing in unemotional language the basis of many dramatic situations. For example, in *The Day of the Jackal*, de Gaulle's life is saved by the French Secret Service who obtained vital information by means of torture. Was this justified? Should we praise the brave German soldiers who laid down their lives for the sake of a criminal lunatic?

When a person acts rationally he uses his own utilities. If society is perfectly well organized the person will perform the same acts whether he uses his own utilities or those of the society. If a person seems to sacrifice his more obvious advantages for the sake of other people, then those other people would call him ethical. This would sometimes be because the interests of others are built into his personal utilities, and sometimes indirectly out of long-term self-interest.

Some people and some societies put more or less emphasis on different aspects of the Good, such as honesty, duty, love, loyalty, kindness, humility, religious feeling, bravery, and fairness or justice. The utilitarian regards all these aspects as derivative. For example, justice is regarded by the utilitarian as a useful concept because it makes a scheme of incentives more credible and so encourages legal, and perhaps ethical, behaviour. Similarly the justification of loyalty is that it encourages the leaders to be benign, and the main objection to terrorism is that it increases the probability of a ruthless Government. If a completely formalized mathematical theory of utility could be produced, then these derivative concepts would emerge in the form of theorems.

It might seem that a utilitarian must believe that the ends justify the means. Although he would certainly recognize the relevance of outcomes of acts, as would even most intuitionists, he might still agree, for example, with Aldous Huxley that the means are likely to *affect* the ends.

Possible Meanings for an Ethical Machine

In a sense, any machine, such as a pocket calculator, in good working order, is ethical if it is obedient. A slightly more interesting example is a homing missile because it has a little intelligence and is more like a kamikaze. Obedience by a person to the terms of a contract can certainly involve ethics, and obedience is also a quality that enables prisoners to earn remission of sentence, but it is not much of a criterion by itself. After all, most mobsters and Nazis are or were obedient, so we need something more than obedience before we can feel happy about calling a machine ethical.

Another interpretation of an ethical machine is one that helps a person to be ethical by fairly straightforward information retrieval. Examples of such machines or programs, are:

(i) A machine that retrieves legal information. This enables an attorney to defend his client, or a judge to decide on sentences similar to those given in the past. Some judges have been guilty of exceedingly unethical behaviour, amounting almost to murder, through not having this kind of information or perhaps by pretending that they did not have it.

(ii) A machine that retrieves medical information.

Warren McCulloch (1956) defined an "ethical machine" as one that learns how to play a game by playing, but without being told the rules. He finishes his article by describing a man as "a Turing machine with only two feedbacks determined, a desire to play and a desire to win".

My concept of an ethical machine is somewhat different. I envisage a machine that would be given a large number of examples of human behaviour that other people called ethical, and examples of discussions of ethics, and from these examples and discussions the machine would formulate one or more consistent general theories of ethics, detailed enough so that it could deduce the probable consequences in most realistic situations.

As an example of this kind of machine or program let us consider the implicit utilities of medical consultants. This example was discussed by Card & Good (1970). The idea is that a team of medical consultants is to be asked what decisions they would make under various circumstances. These circumstances are defined by a set of indicants, and the probabilities of various outcomes are to be estimated independently of the decisions of the consultants. The probabilities and the decisions form the data for the calculations. A complication is that there might be inconsistencies in the decisions. It should be possible then, by an algorithm described in the article, to infer the implicit utilities that the consultants assign to the various outcomes. I don't know whether the algorithm has yet been applied in practice. It was not part of the investigation to assume different scales of fees to be paid to the consultants, nor to examine the effects of malpractice suits.

Concluding Remarks

A somewhat similar investigation has been carried out by Jones-Lee (1976) concerning the value of human life. (See also, for example, Mooney 1970.) The point of such investigations is to help decision-making in connection with, say, road safety. Some people object to such calculations on the grounds that life is priceless, overlooking that money saved on road safety can be spent, for example, on hospitals. It seems, however, inescapable that computer aids to administrative decision-taking will soon of necessity be performing calculations of this nature. So the problem of the ethical machine is already upon us.

REFERENCES

Abelson, R. & Nielsen, K. (1967). "Ethics, history of" in *The Encyclopedia of Philosophy*, vol. *3* (New York: Macmillan & The Free Press), 81–117. (Abelson wrote the part up through the 19th century.)

Asimov, Isaac (1950). *I Robot* (Garden City, New York: Doubleday, 1963 edn.).

Card, W. I. & Good, I. J. (1970). "The estimation of the implicit utilities of medical consultants", *Mathematical Biosciences* 6 (1970), 45–54.

Good, I. J. (1976). Pbi #322 in "Partly-baked ideas", *Mensa Journal International*, No. 193 (Jan. & Feb.), p. 1.

Jones-Lee, M. W. (1976). *The Value of Life: an Economic Analysis* (London: Martin Robertson).

Mooney, G. H. (1970). "The value of life and related problems", U.K. Ministry of Transport; mimeographed, 84 pp.

Ramsey, F. P. (1931). "Truth and probability" (1926), and "Further considerations" (1928) in *The Foundations of Mathematics and Other Logical Essays* (London: Kegan Paul).

Rawls, J. (1971). *A Theory of Justice* (Cambridge, Mass.: Harvard University Press).

Savage, L. J. (1954). *Foundations of Statistics*, New York: Wiley (2nd edn; Dover Publications, 1972).

Thomas, L. (1980). "Notes of a biological watcher. On aritificial intelligence", *New England J. Medicine* (Feb. 28), 506–507.

AUTHOR INDEX

(Page numbers are in roman type for text references, italic for bibliography entries. Chapter numbers preceded by CH.)

561

SUBJECT AND NAME INDEX

(Page numbers are in roman type, CH. precedes chapter numbers. Names only appear which are in no sense bibliographic references; otherwise they are to be found in the author index.)

THE MACHINE INTELLIGENCE SERIES...

The Machine Intelligence Series occupies a unique and universally recognised position in the world literature. The books have evolved from the unbroken sequence of now-famous Workshops conducted by the editor-in-chief Donald Michie, each planned to its own theme and organised as a carefully structured and cohesive source book.

No rigid demarcations are imposed between new results and tutorial overviews, which two elements are so blended as to stimulate and at the same time to instruct.

Novel discoveries and trends are set into a solid background of exposition, and related to previous knowledge in such a way as to serve an advanced tutorial function. No work can be a classic at the time of its publication, but some of the contributions are classics in the making.

The combined bibliographies put into the reader's hands the keys to virtually everything which is yet known in this subject.

MACHINE INTELLIGENCE

Editor-in-chief: Professor Donald Michie, Professor of Machine Intelligence,
                   University of Edinburgh

Volumes 1–7 published by Edinburgh University Press, and in the USA by Halsted Press (a division of John Wiley and Sons, Inc.).

Volume 8 onwards published by Ellis Horwood Limited, Chichester, and in the USA by Halsted Press (a division of John Wiley and Sons, Inc.).

MACHINE INTELLIGENCE 1 (1967)
Contents: Abstract Foundations
            Theorem Proving
            Machine Learning and Heuristic Programming
            Cognitive Processes: Methods and Models
            Pattern Recognition
            Problem-Oriented Languages

MACHINE INTELLIGENCE 2 (1968)
Contents: Abstract Foundations
            Mechanised Mathematics
            Machine Learning and Heuristic Programming
            Cognitive Processes: Methods and Models
            Problem-Oriented Languages

MACHINE INTELLIGENCE 3 (1968)

Contents: Mathematical Foundations
Theorem Proving
Machine Learning and Heuristic Programming
Man-Machine Interaction
Cognitive Processes. Methods and Models
Pattern Recognition
Problem-Oriented Langauges

MACHINE INTELLIGENCE 4 (1969)

Contents: Mathematical Foundations
Theorem Proving
Deductive Information Retrieval
Machine Learning and Heuristic Programming
Cognitive Processes: Methods and Models
Pattern Recognition
Problem-Oriented Languages
Principles for Designing Intelligent Robots

MACHINE INTELLIGENCE 5 (1970)

Contents: Prologue
Mathematical Foundations
Mechanised Reasoning
Machine Learning and Heuristic Search
Man-Machine Interaction
Cognitive Processes: Methods and Models
Pattern Recognition
Principles for Designing Intelligent Robots
Appendix

MACHINE INTELLIGENCE 6 (1971)

Contents. Perspective
Program Proof and Manipulation
Mechanised Reasoning
Heuristic Paradigms and Case Studies
Cognitive and Linguistic Models
Approaches for Picture Analysis
Problem-Solving Languages and Systems
Principles for Designing Intelligent Robots

MACHINE INTELLIGENCE 7 (1972)

Contents: Prehistory
Program Proof and Manipulation
Computational Logic
Inferential and Heuristic Search
Perceptual and Linguistic Models
Problem-Solving Automata

MACHINE INTELLIGENCE 8: Machine Representations of Knowledge (1977)

Contents: Knowledge and Mathematical Reasoning
Problem-Solving and Deduction
Measurement of Knowledge
Inductive Acquisition of Knowledge
Programming Tools for Knowledge-Representation
Dialogue-Transfer of Knowledge to Machines
Dialogue-Transfer of Knowledge to Humans
Case Studies in Empirical Knowledge
Perceptual Knowledge
World-Knowledge for Language-Understanding

MACHINE INTELLIGENCE 9: Machine Expertise and the Human Interface (1979)

Contents: Abstract Models for Computation
Representations for Abstract Reasoning
Representations for Real-World Reasoning
Search and Problem Solving
Inductive Processes
Perception and World Models
Robot and Control Systems
Machine Analysis of Chess
Knowledge Engineering
Natural Language

MACHINE INTELLIGENCE 9:
Machine Expertise and the Human Interface

Preface by Professor Andrei Ershov, USSR Academy of Sciences

Edited by: J. E. Hayes, University of Edinburgh
D. Michie, Professor of Machine Intelligence, University of Edinburgh
and
L. I. Mikulich, Artificial Intelligence Council of USSR Academy of Sciences

MI9 emanates from an East-West forum when leading experts in Western Europe and North America joined forces with their Soviet counterparts at the 9th International Machine Intelligence Workshop at Repino near Leningrad in 1977. Work of the Soviet school (approximately half the book) in this explosively growing area of machine intelligence is thus made accessible for the first time to Western readers, in addition to the latest Western advances.

The emergent theme of knowledge-representation is supported on the theoretical and experimental sides by recent work in inductive inference and theory-formation. New results and authoritative summaries concern abstract models for computation, machine reasoning and problem-solving, perception, robotics, computer game-playing, interactive knowledge systems, and programs for understanding natural language text. The comprehensive and international bibliography (including a complete listing of the major papers in computer chess) gives guided access to the current world literature, including little-known recent Soviet research. It is thus invaluable for professional reference or for reading material for course study.

Readership: Advanced undergraduates, graduates and professional workers in the fields of

Computer and Information Science
Psychology
Linguistics
Philosophy
Mathematics
Brain Science

ISBN 0-85312-1125

575

THE ELLIS HORWOOD SERIES IN
COMPUTERS AND THEIR APPLICATIONS

Series Editor: BRIAN MEEK
Director of the Computer Unit, Queen Elizabeth College, University of London

The series aims to provide up-to-date and readable texts on the theory and practice of computing, with particular though not exclusive emphasis on computer applications. Preference is given in planning the series to new or developing areas, or to new approaches in established areas.

The books will usually be at the level of introductory or advanced undergraduate courses. In most cases they will be suitable as course texts, with their use in industrial and commercial fields always kept in mind. Together they will provide a valuable nucleus for a computing science library.

INTERACTIVE COMPUTER GRAPHICS IN SCIENCE TEACHING
Edited by J. McKENZIE, University College, London, L. ELTON, University of Surrey, R. LEWIS, Chelsea College, London.
INTRODUCTORY ALGOL 68 PROGRAMMING
D. F. BRAILSFORD and A. N. WALKER, University of Nottingham.
GUIDE TO GOOD PROGRAMMING PRACTICE
Edited by B. L. MEEK, Queen Elizabeth College, London and P. HEATH, Plymouth Polytechnic.
CLUSTER ANALYSIS ALGORITHMS: For Data Reduction and Classification of Objects
H. SPÄTH, Professor of Mathematics, Oldenburg University.
DYNAMIC REGRESSION: Theory and Algorithms
L. J. SLATER, Department of Applied Engineering, Cambridge University and H. M. PESARAN, Trinity College, Cambridge
FOUNDATIONS OF PROGRAMMING WITH PASCAL
LAWRIE MOORE, Birkbeck College, London.
PROGRAMMING LANGUAGE STANDARDISATION
Edited by B. L. MEEK, Queen Elizabeth College, London and I. D. HILL, Clinical Research Centre, Harrow.
THE DARTMOUTH TIME SHARING SYSTEM
G. M. BULL, The Hatfield Polytechnic
RECURSIVE FUNCTIONS IN COMPUTER SCIENCE
R. PETER, formerly Eötvos Lorand University of Budapest.
FUNDAMENTALS OF COMPUTER LOGIC
D. HUTCHISON, University of Strathclyde.
THE MICROCHIP AS AN APPROPRIATE TECHNOLOGY
Dr. A. BURNS, The Computing Laboratory, Bradford University
SYSTEMS ANALYSIS AND DESIGN FOR COMPUTER APPLICATION
D. MILLINGTON, University of Strathclyde.
COMPUTING USING BASIC: An Interactive Approach
TONIA COPE, Oxford University Computing Teaching Centre.
RECURSIVE DESCENT COMPILING
A. J. T. DAVIE and R. MORRISON, University of St. Andrews, Scotland.
PROGRAMMING LANGUAGE TRANSLATION
R. E. BERRY, University of Lancaster
MICROCOMPUTERS IN EDUCATION
Edited by I. C. H. SMITH, Queen Elizabeth College, University of London
STRUCTURED PROGRAMMING WITH COMAL
R. ATHERTON, Bulmershe College of Higher Education
PASCAL IMPLEMENTATION: The P4 Compiler and Compiler and Assembler/Interpreter
S. PEMBERTON and M. DANIELS, Brighton Polytechnic
PRINCIPLES OF TEXT PROCESSING
F. N. TESKEY, University of Manchester
ADA: A PROGRAMMER'S CONVERSION COURSE
M. J. STRATFORD-COLLINS, U.S.A.
REAL TIME LANGUAGES
S. YOUNG, UMIST, Manchester
SOFTWARE ENGINEERING
K. GEWALD, G. HAAKE and W. PFADLER, Siemens AG, Munich